D1736387

Rules and Regulations of Brahmanical Asceticism

SUNY Series in Religion
Harold Coward, Editor

Rules and Regulations of Brahmanical Asceticism

Yatidharmasamuccaya
of
Yādava Prakāśa

Edited and Translated
by

Patrick Olivelle

STATE UNIVERSITY OF NEW YORK PRESS

Published by
State University of New York Press, Albany

© 1995 State University of New York
All rights reserved

Printed in the United States of America

No part of this book may be used or reproduced in any manner whatsoever without written permission. No part of this book may be stored in a retrieval system or transmitted in any form or by any means including electronic, electrostatic, magnetic tape, mechanical, photocopying, recording, or otherwise without the prior permission in writing of the publisher.

For information, address State University of New York Press,
State University Plaza, Albany, NY 12246

Production by Marilyn P. Semerad
Marketing by Bernadette LaManna

Library of Congress Cataloging-in-Publication Data

Yādavaprakāśa, 11th cent.
[Yatidharmasamuccaya]
Rules and regulations of Brahmanical asceticism :
Yatidharmasamuccaya of Yādava Prakāśa / edited and translated by
Patrick Olivelle.
p. cm. — (SUNY series in religion)
ISBN 0-7914-2283-6 (hc: alk. paper). — ISBN 0-7914-2284-4 (pb: alk
paper)
1. Asceticism—Brahmanism—Early works to 1800. 2. Brahmans—
Early works to 1800. 3. Dharma—Early works to 1800.
4. Asceticism—Hinduism—Early works to 1800. I. Olivelle, Patrick.
II. Title. III. Title: Yatidharmasamuccaya. IV. Series.
BL1239.5.A82Y35 1994
294.5'447—dc20

94-36124
CIP

10 9 8 7 6 5 4 3 2 1

BL
1239.5
.A82
Y35
1995

for my mother
1902—1993

उपाध्यायान्दशाचार्य आचार्याणां शतं पिता ।
सहस्रं तु पितॄन्माता गौरवेणातिरिच्यते ।।
Manu 2.145

WILLIAM T. BOYCE LIBRARY
FULLERTON COLLEGE
FULLERTON, CALIF. 92634

Contents

Text

Preface

In his review of my edition and translation of Vāsudevāśrama's *Yatidharmaprakāśa*,[1] Professor J. W. de Jong remarked: "It is to be hoped that other works of this class will be edited and translated, above all Yādavaprakāśa's *Yatidharmasamuccaya*, which Sprockhoff praised so highly." It was this remark that first prompted me to undertake this project. Many factors, including the difficulty of obtaining the manuscripts and other research projects, postponed its completion. Fifteen years after de Jong's suggestion, I am delighted that the critical edition and translation of this important work is finally completed.

I started the manuscript search while I was at Indiana University, Bloomington. A generous grant from the University permitted me to travel to India in the summer of 1990 to microfilm the manuscripts used in this edition. The staffs of the Adyar Library, the Government Oriental Manuscripts Library, Madras, and the University of Mysore Oriental Research Institute were generous with their time and assistance. The Center for Asian Studies of the University of Texas at Austin provided the computer facilities and funding for the preparation of this volume. Dr. David Pingree deciphered for me several dates given in the manuscripts, and Dr. H. v. Stietencron helped me to obtain several manuscripts from German libraries. Dr. Madhav Deshpande created the beautiful computer fonts in which this book is set. To all these institutions and individuals, and in a special way to Dr. Kunjunni Raja of the Adyar Library, and to Dr. Richard Lariviere, my colleague at the University of Texas, a heartfelt thank you for their generosity and kindness. I want to thank the State University of New York Press, and in a special way Mr. William Eastman, its director, for undertaking to publish a work such as this, whose scholarly significance will probably be not matched by its market success. I thank also the anonymous reader for the Press who read the manuscript with greater care than usual and made numerous and excellent suggestions.

[1] *Indo-Iranian Journal,* 21(1979), 294–95.

My mother, who lived a long, generous, and productive life, died before this book could be completed. To her it is dedicated. My wife, Suman, read the manuscript several times. She has an eye for the detail and caught many of my blunders. To Suman and Meera, my daughter, a big thank you for their love and friendship.

Introduction

The Author: His Life and Works

In the introductory verses to the *Yatidharmasamuccaya* ("Collection of Ascetic Laws"), the author refers to himself in the third person as Yādava (Ch. 1.3). The conclusions of the first and eleventh chapters identify the author as Yādava Prakāśa, an ascription that is also made in several manuscripts at the conclusion of every chapter. This ascription is confirmed by Vedānta Deśika, who refers to and cites from "the ascetic rules collected by" Yādava Prakāśa.[1]

The Śrī-Vaiṣṇava tradition identifies Yādava Prakāśa as a teacher of Rāmānuja during the early years of his education in Kāñcī.[2] In these accounts Yādava is depicted not only as a teacher of a monistic form of Vedānta philosophy but also as a rather nasty and vindictive individual. When his pupil Rāmānuja disagreed with him in the interpretation of an Upaniṣadic passage, Yādava plotted to kill his young charge. Rāmānuja escaped but was later reconciled with his teacher. Rāmānuja was finally expelled when he rejected another of Yādava's Upaniṣadic interpretations. In the end, Rāmānuja converted his former teacher to the teachings of Śrī-Vaiṣṇavism and to the philosophy of distinguished nondualism (Viśiṣṭādvaita) after defeating him in debate (Singh 1958, 132).

It is impossible to determine the historical accuracy of these stories. At least some elements of the Yādava legend are no doubt intended to demonstrate Rāmānuja's victory over the teachers and teachings of nondualist forms of Vedānta. What better way to demonstrate his final triumph than to depict him as becoming the teacher of

1. The Sanskrit expression "*tatsamuccitasyaiva yatidharmasya*" (Ybh 42 see p. 6, n. 12) must surely be an indirect reference to the title of Yādava's work. For Vedānta Deśika's date and his citations from the Ysam in his *Śrīpāñcarātraparīkṣā*, see p. 191.

2. For accessible accounts of Yādava's life as depicted in these accounts, see Dasgupta 1922, 100–102; Singh 1958, 132.

his own teacher? That the kernel of this story, nevertheless, has a historical basis is evidenced by the comments of Vedānta Deśika, who assumed a leadership role in the Śrī-Vaiṣṇava church within two centuries of Yādava and Rāmānuja. Deśika opposed the practices of abandoning the sacrificial string and shaving the entire head including the topknot, which were common among renouncers belonging to the Advaita tradition (Olivelle 1986–87). He cites texts that prescribe penances for ascetics who follow those customs and presents the case of Yādava as an example.

> When, moreover, the Venerable Yādava Prakāśa, who had abandoned his sacrificial string without considering the repercussions and who, after considering them, became repentant and legitimately questioned the learned men and the inhabitants of various regions who had come to the festival of Vāsudeva, they replied by prescribing for him a penance. (Ybh 41)

The brevity of the allusion to this episode of Yādava's life indicates that Deśika expected his readers to be aware of it. Yādava, according to Deśika, had given up the sacrificial string when he became an ascetic. When he realized his mistake, he asked learned men to prescribe the appropriate penance. Nothing is said about Yādava's association with Rāmānuja, but Deśika's comments at least support the elements of the story regarding Yādava's conversion to the Vaiṣṇava form of ascetic life.

A close examination of the Ysam makes it clear that the work is composed from a Vaiṣṇava standpoint. On the contentious issue of whether an ascetic should discard the sacrificial string, Yādava is clear and firm: all Brahmins are required to wear one, and ascetics are no exception (Ch. 3.9). Yādava cites a text of Atri that specifically prescribes a sacrificial string for ascetics (3.10) and concludes by citing Uśanas:

> By discarding his sacrificial string, a vedic student, a householder, a forest hermit, and even a wandering ascetic will fall. Let no one, therefore, abandon it. (Ch. 3.11)

In an apparent autobiographical reference, Yādava cites several texts that prescribe the appropriate penances for discarding the sacrificial string (Ch. 8.50–58) and comments that these penances apply specifically "to those who have taken to the form of ascetic life that requires the abandonment of the sacrificial string" (Ch. 8.54). It appears, therefore, that Yādava wrote the Ysam after he had converted to the Vaiṣṇava form of asceticism.

Apart from events related to his alleged association with Rāmānuja, little is known with any certainty regarding the life of

Yādava Prakāśa. Even his date has to be estimated from that association. According to tradition, Rāmānuja was born in 1017 C.E. and died in 1137. The length of his life may well have been exaggerated, but it seems fairly certain that Rāmānuja lived approximately during this period. Dasgupta estimates that he became a pupil of Yādava in 1033 and became a Vaiṣṇava ascetic at Śrīraṅgam in 1049, at the age of thirty-two. Yādava's conversion must have taken place some time after this. Under the assumption that Yādava must have been at least thirty years old when Rāmānuja came to study under him, he must have been born before 1003. Even if we assign him a life of seventy years, his death must have taken place before 1073. We may not be too far wrong, therefore, in assigning the writing of the Ysam to the third quarter of the eleventh century C.E.

Very little scholarly work has been done regarding the works and thought of Yādava Prakāśa.[3] Besides the Ysam, Yādava appears to have authored at least two other works. Vedānta Deśika, in his subcommentary on Rāmānuja's commentary on the *Bhagavad Gītā*, makes several reference to a commentary on the *Gītā* by Yādava (Singh 1958, 132, 491). According to one of Deśika's citations, Yādava acknowledged only the first fifteen chapters of the *Gītā* as authentic and considered the final three as supplementary chapters containing sundry material.[4] Vedānta Deśika also alludes to a commentary by Yādava on the *Vedāntasūtra*s (Singh 1958, 132). None of these works has been discovered thus far.

From the little we can gather regarding Yādava's theological ideas, it appears that before his conversion he subscribed to some form of nondualist Vedānta that maintained both the oneness of reality and the real existence of the world. In this view, Brahman transforms itself into the world, in the same way as clay is transformed into a pot. Brahman is thus the material cause of the universe. The emergence of the world from Brahman here parallels the evolution of the material world from *prakṛti*, the primal nature, within the Sāṃkhya cosmological system. Yādava's views in these matters fall broadly within the Vedāntic tradition that goes by the name of *bhedābheda* ("nondifference within difference"), a prominent exponent of which

3. Passing references to Yādava's works and philosophy are made by Dasgupta (1922); Singh (1958); and S. M. Srinivasa Chari (1961). P. N. Srinivaschari (1934, 143–54) devotes a full chapter of his book to Yādava's thought. Two articles devoted to Yādava are Varadachari 1959 and Matsumoto 1968.

4. *etena "samāptaṃ pañcadaśe'dhyāye śāstram uttarais tribhiḥ khilādhyāyaiḥ pariśiṣṭā nānādharmā nirūpitā" iti yādavaprakāśakalpanāpi nirastā.* Cited from Singh 1958, 491.

was Bhāskara.[5] As Matsumoto (1968, 21) himself admits, much of the reconstruction of Yādava's thought that he and others have attempted depends on identifying certain opinions refuted by Rāmānuja in his *Vedārthasaṃgraha* and in his commentary on the *Vedāntasūtra*s as being those of Yādava. Rāmānuja himself does not identify his opponent, and their ascription to Yādava is made only by Sudarśana Sūri[6] in his subcommentary written several centuries later. This ascription is by no means certain. There is no doubt, however, that the *bhedābheda* tradition paved the way for the Rāmānuja's theology of *viśiṣṭādvaita* ("distinguished nondualism"). The Śrī-Vaiṣṇava tradition, indeed, claims Bhāskara and Yādava as its spiritual ancestors in their opposition to the absolute monism of Advaita and to its understanding of ascetic renunciation.

The Ysam, written after Yādava's conversion, is very much Vaiṣṇava in orientation, but there is little opportunity in this text to undertake deep philosophical or theological discussions. Nevertheless, in the extensive discussion of the legitimacy of renunciation carried out in the first chapter, Yādava demonstrates his thorough knowledge of Vedic texts and Vedic exegetical principles.

Yatidharmasamuccaya and the Ascetic Literary Tradition

The Ysam falls into the broad genre of medieval Indian literature known as *nibandha*, which is a subcategory of the Brahmanical literature dealing with *dharma*, including religious, civil, and criminal law. The early technical writings on *dharma* (Dharmaśāstras) were eponymous in nature and came to be regarded as sacred texts or *smṛti*. Medieval India produced numerous commentaries on these root texts. The *nibandha*s, on the other hand, were original compositions not directly tied to root texts and dealt either with the entire spectrum of *dharma* or with selected topics. Such topics included criminal law, ordeals, inheritance, pilgrimage, installation of divine images, sacraments, funeral offerings (*śrāddha*), and penances. One topic of specialized *nibandha*s was the *dharma* of ascetics (*yatidharma*).[7] The old-

5. Bhāskara probably lived in the late eighth or early ninth century C.E.; see Raghavan 1967; Srinivasachari 1934.

6. He was an older contemporary of Vedānta Deśika, and Singh (1958, 26) places him in the first part of the fourteenth century.

7. Several of these works have been published, including the Ypra and Ydhs.

est such text that is still extant or regarding which we have some information is the Ysam of Yādava Prakāśa.

Yādava, however, stands within a long tradition of writings on the life, ideals, practices, and rules of Brahmanical ascetics.[8] Between the fifth and third centuries B.C.E., independent texts appear to have been written in the aphoristic *sūtra* style dealing with the rules of mendicant ascetics. The great Sanskrit grammarian Pāṇini, generally assigned to the fourth century B.C.E., refers to such *sūtra*s authored by Pārāśarya and Karmanda.[9] Except for the group of documents commonly called the Saṃnyāsa Upaniṣads (SUS; Olivelle 1992), however, no independent Brahmanical treatise on ascetic life written prior to the Ysam has come down to us. When the ascetic mode of life became incorporated into the Brahmanical *dharma* within the context of the *āśrama* system (Olivelle 1993), rules and regulations governing Brahmanical ascetics became a province of *dharma* and came to be included within the Dharmaśāstras. It is only with the emergence of the *nibandha* genre of *dharma* literature that independent treatises on ascetic life and practices came to be written. The Ysam, therefore, stands at the head of a long line of such texts dealing with all or some aspects of ascetic practice. Most of these texts are still in manuscript and await publication and study (see Kane I, 1091–92, 1139–40).

The Ysam soon assumed an authoritative position in matters relating to ascetic behavior, at least within the Śrī-Vaiṣṇava community. Vatsa Varada, the grandson of Rāmānuja's nephew, writing in the first half of the thirteenth century C.E.,[10] lists Yādava Prakāśa alongside Bhāskara, Maskarin, and Vijñāneśvara as authorities in matters of ascetic law.[11] According to Varada, any text not mentioned by these

8. For more detailed accounts on the history of Brahmanical literature on asceticism, see Olivelle 1992, 11–18, and my introduction to Part 2 of the Ypra, pp. 21–26.

9. *Aṣṭādhyāyī*, 4.3.110–11. For a discussion of these, see Shastri 1972.

10. Dasgupta (1922, 111, 114), I believe, is incorrect when he calls Vātsya Varada the nephew (sister's son) of Rāmānuja. If he was so closely related to Rāmānuja, it is impossible for him to have been the teacher of Ātreya Rāmānuja (1221–95 C.E.), who was Vedānta Deśika's teacher and maternal uncle, or for Deśika to have met Varada in the company of his teacher (Singh 1958, 127). Colophons to several of Varada's work call him instead the grandson of Rāmānuja's sister's son (*bhaginīsutapautra* or *bhāgineyapautra*); see Olivelle 1986, 23. Singh (1958, 132) gives Varada's dates as 1165–1275 C.E.

11. Yls I.78; see also Yls I.1. Maskarin is the author of a commentary on the GDh, and Vijñāneśvara (early twelfth cent. C.E.) commented on the YDh. Kane (I, 37) assigns Maskarin to the period 900–1100 C.E. Yādava's citation of Maskarin (see Ysam 9.81), however, shows that he was a well-known author in the middle of the eleventh century and pushes his date back to at least the first half of that century.

authors is to be considered spurious. A similar claim is made on behalf of Yādava by Vedānta Deśika (Ybh 100, 129; Abh 55). The books by Yādava and Bhāskara are said to contain the elixir that expunges erroneous ways (Abh 29). Deśika claims, moreover, that only Yādava's collection of ascetics laws "is unanimously accepted by the learned, just as the law book of Manu."[12] The comparison with the *Manusmṛti*, of course, is the greatest compliment that one can pay to an author of a treatise on *dharma*.[13]

Medieval works on asceticism, including the Ypra and the Ydhs, frequently cite passages from works identified as *Yatidharmasamuccaya*.[14] I have been unable to trace any of these passages in the Ysam. In all likelihood, several texts bearing the name *Yatidharmasamuccaya* must have existed in medieval India. These citations must be taken from a work (or works) bearing that somewhat common name and originating within the Advaita tradition to which many of the authors who cite it belonged.

Structure and Contents

At the very beginning of his work, Yādava declares that he has "collected all the vedic and scriptural (*smṛti*) passages pertaining to renunciation" (Ch. 1.3). This statement is nothing remarkable, because the Vedas and the *smṛti*s constitute the two authoritative classes of Brahmanical literature. Later in his introductory remarks (Ch. 1.5), Yādava claims to "present systematically the Law of ascetics culled from the Law Books (Dharmaśāstras)." After listing the authors of these books, he goes on to make this somewhat startling proclamation: "The Law that I present here has been gathered solely from those sections of their books devoted to the topic of renunciation and not from other sections of those books or from the Epics and Purāṇas" (Ch. 1.5–10). Yādava apparently saw the Dharmaśāstras as

12. *tatsmuccitasyaiva yatidharmasyādyāpi mānavādivad avigītaśiṣṭaparigrahāt*—"Because only the law of renouncers collected by him is unanimously accepted by the learned, just as Manu's law book and the like" (Ybh 42). Deśika gives this reason to support his thesis that Yādava has not fallen from his caste even though he once discarded his sacrificial string. Yādava regained his purity by performing the appropriate penance.

13. Indeed, Deśika invokes Yādava's authority in matters of ascetic practice on at least two occasions; see below, p. 191.

14. See, for example, Ydhs pp. 25, 32, 85, 95, 98, 124; Ypra 4.67; 19.39; 23.59; 46.32; 53.31; 57.56; 64.7; 69.18.

having greater authority than other types of *smṛti* texts, such as the Epics (*itihāsa*) and the Purāṇas. Surely Yādava was not presenting here a personal preference; he must have been attempting to bolster the authority of the book he was composing. If so, he was probably reflecting a view widespread at least in Yādava's milieu, namely, that the most authoritative statements on *dharma* were contained in the Dharmaśāstras. Another reason to avoid the Purāṇas may have been the bad condition of their manuscripts even during the Middle Ages, a condition that made it easy for sectarian authors to interpolate passages. Vedānta Deśika, for example, accuses his Advaita adversaries of just such corrupt practices:

> There are other passages which are not found in acknowledged Vedas and *smṛti*s. Sinful people, because of their devotion to opinions that accord with their conduct, first interpolate them and then claim to find them in some Purāṇas that are not well known, or whose collections are lost, or whose beginnings and ends are not determined. (Abh 369)

Yādava's comments on the Purāṇas and the Epics, therefore, are significant for the history of the use and acceptance of sacred texts in medieval India (Olivelle 1986, 66–76).

Yādava further states in his introductory remarks that his book consists of eleven chapters and gives a list of the contents of each (1.4–5). By and large the subjects Yādava deals with are ones common to other texts of this genre. There are, however, a couple of exceptions both in what he chooses to include and in what he omits.

In the very first chapter, Yādava discusses whether the *āśrama* of an ascetic is authorized by the Vedas. Most medieval texts of this type deal very briefly with this topic, citing vedic and *smṛti* passages in support of renunciation. Yādava, on the other hand, spends a great deal of time in presenting objections against the legitimacy of renunciation and in refuting them. Indeed, as I have shown in greater detail elsewhere (Olivelle 1993, 237–43), the legitimacy of the renouncer's *āśrama* was never fully resolved within the Brahmanical tradition, and debates on this issue raged on even during the medieval period. Yādava presents the opponent's arguments in great detail. The opponent argues in the traditional manner that there are explicit vedic injunctions regarding procreation and the payment of debts (see Ch. 1.14) that make marriage and domestic life obligatory for all Brahmins and that preclude the possibility of celibate asceticism. He asks whether the ascetic life is intended to procure heaven or liberation. It cannot be the first, because the ascetic life is always discussed within the context of liberation, and it cannot be the second, because liberation is achieved only through knowledge. He also dismisses the objection that the ascetic life is a necessary condition for achieving the liberating knowledge, because even householders are capable of acquiring that knowledge. The conclusion of the opponent is that the ascetic life cannot be a separate *āśrama*; it must, at most, be a special vow performed by very holy householders. In his reply, Yādava distinguishes two types of people: those who devote themselves solely to the discipline of knowledge (*jñānayoga*) and those who pursue both knowledge and activities (*jñānakarmasamuccaya*). The first type of people consists of ascetics; the second, of householders. Vedic injunctions regarding procreation and sacrifice are directed only at the second group. Vedic statements enjoining the pursuit of knowledge, on the other hand, are directed at ascetics and provide the vedic basis for Brahmanical renunciation.

In discussing the age at which a person becomes eligible for renunciation (Ch. 2), Yādava presents the two traditional opinions, the one requiring marriage and the payment of the debts before renouncing and the other permitting renunciation at any time as long as a person is detached from worldly things. Yādava clearly favors the latter position. He dismisses the view of those who restricted renunciation to people who are disqualified from performing rites, such as the blind, the lame, and eunuchs, because those very handicaps would disqualify such people from becoming ascetics.

In discussing the proper time for renunciation, Yādava presents the views of the authors of early Dharmasūtras, such as Āpastamba, Gautama, and Vasiṣṭha, regarding the *āśrama*s. He understands these authors as permitting a young man who has completed his vedic studentship to freely choose one of the four *āśrama*s. This is what I have called in my recent study "the original *āśrama* system." Yādava is one of a handful of medieval theologians to recognize the existence of this original formulation, which regarded the *āśrama*s as permanent and lifelong vocations to be freely chosen by a young adult (Olivelle 1993, 159).

A question that Yādava does not explicitly raise with regard to eligibility (*adhikāra*) is whether renunciation is open to all twice-born classes (*varṇa*) or restricted to Brahmins, although at the very end of Chapter 2 he cites a text that allows only Brahmins to carry the triple staff (2.65). This is an issue that looms large in medieval discussions and is dealt with in almost all Brahmanical texts on renunciation (Olivelle 1993, 190–201). The reason for Yādava's reticence is unclear; he may well have taken for granted that only a Brahmin can be a renouncer. Indeed, when one reads the Ysam carefully it becomes apparent that for Yādava a renouncer is always a Brahmin (see Ch. 6.174 n. 49). He cites, for example, a passage (Ch. 8.45) that prescribes a penance for accepting a staff or a similar article from Śūdras, Vaiśyas, Kṣatriyas, and fallen Brahmins, a prescription that is meaningful only if the renouncer is assumed to be a Brahmin.

In general, moreover, texts on renunciation have extended discussions on the procedure for becoming an ascetic and on an ascetic's funeral. Yādava, on the other hand, has very brief chapters on these topics. It is clear that his priority was not to describe in detail these ritual procedures but rather to focus on the daily and the annual ritual cycles of an ascetic's life. Yādava describes in great detail the daily duties and practices, the care of the articles an ascetic possesses—especially the staff, water strainer, begging bowl, and water pot—and the penances associated with the breach of proper conduct.

Another distinctive feature of Yādava's composition is the fifth chapter, "Principal Activities." Here he presents a twofold classification of all four *āśrama*s, saying that "Manu has declared only a twofold division of people belonging to the four orders of life" (Ch. 5.4). The two types of ascetics in this classificatory scheme are mendicant renouncers (*bhikṣusaṃnyāsin*) and renouncers who abandon vedic rites (*vedasaṃnyāsika*). Indeed, Manu introduces the second category after his treatment of the normal ascetic, even though he does not use the term *bhikṣusaṃnyāsin* for the latter.[15] Yādava, moreover, claims that according to some (and Yādava appears to favor this view), the traditional division of ascetics into four classes—Kuṭīcaka, Bahūdaka, Haṃsa, and Paramahaṃsa—is based on nonvedic texts of Pāñcarātra and Sāṃkhya.

The principal activities discussed by Yādava in Chapter 5 focus primarily on the mendicant renouncer. Ascetics, according to Yādava, engage in two types of activities. One type consists of such ordinary activities as twilight worship, begging, bathing, and purification. These activities outwardly mark a person as belonging to the renouncer's *āśrama*. They do not constitute the essence of that state. The second type of activities is the essential core of a renouncer's way of life:

> Sāṃkhya, Yoga, devotion to Viṣṇu, vigilance, detachment: these are what is essential, while duties other than these are said to characterize it as an order of life. (Ch. 5.23)

15. See MDh 6.86. For a detailed discussion of the *vedasaṃnyāsin* and of Manu's use of the term "*saṃnyāsa*," see Olivelle 1993, 137–42.

By medieval times Sāṃkhya cosmology in some form or another was incorporated into the cosmologies of almost all sects and traditions, including the Vaiṣṇava. Yādava considers it important for an ascetic to acquire a sound knowledge of the Sāṃkhya cosmological categories. Indeed, all the passages cited by Yādava are taken not from Sāṃkhya texts but from dharmaśāstric works. "One should likewise explore," Yādava advises, "also other texts, such as the Epics, the Purāṇas, the legal works of Manu and others, as well as the Vedāntas, to gain an understanding of the cosmic categories, an understanding that is expressed by the term 'Sāṃkhya'" (Ch. 5.46).

In his discussion of Yoga, Yādava cites directly from Patañjali's *Yogasūtras* (Ch. 5.47). Within this discussion Yādava explores both the virtues falling under the first two steps (*yama* and *niyama*) of the yogic path and the meditative exercises proper. In Yādava's scheme, however, yogic meditation is directed at attaining a deep knowledge and love of Viṣṇu.

> A pure yogin abiding in trance, who has cut all ties and become like the spotless sky—his is the highest Vaiṣṇava state.
>
> People who are stainless like pure crystal, bright like the sun, moon, and fire, cross beyond the reach of darkness when they gladden Viṣṇu with the components of yogic discipline.
>
> The fire of yogic discipline burns up all sins of mind, speech, and body committed through ignorance or negligence, as fire burns a bundle of straw. A man of devotion always sees Viṣṇu with the lamp of yogic discipline. (Ch. 5.119–21)

Yādava, anticipating the division of *bhakti* into *saguṇa* and *nirguṇa* that would emerge several centuries later within Vaiṣṇavism, provides a form of yogic meditation for ascetics who find it impossible to meditate on Brahman without attributes (Ch. 5.123). Such a person should focus his mind on the embodied froms of Brahman as Brahmā, Śiva, and Viṣṇu:

> Let him practice these three moments of breath control repeatedly: inhalation, retention, and exhalation. By meditation on Brahmā, Viṣṇu, and Śiva, a man is freed from bondage.
>
> Let him contemplate Brahmā, the Grandfather, as red in color, Viṣṇu as having the color of a blue lotus, and Śiva as white and with three eyes—they are the boats to cross the ocean of saṃsāra.
>
> The ascetic who lives in this manner totally devoted to yogic practice achieves complete detachment and attains the highest state. (Ch. 5.127–29)

The most complete bodily manifestation of Brahman, however, is in the form of Nārāyaṇa, and it is on the mental image of Him that the ascetic should focus his mind:

> Vāsudeva is the highest Brahman, he is the highest self, and he contains the whole universe. They [Brahmā, Viṣṇu, and Śiva] are indeed his embodiments, for they are differentiated by name into three.
>
> Every day let him meditate with devotion on Nārāyaṇa, the creator of the universe, on Hari, the Lord of all creation.
>
> Let him contemplate Him carrying the conch and discus, auspicious with four arms, wearing a crown, bearing the Śrīvatsa mark and the Kaustubha jewel on his breast, and adorned with divine gems.
>
> Let him contemplate Him dressed in yellow, tall in stature, with a face as pleasing as the moon, dark-skinned, lotus-eyed, and wearing earrings shaped like gleaming crocodiles.
>
> Let him contemplate Him as removing afflictions instantly, risen like the cloud at the end of time, shining with all brilliance, holy, and giving protection to those who seek it.
>
> Let him meditate fervently on Nārāyaṇa as lotus-eyed and salubrious, duly worshipping Him in his mind with the sixteen services. (Ch. 5.130–35)

As these passages suggest, Yādava writes from a Vaiṣṇava standpoint. This perspective is evident especially in the third chapter, in which he discusses the insignia of the renunciatory state, such as staff, ochre garment, begging bowl, water pot, and various other articles that an ascetic is expected to carry. Nevertheless, his position on these points of controversy between Advaita and Śrī-Vaiṣṇava ascetic traditions is much less dogmatic than that of later theologians of the two traditions.[16] Only on the question of the sacrificial string does Yādava side totally with the Vaiṣṇava position, condemning the Advaita practice of discarding the string during the rite of renunciation (Ch. 3.9–11). With regard to the topknot, on the other hand, he recognizes two divergent traditions within sacred literature and permits an ascetic the option of either keeping the topknot or shaving it (Ch. 3.9).[17] Yādava

16. In the Advaita tradition an ascetic is expected to discard the sacrificial string and to shave the topknot, a practice condemned by the Vaiṣṇavas. The Vaiṣṇava tradition also expected all types of ascetics to carry triple staffs (that is, three bamboo sticks tied together), whereas in the Advaita tradition the triple staff was limited to the lowest types of ascetics, while the highest type, Paramahaṃsa, carried a single bamboo staff.

17. Here Yādava is following a long-established rule of interpretation according to which an option arises when two texts of equal authority prescribe contrary courses of action. See Olivelle 1993, 74–77, 83–86, 134–36.

is similarly circumspect with regard to the issue of the single versus the triple staff, again permitting a choice between the two types of staff (Ch. 3.60). Nevertheless, he clearly favors the triple staff, calling it more praiseworthy (Ch. 3.9).

In explaining why it is better to carry a triple rather than a single staff, Yādava introduces two somewhat novel hermeneutical principles. He favors the triple staff because it is enjoined in more sacred texts and because it is the more difficult course (Ch. 3.60). The latter principle becomes further refined by later Vaiṣṇava writers. Varada, for example, states that there can be no option between an easy and a difficult course, because nobody would follow the difficult course, thus rendering the texts enjoining it meaningless (Yls I.54; II. 41). This appears to be an extension of the ancient principle that an option arises only when texts of equal authority enjoin different things (GDh 1.4). Here the equality is extended to the relative difficulty of the two courses of action. Vedānta Deśika explicitly ascribes this principle to Yādava Prakāśa (Ybh 134). According to Deśika, when authoritative texts enjoin two course of action, the one difficult and the other easy, the former should be regarded as the principal course and the latter as the secondary (Ybh 135). Thus, in the case of the triple and the single staff, the former is the principal course, which normally should be followed. If, however, a triple staff is not available, the ascetic may use a single staff until he is able to procure a triple staff (Ysam 3.62; Yls II. 36–39; Ybh 138). Yādava used this principle only to declare the difficult course more praiseworthy. In the hands of later theologians, however, it was transformed into a hermeneutical principle for resolving textual conflicts without the need to permit an option.[18]

The Domestication of Asceticism

From the time of the early Upaniṣads, debates that contrasted the ascetic life to the married life of a householder within society were couched in terms of the opposition between their respective geographical locations, the wilderness and the village (Olivelle 1990). The image of the wild in the Indian mind was associated with danger and impurity. Within this contrast the ascetic life is presented as the complete abandonment of all social life. This is no doubt a contrast between two ideal types. Indian ascetic traditions, of course, were never

18. On the increasing distaste within the Brahmanical tradition over permitting choice in matters of *dharma*, see Olivelle 1993, 134–36.

totally asocial or antisocial; even the traditions that departed radically from the Brahmanical mainstream, such as Buddhism and Jainism, maintained strong connections with society and vied with each other for economic and political patronage. Nevertheless, Indian ascetic traditions in their rhetoric, images, and rituals tended to accentuate their separation from familial and social life. I use the term "domestication" to refer to the process whereby that rhetoric and those images and rituals were transformed to reflect the absorption of asceticism at least partially into the life of society.

The Character of Ancient Indian Asceticism

Ascetic traditions entailing life-long celibacy, homeless wandering, and mendicancy emerged in the Gangetic valley at least by the sixth century B.C.E. Although these traditions did not share a uniform ideology, it is clear that they were rooted in a belief system that included the conception of *saṃsāra* (rebirth, life as suffering) and the aspiration for personal liberation. For the most part these traditions were also anti-ritual, at least in the sense that they rejected the Vedic sacrificial ideology and practice. This is the reason why mendicant ascetics of India gave up the use of fire, the principle element of the Vedic sacrifice.

This radical contrast between the vedic religion and the ancient ascetic ideology and practice has prompted scholars to trace the origin of Indian asceticism to non-Brahmanical or even to non-Aryan sources. Belvakar and Ranade (1927, 401), for example, see the emergence of asceticism as a result of the "contact of the Aryans of the Brāhmaṇa period with peoples of a different culture whom they encountered in the course of their march into the interior of India."[19] Bronkhorst (1993) has recently revived this thesis in a somewhat different form by proposing two sources, the one Brahmanical and vedic and the other *śrāmaṇa*, which appears to include both non-Aryan and non-Brahmanical (e.g. Kṣatriya) elements. Bronkhorst's attempted synthesis of the various viewponts on the origin of Indian asceticism is, at least partly, a response to Heesterman's (1964) contention that renunciation is a logical and internal development of the vedic sacrificial theology.

I remain unconvinced by both sides of this argument, not because they do not contain some elements of truth, but because all by and

19. For a more detailed examination of this issue, see Olivelle 1993, 68–70.

large ignore the social and economic factors that underlie the emergence of these new religious forms (see Olivelle 1993, 55–58). That the Indian society in the Gangetic valley was composed of diverse ethnic groups, many of which were of non-Aryan origin, is obvious. It is equally obvious that the religious beliefs and practices of these groups must have influenced the dominant Aryan classes. It is quite a different matter, however, to attempt to isolate non-Aryan traits at a period a millennium or more removed from the initial Aryan migration. The most we can say is that the ascetic traditions contain beliefs and practices not contained in the early vedic literature, and that they are in many ways opposed to the central vedic ideas.

This contrast cannot be reduced to some presumed opposition between Aryan and non-Aryan, or between Brahmanical and non-Brahmanical, or even between orthodox and heterodox. As I have shown elsewhere (Olivelle 1993), the challenges to the traditional vedic views are found across a broad spectrum of religious literature, including some of the most authoritative texts of Brahmanism.

It is this contrast between the vedic and the ascetic, however, on which I want to focus here. Now, ascetic elements are present in almost any religious or cultural institution. Indeed, Harpham (1987, xi) has recently argued that asceticism is not only an invariable constant in all cultures but only the defining element of culture.

> I have begun with the premise that asceticism has, even today, a certain descriptive resonance. While the term can plausibly "cover" early Christianity, the concept of asceticism exceeds the ideological limitations of that culture; it may best be considered as sub-ideological, common to all cultures. In this large sense, asceticism is the "cultural" element in culture; it makes cultures comparable, and is therefore one way of describing the common feature that permits communication or understanding between cultures. As a new computer-literate, I find myself thinking of asceticism as a kind of MS-DOS of culture, a fundamental operating ground on which the particular culture, the word processing program itself, is overlaid. Where there is a culture there is asceticism: cultures structure asceticism, each in its own way, but do not impose it.

Harpham brings new and interesting insights into the nature of both culture and asceticism which permit us to see ascetic elements as part of, rather than as aberrations of, human nature and culture. Nevertheless, a more restrictive definition of asceticism is required if we are to distinguish the ascetic traditions in the strict sense of the term from other aspects of society, culture, and religion. Otherwise, the very term would cease to have any function in describing a particular sort of religious behavior.

It is clear that ascetic elements are present within the vedic religion. Terms such as *śrama* ("toil") and *tapas* ("heat" and "bodily torture") play central roles in the vedic vocabulary; they are essential elements in almost all descriptions of creation and sacrifice. The strictly ascetic tradtions that emerged in India around the sixth century B.C.E., however, cannot be viewed as merely extentions of this vedic asceticism. I want to point out here some of the defining elements of those ascetic traditions that placed them in stark oppositon to vedic ideology and practice.

In India there existed a wide variety of ascetic traditions. Brahmanical taxonomists often reduce this variety to two broad categories. One is the forest hermit, who leaves the physical bounds of society and withdraws from civilized geography into the wild to subsist on forest produce. The other is the world renouncer, who is an itinerant mendicant maintaining by that very practice close contact with the society from which he has cut himself off. I am interested here only in the second, because it is the tradition to which Yādava belongs. Within the context of ancient and medieval Indian asceticism, I offer the following as its defining elements.

1. Cutting social and kinship ties.
2. Living an itinerant life without a fixed home.
3. Mendicancy associated with the abandonment of socially recognized economic activities and the ownership of property, especially of food.
4. Abandoning ritual activities customary within society.
5. Celibacy.

I am not suggesting that these elements were actually present among all ascetics. The reality hardly ever corresponds faithfully to the norm. These, however, are the central elements of ascetic rhetoric, images, and rituals that seek to define this way of life and to contrast it to that of ordinary people of society.

These elements of asceticism stood in sharp contrast especially to the Brahmanical ideology and values. Indeed, the opposition was not so much between the renouncer and the "man-in-the-world," as proposed by Dumont (1960), but between the renouncer and the ideal-typical Brahmin householder and between the respective value systems embodied by the two. The domestication of asceticism I discuss here is concerned exclusively with the ways in which Brahmanism incorporated the renouncer and his values into the framework of its theology, ethics, and legal code.

The *Āśrama* System as a Structure for Inclusion

It has been a common scholarly assumption that the *āśrama* system was created by conservative Brahmins with the intention of resisting the new religious movements and of safeguarding the Brahmanical religion by incorporating the renunciatory life into a scheme that would lessen its impact and reduce or eliminate the conflict between it and the life of the householder. T. W. Rhys Davids's (1903, 249–50) remarks is typical of this scholarly assumption:

> Unable therefore, whether they wanted or not, to stay the progress of newer ideas, the priests strove to turn the incoming tide into channels favorable to their Order. They formulated—though this was some time after the rise of Buddhism—the famous theory of the *Āśramas*, or Efforts, according to which no one could become either a Hermit or a Wanderer without having first passed many years as a student in the brahmin schools, and lived after that the life of a married householder as regulated in the brahmin law-books.

I have shown elsewhere in greater detail (Olivelle 1993) that this assumption is historically untenable. The earliest formulation of the *āśrama* system as we find it in the Dharmasūtras envisages it not as stages of life through which a person passes as he grows old but as four vocations of life, one of which a young adult may freely choose. The authors of this system was certainly not conservative Brahmins but either Brahmanical renouncers or Brahmanical thinkers sympathetic to the renouncer ideology. By creating this novel theological scheme of four *āśrama*s they were attempting to incorporate the ascetic life style into the Brahmanical *dharma*. In other words, we have here an early example of the domestication of asceticism within Brahmanical theology. In the *āśrama* system these theological innovators created a new and bold structure for including within the expanded umbrella of Brahmanical *dharma* an ideology and life style at variance with the vedic value system centered on the married householder.

The domestication of asceticism was carried out in a more thorough way when this original formulation of the *āśrama* system gave way to its classical counterpart. The classical system eliminated choice and selection of an *āśrama*. The *āśrama*s were envisaged instead as stages of a man's life. In youth a person undergoes vedic initiation and begins a period of study in preparation for assuming adult responsibilities. This is the first *āśrama*, that of a student. After completing his studies the young adult gets married and spends the mature years of his life in pursuing the vedic ideals of procreation and sacrifice, engaged in economically and socially productive activities. The two types of ascetic life styles—forest hermit and renouncer—are thus relegated to old age. After a man has completed his familial and social responsibilities he is free to undertake the ascetic modes of life. As the institution of forest hermit became obsolete at least by the early centuries of the common era, renunciation became the mode of life suitable, according to Brahmanical theology and law, for old age and retirement.

Brahmanical hermeneutics was thus able to resolve the opposition between the value systems centered around the renouncer and the householder by showing that they were not truly opposed because they represented the proper *dharma* (the *svadharma*) of people belonging to different age groups.

The Domestication of Asceticism in Yādava

The Brahmanical law books present the renunciatory life (*saṃnyāsa*) as an *āśrama* common either to all Brahmins or to all twice-born classes. In reality, however, the Brahmanical ascetic tradition became organized into monastic establishments divided along sectarian lines at least by the eighth century C.E. Although they all accepted the authority of the rules of ascetic practice formulated in the Brahmanical law books, these sectarian monastic enterprises developed their own distinctive customs. We have seen how the Vaiṣṇava ascetic tradition differed substantially from the Advaita ascetic tradition of Śaṃkara (see Olivelle 1986–87). The Vaiṣṇavas espoused a much less radical form of ascetic life than the Advaita and retained many of the rules and customs of Brahmanical householders. Yādava is one of the oldest representatives of the Vaiṣṇava tradition.

Yādava's work is a fertile ground for exploring the process of domesticating asceticism within the Vaiṣṇava tradition, because the Ysam, more than most other medieval works on asceticism, integrates ascetic life into the normal ritual life of Brahmanism. This integration is evident in the principle clearly enunciated by Yādava at the beginning of the sixth chapter, which deals with daily practices: any practice not mentioned in connection with ascetics should be gathered from corresponding practices of householders or vedic students (Ch. 6.1). Penances for ascetics, likewise, can be gathered from those prescribed for householders (Ch. 10.156). Reading Yādava's work closely, one gets the distinct impression that the Brahmanical ascetic is a very exalted type of Brahmanical householder rather than a figure who contradicts the value system represented by domestic life. Whatever is prescribed for a Brahmin in general applies also to an ascetic. Since the scriptures, for example, prescribe for all Brahmins the sacramental rites (*saṃskāra*) beginning with the impregnation ceremony and ending with cremation, the son of an ascetic is required to perform the cremation of his renouncer father in the appropriate manner (Ch. 11.25).

We see similar subtle changes introduced into the ancient ascetic laws. Two of the most ancient of such rules are the prohibition on the use of fire and on a stable residence outside the rainy season. Ancient texts use the epithet *anagni* "fireless man" with reference to ascetics (ApDh 2.21.10). Yādava, citing a text of Kapila, however, permits an ascetic who is unable to bear the cold to light a fire (Ch. 7.100). The prohibition on staying in one place for more than a few days is repeated in most medieval texts, despite the clear fact that most Brahmanical ascetics, like their Buddhist counterparts, lived in settled monastic communities. The legal fiction of ceaseless wandering is maintained in both Buddhist and Brahmanical codes. Yādava, however, finds a way explicitly to permit permanent residence.

> Unless he is blind, sick, or lame, he should not spend six nights in any one place. If his mind is totally focused on his duties, however, and if he comes from a different region, he may optionally reside in one place all the time. (Ch. 9.9)
>
> He may, indeed, live in one place even outside of the rainy season. (Ch. 9.13)

Ascetics who have achieved eminence in virtue may also live in one place; wandering ceaselessly is obligatory for others:

> If a man is eminent in virtue, however, he may reside in one place until death. Otherwise, he should cultivate the habit of wandering. This is the opinion of the venerable teachers. (Ch. 9.14)

At another place Yādava says that only the old and the weak should live in monastic establishments, whereas the young and the healthy are required to wander (Ch. 6.291–92). Changes in rules brought about for a variety of reasons are often presented, not only here but also in other areas of *dharma*, as exceptions or as intended for emergencies (*āpaddharma*). Such exceptions often became the norm in practice, if not in law.

Beyond the changes we detect in rules and in the way of life, the most interesting aspects of the domestication of asceticism are in the areas of ritual and purity, especially as they relate to the body. Rituals pertaining to the body and the concerns about maintaining bodily purity expressed within these rites have been the focus of serious scholarly attention in recent years.[20] Bodily appearance, movements, and functions—from issues of dress, hair, food, and toilet to those of excrement, sexual fluids, and menstrual discharge—are given culturally and socially determined meanings that are often encoded in rituals and rules of etiquette. This culturally created human body stands as the primary symbol of the social body. The anthropologist Mary Douglas has argued this point cogently and convincingly in many of her writings:

> The body is a model which can stand for any bounded system. Its boundaries can represent any boundaries which are threatened or precarious. The body is a complex structure. The functions of its different parts and their relation afford a source of symbols for other complex structures. We cannot possibly interpret rituals concerning excreta, breast milk, saliva and the rest unless we are prepared to see in the body a symbol of society, and to see the powers and dangers credited to social structure reproduced in small on the human body. (Douglas 1984, 115)

If, with Mary Douglas (1984), we define dirt as matter out of place, then it seems that, at least as far as the social perception of the human body is concerned, dirt gathers predominantly on its margins and in a special way at the openings that let the inside of the body meet the outside, both by letting bodily excreta and fluids flow out and by permitting outside elements—especially food and water—to come inside. The protection of these boundaries has been a major preoccupation of the Brahmanical tradition; maintaining the purity of the body was and continues to be a major element of Brahmanical ritual and morality. Mary Douglas (1982) again has argued, convincingly I believe, that anxiety about bodily margins and the preoccupation with keeping them clean express anxieties about social integrity and concern for maintaining social order. This anxiety and the resultant preoccupation with bodily purity increase with the increase in the perceived threat to the integrity of the social body. As throughout their history the Israelites were a minority threatened with the loss of group identity, so each Hindu caste—especially the Brahmins—was a minority vis-à-vis the larger society. Both the Jews and the Brahmins show a similar anxiety about the body and bodily fluids. The Brah-

20. See Turner 1984 for a detailed bibliography of recent scholarship in sociology and social-anthropology on the cultural construction of the human body. My own views have been strongly influenced by the works of Mary Douglas (especially 1982 and 1984).

min anxiety has to varying degrees pervaded other castes of Indian society.

In Brahmanical ideology the body is by definition a pure structure constantly threatened at its boundaries with impurity both through the discharge of bodily fluids and excrement and from contact with impure substances and individuals. There are thus minute prescriptions regarding the maintenance of bodily purity: when and how to bathe; how to purify after eating, defecating, and urinating, after sexual intercourse and menstruation, and after touching anything or anybody impure; what to eat; from whom to accept food; with whom one can have sexual, social, or physical contact; and so on. These concerns for guarding the bodily boundaries can be translated as concerns for safeguarding the integrity of the Brahmanical social group. Mary Douglas (1982, 14) has posited that the centrality given to ritual activities in a given society increases in direct proportion to the experience of strong and closed social groups:

> The most important determinant of ritualism is the experience of closed social groups. The man who has that experience associates boundaries with power and danger. The better defined and the more significant the social boundaries, the more the bias I would expect in favour of ritual. If the social groups are weakly structured and their membership weak and fluctuating, then I would expect low value to be set on symbolic performance. Along this line of ritual variation appropriate doctrinal differences would appear. With weak social boundaries and weak ritualism, I would expect doctrinal emphasis on internal emotional states. Sin would be more a matter of affect than of transgression; sacraments and magic would give way to direct, unmediated communion, even to the sacralisation of states of trance and bodily dissociation.

The doctrines and practices of at least some forms of early Indian asceticism show clear signs of what Douglas terms the experience of weak social boundaries. In several of these traditions we note a deep aversion to ritual, an emphasis on internal motive as the determinant of virtue and sin, an ethic based on inner virtue rather than on ritual purity or social status, and the exaltation of altered states of consciousness with accompanying methods of mental training. The anti-ritual stance of early asceticism was symbolically expressed in the abandonment of and the refusal to use fire, the primary element of the vedic ritual religion. The focus on the renunciation of fire as the primary element of the ascetic life is evident especially within the Brahmanical ascetic tradition. As I have shown elsewhere (Olivelle 1981), the very term *saṃnyāsa*, which became the most common

Brahmanical term for renunciation, originally referred to the abandonment of the ritual and of ritual accessories, such as the sacred fire.

Ascetic rhetoric and symbols played on the Brahmanical obsession with bodily purity and rituals of purification, especially bathing and washing. Guarding the bodily boundaries and openings implies that the internal structure of the body is pure, just as protecting the boundaries of society makes sense only if that society is regarded as a valuable structure. Ascetic discourse pictures the body as internally and essentially impure and loathsome, making any attempt to protect it from the outside a futile enterprise. Bathing can remove dirt on the skin, but how can one remove the dirt within the body? In a tongue-in-cheek parody of the Brahmanical obsession with bathing, an ascetic text comments on its futility.

> Made with its mother's and father's filth, this body dies soon after it is born. It is a filthy house of joy and grief. When it is touched a bath is ordained.
>
> By its very nature, foul secretions continuously ooze out from its nine openings. It smells foul and it contains awful filth. When it is touched a bath is ordained.
>
> Through its mother the body is impure at birth; in birth-impurity it is born. It is impure also through death. When it is touched a bath is ordained. (*Maitreya Upaniṣad*, in SUS 113–14)

The body is depicted as a bag of skin filled with filth or as a house built with impure materials.

> Lord, this body is produced purely through sexual intercourse and is devoid of consciousness; it is a veritable hell. Born through the urinary canal, it is built with bones, plastered with flesh, and covered with skin. It is filled with feces, urine, wind, bile, phlegm, marrow, fat, serum, and many other kinds of filth. In such a body do I live. (*Maitreya Upaniṣad*, in SUS 108)
>
> Let him abandon this impermanent dwelling place of the elements. It has beams of bones tied with tendons. It is plastered with flesh and blood and thatched with skin. It is foul-smelling, filled with feces and urine, and infested with old age and grief. Covered with dust and harassed by pain, it is the abode of disease. If a man finds joy in the body—a heap of flesh, blood, pus, feces, urine, tendons, marrow, and bones—that fool will find joy even in hell. (NPU 144)
>
> Those who take delight in this collection of skin, flesh, blood, tendons, marrow, fat, and bones, stinking with feces and urine—what difference is there between them and worms? (NPU 160)

The body depicted here is not a single bounded reality whose boundaries are threatened with contamination and need to be carefully protected. It is simply an aggregate of substances that are in themselves impure and loathsome. The body is often likened to a corpse: a corpse lays bare the filth that the living body normally attempts to hide. These filthy substances are contained in a bag of skin with nine openings out of which they continuously ooze. And we call it our body! Only one kind of attitude and feeling is appropriate with regard to such a thing: a feeling of disgust accompanied by a desire to be rid of it.

The Ysam itself contains passages that echo similar attitudes toward the body. That is only to be expected, because Yādava uses freely images and texts from the ascetic literature he inherited. Nevertheless, Yādava's discussion of an ascetic's life provides a sharp contrast to the views expressed in those ascetic texts. He presents that life as being concerned with rituals relating to bodily functions and with the maintenance of bodily purity. A careful reader of Chapters 6 and 10 cannot fail to notice Yādava's attention to every detail of an ascetic's daily rituals, especially of those relating to bodily purity. Purity is clearly the central concern in Yādava's description of an ascetic's day and in his prescription of various penances aimed at restoring lost purity.

We can understand this concern, because one of the central activities of an ascetic is begging food whose purity he is unable to ensure or ascertain. There is, of course, the legal fiction that begged food is by definition pure. As the almsfood is being given, an ascetic should not ponder "whether it is pure or impure" (Ch. 6.110), because "purity and impurity melt away as the almsfood falls into the bowl" (Ch. 6.109). Yet Yādava himself cites text after text where the concern regarding the purity of almsfood is paramount. In general, the ascetic tries to obtain his food from Brahmins:

> He may beg his food from Brahmins, Kṣatriyas, and Vaiśyas. Even among them, one should beg from people of each subsequent class only when those of the preceding class are unavailable. (Ch. 6.105)

He is allowed to beg from Śūdras only if he is unable to obtain food from the upper classes for a whole day, and even then he is expected to perform a penance to regain his lost purity (Ch. 6.106–08). Yādava gives detailed rules as to the people from whom an ascetic should not accept food, and most of these restrictions are related to purity. An ascetic avoids Śūdras, menstruating women, and those fallen from their caste (Ch. 6.129–35). He is expected not to beg from a house that has become impure due to a birth or a death:

> Whether it belongs to a person of one's own lineage or to someone else, a house in which a birth has taken place does not regain its purity until ten days have passed.
>
> Rites for gods, ancestors, and the like are never performed in such a house. Neither should a mendicant beg almsfood there. If he begs, he should observe a lunar fast. (Ch. 6.138–39)

Begging food thus parallels the paradigmatic ritual acts of oblations to gods and ancestors.

Even though this point is never explicitly made, the rules of begging imply that the donor is normally a woman. Accepting food from a woman brings to the forefront another set of concerns regarding purity. The following detailed list of women from whom food should not be accepted exemplifies these concerns:

> A mendicant should not beg almsfood from a naked woman; a virgin; a woman who is pregnant, menstruating, mad, intoxicated, or angry; a woman who is getting ready to eat or who hates her children or husband; a woman who is independent or lives as she pleases; a woman who is without a husband, suffering from leprosy, or blind; a woman who has married a second time or who has been adopted; a woman with loose hair or seated at ease; a lustful woman; a woman astonished; a woman who is deceitful or distressed; a woman of evil conduct; a woman who is sweating or afflicted with a sickness; a shameless woman; a harlot; a tired woman; a servant; a transvestite; a very cruel woman; and a woman who is breastfeeding her baby. (Ch. 6.143–46)

If, despite all his efforts, he finds that the food he is eating is in some way contaminated, penances are prescribed to regain his purity:

> If an ascetic eats food that has been contaminated by dogs, mice, cats, crows, hair, worms, bones, or clothes, he is purified by eating the five products of a cow. (Ch. 10.67)

Concern for purity is also evident in the rituals associated with eating. Before eating an ascetic should wash his hands and feet, making three applications of earth on each; sip water; and sprinkle water on the food while reciting OṂ (Ch. 6.203–06). He should not touch his food with his left hand or, while he is eating, touch his feet, head, or private parts (Ch. 6.207).

Purity is also the central concern in the rites of purification and bathing that Yādava describes in great detail. Immediately after he gets up in the morning, an ascetic goes out to answer the call of nature. Elaborate procedures of purification follow. Here is an example of these rules:

> To start with, we will describe the purification after passing urine. Filling each time the three joints of his fingers with earth, he should clean the pe-

> nis four times, the left hand twelve times, and both hands eight times. Having purified his penis in the manner prescribed after urinating, he should perform the purification of the anus. He should apply first one handful of earth, and half that amount the second and the third time. Applying earth in this manner, he should purify his anus twenty times, his left hand twice that many times, and both hands twenty-eight times. He should clean his feet, as well as his hands, by applying earth three times. Finally, he should sip some water, control his breath three times, and sip water again. If, when earth is unavailable, a person uses sand for purification, then he should apply it twice the number of times prescribed above. A mendicant in good health should not be remiss in his purifications. If he is remiss, he commits a sin. To remove such a sin, he should control his breath three times and sip water again. (Ch. 6.5–6)

Eating and defecating are the two most problematic activities with regard to purity; at these times a person becomes most vulnerable to pollution. These two activities become doubly dangerous when done together, and in this regard the Brahmanical concern appears, at least to the modern eye, to become extreme. Yādava, for example, gives this remedy when an ascetic has a bowel movement or diarrhea while he is eating:

> If it ever happens that a Brahmin has a bowel movement while he is eating, he becomes impure on account of both the remnants of food and the voiding of excrement. How does he purify himself?
>
> He should first perform the purification, then sip water, fast for a day and a night, and finally take a bath. He is then purified by eating the five products of a cow. (Ch. 10.70–71)

After he has finished the purification following his morning toilet, an ascetic is expected to bathe.

> With its nine openings, the body is extremely dirty. Day and night it continuously oozes through them. It is the morning bath that purifies it. (Ch. 6.25)

Unlike ordinary people, ascetics are required to bathe three times a day, in the morning, at noon, and in the evening. In all matters relating to purity and penance, ascetics are expected to do more than laymen. An oft-repeated verse states:

> A man who wants to purify himself should apply earth once on the penis, thrice on the anus, ten times on the left hand alone, and seven times on both hands. This is the purification for householders. Twice that amount is prescribed for vedic students, three times for forest hermits, and four times for renouncers. (VaDh 16.18–19; MDh 5.136–37; ViDh 60.25–26)

The concern for purity extends from the ascetic's body to the articles that he is expected to carry. Great attention is paid especially to the staff. No other article is permitted to come into contact with it, with the exception of the water strainer, which is pure by definition and is normally tied to the top of the staff.

> Let him never tie a loincloth or a waistband to the triple staff. By foolishly tying them to it, one shows disrespect to the triple staff.
>
> If a mendicant carelessly lets his triple staff come into contact with the other staff, he should wash the triple staff with earth and water and control his breath three times. (Ch. 3.68–69)
>
> A mendicant should discard a staff that has come into contact with marrow, urine, excrement, semen, serum, or blood. When it comes into contact with other types of impure substances, it ought to be purified. (Ch. 8.31)

The "other staff" is used to carry articles such as the begging bowl and clothes that have a lower degree of purity. An ascetic should be careful not to let an impure person or animal pass between himself and his staff:

> If a woman or a Śūdra passes between him and his staff, he should control his breath three times. If a donkey or a camel passes between, he should control his breath six times. If a dog, a pig, or an outcaste passes between, he should control his breath twelve times. (Ch. 8.38)

An ascetic is expected to maintain the purity of his other articles as well, especially that of the begging bowl in which he collects his food.

> An ascetic should discard a bowl if it comes into contact with pus, blood, flesh, urine, excrement, semen, tears, or phlegm.
>
> If, while carrying a bowl, he comes into contact with a dog, crow, rat, bull, camel, jackal, monkey, or outcaste, or with a man fallen from his caste, he should discard that bowl. (Ch. 8.29–30)

Examples of this type can be multiplied, such as the fear of the pollution created by involuntary seminal discharge either during the day or in sleep (Ch. 10.89–96) or when worms emerge from a wound in the body (Ch. 10.64) or lice infest the body (Ch. 10.149). The above examples, however, suffice to show the intense ritualization of an ascetic's daily life centered around the protection of his body and his belongings from contamination. This is surely a far cry from the type of ascetic rhetoric that considered the body itself as putrid and a corpse and any effort to purify it as futile.

If we follow Mary Douglas's line of reasoning, the type of social experience underlying medieval asceticism as described by Yādava must have been very close to that of the ordinary Brahmanical community. The ascetic is not an outsider to that community but a significant and integral part of it. The ascetic is not in the wilderness removed from the social group; he has truly reentered the village. This is what I have called the domestication of asceticism. This domestication was more thorough within the devotional (*bhakti*) traditions in general and in the Vaiṣṇava tradition in particular. With its doctrine of total inner surrender to divine love (*prapatti*) and the supremacy of divine grace in the work of human salvation, a householder and an ascetic have equal access to God. Even though Yādava still speaks in hyperbolic terms about the superiority of the ascetic over the householder (see Ch. 6.296–308), the Śrī-Vaiṣṇava tradition would gradually drift away from the centrality assigned to mendicant asceticism. Rāmānuja became an ascetic after he had been married for some time. Less than two centuries later, however, the leadership of his church went to Vedānta Deśika, a proud householder who had a son when he was forty-six years old and maintained a domestic life until his death.

Translation

CHAPTER ONE

The Rule Sanctioning Itinerant Asceticism

1. OṂ—at the time of meditation we hear
   it proclaim Him!
   Vedas, that string of texts, are a ladder
   to reach Him!
   He is Hari!
   In Him we take refuge!
2. Śrī is His wife, the eagle is His banner.
   Lord of the Universe,
   victory is yours!
   Once He took up the ascetic emblem,
   and from heretic assaults He protected
   the Threefold Veda.[1]

3. I, Yādava, have collected all the vedic and scriptural[2] passages pertaining to renunciation, and I am now setting out to compose this "Collection of Ascetic Laws." 4–5. It consists of eleven chapters: Rule, Age of Candidate, Insignia, Procedure, Principal Activity, Daily

1. There appears to have been a myth according to which Viṣṇu, incarnate as a triple-staffed Brahmin renouncer, once protected the vedic tradition from heretical attacks; cf. Ch. 6.303. The historical reference, if any, of this statement, however, is unclear.

2. Throughout this book, I have translated the term "*smṛti*" as "scripture" or "scriptural" and the terms "*veda*" and "*śruti*" as "Veda(s)" or "vedic." The first refers to a variety of traditionally authoritative texts, including the technical literature on ritual and law, the Purāṇas, and the Epics. Yādava, by and large, reserves this term for the Dharmaśāstric texts.

Practices, Proper Conduct, Rules on Insignia, Wandering and Residence, Penances, and Funeral. In it I present systematically the Law of ascetics culled from the Law Books. 6–9. The authors of these Law Books are Manu, Viṣṇu, Yama, Aṅgiras, Vasiṣṭha, Dakṣa, Saṃvarta, Śātātapa, Parāśara, Kātyāyana, Uśanas, Vyāsa, Āpastamba, Bṛhaspati, Hārīta, Śaṅkha, Likhita, Yājñavalkya, Atri, Gautama, Bodhāyana, Dakṣa the Elder, Kāśyapa, Kapila, Kratu, Śāṇḍilya, Jābāla the Elder, Dattātreya, Devala, Gārgya, Vasiṣṭha the Elder, Viśvāmitra, Gālava, Medhātithi, Bharadvāja, Jamadagni, Śaunaka, Paiṭhīnasi, Satyakāma, Vāyu, and so forth. 10. The Law that I present here has been gathered solely from those sections of their books devoted to the topic of renunciation and not from other sections of those books or from the Epics and Purāṇas.

11. To begin with, I will examine whether in fact there exists a rule authorizing renunciation.[3]

Opponent's Position

12. Some claim that there indeed is no such rule, because one is not found in the Veda, and because scriptures that contradict the Veda are without authority. 13. That is the view of Gautama:[4]

> There is, however, only one order of life according to the Venerable Teacher, because the householder's life is expressly prescribed. [GDh 3. 36]

3. It is a basic assumption in Brahmanical theology and exegesis that there has to be a specific and identifiable vedic rule authorizing a given practice or rite for it to be considered part of *dharma*. Regarding the long-standing controversy on the legitimacy of ascetic and celibate modes of life, see Olivelle 1993.

4. For a detailed discussion of Gautama's and Bodhāyana's views on the orders of life, see Olivelle 1993, 83–91. The basic argument of both is that only the householder's life is explicitly prescribed in currently available vedic texts ("express vedic texts": see Ch. 1.16). It is a well-known principle of Brahmanical hermeneutics that the Veda is the supreme authority in matters of *dharma*. Other scriptures (*smṛti*) are considered authoritative because they are, at least in principle, based on the Veda. An express vedic text (*pratyakṣaśruti*) is a vedic passage that is preserved within a vedic school (*śākhā*) and available for examination. A purported scriptural (*smṛti*) passage that contradicts such a text is judged null and void. If no express vedic text exists to support a scriptural statement, then the latter retains its authority and is supposed to be based on a lost or unavailable vedic text. In such cases a vedic text is presumed—or more technically, inferred—to exist, although it is currently unavailable. Such a presumed vedic text—technically called *anumitaśruti* or "inferred vedic text"—is never allowed to contradict an express vedic text. Since the acceptance of celibate orders of life contradicts the vedic injunction to marry and to procreate, Gautama and Bodhāyana argue, scriptural passages authorizing such states are without authority.

14. Bodhāyana states:

Some maintain that there is a fourfold division of this very Law.

> Four [paths leading to the gods traverse between heaven and earth. Place us on that among them, all you gods, which will bring us unfailing prosperity]. [TS 5.7.2.3]

This text has only an invisible purpose[5] and, therefore, refers to categories of rites, namely, vegetable offering, soma offering, animal offering, and offering with a ladle.

Now, these orders are student, householder, forest hermit, and wandering ascetic. A student serves his teacher until death. A forest hermit kindles his fire according to the procedure for ascetics[6] and lives in the forest, conducting himself in accordance with the Book on Hermits,[7] eating roots and fruits, and practicing austerities. He should bathe at dawn, noon, and dusk, and subsist on wild produce.[8] He may also subsist on almsfood, but he should never enter a village. Wearing matted hair and clothed in bark or deer skin, he shall not eat what has been stored for over a year.

5. This passage from the BDh differs considerably from the critical edition. That edition here reads *adr̥ṣṭatvāt*, which according to Bühler and the commentator, Govinda, means "Because no other meaning is to be found." This, according to Bodhāyana, is the reason for interpreting the vedic text "Four paths leading to the gods . . ." (TS 5.7.2.3) as referring to the four types of sacrifices and for rejecting the interpretation made by the proponents of the system of four orders, according to whom the "four paths" refer to the four orders of life. The variant reading recorded by Yādava appears, on the contrary, to be a reference to the well-known principle of Brahmanical hermeneutics that the Vedas, and therefore *dharma*, must always have an invisible purpose or aim; their results are manifested after death. According to this interpretation, Bodhāyana argues against the opponent's interpretation because the vedic text, having by definition an invisible purpose, can refer only to sacrifices. The implication appears to be that the various modes of life subsumed under the four orders serve only worldly purposes. This appears also to be the point made a little later on with the expression "*dr̥ṣṭārthatvāt* ", "For they have a visible purpose."

6. Technically called *śrāmaṇaka*, this is a special ritual procedure for establishing a sacred fire before a forest hermit leaves for the forest. A version of this procedure is given in the VaiDh 2.1. The fire of a hermit itself is often referred to as "Śrāmaṇaka fire", see VaiDh 2.1–5.

7. Bühler, following Govinda, takes "*vaikhānasaśāstra*" to be a treatise composed by the sage Vikhanas, regarded as the founder of the institution of forest hermits. I prefer to translate this expression as referring merely to a treatise on hermits. It is also possible that it refers to such treatises in general rather than to a specific one.

8. Literally, "what is not grown in a village." The total physical separation of forest hermits from society is highlighted by their abstention from using anything mediated by civilization, whether it be cultivated food or manufactured clothing. One law book prohibits them from "stepping on plowed land" (GDh 3.32), the prime symbol of civilized geography.

> A wandering ascetic should forsake his kin and wander about without possessions. After going to the wilderness, he should shave his head completely or keep only his topknot, wear just a loincloth, and reside in one place during the rains. Clothed in an ocher garment, he should beg for food when pestles have been set aside and embers extinguished, when the people have finished their meals and removed the dishes. He shall not hurt any creature by verbal, mental, or physical acts of hostility. He should carry a water strainer for use in purifications and use for ritual purposes only water that has been drawn out.[9] They proclaim: "We stick to the middle, rejecting the fire sacrifices to the gods and separating ourselves from both sides."[10]
>
> There is, however, only one order of life according to the Venerable Teacher, because a person does not bear children in the others. In this connection, they quote:
>
> > There was once a demon named Kapila, the son of Prahlāda. It was he who made these divisions in his effort to compete with the gods. A wise man, therefore, should pay no heed to them.
>
> For they have a visible purpose. On this point, when they quote[11]

9. Flowing water, such as that of a river, is always pure and can be used without straining. Stagnant water (for example, in wells and ponds) must be drawn out in a vessel, strained with a cloth, and poured from the vessel to make it run before it can be used for ritual purposes. See Ch. 6.41–44.

10. "We" probably refers to wandering ascetics. The meaning appears to be that ascetics take to their path with this type of belief or proclamation. The meaning of "both" (sides, ends, or extremes?) and "the middle" is unclear, however. Govinda, followed by Bühler, takes "both" to mean this world and the next and "middle" to mean Brahman. In a forthcoming article entitled "The Earliest Brahminical Reference to Buddhism?" Richard Gombrich has suggested that the middle may be a reference to the Buddhist "middle way" (the critical edition of BDh reads, in fact, *madhyamaṃ padam*, middle state or path). It may, however, be possible to interpret this difficult phrase within the context of the RV (10.71.9) passage cited later. There, people who do not participate in ritual are said to "proceed neither to this side nor to the other side." The meaning, at least within Bodhāyana's understanding of this text, appears to be that such people do not gain prosperity in this world or in heaven after death, two major goals of the vedic ritual. In this light, one may see the ascetics as rejecting both those goals in favor of the "middle," which may refer to the goal of final liberation.

11. See n. 5. The line of Bodhāyana's argument is that when supporters of celibate asceticism cite vedic proof-texts such as this from the TB, a passage that is also cited in the BaU 4.4.23 in support of Upaniṣadic doctrines, the upholders of marriage and ritual religion can quote many other texts that argue against celibacy. This is an excellent example of the internal controversies regarding proper belief and proper action that went on within the Brahmanical tradition itself. The targets of the legal authors' critique were mainly their colleagues who espoused different and often ascetic ideas, rather than Buddhists and other heretics, as it is often supposed.

> This eternal greatness [of a Brahmin is neither increased nor reduced by rites. The self knows that greatness of his. When someone knows it, he is not stained by evil deeds]. [TB 3.12.9.7–8]

one should reply by quoting

> At the time of death [a man without the knowledge of the Veda does not turn his mind to that great all-perceiving self], set ablaze by whose power the sun gives warmth [and a father in his son is provided with a father from generation to generation].[12] [TB 3.12.9.7]
>
> These people who proceed neither to this side nor to the other side, who are neither Brahmins nor participants at Soma sacrifices—they make use of speech in evil ways and weave their web in ignorance.[13] [RV 10.71.9]
>
> Through offspring, O Fire, may we obtain immortality. [RV 5.4.10]
>
> At his very birth a Brahmin is born with three debts: a debt of vedic studentship to the seers, a debt of sacrifice to the gods, and a debt of offspring to the forefathers. [TS 6.3.10.5]

There are innumerable such statements on people's association with debts, as well as direct prohibitions.[14] [BDh 2.11.9–33]

15. Āpastamba says:

> Study of the triple Veda, studentship, procreation, faith, austerity, sacrifice, gift giving—we are with those who perform these. Those who commend other things will become dust and perish. [ApDh 2.24.8]

16. Therefore, no celibate orders of life exist, because they are not sanctioned in the Veda and because scriptural texts lose all authority when they contradict an express vedic text [see Ch. 1.13 n. 4].

12. The statement about the father becoming a father (*pitṛmān*) through his son is not altogether clear. It is clear, however, that it resonates with other vedic statements regarding the importance of procreation. In another place the TB (1.5.5.6) affirms that "in your offspring you are born again; that, O mortal, is your immortality." The *Aitareya Āraṇyaka* (2.5) claims that a father is born a second time in his son, and the *Aitareya Brāhmaṇa* (7.13.1) asserts that a father attains immortality when he sees the face of his living son. The point of all this for Bodhāyana's argument is that the celibate state authorized by the system of the orders of life (*āśrama*) goes against explicit vedic statements on the necessity of begetting children, especially sons.

13. The meaning of this very difficult verse is unclear, especially the last phrase containing the hapax legoumenon *sirī*. The reason for its citation here, however, is clear. The verse, as Bodhāyana understands it, condemns those who reject ritual practices and use speech (*vāc*), probably meaning the vedic texts, in evil ways. This, according to Bodhāyana, is precisely what the creators of the *āśrama* system did by using vedic proof-texts in support of their theory.

14. The vedic passages dealing with debts implicitly prohibit celibate states of life. Bodhāyana, further, affirms that the Vedas contain injunctions that directly and explicitly prohibit such modes of life. This last statement does not appear in the critical edition of the BDh.

Objection

17. Now someone may object that there indeed exists an express vedic text among the followers of the White Yajurveda:

> Desiring this very world, wandering ascetics depart for the ascetic life. [BaU 4.4.22]

And also:

> Eschewing erudition, therefore, let a Brahmin live like a simpleton. Eschewing both erudition and simplicity, then, he becomes a sage. [BaU 3.5.1]

18. That text points out also the conduct:

> On knowing this, indeed, the people of old did not wish for offspring, for they thought: "Our self is our world; so why should we need offspring?" [BaU 4.4.22]

And also:

> They did not offer the daily fire sacrifice. [?]

Reply

19. We answer this objection with a question: is itinerant asceticism enjoined for the benefit of the agent or, like rites such as holding the hand, for the benefit of some other ritual act?[15] If, on the one hand, it is for the agent's benefit, then, according to the maxim "It should be heaven," its purpose has to be either heaven or something else.[16] Now, its purpose cannot be heaven, because that would negate its inclusion within the subject of liberation, for obviously every treatise that enjoins itinerant asceticism does so exclusively within the section devoted to the subject of liberation. Consequently, we are compelled to affirm some degree of correlation between it and the subject of lib-

15. Brahmanical hermeneutics divides all ritual acts into those that directly benefit the ritual actor (*puruṣārtha*) and those that are required only by the rite itself and therefore perform a merely ritual purpose (*kratvartha*). In the example alluded to, the marriage ceremony as a whole serves the purpose of the ritual actors—the bride and groom—but the groom's particular act of taking the bride's hand serves a merely ritual purpose. For this hermeneutical principle, see PMS 4.1.2. In this entire discussion by Yādava, the terms for asceticism and renunciation (*pārivrajya, saṃnyāsa,*) are taken to refer directly to the rite for becoming an ascetic rather than to the ascetic life in general. It is only within this context that the analogy to other vedic rites makes sense.

16. This maxim deals with an abstruse exegetical principle spelled out in PMS 4.3.7.13–16. Simply stated, the maxim asserts that the single goal of the various rites prescribed in the Veda is heaven. If we follow this maxim, then the rite of renunciation—if it qualifies as a vedic rite—should have heaven as its goal. If not, then the opponent has the burden of presenting something else as its specific goal.

eration. It is impossible, however, to make such an assertion, because the Vedas clearly teach that liberation is achieved only through knowledge:

> Upon knowing him in this manner, one transcends death. There is no other path along which to travel. [VS 31.18]

> Sacrificial presents do not reach there, nor do those who practice austerities but lack knowledge. Only through knowledge does a man reach that place where desires are vanquished. [SB 10.5.4.16]

20. Now, some claim that itinerant asceticism is enjoined as a necessary adjunct to the acquisition of knowledge. That is not true. Since the acquisition of knowledge is open to householders as well, it is improper to assume that there is an injunction establishing a separate order of life for that purpose. Even if we were to so assume, it would not establish a separate order of life. On the contrary, it would only institute a particular vow called "itinerant asceticism" intended exclusively for householders, in a manner similar to the vow of maintaining three sacred fires.[17] And we understand it to be a particular observance entailing the abandonment of attachments, an observance that is not incompatible with the household life one has already undertaken. Practices found in the scriptural texts are not to be accepted when they contradict the Veda. The very term "itinerant asceticism," moreover, is not noted elsewhere as referring to a separate order of life, for if it were, that order would be rendered nonvedic. So we must conclude that this vedic text contains only an illustrative reference[18] to itinerant asceticism, an institution well known in the scriptures, and that the intention of that text here is only to praise knowledge—saying, in effect, that knowledge is so great that by its power people do not fall into sin even when they relinquish rites that have been enjoined on them.

17. Three sacred fires are required for the performance of several vedic sacrifices. Although all Brahmins were expected ideally to maintain all three fires continuously in their homes, from early times on only exceptional people who were professional priests did so. Such persons were referred to by the technical term "*āhitāgni*." By the middle ages this practice appears to have become so rare as to be considered a special and extraordinary vow. According to the argument of Yādava's hypothetical adversary, renunciation should be considered a similar vow that exceptional householders may undertake voluntarily.

18. The reference is to the texts of the BaU that the opponent had cited in support of renunciation as constituting a separate order of life; see Ch. 1.17–18. "Illustrative reference" (*anuvāda*) is a technical term in vedic exegesis and refers to statements that have no injunctive power of their own but merely repeats by way of illustration or commendation rules that have already been laid down. The opponent's intent is to deny any injunctive force to this vedic text with regard to renunciation.

21. Thus, some teachers hold that there is no order of life called itinerant asceticism, because [a] there is no exclusive vedic observance that is not open to householders and constitutes a special order of life, an observance that would parallel, for example, the daily fire sacrifice,[19] and [b] customs such as begging for food are just elements of good conduct, in much the same way as twilight worship and the like, and as such they are intended to promote observances that do constitute an order of life and are not observances that could on their own constitute an order of life.

Author's Position

22. To all this we reply. There is an exclusive observance known as the yoga of knowledge. The following vedic text, accordingly, notes at the outset the rites beginning with "truth" and ending with "mental,"[20] goes on to prescribe renunciation: "They say that renunciation, therefore, surpasses these austerities" [MNU 538], and finally enjoins the yoga of knowledge as what is expressed by the term renunciation: "One should attach oneself to the self" [MNU 540]. Now, the yoga of knowledge consists in the sole pursuit of knowledge. Such a pursuit, evidently, is not possible for householders, because they are required to perform in addition rites such as the daily fire sacrifice. Only the yoga of rites, consequently, is applicable to them. Now, the yoga of rites consists in the simultaneous pursuit of both knowledge and rites, from which pursuit its practitioners obtain liberation. Wandering ascetics, on the other hand, attain liberation solely through the yoga of knowledge. Because they do not perform rites, therefore, the same text in a subsequent passage shows how they accomplish the ritual and prescribes that a wandering ascetic should carry it out every day without fail: "In the case of a man who knows the sacrifice in this manner, [his self is the sacrificer, faith is his wife, his body is the fire

19. The daily fire sacrifice (*agnihotra*) is both a vedic observance and a practice that is meant exclusively for householders. The argument here is that such an exclusive practice meant solely for renouncers is not found in the Veda.

20. The reference is to section 505–15 in the MNU. These eleven statements define the "ultimate" (*param*) progressively as truth, austerity, control, tranquility, generosity, virtue (*dharma*), procreation, fires, fire sacrifice, sacrifice, and mental (offering).

wood . . .]."[21] This is not merely a laudatory statement but a true injunction, because it has no precedent.[22]

23. Is it not true that even wandering ascetics perform rites such as the twilight worship? Certainly, but they are customary practices, and as such they are performed solely to promote the duties of one's order of life and not to obtain liberation. Only the yoga of knowledge aims at liberation. Practices such as twilight worship foster that yoga, because, as stated in the following scriptural passages, a person who does not perform the twilight worship is not qualified to perform such yoga:

> A man who does not perform the twilight worship is always impure and is unfit to perform any rite.

And:

> The Vedas do not cleanse a man who pays no heed to good conduct.

We will point out, moreover, that practices such as silent prayer, austerity, and begging are included within restraints and constraints.[23] Now, all branches of learning recognize that restraints, constraints, and the like are elements of yoga. Those practices, therefore, must also be included within the yoga of knowledge.

24. It is thus established that the yoga of knowledge pertains to wandering ascetics, while the yoga of rites pertains to householders. The Veda accordingly declares that a person can attain immortality only by abandoning rites:

21. This long passage (MNU 543–50) is an extensive allegory of the sacrifice that a renouncer performs internally. At this sacrifice his own body, bodily functions, and the act of eating are homologized with the various elements of the sacrifice. Such a renouncer performs a continuous and daily sacrifice by his very existence and by the daily activities he performs.

22. Here we encounter a bit of abstruse hermeneutical ratiocination. The issue addressed is whether the MNU passage cited here regarding the internal sacrifice has true injunctive power or is merely a laudatory statement. The latter type of vedic statements falls under the category known as *anuvāda*, or illustrative statements (see Ch. 1.20 n. 18). These are not injunctions in their own right but are authoritative only because they refer to *already-established* injunctions. The author denies that the passage in question can be such a noninjunctive statement by saying that it has no precedent, i.e., that there is no previously established injunction of which it can be an illustration or praise. Consequently, it must be what Brahmanical hermeneutics calls an "original injunction" (*apūrvavidhi*), that is, an injunction that prescribes a practice for the first time.

23. Restraints (*yama*) and constraints (*niyama*) are the first two steps of the eightfold yogic path: see Ch. 5.47f. The author wants to point out that the common practices of renouncers, such as begging for food, are in fact part and parcel of their yogic endeavor and are therefore also a part of their yoga of knowledge.

> Not by rites, not by offspring, and not by wealth—but by renunciation did some people attain immortality. [MNU 227]

And also:

> Firmly grasping the import of Vedāntic wisdom, their hearts purified by the practice of renunciation, all these ascetics attain at the end of time in the world of Brahmā final liberation from the highest immortality.[24] [MNU 229–30]

The Blessed Vāsudeva, likewise, declares:

> [I have formerly taught, my dear, a twofold method of perfection:] the yoga of knowledge for followers of Sāṃkhya and the yoga of rites for yogins. [BhG 3.3]

25. Consequently, because an exclusive practice does exist [see Ch. 1.21 n. 19], we posit the existence of an order of life called "itinerant asceticism" that is sanctioned by the Veda. Because they are based on the vedic texts providing that sanction, moreover, the scriptural passages on this topic retain their authority. Now, practices connected with this order are not appropriate for householders, because, in the statement "They beg for their food" [BaU 4.4.22], the Veda enjoins on all ascetics the abandonment of property.[25]

It is established, therefore, that itinerant asceticism is a clearly distinct order of life.

26. That ends the first chapter, entitled "The Rule Sanctioning Itinerant Asceticism," of the *Collection of Ascetic Laws* composed by Yādava Prakāśa.

24. The meaning of this phrase is unclear. It may mean that these ascetics first attain the world of Brahmā, defined here as "highest immortality," and from there are finally liberated (*mokṣa*) at the end of time. This verse occurs also in the *Muṇḍaka Upaniṣad* (3.2.6) and in the *Kaivalya Upaniṣad* (1.4), where the reading is *parāmṛtāḥ* (this reading is also found in some recensions of the MNU). The translation thus would be ". . . at the end of time, being supremely immortal, attain final liberation in the world of Brahmā."

25. The argument is that begging is enjoined on all wandering ascetics. Begging implies abandoning all possessions. Such an abandonment is impossible for householders, both because of family responsibilities and, more importantly from a hermeneutical standpoint, because their obligation to perform rites requires that they possess the wealth needed to perform them. Consequently, the *dharma* of renouncers is exclusively theirs and cannot be practiced by householders. This supports the author's claim that renunciation constitutes an order of life distinct from that of the householder.

CHAPTER TWO

Age of Eligibility of a Candidate for Itinerant Asceticism

1. We will now consider the candidate's age of eligibility.

Renunciation after Marriage

2. According to one opinion, itinerant asceticism is permitted only after a person has lived as a forest hermit and not while a person is still a vedic student. 3. This view is supported by the following vedic texts:

> After giving to the teacher a gift that would please him, let him not cut off his line of offspring. [TU 1.11.1]
>
> 4. At his very birth a Brahmin [is born with three debts]. [TS 6.3.10.5: see Ch 1.14]
>
> Procreation is the very foundation. Spinning out well the thread of progeny, a man becomes free from his debt to the forefathers. [MNU 525]

5. Manu, likewise, states:

> Only after paying his three debts should a man set his mind on renunciation.[1] Should he take to renunciation without paying them, he will fall.[2] [MDh 6.35]

6. Yājñavalkya says:

> No one but a man who has studied the Veda, recited silent prayers, fathered sons, distributed food, established the sacred fire, and offered sacrifices according to his ability may set his mind on renunciation. [YDh 3.57]

1. The term "*mokṣa*" (lit., "liberation") in Manu and in Yājñavalkya (below, Ch. 2.6) refers specifically to the renunciatory mode that constitutes the fourth order of life devoted exclusively to the pursuit of personal liberation. For an extensive discussion of the meaning of this term in Manu, see Olivelle 1993, 137–42.

2. The meaning of "fall" here (and in similar co ntexts elsewhere) is not clear. It may refer to the falling into hell after death, to the fall from caste, or more generally to falling into a state of sin.

7. Śaṅkha and Likhita state:

> After he has lived as a forest hermit and has reached an advanced age, a man may freely take to itinerant asceticism.

8–10. Medhātithi says:

> Detached from ties to sons, wife, home, fields, cows, gold, and the like, as well as from human and divine pleasures revealed in the Vedas; freed from sin by reciting the Vedas and by performing sacrifices and austerities; with his heart made pure and his senses subdued through religious practices carried out over many lifetimes; and counseled by the Epics, Purāṇas, and the Veda—he strives after the highest state. Because he strives, he is called an ascetic.[3] Only such an ascetic attains this highest bliss, and no one else.

Renunciation Permitted at Any Time

11. Some, on the other hand, are of the opinion that a person may take to itinerant asceticism freely either while he is a vedic student or from home or the forest. 12. This position is supported by a vedic passage from the *Jābāli:*

> After completing his vedic studies, he should become a householder. After he has been a householder, he should become a forest hermit. After he has been a forest hermit, he should depart for the ascetic life. Or rather, he may depart for the ascetic life while he is still a vedic student, or from home or the forest. [JU 64]

13. Yama says:

> After he has observed his vedic vow,[4] a learned Brahmin who is impartial toward all creatures, both the mobile and the immobile, may devote himself to renunciation [see Ch. 2.5 n. 1].
>
> 14. Or else, a householder who has fathered sons and subdued himself and his senses, who yearns not for any pleasure, and who has done all he has to do may become a wandering ascetic.

15. We gather from this passage that, if someone is a vedic student, he should depart for the ascetic life only after he has completed his vow; if he is a householder, he should depart only after he has fathered a son—because it was already stated, ". . . one who has performed sac-

3. The author derives *yati* ("ascetic") from *yatana* ("striving"). The etymological connection between the two is uncertain, but it was a common practice in ancient India for an author to use such phonetic similarities to point out what he may have regarded as the essential nature of some institution or practice.

4. The vedic vow refers to the period of vedic studentship following a boy's vedic initiation.

rifices, after drawing his sacred fires into his heart . . .";[5] and if he is a forest hermit, he should depart only after he has performed austerities. This interpretation should be applied to what follows as well.[6] This is also the object of Manu's statement: "Only after paying his three debts . . ." [see Ch. 2.5]. 16. Some declare:

> After he has truly come to know the highest Brahman, a vedic student, a widowed householder, or a forest hermit should give up attachments and become a wandering ascetic.

17. From this passage we gather that, if he is detached, itinerant asceticism is open to a widowed householder even before he has completed such duties as fathering a son. 18. Bṛhaspati says:

> Seeing that saṃsāra is without any substance and longing to see the true substance,[7] a man imbued with deep detachment should depart for the ascetic life even before he has married.
>
> 19. Or someone may do so after he has fathered children and offered a variety of sacrifices, while another may do so after his "half-body" has died, and yet another from the forest.

20. "Half-body" means wife, according to the statement:

> When a man's wife drinks liquor, half his body dies. [VaDh 21.15]

and according to the vedic text:

> The wife is a full half of a man's body. [TS 6.1.8.5]

21–24. Śaṅkha states:

> Having thus spent some time in the forest, a twice-born man should enter the celibate order of life.[8] Even a vedic student may do so, however, if he has attained a high intensity of detachment by his knowledge of various Upaniṣads; if he has withdrawn all his senses and keeps them far from sensual objects; if he finds delight only in himself; if with his mind he

5. It is unclear where this statement was already made. No manuscript records it in any other section of the work. It may well refer to that part of Yama's text which Yādava does not include in the citation made here. Yādava may just be assuming that his readers are aware of this passage.

6. This means that when a text permits a student, householder, or forest hermit to renounce, we should assume that its author means that such people are eligible to renounce only when they have completed the duties of their respective states.

7. There is a play here on the Sanskrit word "*sāra*" ("pith" or "substance"). Saṃsāra, if one ignores the nasal, can mean "with substance." In reality, however, saṃsāra is *asāra* (or *niḥsāra*), that is, "without substance." The true substance that he seeks is Brahman; see also NPU 139. This is another example of the phonetic etymology I commented on in n. 3.

8. The expression "*brahmāśrama*" may also mean the order devoted to (acquiring the knowledge of) Brahman. In either case, it clearly refers to the last order of life, i.e., renunciation.

has vanquished his adversaries; if he has got hold of his self and keeps it securely fastened by repeatedly engaging in yogic practices; if he has banished all attachments; and if he adheres strictly to his vow. Or even a twice-born householder, if he possesses the above qualities, may enter the celibate order of life after he has offered a sacrifice to Prajāpati, given all his possessions as a sacrificial gift to the priests according to the prescribed rules, and deposited his sacred fires in himself.

Renunciation before Marriage Only for the Handicapped

25. In this manner, some vedic and scriptural texts advocate itinerant asceticism directly from vedic studentship, while others permit it only after a man has paid his debts and fulfilled other similar obligations. Given the resultant contradiction,[9] some argue that the vedic and scriptural statements advocating renunciation directly from vedic studentship are made with reference to people such as the blind and the lame who are disqualified from performing rites. 26. This is supported by Likhita:

> As a result of merits he has accumulated over ten million lifetimes or by divine intervention, a man may become detached and display a strong yearning for Brahman.
>
> 27. After he has learned the true meaning of the Veda, it may become impossible for such a man to live at home. So he may depart for the ascetic life either while he is a student or, when he is old, from home or the forest.

9. The contradictions that result when vedic or scriptural texts prescribe mutually exclusive actions provided much of the grist for the hermeneutic mill of Brahmanical exegetes. Briefly, the hermeneutic rules provided three avenues to resolve contradictions: (a) A person could show that one of the statements in question is less authoritative than the other, either because one is vedic and the other is not (see Ch. 1.13 n. 4), or because there is some doubt regarding the injunctive power of one (see Ch. 1.20 n. 18). According to a well-known exegetical maxim, only statements of equal authority that contradict each other's provisions can give rise to an option (GDh 1.4). (b) One could show that the contradiction is only apparent by demonstrating that the provisions of the two have in view two different groups of individuals or two different periods of the same individual's life. This is called "restrictive option" (*vyavasthitavikalpa*), even though there is no true option here at all. This is by and large the preferred method of conflict resolution in Brahmanical hermeneutics (see Ch. 2.28 n. 10) and the one advocated by those who would restrict renunciation to ritually handicapped people. (c) When the first two avenues fail, the contradiction between equally authoritative texts creates an option. An individual may choose to follow either one. In the discussion below, and in general throughout the book, we will see these methods of conflict resolution used by various factions to buttress their own positions and to invalidate those of their opponents.

28. A young and healthy man should live diligently as a householder, while the blind, the lame, the old, and lepers should resort to asceticism.[10]

Renunciation before Marriage for Detached People

29. Others, however, argue as follows: "Should we rather not assume that there is no real contradiction in either the vedic or the scriptural passages? Unable as he is to undertake itinerant asceticism, why should not a man who is not detached become a householder? For surely it is impossible for a man who is not detached to undertake itinerant asceticism." 30. Their position is supported by Dakṣa:

> Even those beings who are endowed with the highest virtue[11] fall under the control of sensual things. How much more, then, creatures with paltry virtue? And need we even talk about human beings?
>
> 31. Only a man whose passions have been extinguished, therefore, should take up the staff.[12] Others do not have the capacity to do so, attracted as they are to sensual things.
>
> 32. There are a lot of twice-born men who make a living by using the emblem of the triple staff. According to scripture, however, a man who does not know Brahman is not worthy of the triple staff.

33. Likhita:

> After a twice-born man has performed the rite at which he renounces all things, if he returns to the world, the king should brand him with a dog's paw and make him a slave.
>
> 34. A man should renounce, therefore, only after he has first examined the purity of his heart for a long time and ascertained that his mind will not waver from the Law.

10. The first two verses of this quotation appear to contradict the view they are expected to support. If we were to argue in the manner of a Brahmanical exegete, however, we could take the last verse as qualifying the injunction that permits a detached person to renounce either before or after marriage. Thus, a detached man should get married if he is young and healthy, while he may renounce if he is old or handicapped. The option given in the injunction is thus not a true option, since the two alternatives refer not to the same but to different individuals. See the alternative (b) in the previous note.

11. The term "*sattva*" is used in Sāṃkhya cosmology as the highest of the three strands (*guṇa*), which constitute material reality. The term here may have a cluster of meanings, including goodness, power, wisdom, and purity. It is unclear who these beings are, but their opposition to humans suggests that they are supernatural beings such as gods and seers.

12. This is a reference to the renunciatory rite at which the ascetic takes a bamboo staff as the emblem of his new state. See Chs. 3 and 4.

35. Yama:

> Only when a man has quenched his passion and lust, attained perfect tranquillity, and become totally intent on Brahman does he become qualified to be a renouncer. Others do so just to gain a living.

36. There is no justification, moreover, for assuming that the vedic passage prescribing immediate renunciation[13] is directed at those who are disqualified, because later on in the following passage the same text prescribes it separately for them:[14]

> Further, regardless of whether he has taken the vow or not, whether he has graduated or not, and whether he has a sacred fire or not, [let him renounce on the very day that he becomes detached].[15] [JU 64]

37. Jābāli the Elder states:

> Regardless of whether he has taken the vow or not, whether he has graduated or not, whether he has the domestic fire or not, whether he offers the daily fire sacrifice or not, let him fetch some fire from the village and. . . .[16]

38. Now, the statement "the blind, the lame, the old, and lepers should resort to asceticism" [Ch. 2.28] does not contradict our position, because the terms "blind" and so forth have been explained in a different way.

39. Thus, for instance, Medhātithi says:

> When a man remains as unmoved when he sees a sixteen-year-old young lady as when he sees a newborn girl or a hundred-year-old woman, he is called a "eunuch."

13. I believe that the technical meaning of the term "*utthānaśruti*" (lit., "vedic text on rising up") is that the text prescribes immediate departure from society without regard to any other condition. See, for example, Ch. 2.25 above, where the same term is used with reference to texts that advocate renunciation directly from vedic studentship. The term *vyuthāna* is used with this meaning by Śaṃkara in his commentary on BaU 3.5.1: see Olivelle 1986, 79–91. The text to which Yādava refers here is the *Jābāli* cited at Ch. 2.12.

14. The referent of "them" is unclear, but in all likelihood the author means that in the following passage the *Jābāli* enjoins immediate renunciation specifically on those who are totally detached. "Separately" may signify the following: In the earlier passage (Ch. 2.12) immediate renunciation while a person was still a student was presented within the context of prescribing renunciation within the sequence of the orders of life for ordinary people. In that context there may be some justification in taking the rule of immediate renunciation as directed at those who are disqualified from marriage. In this text, on the other hand, no such doubt is possible, because the text speaks specifically and solely of those who are detached.

15. "Vow" refers to vedic initiation, and a *snātaka*, here translated as one who has graduated from vedic school, is a young adult who has performed the ceremony that concludes the period of vedic studies. This ceremony concludes with a ritual bath, and hence the graduate is called *snātaka*, "one who has taken the bath."

16. The author cites only the beginning of the passage, a common practice in this type of literature. He expects his reader to be familiar with these citations. I have been unable to trace the rest of this passage.

> 40. When a man walks only to beg food and to answer nature's calls, and even then does not travel beyond a league, he is called "lame."
>
> 41. When a wandering ascetic, as he stands or walks, does not look beyond six feet in front of him, unless there is some danger, he is said to be "blind."
>
> 42. As he hears words that are kind or unkind, soothing or scathing, when a man remains as if he had not heard them, he is said to be "deaf."[17]

43. The blind, moreover, are not qualified to become wandering ascetics because of the rule "He should place his foot on the ground after determining its purity by inspection."[18] 44. Neither are the lame or lepers, because of rules such as the following:

> Traveling to holy bathing places and temples, let him roam the earth like a worm along the path pointed out by the sun.[19]

45. The rule of celibacy disqualifies eunuchs from itinerant asceticism, for celibacy is abstention from sex. Now abstention from sex does not arise at all in the case of a eunuch, because, remaining unmoved like a pillar, he does not have the capacity to engage in sex. Clearly abstention becomes a vow only for those who have the capacity.

46. Consequently, the vedic passage on debts is directed at those who are not detached. For those who are detached, on the other hand, only one path is open, and that is itinerant asceticism. 47. Accordingly, Bṛhaspati states:

> . . . a man imbued with deep detachment should depart for the ascetic life even before he has married. [see Ch. 2.18]

48. Kratu:

> After he has truly come to know the highest Brahman, a vedic student, a widowed householder, or a forest hermit should give up attachments and become a wandering ascetic.

49. Śaṅkha:

> Even a vedic student may do so, however, . . . if he has banished all attachments; and if he adheres strictly to his vow.

17. These verses and other similar ones are contained in the NPU 146–47; see also Ch. 7.130–36.

18. MDh 6.46. The verse literally means that he should place his foot purified by his gaze; that is, he should look carefully to see whether there are any insects or bugs before putting his foot down as he walks, lest he kill them. Jain mendicants use brooms to brush insects from their path. The point here is that this rule of Manu disqualifies the blind because they cannot visually inspect the ground.

19. The second half of the verse is found in the MBh 14.46.32. The point of the argument is that the lame would not be able to roam the earth or to visit holy places. How this text would disqualify lepers is less clear. Perhaps they would not be allowed to enter temples or sacred bathing places (*tīrtha*).

50. Or even a twice-born householder, if he possesses the above qualities, may enter the celibate order of life after he has offered a sacrifice to Prajāpati, given all his possessions as a sacrificial gift to the priests according to the prescribed rules, and deposited his sacred fires in himself. [see Ch. 2.23-24]

51. Dattātreya:

The triple staff is the emblem of Viṣṇu. It is the means of liberation for twice-born people and signals the cessation of all rules.[20] That is the teaching of the Veda. It was prescribed of old by the Self-Existent One for those who had become disaffected with household life.[21]

52. The teachers[22] are of the opinion that a temporary vedic student[23] is free to choose[24] any of the four orders of life. 53. Vasiṣṭha accordingly states:

There are four orders of life: vedic student, householder, forest hermit, and wandering ascetic. After studying one, two, or all the Vedas, a student who has not violated his vow of celibacy may enter whichever of these he prefers. [VaDh 7.1.3]

54. Āpastamba also says:

After learning the rites, he may undertake whichever he likes. [ApDh 2.21.5]

20. The term "*dharma*" in this context probably refers to the duties and laws of castes and orders of life. The renunciatory life is often depicted as transcending *dharma*.

21. The referent of "it" is unclear, but in this context it may refer to the triple staff. This half-verse is given within a different context in the Yls 2.32 (Olivelle 1987, 50, 65).

22. This could, of course, be an honorific plural. In this type of literature such plurals invariably refer to authoritative figures of old whose views support those of the author. It also may be a literary device rather than an actual reference to a particular teacher.

23. Such a vedic student is distinguished from one who resolves to live as a student all his life. According to the original formulation of the *āśrama* system, which is presented here by Yādava, it was the temporary student who, at the completion of his period of study, chose an order in which he would spend his entire adult life. The first order in this scheme is permanent studentship, which, among others, the temporary student may choose. The choice of an *āśrama* was limited to this crucial period of a man's life when he is about to assume adult responsibilities. On the original *āśrama* system and for a discussion of the texts cited here, see Olivelle 1993, 73–101.

24. The term "*icchāvikalpa*," "free or unrestricted option," means that any student may freely choose an order of life he prefers. This type of option is different from the *vyavasthitavikalpa*, which restricts the choice to a particular group or class of people. See Cg. 2.25 n. 9.

55. The Blessed Vyāsa states:

> After duly acquiring vedic knowledge by serving his teacher, a twice-born man should give a gift of a cow to the teacher and, with his permission, take the ritual bath.
>
> 56. Then, that learned Brahmin may live in whichever order of life he prefers, either as a permanent student, or as a sage, or else as a wandering ascetic.[25]

57. Gautama declares:

> For him, some assert, there is a choice of orders.[26] [GDh 3.1]

58. Now with regard to the statement "Only after paying his three debts . . ." [see Ch. 2.5], that too—when we interpret it within the restrictions imposed on it by vedic and scriptural statements enjoining itinerant asceticism straight from vedic studentship for those who are detached—must refer exclusively to people with attachments. Alternatively, it may intend to point out that debts once assumed must be paid.[27]

59. It is established, therefore, that a man who is detached may become a wandering ascetic while he is still a student, or from home or the forest. 60. Bṛhaspati accordingly states:

> When a man is attached to the Supreme Self and detached from all else, and when he is freed from all desires, he is fit to eat almsfood. [see NPU 139]

25. Only three of the four orders are listed here explicitly. However, the term "*muni*" ("sage") is ambiguous. It may refer to a householder or a hermit, and here it may perhaps include both.

26. "For him," that is, for a temporary student who has completed his vedic studies.

27. Yādava's intention is to show that Manu's passage must refer to people who are not detached, for otherwise it would be rendered null and void by contradicting vedic texts. Alternatively, Manu may intend to state only that those who have assumed debts must pay them before taking to renunciation. As Vijñāneśvara, another great medieval theologian, points out (commenting on YDh 3.56–57), it is foolish to think that a person is literally born with these debts. One assumes them when one becomes qualified to pay them by undertaking a particular mode of life. Thus, when a man is initiated he assumes the debt to study, as when a man gets married he assumes the debts to procreate and to offer sacrifices. According to this interpretation, Manu's statement does not contradict other texts that permit a detached man to renounce before he gets married, because before marriage he is not burdened with the debts of procreation and sacrifice. For an extensive discussion of this point, see Olivelle 1993, 177–82, 237–43.

Renunciation When Death Is Imminent

61. Aṅgiras permits itinerant asceticism also for those facing imminent death:[28]

> One who is tired of forest life may depart for the ascetic life after performing the appropriate rite. A twice-born man may renounce if he is afflicted with a disease, if he is detached, or if he has acquired the knowledge of Brahman.
>
> 62. A man may depart for the ascetic life while he is vedic student or from home or the forest if he is learned or if he is sick and in great pain.
>
> 63. The sage Aṅgiras has ordained renunciation for a man overcome by fear at the sight of a robber, a tiger, and the like or when a dreadful peril is at hand.

64. Śātātapa likewise states:

> If a man says, "I have renounced," even with his last breath, he will obtain a reward equal to one thousand sacrifices.

65. Dattātreya declares:

> The practice of carrying the emblem of Viṣṇu is the prerogative of those born from the mouth, and not of those born from the arms or the thighs.[29]

66. That ends the second chapter, entitled "Age of Eligibility of a Candidate for Itinerant Asceticism," of the *Collection of Ascetic Laws*.

28. The term "*ātura*" generally refers to a person who is sick or infirm. Within the context of renunciation, however, it acquires a technical meaning and refers to a person who is in danger of imminent death either through sickness or when attacked by robbers or wild animals. A definition of this term is given at Ch. 4.42. For the procedure of renunciation in such an emergency, see Ch. 4.39–47.

29. The reference is to the cosmogonic hymn of the *Ṛgveda* (10.90), which portrays the Brahmins as originating from the mouth of the primeval man dismembered in sacrifice and the Kṣatriyas and Vaiśyas from the arms and the thighs, respectively. The eligibility of non-Brahmins for renunciation is a hotly debated point of medieval Brahmanical theology, a topic, however, that Yādava does not address explicitly.

CHAPTER THREE

Examination of the Insignia

1. Now we will examine the insignia, which are of two types: the external and the bodily. The bodily insignia consist of the sacrificial string and having the head completely shaved or wearing just a topknot, while the external insignia are the staff, the water pot, and other such items. With reference to external insignia we employ the term "article."[1]

Bodily Insignia

2. I will first describe the bodily insignia. Vasiṣṭha states:

> Wearing a sacrificial string and carrying a water pot in his hand. . . . [VaDh 10.31]

and:

> Let him be shaven-headed, free from pride and anger, and without possessions. [VaDh 10.6]

3. Yama:

> He should always sleep on the bare ground and never stay long in the same place. His head shaven and always living in the wilderness, let him turn his mind incessantly to knowledge.

4. Paiṭhīnasi:

> A sage is homeless and shaven-headed, unselfish and without possessions.

1. The Sanskrit word "*mātrā*" is used in ascetic literature as a technical term referring to the external articles, such as garment, staff, and begging bowl, that a renouncer is required to carry. Here the author defines that term as referring only to those articles that constitute the external insignia and not to those, such as the sacrificial string, that are viewed as constituting his bodily insignia. According to this view, the sacrificial string, which is an external article, is viewed as almost a bodily mark like the shaven head.

5. Bodhāyana:

> Going to the wilderness, he should either wear a topknot or have his head completely shaved. [BDh 2.11.17–18].

6. Kratu:

> After chanting the three hymns—Mind,[2] Viṣṇu, and Puruṣa[3]—in praise of the Highest Spirit, let him depart from home robed in ocher, carrying a bowl and a staff, and with his head completely shaved or wearing just a topknot.

7. Sumantu

> A sage is shaven-headed and without possessions.

8. Gautama:

> He should have his head completely shaved or wear just a topknot. [GDh 3.21]

9. Consequently, one may choose either to shave the head completely or to wear just a topknot.[4] All ascetics without exception, however, are required to wear a sacrificial string. 10. Accordingly, with specific reference to itinerant asceticism, Atri declares:

> Those Brahmins who, subsisting by sophistry, foolishly discard the sacrificial string sacred to the triple divinity—Brahmā, Viṣṇu, and Śiva—will undoubtedly fall both from the path to heaven and from the path to liberation.

11. Uśanas:

> By discarding his sacrificial string, a Vedic student, a householder, a forest hermit, and even a wandering ascetic will fall. Let no one, therefore, abandon it.

2. The Mind-hymn is probably the same as the Śivasaṃkalpa (VS 34.1–6; see Ch. 6.64, n. 32), which contains the words *tan me manaḥ śivasaṃkalpam astu*. The commentator Mahīdhara calls these verses *manodevatāḥ*.

3. The meaning of the expression "*vaiṣṇavapauruṣa*" is unclear. I have taken it to mean hymns connected with Viṣṇu and Puruṣa, the two often being identified in Vaiṣṇava literature. The identity of the three hymns is also unclear. They certainly include the famous Puruṣa hymn (RV 10.90), and perhaps the so-called Viṣṇusūkta, which according to Paṇḍit Daulatarāma (*Nirṇayasindhu*, Vārāṇsī: Ṭhakurprasād & Sons, 1975, p. 1324) consists of the four verses *viṣṇor nu kam* (RV 1.154.1–4), the two verses *viṣṇoḥ karmāṇi* (RV 1.22.19–20), and the two verses *trīṇi padā* (RV 1.22.18–19; the latter is thus listed twice). A somewhat different version is given in the *Śuklayajurvedīyamādhyandinavājasaneyināṃ Nityanaimittikakarmasamuccayaḥ* (Bombay: Nirṇayasāgara Press, 1952), p. 411.

4. The reason for the choice is the diversity of opinions given in the authoritative texts cited. See Ch. 2.25 n. 9.

External Insignia

12. I will now describe the external insignia. Dakṣa states:

A Vedic student is recognized by the girdle, antelope skin, staff, and the like; a householder by the staff, sacrificial broom, and the like; a forest hermit by long nails and hair; and an ascetic by the triple staff. These are their respective marks.

13. Bṛhaspati:

After he has thus performed the rite of renunciation, let him take a triple staff tied with a water strainer and reaching up to his hair, as well as a bowl and a water pot.

14. Śaṅkha and Likhita:

Abandoning all undertakings,[5] he relies on the use of a triple staff, a water pot, fine thread, and a water strainer, shaves his head, wears ocher clothes, and subsists on begging.

15–16. Aṅgiras:

I shall declare the insignia by which an ascetic is recognized: a sacrificial string, a triple staff, a cloth to strain insects, a sling, a begging bowl, a stool, a loincloth, and a waistband. Only a man who possesses these insignia is a true ascetic, and no one else.

17. "Stool" means the "tortoise seat."[6] Devala says:

The articles[7] consist of an ocher garment, a shaven head, a triple staff, a water pot, a bowl, a water strainer, a pair of sandals, a seat, and a ragged shawl.

18. Gālava:

Now, a wandering ascetic bears the insignia; is shaven-headed or wears a topknot, always wears a sacrificial string, and dons a ragged ocher garment. Let him use a cloth to cover his nakedness but not wear an upper garment. He carries a triple staff, a water strainer, a water pot, a bowl, and a ragged shawl.

19. Likhita:

Let him wear a ragged shawl and an ocher garb of cotton, bark, antelope skin, Kuśa grass, or hemp.

5. The term "undertakings" (*ārambha*) refers in a special way to ritual activities. The GDh (3.25), for example, calls a renouncer an *anārambhin*, "one who does not undertake ritual activities."

6. This is a low stool carried by ascetics and used both as an ordinary seat and to sit down while performing ritual purifications. See Ch. 3.79.

7. For the technical meaning of the term "article" (*mātrā*), see Ch. 3.1 n.1. In spite of that definition of this term, the shaven head is here listed as an article.

20–21. A sling and a bowl with a lid hung from a tripod,[8] a triple staff tied with a water strainer, a round stool, a topknot, a sacrificial string, and also a water pot for use in purifications: whether he is walking or is seated, a pure man should always carry these.

22. Yama:

Needle and thread, a tripod, a pair of sandals, a pot, a sling made of string, a begging bowl, a stool, a ragged shawl, a tattered garment, and a staff: this is the short list of articles he should possess.

23. Uśanas:

A bowl and its lid, a sling, a triple staff tied with a water strainer, a stool, a waistband, a loincloth, a sacrificial string, and a ragged shawl: let him take these and abandon everything else.

24–25. Kratu:

He may carry twenty or ten articles, but he should always carry at least five. The following are the twenty items called articles laid down by the scriptures: ragged shawl, needle, antelope skin, umbrella, water strainer, water pot, stool, bowl, sling, rosary, sacrificial string, spade, a pair of sandals, loincloth, tripod, a pair of shoes, staff, fine thread, yoga band,[9] and outer garment.

26. Of these twenty articles, five are obligatory. They are the sacrificial string, triple staff, water strainer, bowl, loincloth, and waistband.[10] 27. Viṣṇu, likewise, states:

Sacrificial string, triple staff, bowl, water strainer, loincloth, and waistband—one should not abandon these as long as one lives.

8. The sling, which resembles present-day macramé pot-hangers, is tied to the top of the tripod. The bowl is suspended in the sling. When the tripod is set up, the bowl in the sling hangs from its center. The tripod, like a present-day camera tripod, is collapsible. When folded up, it can be held by the bottom, with the top resting on the shoulder and the sling with the bowl hanging behind the shoulder. It appears that in the early period the tripod was used to carry a water pot rather than a begging bowl. For an extended discussion about the triple staff and the tripod, see Olivelle 1986, 42–52, and von Hinüber 1992, 51–67.

9. This is a strip of cloth stitched to form a loop. Iconographic representations of ascetics show them wearing it around their thighs and the back, thus supporting the legs as they sit on their haunches. Later texts give great prominence to the investiture of an ascetic with the yoga band, presenting it as a type of higher ordination. After this ceremony an ascetic is permitted to teach and to initiate others into the ascetic order. For a description of this rite, see Ypra 66.

10. If the loincloth and waistband are counted as separate items, the list contains six rather than five articles. This anomaly may be why the bowl is omitted in several manuscripts. In all likelihood, however, the loincloth and waistband are counted as a single item, just as the needle and thread are (see Ch. 3.28). That the bowl was originally part of this list is confirmed by the statements that follow (Ch. 3.27–28).

28. The fact that one takes a bowl necessarily implies that one has to take also its accessories: a sling, a cover, and a tripod. The ten articles are those listed in the scriptural passage beginning "Needle and thread . . ." [see Ch. 3.22], where we count ten articles by taking the needle and thread as a single item.

29. Now, there are two types of wandering ascetics. The one is devoted to training himself in knowledge and seeks to become proficient in yoga, whereas the other, who has already mastered yoga and knows the truth, lives without visible insignia, keeps his conduct concealed, and although sane, behaves like a madman.[11] 30. Kratu, likewise, points out the two types:

> A yogin should go around in the forenoon, while a person who possesses the true knowledge should go around in the afternoon.[12]

31. Kratu himself makes the following comments with reference to the ascetic who possesses the true knowledge:

> Virtue, good conduct, learning, knowledge, detachment—that is the definition of the Law. What is the use of articles for a man who has gained complete control of himself?[13]
>
> 32. Meditation, purification, austerity, worship, control of breath, silent prayer, divine praise, twilight worship, begging food, and divine service: he should perform these until death.

33. Even those who possess the true knowledge are without exception required to carry the five articles [see Ch. 3.26], because of the injunction ". . . should always carry at least five" [see Ch. 3.24] and because of the rule requiring them to beg their food.[14]

11. This is the stock description of a renouncer at an advanced state of holiness. See VaDh 10.18–19; JU 69.5–6.

12. The reason for the "going around" is to beg (see Ch. 6.98). This is an interesting observation regarding ascetic practice. Brahmanical ascetics are expected to beg late in the afternoon, after the people have finished their meal (see Ch. 6.97–100). Neither Kratu nor Yādava (see Ch. 6.98) reveals the identity of the "yogin." Buddhist monks, however, are not allowed to eat in the afternoon and beg their food in the morning. Kratu's statement may thus be an implicit relegation of Buddhist monks to a lower level of asceticism. It is, however, the only such distinction in the time of begging that I have encountered.

13. The reference is probably to yogic powers, such as the knowledge of previous births and others' thoughts, listed in the *Yogasūtra* (3.16–55).

14. The reasoning here is that the ritual of begging requires the mendicant to be equipped with a begging bowl, a triple staff, and the like. See Ch. 6.151–71.

Description of the External Insignia

34. In what follows I will describe the specifications of a sacrificial string and the other items on the list of articles.

Sacrificial String

I take up first the specifications of a sacrificial string. 35. With special reference to itinerant asceticism, Dattātreya and Atri state:

> The cotton string should be made by twisting three pieces of thread upward and three pieces downward, with an outer one twisted the same way.[15]
>
> 36. The sacred string of Brahmins, according to scripture, is made of nine pieces of cotton thread divided into three groups of three, with three pieces twisted downward and three twisted upward.
>
> 37. Wearing this ninefold string is the means of liberation for twice-born people; without it one is forthwith excluded from all aspects of sacred law.

Staff

38. I will now describe the specifications of a staff. Kapila states:

> Let him carry one or several bamboo staffs[16] three-fourths of an inch thick, straight, and reaching up to his nose or as tall as himself. 39. Now, they also cite these verses:
>
> > In this text we define a joint as the spot where one sees fine sprouts with emergent leaves and the middle as what is in-between.
> >
> > 40. They say that an ascetic's staff should be one that does not contain three, five, seven, nine, or eleven joints.[17] Below its bottommost joint, moreover, and above its uppermost it should extend one and a half inches.

15. This outer string is also made by twisting three pieces of thread. On the way sacrificial strings are manufactured, see Kane, II, 287f.

16. The plural here probably refers to the triple staff made by tying three bamboos together (see Ch. 3.44–47). The triple staff is preferred by the Vaiṣṇava ascetics. On the controversy regarding the staff, see Olivelle 1986, 56–54.

17. It appears that ascetics avoided staffs with an odd number of joints. Another work recommends staffs with six, eight, ten, twelve, and fourteen joints and gives such staffs respectively the following names: Sudarśana, Nārāyaṇa, Gopāla, Vāsudeva, and Ananta; see *Saṃnyāsāśramapaddhati* (Prājña Pāṭhaśālā Library, ms serial no. 4992), folio 33b (see Olivelle 1986, 155 n. 56). It is unclear how universal this attitude was, because a half-verse cited in the PaM (I.2, 157–59) recommends staffs with eleven, nine, seven, four, three, and two joints, and that half-verse is given here in the variant reading of several manuscripts.

41. This provision holds good also for householders. Dattātreya states:

He should carry three bamboo staffs, each three-quarters of an inch thick, reaching up to top of his head, with their bark intact, unblemished, pleasant, without holes or cracks, and containing six, eight, or ten evenly spaced and unprotruding joints.

42. Dakṣa:

An ascetic should carry three bamboo staffs with evenly spaced joints and reaching up to his hair.

43. Dakṣa the Elder:

Let a wise man carry a triple staff with a water strainer tied to its top.

44. Hārīta:

He should mark off five equal sections on his triple staff and bind it above the third section with a string of black cow's hair to a width of three inches.

45. Containing a series of three knots and with a water strainer tied to its top, he should take it in his right hand while reciting the appropriate mantra when his teacher hands it to him.[18]

46–47. Dakṣa the Elder:

He should tie the triple staff with a string at the top and the bottom between the joints.[19] Below the second section from the top[20] also he should tie a cow's hair string to a width of three inches. Or else he may mark off five equal sections and tie it five times with a string.

48–49. In the Pāñcarātra text *Tattvasāgarasaṃhitā* it is stated:[21]

Let an ascetic think of the top section of the triple staff as Parameṣṭhin, the second section as Puruṣātman, the mid-section as Viśvātman, the fourth

18. For the mantra that is recited when a new ascetic formally takes up his staff, see Ch. 4.19, 38. The knots that tie the three bamboos are called *mudrā* (the term usually used for hand gestures with mystic significance) and given different symbolic values. Often, five such knots or *mudrās* along the staff are mentioned (see Ch. 3.46–47), relating to serpent, cow, ax, conch, and Brahmā. For an account of these *mudrās*, see Ypra 35.7–29.

19. I have translated *madhye* as "between the joints" in the light of the statement made above at Ch. 3.39. If it means simply "in the middle," the translation would be "at the top, the bottom, and the middle." My interpretation is more likely, since the middle binding is referred to in the next half-verse.

20. As stated at Ch. 3.44, one marks off five equal sections. The middle binding is done just below the second from the top, i.e., at the beginning of the third section.

21. Contrary to his opening remark that he limits himself to Dharmaśāstric texts (Ch. 1.10), Yādava here cites from a Pāñcarātra text. Smith does not list the *Tattvasāgarasaṃhitā* among the extant texts, although it is found in a couple of ancient lists of Pāñcarātra texts; see Smith 1975, 243, 262.

section as Nivṛttipuruṣa, and the fifth section as Sarvātman.[22] Let him envisage the triple staff in its entirety as an image of Viṣṇu.

50. Hārīta:

An ascetic should carry at all times the image of Viṣṇu that is called the triple staff.

51. Śaunaka:

The short is the staff of knowledge, the medium is the staff of the self, and the long is the staff of Viṣṇu—let an ascetic carry the triple staff.[23]

52. Pracetas:

An ascetic should carry the sacred string and the triple staff by himself, just as he does the topknot. If he gets someone else to carry them, he should undergo the following penance.

53. After sprinkling the triple staff with water as he recites the Puruṣa hymn and the seven verses to Viṣṇu,[24] he should control his breath one hundred times.

54. Let him place his staff near by[25] when he bathes, when he answers the calls of nature, when he eats, when he engages in silent prayer and private vedic recitation, and when he sleeps.

55. An ascetic should always take with him a triple staff, as well as a single bamboo staff to carry articles such as the loincloth and the waistband.

56. If an ascetic voids urine or excrement while holding the triple staff, to restore purity he should perform the rite of sipping water with the staff in his hand.[26]

57. Jābāli the Elder:

22. In Vaiṣṇava theology, these are names given to different aspects of the supreme god Viṣṇu.

23. It is unclear whether the author is referring to triple staffs themselves or to the three bamboos that constitute a triple staff (the variant *tridaṇḍān*, "three staffs," in ms A4 appears to support the latter). If it is the latter, then one of the three must have been long, one of medium length, and one short. I have not encountered any other reference to such a distinction in lengths either of the bamboos or of staffs themselves, although sources specify various lengths, such as reaching the nose or hair or being as tall as one's body.

24. The Puruṣa hymn is RV 10.90. The seven verses to Viṣṇu may be the same as the hymn to Viṣṇu: see Ch. 3.6 n. 3.

25. I am not quite sure of the exact meaning of the expression "*upa daṇḍena bandhayet*," which I assume to mean that he should place the triple staff near him when he engages in these activities, as indicated in Ch. 8.23.

26. The wording makes it unclear whether the purification is intended for the staff, for the ascetic, or for both.

After filling his cupped hands with water and pouring it down, and taking one or [three] staffs. . . .[27]

58. Bodhāyana:

And thereafter he should not wear a white garment. He may carry a single or a triple staff. [BDh 2.17.44–18.1]

59. Yājñavalkya:

Or he may carry a single such staff, in which case it should not be tied with a cow's hair string.

60. One has a choice, therefore, with regard to the type of staff one carries. Yet, both because it entails a greater effort and because it is mentioned in a larger number of texts, carrying a triple staff is more praiseworthy than carrying a single staff. 61. This position is supported by the Blessed Vyāsa:

Carrying a triple staff is commended, and likewise living in solitude, eating little, and living without worries. For ascetics these are the means to liberation.

62. This difference in the type of staff does not entail corresponding differences with regard to either the other articles or duties such as twilight worship. Some texts, on the other hand, prescribe a single staff when the triple staff is damaged.[28] 63. Atri and Jābāla state:

When the water strainer or the triple staff is inadvertently damaged, he should take a single bamboo staff or, as an inferior alternative, a Palāśa staff.

64. When even these are not available, let him go around carrying a Palāśa leaf or a tuft of Kuśa grass until he obtains a better staff.[29]

65. Hārīta:

When the water strainer or the triple staff is inadvertently damaged, he should take a single bamboo staff or, as an inferior alternative, a Palāśa staff and proceed until he obtains a triple staff.

27. Only the first words of this citation are given. I have been unable to trace the rest of the passage. See Ch. 2.37 n. 16.

28. The Sanskrit term "*naṣṭa*" has several shades of meaning, including damaged, lost, spoiled, and corrupted. All these may be intended here. A renouncer is expected to throw into water a staff that is broken or damaged, as well as one that has come into contact with impurities, such as liquor, urine, excrement, and blood. A staff is likewise to be abandoned when the water strainer normally tied to its top is similarly damaged. See Ch. 8.24–31; Ypra 68.78–80.

29. Palāśa is the tree *Butea frondosa*, and Kuśa is a type of grass (*Poa cynosuroides*) used for ritual purposes.

66. Ever vigilant and composed, he should vigorously search for a triple staff, and when he finds one, he should take it, after tying a water strainer to its top.

67. Medhātithi:

As long as he does not have three staffs, he may go around with one. Even then he should tie a water strainer to its top for use in purifying water.

68. Jamadagni:

Let him never tie a loincloth or a waistband to the triple staff. By foolishly tying them to it, one shows disrespect to the triple staff.

69. If a mendicant carelessly lets his triple staff come into contact with the other staff,[30] he should wash the triple staff with earth and water and control his breath three times.

Pot

70. In the age of Kali one should not carry a pot. Accordingly, Devala states:

In the Dvāpara and similar ages an ascetic may eat from a begging bowl. In the Kali age, however, he should never eat directly from his begging bowl, nor should he carry a pot.[31]

Water Strainer

71–72. Medhātithi gives the specifications of a water strainer:

One should understand that a water strainer should be smooth,[32] white, and untouched; that it should be nine inches long on both sides, or two or three times that long, or six inches long on all sides, or a full span; that it should be without holes, soft, and made of cotton; and that it should not be made by an outcaste or a similar person.

30. The other staff refers to the pole used to carry an ascetic's personal belongings (see Ch. 3.20–21 n. 8 and 3.55). Coming into contact with the loincloth and other impure articles renders it impure. The purity of the triple staff is indicated by its contact with the water strainer.

31. As we shall see in Ch. 6.206, a renouncer begs food in a begging bowl but transfers it into a different dish, often a leaf, when he eats. The meaning of "pot" (*kuṇḍikā*) and the significance of its prohibition are unclear. It must be something different from the water pot (*kamaṇḍalu*) that ascetics are required to carry. At Ch. 3.22, however, the *kuṇḍikā* is listed among the ten articles an ascetic should carry, and this term has given the *Kuṇḍikā Upaniṣad* its title. For further details, see Sprockhoff 1976, 44–46, and von Hinüber 1992, 51–67..

32. The meaning of the term "*vikeśa*" in this context is unclear. I have taken it to mean a piece of cloth that is not shaggy. It may also mean "without hair," that is, without hair sticking to it, but since the term is listed under specifications, this meaning seems less likely.

The term "untouched" means not previously used. 73. Aṅgiras states:

> There are only three white things that ascetics always have: sacrificial string, teeth, and a cloth to strain insects.

Begging Bowl

74. Atri describes the bowls:

> A bowl may be made of clay, wood, bottle-gourd, bamboo, thread, stone, grass, or linen, or it may be a funnel fashioned out of a leaf.
>
> 75. He should take one of these according to his ability. If he thereafter takes a different bowl out of greed, he should control his breath ten times.

76. Kratu:

> One should take a bowl made of bamboo, wood, stone, bottle-gourd, grass, leaves, clay, or linen, according to one's ability.

77. Manu:

> Manu, the son of Svayambhu, has declared that bowls made of bottle-gourd, wood, clay, and bamboo are suitable for ascetics. [MDh 6.54]

Sling

78. Hārīta gives the specifications of a sling:

> These are the specifications of a sling. It is made by knotting linen strips, Kuśa fibers, or cotton strings and is shaped like a lotus, with five or six sections.[33]

Seat

79. The same author gives the specifications of a seat:

> It is laid down that the seat of an ascetic should be round and equipped with a handle and that it should be made of wood. Sages in ancient times created it both for purification and for sitting down.

Spade

80. Kapila gives the specifications of a spade:

> There is no fault in having a three-inch spade for digging the earth.

81. That ends the third chapter, entitled "Examination of the Insignia," of the *Collection of Ascetic Laws*.

33. The term "*muṣṭi*" (lit., "clenched fist") here probably refers to the sections of a sling; see Ch. 3.20–21 n. 8 and Ypra 8.9–11.

CHAPTER FOUR

The Procedure of Renunciation

1. I will now describe the procedure of renunciation, explaining at the outset the procedure given by Śaunaka. In the course of this explanation I will point out at the appropriate places certain indispensable details of the procedure not found in Śaunaka but given elsewhere. 2. Kātyāyana gives its preliminary rites:

> People living outside the orders of life should perform four Kṛcchra penances, while those living within an order should perform a single Kṛcchra penance.[1] In this manner one becomes fit for renunciation. On the twelfth day of the bright fortnight or on the full moon, he should announce his intention[2] and get his head shaved. He should then perform the Śrāddha oblations—first to the gods, second to the seers, third to the divine beings, fourth to the male ancestors, fifth to the female ancestors, sixth to human beings, seventh to the elements, and eighth to the self.[3]

3. Blessed Vasiṣṭha the Elder says the same thing, with an identical statement beginning with "on the full moon day."[4] 4. Śaunaka states:

1. Those living outside the four orders of life are people such as bachelors who have completed their Vedic studentship and widowers. Four Kṛcchra penances constitute what is technically known as a Prājāpatya penance (see MDh 11.211; YDh 3.319). It consists of taking one meal a day for six days—a morning meal the first three days and an evening meal the second—eating what is received unasked during the next three days, and fasting during the last three. See GDh 26.1–5; ApDh 1.27.7; BDh 2.2.38; 4.5.6. A single Kṛcchra penance is a quarter of the Prājāpatya, that is, doing the same four austerities for only one day each. Such a penance is called *pādakṛcchra* ("quarter penance") at YDh 3.318. Regarding the "hot penance" (*taptakṛcchra*) that some sources prescribe here, see Ch. 10.44 n. 9, and my translation of Ypra 6.2–3n.

2. This is the formal and open declaration that he will perform the rite of renunciation. Such a formal declaration is a prerequisite of all Brahmanical rites.

3. For a detailed procedure of these oblations, see Ypra 7 and Sp 3–4. Śrāddha oblations are generally funerary offering made to deceased ancestors. Here these oblations are extended to other inhabitants of the universe.

4. The author appears to be saying that Vasiṣṭha the Elder gives the same procedure and that his text reproduces verbatim the section of Kātyāyana's text beginning with "on the full moon day."

On the day preceding the rite of renunciation, he should offer a Śrāddha oblation to the ancestors with happy faces[5] and feed the invited Brahmins. Then he should get them to announce that the day is auspicious and to proclaim success and prosperity, after which he should get his hair and beard shaved and his nails clipped.

5. Blessed Jāmadagnya also speaks to this:

He should get his hair and beard shaved and his nails clipped.

6. Śaunaka:

Then he should bathe in the prescribed manner and give away all his possessions with the exception of things required for the sacrifice and other similar rites.[6]

7. Bodhāyana:

Staffs, sling, water pot, water strainer, and bowl: taking these. . . .[7]

8. Vasiṣṭha:

Triple staff, seat, ragged shawl, sling, bowl, and water pot—a wise man should take these six and abandon other possessions.

9. He is enjoined to cleanse his impurities and to get rid of his possessions. One should never admit to renunciation a man who has not forsaken his sons and his wealth.

10. Kātyāyana:

Triple staff, water strainer, sling, bowl, loincloth, and ocher garment—he should place these in front of the fire; a man without a sacred fire should set one up.

11. Bodhāyana:

A man without a sacred fire is to set one up and to follow the procedure prescribed for a person with a single fire.[8]

5. Ancestors with happy faces (*nāndīmukha*) are those beyond the three most recently deceased forefathers, namely, the father, paternal grandfather, and paternal great-grandfather. These three are called "teary-faced" (*aśrumukha*). Oblations to the former ancestors are offered on auspicious occasions, such as a birth or a marriage, and follow a somewhat different procedure. See Ypra 7.3–4n, 7.5n.

6. As part of the renunciatory rite, the candidate offers a final sacrifice to Prajāpati or to Agni Vaiśvānara and gives gifts to the officiating priests; see Ch. 4.26, 28.

7. The rest of Bodhāyana's statement reads: "he should go to the outskirts of the village, to the village boundary, or to a fire stall, eat the triple mixture of ghee, milk, and curd, and observe a fast" (BDh 2.17.11–12.).

8. A person with a single fire maintains the domestic fire called *āvasathya* and performs all the rites in that fire. He is distinguished from a man who maintains the three Vedic fires, who is called *āhitāgni*. These fires are the east fire (*āhavanīya*), householder's or west fire (*gārhapatya*), and south fire (*anvāhāryapacana*). Some sources list five fires, adding a hall fire (*sabhya*) and domestic fire (*āvasathya* or *aupāsana*). See Ypra 7.30–49; 10.5. The modifications of the renunciatory ritual for people without a fire and for those with the three Vedic fires are given in Sp 16–17.

12. Śaunaka:

Then, after getting together the staff and the other articles, he should go to a temple, to the village boundary,[9] to the outskirts of the village, to the bank of a river, or to a holy place, and, joining his hands in prayer, he should silently recite:

> Homage to Brahman! Homage to Indra! Homage to the Sun! Homage to the Self!

He should then sip some water and, taking some sacred Darbha grass in his folded hands, silently recite the Vedas and the like. Then he eats a handful of barley meal and sips some water. Next, he should consecrate the region of his navel with this mantra:

> To the self, svāhā! To the inner self, svāhā! To Prajāpati, svāhā!

Then he should eat the triple mixture of milk, curd, and ghee, sip some water, and observe a fast. Or else he may drink some water. And he should silently recite:

> OṂ Earth, I enter Sāvitrī. That excellent [glory] of Savitṛ.
> OṂ Atmosphere, I enter Sāvitrī. The glory of god we meditate.
> OṂ Heaven, I enter Sāvitrī. That he may stimulate our prayers.[10]
> OṂ Earth, I enter Sāvitrī. That excellent glory of Savitṛ, the god, we meditate.
> OṂ Atmosphere, I enter Sāvitrī. That he may stimulate our prayers.
> OṂ Heaven, I enter Sāvitrī. That excellent glory of Savitṛ, the god, we meditate, that he may stimulate our prayers.
> OṂ Earth, Atmosphere, Heaven, I enter Sāvitrī. That excellent glory of Savitṛ, the god, we meditate, that he may stimulate our prayers. [RV 3.62.10]

It is acknowledged that a person thus betakes himself to another order of life and becomes one with Brahman. Thus they quote:

> Having gone from one order of life to another, a man who has offered sacrifices and subdued his senses becomes a mendicant when he gets tired of giving alms and offering oblations.

Such a mendicant, indeed, is fit for immortality.

13. Śaunaka:

Then, before sunset, he should melt some butter, strain it, and offer four ladlefuls in the blazing fire, saying, "OṂ svāhā!" He then performs the evening fire sacrifice, spreads some grass to the north of the fire, places the vessels on that grass, spreads some sacred Darbha grass to the south of the

9. All the manuscripts have the reading *grāme* ("in the village"), but I think the intention is to indicate a place removed from the village. In most similar contexts, sources use the word *grāmānte* ("at the boundary of a village").

10. The candidate here internalizes the Gāyatrī verse by first reciting each of its three feet separately. Given the difference in the syntax, it is impossible to accurately reproduce the three feet separately in English.

fire at the seat of the Brahman priest,[11] covers them with a black antelope skin, and, sitting there, keeps awake that night. Rising at the hour sacred to Brahman,[12] he bathes according to the rule and performs the morning fire sacrifice. Then, after reciting the Great Utterances,[13] he should stand in the middle of the water and recite softly the hymn "Swift runs this giver of delight" [RV 9.58]. Thereafter, he gratifies some Brahmins with food, gets them to announce that the day is auspicious and to proclaim success and prosperity, adds fuel to the fire, and makes an offering of ghee, saying,

> To the in-breath, svāhā! To the out-breath, svāhā! To the diffused breath, svāhā! To the up-breath, svāhā! To the middle breath, svāhā!

After that, as he recites the Puruṣa hymn [RV 10.90], he offers a piece of firewood, ghee, and porridge[14] at each verse. Then, after silently reciting the Puruṣa hymn and arranging the goblet of holy water, he offers the oblation to Agni Sviṣṭakṛt.[15] He offers according to his wish the oblations Jaya and the like to Agni Sviṣṭakṛt.[16] He should then present to his teacher a cow, gold, and a bowl of ghee, as well as anything else that he might be inclined to give, and pay his respects to the teacher, saying, "May the Maruts pour down on me . . ." [TA 2.18.1]. Thereupon, he should deposit the fires in himself, saying, "Come, O fire, with that body of yours worthy of sacrifice . . ." [TB 2.5.8.8]. Then, standing before the fire or in water, he recites three times softly, three times in a medium voice, and three time aloud,

> OṂ Earth, Atmosphere, Heaven! I have renounced!

Facing the east, then, he fills his cupped hands with water and pours it down, as he says:

> I grant safety to all being!

14. Likewise, Bodhāyana also, after giving the passage beginning with "OṂ Earth, Atmosphere, Heaven! I have renounced!" until "pours it down," goes on to say:

11. At Vedic sacrifices this priest sits silently to the south of the east fire and rectifies any errors committed by the other priests.

12. This is the period from first light to sunrise; see Ypra 8.34–35n.

13. The Great Utterances (*vyāhṛti*) are either three (*bhūḥ, bhuvaḥ, svaḥ*) or seven (with the addition of the four other worlds: *mahar, janas, tapas,* and *satya*).

14. The porridge (*caru*) is made by boiling rice and barley in milk.

15. This is the aspect of the fire god that "makes a sacrifice properly offered," i.e., it makes the sacrifice successful and fruitful. This oblation is offered at the conclusion of every sacrifice.

16. Three supplementary oblations called Jaya, Rāṣṭrabhṛt, and Abhyātana may be offered by a sacrificer to obtain specific desires, such as success. See TS 3.4.6.2 and Śabara's commentary on the PMS 3.4.9.25. For a description of the rites, see *Śrautakośa*, English Section, I.1, pp. 201–205. The reading of this and the previous sentence, as one can see from the variants given in the critical edition, is quite uncertain.

No being will ever pose a danger to a sage who wanders after he has given safety to all beings. [BDh 2.17.27–30]

15. Vasiṣṭha the Elder:

When, according to the sequence of tone,[17] a man utters three times the words "I have renounced," by that very renunciation he frees forthwith from hell thirty generations of forefathers before him and a further thirty beyond them, as well as thirty generations that will come after him.

16. For, when it sees a twice-born man who has renounced, the sun swerves from its place, thinking, "This man will split my orb and proceed to the highest Brahman."[18]

17. If a learned Brahmin who has become detached and who has a desire to enter the renouncer's order happens to die, he will never again come into being, irrespective of the order in which he lived.[19]

18. The same author states:

A man who has not maintained the three Vedic fires [see Ch. 4.11 n. 8], as well as a widower, should perform the rite of renunciation in this manner.

19. Śaunaka:

He then takes the ocher garment, saying, "Well-dressed and covered has come the youthful one . . ." [RV 3.8.4]; the triple staff, saying, "Friend, protect me"; and the sacrificial string, with the words "That health and well-being we choose. . ." [TS 2.6.10.2]. He takes the sling, saying, "May that bright light born beyond this atmosphere . . ." [TS 4.2.5.2]; the bowl, saying, "OṂ"; the water strainer with the words "The purifier with which the gods ever cleanse themselves . . ." [TB 1.4.8.6]; and the water pot with the words "The light by which the gods rose up . . ." [TS 5.7.2.2].

20. Kātyāyana, on the other hand, states:

He takes the bowl, reciting the seven Great Utterances.

21. Vasiṣṭha:

He takes the sacrificial string, saying: "Wear the white sacrificial string . . ." [PG 2.2.10; BU 85],[20] and the five items beginning with the triple staff with the mantras "The swan seated in purity . . ." [RV 4.40.5], "His rays lift it up high for all to see . . ." [RV 1.50.1], "The splendid face of the gods has risen . . ." [RV 1.115.1], "That bright eye, divinely ordained . . ." [RV 7.66.16], and "Homage to Mitra's and Varuṇa's eye . . ." [RV 10.37.1]. He

17. That is, in a soft, medium, and loud voice; see Ch. 4.13.

18. The belief that the sun, and sometimes the moon, acted like a door shutting off this world from the immortal world beyond is expressed in several Upaniṣads: BaU 6.2.15; ChU 5.10.1; KauU 1.2.

19. The syntax is problematic, but the meaning appears to be that he will not be reborn in saṃsāra even if he were to die before he could actually become a renouncer.

20. Since only the first word of this verse (*yajñopavītam*) is given, I cannot be absolutely sure that this is the intended verse. For another formula with the same first word and coming directing after this in the PG 2.2.10, see Ch. 4.27 below.

should then worship the fire with the mantra "Member by member, joint by joint . . ." [RV 10.97.12] and discard the fire with the two mantras beginning with "Set ablaze. . . ." [RV 6.15.7]. He should then go to the outskirts of the village and take the three staffs with the words "The bull roars aloud, bound with a triple bond" [RV 4.58.3]. After silently reciting the four purificatory verses and the triple prayer,[21] he should take three steps, saying, "Three steps did Viṣṇu take . . ." [RV 1.22.18]. After worshipping with the formula "That highest step of Viṣṇu . . ." [RV 1.22.20], he should softly recite "You are self-existent . . ." [VS 2.26]. He should then give safety to all living beings—to the creatures of the water such as fish and to animals on land such as cattle, deer, and reptiles—and thereafter refrain from picking flowers, roots, and fruits, from cutting trees, from honey, meat, and falsehood, and from giving and taking.

22. Kātyāyana states:

Abandoning his own village and relatives, he should go to another village and devote himself to silent prayer and meditation. He may subsist on almsfood that he solicits or receives unasked. He should avoid love, anger, lust, and hatred. Living in this manner all his life, he attains Brahman and is not reborn.

23. Śaunaka:

Then, without looking around and in silence, he should walk toward the east or the north. He should zealously cultivate tranquillity, self-control, and similar virtues. He should engage in study, reflection, and meditation and always recite the syllable OṂ.

24. That concludes the procedure of renunciation given by Śaunaka.

25. Kapila states:

A man who has not maintained a sacred fire, however, after shaving his head completely or wearing just a topknot, should fast a day and a night, take a bath, and with his hand offer some water into the water, saying,

> Waters indeed are all the gods. I offer to all the gods, svāhā! I have risen above the desire for sons, the desire for wealth, and the desire for worlds, svāhā!

Then he says three times softly, three times in a medium voice, and three times aloud:

> OṂ Earth, Atmosphere, Heaven! I have renounced!

For it is said that gods are triply true [see BDh 2.17.28.]. Then he fills his cupped hands with water and pours it on the ground, saying,

> Safety from me to all creatures, svāhā!

21. The Sanskrit is unclear. It may also mean "the fourfold and triple purificatory verse." In any case, I am not sure what the four verses are. The triple verse (*trika*) is the syllable OṂ, the three great utterances, and the Gāyatrī verse. See Ch. 5.82.

He then takes one or more staffs [see Ch. 3.38 n.16], a water strainer, a water pot, a sling, and a bowl and, in the presence of the fire, forsakes his sons, friends, enemies, and relatives.

26. Vasiṣṭha the Elder states:

Now, a man who has maintained the three Vedic fires should rise at dawn and make one of the following sacrifices using rice and barley: Vaiśvānarī, Pāthīkṛtī, or Tantumatī.[22] Then, going up to the east fire, he should offer in it the sacrificial vessels,[23] saying, "To the heavenly world, svāhā!" and deposit that fire in himself, reciting the mantra "This is your proper womb . . ." [TS 1.5.5.2]. Then, going up to the south fire, he should offer in it the mortar and pestle, saying, "This Agni in the land is rich . . ." [VS 3.40], and deposit that fire, reciting the mantra "This is your proper womb . . ." [TS 1.5.5.2]. Then, going up to the householder's fire, he should offer in it the fire drill, saying, "He is the householder, this Agni of the householder . . ." [VS 3.39], and deposit that fire, reciting the mantra "This is your proper womb . . ." [TS 1.5.5.2]. Standing in the middle of the altar, then, he should silently recite the hymn "A thousand heads has Puruṣa . . . [RV 10.90] and offer worship with the mantra "From the waters he was born . . ." [TA 3.13.1].[24] He should then worship the self, saying, "I know this great Puruṣa . . ." [TA 3.13.1], and offer rice balls to his ancestors in the following manner:

In the eastern direction: "May my ancestors together with Indra become sated." After worshipping them with the mantra "Indra the rescuer . . ." [RV 6.47.11], he should offer the rice balls to his ancestors.

In the south-eastern direction: "May my ancestors together with Agni become sated." After worshipping them with the mantra "Agni is the head . . ." [RV 8.44.16], he should offer the rice balls to his ancestors.

In the southern direction: "May my ancestors together with Yama become sated." After worshipping them with the mantra "You are Yama . . ." [RV 1.163.3], he should offer the rice balls to his ancestors.

In the south-western direction: "May my ancestors together with Nirṛti become sated." After worshipping them with the mantra "This is your share, Nirṛti . . ." [TS 1.8.1.1], he should offer the rice balls to his ancestors.

22. Vaiśvānarī is an offering to Agni "present in all men." This is the sacrifice normally enjoined prior to renunciation. A detailed description of it is given in Sp 16. Pāthīkṛtī is an offering to Agni, "who prepares the way." It is prescribed as a penance for one who has neglected to offer the full-moon and new-moon sacrifices (MK 5.2430; Rudradatta, commenting on ApSr 9.8.5). Tantumatī is an offering to Agni Tantumat (probably meaning "uninterrupted like a thread"), again recommended as an expiation for neglecting ritual obligations (SanGr 5.4.1–2).

23. Other sources specify that he should throw in the fire only the wooden utensils. Those made of stone or metal are given away to the priests.

24. This is the beginning of the so-called Uttaranārāyaṇa hymn, which gets its name from the fact that it follows the Puruṣa (here identified with Nārāyaṇa) hymn both in the VS (31.17) and in the TA.

In the western direction: "May my ancestors together with Varuṇa become sated." After worshipping them with the mantra "A broad path indeed has Varuṇa made . . ." [RV 1.24.8], he should offer the rice balls to his ancestors.

In the north-western direction: "May my ancestors together with Vāyu become sated." After worshipping them with the mantra "A hundred horses, O Vāyu, . . ." [RV 4.48.5], he should offer the rice balls to his ancestors.

In the northern direction: "May my ancestors together with Soma become sated." After worshipping them with the mantra "King Soma . . ." [VS 19.72], he should offer the rice balls to his ancestors.

In the north-eastern direction: "May my ancestors together with Īśāna become sated." After worshipping them with the mantra "Lord of this world . . ." [RV 7.32.22], he should offer the rice balls to his ancestors.

In the direction of the zenith: "May my ancestors together with Brahmā become sated." After worshipping them with the mantra "Brahman of old was born in the east . . ." [TS 4.2.8.2], he should offer the rice balls to his ancestors.

In the direction of the nadir: "May my ancestors together with the snakes become sated." After worshipping them with the mantra "Homage to the snakes . . ." [TS 4.2.8.3], he should offer the rice balls to his ancestors.

27. After completing the offering of rice balls, he tells his relatives, "Give your approval," and takes a hundred blades of sacred Darbha grass. The rest of the procedure should be gathered from Śaunaka's statement beginning "You are the sacrificial string . . ." [PG 2.2.10].[25]

28. Kapila mentions a special feature applicable only in the case of a man who has maintained the three Vedic fires:

If he has maintained the three Vedic fires, he should perform a sacrifice to Prajāpati at which he gives all his possessions as a sacrificial gift to the priests. He should then deposit the fires in himself, reciting the mantra "This is your proper womb . . ." [TS 1.5.5.2], and, standing in the middle of the altar, contemplate Viṣṇu, the god Nārāyaṇa, carrying a conch, discus, and mace, robed in yellow, and wearing a crown, bracelet, and earring. Receiving his teacher's permission, then, he should recite the Praiṣa mantra.[26]

25. This passage of Śaunaka is not given by Yādava, but must have been known to his readers for him to mention only its beginning. A passage with a similar beginning is given at Ch. 4.21 but ascribed there to Vasiṣṭha.

26. Praiṣa is the technical term for the mantra "I have renounced," which is considered to be the essential element of the renunciatory rite (Olivelle 1975).

29. Jāmadagnya:

A twice-born man who is free from debt may undertake the rite of renunciation after reciting for twelve days the hymn "Order and truth . . ."[27] and learning the meaning of the Vedas in the prescribed manner.

30. He should get his hair and beard shaved and in silence observe a fast at a holy place of water, keeping awake that night of the changing moon.[28]

31. He should perform a sacrifice to Prajāpati at which he gives all his possessions as a sacrificial gift to the priests and deposit the fires in himself, reciting the verse "Come, O Agni, with that body of yours worthy of sacrifice . . ." [TB 2.5.8.8].

32. The Brahmin should stand within the sacrificial enclosure and recite "I am the mover of the tree . . ." [TU 1.10.1]. The Veda is really the tree of Brahman. He becomes fit for Brahman.

33. The son or the pupil is admonished: "Speak the truth [TU 1.11.1]. One should never seek to obtain almsfood by giving advice or taking part in debates."[29]

34. He says three times softly, three times in a medium voice, and three time aloud, "OṂ Earth, Atmosphere, Heaven! I have renounced." For the exponents of the Veda declare that gods are triply true.

35. The ascetic should then take the triple staff, saying, "Three steps did Viṣṇu take . . ." [RV 1.22.18], and, if he is wise, he should take as well the staffs of mind, speech, and body.[30]

36. "Agni is the divinity, and Gāyatrī is the meter": with this mantra[31] the twice-born mendicant should take a bowl made of bottle-gourd or wood. He should take the water strainer with the verse "With the golden strainer sacred to Prajāpati . . ." [TB 1.8.6]. A sage should be equipped with a strainer and drink water purified with it.

27. This is the Aghamarṣaṇa hymn (RV 10.190) recited to remove sins. See MNU 143-48, together with Varenne's note there, and Ch. 6.34 n. 16.

28. The term *parvan* refers to the days of the full and new moon, as well as to the eighth and fourteenth days of the lunar fortnight. However, most sources recommend that the rite of renunciation be performed on the full moon. "Place of water" refers to any body of water that one can enter to bathe, such as a lake, river, or tank.

29. The verse is somewhat unclear. It is unlikely that these words would be spoken by the man undergoing the initiation It is more likely that they are addressed to him by his father or teacher. I have included the second half of the verse as part of the instruction. If it stands outside, it would be quite out of place within the context. The second half of the verse is found also in VaDh 10.21 and MDh 6.50 (see Ch. 7.8).

30. This is a common allegory of the three staffs of an ascetic. The Sanskrit term "*daṇḍa*" ("rod") can mean staff, rod, punishment, and restraint. The control of one's mind, speech, and body are thus considered the true triple staff.

31. I am not altogether sure about this reading. Generally, one announces the divinity, the meter, and the seer connected with a particular mantra, but that announcement itself is not regarded as a mantra. In Ch. 4.19 the mantra at the taking of the bowl is OṂ.

37. No being will ever pose a danger to a man who gives the gift of safety as he pours water from his cupped hands, saying, "To all beings, svāhā!"

38. Going silently toward the east or the north of the village, he should bathe in the prescribed manner and control his breath six times.

39. He then offers the sacrificial string in water with the words "Earth, svāhā!" and takes the triple staff, saying, "Friend, protect me." In the Supplement there is a statement enjoining the disposal of the sacrificial string worn previously.[32]

Renunciation When Death Is Imminent

40. We will describe next the procedure of renunciation at a time of imminent death [see Ch. 2.61 n. 28]. 41. With reference to this, Jābāli states:

> If a man is in mortal danger, he may renounce orally or mentally. This path has been prescribed here for Brahmins. [JU 68–69]

42. Aṅgiras:

> There is an exception in the case of those who are in moral danger: they need not follow the normal procedure or perform any rites. The rule for people in mortal danger is that they can renounce by merely reciting the Praiṣa [see Ch. 4.28 n. 26].

43. Likhita:

> When a man is about to be killed by a tiger, fire, a robber, or a snake, or when a man suffering from a serious sickness wishes to die, he should take to renunciation either following or disregarding the normal procedure.
>
> 44. If a man says "I have renounced," even with his last breath, he will rescue his forefathers and place himself on the path to liberation.
>
> 45. After he has thus renounced, the twice-born man who reverts to lay life when the danger of death has passed, as well as those who maintain social contact with such a man—all of them become outcastes by their actions. No expiation is possible for such people.

32. It is unclear which supplement Yādava means. The Vaiṣṇava tradition that required its renouncers to wear a sacrificial string interpreted scriptural statements enjoining its abandonment as referring to the sacrificial string worn previously while the renouncer was a householder or a student. Such a text is cited anonymously in the Yls I.50–58 (Olivelle 1987, 59–60): "Having clipped his nails, he should discard the old sacrificial string, garment, and water pot, and, taking new ones, enter the renouncer's order." The implication is that the candidate takes a new sacrificial string at his renunciatory rite. For the controversy concerning the sacrificial string, see Olivelle 1986 –87.

46. After he has thus renounced, if the danger of death passes, he should receive in the presence of the teacher the triple staff and other articles while reciting the appropriate mantras. And taking them, he should engage in the practice of yoga.

47. When any of these articles is damaged [see Ch. 3.62 n. 28] and he finds a new one, hc should take it himself while reciting the appropriate mantra. He should throw the damaged ones in water, saying, "Go to the ocean, svāhā!" And he should learn the laws pertaining to ascetics—that is the teaching of Likhita.

48. Three methods of renouncing are given for people in danger of death, according to the statement ". . . either following or disregarding the procedure" [see Ch. 4.42]. The proper procedure should be followed if a person is somehow able to perform it. If he is unable, he should recite orally just the Praiṣa: "I have renounced." If he is unable even to do that, he should just mentally abandon attachments. That concludes the procedure of renunciation at a time of imminent death.

49. That ends the fourth chapter, entitled "The Procedure of Renunciation," of the *Collection of Ascetic Laws*.

CHAPTER FIVE

Principal Activities

1. Next I will discuss the principal activities of ascetics. 2. In this connection, Uśanas writes:

> There are two kinds of vedic students, according to the scriptures: the temporary and the permanent; and likewise, two kinds of hermits: those who take their wives with them and those who leave their wives behind.
>
> 3. Mendicants likewise are of two types: mendicant renouncers and renouncers who abandon vedic rites; while there are numerous divisions of householders, such as Śālīna.[1]

4. Manu has declared only a twofold division of people belonging to the four orders of life. Out of these, listen now to the description of a mendicant renouncer.

> 5. When a twice-born man becomes detached from the pleasures of this world and the next, he may depart for the ascetic life after offering a sacrifice to Agni Vaiśvānara at which he gives all his possessions to the priests as their sacrificial fee [see Ch. 4.25 n. 22].

6. So, on the twofold division of wandering ascetics there is agreement. 7. Some, nevertheless, report a fourfold division:

> There are four kinds of mendicants: Kuṭīcaka, Bahūdaka, Haṃsa, and Paramahaṃsa, listed in an ascending order of eminence.

8. Others, however, claim that this division is authorized not by the Vedas but by the texts of Pāñcarātra and Sāṃkhya.[2] 9. And Āpastamba refutes that view:[3]

1. For an extensive discussion of the various classifications of these four institutions, see Olivelle 1993, 161–73.

2. In Yādava's eyes, these texts were clearly inferior and could not be completely trusted. See his opening comments (Ch. 1.10) that his treatise is based solely on the Dharmaśāstras and not on the Epics and Purāṇas.

3. It is not altogether clear what that view is. I think that Yādava is firmly opposed to the fourfold division given above, not so much because it contains four

Some require him to go completely naked. Abandoning truth and falsehood, pleasure and pain, the Vedas, this world and the next, he should seek his self. When he comes to know it, he attains liberation.

That is forbidden by the sacred texts. Moreover, if a man attains liberation upon knowing it, then he would not experience pain even in this life. This explains what follows.[4] [ApDh 2.21.12-17]

10. Atri:

Some mendicants, the Vedas note, wear topknots, while others have their heads completely shaved. There are four kinds of Brahmin mendicants, but all of them carry triple staffs.

11. Parāśara:

Now, there are four kinds of wandering ascetics: Kuṭīcaka, Bahūdaka, Haṃsa, and Paramahaṃsa. Of these, Kuṭīcakas are those who get a son of theirs or a similar person to build them a hut; give up lust, anger, greed, delusion, pride, envy, and the like; and renounce in the prescribed manner. They carry a triple staff and a water strainer, wear an ocher garment, and devote themselves to bathing, purification, sipping, silent prayer, private vedic recitation, chastity, and meditation. At the time for begging, they obtain food only from a son of theirs or from a similar person just sufficient to sustain life and always dwell in that hut. Thus they liberate themselves.

Bahūdakas are those who carry a triple staff, a water pot, a water strainer made of fine thread, and a sling, and wear an ocher garment. They explain the meaning of the Vedāntas and beg almsfood from virtuous Brahmins. Thus they liberate themselves.

Haṃsas are those who carry a triple staff, a water strainer, and a sling and wear a sacrificial string. They consume cow's urine and cow dung and observe vows such as the following: fasting for one or three nights, or for a month or a fortnight, the Kṛcchra penance, the lunar fast, and the Sāntapana, Mahāsāntapana, Parāka, and Tulāpuruṣa penances.[5] They live in

---

classes of ascetics but because it presents them in a hierarchy with the Paramahaṃsa at the top. This is precisely the arrangement preferred by Advaita (see Olivelle 1986–87). Yādava sees Āpastamba's comments as refuting the Advaita claim that their highest ascetics are liberated while still alive (*jīvanmukta*) and are free from many of the rules of Brahmanical etiquette and ethics.

4. The reference is unclear. The commentator, Haradatta, explains that even after attaining knowledge, one must perform the yogic exercises in order to eliminate pain, including the pain a man will suffer in afterlife. The intent clearly is to preclude the possibility of someone living an antinomian life by claiming that he has attained the liberating knowledge.

5. For *kṛcchra*, see Ch. 4.2 n. 1. Unless the night is specifically indicated by the context, in Sanskrit the term "night" often stands for a full twenty-four-hour day. The "lunar fast" consists of increasing and decreasing by a mouthful the quantity of food eaten each day, according to the waxing and waning of the moon. One eats fif-

sacred areas abounding in cows and Brahmins. Thus they liberate themselves.

Paramahaṃsas are those who carry a triple staff, a water strainer, and a sling. They wear a sacrificial string, as well as an under- and an overgarment. They spend a single night in a village and five nights in a town, at a sacred bathing spot, or in a religious house. At the proper time for begging, they make a funnel out of dried leaves and beg almsfood only from Brahmin households, eating just eight mouthfuls. They are faithful to the twilight worship, and they always live at the foot of a tree. Thus they liberate themselves.

Renouncers Who Abandon Vedic Rites

12. Speaking of the two types of renouncers, Manu describes the renouncer who abandons vedic rites:

> I have explained this distinct law of self-controlled ascetics; listen now to the ritual discipline of renouncers who abandon vedic rites. [MDh 6.86]

13. In some regions they read at this place the three verses beginning with "Only after paying his three debts . . .".[6]

> Vedic student, householder, forest hermit, and mendicant: these four distinct orders of life are rooted in the householder.
>
> 14. Now, when a Brahmin acts as prescribed and undertakes these in the proper sequence as spelled out in the sacred texts, each and every one of them[7] leads him to the highest state.
>
> 15. Yet, following the directives of the Vedas, the householder is proclaimed to be the best of all these, for he supports the other three.

---

teen mouthfuls on the day of the full moon and decreases the amount of food by one mouthful a day until the new moon, on which day one observes a total fast. The intake of food is similarly increased during the second half of the month. At the Sāntapana a person subsists on the urine of cows, cow dung, milk, sour milk, ghee, and a decoction of Kuśa grass. The penitent may eat all of them on one day and fast on the next day or subsist on each of these six products on six consecutive days and fast on the seventh. The latter is called Mahāsāntapana, "great Sāntapana." At the Parāka one fasts for twelve days, whereas at the Tulāpuruṣa, according to one description, the penitent subsists on oil-cake, the scum of boiled rice, buttermilk, water, and barley meal, eating each substance in succession on only one day and observing a total fast on the final day. For sources, see Olivelle 1986, 130 nn. 39, 42, and Olivelle 1987, 56 n. 17.

6. The three verse are MDh 6.35-37; see Ch. 2.5. Yādava appears to be referring to a recension of Manu in which these verses are given immediately after MDh 6.86.

7. The Sanskrit term *api* ("also") appears to have a concessive force here. As several commentators point out, the intention is to assert not that a person must undertake all four orders in succession if he is to attain the highest state but that each of these four (this appears to be the sense of *sarve 'pi*: "all") can lead to that state.

16. As all rivers and rivulets ultimately end up in the ocean, so people in all orders of life ultimately end up with the householder.[8]

17. All twice-born people who belong to any of these four orders should observe the ten-point Law diligently and unfailingly.

18. Resolve, forbearance, self-control, honesty, cleanliness, mastery of the senses, modesty, learning, truthfulness, and suppressing anger: these are the ten points of the Law.

19. Those Brahmins who learn and then observe the ten points of the Law attain the highest state.

20. If a twice-born man has steadfastly followed the ten-point Law and is free from debt, he may renounce after he has learned the Vedānta in the prescribed manner.

21. After he has renounced all ritual activities, thus avoiding their inherent dangers,[9] let him live at ease under the care of his sons and devote himself to the recitation of the Veda. [MDh 6.87–95]

22. Some propose that a Kuṭīcaka live in the very same manner. By using the term "points" in the statement "ten points of the Law" [Ch. 4.19], the author intends to point out that they are supplementary to the Law pertaining to the orders of life. The meaning, therefore, is that, as they follow their respective Law, people belonging to all the orders should be in the habit of practicing the ten points of the Law beginning with resolve.

Mendicant Renouncers

23. Next, we will describe the Law pertaining to the order of mendicant renouncers. Kratu states:

> Sāṃkhya, Yoga, devotion to Viṣṇu, vigilance, detachment: these are what is essential, while duties other than these are said to characterize it as an order of life.

24. This is what the text intends to say. "Sāṃkhya" is the knowledge of the cosmological principles. "Yoga" may be either the one with

8. The meaning of "end up in" appears to be as follows. The existence of rivers depends on their connection with the ocean: it provides them initially with their water and into it they finally merge. Similarly, the existence of people in other orders depends on the householder in a variety of ways: the others obtain food from householders, and new recruits are either householders or their children (see MDh 3.77–78). In a more pregnant sense, however, they end up with the householder, because in the rebirth process they become transformed into the semen of the householder through whom they receive their new birth.

9. Ritual duties as well as normal household activities entail violence and injury to living beings. On the dangers of household life, see MDh 3.68; 5.39–41.

eight components or the one with six.[10] "Devotion to Viṣṇu" is the worship of the Lord, namely, love of the Supreme Self. "Vigilance" is to remain constantly alert. "Detachment" is not to be attached to sensual objects. 25. Accordingly, Bṛhaspati remarks:

> When a man is attached to the Supreme Self and detached from all else, and when he is freed from all desires, he is fit to eat almsfood. [cf. NPU 139]

26. The meaning of the statement "these are what is essential, while duties other than these . . ." [Ch. 4.23] is as follows: These alone constitute the principal Law of that order of life. Duties other than these, for example twilight worship, merely characterize it as an order of life, while the Law of that order constitutes its true essence. A person who is steadfast in the performance of those duties is merely steadfast in his order; he is not steadfast in the Law of his order. Activities such as twilight worship are thus reduced to the level of accessories to the Law of that order; they themselves are not part of the Law.[11] 27. This position is supported by Dakṣa:

> A man who does not perform the twilight worship is always impure and is unfit to perform any rite. Whatever other rite he may perform, he will not reap its reward.

Sāṃkhya

28. Of those essential duties, I now describe Sāṃkhya. Yama states:

> No matter what order of life he may be devoted to, when a man knows the twenty-five cosmological principles—that is, the primary substances and the transformations—he is freed from sorrow.

10. Yādava discusses (Ch. 5.47-89) the former, which is the traditional Yoga system, but not the latter, which the Pāñcarātra text *Viṣṇusaṃhitā* calls "Bhāgavatayoga" (30.1–2). It lists the six components as control of breath, withdrawal of senses, concentration, reasoning (*tarka*), trance, and meditation (30.57–58).

11. Kratu's text and Yādava's commentary on it are far from clear. The lack of clarity, no doubt, has caused the bewildering variety of readings obtained in the manuscripts. I believe the text of the critical edition is correct. An inability to follow Yādava's thought appear to have caused several of the scribes/editors to emend his commentary. Yādava distinguishes the outward manifestations of a particular order of life from its inner core or essence. The former he refers to as mere "order of life" (*āśrama*), while he characterizes the latter as "the Law of the order" (*āśramadharma*). The Law consists of the five points mentioned by Kratu, while other duties, such as twilight worship, constitute what Yādava terms *āśrama*, that is, activities that outwardly mark a particular order of life. I assume that begging and carrying a triple staff—indeed most of the customs discussed in Chapter 6—fall into the latter category. Chapter 5, on the other hand, is devoted to the description of the former five points (especially the first three), which according to Yādava constitute the "principal duties" (*mukhyakarma*) of an ascetic. See also Ch. 1.23.

29. Mind, intellect, ego, ether, air, fire, water, and earth are the eight primary substances. The remaining sixteen are the transformations.

30. Ears, eyes, tongue, nose, skin, ideas, sound, form, taste, touch, smell, speech, hands, anus, sexual organs, and feet are, according to the scriptures, the sixteen transformations.

31. "Ideas" refers to the activities of the mental organs.

Sages call this the knowledge of the twenty-four. The twenty-fifth is the unmanifest,[12] and the twenty-sixth is the Supreme Lord. When they come to know this, ascetics with calm minds attain liberation.

32. Without sound or taste, beyond touch or smell, formless and pure, transcending pleasure and pain—that is the highest step of Viṣṇu.

33. It is unborn, immaculate, and calm, it is unmanifest and imperishable, it is without beginning or end, it is knowledge, it is Brahman—that is the highest step of Viṣṇu.

34. Bṛhaspati:

This here is the highest being, from which manifold beings arise and into which they return, like pots from clay.

35. This here is the highest light, of which others are like sparks. It is scattered in the sun, moon, fire, lightning, stars, planets, and the like.

36. This here is supreme bliss; others, mere specks of joy. From it they drink who do meritorious deeds—Brahmā, Indra, ancestors, and men.

37. In His aspects of unity and multiplicity, the Lord resides in all beings. This is the highest unity—the highest being, the highest goal.

38. After this opening statement, Bṛhaspati goes on to state in closing:

When, in this manner, a man comes to know Brahman, he is freed from saṃsāra.

39. Śaunaka:

Earth, water, fire, wind, and ether—a learned man should recognize these as the five elements.

40. Ears, eyes, skin, tongue, and nose—one should recognized these as the five organs of cognition within this body.

41. Mind, intellect, and self, as well as the unmanifest—these, they say, are the four that are said to be beyond the sense organs.

42. Sound, form, touch, taste, and smell—a wise man should always recognize these as the objects of the sense organs.

43. Hands, feet, organ of generation, tongue, and anus—he should always recognize these as the five organs of action within this body.

12. This probably refers to the Sāṃkhya category of primal nature (*prakṛti*). In classical Sāṃkhya there are only twenty-five principles, including spirit, primal nature, and the twenty-three products of primal nature.

44. These twenty-four are said to be the cosmic principles. Transcending them stands the Male Principle that one understands as the self.

45. When they come to know this, ascetics with calm minds attain liberation. This here is the supreme secret, this is the highest imperishable state.

46. The rest of this text beginning with "Without sound or taste, beyond touch or smell, formless . . . ," is identical to the passage of Yama [see 5.32-33]. One should likewise explore also other texts, such as the Epics, the Purāṇas, the legal works of Manu and others, as well as the Vedāntas, to gain an understanding of the cosmic categories, an understanding that is the expressed by the term "Sāṃkhya."

Yoga

47. Next, I describe the yogic discipline for a person who has an understanding of the cosmic categories. The yogic discipline with eight components is given in the work of Patañjali [Ys].

The eight components are restraints, constraints, siting posture, control of breathing, withdrawal of senses, concentration, meditation, and trance [Ys 2.29]. The restraints are to abstain from injuring, to tell the truth, to refrain from stealing, chastity, and poverty [Ys 2.30]. The constraints are purification, contentment, austerity, vedic recitation, and contemplation of the Lord [Ys 2.32]. The siting posture is a position that is stable and comfortable [Ys 2.46]. The control of breathing is the suspension of the breathing process [Ys 2.49]. The withdrawal of senses is when the senses do not come into contact with their respective objects, thereby coming to truly resemble the nature of the intellect [Ys 2.54]. Concentration is to focus the mind on a particular object [Ys 3.1]. The uninterrupted focusing of one's thought on that object is meditation [Ys 3.2]. That very meditation, when it reveals just the object and becomes bereft, as it were, of its own nature, is trance [Ys 3.3].

48. Of these eight components, those beginning with the withdrawal of senses are essential, like the hands and other limbs of Devadatta, while the rest are considered components because of their instrumentality.[13] When some of these come into conflict with other more intrinsic components, one should observe the more intrinsic components. 49. Accordingly, the Blessed Vyāsa declares:

13. The meaning appears to be that the three components—withdrawal, concentration, and trance—are true components (lit., "bodily parts") of the yogic discipline of the mind, just as hands and feet are essential parts of the body. The first six components, on the other hand, are not essential but serve only to promote the discipline of the mind.

> A wise man should always practice the restraints, even if he has to disregard the others. A man falls if he neglects the restraints and devotes himself solely to the constraints.

50. These same components are described in many different ways in scriptural texts. To begin with, Kratu, after stating "or else with the components of yoga such as restraints" [Ch. 6.23], goes on to say:

> Resolve, forbearance, self-control, honesty, purity, mastery of the senses, modesty, learning, truthfulness, and suppressing anger—this is the hallmark of the Law.
>
> 51. Abstention from injuring, equanimity, and honesty; forbearance, self-control, tranquillity, and the like; contentment, and freedom from malice, deceit, and hostility—the scriptures call these the restraints.
>
> 52. Doubt, pride, sloth, attachment, desire for results from actions, fear, possessions, and selfishness—the abandonment (of these), the scriptures say, constitutes the minor restraints.
>
> 53. Lust, passion, strife, sleep, delusion, hunger, sinful thoughts, hate, egotism, and greed—victory over these, the scriptures say, constitutes the controls.
>
> 54. Humility, virtue, belief,[14] yogic discipline, good conduct, learning, rites, impartiality, gentleness, firmness, and detachment—these are the higher restraints.
>
> 55. Meditation, tranquillity, amiability, and silence, as well as to refrain from entreating, yearning, touching, or looking—these are said to be the constraints.

56–57. Śaunaka:

> Ten vows are enjoined on all ascetics: not to injure, to tell the truth, honesty, chastity, poverty, to suppress anger, obedient service of the teacher, cleanliness, to refrain from wrongful conduct in mental, verbal, and physical activities, and to avoid carelessness.

58. Bodhāyana:

> Now there are these vows: not to injure, to tell the truth, honesty, to refrain from sex, and renunciation.[15] There are also five secondary vows: to suppress anger, obedient service of the teacher, to avoid carelessness, cleanliness, and purity in food. [BDh 2.18.2-3]

14. The term "*āstikya*" (lit., "the condition of one who says 'It is'") has a range of meaning, including the belief in an afterlife, in the operation of *karma*, and in gods.

15. The last item is *tyāga*. The commentator Govinda and, following him, Bühler take it to mean giving gifts or liberality. I think this is less likely, given the general prohibition against the giving of gifts by ascetics. I prefer to take it as a general reference to the ascetic attitude of renunciation or abandonment with regard to all possessions and relationships.

59. Yama:

> Now King Yama, the son of Aditi, has proclaimed the duties prescribed for devout ascetics, as well as for renouncers who abandon vedic rites.
>
> 60. Not to injure, to tell the truth, to suppress anger, chastity, austerity, learning, honesty, to avoid transgressions—this, the scriptures say, is the tenfold Law.

61. The Law becomes tenfold because austerity is distinguished into mental, verbal, and physical.[16]

> Contentment, obedient service of the teacher, avoiding carelessness, forbearance, compassion, silence, purity in food, and cleanliness—these are the eight vows.

62. Since there are different types of injury, we must undoubtedly distinguish also different types of non-injury. Now there are ten types of injury: causing anxiety, causing pain, causing someone to weep, drawing blood, calumny, destroying someone's happiness, conquest, making someone grovel, obstructing someone's welfare, and killing. 63. Jābāli the Elder, moreover, gives distinctions that are not well known:

> The man who does the killing, the man who gives his consent, the man who butchers the carcass, those who buy and sell, the cook, the one who assists in the cooking, and the eater: these are the eight types of killers.

64. Vāyu describes truthfulness:

> Wise men assert that a lie in the service of righteousness causes no harm. In spite of that, one should not tell a lie. Such an inclination is fraught with danger.

65. The same author describes honesty:

> An ascetic who seeks to be righteous should not tell what is untrue. Even if he is in dire straits, moreover, he should never succumb to stealing.

66–67. Bṛhaspati gives the different types of chastity:

> To remember, to recount, to engage in amorous play, to look at, to speak in secret, to formulate an intention, to make a firm resolve, and to perform the act—wise men present these as the eight types of sexual relationships. Their opposite is chastity, and it, likewise, is of eight types.

68. Likhita describes poverty:

> He should not speak in Sanskrit but should behave like a man who is childish and dumb. He should not accumulate possessions, not even the articles of an ascetic, for use at a future date.

16. Yādava here intends to show how the Law is tenfold even though only eight items are listed, because austerity is further divided into three types.

69. I will cite later [Ch. 6.5–8] Garga's description of purification.

70. Yama describes vedic recitation:

> When he is tired of meditation, an ascetic shall always spend his time in silent prayer, and when he is tired of silent prayer, in meditation. He should thus continue this process, meditating sometimes and praying silently at other times.
>
> 71. The four cooked offerings along with the vedic sacrifices—all those taken together are not worth a sixteenth portion of the sacrifice of silent prayer.[17] [cf. MDh 2.86]
>
> 72. A sacrifice of silent prayer is ten times better than a vedic sacrifice; that prayer is a hundred times better, the scriptures say, when it is said inaudibly, and a thousand times better when it is recited mentally. [cf. MDh 2.85]

73. Manu:

> He should always recite silently the vedic texts pertaining to the sacrifice and to the gods and those pertaining to the self, as well as what is expressed in the Vedāntas. [MDh 6.83]

74. "What is expressed in the Vedāntas" is OṂ.[18] Āpastamba:

> He speaks only during his private vedic recitation. [ApDh 2.21.10]

75. Bodhāyana:

> Morning and evening let him recite silently the mantras used at the daily fire sacrifice [BDh 2.18.20]. This is the rule when a man who had been in the habit of offering the daily fire sacrifice departs for the ascetic life.

76–77. Kapila describes the contemplation of the Lord:

> Bathing at dawn, silent prayer, silence, the habit of living always in solitude, paying homage, fasting, devotion to Viṣṇu and to one's teacher, belief [see Ch. 5.54 n. 14], constant recitation of the Veda,[19] being faithful to the control of breath, and worshipping Viṣṇu at dawn, noon, and dusk—that is the highest means of liberation.

78. Atri:

> At dawn, noon, and dusk, let him worship Viṣṇu, as well as the gods who share His nature; let him never pay homage to or worship anyone else.

17. The four cooked offerings are four of the five great sacrifices that a Brahmin is expected to offer every day—the offerings to gods, ancestors, spirits, and men. The *vidhiyajña*, which I have translated as "vedic sacrifices," are the major oblations offered according to the rules set forth in the vedic texts.

18. The original passage of Manu appears to refer to the vedic texts pertaining to the self found in the Vedāntas. This is the interpretation of the commentators, which is followed by Bühler. Yādava, however, takes the expression *vedāntābhihitam* as a separate entry referring to OṂ.

19. The meaning of *brahmasaṃsparśa* is not altogether clear. It may mean close contact or intimacy with *brahman*, which in this context probably refers to the Veda or perhaps to the syllable OṂ (see Ch. 5.95).

79. Kratu:

The Blessed Lord Viṣṇu, who is the Highest Self, the great unborn one, the single ruler of what moves and of what moves not—He is the highest goal of ascetics.

80. The same author states again:

After he has resorted to the emblem of Viṣṇu [see Ch. 3.48–51], if a man meditates on or worships another deity, he will have no happy afterlife for a thousand million eons.

81. The same author says further:

Let him conduct his worship with the Puruṣa hymn [RV 10.90] and his praise with the hymns to Viṣṇu[20] and meditate on the single syllable OṂ. Let him silently recite the vedic texts pertaining to the sacrifice, as well as the triple and the fourfold prayer, as he controls his breath.

82. The triple prayer consists of OṂ, the Great Utterances, and the Gāyatrī verse; the same three together with the Śiras formula constitute the fourfold prayer.[21] Śaṅkha describes the sitting posture:

He should sit with a serene mind in an abandoned house, a temple, a cave, or a mountain cavern, or in a place that he finds pleasant.

83. Assuming a sitting position in the manner prescribed in the yogic texts, he should always engage in yogic meditation, but especially during twilight.[22]

84. Viśvāmitra:

Then, in a sheltered and agreeable place where the ground is flat he should place, one on top of the other, Kuśa grass, an antelope skin, and a clean cloth.

85. Sitting there in the lotus position, he should bring his limbs into equilibrium. Mentally composed, then, he should control his breathing for a while.

86. Śaṅkha describes the characteristics of breath control, withdrawal of the senses, concentration, and meditation:

A man burns up his faults through the control of breathing, his sins through concentration, his attachments through the withdrawal of the senses, and his ignoble qualities through meditation.

20. The identity of these hymns is uncertain. They may be the same as the verses going under the name of Viṣṇusūkta; see Ch. 3.6 n. 3.

21. For the great utterances, see Ch. 4.13 n. 13. The Gāyatrī verse, also known as Sāvitrī (RV 3.62.10), is given at Ch. 4.12. The Śiras formula is "OṂ The waters, the light, the taste, the immortal, Brahman! Earth, Atmosphere, Heaven! OṂ"—*oṃ āpo jyotī raso 'mṛtaṃ brahma bhūr bhuvaḥ suvar oṃ* (MNU 241–42).

22. This may mean at dawn and dusk, but it could also refer to the three junctures of the days, including noon, which is the juncture between forenoon and afternoon.

87. When a person recites three times the Gāyatrī verse together with OṂ, the Great Utterances, and the Śiras formula, as he controls his breathing, it is called the control of breath.

88. The curbing of the sense organs is called the withdrawal of the senses. The curbing of the mind knowledgeable people term concentration.

89. The vision of the God of gods within Brahman through meditative practice is called meditation. I will tell you of a meditative practice even better than that.

90. "Meditation" here refers to trance, while meditative practice refers to meditation proper. The author points this out:

In the heart abide all the gods. The breaths are fixed within the heart. In the heart abide the sun and celestial lights. Everything is established within the heart. [cf. BU 84-85]

91. Make your body the lower slab and the syllable OṂ the upper fire drill. Churn it continuously in meditation. You shall then see Viṣṇu abiding in your heart. [SvU 1.14]

92. The meaning here is that one should meditate on Brahman by means of OṂ, giving up words and other such means. The Vedas likewise state: "OṂ—thus should a man link himself with the Self" [MNU 540]. 93. Similarly, after stating, "Put away other words" [MuU 2.2.5], the text goes on to say, "OṂ—thus alone should a man contemplate the Self" [MuU 2.2.6]. And also: "One should not ponder over a lot of words" [BaU 4.4.21]. 94. Yama states:

There are two forms of Brahman that one must know: the Brahman of speech and the Supreme Brahman. After a man has immersed himself in the Brahman of speech, he attains the Supreme Brahman.

95. The Brahman of speech is OṂ. Yama and Śaṅkha state:

The moon abides at the center of the sun, and fire at the center of the moon. The real abides at the center of fire, and Viṣṇu at the center of the real.

96. Viśvāmitra:

After controlling his thoughts until his mind has become calm, he should contemplate the orb of the sun shining at the center of his heart.

97–98. And abiding at the center of the sun's orb he should contemplate the moon, fire, and the Brahman of great light. To get rid of all obstacles, he should contemplate god Viṣṇu abiding within the lotus of his heart, envisaging Him as four-armed and brilliant like pure crystal. Then, he should tirelessly contemplate Him as without attributes, preceded by Brahman.[23]

23. Two types of contemplating God are presented here (cf. Ch. 5.104). In the first, a person imagines Viṣṇu as having physical attributes, which is almost an icono-

99. "Preceded by Brahman": "Brahman" here means the syllable OṂ; the meaning is that he should contemplate Nārāyaṇa, reciting first the syllable OṂ.

Over and over again he should contemplate Him as abiding in his heart—He who is the reality, the all, the self of all, the highest state called Viṣṇu, immaculate and salubrious.

100–101. I myself am that Brahman, pervading all and surpassing the self. The kind of mind a person has when he has given up the attachment to sensual objects and confined the mind within the heart—that is his highest state. Let him again take the intellect that he has thus discerned into the Supreme Self.

102. When a sage is unable to attain equanimity, let him suppress his mental activities until they dissolve within his heart.

103. This alone is knowledge and meditation. All else is just a lot of words. When the sense organs are under check and the mind does not stir, then the self shines in all its purity as calm and pure consciousness.

104. Likhita:

Imbued with love after examining the Purāṇas and the Vedāntas, he should always contemplate in his heart Viṣṇu both with a physical appearance and as without attributes.

105. The contemplation of the self through yogic discipline is the highest of all duties. One should give up everything else that impedes it, with the exception of what is absolutely necessary.[24]

106. Bṛhaspati:

Forbearance is a sacred bathing place, and self-control is a sacred bathing place—and so are the control of the sense organs and compassion toward all creatures. Meditation is the most excellent of all sacred bathing places.

107. These five sacred bathing places, as well as truthfulness, which is the sixth, always and everywhere reside in one's body. It is in them that one should bathe.

108. A man who bathes at Puṣkara, in the Ganges, and in the Kuru forest is not freed from his sins as completely as a man who bathes at the sacred bathing places consisting of forbearance and the like.

109. Wherever a man lives with all his sense organs controlled, that very place is Kurukṣetra, it is Naimiṣa, and it is Puṣkara.

---

graphic imagination of Viṣṇu. In the second, Viṣṇu is identified with the absolute Brahman, who is without parts and attributes. See the concession made to people who are unable to engage in this type of abstract contemplation at Ch. 5.123.

24. The term *āvaśyaka* may also mean a call of nature. In that case, the translation would be ". . . impedes it, unless it is a call of nature."

110. Pilgrimages to sacred bathing places, as well as the fruits accrued from them, are prescribed for those people who make the distinction, "This is a sacred bathing place, and this is not."

111. For a man who knows that everything is Brahman, there is nothing that is not a sacred bathing place. Whether he is awake, dreaming, or in deep sleep, he always abides in Brahman alone.

112. This is the highest Law. All others—sacrifices, gifts, austerity, and Vedas—are mere drops from it, established here under the guise of sacred bathing places.

113. Kratu praises Yoga, as well as the components of yogic practice, such as control of breathing, withdrawal of senses, concentration, meditation, and trance:

If a man fills the entire universe with jewels and gives it to people learned in the Vedas, the reward he will receive is perishable, but not that of calling to mind Viṣṇu just once.

114. People who stand in the middle of five fires or in water, people who stand in open air, and people who consume fire and smoke—these are not worth a sixteenth part of a man who performs the control of breath.

115. By subsisting on bark, leaves, flowers, vegetables, water, fruits, roots, and air, a man achieves purity of heart in twelve years, while he does so in one year through the withdrawal of senses.

116. It is easy for a man to engage in yogic concentration when he is devoted to Viṣṇu in the company of His consort and carrying a discus, sword, and quiver; it is difficult for people who are undisciplined. [cf. MBh 12.289.54]

117. They may be able to endure fire, snow, war, vedic recitation, austerities, and vows, but they are unable to remain even for a moment in the condition that destroys sins.

118. In this world people put up with leprosy, fever, poison, and illness, but they find it difficult to bear those who bring about yogic tranquillity.

119. A pure yogin abiding in trance, who has cut all ties and become like the spotless sky—his is the highest Vaiṣṇava state.

120. People who are stainless like pure crystal, bright like the sun, moon, and fire, cross beyond the reach of darkness when they gladden Viṣṇu with the components of yogic discipline.

121. The fire of yogic discipline burns up all sins of mind, speech, and body committed through ignorance or negligence, as fire burns a bundle of straw. A man of devotion always sees Viṣṇu with the lamp of yogic discipline.

122. Hārīta comments on the conclusion of yogic practice:

One is advised to undertake meditation until one obtains the bliss arising from knowing the self. Even after that, however, one should continue to perform the actions prescribed in the Vedas and the scriptures.

123. Bṛhaspati presents the type of meditation to be undertaken by those who are unable to meditate on Brahman without attributes:

> If a person is unable to meditate on the formless Brahman, let him purify himself by controlling his breath and meditating on His embodied form.
>
> 124. When a person recites three times the Gāyatrī verse together with OṂ, the Great Utterances, and the Śiras formula [see Ch. 5.82 n. 21], as he controls his breathing, it is called the control of breath.
>
> 125. A man burns up the faults of mind, speech, and body through the control of breathing, his attachments through the withdrawal of the senses, and his ignoble qualities through meditation.
>
> 126. As the impurities of metals are removed by blowing (with bellows in a furnace), so the sins committed by the senses are burnt up through the control of breath.
>
> 127. Let him practice these three moments of breath control repeatedly: inhalation, retention, and exhalation. By meditation on Brahmā, Viṣṇu, and Śiva, a man is freed from bondage.
>
> 128. Let him contemplate Brahmā, the Grandfather, as red in color; Viṣṇu as having the color of a blue lotus; and Śiva as white and with three eyes—they are the boats to cross the ocean of saṃsāra.
>
> 129. The ascetic who lives in this manner totally devoted to yogic practice achieves complete detachment and attains the highest state.
>
> 130. Vāsudeva is the highest Brahman, he is the highest self, and he contains the whole universe. They are indeed his embodiments, for they are differentiated by name into three.[25]
>
> 131. Every day let him meditate with devotion on Nārāyaṇa, the creator of the universe, on Hari, the Lord of all creation.
>
> 132. Let him contemplate Him carrying the conch and discus, auspicious with four arms, wearing a crown, bearing the Śrīvatsa mark and the Kaustubha jewel on his breast, and adorned with divine gems.
>
> 133. Let him contemplate Him dressed in yellow, tall in stature, with a face as pleasing as the moon, dark-skinned, lotus-eyed, and wearing earrings shaped like gleaming crocodiles.
>
> 134. Let him contemplate Him as removing afflictions instantly, risen like the cloud at the end of time, shining with all brilliance, holy, and giving protection to those who seek it.
>
> 135. Let him meditate fervently on Nārāyaṇa as lotus-eyed and salubrious, duly worshipping Him in his mind with the sixteen services.[26]

25. The meaning is that all three embodied gods who are the subject of this type of meditation—Brahmā, Viṣṇu, and Śiva—are in fact three aspects with different names of the one ultimate god, here referred to as Vāsudeva.

26. The services are rendered mentally rather than externally during yogic meditation. The sixteen services are invitation, seat, water to wash the feet, water given to

136. Dattātreya:

People who seek liberation worship with the eighteen offerings the Blessed Puruṣottama as abiding in the heart, in fire, and in the sun.

137–41. The worship of Viṣṇu with Palāśa leaves [see 3.64 n. 30] and lotus blossoms is said to be praiseworthy. After thus tirelessly worshipping Nārāyaṇa, the king of gods, let a yogin contemplate with a collected mind His appearance while reciting OṂ. Or, according to his special yogic practice, he should always envisage him with a bodily form—

He is a male, colored like the sun,
lotus-eyed, dressed in spotless gold,
conch, discus, and mace in his hands;
adorned with a crown,
with lovely bangles and bracelets;
The husband of Śrī,
his chest resplendent with jewel and Śrīvatsa mark,
Hṛṣīkeśa! Acyuta!
dark-skinned and lotus-eyed;
standing or seated in the middle
of the lotus that is my heart.

142. Let him contemplate in this manner the God who is the supreme Lord of the whole universe, who wipes out all afflictions, and who pervades causes and effects.

143. Śaṅkha explains the reward of practicing yoga:

A yogin, versed in all the yogic and Vedāntic texts, should always contemplate Brahman in conformity with its qualities as specified in each.[27]

144. Nevermore dejected, he definitely attains that light. As he becomes one with it,[28] he attains the bliss, happiness, and nonduality that is revealed by it in manifold ways and achieves the highest freedom.

145. Yājñavalkya:

Sacrifice, good conduct, self-control, abstaining from injuring, gifts, private vedic recitation—of all these activities, the highest duty is to obtain the vision of the self through yogic practice.

146. Viśvāmitra:

The supreme Brahman, which is nondual and happiness itself as proclaimed in Sāṃkhya, reveals itself to the yogin who meditates in this manner and who is established in Brahman.

---

a valued guest, water for sipping, bathing, garment, sacrificial string, perfume, flowers, incense, lighted lamp, food offering, obeisance, circumambulation, and farewell. The list of eighteen services contains in addition ornaments and betel leaves. See Kane, II, 729.

27. The meaning appears to be that the yogin should meditate on Brahman as endowed with the qualities that the yogic texts and the Vedāntas ascribe to Brahman.

28. Probably becoming one with Brahman, here identified as the light.

147. When the ultimate reality reveals itself wise men attain liberation. It is not attained by anyone else who is not devoted to yogic practice and to ritual activities.

148. Therefore, one should also perform rites every day at the proper time. These rites are associated with knowledge, and they should be performed by those who desire liberation.

149. Bṛhaspati:

As he meditates in this manner, the lamp of knowledge rises and the mental impressions derived from his past lives disappear, like darkness at the rising of the sun.

150. With all that he should purify his impure mind, for only when it is rendered immaculate does a man disappear into Brahman.

151. Medhātithi describes the nature of liberation:

A liberated man joins the ultimate as rivers join the ocean. He becomes that, he receives its name, and he is not born here again.

152. For he becomes the self of all beings—beings belonging to the realms of matter, gods, sacrifice, and the self.

153. He is Brahmā; he is Viṣṇu; he is Śiva; he is Sun and Yama; he is Fire and Nirṛti; he is Wind and Īśāna—he is the king of all beings.

154. He is the Vedas; he is the sacrifices; he is the gods; he is cattle, sacrificial gifts, and the like; he is also faith and the like; he is the oblation; he is time; he is the rite and the performer of the rite; he is resolve; and he is the rule. Of all he is the self and the haven—he is the lord of all beings.

155. Kratu describes Sāṃkhya and Yoga, as well as their rewards:

Let him cleanse the organs of action with his mind and his intellect with knowledge. Let him purify his mental dispositions with that very purification, and his knowledge and ignorance by means of his teacher's words.

156. In his imagination let him appoint the intellect as his queen, virtue as his minister, the mind as the doorkeeper, and the ego as the general.

157. Those among them who are without desire he should appoint as superintendents over ten villages. The great fort is surrounded by three ramparts and made up of the five elements.[29]

158. The soul remains like the king seated on the throne of yogic might; he remains like a witness knowing everything and observing the disparity of qualities.

29. The verse is elliptical and somewhat obscure. It is not clear to what internal organs the ten superintendents correspond, but they may be the ten organs of sensation and action. The three ramparts are probably the three strands of Sāṃkhya—goodness, energy, and darkness.

159. Let him give up musing, imagining, anxiety, fear, and perplexity and abandon social relationships and the quest for wealth and righteousness relating to a place, a caste, or personal excellence.

160. Abandoning all thoughts and emotions, let him just think "I am being." Living in solitude, let him always keep that in mind day and night. Thereafter, when his passions have been extinguished, the self immediately enters the highest state.

161. That ends the fifth chapter, entitled "Rules Regarding the Principal Activities," of the *Collection of Ascetic Laws*.

CHAPTER SIX

Daily Practices

1. I describe next the daily practices of ascetics. If someone needs to find out about a practice that is not dealt with here, he should gather it from the corresponding practice of vedic students, following the rule that "when they do not run counter to the specific requirements of a particular order of life, these duties of vedic students apply also to people in other orders" [GDh 3.10].[1] When something is not found even there, one should gather it from the practices of householders. 2. Accordingly, the Blessed Vyāsa states:

> When they are not mutually exclusive, all the practices of every order of life are applicable to every other order of life.

Morning Duties

3. Viśvāmitra:

> Rising in the morning, he should purify himself according to the rules.[2] Then, after he has sipped some water, he should diligently use a toothstick to clean his teeth, except on days of the lunar phases.[3]

1. This is a free and long translation of Gautama's pithy aphorism (lit., "That also for others when not in contradiction."). After listing the duties of a student, Gautama offers this comment to indicate that the duties of a student, which he describes in detail, apply also to other orders of life when those duties do not contradict specific requirements of each order.

2. This is probably an allusion to answering the call of nature in the morning. After going to the toilet one performs the required purification before engaging in other activities.

3. These are the full moon and the new moon, as well as the eighth and fourteenth days of the lunar month. The term "*parvan*" may also refer to other astronomical phases, such as the equinox and the solstice. Toothsticks are made from small twigs of a variety of medicinal trees (see Kane II, 655). The tip of the twig is crushed to form a brush for cleaning the teeth.

4. After bathing, he should pray silently until the sun comes into view. The mantra prescribed at sunrise begins "Rise up, O Brahmaṇaspati!"[4]

5. Garga:

We will now explain the purifications relating to the observances and disciplines of mendicants, as well as the corresponding expiations.[5] To start with, we will describe the purification after passing urine. Filling each time the three joints of his fingers with earth, he should clean the penis four times, the left hand twelve times, and both hands eight times. Having purified his penis in the manner prescribed after urinating,[6] he should perform the purification of the anus. He should apply first one handful of earth, and half that amount the second and the third time. Applying earth in this manner, he should purify his anus twenty times, his left hand twice that many times, and both hands twenty-eight times. He should clean his feet, as well as his hands, by applying earth three times. Finally, he should sip some water, control his breath three times, and sip water again.

6. If, when earth is unavailable, a person uses sand for purification, then he should apply it twice the number of times prescribed above. A mendicant in good health should not be remiss in his purifications. If he is remiss, he commits a sin. To remove such a sin, he should control his breath three times and sip water again.

7. Rising at the time sacred to Brahmā,[7] he should contemplate the Highest Self in his heart every day, reciting the mantra that begins "Delighting in wealth, you are powerful" [MNU 539].

8. Then, having first taken some earth, he should answer the call of nature and perform four times the purification prescribed for householders. If he takes the earth after he has answered the call of nature, however, he should bathe by entering the water fully clothed.

9–12. Devala:

A single portion of earth, according to the scriptures, is the amount that would fill the three joints of one's fingers. He should clean the penis four times, the left hand twelve times, and both hands eight times. Then he

4. According to the variant recorded in mss A1 2 R1, the mantra is taken from TA 4.2 and extends up to the words *anu me'maṃ sāthām.*

5. The text here is obscure and possibly corrupt. The exact meanings of the Sanskrit terms "*niyama*" and "*saṃyama*" here are unclear, but they probably refer to the disciplinary practices of ascetics. The compound word may also be translated as ". . . explain the observances, disciplines, purifications, and expiations of mendicants."

6. The meaning appears to be as follows. When a person voids excrement, he should first perform the purification of the penis in the same way as he would after he has urinated and then undertake the purification of the anus.

7. This time of the morning sacred to Brahmā is defined in different ways. In general, it is the time between the first light and sunrise. See Ypra trans., 8.34n.

should do the purification of his anus by applying earth on it twenty times; the first time he should apply a handful, and half that amount at each subsequent time. He should then clean his left hand forty times, both hands twenty-eight times, and each of his feet three times. If sand is used, then the number of cleansings is doubled. Having sipped water twice, and then three times, he should sip again after controlling his breath.[8]

13. The same author states:

He should always take the earth before he goes out to void urine or excrement. If he takes it afterward, he should bathe by entering water fully clothed.

14–15. Jamadagni:

One method of purification is prescribed for the daytime and another for the night, and yet another at times of difficulty. The prescribed method applies to persons in good health and in daytime. Half the prescribed purification is to be performed during the night, half that of the night when one is sick, and half that of the sick when one is on the road.

16. Devala:

After voiding urine or excrement, an ascetic should control his breath once, twice, or three times, depending on the place, the time, and the like.

17. The same author states:

Meditation, divine worship, eating, brushing the teeth, answering the calls of nature, and bathing: at these six times silence is enjoined.

18. Vāyu:

Even when he sips water properly, a man becomes impure if he does so with his head covered up to the ears, while he is in water or on a vehicle, while he is standing or talking, or with unwashed feet or untied topknot.

19. Devala:

When someone has diarrhea, vomits, or voids urine or excrement during the morning or evening twilight worship, he should bathe in the middle of that worship, conclude the worship of the sun, and control the breath three times.[9]

20. Scriptures prescribe that control of breathing is done at night with just a single recitation of OṂ and at midday while reciting it several times. An ascetic should not sip water while he is seated on a wooden bench.[10]

8. Following the description of the rite at Ch. 6.5, it may be possible to emend the edited text by changing the second *ācamya* to *āyamya*. The verse would then read *dvir ācamya trir āyamya prāṇān apy ācamet punaḥ*: "Having sipped water twice, he should sip again after controlling his breath three times."

9. The reading of this verse is unclear and possibly corrupt. The translation is tentative.

10. The meaning of *kāṣṭha* is unclear. I have taken it to mean a wooden seat, because there is a general prohibition against sipping water while sitting on a seat (see

21. Garga:

Vedic students and ascetics should not wash the inside of the penis. If they do so, they should observe a lunar fast.[11]

22. Then, after brushing his teeth, he should bathe. Kratu states:

Ascetics, yogins, students, people who are a hundred years old, those who speak the truth, those who keep vows, good women, and people devoted to giving gifts—they are always purified by bathing.

23. A man should never bathe before he has purified himself after going to the toilet. For the old and the sick, a bath consisting of the recitation of mantras, or with the use of hot water, or else with the components of yoga such as restraints [see Ch. 5.47] is prescribed. An ascetic should always perform the Varuṇa bath using the mantra "Waters, you bring delight."[12]

24. Dakṣa:

When morning comes, he should purify himself according to the rules, brush his teeth, and then take a bath.

25. With its nine openings, the body is extremely dirty. Day and night it continuously oozes through them. It is the morning bath that purifies it.

26. A bath taken after the first light, at dawn, or even after sunrise is equal to a Prājāpatya penance [see Ch. 4.2 n. 1]; it erases all sins.

27. A Brahmin who gets up at dawn and takes the morning bath will expiate in three years the sins he has committed over seven lifetimes.

28. When he performs rites such as bathing, he should meditate on the god Nārāyaṇa; for, as the Vedas say, it expiates all evil deeds.[13]

29. A holy man given to bathing possesses ten qualities: beauty, majesty, strength, purity, longevity, good health, freedom from desires, elimination of bad dreams, austerity, and wisdom.

30. Kapila:

A person who is unable to take the morning bath should wash the body below the navel, clean the body and the head with a wet piece of cloth, change the underwear, and perform the twilight worship. He should al-

---

Devaṇṇabhaṭṭa, *Smṛticandrikā*, āhnikakāṇḍa, p. 102). The normal posture for sipping is sitting on one's haunches with the elbows between the knees.

11. Washing the inside of the penis probably means washing inside the foreskin. For the lunar fast, see Ch. 5.11 n. 5.

12. This formula is found at RV 10.9.1–3 and TS 4.1.5.1. The normal bath with cold water is called the Varuṇa bath, for which there are several substitutes. The bath by reciting vedic mantras (*brāhmasnāna* or *mantrasnāna*) consists of sprinkling oneself with water while reciting the mantra "Waters, you bring delight." For the various types of baths, see Ypra 37.

13. The meaning could also be that meditating on Nārāyaṇa rectifies any rite that is not properly performed.

ways bathe either before or after midday. Then, after he has sipped some water, he should control his breath three times and sip water again.

31. Viśvāmitra:

> If a person is unable to take the morning bath, he should perform the Kapila bath.[14] One who is unable to do even that should perform the bath consisting of mantras.

32. Aṅgiras:

> When the time for the bath has come, he should put on half the normal amount of clothes, and half the latter amount—that is, just a loincloth—during the time of silent prayer.

33. In this manner, he should bathe at dawn, noon, and dusk. The mantras recited while sprinkling oneself[15] are "We appease your anger, O Varuṇa . . ." [TS 1.5.11.3]; "Loosen the upper, the middle, and the lower noose, O Varuṇa . . ." [TS 1.5.11.3]; and "I have sung the praise of Dadhikrāvan . . ." [TS 1.5.11.4], together with the three verses beginning "Waters, you bring delight" [RV 10.9.1–3]. The four mantras beginning with "Golden colored . . ." [TS 5.6.1] and the lesson that begins "The purifier . . ." [TB 1.4.8] are prescribed at this sprinkling.

34. Next, the sipping of water while reciting mantras. In this regard, Kratu states:

> After sipping water while reciting the fourfold mantra, he should sprinkle himself with purified water as he recites the Aghamarṣaṇa hymn[16] and the verse "Freed from the post, as it were . . ." [TB 2.4.4.9] and offer libations of water to gods and ancestors.

35. The meaning of this is that he should sip water four times reciting each time the fourfold mantra. Manu states:

> The Gāyatrī verse accompanied by ten recitations of OṂ, preceded by the seven Great Utterances, and followed by the Śiras mantra[17] is said to be the destroyer of sins.

14. The Kapila bath is described in the previous verse. The inability to bathe normally is due to sickness or old age.

15. Technically called *mārjana* ("washing"), this is part of the twilight worship and consists of sprinkling oneself with water as one recites the mantras listed.

16. This hymn (RV 10.190) is considered to be specially efficacious in destroying sins. The term "Aghamarṣaṇa" is also used for a particular rite for erasing sins. A person takes water in the right hand cupped like a cow's ear and holds it near the nose. He then breathes onto the water while reciting the above hymn and throws the water to the left.

17. This mantra is found at MNU 342: "OṂ The waters, the light, the taste, the immortal, Brahman! Earth, Atmosphere, Heaven! OṂ!"

36. This lesson hidden in the Vedas is the fourfold mantra. Some maintain that the fourfold mantra consists of the syllable OṂ, the Great Utterances, the Gāyatrī verse, and the Śiras mantra.[18] Devala:

> Having sprinkled water on his body while reciting the Gāyatrī verse and the Aghamarṣaṇa hymn, he should offer handfuls of water as libations to Viṣṇu as he recites the twelve names of Viṣṇu.
>
> 37. An ascetic, after he has purified himself, should first offer libations of water with one hand—one libation per name—as he recites the twelve names of Viṣṇu, each preceded by OṂ and followed by the word "Homage!"

38. These mantras read as follows: "OṂ Homage to Keśava!"[19] Next, he offers libations to gods and ancestors.

> Taking in his cupped hands water sufficient to fill a bull's horn, he should offer a libation to the gods. In like manner and with his hands properly joined, he should then offer a libation to his ancestors.
>
> 39. He should offer the libation to the ancestors wearing the sacred string in the sacrificial position and using the part of the hand sacred to the gods.[20] At the conclusion, moreover, he should say "Glory! Homage!" and utter the words "I satiate."

40. "OṂ Earth, I satiate! OṂ Atmosphere, I satiate! OṂ Heaven, I satiate! OṂ Earth, Atmosphere, Heaven! Glory! Homage! I satiate! OṂ Earth, svadhā OṂ! OṂ Atmosphere svadhā OṂ! OṂ Heaven svadhā OṂ! OṂ Earth, Atmosphere, Heaven! Glory! Homage! Svadhā OṂ!" This mantra ends with the exclamation "svadhā."[21] 41. After conclud-

18. It is unclear what the lesson hidden in the Vedas refers to and how that is different from the latter view. The fourfold mantra as described here is given at MNU 340–42.

19. The twelve names are Keśava, Nārāyaṇa, Mādhava, Govinda, Viṣṇu, Madhusūdana, Trivikrama, Vāmana, Śrīdhara, Hṛṣīkeśa, Padmanābha, and Dāmodara. Thus, the first mantra would read *oṃ keśavāya namaḥ* —"OṂ Homage to Keśava!" The others are formed by inserting the other eleven names.

20. At divine sacrifices the sacred string is worn looped around the left shoulder and resting on the right hip. When offering libations (and when sipping water), different parts of the hands are used. These parts are considered appropriate for various divinities. Although sources are not unanimous, in general the extremity of the palm (i.e., the tips of the fingers) is used to pour water for the gods, while the root of the index finger (i.e., between thumb and index finger) is used in rites for ancestors (cf. Kane II, 652). Likewise, at ancestral rites the sacred string is worn from the right shoulder extending toward the left hip. Ascetics, on the other hand, are not expected to make ancestral offerings. Thus, even in rites intended for the ancestors, ascetics use ritual modes appropriate for the gods.

21. The author here gives the actual mantras used in the offering of libations to the ancestors. The exclamation "svadhā" is used at the conclusion of mantras used in offerings for ancestors. Its counterpart, used for gods, is "svāhā."

ing the bath and controlling his breath three times, he performs as before rites such as the sipping of water while reciting mantras and the twilight worship. A water strainer is closely associated with the five rites beginning with the sipping of water.[22] If, when a water strainer is available, a man performs the rites of sipping, sprinkling water, offering libations, worshipping the sun, filling the water pot, and silently reciting the Gāyatrī using something else, all those rites will become fruitless for him. 42. Medhātithi:

> Let him use that [i.e., water strainer] at sipping, sprinkling, offering libations, worshipping the sun, and filling the water pot.

43. Gālava:

> If an ascetic fails at any time to use a water strainer at sprinkling, sipping, offering libations, and worshipping the sun, all those rites will become fruitless for him. He should, moreover, perform an expiatory penance.

44. Atri:

> Water that has been drawn out, water that flows, and water in an unsullied lake—such water is pure, the Vedas declare, and should not be filtered with a cloth strainer [see Ch. 1.14 n. 9].

45–46. Hārīta:

> After he has bathed and sipped water according to the rules, he should perform the twilight worship before sunrise and in the prescribed manner, reciting silently the triple prayer.[23] He does so either standing or seated and carrying in his two hands a water strainer and the rosary of Rudrākṣa beads, as well as two purificatory rings made of cow's hair, rings that destroy sins.[24]
>
> 47. He should then worship the sun—in the morning reciting the three mantras beginning "The fame of Mitra . . ." [TS 3.4.11.5] and in the evening reciting the five mantras addressed to Varuṇa.[25]
>
> 48. An ascetic, being totally devoted to the Highest Self, should make an offering of water to the sun at dawn, noon, and dusk, as well as after he has finished his meal.

22. The five rites are sipping, sprinkling water, offering libations, worshipping the sun, and filling the water pot. The meaning is that he uses the water strainer to purify the water used at these rites.

23. The triple prayer consists of the syllable OṂ, the three Great Utterances (*bhūr bhuvaḥ svaḥ*), and the Gāyatrī verse; see Ch. 5.82.

24. These rings are generally made of the sacred *darbha* grass (although here cow's hair is specified) and are worn at certain rites. They are intended to purify the performer. One stands while performing the morning twilight worship and is seated during the everning worship.

25. These mantras follow immediately after the three to Mitra at TS 3.4.11.5–6. See also BDh 2.18.21.

49. At the worship following the meal he uses the mantra "Gazing up from the darkness . . ." [TS 4.1.7.4], while at the time of begging he uses the Haṃsa mantra.[26]

> At sunrise he should make an offering of water with a collected mind as he recites the Gāyatrī verse. If the sun sets while he is engaged in silent prayer, he should make the water offering at the end of his silent prayer.

50. Devala:

> He should worship the sun at dawn, noon, and dusk. Then, after making a circumambulation clockwise, he should pay reverence by bending his knees and bowing his head.
>
> 51. He should pay obeisance to the sun without mentioning his name. Then, after offering a libation as before, he should duly engage in silent prayer with a collected mind.

52. Bodhāyana:

> He should perform the evening twilight worship using the mantras addressed to Varuṇa and the morning worship using the mantras addressed to Mitra. [BDh 2.18.21]

53. Śaunaka:

> He should meditate as soon as he gets up from sleep. Then, after he has answered the call of nature, he should purify himself, and sip water. After brushing his teeth, he should bathe before sunrise in the prescribed manner and sprinkle water on himself as he recites the three mantras beginning "Waters, you bring delight" [RV 10.9.1-3] together with the water mantras.[27] Facing the east, then, he should throw upward some water while reciting the Gāyatrī verse. Holding Darbha grass in his hand, he should remain standing as he recites the Gāyatrī verse until sunrise. He should spend the rest of the day engaged in silent prayer, meditation, and divine praise.

54. Kapila:

> Planting his feet firmly on the ground, he should undertake silent prayer, offering nourishment,[28] and worship. Then, standing or seated facing the east and holding purificatory rings in his hands, he should silently recite the triple prayer according to his ability, using either his fingers or a Rudrākṣa rosary. He should control his breath three times at dawn, noon, and dusk. To purify himself of the sins he may have committed by unknowingly killing living creatures, he should use a water strainer at sip-

26. This mantra is RV 4.40.5, which also occurrs at TS 1.8.15.2; see Ch. 6.151.

27. The identity of these mantras is unclear. For the mantras that precede the three mentioned here, see above Ch. 6.33.

28. The term *bhojana* literally means eating or feeding. In this context, however, it probably refers to the offerings of libations to the sun.

> ping, sprinkling, offering libations, and filling the water pot. He should perform the worship of the sun with his cupped hands filled with water.

55. After he has thus performed the twilight worship, he should engage in the yogic practice described before [Ch. 5.47f]. Viśvāmitra says this in the passage that begins

> After he has bathed, he should engage in silent prayer until the sun comes into view [Ch. 6.4]. Then, in a sheltered and agreeable place where the ground is flat. . . .[29]

56. Having thus performed the yogic practice and likewise completed the ritual procedure given in the text that begins "For a man who performs a sacrifice knowing this . . . ,"[30] he should then end the yogic exercises and offer a silent prayer. He should then leave that place and, if he observes the vow of spending just one night in a village, go to another village. This is stated by Śaṅkha:

> After meditating until he has obtained the bliss arising from the knowledge of the self, he should gradually end his yogic exercise. After silently reciting OṂ and completing his private vedic recitation, he should leave that village and go to another. This is the settled rule.

57. If he does not go to another village, he should remain there engaged in divine praise, silent prayer, meditation, and the like. This is stated by Bṛhaspati:

> Rising before dawn, he should answer the call of nature and purify himself. Then he should remain reciting the Gāyatrī verse until sunrise.
>
> 58. He should spend the remainder of the day engaged in controlling the breath, silent prayer, meditation, and divine praise, as well as in reciting epic and purāṇic texts that have vedic sanction.

59. That concludes the description of the morning duties.

Midday Duties

60. Next, I will describe the midday[31] duties. In this connection, Śaunaka states:

> Then, after bathing in the prescribed manner, he should sip water, and sprinkle himself with water as he recites the three mantras that begin "Waters, you bring delight" [RV 10.9.1–3]. Standing in water, then, he

29. The entire passage is given at Ch. 5.84–85.

30. This text of the MNU (543) homologizes various parts of the ascetic's body as well as his daily activities with corresponding objects and operations of a sacrifice. The meaning here appears to be that the ascetic by reciting this text performs a mental sacrifice, transforming his entire existence and activities into a continuous ritual process.

31. For a definition of "midday," see Ch. 6.99.

should control his breath sixteen times while reciting the Aghamarṣaṇa hymn [see Ch. 6.34 n. 16]. Coming out of the water, he should wash his garment, clean his loins with earth and water, and wear a clean fresh loincloth and outer garment. He should then sip water and take the water strainer while reciting "OṂ Earth, Atmosphere, Heaven!" Then he offers libations, saying, "OṂ Earth, I satiate!"

61. The rites described above up to thc statement "In like manner and with his hands properly joined, he should then offer a libation to his ancestors" [see Ch. 6.38] are performed as before. Then he worships the sun, reciting the two mantras "His rays raise him up . . ." and "The bright face of the gods . . ." [TS 1.4.43.1]. After controlling his breath six times, he should silently recite the Gāyatrī verse one hundred and eight times. 62. Bodhāyana:

He worships the sun with the two mantras: "His rays raise him up . . ." and "The bright face of the gods . . ." [TS 1.4.43.1]. "OṂ is Brahman. Brahman, indeed, is this light. This thing that glows warmly is this Veda. This thing that glows warmly is what we must come to know"—with these very words he satiates the self, and he worships the self. For the self is Brahman, the self is the light. He should then recite the Gāyatrī verse one hundred times, one thousand times, or an unlimited number of times. Taking the water strainer with the words "OṂ Earth, Atmosphere, Heaven!" he fetches water. [BDh 2.17.39–42]

63. Hārīta:

After bathing and sipping water according to the prescribed rules, he should offer libations with water purified through a water strainer and worship the sun as he recites the appropriate mantras.

64. Kratu:

After bathing, a mendicant should silently recite the following in front of the sun: "His rays raise him up . . . , " "The bright face of the gods . . ." [TS 1.4.43.1], "That bright eye ordained by the gods . . ." [RV 7.66.16], the Śivasaṃkalpa verses,[32] the Puruṣa hymn [RV 10.90], and the Viṣṇu hymn.[33]

65. In the morning he should worship the sun with mantras addressed to Mitra and in the evening with those addressed to Varuṇa. After the people in the village have finished their meal, he should go on his begging round during the day reciting the Haṃsa mantra.

32. These are the group of six verses that begins "That which rises far when people are awake . . ." (VS 34.1–6).

33. There is no consensus regarding this particular hymn: see Ch. 3.6 n. 3.

66. After sprinkling himself with well-purified water as he recites the three Pāvamānī and the three Aghamarṣaṇa verses with explicit meanings,[34] he should silently recite the Gāyatrī verse one hundred and eight times.

67. Viśvāmitra:

Then, after he has taken his midday bath, the wise man should recite the Gāyatrī silently and with a collected mind and also recite a few vedic texts.

68. To purify himself, moreover, he should silently recite the following: the Viṣṇu hymn, the Pāvamāna verses, the mantras addressed to Varuṇa, Rudra, and the sun, and the Upaniṣad.[35] Then, after he has done his meditation as prescribed, he should go on his begging round.

69. Hārīta:

Sitting down facing the east, he should silently control his breath three times. After reciting the Gāyatrī verse as many times as he is able, he should contemplate the highest state. Then, to sustain his life he should always go on his begging round.

70. Devala:

Facing the east, an ascetic should silently recite the mantras and hymns of praise.[36] There is no time when their recitation is suspended, for scriptures consider that recitation to be an obligatory daily rite.

71. Then he should worship Viṣṇu in the manner prescribed in the Vedas; if he is unable to use vedic mantras, however, he may optionally use those given in the Pāñcarātra texts.

72. Manu:

Day and night an ascetic injures living creatures without being aware of it. To cleanse himself of those sins, he should bathe and control his breath six times [MDh 6.69].

73. Now, there is a question as to how he should perform divine worship. Since a penance is prescribed when an ascetic plucks fruits or flowers, he should perform the worship with water or with articles

34. This is a tentative translation of the unclear expression "*vācyaliṅga*." The Pāvamānī are, according to some, the purificatory verses found in the ninth book of the RV, while others take them to refer specifically to RV 9.67.21–27 (Kane II, 317 n. 755). If the word "*pāvamānī*" is taken adjectivally, however, the translation would be "the Aghamarṣaṇa verses that bestow purity."

35. The Pāvamāna verses may be the same as the Pāvamānī (see n. 34). For the mantras addressed to Varuṇa, see Ch. 6.47 n. 25. Those addressed to Rudra are probably the Rudrādhyāya (TS 4.5.1–11). See Ch. 6.267 n. 62, for the mantras addressed to the sun. I am unable to identify the Upaniṣad referred to here.

36. This appears to be an unusual meaning of "*stoka*," which usually means "little." The context requires a meaning similar to the one adopted.

brought by others, reciting the Puruṣa hymn and other mantras contained in the Vedas. 74. Āpastamba:

> Speaking only during his private vedic recitation, and gathering from a village just enough food to sustain his life, he should go about without regard for this world or the next. The rule is that he should wear discarded clothes; some require him to go completely naked. [ApDh 2.21.10–12]

75. Manu:

> He should always recite silently the vedic texts pertaining to the sacrifice and to the gods, and those pertaining to the self, as well as what is called Vedānta. [MDh 6.83; see Ch. 5.74 n. 18]
>
> 76. Let him reflect on the union, the separation, and the means of separation and contemplate the true nature of the soul, the Lord, and primal matter.[37]
>
> 77. He spends the time until noon engaged in study, meditation, and the recitation of the Epics and Purāṇas. At midday, too, the same procedure applies.
>
> 78. After concluding the rites relating to the bath, he should make the offering of water as prescribed. Then, after worshipping the sun while reciting the two mantras "His rays raise him up . . ." and "The bright face of the gods . . ." [TS 1.4.43.1], he should engage in silent prayer.

79. That concludes the description of midday duties.

Begging

80. Next, I describe the procedure of begging. In this regard, Uśanas states:

> Scriptures have proclaimed five types of almsfood: *mādhūkara* ["begging in the manner of a bee" from many houses] not deliberately selected, *prākpraṇīta* ["offered in advance"], *ayācita* ["unsolicited"], *tātkālika* ["contemporaneous"], and *upapanna* ["offered"].
>
> 81. *Mādhūkara*, the scriptures say, is food begged in the manner of a bee[38] by going to three, five, or seven houses that have not been deliberately selected.

37. In Yoga cosmology, the present condition of humans is created by the union of souls with primal matter (*prakṛti* or *pradhāna*). Separation of the two constitutes liberation, and the yogic techniques are the means of that separation.

38. The comparison with the bee is instructive in at least two ways. A bee gathers nectar from many flowers and does not injure them in the process. Likewise, an ascetic does not become a burden on any single householder by begging a little food from several houses.

82. *Prākpraṇīta*, the blessed sage Uśanas has said, is what devout people offer to someone even before he has risen from bed.

83. *Ayācita* is the almsfood offered by somebody before one sets out on the begging round. Manu has said that it may be eaten.

84. *Tātkālika* is said to be what is proclaimed by a Brahmin as almsfood as one approaches him. That too may be eaten by a man seeking liberation.

85. *Upapanna*, sages aspiring to liberation declare, is the cooked food brought by devotees to a monastery.

86. These are the five types of almsfood, and scriptures proclaim that they are equal to drinking Soma juice. A man becomes pure by subsisting on any one of them.

87. Viśvāmitra:

> *Mādhūkara* being the fixed practice, these others are regarded as its substitutes. If an ascetic capable of begging in the *mādhūkara* manner practices any of the others, he commits a sin.

88. Prohibitions contained in statements such as "A full meal from a single house, honey, meat . . ." [see Ch. 10.59] are syntactically related to the above statement.[39] Therefore, they should be regarded as directed only at those who are capable of begging in the *mādhūkara* manner. Even if one is so capable, it is not wrong for him to eat a full meal from a single house when it is done as an act of kindness.

89. Medhātithi thus declares:

> He should not eat a full meal from a single house, the food given by a Śūdra, or an excessive amount of food. He may eat a full meal given by a Brahmin either if he is weak or as an act of kindness.

90. Kātyāyana:

> An ascetic may subsist on almsfood that he solicits or receives unasked.

91. Aṅgiras:

> It is not a sin for ascetics who are sick, old, or suffering from a long illness to eat a full meal from a single house.

92. Bodhāyana:

> He should eat only as much as is needed to sustain his life. [BDh 2.18.12]

39. A central principle of Brahmanical hermeneutics is that conflicts between injunctions should be avoided as far as possible (see Ch. 2.25 n. 9). Many strategies were devised for this purpose. One of them is called *ekavākyatānyāya*, the maxim that rules of apparently different provenance form a syntactic or meaningful whole (i.e., a single complete sentence) and that their meanings should be derived within this larger context. In the present case, the prohibitions given at Ch. 10.59 are considered as referring to ascetics capable of practicing the *mādhūkara* type of begging and not to the old and the sick.

93. Kapila:

> He should eat commendable types of food, such as food received randomly or given spontaneously as soon as he approaches. An ascetic should avoid food that has been offered to deceased ancestors.

94. Yama:

> An ascetic may beg food in the manner of a bcc even from the house of a barbarian. But he shall not eat a full meal even from a man equal to Bṛhaspati.
>
> 95. There is no man higher than a Brahmin; there is no god higher than Vāsudeva; there is no law that excels the law of classes and orders; there is no scripture that equals the Vedas; there is no purity equal to that of almsfood; and there is no austerity superior to fasting.
>
> 96. Almsfood begged in the manner of a bee destroys even the most heinous sins. On such almsfood, therefore, should an ascetic subsist, receiving it in a clean and undamaged bowl.

97. Next, I will describe the rules of begging in the manner of a bee. Manu specifies the time:

> An ascetic should go on his begging round only when the smoke has stopped rising, the pestles have stopped pounding, the meal has come to an end, and the dishes have been put away. [MDh 6.56]

98. Kratu:

> A yogin should go around in the forenoon, while a person who possesses the true knowledge should go around in the afternoon [see Ch. 3.30 n. 12]. A mendicant surely commits a sin if he goes around begging at midday.

99. Midday consists of the one and a half hours after the sixth hour following sunrise, according to the definition "The time after midmorning and before noon."[40] 100. Kapila:

> A man who is extremely hungry need not wait until the very last moment to beg.

101. Bodhāyana addresses the issue of the restrictions as to the place of begging:

40. Within the fivefold division of the day into morning (*prātaḥ*), midmorning (*saṅgava*), midday (*madhyāhna*), afternoon (*aparāhṇa*), and evening (*sāyāhna*), each division is given three *muhūrta*s or six *ghaṭikā*s (approximately 2 hours and 24 minutes). According to this reckoning, midday extends from 4 hours and 48 minutes until 7 hours and 12 minutes after sunrise. The time given by Yādava is somewhat different.

Next, the rules for begging. He should seek to obtain almsfood from Brahmins who follow the mode of life of Śālīnas or Yāyāvaras, after they have completed their Vaiśvadeva offering.[41] [BDh 2.18.4]

102. Viṣṇu:

He should beg food from the houses of Yāyāvara householders. The advice of this book is that he should regard this first mode of begging as the best.

103. Going beyond those, an ascetic may beg from householders who maintain the sacred fires, who have faith, who are subdued, who are learned in the Vedas, and who are magnanimous.

104. Going beyond even those, an ascetic may beg from people who are not Śūdras, who are not wicked, and who have not fallen from their caste. These are the three modes of begging prescribed for him.

105. Medhātithi:

He may beg his food from Brahmins, Kṣatriyas, and Vaiśyas. Even among them, he should beg from people of each subsequent class only when those of the preceding class are unavailable.

106. When no one belonging to any of these classes is available, and he has gone three meal times[42] without eating, an ascetic may accept almsfood even from a Śūdra, for it is said that an ascetic must preserve his life by means of almsfood.

107. Life is what permits people to pursue the goals of duty, wealth, pleasure, and liberation. Does not a man who destroys life destroy also those goals? And a man who safeguards life, does he not safeguard also those goals?

108. If in an emergency an ascetic begs food from a Śūdra, or a Vaiśya, or a Kṣatriya, he should purify himself by controlling his breath a hundred times, fifty times, or twenty-five times, respectively. If he begs from such people without knowing it, the penance for regaining purity is half the listed amounts.

109. Kratu:

When an ascetic begs in the manner of a bee, he should not make inquires regarding the donor's ritual practices, religious activities, behavior, virtue, conduct, learning, and lineage, as well as whether the donor is pure

41. Śālīna (lit., "people with large houses") and Yāyāvara (lit., "itinerant") were two ancient classes of holy householders (see BDh 3.1). The Vaiśvadeva (lit., "all gods") offering is an oblation of food obligatory before any meal.

42. Morning and evening are considered meal times for people. So, not eating for three meal times means that a person has not eaten for a whole day and the morning of the next. Since ascetics are expected to eat only once a day in the evening, this provision boils down to not eating for a whole day.

or impure, auspicious or inauspicious. Purity and impurity melt away as the almsfood falls into the bowl.

110. Jābāli the Elder:

He should not inquire after the donor's class or ask whether the donor is auspicious or inauspicious. When the almsfood falls into the bowl, let him not think whether it is pure or impure.

Another reading of this text is ". . . into the bowl, purity and impurity melt away." 111. Atri:

He should not beg from families that are related to him. Even if he is offered almsfood in the houses of his pupils, enemies, relatives, and kings, or in houses where a death or a birth has recently taken place, he should not accept it. He should avoid any food that he has prepared himself or if accepting it would cause hardship to someone.

112. Kapila:

If someone is extremely old, weak, sick, feeble, or physically impaired, he may beg his almsfood from his pupils, relatives, sons, brothers, or friends.

113–14. When an ascetic seeks to obtain external goods such as horses, beds, and seats; when he officiates at sacrifices, teaches, and explains texts and receives in return clothes and vessels; and when he looks at and thinks about women and has sex with them, he becomes guilty of commingling the duties of different orders.[43] Whether he lives in a house or in the wilderness, therefore, an ascetic should seek to obtain his almsfood from his son.

115. The same author states:

If someone is extremely old, very weak, sick, a hundred years old, or physically impaired, he may beg his almsfood from his pupils, relatives, sons, brothers, or friends.

116. People who are humpbacked, dwarfs, maimed, crippled, lame, blind, or sick are not tainted by any fault relating to their almsfood, as also when a king no longer rules the country.

117. Vasiṣṭha specifies the number of houses:

Clothed in a single garment or an antelope skin, he should go to seven houses that he has not selected beforehand when the smoke has stopped rising and the pestles have stopped pounding. [VaDh 10.7–9]

43. This is a very tentative translation of a grammatically obscure verse. I have taken "*saṃkarī*" to mean the confusion of the different orders of life, which parallels the more common fault of causing the mixture of castes.

118. Devala:

When the aforementioned people are unavailable [see Ch. 6.106], he may go to any house in the entire village, after purifying himself and observing silence. He should, nevertheless, avoid people of ill repute.

119. After careful scrutiny, the gods once determined that the food of a learned Brahmin who is a miser and that of a usurer who is liberal are of the same quality.

120. But Prajāpati told them: "Do not create an equality between unequal things. The food of the liberal man is purified by faith, while that of the other is corrupted by lack of faith."

121. A prudent man should not accept forbidden food even when it is offered to him, as well as food that makes one sick or that has been thrown away by someone.

122. Atri:

Now I shall describe the rules of begging in their entirety, as well as the types of food one should avoid. An ascetic who neglects them falls quickly, while one who observes them finds release.

123. He should live by the beelike method of begging and never practice the other methods. All these are contemptible means of livelihood, except when he is advised that they are appropriate for him.

124. Food begged in the manner of a bee from houses that have not been preselected or what is given spontaneously—let him eat that irreproachable food with a mind free from greed.

125. A mendicant may always visit three, six, seven, or eight houses—this is the method of begging in the manner of a bee, clearly the most excellent. If he wants he may visit even a larger number of houses.

126. Let him collect almsfood containing every good taste, including such items as rice, barley, oil-cakes, vegetables, buttermilk, milk, and curd, but not anything that would involve an injury to a living being.

127. Whatever food that does not violate a man's vow may be properly eaten by him. He should always eat healthy food that digests easily, but in moderation. An ascetic should avoid foods that would inflame the humors.

128. He should avoid houses with large families or with greedy people, because such people give food with great pain.

129. Whenever there are signs of fraud or misery in a house, a mendicant should avoid it as he would an oblation pecked by a crow.

130. An ascetic should avoid any food presented by a menstruating woman and the food of a twice-born person when presented to him by a Śūdra, as well as any food placed in a vessel made of iron or in a part of an animal.[44]

44. This probably refers to a bowl or a plate fashioned out of bone, horn, or skull (see Ch. 6.247).

131. An ascetic should refrain from accepting as alms food that had been prepared either as an offering to the ancestors or the gods or for some other purpose, as well as when it would cause hardship to someone.

132. A mendicant should not eat from the house of a couple who have failed to produce any children. If he eats, he should observe a lunar fast [see Ch. 5.11 n. 5].

133–34. When (the food) has been looked at by,[45] abortionists, heretics, people afflicted with leprosy and the like, menstruating women, dogs, eunuchs, crows, outcastes, or people of the lowest castes, as also when he sees them somewhere, he should not beg there. If he begs, he should observe a lunar fast. He should not even talk with them, except to ask for directions or when there is a danger.

135. In all social interactions, but especially in begging food, he should avoid all those guilty of heinous crimes or fallen from their castes.

136. When an individual commits an offense, an ascetic should abandon the entire region in the Kṛta age, the village in the Tretā age, the family in the Dvāpara age, but just that individual in the Kali age. After abandoning him, the ascetic may go on his begging round.

137. The man who does the act, the man who gives his consent, the man who instigates the act, and the man who approves of the act—all these reap the reward of the action, be it merit or sin. [cf. ApDh 2.29.1]

138. Whether it belongs to a person of one's own lineage or to someone else, a house in which a birth has taken place does not regain its purity until ten days have passed.

139. Rites for gods, ancestors, and the like are never performed in such a house. Neither should a mendicant beg almsfood there. If he begs, he should observe a lunar fast.

140. A mendicant should never seek to obtain almsfood from the family of a relative, from a royal household, or from pupils, relations, friends, and the like.

141. Gods and ancestors do not eat the food given by a husband of an outcaste woman or by a man ruled by his wife. A mendicant should likewise abstain from such food.

142. The special law pertaining to each class and order of life is given the name "hero." Those who abide by it are declared to be heroes, whereas a man who violates it is a murderer of a hero, whom an ascetic should shun.

143–46. A mendicant should not beg almsfood from a naked woman; a virgin; a woman who is pregnant, menstruating, mad, intoxicated, or angry; a woman who is getting ready to eat or who hates her children or husband; a woman who is independent or lives as she pleases; a woman who is

45. The syntax of this sentence (especially of "*dṛṣṭam*") is unclear. The translation assumes that it is an ellipsis.

without a husband, suffering from leprosy, or blind; a woman who has married a second time or who has been adopted; a woman with loose hair or seated at ease; a lustful woman; a woman astonished; a woman who is deceitful or distressed; a woman of evil conduct; a woman who is sweating or afflicted with a sickness; a shameless woman; a harlot; a tired woman; a servant; a transvestite; a very cruel woman; and a woman who is breast-feeding her baby.

147. Kapila:

He should not enter a house with a large family or when the doors are shut. He should not beg almsfood from a woman who is asleep, mad, wanton, intoxicated, sweating, seated at ease, pregnant, sick, in sexual intimacy with her husband, lustful, getting ready to eat, or breast-feeding her baby. He should neither beg nor accept the almsfood offered by a menstruating woman, given contemptuously, handed to him by a naked woman, or brought by a virgin.

148. Kratu:

He should avoid salt given separately,[46] meat, honey, the food given at a house defiled by the impurity caused by a death or a birth, and the food given by fools, sinners, transvestites, and people fallen from their caste.

149. He should never beg from a woman who is foolish, independent, or a leper, from a woman who hates her children or husband, from a virgin or a midwife, from a woman who has married a second time, or from a naked woman.

150. Jābāli the Elder:

One may eat the food of people belonging to only two orders of life, the householder's and the hermit's. The food of people belonging to other orders is not to be eaten, as also the food of other ascetics.

151. Next, I will describe the procedure of begging. With regard to this, Śaunaka writes:

Then, after cleaning his begging bowl with water and a cord of cow's hair while reciting the seven Great Utterances, and after worshipping the sun with the mantra "The swan seated in purity . . ." [TS 1.8.15.2], he should travel silently and with a serene mind.

152. Śaṅkha and Likhita:

A begging bowl may be made of any of the following: wood, gourd, cane, and clay. He should scrub it with his hand using water and a cord of cow's hair and then go out to beg almsfood from Brahmins of good conduct.

46. Salt used in cooking is not forbidden to an ascetic, but ascetics are not allowed to have a separate portion of salt on their plates, a practice common at an Indian meal. Such salt is given the technical term "*pratyakṣalavaṇa*," "visible salt."

153. Atri:

Taking the bowl in his left hand and the triple staff in his right, he should worship the sun, meditating on the unity of the self.

154–55. Meditating on God with a collected mind, he should silently recite the mantra of purity.[47] The person in the sun called by the name Viṣṇu, who abides within the heart—I am He, the god Nārāyaṇa, the person who is the witness of the world. Let him by himself thus meditate on the self, the person who is the creator of all.

156–57. Then, after performing a circumambulation clockwise, he should worship the sun, the destroyer of darkness. After worshipping it, he should again put on his sandals when he walks on the ground for the sake of purity. He should never discard his sandals, for the water pot and the almsfood become defiled when he walks without sandals.

158–63. Putting on his sandals, a mendicant should walk, meditating on Viṣṇu:

May Viṣṇu guard me from the sides,
from above and from below;
and Vaikuṇṭha from every direction!
May Rāma, bow in hand, guard me from all sides;
and Keśava, discus in hand!
May Govinda protect me,
he who drinks soma and eats
what's offered to manes and gods;
Viṣṇu, seated on Garuḍa,
Ananta, discus in hand,
bearing the aspect of a dwarf;
Supreme Self, subtle, pervading all, eternal;
without parts or attributes, imperishable,
bearing a form all white;
without beginning or end;
Ever sleeping on Ananta decked with jeweled hoods,
at the center of the ocean of milk;
May that Mādhava protect me!
May he protect my entire body, within and without,
from the crown of my head to the soles of my feet!
May the Garuḍa-bannered god guard me,
bearing every weapon, possessing every power!
The self of all, the supreme lord,
from the lotus of whose navel was born
Brahmā, the lord and creator of all;
May that Mādhava protect me!

47. This long mantra is contained in MNU 440–56. In some sources this mantra plays a major role in the rite of renunciation; see Ypra 14.

164. Meditating in this manner, he should go around wearing a single garment and a sacrificial string. For the garment was created by Brahmā for the success of all duties. No rite bears fruit, it is said, when it is performed without wearing a garment.

165. Devala:

He should first make his body the dwelling place of the true essence of Brahman and worship with the mantras beginning "Homage to Brahman!"[48] He should then silently recite the mantra of purity, perform a circumambulation clockwise as he recites "Coming with true light . . ." [TS 3.4.11.2], and silently recite the mantra "Your ancient paths . . ." [TS 7.5.24.1]. Then, he should go around silently.

166. Yama:

After purifying himself, he should always go around silently in the evening to beg for pure almsfood. He should wear a single garment or go naked and walk slowly, keeping his gaze within six feet in front of him.

167. He should beg alone and without greed, his gaze fixed on one point. Living without a fire or a home, he should not seek to indulge himself.

168–71. Medhātithi:

He should wear one garment from his navel to the knees and a second as an undergarment. Then, after worshipping the sun, he should go to houses to beg for almsfood carrying a begging bowl and a triple staff. After requesting almsfood, he should stand at the door with his head lowered so that he can be seen. Silently and with a totally serene mind, he should stand there in meditation, as if asleep even though it is day. When he sees that no one is responding, he should remain silently for about as long as it takes to milk a cow. If no one offers him anything even after they have seen him, he should proceed to another house. If someone responds, he should wait until the almsfood is given.

172. Kratu:

He should walk silently and with a serene mind, detached and self-controlled, as if he were asleep, placing his feet on the ground after determining its purity by inspection, wearing a single garment, and carrying a single bowl.

173. An ascetic should live by eating at the fourth, sixth, or the eighth mealtime [see Ch. 6.106 n. 42], or by observing the lunar fast [see Ch. 5.11 n. 5], or by begging food from five or seven houses of people who are strict in their ritual practices.

174. Standing with his head lowered, he should ask for almsfood just once, placing the word "Lady" at the beginning of the request.[49] He

48. The identity of these mantras is unclear. See TU 1.1; Ypra 21.43.

49. The wording of the request is *bhavati bhikṣāṃ dehi*—"Lady, give almsfood." At Ch. 6.185 the ascetic is instructed to place the syllable OṂ at the very beginning of

should wait for about as long as it takes to milk a cow. After he has left a house, he should not return to it.

175. Bodhāyana:

He should make the request, placing the word "Lady" at the beginning. Let him wait for about as long as it takes to milk a cow. [BDh 2.18.5–6]

176. Devala:

Ascetics are always required to carry an umbrella on their begging rounds when it is raining, but not to shelter themselves from the sun's heat.

177. Atri:

An ascetic should always go alone, wearing a single garment and carrying a single bowl. He should go out to beg just once a day, and never beg again later on.

178. As he walks, an ascetic should not look up, around, or afar. A mendicant should walk casting his eyes on the ground just six feet in of him.

179. He should not peek inside a house through the opening of the door with the desire of getting almsfood. Neither should an ascetic make a loud noise there or knock on the door.

180. After first skipping a house, he should not return there again. If he returns and receives almsfood from there, he should control his breath thirty times.

181. As he begs, he should never visit houses both to the left and to the right. If he skips a house that is without blame, he should control his breath a hundred times.

182. He should enter a house that he has not selected beforehand and whose door is left open by the owner, taking into account the differences in time and place, as well as the ability of the donor.

183–85. He may enter a house to beg if another mendicant has not been there before. After he enters a house, the mendicant should stand with an unflinching mind either in the fire stall or where the housewife can see him. Taking the bowl in his left hand and the triple staff in his right, he should make the request, prefacing it with OṂ and placing the word "Lady" at the beginning. After making the request for almsfood, an able-bodied ascetic should not sit down anywhere.

186–87. He should not beg for any other thing, greedy for gratification. Purifying with his gaze the almsfood carried in the donor's hand, the ascetic should place his triple staff against his right shoulder with his hand and take the lid off the begging bowl with his right hand. The bowl should always be placed in the left hand and never in the right.

---

the request. Placing the word "Lady" at the beginning is prescribed for Brahmin students, while Kṣatriyas and Vaiśyas place it in the middle and end of the request, respectively; see MDh 2.49. The assumption is that the donor is always the housewife. The present injunction assumes, moreover, that the ascetic is a Brahmin.

188. Likhita:

Even if he is about to die, he should never eat a full meal given by one person. Let him live by begging in the manner of a bee even from an outcaste, for it purifies the mind.

189. If he has been refused once, he should never again enter that house at the time for begging. Even from a different house, moreover, he should never accept as alms any food that has already been prepared for another purpose [see Ch. 6.131].

190. Kāśyapa:

Entering just three inches inside, he should stand motionless and evenly on both feet. Unless it contains sticks, stones, or bits of pottery, he should not consider any almsfood as impure and despise it. Rather, he should regard it as pure and accept it. He should never look at the face of the donor, but only at the hands. He should cast his glance not more than six feet in front of him and not look constantly sideways or behind. He should enter houses with open doors and never those where the doors are shut. He should neither knock at a door nor make a loud noise. He should not leave too quickly or stay too long.

191. Devala:

If at any time an impediment arises after he has entered a village to beg and as a result he leaves that village, he should not go out to beg again.

192. Jamadagni:

If an ascetic does not receive almsfood from a particular house for five or seven days, he should always avoid that house as if it were a house of an outcaste.

193. Every day that a mendicant leaves a house hungry and without food, he takes with him all the merit that that householder has acquired through daily vedic recitation, sacrifice, and giving gifts.

194. The same author states:

An ascetic should not take as alms anything besides food, and he should not even take cooked food improperly. One who does so deserves to be punished like a thief.

195. Jābali the Elder:

One should eat using a single bowl—this is declared to be the highest vow. If a person is infirm or sick, there is no harm in using two bowls.

196. If an able-bodied and healthy ascetic subsists by using more than a single bowl, that wicked man, greedy for bowls, will end up in hell.

197. When a greedy mendicant asks a donor to fill his bowl, the donor attains heaven, while the eater eats sin.

198. If a renouncer exhibits any greed when he begs almsfood after receiving an invitation, he will undoubtedly fall.

199. When a man says "Give me more! Give me more!" or asks for salt or condiments, that almsfood becomes equal to cow's meat. After eating such food, one should observe a lunar fast [see Ch. 5.11 n. 5].

200. If a man foolishly refuses to accept what a housewife carries in her hands to give him, he will be born in the wombs of crows.

201. Kapila:

After requesting almsfood, he should not tarry long. When someone says "No," he should leave without ill will. He should not ask anyone to fill his one bowl.

202. Bharadvāja:

After reciting silently the mantra "O ladle, fly away filled . . ." [TS 1.8.4.1], he should leave, saying, "Homage!"

Procedure of Eating

203. Next, I describe the procedure of eating. Śaunaka explains it:

Then, after returning from begging, he should place the bowl in a clean place, wash his feet, sip some water, and control his breath three times. Afterward, he should sip water again, sprinkle water on the almsfood while reciting OṂ, consecrate it with the Gāyatrī verse, and offer an oblation to Viṣṇu with the mantra "Viṣṇu traversed this . . ." [TS 1.2.13.1–2]. He should then make offerings to the sun with the two mantras "His rays raise him up . . ." and "The bright face of the gods . . ." [TS 1.4.43.1], to Brahmā with the mantra "Brahman was first born in the east . . ." [TS 4.2.8.2], and to living beings with the mantra "Homage to beings!" [MNU 463]. He should then eat what remains as if it were medicine.

204. Bodhāyana:

Then, after returning from begging, he should place the bowl in a clean place, wash his hands and feet, sip some water, and make an offering in front of the sun with the mantras "His rays raise him up . . ." and "The bright face of the gods . . ." [TS 1.4.43.1]. He should likewise make offerings to Brahmā with the mantra "Brahman was first born in the east . . ." [TS 4.2.8.2], to Viṣṇu with the mantra "Viṣṇu traversed this . . ." [TS 1.2.13.1–2], and to living beings with the mantra "Homage to beings!" [MNU 463]. It is recognized that after an ascetic's final sacrifice the sacred fires reside in the sacrificer himself. His in-breath is the householder's fire [see Ch. 4.11 n. 8], his down-breath is the south fire, his diffused breath is the east fire, his middle breath is the hall fire, and his up-breath is the domestic fire. These five fires indeed abide in the self; hence, he offers only in his self. It is recognized that this is the sacrifice which is offered in the self, which abides in the self, which is founded on the self; and that it leads the self to bliss. After making offerings to living beings with compassion, he should sprinkle the remainder of the food with water and eat it as if it were medicine. [BDh 2.18.7–10]

205. Yama:

He should neither eat out of the begging bowl nor use the bowl to sip water. In the Kṛta, Tretā, and Dvāpara ages an ascetic may eat directly out of his begging bowl, but in the Kali age he should not eat out of the bowl or carry a pot [see Ch. 3.70 n. 31].

206. Bharadvāja:

He should make a plate out of an old leaf that has fallen down and eat in it but never eat in a metal dish. If he eats out of a metal bowl, he should perform a Prājāpatya penance [see Ch. 4.2 n. 1]. He should eat the food after going to a deserted spot outside the village, or to the wilderness, or to a deserted bank or sandy shore of a river, or to a lotus pond. Washing it at a sacred bathing place, he should place the bowl in a sheltered spot. After washing his feet with three applications of earth and likewise also the hands, he should sip some water and control his breath six times. After reciting the hymn to food[50] together with OṂ and the Gāyatrī verse, and thinking of the food as having the nature of the Highest Self, he should drink some water, saying, "You are an underlayer for ambrosia," and make an offering of food in his breath. If, while he is eating, he finds some food contaminated with tiny bits of hair or insects, he should throw away just that portion, wash his hands, and continue eating. If a hair gets into his mouth, he should discard that mouthful immediately from his mouth, rinse his mouth twelve times with water, and continue eating.

207. Bṛhaspati:

After completing his daily duties and with his speech, mind, eyes, and sex organs under complete control, he should gather almsfood in a subdued manner and eat it in a secluded place.

208. While he is eating, he should never touch the food with his left hand or with his feet, nor should he touch his feet, head, or private parts.

209. Outside mealtime, an ascetic should not take anything into his mouth except medicine and the toothstick.

210. Viṣṇu:

He may eat as almsfood barley meal, milk, ghee, well-ripened fruits and roots, vegetables, oil-cakes, or grist.

50. The identity of this hymn is uncertain. The Ypra (58.46–47) gives the following mantra: "Food is Brahmā, the taste is Viṣṇu, and the eater is Śiva. A twice-born man who eats as he meditates in this manner is not tainted by the defilements of food." A longer hymn in praise of food is given in Vidyarnava 1979, 165, the first section of which is TA 8.2.

211. These are the different types of food that bring success to a yogin. One should eat them daily with a totally focused mind.

212. When he is about to eat, the ascetic should first take one drink of water silently and with a collected mind and then eat the first oblation, saying, "For the in-breath, svāhā!"

213. He should eat the second, saying, "For the down-breath, svāhā!"; the next, saying, "For the diffused breath, svāhā!"; thc fourth, saying, "For the up-breath, svāhā!"; and the fifth, saying, "For the middle breath, svāhā!"

214. After offering in this manner the oblations in the breaths, he should eat the remainder in silence. He should then drink water again once, sip some water, and touch his heart.

215–16. Yama:

A mendicant should go out to beg when the smoke has stopped rising and the pestles have stopped pounding and when the sacrifice has been completed. He should not go to a place filled with people who live like dogs[51] or packed with hermits, or when the people have not yet taken their meal. He should take only what would sustain his life, and not eat as much as he can get. Let him never eat for the pleasure of it.

217. When one eats almsfood that is pure in its origin and has been sprinkled with water, and from which oblations have been offered, each mouthful becomes equal to a sacrifice.

218. It is sprinkled with water while reciting OṂ, and it is offered in the internal fires of one's self consisting of the five breaths, while saying "svāhā" at each offering.

219–20. The in-breath is the eye, the day, and the sun. The diffused breath is the ear, the night, and the moon. The down-breath is speech, mind, and fire. The middle breath is water, mind, and lightning. And the up-breath is wind and space. Offering food to these breaths with a collected mind, he becomes sated; becoming sated by eating, he is freed from his triple debt [see Ch. 1.14].

221. It is stated everywhere that one should eat the almsfood after sprinkling it with water. Saṃvarta states:

Gathering five, seven, or eight morsels of almsfood, a sage should sprinkle it with water and eat all of it with a collected mind.

51. This may refer to either of two groups of people. The first group consists of people of a very low caste, who are depicted as *śvapāka*, or cooking dog's meat. The second is a class of ascetics who are said to imitate the habits of dogs or observe the "dog vow" (*kukkuravrata*). See *Dīgha Nikāya*, III, 6–7.

222. Kapila:

Returning then from the village with a single bowl, he should sprinkle the almsfood with water and eat it immediately. He should not speak at all with anyone. He should not beg for anything else other than medicine. Living in this manner all his life, a mendicant will become liberated.

223. One should consider the following if there is a suspicion of some flaw. Kratu states:

He should sprinkle the almsfood with water with the fourfold mantra [see Ch. 5.82], make offerings to Viṣṇu, Brahmā, the sun, and living beings with mantras containing their respective marks [see Ch. 6.204], and give some food to the needy.

224. He should make the lotus of his heart turn its face upward by controlling the in-breath and the other breaths through the suppression of inhalation and the like and offer the food in the fire of Brahman, which is the size of a span—he is thus freed from all defilements.[52]

225. He should neither taste the food nor talk about the six tastes while he eats. Remaining the same whether the food is cooked well and badly, he should not take delight in the one or despise the other.

226. The same author states:

He should not throw food away or eat too much; he should neither speak ill of any food or collect too much of it. Let him not treat with contempt cows, Brahmins, the sun, the moon, fire, wind, and water.

227. Kapila:

If it does not go against his vow, he may accept even any stale food. If he entertains the desire to put on fat, he should control his breath three times and sip water again. He should place the bowl on a support or on a spot he has cleaned two or three times; sprinkle that bowl with water reciting OṂ; and consecrate the almsfood with the triple prayer [see Ch. 5.82]. He should at least worship a mouthful of food with the mantra "Viṣṇu traversed this . . ." [TS 1.2.13.1–2]. He should not eat without making a food offering. Making food offerings to living beings and similar practices, as well as sharing one's food with the needy, are praiseworthy.

228. Sages subsisting on almsfood live happily like bees without causing harm to any living being.

229. "May the moon alone eat the food": the person who eats food reflecting in this manner eats immortality. He eats food in his in-breath, saying, "For the in-breath, svāhā!" He eats food in his down-breath, saying, "For the down-breath, svāhā!" He eats food in his diffused breath, saying, "For

52. This is a rather tentative translation of an elliptical passage with Tantric overtones. The breath is controlled by making the moments of inhalation, retention, and exhalation even and progressively longer.

the diffused breath, svāhā!" He eats food in his up-breath, saying, "For the up-breath, svāhā!" He eats food in his middle breath, saying, "For the middle breath, svāhā!" Whoever eats food is fire. Whatever food one eats, all that is the moon. He should wash the bowl and take it after consecrating it with the triple prayer. After eating thus he is freed from sin.

230. Viśvāmitra:

An ascetic who practices begging in the manner of a bee should offer food to the first four; he should not, however, make offerings to the remaining four.[53]

231. He should offer to the sun reciting the two mantras "His rays raise him up . . ." and "The bright face of the gods . . ." [TS 1.4.43.1]; to Brahmā while saying, "Brahman was first born in the east . . ." [TS 4.2.8.2]; and to Viṣṇu with the mantra "Viṣṇu traversed this . . ." [TS 1.2.13.1–2].

232. Then he should make a fourth offering to all living beings. He should make offerings the size of a mouthful to the sun and so forth in the proper order.

233. An ascetic who gathers daily the food belonging to others and makes offerings of it commits a sin and has to perform a penance.[54]

234. For what reason should he give alms? And what reward does he reap by giving? Both the one who gives and the one who receives will go to hell.

235. Hārīta:

Placing the begging bowl in his left hand, he should take the lid off and clasp the bowl with his right.

236. He should beg as much almsfood as would satisfy his hunger. Returning, then, he should set down the bowl and sip some water in full control of himself.

237. Taking a mouthful of food mixed with all the condiments, an amount that would cover the four fingers, he should place it separately in the bowl with a collected mind.

238. He should then make offerings of food to the deities beginning with the sun and to living beings. Sprinkling the food with water, the ascetic should silently eat the food from a plate made of leaves but never out of the begging bowl.

53. The text does not specify the identity of the two sets of four. The first set clearly refers to the sun, Brahmā, Viṣṇu, and living beings. The second set appears to include gods, ancestors, and human beings.

54. The Sanskrit "*tyajati*" means literally "he abandons or discards." Within the context, it refers in all likelihood to the "abandonment" of food in a sacrifice or oblation; the depositing of a sacrificial offering is often referred to as its abandonment (*tyāga*). These offerings may include oblations to ancestors and alms to other people; see Ch. 6.251–52.

239. However, he should never eat from a plate made of the leaves of the following: banyan, sun plant, bo tree, Kumbhī plant, and Tinduka and Karañja trees.[55]

240. Even in an emergency, however, he should never eat out of a brass plate. All ascetics who eat out of brass plates are referred to by the name Palāśa.[56]

241. An ascetic who eats out of a brass plate takes upon himself all the sins of both the tinker who made it and the householder who owns it.

242. Yama:

Vessels made of gold or iron are not appropriate bowls for ascetics either for collecting alms or for eating.

243. When almsfood is put in a bowl made of gold, silver, copper, brass, or iron, the donor gets no merit and the receiver goes to hell.

244–45. Likhita:

He should neither eat out of the begging bowl nor use the bowl to sip water. In the Kṛta, Tretā, and Dvāpara ages an ascetic may eat directly out of his begging bowl, but in the Kali age he should not eat out of the bowl or carry a pot [see Ch. 3.70 n. 31]. He should rather eat from a plate made of leaves but never put the food on the back side of the leaves

246–47. When the leaves of Palāśa,[57] lotus, or banana are unavailable, he should forgo eating. Even when other leaves are unavailable, he should refrain from eating food placed on Kuśa or some other type of grass or on the ground, or out of vessels made of gold, silver, brass, copper, iron, or a part of an animal [see Ch. 6.130 n. 44].

248. He may eat off of a Palāśa leaf or, in an emergency, directly out of his hand. A householder who eats off of a Palāśa or a lotus leaf should observe a lunar fast [see Ch. 5.11 n. 5]. An ascetic and a forest hermit who do so, however, reap the reward of a lunar fast.

249. Medhātithi:

A mendicant does not commit a sin by eating from plates made of gold, silver, copper, brass, shell, or stone; he does commit a sin if he accepts any of them.

250. Yama and Likhita intend to point out that an ascetic is not allowed to take for his own use, whether it is to collect almsfood or for eating, vessels made of gold and the like. Medhātithi's view, on the

55. The respective botanical names of these are *Ficus indica, Calotropis gigantea, Ficus religiosa, Bignonia suaveolens* (the name Kumbhī, however, applies to a variety of trees), *Diospyros embryopteris*, and *Pongamia glabra*.

56. A class of demons (Rākṣasa) are known by the name Palāśa, which literally means "flesh eater."

57. *Butea frondosa*.

other hand, is that an ascetic commits no sin when in an emergency he takes for his own use such vessels and eats from them, so long as they belong to someone else. When even such vessels belonging to others are unavailable, he should eat directly out of his hand. One should not eat from vessels made of brass and the like merely because leaves are unavailable. Rather, one may eat from them only when there is an imminent danger of death,[58] according to Hārīta's statement: "Even in an emergency, however . . ." [Ch. 6.240]. 251. Atri gives the rule regarding the disposal of the food offerings:

> He should not give a food offering to a needy person or throw it away as he pleases. A wise man should throw it in water or bury it in the ground.

252. Kratu speaks about giving almsfood to others and about the disposal of that food when the ascetic is prevented from eating it:[59]

> A person who collects almsfood in the manner of a bee and then gives it to Brahmins goes to a terrible hell; one who eats such food should observe a lunar fast.
>
> 253. Almsfood is permitted to twice-born people when they are performing a penance or a vow and in a time of distress. For others such a gift constitutes a theft, while for ascetics it is equal to a sacrifice

254. Śāṇḍilya declares that ascetics should eat only once a day:

> Going to a village in the evening, he should silently collect almsfood. Just once every day he should eat eight mouthfuls of food.

255. Jābāli the Elder:

> He should never eat at night or eat again after he has eaten. A renouncer who eats at night undoubtedly falls.
>
> 256. If, after the time for the twilight worship has passed, an ascetic eats at night, all his religious activities—worship, silent prayer, control of breath, and food offerings—will become fruitless; a penance is ordained for him.

257. Vasiṣṭha speaks about eating twice:

> He may eat in the morning and in the evening what he receives from a Brahmin household, with the exception of honey and meat. He should not eat until he becomes satiated. [VaDh 10.24–25]

This provision applies to the infirm.

58. The meaning is that an ascetic who fears that he will die if he continues to fast may eat to save his life and do so even from a forbidden vessel.

59. The text here appears to be corrupt, and the manuscripts give widely divergent readings. The two verses that follow deal only with the prohibition about giving away almsfood. They do not deal with the disposal of uneaten food.

Rites Following the Meal

258. Next, I explain the rites that follow the meal. In this regard, Śaunaka states:

> After eating he should sip some water and silently recite the mantra "May my speech be in my mouth, my breath in my nose . . ." [TS 5.5.9.2]. Then, after sipping water, he should worship the sun with the mantra "As we gaze from the darkness . . ." [TS 4.1.7.4], clean the bowl with water and a cord of cow's hair while reciting the seven Great Utterances, control his breath three times, and silently recite the Gāyatrī verse one hundred and eight times. He should spend the rest of the time engaged in silent prayer and meditation. Then, at the evening twilight when the sun has set, he should silently recite the Gāyatrī verse while he is seated until the stars appear. Thereafter, he should meditate until he falls asleep. He should meditate also when he is awakened from sleep.

259. Yama:

> Things made of gold and silver, vessels used in sacrifices, and the bowls of ascetics—the rule is that these are purified with just water.

260. Likhita:

> After worshipping the sun following his meal, he should always read the Purāṇas. Reading the Purāṇas purifies the heart and thus develops the love of Viṣṇu.

261. Śaṅkha and Likhita:

> A begging bowl may be made of one of the following: wood, gourd, cane, and clay. It is cleaned using water and a cord of cow's hair. It is to be cleaned every day. While he does this, it is not necessary to sip water. He should not throw the bowl on the ground or permit it to come into contact with something impure. After the meal he should sip water, sip once again, and sprinkle water on the articles.[60] It is not inconsistent to carry a sling of cord, in the same way as other articles.[61]

262. Śaṅkha:

> After worshipping the sun following his meal and sitting down on his seat, he should control his breath, silently recite the Gāyatrī verse one hundred and eight times, and again meditate on Nārāyaṇa.
>
> 263. He should spend the rest of the day reading the Purāṇas and occupied in other similar activities. Then, after performing the evening twilight worship, he should engage in yogic exercises; he should do so also when he wakes from sleep.

60. The Sanskrit term "*dravyāṇi*" is rather vague. In all likelihood, the water is sprinkled on the ascetic's belongings, such as the bowl.

61. This elliptical sentence is far from clear. The meaning may be that, as an ascetic is permitted to possess other articles, so he is permitted also to have a sling for carrying the water pot.

264. When every day a man thus performs meditation as his principal activity but also does his ritual duties, he is fit for becoming Brahman.

265. Viśvāmitra:

After his meal he should worship the sun with the mantra "As we gaze from the darkness . . ." [TS 4.1.7.4]. I have declared the five ways of begging for mendicants [see Ch. 6.80].

266. A mendicant who lives in this manner is truly an ascetic; he truly belongs to an order of life. After performing the twilight worship in the prescribed manner, he should engage in meditation.

267. The morning twilight worship is performed using the verses addressed to Mitra; the midday worship, using the verses addressed to the sun; and the evening worship, using the verses addressed to Varuṇa.[62]

268. The twilight worship of the rising sun is known as Sārasvatī, while the midday worship is called Śāṅkarī, and the evening worship, Vaiṣṇavī.

269. A Brahmin, if he is wise, should always perform the meditation in this manner. This meditation has been taught by me for achieving success in silent prayer and sacrifice.

270. If a man performs the twilight worship wearing purificatory rings made of cow's hair, every evil deed he has performed will be washed away at once.

271. Seated facing the east on Darbha grass and holding Darbha grass in his hands, he should recite the Gāyatrī verse one thousand times or one hundred times with a fully collected mind.

272. The three immaculate Great Utterances preceded by OṂ and the Gāyatrī with three feet—these are known as the highest state.

273. He should always wear a purificatory ring made of Kuśa grass in his right hand, especially when he is eating. He is thus not defiled by the flaws in the food.

274. Wearing a sacrificial string and a top knot, carrying a triple staff, and furnished with a seat and a water pot, he should perform all the rites prescribed in the Vedas and the scriptures. An ascetic achieves success if he always performs yoga; he does not achieve it by any other means.

275. Medhātithi:

After his meal he should himself wash his bowl with water and a cord of cow's hair as he recites the Great Utterances, the Gāyatrī verse, or the syllable OṂ.

62. For the verses addressed to Mitra and Varuṇa, see Ch. 6.47. According to the *Bodhāyanīyabrahmakarmasamuccaya*, p. 54, the mantras to be recited at midday are the following five: "As we gaze from the darkness . . ." (TS 4.1.7.4), "His rays raise him up . . . ," "The bright face of the gods . . ." (TS 1.4.43.1), "That eye favorable to the gods . . . ," and "Who arose from the mighty ocean . . ." (TA 4.42.5).

276. Then he should control his breath three times and silently recite the Gāyatrī verse one hundred and eight times. If he needs to speak at all, he should say only something useful.

277. He should then calmly spend the rest of the day in meditation. He should engage in twilight worship when the sun glows red until the appearance of stars.

278. He should again engage in meditation until he falls asleep. When he wakes from sleep he should meditate again and, while standing, silently recite again the mantras of the morning twilight worship.

279. Bharadvāja:

After sipping a handful of water, saying, "You are the cover of ambrosia," he should brush his teeth while reciting OṂ. He should throw the remainder of the food together with the plate into water, sip some water, control his breath three times, sip water again, and silently recite the mantra "May my speech be in my mouth, my breath in my nose . . ." [TS 5.5.9.2]. He should then sprinkle himself with the mantra "Waters you bring delight" [RV 10.9.1-3] and carry out the worship with the mantra "As we gaze from the darkness . . ." [TS 4.1.7.4]. Then, he should wash his begging bowl while reciting OṂ, silently recite the Gāyatrī verse one hundred and eight times, and, taking a cord of cow's hair, rub the dry begging bowl with it while he again recites OṂ. After tying it as he recites the mantra "The quarters, the directions . . ." [TS 1.3.10.2], he should set the bowl down while reciting the Gāyatrī verse and worship the sun glowing red. A mendicant who thus takes his meal in the prescribed manner attains the highest goal.

Evening Duties

280. I describe next the evening twilight worship. On this point Śaunaka writes:

Rites such as bathing are done in the evening in the same way as before. After completing that entire set of rites, he should make an offering of water to the sun glowing red in the same manner as before.

281. Then he should worship the sun with the verses addressed to Varuṇa and complete the rites connected with twilight worship. Remaining seated, he should engage in meditation until he becomes sleepy. If he awakens he should again meditate. Such a man is fit for becoming Brahman.

282. Hārīta specifies the place where an ascetic should spend the night:

After eating in the bowl, he should wash it while reciting a mantra. That bowl of his is not defiled like a cup at a sacrifice.

283. Then, after sipping some water and controlling his breath, he should worship the sun. He should spend the rest of the day engaged in silent prayer, meditation, and reading the epics. Then, after performing the twilight worship, he should spend the night in a temple or a similar place.

284. Śāṇḍilya:

He should renounce all ritual activities, with the exception of the Veda. Building a hut outside the village, then, he should live there or at the foot of a tree.

285. Kratu:

Free from attachments and doubts, undefiled and practicing yoga, he should live in a deserted house, a cave, a fire stall, or a temple.

286. Vasiṣṭha speaks about the prohibition of couches and the like, the covering for the body, and the obligation to sleep on the ground:

He should always spend the night wearing a single garment, covering his body with an antelope skin or with grass that has been nibbled by cows, and sleeping on the ground.[63] He should do so in the outskirts of the village, in a temple, in a deserted house, or at the foot of a tree. Mentally rehearsing his daily vedic recitation, he should always live in the wilderness and not roam in the vicinity of village cattle. [VaDh 10.9–16]

287. The same author comments:

He should not eat until he becomes satiated. He may live within a village. He should not be crooked, deceitful, or irresolute. [VaDh 10.25–27]

288. Dakṣa addresses the issue of living without a companion and the question of who is entitled to live in a religious house and who is not:

One is a true mendicant, two are said to form a sexual pair, and three are called a village. When they are more than that, they constitute a city.

289. A mendicant should not form a city, a village, or even a pair. If an ascetic forms these three, he falls from his duty.

290. In such groups gossip about kings, almsfood, and the like become rampant. Close association inevitably breeds love, calumny, and envy toward each other.

291. Mendicants who have become weak by performing austerities and silent prayers, who are sick or old, who are under evil planetary influence, and who suffer from a physical handicap are entitled to live in a religious house.

63. The critical edition of the VaDh has the reading *anityāṃ vasatiṃ vaset*, which translates as "He should not have a stable residence." In the citation by Yādava, however, the passage is intended to show how an ascetic should spend the night, hence my somewhat nonliteral translation of *nityaṃ vasatiṃ vaset* as "he should always spend the night." In this context, moreover, covering the body appears to refer to an ascetic substitute for a bed sheet.

292. A mendicant who is healthy and young is not entitled to live in a religious house. If, for example, such a mendicant engages in sexual activity while living in a religious house, he defiles that place and also causes distress to the old people living there.

293. Kapila, on the other hand, approves of living with companions:

> He should greet respectfully teachers, old people, and those given to austerities who visit him. He should regard them as Viṣṇu himself. The practice of sharing what he has with them according to his ability in the performance of religious rites is also recommended as praiseworthy. He should live in the company of ascetics who are not cantankerous and follow common customs.

294. Śaunaka:

> He should neither build a house himself nor have one built for him. He should occupy one that is already built. Then, he should meditate on Brahman and keep his mind focused only on Brahman as he falls asleep. Or he may enter a temple free of heretics and somehow spend the night there, either keeping awake or sleeping. Then, sitting down, he should sip some water, control his breath three times, and sip again. At night he should sip water taken from a water pot placed on a wooden plank, while during the day he should use flowing water. He should not leave a holy place that is pleasant and has a lot of water. He should not develop an intense attachment to a sacred bathing place.

295. Vāyu:

> At the end of the night water is to be drawn in the prescribed manner into a clean pot. He should himself throw away water that has remained in a pot a day and a night, even though it may be pure.

Behavior toward Ascetics

296. Next, I will explain what a householder should do when a mendicant visits him for food or lodging. In this connection, Jābāli the Elder writes:

> Even though a Brahmin may have mastered all four Vedas, offered Soma sacrifices, and performed a hundred sacrifices, an ascetic is far superior to him; they are as different as a sesame seed and Mount Meru.
>
> 297. If a man does not get up from his bed or chair when he sees an ascetic, on account of that deed that foolish man will be reborn in animal wombs after death.
>
> 298. One should not denigrate an ascetic, be he virtuous or sinful. People who are malevolent toward ascetics end up in hell.

299. Dattātreya:

A Brahmin who carries the emblem of the triple staff is Nārāyaṇa himself in visible form. So, when a man worships him, he thereby worships Viṣṇu himself.

300. Non-mendicants should worship a mendicant who is totally devoted to his duties, irrespective of whether he is virtuous or vile, or whether he has taken his vows a long time ago or just recently.[64]

301. An ascetic who carries the triple staff is an image of Viṣṇu. One should always worship him with a devout heart using the eight-syllable mantra containing the name of Nārāyaṇa.[65]

302. The triple staff is the emblem of Viṣṇu. It is the means of liberation for twice-born people and signals the cessation of all rules [see Ch. 2.51 n. 20]. That is the teaching of the Veda.

303. The law contained in the triple Veda was once assaulted by Buddhists, heretics, and the followers of Kaṇāda, and it was protected by Viṣṇu carrying a triple staff [see Ch. 1.2 n. 1].

304. Jamadagni:

If someone gives to an ascetic food that has dried out and that had been cooked separately, the fool will go to hell on account of that sin.

305. An ascetic and a vedic student are both entitled to receive cooked food. If a man eats without giving food to these two, he should observe a lunar fast.

306. One should first pour water on the ascetic's hand, then give the almsfood, and finally pour water on his hand again. That almsfood is equal to Mount Meru, and that water is comparable to the ocean.

307. Viṣṇu himself eats in the house of a man where an ascetic eats. The triple world eats in the house of a man where Viṣṇu eats.

308. All the sins that a householder may have accumulated during his entire life are reduced to ashes when an ascetic spends a single night with him.

309. If a man ignores those who do not cook and feeds people who do cook, all his labor with regard to divine and ancestral rites will be in vain.

310. If a man turns away a good ascetic who is neither defiled nor sinful, he will hand over his merits to that ascetic and take over the ascetic's sins.

311. Whether he is a saint or a sinner, a fool or a sage, an ascetic should be honored, O Yudhiṣṭhira, even if he simply wears an ocher robe and carries a staff.

64. I have tried to make some sense of this somewhat unclear and possibly corrupt verse by assuming an *avagraha* before *bhikṣubhiḥ*.

65. This mantra is *oṃ namo nārāyaṇāya*—"OṂ Homage to Nārāyaṇa!"

312. Atri:

One who is giving the almsfood should first pour water on the mendicant's right hand and then put the almsfood in the bowl that is carried in his left hand.

313. The pouring of water while giving almsfood has been ordained to satiate the gods and ancestors. They become sated indeed when that food is given.

314. Even if a man gives the entire earth, it would not equal the merit of preparing almsfood and giving it to a mendicant, who is an image of Viṣṇu.

315. When man gives to a renouncer a begging bowl, a seat, a staff, a sling, or a water strainer, he reaps the reward of giving a cow.

316. If a man builds a hermitage to house sick mendicants or cares for them with healthy food and the like, he obtains an eternal reward.

317. Jābāli the Elder:

Almsfood that has been kept aside, licked by cats and mice, left open to the wind, or dried up is equal to honey and meat.

318. The person who accepts almsfood that is stale or that had been previously offered to gods does not commit sin, but the donor goes to hell.

319. One should first pour water on the mendicant's hand, then give the almsfood, and finally pour water on his hand again. That almsfood is equal to mountains, and that water is comparable to the ocean. Almsfood given in this manner satiates the gods.

320. Jābāli:

If a man ever robs something from the hands of an ascetic, the fool will go to hell on account of that sinful deed.

321. When a man gives to a renouncer a triple staff, a water strainer, a begging bowl, or a seat, he reaps the reward of giving a thousand cows.

322–23. When a man gives to a triple-staffed ascetic a begging bowl of one of the four kinds furnished with all requisites after filling it with sacrificial food and offers himself as well, he rescues all those abject sinners who are burning in hell and, raising himself by himself, attains the highest state.

324. As many bowls and as much food as he gives, for that many thousands of years he will rejoice in heaven.

325. That ends the sixth chapter, entitled "Daily Practices," of the *Collection of Ascetic Laws.*

CHAPTER SEVEN

Proper Conduct

1. Now I will explain the rules of proper conduct. Manu writes in this connection:

> A sage should live without fire or house and enter a village to obtain food. He should remain disinterested, not acquisitive, and mentally composed. [MDh 6.43]
>
> 2. A begging bowl, dwelling at the foot of a tree, ragged clothes, a solitary life, and equanimity toward all—these are the marks of a renouncer.[1] [MDh 6.44]
>
> 3. Let him long neither for death nor for life and await his appointed time, as a servant awaits his wages. [MDh 6.45]
>
> 4. He should place his foot on the ground after determining its purity by inspection. He should drink water that has been purified with a cloth strainer. He should speak words that are pure because true. And he should conduct himself with a pure heart. [MDh 6.46]
>
> 5. Let him bear insults patiently and never treat anyone with contempt. Let him, moreover, never quarrel with anyone just for the sake of this body. [MDh 6.47]
>
> 6. Toward a man who is angry at him let him not show anger in return; let him say kind words to those who revile him. In connection with any of the seven doors,[2] moreover, let him not speak an untrue word. [MDh 6.48]
>
> 7. Finding joy in activities pertaining to his inner self, he should sit in meditation, free from concerns and desires, and go about alone during the day for the sake of bodily comforts.[3] [MDh 6.49]

1. Manu uses the term *mokṣa* (lit., "liberation") as a technical term for the order of life (*āśrama*) devoted to liberation, namely renunciation (see Ch. 2.5). The term "*mukta*" (lit., "liberated") thus refers to one who has renounced. The most appropriate translations of these two terms, therefore, are "renunciation" and "renouncer." For a more detailed discussion of Manu's use of this term, see Olivelle 1993, 137–42.

2. The identity of the seven doors is uncertain, and the commentators of Manu offer a variety of interpretations. The seven are most likely the five senses, together with the mind and the intellect; see Ch. 5.40–41.

3. I interpret the elliptic phrase "*sukhārtham*" as search for bodily comforts, such as food. The reason ascetics go about during the day is to beg for food, and the

8. He should never seek to obtain almsfood by interpreting portents and omens, by practicing astrology or palmistry, by giving advice, or by participating in debates. [MDh 6.50]

9. Let him not visit a house crowded with hermits, Brahmins, birds, or dogs, or even with other mendicants. [MDh 6.51]

10. He should always disdain food given with a great show of respect, for when he accepts such food, even a liberated ascetic slips into bondage. [MDh 5.58]

11. By eating little and by living in an isolated place he should restrain his senses as they are being drawn by sensual things. [MDh 6.59]

12. By bringing his senses under control, by eradicating love and hate, and by not causing harm to any creature, he becomes fit for immortality. [MDh 6.60]

13. Let him reflect on the diverse destinies of people resulting from evil deeds, their descent into hell, and their suffering in Yama's abode. [MDh 6.61]

14. Let him reflect on how they are separated from the ones they love and united with the ones they hate and on how they are overtaken by old age and oppressed by disease. [MDh 6.62]

15. Let him reflect on how they depart from this body and start a new life in a womb and on how this inner self migrates through untold millions of wombs. [MDh 6.63]

16. Let him reflect on how the embodied souls are subjected to suffering on account of sins and how they experience unending happiness by pursuing righteous goals. [MDh 6.64]

17. Let him reflect on the subtle nature of his inner self through yogic concentration and on how it takes birth in the most excellent of bodies, as well as in the vilest. [MDh 6.65]

18. Viṣṇu:

Respect and disrespect—these two produce joy and anger in people, but in promoting the success of those engaged in yogic practice, their effects are exactly the opposite.[4]

19. Respect and disrespect—they call these two poison and ambrosia. Of the two, disrespect is ambrosia, while respect is deadly poison.

20. The same author states further on:

---

very next verse deals with begging. The editions of MDh read "*iha*" ("in this world") for "*divā*," and most commentators of Manu take the phrase to mean the desire to attain the bliss of final liberation.

4. This and the following verses ascribed to Viṣṇu are found in the forty-first chapter of the *Mārkaṇḍeya Purāṇa*.

Let a yogin, his mind concentrated, behave in such a way that people would scorn and despise him, taking care not to cause harm to the practices of good men.

21. Once again the same author states:

He should engage in that essential activity by which he will attain liberation, for other rites in numerous ways create obstacles on the path of yoga.

22. Abandoning all rites that are either voluntary or forbidden, let him practice just the obligatory rites.

23. Yama:

If one man rubs sandalwood paste on his right arm, while another cuts off his left, he should look upon them with equal eyes.

24. This should always be his disposition in the face of pleasant and unpleasant things. Under all circumstances, whether desirable or disagreeable, he should always remain the same.

25. He should be the same to friend and foe, to the good and to the bad; freed from attachments, he should remain the same in cold and heat, in pleasure and pain.

26. He is neither elated when he is praised nor angered when he is abused. A man who is the same when he is loved or hated is a sage without desire for anything.

27. When a man is neither elated nor dejected at anything he might hear, touch, see, taste, or smell, he should be regarded as one who has vanquished his senses.

28. He should not be fickle in anything he does, whether it be with his hands, feet, eyes, or speech. That is the mark of a cultivated man.

29. The same author likewise states:

Food that is pure, that comes from a pure source, and that is not especially savory produces a pure mind, while impure food produces an impure mind.

30. The body is a lump of flesh and blood, a pile of marrow, fat, and bones. Equipped with hair and nails, it contains fat and other kinds of filth.

31–32. Enveloped by skin and filled with urine and feces, it stinks. An abode for the winds[5] and a vessel of impurities, the body is without substance, like a picture on a wall or foam on water. Containing both perishable and imperishable parts, it is a place for collecting love and hate.

33–34. The body is like a fort with a single column, nine gates, and three pillars. It is constructed with the five elements. Joys are its ramparts; the

5. Winds constitute one of the three bodily humors, the other two being bile and phlegm.

mind is its mighty ruler. The ten senses are the soldiers who surround it, diseases are the wild beasts that infest it, and the potent sense objects are the powerful provinces that attack it, as it is being ruled by the intellect.[6]

35. The body is the painful abode of disease, subject to old age and sorrow. Let a man abandon this impure and impermanent dwelling place of elements.

36. Bathing, silent prayer, meditation, purification, light meals—only a man who performs these five will become liberated.

37. He should engage in the daily practice of listening to the Purāṇas with devotion, for by listening to the Purāṇas even a fool acquires devotion.

38. Devotion that continues uninterrupted brings release. Therefore, one should recite the Purāṇas. By reciting them a sage attains the state of the supreme Brahman.

39. Vasiṣṭha:

A wandering ascetic should set out after giving a promise of safety to all creatures [VaDh 10.1]. Now they also cite these verses:

> When a sage goes about after giving a promise of safety to all creatures, he too will have nothing ever to fear from any creature. [VaDh 10.2]
>
> 40. But if he takes to the ascetic life without giving a promise of safety to all creatures, he kills creatures born and yet to be born, as he does also when he accepts gifts. [VaDh 10.3]
>
> 41. The single syllable OṂ is the highest Brahman, and the control of breath is the highest austerity. Eating almsfood is better than fasting, and compassion is superior to giving gifts. [VaDh 10.5]

42. Likewise, the same authors state later on:

He keeps his emblem and his conduct concealed. Although sane, he assumes the appearance of a madman. Now, they also cite these verses:

> Liberation is not possible for individuals who are passionately devoted to grammar, who delight in captivating people's hearts, who are preoccupied with food and clothing, or who are fond of lovely houses. [VaDh 10.18–20]
>
> 43. He should never study, or speak, or even listen. No one but a man who is already equipped with these qualities is an ascetic.
>
> 44. If, after assuming the ascetic life, a man fails to live according to its rules, the king should brand him with the mark of a dog's foot and expel him from the kingdom.

6. Some of these analogies are easy to follow. The single column is probably the spine; the nine gates are the openings of the eyes, ears, nostrils, mouth, anus, and urinary canal; and the three pillars the three strands of goodness, energy, and darkness.

45. Further on, he states:

They expound teachings and acquire disciples for profit and adulation. These and other similar tricks, great in number, are used by false ascetics.

46. Meditation, purification, mendicancy, living always in solitude—these are the four activities of a mendicant, and there is no fifth.

47. A person would undertake the recitation of texts and the study of a lot of books only if he regards something in this world as a second reality besides himself

48. A twice-born man should depart for the ascetic life after he has deposited his sacred fire in himself. He should always be devoted to the recitation of the Vedas and intent on gaining the knowledge of the self.

49. After he has followed all the orders of life, overcome anger, and vanquished his senses, a twice-born man who has come to know the meaning of the Vedas will attain the world of Brahmā. The rule of lifelong commitment is prescribed with regard to all the orders of life.[7]

50. Śātātapa:

If an ascetic lapses after he has assumed the final duty, I cannot see a penance that would purify that slayer of the self.[8]

51. If, after he has become a wandering ascetic, a man becomes a householder once again, he will be reborn as a worm living in excrement for sixty thousand years.

52. After he has formally declared in this world his intention to renounce, if a man does not carry out the rite of renunciation, he will sink into the depth of darkness, consumed by the fire of his false promise.

53. If, after he has become a wandering ascetic, a man continues to engage in sexual activity, he will be reborn as a worm living in excrement for sixty thousand years.

54. Then he will become a horrible mouse living in frightful abandoned houses. Soon he will reenter a womb[9] and be reborn as a dog during twelve lifetimes.

55. He will then become a vulture for twenty years and a pig for nine, after which he will be reborn as a tree full of thorns without flowers or fruits.

7. The meaning appears to be that a person may legitimately decide to spend all his life following the duties of any one order of life. For this provision and for the history of the institution of the four orders of life (*āśrama*), see Olivelle 1993.

8. "The final duty" refers to any lifelong vocation, such as perpetual studentship. In ascetic literature it often refers specifically to the renunciatory state that is both lifelong and final, because it is the last order of life. The expression *ātmahā*, here translated as "slayer of the self," can also mean a suicide.

9. This may imply that becoming a mouse does not involve conception in a womb. Mice may have been imagined as spontaneously produced within piles of rubbish.

56. Thereafter, he will becomes the stump of an Aśoka tree burnt by a forest fire, and he will remain without consciousness for one thousand years.

57. At the end of those one thousand years he will be born as a demonic Brahmin tormented by hunger and thirst, eating raw flesh, and drinking blood. He will gain release gradually from that state, but at the cost of his family's destruction.

58. A man who causes the apostasy of a renouncer, a man who admits a fallen man into renunciation, and a man who places obstacles on the path of renunciation—all these three the scriptures declare to be fallen.[10]

59. There are outcaste Caṇḍālas called Bindula, who wear the outward marks of wandering ascetics.[11] Children born to them should be made to live with Caṇḍālas.

60. Hārīta:

After a man has performed the rite of renunciation with full knowledge and in the prescribed manner, if he again becomes a householder, he is indeed an apostate and is excluded from all religious activities.

61. If a man forsakes the ascetic life to become a householder once again, he will be reborn as a worm living in excrement for sixty thousand years.

62. The text from here onward follows the reading of Śātātapa.[12]

An apostate kills ten generations of his ancestors before him and ten generations of his descendants after him, while those same generations are rescued by a twice-born ascetic who remains faithful to his vows.

63. Therefore, an ascetic should make every effort to carry the triple staff. If he faithfully carries out the duties of an ascetic, he will not be born again on earth.

64. The triple-staffed ascetic belongs to the highest of all the order's of life. He should indeed be worshipped with devotion by people who follow the true path.

65. A Brahmin who carries the emblem of the triple staff is Nārāyaṇa himself in visible form. When a man worships him, he thereby worships Viṣṇu himself.

66. An ascetic who carries the triple staff is an image of Viṣṇu. One should always worship him with a devout heart using the eight-syllable mantra containing the name of Nārāyaṇa [see Ch. 6.301 n. 65].

10. The meaning of "fallen" (*patita*) in this type of literature is always rather vague. In its strict legal sense, this term refers to a man who has fallen from his caste due to a serious sin or violation of caste rules. In a broader sense, it may refer to anyone guilty of a major crime or sin.

11. The statement does not clearly identify these people. It may refer to people who claim to be ascetics but live with families. Many such groups of householder ascetics are recorded in Indian history. See Bouiller 1979; Derrett 1974.

12. The author appears to omit a section of Hārīta's passage that follows verbatim the text of Śātātapa given above; see Ch. 7.51.

67–68. I have thus explained to you, O Brahmins, this eternal path of truth. But when the age of Kali comes, there will arise ascetics wearing vile emblems different from this. They will all be inflamed by the fire of Gautama.[13] In the Kali age, moreover, they will explain the meaning of the Veda in an entirely different way.

69. These naked ascetics are Buddhists in disguise, and they will revile the triple Veda. These dimwits will recite the Upaniṣads at night.

70. "We are liberated!"—with this conviction, they will eat the food of Śūdras. In the age of Kali they will sway even those who are committed to the duties proper to them.

71. There are many twice-born men who gain a living by the strategy of carrying a single staff. Because they have forsaken rites, they fall into the dreadful Raurava hell.[14]

72. Therefore, let a wise man not talk with, or even look at, such ascetics. When someone looks at them, he is purified by looking at the sun.

73. If a man feeds a twice-born ascetic who is naked or who is without a sacrificial string at a funerary repast, he thereby offers to his ancestors semen, urine, and excrement.

74. If a man resorts to a single staff either because he has been talked into it or because of greed and afterward regains the spirit of detachment, he should carry a triple staff like a wise man.

75. Parāśara:

These two men go through the sun splitting its orb apart—a wandering ascetic who is absorbed in meditation and a soldier who goes fearlessly to death in battle.

76. When it sees a twice-born man who has renounced, the sun swerves from its place, thinking, "This man will split my orb and proceed to the highest Brahman." [see Ch. 4.16 n. 18]

77. Kātyāyana:

He should avoid love, hatred, and other such faults all his life. An ascetic who always lives in this manner will reach Brahman.

78. Uśanas:

Casting off all attachments, overcoming hatred, eating little, and subduing his senses, he should shut his doors [see Ch. 7.6 n. 2] with his intellect and turn his mind to meditation.

13. This is clearly a reference to Buddhist ascetics, although Brahmanical ascetic literature of this period tends to conflate all types of non-Brahmanical ascetics into a single category.

14. This verse touches on the medieval controversy between the Advaita ascetic tradition, which prescribed a single staff, and the Śrī-Vaiṣṇava ascetics, who carried triple staffs. The latter often accused the Advaitins of being Buddhists pretending to follow the Brahmanical law. On this controversy, see Olivelle 1986–87.

79. Vyāsa:

Casting off all attachments and possessing the knowledge of all things, he should practice zealously all that I have taught before regarding the knowledge of the self.

80. A man whose mind is set on the self should make every effort to shun worldly affairs. He should fervently recite the various Upaniṣads that bring about liberation.

81. Āpastamba:

Next, the rules for a wandering ascetic. Immediately thereafter,[15] from the state of a vedic student, he departs as a wandering ascetic. For such a person they prescribe the following. A sage should live without fire or house, without comfort or protection. He speaks only at his daily vedic recitation. Gathering from a village just enough food to sustain his life, let him wander about without longing for anything in this world or the next. [ApDh 2.21.7–10]

82. Bṛhaspati:

Householders observe the vow of celibacy by being faithful to their wives, whereas total abstinence is demanded of those who belong to the other three orders of life.

83. Later on the same author states:

He should not mingle with his relatives, children, friends, and the like, or with eminent men among the twice-born people, even when he meets them in a different region. Such mingling will undoubtedly lead to lust, hatred, and the like.

84. The same author further states:

An ascetic should not live permanently at a sacred bathing place or devote himself totally to fasting, study, or teaching.

85. Śaṅkha:

If one man rubs sandalwood paste on one of his arms while another cuts off his other arm, he should not feel kindly toward the one and unkindly toward the other. With a friendly disposition and seeking the welfare of all creatures, he regards a clod, a stone, and a piece of gold as the same.

86. Likhita:

He should not be fond of books that do not deal with spiritual matters or become an astrologer. He should not treat people who are sick, poisoned, or possessed, even if it is done for a religious reason.

87. He should not gather a lot of disciples, broadcast his knowledge, or speak in Sanskrit, but should go about like a simpleton and a mute.

15. This means he departs immediately after completing the period of studentship following vedic initiation. Regarding Āpastamba's view on the time for becoming an ascetic, see Olivelle 1993, 74–82.

88. Later on the same author states:

If, after he has renounced, a man observes the duties of an ascetic for three years, devoting himself continuously to yogic practice, he will attain liberation after death.

89. Therefore, a man should seek to attain sovereignty, the highest step of Viṣṇu. A twice-born man should enter the order devoted to liberation and seek to live in it for even a day.

90. Śaṅkha and Likhita state:

An ascetic should subsist on almsfood and not be fond of sharing it with others. He should avoid begging from public sinners and from people fallen from their caste and live on humble and disparaged food. He should be satisfied with wearing just a loincloth. With his passions totally extinguished, he awaits his appointed time, constantly absorbed in meditation. Finding delight in himself, he is in the habit of living in secluded places. Free from deception, hypocrisy, and deceit, he never resides in the same village. Giving up the faults inherent in attachment, he should cultivate the habit of wandering. Adept at understanding the self and distinguishing it from other things, he should not be fond of staying in one place outside the rainy season. He should perform the purifications after voiding urine and excrement, as well as the ritual sipping, with water that has been drawn out.

91. The same authors state further:

When a man bears patiently the barbed words evil people may hurl at him and maintains a joyful spirit without getting angry, it constitutes his self-control generated by his mind.

92. When a man bears patiently cold, heat, and other such dualities, as well as attacks by evil people, the scriptures call it patience and forbearance.

93. When a man has attained supreme wisdom and remains completely calm in the face of every event, whether it is desirable or undesirable, calamitous or propitious, he possesses tranquillity and self-control.

94. When man possessing austerity, knowledge, self-control, and power does not get angry at barbed and cutting words hurled at him—that wise man will not be confounded in this world.

95. If an ascetic with a gentle heart follows in this world the rules of the order devoted to liberation, he will soon cast off the bonds of rebirth and become fit for immortality.

96. The same authors state further:

Avoiding people who have fallen from their castes and keeping his senses, speech, and eyes under control, he should beg almsfood from the four classes. Among these, however, he should avoid people of each lower class when those belonging to a higher one are available.[16]

97. Dakṣa the Elder:

An ascetic comes to possess a staff by acquiring the staffs of speech, mind, and deed and not just because he carries a bamboo stick.[17]

98. The staff of speech is the practice of silence, the staff of mind is the control of breath, and the staff of deed is not injuring any living being.

99. Kapila:

An ascetic should abstain from uttering words of greeting or blessing. He should neither build a house himself nor have one built for him. He should occupy one that is already built. Then, he should meditate on Brahman and keep his mind focused only on Brahman as he falls asleep. Or he may enter a temple free of heretics and somehow spend the night there, either keeping awake or sleeping. Then, sitting down, he should sip some water, control his breath three times, and sip again. At night he should sip water taken from a water pot placed on a wooden plank, while during the day he should use flowing water. He should not leave a holy place that is pleasant and has a lot of water or be exceedingly attached to such a place. He should not be given to explaining epic and purāṇic texts.

100. Later on the same author states:

If he is unable to bear the cold,[18] he may light a fire using pieces of wood that have fallen on their own from trees and that do not harbor insects. There is no fault in his eating roots and fruit that do not contain larvae. Let him not hurt anything, whether it has consciousness or not, for little cause. There is no fault in his possessing such things as a water pot, a water strainer, and metal articles given to him on loan. Let him not get angry even when he is provoked or become elated even when he is flattered. Let him desire neither to die nor to live. He should not throw away a bowl that is not damaged by fire. After answering a call of nature, he should immediately, without waiting even a moment, go to a nearby place of water to purify himself and silently recite the appropriate prayers.[19] Then he should turn his mind to Viṣṇu. He should not, however, show partiality to one god. He should give up a dwelling that is in close proximity to others and has patrons. He should not continue looking when he sees a pretty woman but shut his eyes. He should recite OṂ and not become alarmed.

16. This is an expanded translation of the pithy statement following similar provisions given elsewhere; cf. Ch. 6.105.

17. The author plays on the dual meaning of the Sanskrit term "*daṇḍa*," both staff and control or punishment; see Ch. 4.34 n. 30.

18. Although cold is not mentioned, it appers to be implied.

19. As I have indicated in the critical edition, the readings preserved in the manuscripts are all corrupt. The translation given here is, therefore, very tentative.

101. The same author states further:

An ascetic who seeks final bliss should vigilantly shut off all his senses, thereby erasing what he has perceived.

102. When a man is in the habit of singing songs of divine praise and is given to controlling his breath, then even the sins he may have committed during previous lifetimes cease to affect him at all.

103. Kratu:

Destroying living organisms, using a metal bowl, ejaculating semen, wearing white clothes, sleeping during the day, and speaking idly—these are the seven causes of an ascetic's fall.

104. He should avoid things that have been stored for a long time, as well as activities such as hoarding. Grass, earth, wood, water, stone, leaves, roots, and fruit—he should not take them unless they are given to him, and even when they are given, he should not accumulate them.[20]

105. Male and female slaves, houses, carriages, cows, fields, grain, money, and gold:[21] by accepting such forbidden things a man destroys two hundred generations of his family.

106. Jābāli the Elder:

An ascetic who is self-possessed should not attend receptions, ancestral rites, sacrifices, and events in honor of gods such as processions and festivals, as well as any kind of entertainment.

107. Further on the same author states:

An ascetic who is intent on giving gifts, as well as one who accumulates clothes and other such goods—both will end up in the putrid hell because of their stupidity.

108. Dattātreya:

If, after he has taken up the emblem of Viṣṇu, a man foolishly abandons it, he will go to a hell that is fearsome, violent, narrow, and cruel.

109. Devala:

These are the rules of an ascetic—to regard friend and foe alike; not to accumulate possessions; to practice celibacy; to behave in a pleasant manner; to keep himself pure; not to participate in occupations and arts; and to avoid jewels, money, grain, sensual enjoyments, social intercourse, jealousy, pride, duplicity, delusion, excitement, strife, astonishment, quarrels, fear, debate, and the like.

20. This verse is elliptical and unclear, and the reading may be corrupt. Mine is a tentative translation.

21. The meaning of the term "*rasa*" in this context is unclear. I have taken it to mean gold, because the list contains items commonly associated with wealth. The term can also mean, among other things, liquor or any sweet drink.

110. An ascetic should beg every day from the houses of virtuous householders food and medicine in such amounts as not to leave a surplus for the next day.

111. If an ascetic accepts for his own use an amount of food or medicine that is more than necessary for that day, he will go to hell.

112. He should accept things that are necessary to carry out his duties from good people who follow an active mode of life. Even by mistake he should not accept anything from those who follow a nonactive mode of life.[22]

113. Garga:

After giving up the duties of every other type of life, a man should take up the duties of an ascetic. Should he lapse from the duties of an ascetic, he will not receive the reward of any duty he may have performed.

114. Vasiṣṭha the Elder:

He should avoid activities such as the following: plucking flowers or fruits, digging up roots, nipping the tips of leaves,[23] eating honey or meat, and exchanging gifts.

115. Medhātithi:

His possessions consist of the following six articles: triple staff, water pot, sling, begging bowl, seat, and loincloth.

116. As an ascetic would not accept urine and excrement, in the same way he should not accept these six things: movable and immovable property, seeds, metal utensils, poison, and weapons.

117. As a man would carry out a sentence handed down by the king, in the same way an ascetic should carry out the following six things: begging almsfood, silent prayer, bathing, meditation, purification, and divine worship.

118. As he would avoid the wife of another man, in the same way he should avoid the following: alchemy, judicial litigation, astrology, buying and selling, and all sorts of crafts.

119. As he would not look at excrement, in the same way he should not look at these six: dances and similar shows, gambling, young women, friends, festive foods, and menstruating women.

120. An ascetic should never live in these six types of places: royal courts, cities, trading posts, granaries, cattle farms, and houses.

22. Within the scheme of the four orders of life, householders belong to the first category and ascetics, and possibly also students, to the second. The position of hermits is unclear, for some sources permit begging from them, while others relate them closely with ascetic modes of life; see Ch. 6.150.

23. The meaning of "*agra*" is not altogether clear. One manuscript reads "*tṛṇāgra*" ("tips of grass"). The sense may be the breaking of the tips of branches, leaves, and the like.

121. These are the six causes of an ascetic's fall: traveling at night, traveling in carriages, talking about women, greed, sleeping on beds, and wearing white clothes.

122. An ascetic should never even think of these six: lust, hatred, pride, arrogance, hypocrisy, and malice toward others.

123. These six are the causes of an ascetic's bondage: residence, lack of a bowl, accumulation, gathering disciples, sleeping during the day, and idle speech.

124. When an ascetic spends more than one day in a village or five days in a city outside of the rainy season, that offense is called "residence."

125. When a mendicant who subsists on almsfood fails to acquire even one of the prescribed types of bowls, it is called "lack of a bowl."

126. When an ascetic takes an additional bowl, triple staff, or similar article for use in the future, it constitutes the "accumulation" of goods.

127. When an ascetic gathers disciples not out of compassion but for the services, profit, and honor they provide and the fame they would bring, it should be recognized as "gathering disciples."

128. Because of its lucidity, knowledge is called day, while ignorance is called night. When someone is negligent in those practices that produce knowledge, he is said to be a man who "sleeps during the day."

129. Conversations relating to spiritual matters, asking for almsfood, divine praise, words of kindness, or asking the way—talking at times other than these is called "idle speech."

130. When he possesses these six qualities, an ascetic surely is called tongueless, a eunuch, lame, blind, deaf, and stupid.

131. When a man, as he eats, does not notice that one thing is tasty and another is not, or that one thing is hot and another is sweet, he is called a "tongueless" man.

132. When a man remains as unmoved when he sees a sixteen-year-old young lady as when he sees a newborn girl or a hundred-year-old woman, he is called a "eunuch."

133. When a man walks only to beg food and to answer nature's calls and even then does not travel beyond a league, he is called "lame."

134. When a wandering ascetic, as he stands or walks, does not look beyond six feet in front of him, unless there is some danger, he is said to be "blind."

135. Upon hearing words that are kind or unkind, soothing or scathing, when a man remains as if he had not heard them, he is said to be "deaf."

136. When in the presence of hostile people a mendicant remains silent and acts as if he were asleep, even though he has the full use of his faculties, he is said to be "stupid."[24]

24. The Sanskrit term "*mugdha*" means both stupor and stupidity.

137. A person who knows these ten sets of six, who is endowed with the highest faith, and who is totally devoted to the Supreme Self will be freed from both the gross and the subtle bodies.

138. Jamadagni:

The fool who plucks grains, breaks trees, creepers, or plants, or damages mobile or immobile creatures will go to hell.

139. One who eats a full meal given by a single person, one who accepts food twice, one who obtains a livelihood through mendicancy, and one who accepts food three times[25]—these four types of ascetics undoubtedly fall.

140. Ascetics, vedic students, and widows should abstain from chewing betel leaves, from anointing their bodies with oil, and from eating out of brass plates.

141. Liquor and betel leaves—these two are of equal strength. Therefore, an ascetic should make every effort to abstain from betel leaves.

142. Śaunaka:

Let him not broadcast his virtues. Let him not get angry even when he is provoked or become elated even when he is honored. He should bathe in the morning, at noon, and in the evening, submerging in the water like a stick. Likewise, he should not jump in or swim across a river. Let him not desire to live or to die. He should not travel at night or at dawn and dusk. He should abstain from chewing betel leaves and not long to eat twice or to anoint his body with oil. He should not attend receptions, ancestral rites, and sacrifices, as well as processions and festivals in honor of gods. He should also avoid friendly contact with hermits and householders in trading posts or at places of assembly.

143. Paiṭhīnasi:

Let him neither rejoice when he is praised nor become angry when he is reviled. Discovering both to be the same through knowledge and austerity, let him live in total equanimity.

144. Satyakāma:

After giving up the duties of every other type of life, a man should take up the duties of the life devoted to liberation. Should he lapse from the duties of the life devoted to liberation, he should perform a purificatory rite.

25. The meanings of these four categories, especially the second and the fourth, are very unclear. The term "*dvipratī*" is, to my knowledge, unknown elsewhere. Even the editor of M considers this corrupt. I have attempted to derive it from "*prati* √*i*," meaning "to accept." Likewise, the term "*trisaṃgrahī*" is unclear; I have taken it as referring to a man who accept food either three times from the same house or three times a day.

145. He should not step on a spot that he has not inspected or travel along a road not pointed out by the sun.[26] Let him not injure any living being in thought, word, or deed.

146. That ends the seventh chapter, entitled "Proper Conduct," of the *Collection of Ascetic Laws*.

26. The meaning is that he should travel without a specific destination, along the way pointed out by the sun.

CHAPTER EIGHT

Rules on Insignia and Related Penances

1. Now I will explain the rules on insignia, such as shaving, as well as the penances associated with them. In this connection, Śaunaka writes:

> He should have himself shaved at the junctures between seasons, without cutting his topknot or shaving the hair of his body.

2. Devala:

> The lunar day that falls between the fourteenth day of the bright lunar half-month and the first day of the dark half-month should be regarded as the juncture between two seasons. A person should have himself shaved on that day.[1]

3. Likhita:

> On every full-moon day falling at the juncture between seasons, except when it occurs during the four months of the rainy season, an ascetic should have his head shaved without cutting his topknot.
>
> 4. If he is sick or threatened by robbers, kings, and the like, or if he lacks the resources, he may have himself shaved on any day between the full moon and the fifth day of the dark half-month.

5. Now, the juncture between seasons should be regarded as the lunar day that falls between the fourteenth day of the bright lunar half-month and the first day of the dark half-month. The meaning is that he should undertake the shaving during the solar day on which falls the juncture between the fifteenth day of the bright half-month and the first day of the dark half-month.[2] 6. Devala:

1. The bright half-month begins with the new moon and the dark half-month with the full moon. An Indian season lasts two months and, according to this reckoning, begins on the day of the full moon of every other month.

2. A lunar day can begin and end at any time during a twenty-four-hour solar day, which according to the Indian reckoning begins not at midnight but at sunrise and concludes at the sunrise of the next day. The author wants to point out that the

Immediately after the conclusion of the four months of the rainy season, he should shave the hair of his head and his beard, but not the body hair below the neck.[3]

7. Manu:

Self-controlled and not hurting any living being, let him always wander with his hair and beard shaved and his nails clipped, carrying a bowl, a staff, and a water pot. [MDh 6.52]

8. Devala:

He should shave his head or, optionally, keep a topknot. If he thoughtlessly violates this rule, there is no doubt that he can be purified only by performing a Prājāpatya penance [see Ch. 4.2 n.1].

9. Gālava:

If a man shaves the three places,[4] he should perform a Prājāpatya penance and then control his breath one hundred times.

10. Jamadagni:

An ascetic should perform a penance if he shaves his armpits, pubic region, and the like. He should perform three Prājāpatya penances and then control his breath one hundred times.

11. This latter penance applies when one shaves the armpits, pubic region, and so forth together at the same time.[5] Medhātithi:

At the juncture between seasons he should get himself shaved, avoiding the armpits, the pubic region, and the topknot. A mendicant should never let three occasions for shaving pass without shaving within a year.[6]

12. Immediately after shaving, an ascetic should bathe with water and earth, control his breath three times, and sprinkle himself with water as he recites the mantras addressed to Varuṇa [see Ch. 6.47 n. 25].

---

shaving should be done on the solar day that contains the passage from the full moon to the first day of the dark half-month.

3. Although the neck is not specified in this text, it appears to be implied; see Ch. 9.64.

4. These three are the topknot, the armpits, and the pubic region.

5. The author is here attempting to show that there is no contradiction between Jamadagni, who prescribes three Prājāpatya penances, and Devala and Gālava, who prescribe just one. If all three places are shaved at the same time, then the penance is tripled.

6. The point of this rule is somewhat unclear. Vāsudevāśrama (see Ypra 61.99) interprets this passage as follows. If a mendicant observes a two-month rain residence, then he should shave at the beginning and end of that period, that is, between the juncture of each season. However, if he keeps a rain residence of four months, then he does not shave during the juncture that falls within that period, because ascetics are forbidden to shave during their rain residence. Instead, he should shave at the third juncture falling at the conclusion of that period.

13. A mendicant becomes impure by the water running down from his loincloth. So, after bathing, he should come out of the water and wash his loins with water and the remainder of the earth.

14. If he voids urine or excrement, he should, when he bathes, carry out twice as much of everything normally prescribed; if he remains without bathing for one and a half hours and eats or drinks during that time, he should carry out six times as much of everything normally prescribed.

15. When a person has taken the staff and the like, he should discard them only if they are damaged [see Ch. 3.62 n, 28]. He should throw damaged ones in water, saying, "Go to the ocean, svāhā!"

16. After throwing away an article, he should take a new one reciting the Gāyatrī verse or the syllable OṂ. He should take a sacrificial string with the mantra "That health and well-being we choose" [TS 2.6.10.2] and the water pot with the mantra "Waters, you bring delight" [see Ch. 6.23 n. 12].

17. An ascetic should place the water pot filled with water and hanging from a sling at a spot at least an arrow's length above the ground; otherwise, he will become defiled.

18. An ascetic is not defiled if he walks a distance of three bow shots without his triple staff in the wilderness, but within a village he is defiled if he goes without it even from one house to another.

19. The same author also states:

If an ascetic discards the triple staff and the like that he has taken before they are damaged, he should fast for one night and control his breath one hundred times.

20. Gālava:

When someone has a water strainer but performs the rites of sipping water, offering libations, and worship without using it, all his rites will bear no fruit. A penance is enjoined on him in the verse "After controlling his breath three hundred times, he should silently recite the triple prayer [see Ch. 5.82] three hundred times." If he drinks water without using the water strainer, he should control his breath ten times.

21. Atri:

If he drinks water that is contaminated—with a bad odor, color, or taste, turbid, or containing hair—without filtering it with a water strainer, he should control his breath ten times.

22. In a verse I have already cited [Ch. 6.44], the same author makes an exception in this regard:

Water that has been drawn out, water that flows, and water in an unsullied lake—such water is pure, the Vedas declare, and should not be filtered with a cloth strainer.

23. Gālava:

He should recite the syllable OṂ both when he takes a water strainer and when he ties it to the staff. He should not separate the water strainer from the staff.[7] Should he do so through negligence, he should sip water, control his breath three times, and sip water again. He should not be without his triple staff when he bathes or eats. Should he be without it through negligence, he should sip water, control his breath three times, and sip water again. He should lay down the triple staff with its top toward the east or the north while reciting the mantra "You are the abode of Viṣṇu" [TS 1.1.12.1]. If it falls down, he should silently recite the mantra "Rise up, O Brahmaṇaspati" [RV 1.40.1]. If he lets his triple staff come into contact with other staffs, he should wash it with the mantra "You are purified by the mind of Viṣṇu" [MS 4.1.5] and control his breath three times [see Ch. 3.69 n. 30]. If he does so accidentally, he should wash it while reciting OṂ and further recite OṂ ten times.

24. Garga:

If he lets his staff come into contact with something impure, he should silently recite the mantra "Lord of the forest, be strong in limb" [TS 4.6.6.5]. He should then wash it with the mantra "You are purified by the mind of Viṣṇu" [MS 4.1.5] and control his breath three times. If he does so accidentally, he should wash it while reciting OṂ and recite OṂ ten times.

25. Gālava:

If the water pot, water strainer, or bowl comes into contact with something impure, the rule is that it should be discarded immediately.

26. Atri:

He should not let his bowl come into contact with anything greasy. If he does so accidentally, he becomes impure.

27. The same author states:

If someone discards a bowl, a triple staff, or a similar article when it is not damaged or defiled, he should fast for a day and a night and recite the Gāyatrī verse one hundred and eight times. If, on the other hand, he continues to carry a bowl after it is damaged, he should fast for three days.

28. Jamadagni:

He should perform a hundred when he breaches a rule of purity, as well as when he breaks his bowl.[8] If his bowl breaks when it is being carried by some other person, however, he should fast for three days.

29. Further on the same author states:

7. It is a general rule that, when he is not using it, an ascetic should always tie his water strainer to the top of his staff.

8. The text is elliptical and does not specify the hundred acts that constitute the penance. In similar contexts, other sources prescribe the control of breathing or the recitation of the Gāyatrī verse or the syllable OṂ.

An ascetic should discard a bowl if it comes into contact with pus, blood, flesh, urine, excrement, semen, tears, or phlegm.

30. If, while carrying a bowl, he comes into contact with a dog, crow, rat, bull, camel, jackal, monkey, or outcaste, or with a man fallen from his caste, he should discard that bowl.

31. A mendicant should discard a staff that has come into contact with marrow, urine, excrement, semen, serum, or blood. When it comes into contact with other types of impure substances, it ought to be purified.

32. Within a village he should not go even from one house to another without his staff. Should he do so, he ought to control his breath several times, as also when he travels in that manner beyond the permitted distance in a forest.

33. If, without a staff, he visits a house or travels beyond three bow shots in a forest, he should control his breath three times for each offense after he returns to his place of residence.

34. He should never be separated from his staff, seat, bowl, and the like. He commits a sin when he separates himself from them, and a penance is enjoined on him.

35–36. When he is separated from them, the scriptures prescribe that he control his breath—one hundred times for the staff, fifty times for the water pot, sixteen times for the bowl, eight times for the water strainer, six times for the sling, and four times for the seat. These are the means of his purification.

37. Satyakāma and Jābāla:

Next, we will explain the penances for mendicants. If someone travels beyond a couple of miles leaving behind his bowl, he is required to undergo a penance. He should control his breath thirty times and silently recite the triple prayer three hundred times. If someone crosses a river that flows into the ocean leaving behind his triple staff, bowl, or seat, he should fast for three days and control his breath one hundred times.

38. Further on the same authors state:

If a woman or a Śūdra passes between him and his staff, he should control his breath three times. If a donkey or a camel passes between, he should control his breath six times. If a dog, a pig, or an outcaste passes between, he should control his breath twelve times. When he violates a prescribed rule, he should control his breath twelve times.

39. Dakṣa:

After leaving behind his triple staff[9] or his bowl, an ascetic should fast for a whole day. Thereafter, he should take the triple staff with the appropriate mantra but discard the begging bowl.

9. In these texts the plural "*daṇḍāḥ*" is frequently used as a synonym of the triple staff (*tridaṇḍaḥ*), especially due to the exigencies of meter. I have regularly

40. Atri:

If someone at any time throws his triple staff or his bowl on the ground, he should control his breath sixteen, twelve, eight, or six times.[10]

41. Devala:

Tell us, O great sage, what someone should do to purify a staff and similar articles when they are spoilt by excrement, fire,[11] and the like.

42. He should carefully wash the triple staff with earth and water twelve times. Then he should silently recite the Puruṣa hymn [RV 10.190] and again wash it with water. With regard to other articles so defiled, O best of kings, the rule is that they are to be thrown away at once.

43. One should throw away a bowl, a water strainer, or a similar article that has come into contact with semen, leavings of food, tears, excrement, urine, phlegm, a Śūdra, cattle, or fire, as well as when they are touched by a thief or similar person.

44. If an ascetic accepts a staff or a similar article from a person belonging to the four classes beginning with a Śūdra, he should control his breath one hundred, fifty, twenty-five, or ten times, respectively.[12]

45. Atri:

If he accepts an article such as sandals, umbrella, garment, or begging bowl from a Śūdra, he should control his breath one hundred times; from a Vaiśya, fifty times; from a Kṣatriya, twenty-five times; and from a debased Brahmin, ten times.

46. Jābāli the Elder:

If a mendicant leaves behind his triple staff and water strainer in some house, he should silently recite the Puruṣa hymn [RV 10.190] and control his breath ten times.

47. Devala:

A householder who eats what others have cooked and a mendicant who neglects having a bowl are reborn in animal wombs for ten thousand years.

---

translated such plurals as "triple staff" so as not to create a confusion for the reader of the translation.

10. It is unclear whether the numbers refer to general alternatives of the penance or, what I believe is more likely, to specific penances for placing directly on the ground the different articles: sixteen for the staff, twelve for the bowl, and so forth. See the similar gradation at Ch. 8.35–36.

11. The term "*kravyāda*" can refer to any animal or bird that eats carrion or raw flesh, as well as to fire, especially the cremation fire that "eats" the flesh of the deceased. Articles are to be discarded when they are damaged or burnt (see Ch. 7.100).

12. The meaning is that he should control his breath one hundred times if he accepts from a Śūdra, fifty times if he accepts from a Vaiśya, and so forth (see verse 45). I have taken "*pañca*" (lit., "five") to be a shorthand for "*pañcaviṃśati*" ("twenty-five") required by the exigencies of the meter.

48. When a bowl is unavailable, an ascetic is required to use a vessel made of leaves. He may use such a vessel until he gets a regular bowl.

49. Kapila:

A frail ascetic may carry the following: needle, nail clippers, water strainer, bowl, undergarment, and outergarment.

50. Atri:

If he discards his sacrificial string, he should perform six Kṛcchra penances [see Ch. 4.2 n. 1] while reciting the Gāyatrī verse. Then he should undergo again the rite of investiture with a sacrificial string.

51. Jābāli the Elder:

If a mendicant devoted to meditation lives without a sacrificial string, then all his activities will bear no fruit. A penance is prescribed for such a man.

52. He should perform six Prājāpatya penances while reciting the Gāyatrī verse. Then he should undergo vedic initiation again and wear a sacrificial string.

53. Without delay, then, he should take a triple staff. He will thus not end up in hell but attain a happy state after death.

54. This same penance applies also to those who have taken to the form of ascetic life that requires the abandonment of the sacrificial string. Hārīta:

I will tell you the penance that will erase the sin committed when someone performs rites such as eating without wearing a sacrificial string.

55. He becomes purified by duly controlling his breath five hundred times for each day that he had performed the rites of eating and the like in that manner.

56. When a man devotes himself in this world to the continuous practice of yoga, even the grievous sins he may have committed are erased. Therefore, a man should devote himself to yoga and always meditate at the conclusion of rites.

57. The same author states:

If a sterling Brahmin inadvertently voids urine or excrement without wearing a sacrificial string, he should control his breath six times.

58. He should at all times wear the string in the sacrificial position, except when he answers a call of nature. When answering a call of nature he should let the string hang from his neck and throw it on his back.[13]

13. In its normal position the string (which is a loop) is worn on the left shoulder, extending across the chest and resting on the right hip. This is the position for all ritual activities, except ancestral rites, when the string is worn on the right shoulder and rests on the left hip. The string is left hanging from the neck like a garland

59. Next, I will discuss the garment. In this connection, Gautama remarks:

> He should wear a garment to cover his loins. According to some, he should use discarded clothes after washing them. [GDh 3.18–19]

60. Bṛhaspati:

> He should wear an old garment to cover his loins. According to some, he should use old clothes that have been thrown outside by others.

61. Hārīta:

> He should take a loincloth, a ragged shawl as protection against the cold, and a pair of sandals. Let him not take possession of anything else.

62. Jābāli:

> Let him wear a cotton garment, a religious habit that is not made with tree bark. Without wearing such a garment, he is not purified when he sips water or when he performs the twilight worship. He should wear only an ocher-colored cotton garment, as well as a ragged shawl.

63. Śaṅkha and Likhita:

> He should carry in his hand a triple staff tied with a water strainer. He should wear a garment made of Kuśa grass, ragged cloth, or tree bark, and have a change of clothes.[14] Some permit also a ragged shawl against the cold.

64. Even though the term ocher is used without further specification, nevertheless one should color the garments with the red chalk known as Gairikā. Jābāli the Elder, for instance, points this out when he prohibits householders from wearing the insignia of the ascetic state:

> He should not wear a garment dyed ocher, or carry a sling or a tripod: this is the characteristic behavior of a graduate.[15]

65. Dattātreya:

> The scriptures prescribe a garment colored with red chalk for people in the order of life devoted to liberation. They should, however, wear a white sacrificial string made of nine strands.

(technically called *nivīta*) when one goes to the toilet. Various strategies are used to prevent the string from contamination. In modern India Brahmins usually wrap the string around the right ear.

14. The meaning of the term "*viparidhāna*" (or of the alternate reading "*viparidhāvana*") is unclear. Because the verb is regularly used with reference to changing one's clothes (see Ch. 6.30, 32), I have taken the noun to mean a spare set of clothes.

15. A graduate is a person who has concluded his period of vedic study (see Ch. 2.36 n. 15). Quite frequently, the legal literature uses the expression with reference to all householders, who by definition have concluded their vedic studentship. Regarding the identity of the tripod and its distinction from the triple staff, see Olivelle 1986, 42–52.

66. An ascetic should not become attached even to those articles that he is required to possess. Devala, accordingly, states:

> Looking upon earth and gold with equal eyes and totally impartial, let him not develop an attachment even to the articles he possesses.

67. Manu:

> He should be free from attachment to the articles he possesses.

68. Vasiṣṭha:

> Hut, water, clothes, tripod,[16] house, seat, food—a man who is not attached to any of these truly knows the path to liberation.[17] [VaDh 10.23]

69. That ends the eighth chapter, entitled "Rules on Insignia and Related Penances," of the *Collection of Ascetic Laws*.

16. The meaning of "*tripuṣkara*" is unclear. The term refers to a famous pilgrimage center with three holy lakes, and Bühler translated it as "the three Pushkaras (holy tanks)." This meaning does not fit the context, which includes a variety of items associated with the life of an ascetic. I have taken the term as referring to the tripod from which hangs the ascetic's water pot. This meaning is very uncertain, but the term *puṣkara* can refer to an arrow, and possibly to any shaft or stick. The association of the water pot with a holy lake, moreover, makes this connection plausible.

17. The Sanskrit expression here is "*mokṣavit*"—literally "one who knows liberation"—but the term "*mokṣa*" in ascetic literature frequently is a synonym of the renunciatory state (see Ch. 7.2 n. 1)

CHAPTER NINE

Wandering and Rain Residence

1. I will explain next the wandering and residence of ascetics. On this point, Gautama remarks:

> He should be celibate and keep a fixed residence during the rains. [GDh 3.11–12]

2. Medhātithi:

> He is seen in one place in the morning, at another place at noon, and at yet another at sunset; like the sun, he should remain without a home and free from attachment.
>
> 3. He should spend the night in one place, either in a temple or in a fire stall, except when he is afraid for his life or when there is a great danger.
>
> 4. He should spend the four months of the rainy season outside a village. The two reasons given above remain valid here also for entering a village.

5. From these passages we gather that an ascetic should reside in one place only during the rainy season and not at other times. Manu makes a small concession here:

> During the eight hot and cold months he should on the whole roam around. Out of compassion for all living beings, he should reside in one place during the rains.

6. Kratu spells out the concession hinted at here by the words "on the whole":

> Residing in one place only during the rains, he should wander along the path pointed out by the sun, spending one day in a village, three days in a town, and five or seven days in a city.

7–8. Likhita:

> Having surrendered himself to the highest Brahman, he should travel to sacred bathing places and temples, as he, full of compassion, continues to perform rites according to his ability and to be totally devoted to the prac-

tice of yoga and to silent prayer. To purify himself, moreover, he should perform Kṛcchra penances, lunar fasts [see Ch. 5.11 n.5], and similar austerities

9. Unless he is blind, sick, or lame, he should not spend six nights in any one place. If his mind is totally focused on his duties, however, and if he comes from a different region, he may optionally reside in one place all the time.

10. It is certain that all ascetics should maintain a fixed residence in one place during the four months beginning with Śrāvaṇa [July–August].

11. Devala:

He should not reside for long in one place outside of the rainy season. The rainy season is the four months beginning with Śrāvaṇa [July–August]. He should not travel during that period.

12. Gālava:

During the rains he should live in one place, either in an abandoned house or at the foot of a tree.

13. Viśvāmitra:

He may, indeed, live in one place even outside of the rainy season.

14. Manu the Elder states:

If a man is eminent in virtue, however, he may reside in one place until death. Otherwise, he should cultivate the habit of wandering. This is the opinion of the venerable teachers.

15. Yama comments on the place and the manner of such residence:

He should spend a single night in a village and five nights in a city. During the four months of the rainy season, however, a sage should reside in one place.

16. On land and in water living creatures abound; the sky is garlanded with living creatures. So during the rains, when the world is packed with living beings, let him reside in one place.

17. His mind serene and controlled, let him roam the earth like a worm along the path pointed out by the sun, without making any provision for the next day.

18. During the night, and at dawn, noon, and dusk, he should not move to a different place except to void urine or excrement or when he fears for his life.

19. Totally unfettered, let him always wander alone, without a companion; for when a man wanders alone his path becomes smooth, but it thwarts him when he does not.

20. He should place his foot on the ground after determining its purity by inspection. He should drink water that has been purified with a cloth

strainer. He should speak truthful words, and he should work for the welfare of all creatures.

21. A mendicant should wear a single garment, eat once a day, use a single bowl, and go around alone to beg in a village—that is the ancient vow of the seers.

22. He should always sleep on the ground and never have a fixed residence. He should shave his head and always live in the wilderness. And he should turn his mind continuously to mediation.

23. A place rich in almsfood, the king, relatives, sons, friends and the like, his wife, and gossip about benefactors—let him not even think about these.

24. A sage, if he is serious about attaining liberation, should not pay respects to any of his friends or tell them "Come! Go! Stay! Welcome!"

25. Every day one should pay obeisance to those ascetics who are senior in their vows[1] and who carry out their duties faithfully, as if they were the images of Viṣṇu.

26. An ascetic should pay obeisance only to a renouncer who was ordained before him and who is his equal in virtue, and to no one else.

27. An ascetic should pay homage only to the gods and to aged ascetics who are faithful to their duties; he should never pay respects to a member of any other order of life, however eminent he may be.

28. Let him not fill himself up morning and evening, or become overly fond of food. Nor should he, out of lust, ever become attached to sense objects.

29. He may ask the way and ask for almsfood. He is allowed to speak only on those two occasions; every other type of speech is forbidden.

30. Atri:

Keeping his virtues hidden and living a life of obscurity, let the wise man, although not a fool, behave like a fool without corrupting the path of virtue.

31. Kapila:

Let him somehow keep a fixed residence, just like the old and the sick.

32. Bṛhaspati:

Except in a time of emergency, an ascetic should never accept provisions for a journey. In an emergency he may accept cooked food so long as it is eaten that very day.

1. The meaning is that junior ascetics should pay their respects to ascetics who are more senior. "Vows" here probably refers to their ascetic ordination. Seniority within the ascetic community is measured according to not the age but the time when each member was ritually admitted into the ascetic order.

33. Jamadagni:

A man is not defiled by having something in his hands when he voids urine or excrement in the wilderness, in a deserted region, or on a road infested with robbers or tigers.

34. Placing that item on the ground, he should purify himself according to the rules, and then, taking it in his lap, he becomes pure by sipping water.

35. Gālava:

If he travels beyond nine miles, he should control his breath twelve times.

Rain Residence

36. Next, I will discuss the four-month period of the rainy season. One begins this period on the full-moon day of Āṣāḍha [June–July] and concludes it on the full moon of Kārttika [October–November]; or one begins it on the full moon of Śrāvaṇa [July–August] and concludes it on the full moon of Mārgaśīrṣa [November–December]. Others, however, maintain that the vow concludes after two months, because the statement "He should keep a fixed residence during the rains" [Ch. 9.1] prescribes one season.[2] 37. Jābāli:

During the eight hot and cold months he should on the whole roam around. Out of compassion for all living beings, he should reside in one place during the rains.

38. With faith and devotion, he should reside in a village during the four months of the rains, for if he does not transgress this rule of residence, he will attain the eternal state.

39. When it rains even out of season, he should not travel beyond a couple of miles from the village limits as long as the ground remains wet.

40. Medhātithi:

He should collect dry and pleasant earth of high quality on the twelfth day of the bright half during lunar month of May–June or June–August, without causing harm to any creature.[3]

2. The argument here is that the expressions "rains" generally refers to a particular season of the calendar year. A season, however, consists of only two months. Therefore, the vow of keeping a fixed residence should apply only to the two months of the rainy season.

3. Even though the terms "*śuci*" and "*śukra*" have somewhat indeterminate meanings, within the context of the four-month rain residence they probably indicate the months of Jyeṣṭha and Āṣāḍha. The earth collected is used much like soap for bathing and cleaning oneself after toilet. During the dry months such earth could be collected at any time, but during the rains there is a danger of killing worms and insects. Therefore, all the earth an ascetic would require for the four months had to be

41. When it rains even out of season, a mendicant who is faithful to his duties should refrain from traveling as long as the ground remains wet. He should keep a fixed residence during the four months from Āṣāḍha [June–July] until the beginning of Kārttika [October–November].

42. Atri:

I will declare the rules regarding the four-month residence of self-controlled ascetics, by following which a man is always sure to attain liberation.

43–44. On any auspicious day from the beginning of Jyeṣṭha [May–June] until the full moon of Āṣāḍha [June–July], or on the day that he makes the ritual declaration of intent,[4] an ascetic should proceed to a public field that is dry, pleasant, sandy, and without gravel, stones, creepers, plants, clods, and the like.

45. Let him call to mind Viṣṇu in the form of a boar as he supported the earth and the purifying earth as she was born by Vāsudeva abiding in the heart of every being.

46. "The Self-existent One abides within you, O goddess, through the holy syllable OṂ, for you have been created by the God of gods as the means of purification.

47. "The holy syllable OṂ, O goddess, likewise abides within you, the earth." Having thus made the divinities abide in the earth with the mantras containing the syllable OṂ, he should then recite:

48. "I bear the earth on my head, O goddess, you who have been traversed by the horse, the chariot, and Viṣṇu. Protect me at every step. You are the earth, the cow, the sustainer, the support of the world, you who were raised up by the black boar with a hundred hands. Destroy my sins, O earth, destroy whatever evil I have done. When you have destroyed my sins, I will live a hundred years. Make me prosperous, O earth, for you are the foundation of all things. She rules over all creatures, she is marked by smell, she is difficult to assail, she is eternally prosperous, she abounds in cow dung—I invoke that goddess of prosperity.[5]

---

collected prior to the rains. This collection became highly ritualized within Brahmanical and other forms of Indian asceticism, as did the four months of enforced residence.

4. Before performing any ritual a person is required to declare formally and publicly his intention to perform that ritual. This declaration is technically called *saṃkalpa*. The declaration is generally done the day prior to the rite—in the present case, the day before the full moon of June–July.

5. The critical edition contains only the initial words of these mantras. They are found in the MNU 89–111. The statement that the earth is marked by smell probably refers to the cosmological view that assigns a particular quality to each of the five elements, earth being assigned the quality of smell. Earth abounding in cow dung is considered doubly pure and purifying.

49. "Viṣṇu, assuming a fierce form, once raised you up, O goddess. May that Keśava, who gives support to you, the supporter of all, join you in protecting me.

50. "You, O goddess earth, are known as the support, the governess, the purifier, and the mother of all creatures, and you grant safety to all.

51. "May the earth along with Viṣṇu protect me from all creatures." With his self composed, let him thus pray to the earth, the supporter of the world, and then continue:

52. "O earth, you have been given by Brahmā at the request of Kāśyapa. Remove, O earth, whatever evil I may have done."

53. He should take that auspicious earth, reciting the two mantras beginning with "Viṣṇu traversed this . . ." [RV 1.22.17–18]. Then, seated facing the east on Darbha grass and carrying blades of Darbha in his hands, he should undertake the vow of the four-month rain residence:

54. "Mādhava, the Lord of the universe, together with his wife Lakṣmī, spends these four months sleeping on the coils of the serpent Śeṣa for the welfare of all creatures.

55. "Until the eternal Lord awakens from his sleep, I too will reside in one place for the welfare of all creatures."

56–57. Then he should recite silently the verse "The sky is firm, the earth is firm . . ." [RV 10.173.4] and touch the earth. A mendicant should follow the very same procedure when he performs the vow either on the twelfth day of the bright half or on the full-moon day of Āṣāḍha [June–July] or, if that full moon is cut short, on the day of the Uttara Āṣāḍha constellation.[6]

58. Fetching some earth while reciting "Viṣṇu traversed this . . ." [RV 1.22.17–18], he should bring it back. Then he should worship the holy bathing places with the same mantra.

59. After he has paid obeisance to the older ascetics in the order of their seniority and in the prescribed manner, an ascetic who is junior should offer some earth to an ascetic who is senior to him.

60–61. He should worship one or two balls of earth with the following mantra: "Accept this ball of earth, O mendicant, which is auspicious and removes all sins. May this goddess along with Viṣṇu protect both you

6. Earlier (Ch. 9.43–44) the author stated that the vow should be performed in May–June, prior to the start of Āṣāḍha. Here he gives alternative days within the month of Āṣāḍha. The expression "*khaṇḍā paurṇimā*" ("full moon cut short") in all likelihood is the same as "*khaṇḍā tithi*," that is, a lunar day that is current at sunrise but ends before midday. On such a day one does not start or conclude a vow (*Nyāyakośa*, p. 255). If the full moon of Āṣāḍha ends before noon, then one commences the rain retreat not on that day but on the lunar day that falls on the constellation called Uttara Āṣāḍha, which falls approximately between the twenty-first and twenty-fifth days of the lunar month.

and me." Having thus taken that earth, he should use it in performing rites such as bathing.

62. He should use the earth that he has collected at this time to perform purificatory rites that require the use of earth during the four rainy months.

63. From the following day, which is the first day of Śrāvaṇa [July–August], he should neither travel nor get himself shaved for four months.[7]

64. He should get himself shaved on the opening and concluding days of the rain residence. Even at these times he should never shave below the neck, or the topknot, eyelashes, or eyebrows.

65. If he is unable to begin his rain residence on the twelfth day or on the full moon because of some difficulty or because he cannot find a place to stay, he may travel on until the fifth day of the dark fortnight.

66. If an ascetic travels after that time, he ought to perform a penance. A mendicant should perform one Kṛcchra penance if he travels in disguise.

67. If he travels beyond a couple of miles from the village limits, he should control his breath thirty times and silently recite the triple prayer three hundred times.

68. The above penance applies to a person who returns the same day. In this connection, Jābāli the Elder gives the penance for a person who stays away overnight:

One should not travel beyond a couple of miles from the village limits. If someone carelessly travels more than a couple of miles, he becomes purified only after he has performed a Prājāpatya penance and controlled his breath sixteen times.

69. Vāyu:

A Brahmin who has been initiated into yoga should not disrupt his rain residence. If he does so, he is cleansed and regains his purity by performing a hot Kṛcchra penance [see Ch. 10.44 n. 9].

70. When he perceives a bodily danger during an emergency, when a famine strikes, or when there is an upheaval in the kingdom, he should leave that place even during the rains.

71. Even during the rains he should quickly abandon a region that is infested with robbers, afflicted with a famine, or plagued by disease, or that has been overrun by another king.

72. Atri:

If someone abandons his residence during the rainy season when there is no crisis, he should silently recite the triple prayer one thousand times and control his breath one hundred times.

7. This verse assumes that the vow of rain residence is performed on the full moon of Śrāvaṇa (July–August), which is given as an alternate date (Ch. 9.10, 36)

73. If someone enters a different place during the rainy season when there is no crisis, he should silently recite the triple prayer one thousand times and control his breath one hundred times.

74. If during the rains someone bypasses many villages that are suitable to reside in, he should perform one Kṛcchra penance for each village he bypasses to free himself from that sin.

75–76. He should consecrate the water with the four mantras beginning with "The waters, the eldest of whom is the ocean . . ." [RV 7.49.1–4] and the Śiras mantra. The head is shaved on all four sides after moistening it with water. He should consecrate the razor with the mantra "Sharpen us . . ." [RV 8.4.16]. It is appropriate for an ascetic who is sick or in some danger to perform rites such as shaving at any time until the fifth day of the dark fortnight.

77. On the twelfth day or the full moon in the month of Kārttika [October–November] he should get himself shaved and throw the remaining earth into water as he recites the mantra "Go along the wide atmosphere . . ." [TS 1.1.2.2].[8]

78. On the next day, that is, on the thirteenth day of the bright fortnight or the first day of the dark fortnight,[9] he should get up and go to any region he wants while reciting the verse "Three steps Viṣṇu made . . ." [RV 1.22.18].

79. The three verses beginning with "Mighty and invincible is the celestial help of the three gods . . ." [RV 10.185.1–3], as well as the verse "The ancient paths of yours . . ." [TS 7.5.24.1]—after he has silently recited these verses, he should go away, walking first toward the east or the north.

80. Gautama:

Outside the season he should not spend a second night in a village. [GDh 3.21]

81. Maskarin [on GDh 3.21] explains: "When the season is over, he should not spend a second night in a village. The meaning is that he should not spend two days in a single village." 82. Viśvarūpa explains:[10] "Even though the statement 'Outside the season . . .' does not specify the season, nevertheless we should take it as referring to the rainy season, according to Śaṅkha's statement: 'A single place of residence is

8. Here the author switches to the conclusion of the rain residence. During the concluding rite the ascetic throws away the earth that he has not used during the rainy season and begins a new chapter in his liturgical calendar.

9. If he concludes his rain residence on the twelfth day, then the following day would be the thirteenth of the bright fortnight, whereas if he concludes it on the full moon, then the following day would be the first of the dark fortnight.

10. Viśvarūpa wrote a commentary on the *Yājñavalkyasmṛti* (YDh), in which I have not been able to trace this citation. There is no mention anywhere else that he wrote a commentary on the GDh.

not prescribed outside the two months of the rainy season.' The two months of Śrāvaṇa [July–August] and Bhādrapada [August–September] apply to those who are weak. Devala [see Ch. 9.11] prescribes four months: 'He should not stay long in one place outside the rainy season. The four months beginning with Śrāvaṇa [July–August] constitute the rainy season.'" 83. Satyakāma and Jābāla:

> When a mendicant arrives in a village, a town, or a city during the rainy season, he should remain there permanently. But when the rains are over he should not remain there even a moment longer. If he remains there inadvertently, he should perform a Prājāpatya penance.

84. Atri once again states:

> . . . after he has silently recited these verses[see Ch. 9.79], he should go away, walking first toward the east or the north. He should spend only a single night in a village, but on some occasions he may reside there longer as if he were blind, stupid, deaf, mad, and dumb [see Ch. 7.130–36].
>
> 85. Should he divulge his name, lineage, and the like; the branch of the Veda he belongs to; the region he comes from; his ancestry, family, learning, and age; and the mode of life, the vows, and the virtues he observes, he will never attain success. Divulging such things, no doubt, causes harm to a pious ascetic.
>
> 86. Keeping his virtues hidden and living a life of obscurity, let the wise man, although not a fool, behave like a fool without corrupting the path of virtue.

87. That ends the ninth chapter, entitled "Description of Wandering and Residence," of the *Collection of Ascetic Laws*.

CHAPTER TEN

Penances

1. Now I will describe the penances. Vāyu writes on this subject:

> Penances should be performed both for sins committed unintentionally and for sins deliberately committed. Even here others make the following observations
>
> 2. Sins, one should know, are of three kinds: sins committed by word, thought, and deed. Spread across day and night, they burn the people here.
>
> 3. Neither rites nor life lasts long—this is the highest truth the Veda teaches. So, while one is still alive, one should practice penances without any delay.
>
> 4. People begin to take delight in sins when they habitually commit them. Thus these sins increase day by day. It is through penance that a man should purify himself of sins committed both habitually and deliberately. He should continue to purify himself thus until his mind becomes serene.
>
> 5. If perchance a yogin inadvertently commits a grievous sin, he should perform just his yogic practice and not undergo any other expiation.
>
> 6. The yogic practices of breath control, withdrawal of senses, and meditation destroy sins committed inadvertently better than any other penitential observance.

7. This passage points out that penitential observances have to be performed for sins committed habitually or deliberately, while yogic practice is prescribed for sins committed inadvertently. This point is made also by Hārīta:

> When a man devotes himself in this world to the continuous practice of yoga, even the grievous sins he may have committed are erased.

8. Atri:

> If an ascetic is unable to perform penances such as Kṛcchra, lunar fast, Parāka, and Sāntapana [see Ch. 5.11 n. 5], he should control his breath.
>
> 9. A sin committed by men that takes a day's fast to erase is undoubtedly erased by silently reciting the triple prayer [see Ch. 5.82] one thousand times.

10. A sin that a twice-born man destroys by reciting the triple prayer one thousand times is completely destroyed by controlling the breath just one hundred times.

11. A sin that twice-born men destroy by controlling the breath one thousand times is completely destroyed at once by meditating on Viṣṇu.

12. Control of breathing, silent prayer, meditation—for a mendicant there is no means of purification other than these. A mendicant, therefore, should perform these alone to purify himself.

13. By these three means a mendicant, if he controls his breath one hundred times every day, frees himself even from the guilt of killing his father and mother.

14. Jamadagni:

When the control of breathing, mediation, and silent prayer are performed continuously, they burn up all sins, as fire burns a kindling stick.

15. Vyāsa:

A man purifies himself of all the minor sins, as well as of the most grievous ones, when he meditates on Brahman during one quarter of the night.

16. Gālava:

The sight of the Lord is the expiation for all sins.[1]

17. Vāyu:

Yoga takes root in a vigilant man; indeed, yoga is thought to be the best. There is nothing more beneficial to men than yoga.

18. It is the greatest of all purifiers, the best of all cleansers. Therefore, the wise recommend it for those who are able to undertake it.

19. Jamadagni:

Alternatively, one should carry out what one's teacher orders without hesitation; in all matters, whether it is assessing punishments or conferring favors, the teacher is the authority.

20. Vāyu:

When a man commits a transgression in thought, word, or deed, he should carry out the collective decision of the assembled judges.[2]

1. The sight of the Lord may refer to either the inner contemplation of the Lord in meditation, as suggested by the preceding statements, or the sight (*darśana*) of the Lord that one receives in a temple.

2. I have taken the term "*sabhya*" in its more technical sense as people sitting in a formal council. It may also be taken to mean any cultured and educated person, in which case the decision regarding the punishment would be made in a less formal way.

21. Atri:

> Eating little, austerity, silence, and bathing at dawn, noon, and dusk are likewise prescribed specifically for a mendicant who has committed a minor sin.
>
> 22. After controlling his breath one thousand times, he should silently recite the syllable OṂ ten thousand times and then the triple prayer twenty-five thousand times in the prescribed manner. A mendicant is purified by performing this vow in the wilderness.

23. Next I will describe the penance for neglecting the twilight worship. Devala comments in this connection:

> If, through carelessness, a person who is not sick fails to perform his twilight worship, he is sure to be purified by silently reciting the triple prayer one thousand times.

24. Garga:

> A mendicant who neglects to perform his twilight worship is required to do a penance. He should silently recite the triple prayer one thousand times and control his breath one hundred times.

25. Gālava:

> He should worship the sun when it is half risen. If he lets that time lapse, he should control his breath twelve times.

26. Next, the penances relating to begging. Devala writes in this regard:

> After announcing himself,[3] he should not remain long. If he remains a long time, he should control his breath sixteen times. After announcing himself, he should not pay reverence to gods, elders, and the like. If he does so out of ignorance, he should control his breath sixteen times. After announcing himself, he should not neglect to accept the almsfood. If he neglects, he should control his breath thirty times. After announcing himself, he should not eat a full meal from a single house. If he eats, he should perform a Prājāpatya penance.

27. Bharadvāja:

> He should avoid conversations. If he does so inadvertently, he should control his breath three times. After taking the bowl in his left hand and the triple staff in his right, he should never change the hand in which each is carried. If he changes inadvertently, he should control his breath three

3. When a mendicant arrives at a house, he announces his presence by saying "Lady, give almsfood"; see Ch. 6.174, 183–85. These penances relate to breaking the rules of etiquette accompanying such a request.

times. He should not let the bowl he carries in his left hand come into contact with the triple staff in his right hand. If he allows them to come into contact, he should control his breath six times. After announcing himself and entering a house, he should not sit down. If he sits anywhere, he should control his breath twelve times. If, through carelessness, a mendicant accepts almsfood at the invitation of a Śūdra or a menstruating woman, he should control his breath sixteen times. He should not beg for or accept almsfood after leaving the triple staff outside a house. If he accepts, he should control his breath sixteen times. He should not let the triple staff out of his hand when begging for or accepting almsfood. If he does so inadvertently, he should control his breath one hundred times.

28–31. Devala and Kāśyapa:

Dogs, donkeys, camels, mice, cats, vultures, monkeys, pigs, blackened wood, a funeral pyre,[4] human bones, village fowl, jackals, ungrateful people, Śūdras, drunkards, people who have discarded the sacrificial string,[5] naked people, twice-born men who have entered heretical sects, traitors, people who speak ill of gods or Brahmins, arsonists, mercenary teachers of the law,[6] dirt piles, hermaphrodites, and Brahmins who act as temple priests[7]—if an ascetic touches any of these, he should place his begging bowl on a pure spot and go to an auspicious place of water [see Ch. 4.29 n. 28].

32. After purifying himself according to the rules, the ascetic should wash with earth and water the part of the body that was defiled, using twelve applications of earth.

33. Then he should wash all that with water and take a bath. Becoming pure again after sipping some water, he should eat and then control his breath six times.

34. After sprinkling himself with water repeatedly while reciting the three mantras beginning "Waters, you bring delight" [RV 10.9.1-3], he should per-

4. The reading of the edition is uncertain and possibly corrupt. I have taken "*agnicayana*" to refer to a funeral pyre, which is the only plausible meaning in the context of human bones, even though that meaning is not standard.

5. This may include those ascetics of the Advaita tradition who discard their sacrificial strings upon becoming renouncers, some of whom also went naked; Olivelle 1986–87.

6. The term "*dharmavikrayin*" literally mean "a seller of *dharma*." I have taken it to refer to Brahmins who teach the Vedas in return for monetary compensation. Teachers traditionally taught at no cost to students, although the students were expected to render services to the teacher and to give him a gift at the conclusion of their period of study.

7. Although the term "*devalaka*" can refer to any priest who performs temple services, it is specially applied in legal literature to Brahmins who earn their living by such services. One source defines such a person thus: "A Brahmin who devotes himself to idol worship for three years to make a living is called a *devalaka*. He is forbidden from taking part in offerings to the gods or ancestors." See Ypra 38.22–23.

form the Aghamarṣaṇa [see Ch. 6.34 n. 16] while standing in the water and bathe once again.

35. He should take the begging bowl after sprinkling it with water while reciting the triple prayer and again immerse it in water together with his hand.[8]

36. In this manner a mendicant's almsfood is purified when it comes into contact with the things listed above. A begging bowl should be purified only when it comes into contact with something else, and not otherwise.

37. If someone continues to use a begging bowl after it has come into contact with a Śūdra, dog, crow, and the like, he should observe a lunar fast.

38. Jamadagni:

If an ascetic comes into contact with a dog, a crow, a pig, a prostitute, excrement, a donkey, or a camel, he is purified by immersing himself in water together with his almsfood and reciting silently the Aghamarṣaṇa hymn.

39. Jābāli the Elder:

If a renouncer touches a dog or an impure thing while he is on his begging round, after collecting the almsfood he should bathe and control his breath six times.

40. He should purify the almsfood by reciting the Gāyatrī verse and the syllable OṂ; it is made pure by sprinkling it with water while reciting the mantra sacred to Varuṇa.

41. Garga:

If someone accepts almsfood after the begging bowl has fallen down, he should control his breath thirty times.

42. Gālava:

One should avoid a house in which fish or meat is cooked. If someone accepts almsfood at such a house, he should control his breath twelve times.

43. Devala:

If someone begs both within a village and outside it and accepts almsfood from both locations, he should perform the Sāntapana observance [see Ch. 5.11 n. 5].

44. Jamadagni:

If, after entering one village to beg and failing to obtain any almsfood there, he begs in a second village, he should perform the hot penance.[9]

8. The syntax of *sakare* is unclear, and my translation, "together with his hand," is tentative. If one separates the words (*sa kare*) and takes *kara* to mean sunlight, one could arrive at ". . . immerse it in water, and (leave it) in the sun."

9. The "hot penance" (*taptakṛcchra*) consists of consuming nothing but hot milk, hot ghee, and hot water and inhaling hot air during an entire day. According to some, each substance is consumed for three days (see MDh 11.214; VaDh 21.21; BDh

45. If, after almsfood has been placed in the bowl, an ascetic eats a full meal from a single house, he should control his breath one hundred times to purify himself.

46. If someone who eats food begged in the manner of a bee[10] fails to make the customary oblations of food to the gods,[11] he is sure to be purified only by performing a Prājāpatya penance.

47. If someone who eats food begged in the manner of a bee offers the oblations of food to the gods and then does not eat the food, he becomes pure only after three nights.

48. Gālava:

If an ascetic eats on the same day both the food given by some individual and the food he has obtained by begging, he should silently recite the Gāyatrī verse ten thousand times.

49. Devala:

If, after setting aside the oblation to the gods in the begging bowl, an ascetic fails to recite the appropriate mantra, he becomes purified by silently reciting the triple prayer one thousand times.

50. When a mendicant comes into contact with a menstruating woman, a corpse, an outcaste, a thief, a naked person, an ascetic who carries a skull as a begging bowl,[12] a person who has fallen from his caste, or a treacherous person, he should discard his almsfood.

51. If an ascetic eats just once the food of a man fallen from his caste, he should perform a penance. He is sure to be purified by performing the Vajra penance three times.

52. One should cook a handful of barley in cow's urine and eat it on the day of the new moon. That is the great Vajra penance.[13]

53. Alternatively, one may perform the Prājāpatya penance for eating the food of a fallen man. If one eats inadvertently from such a man just once, he is purified by a Prājāpatya penance.

54. He should, moreover, control his breath one hundred times and perform the quarter Kṛcchra penance [see Ch. 4.2 n.1]. Or he may drink for three

---

2.2.37), the total penance thus lasting twelve days. For variants, see ViDh 46.11; YDh 3.317.

10. For the various ways in which almsfood can be obtained, see Ch. 6.80–86.

11. For a description of these oblations, see Ch. 6.223–32.

12. The term may more specifically refer to a Kāpālika ascetic of the Śaivite tradition, and the adjective "naked" may indeed be an attribute qualifying such an ascetic.

13. A description somewhat different from this is provided in a text ascribed to Atri and cited by Kane (IV, 149), which says that the penance consists of eating barley fried in ghee and mixed with cow's urine.

nights a decoction made by boiling the Śaṅkhapuṣpa plant[14] and mixing it with milk.

55. Hārīta:

I will teach you how to purify yourself after eating food when a doubt or a confusion arises regarding its purity. Listen as I explain.

56. One should drink a decoction made with the Brahmasuvarcalā plant[15] without adding salt or lime. Or else he should drink a decoction made with the Śaṅkhapuṣpa plant and mixed with milk.

57. Or he should drink a decoction made by boiling the leaves of Palāśa and Bilva, Kuśa grass, lotus leaves, and Udumbara fruits.[16] He will then be purified in three nights.

58. Or he could purify himself after eating a forbidden food by drinking the five products[17] of a tawny cow according to the rules.

59–60. Atri:

A full meal given by a single person, honey, meat, food contaminated by feces and the like, food obtained by paying respects, food offered to the gods, and salt given separately [see Ch. 6.148 n. 46]—if an ascetic eats any one of these, he should perform a Prājāpatya penance. If he eats food containing honey or meat, however, he should perform a Parāka penance [see Ch. 5.11 n. 5] and silently recite the triple prayer one hundred thousand times. If he chooses silent prayer as a penance, he should recite it silently for a year.

61. If, in an emergency, someone consumes pieces of living creatures contained in his water or eats honey or meat, he should silently recite the triple prayer one thousand times and control his breath one hundred times.

62. Jābāli the Elder:

If, out of compassion, someone gives or accepts what has not been given to him, he should perform the great Saumya penance[18] or else a Prājāpatya penance.

63. If a mendicant eats a full meal from a single person out of either kindness or greed, he is purified by performing a Prājāpatya penance and by controlling his breath one hundred times.

14. The botanical name for this plant is *Andropogon aciculatus*.

15. The botanical name for this plant is *Heliantus* or *Clerodendron siphonanthus*.

16. The botanical names are: Palāśa = *Butea frondosa*; Bilva = *Aegle marmelos* (Indian Bel); Kuśa = *Poa cynosuroides*; Udumbara = *Ficus glomerata*.

17. Milk, buttermilk, ghee, urine, and feces.

18. Sources contain different descriptions of this penance. According to the YDh (3.321), it lasts six days. During each of the first five days the penitent subsists on oil-cake, scum from boiled rice, butter milk, water, and barley, respectively. On the last day he observes a total fast. See Kane, IV, 152.

64. Devala:

If worms come out of a wound on his body or if he eats honey or meat, he should fast for three days and control his breath one hundred times.

65. Gālava:

If someone eats honey or meat, he should perform a Parāka penance. If he chews betel, he should fast for a day and a night. If he does so deliberately, he should perform a Prājāpatya penance.

66. Jamadagni:

A full meal given by a single person, honey, meat, food at a funerary offering for a newly deceased person, food at a house where a birth has taken place, and salt given separately—these foods are forbidden to ascetics. To purify oneself after violating the ban on each of these items, one should perform a Prājāpatya penance.

67. Kratu:

If an ascetic eats food that has been contaminated by dogs, mice, cats, crows, hair, worms, bones, or clothes, he is purified by eating the five products of a cow.

68. Bharadvāja observes in the passage beginning with:

If, while he is eating, he finds some food contaminated with tiny bits of hair or insects. . . . [see Ch. 6.206]

69. Devala:

If it ever happens that while someone is eating he finds that he has become impure by eating a piece of meat,[19] he should first throw away that food and then take a bath. Afterward, he should silently recite the triple prayer one thousand times and control his breath one hundred times.

70. Jamadagni:

If it ever happens that a Brahmin has a bowel movement while he is eating, he becomes impure on account of both the remnants of food and the voiding of excrement. How does he purify himself?

71. He should first perform the purification, then sip water, fast for a day and a night, and finally take a bath. He is then purified by eating the five products of a cow.

72. If a mendicant throws away any leftovers of his almsfood, he should control his breath three times for each mouthful that he has thrown away.

73. When he enters a village covered with mud during the rains, he should wash his legs and feet, applying earth three times to the legs and seven times to the feet.

19. The meaning appears to be that the ascetic was unaware of the presence of the meat in his almsfood when he started to eat and took the meat into his mouth inadvertently.

74. Devala:

If water that has touched his hair or beard falls into his bowl, an ascetic should throw away both the bowl and the almsfood in it and observe a fast.

75. Every time he purges, vomits, voids urine or excrement, or eats a meal given by one person, he should, after returning from his begging round, bathe and control his breath three times.

76. Jamadagni:

Whenever someone smells liquor, urine, or excrement or the foul odor emanating from a funeral pyre, he should control his breath three times.

77. If an ascetic happens accidentally to see someone vomit or void urine or excrement,[20] he is purified by controlling his breath once; but if he does them himself, he should control his breath twice.

78. Gālava:

Whenever someone smells the odor of putrid matter, excrement, urine, a funeral pyre, or liquor, he should control his breath.

79–80. He should always observe the constraints and by means of them safeguard the restraints.[21] No transgression of the rules of constraint takes place in a time of emergency or physical infirmity; when drinking water or taking medicine; at a sacrificial offering; when Brahmins desire something; when eating flowers, roots, or fruits; with regard to ghee and milk; in carrying out a teacher's command; with regard to bark and leaves;[22] and in brushing the teeth, as well as when Brahmins permit something.

81. One should perform the rites for removing sins after Brahmins have loudly proclaimed that day to be holy. By doing so one is freed from sins committed without deliberate intent.

82–83. Bodhāyana:

Now they present the following rules for the time when a teacher explains an Upaniṣad:[23] standing; observing silence; sitting down; bathing at

20. Given the opposition between seeing and doing, I think my translation of the first clause is accurate. The phrase literally means ". . . to see vomit, urine, or excrement."

21. The terms "*yama*" and "*niyama*," here translated as "restraints" and "constraints" (see Ch. 5.47), have specific technical connotations within the system of Yoga, but outside that context they are used with widely different meanings. Their exact meanings in this context are unclear. The use of "constraints" with regard to violations of normal rules, however, indicates that the term may here refer to specific restrictive rules. This is the meaning the term "*niyama*" has in the exegetical tradition of Mīmāṃsā.

22. The meaning is unclear, and the reading is quite uncertain, as one can judge from the variety of the readings given in the manuscripts.

23. I am not completely sure of the meaning of this elliptic sentence; nor am I sure whether Bühler in the translation of the BDh or Haradatta in his commentary

dawn, noon, and dusk; observing the vows of eating at the fourth, sixth, or eighth mealtime; keeping the vow of eating grain, oil-cake, barley, curd, and milk.[24] It is said: At that time he should observe silence and speak only when there is a need with teachers and sages who have mastered the triple Veda or with learned people belonging to other orders of life, when there is no danger of breaking his vow; even then he should speak pressing his teeth together and keeping the voice within the mouth. Standing, observing silence, and sitting cross-legged—only one of these should he observe at a time and never all three together. It is said: If one goes there, one may follow a guest only a short distance, so also in times of emergency and when there is no danger of breaking his vow.[25] In the case of a person who observes faithfully the vows of standing; observing silence; sitting; bathing at dawn, noon, and dusk; and eating at the fourth, sixth, or eighth mealtime, the following eight things do not break his vow: water, roots, ghee, milk, sacrificial offering, the wish of a Brahmin, a command of the teacher, and medicine. [BDh 2.18.15-19]

84. Devala:

If someone inadvertently forgets to observe any rule relating to sleep,[26] he is purified for certain by silently reciting the triple prayer one thousand times.

85–86. I describe next the expiation of sins committed at night. In this connection, Jābāli the Elder writes:

If, after the time for the twilight worship has passed, an ascetic eats at night, all his religious activities—worship, silent prayer, control of breath, and food offerings—will become fruitless; a penance is ordained for him. He should fast for one night and control his breath sixteen times.

---

fully understood it. The general context of the passage is the enumeration of various vows an ascetic must observe when he studies the Upaniṣads with a teacher. I have taken the plural *ācāryāḥ* as merely honorific or as a generic statement; in either case, the singular functions better in English.

24. Bühler, following the commentator, understands the ascetic as standing during the day and sitting during the night. A mealtime occurs twice a day. The vows thus refer to fasting for two, three, or four days; see Ch. 6.106 n. 42.

25. The meaning of this elliptic aphorism is extremely unclear. The critical edition of the BDh reads *anuvratayet* in place of *anuvrajet*, but even there the meaning is far from clear. Bühler's rendering follows the commentator, who, I believe, did not have a better idea of what it meant.

26. The term "*svāpacāra*" appears to indicate customs and rules relating to sleeping [see Ch. 6.280–86; Ch. 10.97–99], but I am not sure of either the reading or the exact meaning of this passage.

87. Jamadagni:

When someone eats food at night, scriptures prescribe that he control his breath ten times; he should do the same penance also when he fetches water or earth at night.[27]

88. If what he has collected becomes lost or destroyed, however, he is not defiled by fetching them just once at a flowing river or in a temple.

89. When someone has a seminal discharge at night, he should bathe and control his breath twelve times. By thus controlling his breath, an ascetic recovers his purity completely.

90. Śaunaka:

He should not recall the sexual pleasures he formerly enjoyed. If he inadvertently recalls them, he should sip water, control his breath three times, and sip water again. When he inadvertently looks at a woman, he should control his breath. When he enjoys sexual pleasures in a dream, he should silently recite the triple prayer one thousand times and control his breath twelve times. If he has a seminal discharge while enjoying sexual pleasures in a dream, however, he should control his breath twelve times. If he ejaculates he should control his breath twice as much and sip water again.

91. Kapila:

When someone enjoys sexual pleasures in a dream, he should bathe and silently recite the triple prayer one thousand times. When someone bleeds after scratching himself, he should observe a fast.

92. Gālava:

If someone ejaculates after deliberate masturbation, he should perform three Parāka penances. When one does so involuntarily while having intercourse with a woman in a dream, he should control his breath twelve times. If someone has an involuntary seminal discharge in sleep, he should control his breath twelve times. Every time someone inadvertently sees a woman's private parts, he should control his breath three times, but when he does so in a dream he should perform the Aghamarṣaṇa. Whenever he has an involuntary discharge of semen, he should control his breath sixteen times, but when he ejaculates after voluntary masturbation, he should observe the lunar penance.

93. Jābāli:

If someone ejaculates voluntarily or by masturbation, he should control his breath one hundred times and perform three Parāka penances.

94. If someone inadvertently ejaculates during the day, he should perform the following penance. He should control his breath one hundred times as he fasts for three nights.

27. The meaning is that he should not go out to collect earth or water for purification after toilet during the night. He is expected to gather them during the day for use at night.

95. If he involuntarily ejaculates on seeing a woman because of the weakness of his organ, he should control his breath sixteen times.

96. Vāyu:

If a mendicant ever ejaculates voluntarily, he should perform three Prājāpatya penances and control his breath one hundred times.

97. Parāśara the Elder:

"You remain asleep, O Vāsudeva, until sunrise. I too will do likewise for the welfare of all creatures."

98. "Seven seers are lodged in the body; seven guard the seat vigilantly. Seven waters went to the world where he sleeps and where two gods who never sleep and sit at the sacrifice keep watch."[28]

99. Reciting these two mantras, he should sleep. If he fails to recite them, he should control his breath six times and go to sleep again after reciting them. In the morning he should get up reciting the mantra "Rise up, O Brahmaṇaspati!" [see Ch. 6.4 n. 4]. If he does not recite it, he should control his breath three times and rise up again.

100. Next I describe the penances for transgressing the rules of constraint. In this connection, Vāyu states:

A penance is prescribed every time a mendicant violates either a major or a minor observance.

101. An ascetic should observe a penance when he deliberately engages in sexual intercourse with a woman. He should perform Kṛcchra penances while he controls his breath for one whole year.

102. Then, after he has humbled himself by intently practicing penances and meditation and attained once again total indifference to worldly things, he should diligently beg for almsfood.

103. Kapila:

After engaging in sexual intercourse just once, an ascetic should fast and silently recite the triple prayer one hundred thousand times. If he does so repeatedly for three nights, he should silently recite the triple prayer for a year. If someone has sexual intercourse with a Śūdra woman just once, he should live in the wilderness, eating Bilva[29] and the like that have fallen

28. VS 34.55. This verse contains a riddle that was obscure enough to be included in a very ancient exegetical work, Yāska's *Nirukta* (12.37). Yāska gives two explanations, one with reference to cosmic realities and the other with reference to the human body. Thus, the seven seers are rays of the sun or the senses; the body is the sun or the body; seven waters are interpreted as works; and the two gods are wind and sun or the selves of knowledge and luster. The first interpretation refers to the setting sun, and the second to a sleeping person.

29. This is the Bel fruit (*Aegle marmelos*).

on their own after washing them and reciting the syllable OṂ, until he becomes purified through his own death.

104. Jābāli:

An ascetic should observe a penance when he deliberately engages in sexual intercourse with a woman. Controlling his breath, he should perform Sāntapana penances during one whole year.

105. Gālava:

If someone has sexual intercourse with a prostitute just once, he should observe the penance prescribed for killing a Brahmin.

106. Atri:

An ascetic should do the following to purify himself after committing a grievous sin. The yogin should silently recite the triple prayer one hundred thousand times and control his breath ten thousand times. Then he should silently recite the syllable OṂ one hundred thousand times.

107. When someone foolishly engages in sexual intercourse with a woman just once, he is purified in the above manner. Also, when a person engages in sex deliberately and repeatedly, he is purified through a penance.

108. Vāyu:

What people call wealth is truly the lifebreaths that roam outside. When someone steals the wealth of another man, he steals that man's lifebreaths.

109. When an evil ascetic does such a thing, breaking thereby the code of his order of life, he should, after he again becomes indifferent to worldly things, perform a lunar penance for one year in the manner prescribed in the scriptures. So states the Veda.

110. Then, at the end of that year, when he has become pure once again and recovered his indifference to worldly things, a mendicant may beg for almsfood.

111. Gālava:

If someone deliberately accepts money, cows, land, sesame seeds, and the like, he should perform a penance as if he had fallen from his caste.

112. Jamadagni:

If a man discards something he has accepted, he should fast for three days. By silently reciting the Gāyatrī verse ten thousand times, a man is freed from all grievous sins.

113. The same author states:

When someone sees a wretched ascetic who accepts land, cattle, or gold, he should bathe by entering the water fully clothed.

114. Vāyu:

When someone tells a lie with regard to a fast, he should control his breath one hundred times. An ascetic who desires virtue should never tell a lie.

115. Gālava:

When someone tells a lie, he should fast for three nights. If someone tells a lie for a righteous reason, he should fast for a whole day and control his breath one hundred times.

116. Jamadagni:

When someone causes injury to a mobile or an immobile creature by his speech, mind, or actions, he should purify himself through the organ that caused the injury.

117. When the injury is caused by speech, he should restrain his speech; when it is caused by the mind, he should restrain his breaths; and when it is caused by physical acts, he should restrain his actions. With his mind he should pledge total detachment from worldly things.

118. When a man is lax in restraining his speech, mind, and actions, he destroys his knowledge, his highest goal, and the three worlds, respectively.

119. He should practice silence, the restraint of speech. The restraint of actions is fasting, and the restraint of the mind is the control of breath.

120. When faults are committed, this is the way to expiate them. If he commits them for a very long time, he should perform the stipulated observances twice as long.

121. Gālava:

If someone kills a quadruped, he should observe a lunar fast, whereas he should fast for ten nights when he kills a crab, a brightly colored fish or bird, and the like.[30]

122. If a mendicant deliberately causes injury to cattle or animals, he should perform a Kr̥cchra and an Atikr̥cchra penance or observe a lunar fast.[31]

123. Jamadagni:

If someone causes an injury to a lizard, a fish,[32] a frog, a gecko, or an animal such as an osprey, he should eat half a meal a day for ten days.

124. If someone causes injury to a cat, a mouse, a snake, a large fish, a bird, or an animal such as a mongoose, he should observe a lunar fast. Each time he injures a tiny ant, he should control his breath three times.

125. If a mendicant kills an animal with very small bones, he should perform a penance. He should control his breath thirty times and eat half a meal for one day.

30. The term "*citraroman*" can refer to any animal that has bright or variegated hair or scales. Since quadruped animals have already been mentioned, it appears likely that the term refers to a brightly colored fish or bird.

31. See Ch. 4.2 n. 1 and Ch. 5.11 n. 5. The Atikr̥cchra penance is much like the Prājāpatya, except that the food is limited to just a single mouthful per day.

32. This is just a guess. I do not know what a *kṣīragala* is, and it is not listed in any dictionary. A *kṣīrajāla* is a kind of fish, and this may be a variant of it.

126. Gālava:

If he breaks leaves, roots, sprouts, or flowers, he should control his breath thirty times.

127. Dattātreya:

If someone happens to see accidentally a Brahmin who is either naked or without a sacrificial string, he is purified by bathing fully clothed, making twelve applications of earth.

128. Hārīta:

If someone feeds a Brahmin who is naked or without a sacrificial string at a funerary offering, he offers thereby semen, urine, and excrement to his ancestors.

129. If a man resorts to a single staff either because he has been talked into it or because of greed and afterward regains the spirit of detachment, he should carry a triple staff like a wise man.

130. He should faithfully perform the Prājāpatya penance for a full month, as he bathes at dawn, noon, and dusk, and all the time silently recite the Gāyatrī verse.

131. But if he wants to complete the penance quickly, he should remain for a day subsisting on air and spend the night standing in water until sunrise; he gains thereby the fruit of a Prājāpatya penance.

132. When the sun rises, he should silently recite the Gāyatrī verse eight thousand times. A man is thereby released from all his sins, unless he is guilty of abortion.

133. When every sin imaginable rises up at once, the Gāyatrī verse recited ten thousand times becomes the highest means of purification.

134. When one recites three times the Gāyatrī verse together with the Great Utterances, the syllable OṂ, and the Śiras mantra [see Ch. 5.82], while he controls his breath, it is called "the control of breath."

135. The moment a man performs the control of breath in the manner prescribed and with a composed mind, the sins he has committed during that day and night are destroyed.

136. When a Brahmin sits down at the evening twilight and controls his breath, he is cleared of the sins he has committed during the day by thought, word, and deed.

137. She is a thousand at the highest, a hundred at the middle, and ten at the lowest; the man who always recites this goddess Gāyatrī is not tainted by sin.

138. Controlling the breath sixteen times every day while reciting the syllable OṂ and the Great Utterances purifies even an abortionist within a month.

139. The Kṛcchra penance and the lunar fast destroy all sins, even the greatest, whether they involve wrongful actions or incorrectly performed rites.

140–41. Saṃvarta:

Please listen to the expiation meant for those who have fallen from renunciation. If someone returns to the world after he has renounced, that foolish man should tirelessly perform Kṛcchra penances continuously for six months. This is seen as the means of expiation for a lapsed ascetic.

142. The same author states:

For a man learned in the four Vedas who has killed a Brahmin or his teacher,[33] one should prescribe the penance associated with the causeway to Laṅkā.[34]

143. Walking barefoot and without an umbrella, such a man should beg for almsfood from all four classes near the causeway to Laṅkā, announcing publicly his misdeeds.

144. "I am an abject sinner. I have committed the most heinous of sins. Guilty of killing a Brahmin, I stand outside the doors of houses seeking almsfood."

145. Living in cow pens and settlements of cowherds, in towns and villages, and traveling to sacred bathing places, he will finally arrive at the sacred ocean.

146. Then he will see the causeway that leads across the ocean to Laṅkā, a causeway that is ninety miles wide and nine hundred miles long.

147. After seeing the causeway, he will become immediately purified when he sees the king of the entire world as he performs the horse sacrifice.[35]

148. Devala:

If someone touches a menstruating woman, a prostitute, an intoxicated woman, or a log used to carry a corpse, he should take a bath and silently recite the prayer twice.[36]

149. The same author states:

A penance is prescribed when someone discovers lice on his body. After fasting for one day, he should control his breath six times.

33. The term "*brahmahan*" may here refer also to a man who metaphorically kills the Veda by giving up his life of renunciation. One who does that would also metaphorically kill the teacher who imparted the Veda to him.

34. This is the group of islands extending from Rameśvaram in India to the northeastern coast of Sri Lanka, today commonly referred to as Adam's Bridge. In the mythology of Rāma, this was constructed by Hanuman, the monkey associate of Rāma, to facilitate the invasion of Laṅkā to rescue Sītā from Rāvaṇa.

35. The meaning here is rather unclear. In all likelihood, however, it refers to a penance known as Aśvamedha ("Horse Sacrifice"), in which the sinner takes a bath in the sea or a river at the end of a horse sacrifice performed by a king. This penance is prescribed for the murder of a Brahmin (see Kane, IV, 131).

36. The text does not specify the prayer. In such contexts, it is most often the Gāyatrī or the triple prayer (see Ch. 5.82).

150. Garga:

Mendicants should not accept things from one another. If someone thoughtlessly accepts something from another mendicant, he should silently recite the mantra "The fame of Mitra . . ." [TS 3.4.11.5] and control his breath three times.

151. Gālava:

When someone bleeds after scratching himself, he should fast for a day and a night.

152. Jamadagni:

He should not even think about his mother, father, or son. If ever he experiences a feeling of love toward them, he should control his breath sixteen times.

153. Satyakāma and Jābāla:

If he ever uses the ritual utterances Svāhā, Svadhā, and Vaṣaṭ even once, or has them used,[37] everything he does will bear no fruit. He is further required to undergo a penance. If he uses those utterances himself, he should perform three Prājāpatya penances and control his breath twelve times.

154. Satyakāma gives the penance for those sins not mentioned above:

When someone violates a prescribed rule, he should control his breath twelve times.

155. The more and the less severe penances given here should be understood as referring to people with physical infirmities, taking into account such factors as time and place. Some, on the other hand, hold that, given the conflict between the opinions of the sages, one is free to choose among the different penances listed.[38]

156. Other duties not given here, moreover, as well as the penances for their violation, should be gathered from texts on the duties of householders.

157. That ends the tenth chapter, entitled "Penances," of the *Collection of Ascetic Laws*.

37. These utterances are used at the end of mantras at the moment an offering is made in the fire. Svāhā is used in rites to gods, whereas Svadhā is used for ancestral rites. Ascetics are not permitted to perform either type of rite, or have such rites performed on their behalf. This is the meaning of "use" and "have them used.."

38. Yādava has cited numerous texts that give different penances for the same offence. He explains this difference as relating to the different capabilities of the ascetics. Healthy ascetics should perform the more severe penances, while the more lenient penances are meant for the sick and the weak. This is an example of restrictive option (*vyavasthitavikalpa*) that I discussed earlier (see Ch. 2.25 n. 9). Some would argue, however, that these contradictory penances are an example of textual conflict, permitting a free choice among the various options (*vikalpa*).

CHAPTER ELEVEN

The Procedure of an Ascetic's Funeral

1. I will now describe the procedure of an ascetic's funeral. In connection with this, Bodhāyana states:

> I will describe the complete procedure of an ascetic's funeral. After purifying himself by taking a bath, a householder should perform the funeral of an ascetic.
>
> 2. He should decorate the corpse with perfumes and garlands and place it on a bier. He should carry it toward the east or the north accompanied by the shouts of victory and the sound of drums and take it to a pure place.
>
> 3. On a river bank, under a banyan tree, near a temple or a cow pen, or under a Palāśa tree, he should dig the sacrificial ground that is the grave; he should dig it to a depth equal to the height of the ascetic's staff while reciting the Great Utterances. He should sprinkle the grave with water while reciting the Great Utterances, have the corpse bathed while he recites the Puruṣa hymn [RV 10.90], decorate it with perfumes and the like, and place it in the grave, saying, "O Viṣṇu, protect the oblation" [TS 1.1.3.1]. He then places the staff in the right hand of the deceased ascetic, saying, "Viṣṇu traversed this . . ." [TS 1.2.13.1–2]. Then, he should silently recite the mantra "The swan seated in purity . . ." [TS 1.8.15.2] at the chest of the deceased, the Puruṣa hymn [RV 10.90] between the eyebrows, and the mantra "Brahman was first born in the east . . ." [TS 4.2.8.2] at the crown of the head. He should then split the top of the ascetic's head as he recites the mantra "The earth has gone to the earth . . ." [ApSr 3.20.9; BDh 1.6.7], touching it as he recites the Gāyatrī verse. He should fill the sacrificial ground of the grave, reciting the syllable OṂ, and repeatedly purify the area while reciting the Gāyatrī. If the grave is disturbed by jackals, crows, and the like, the person who performed the funeral would incur a sin and a drought would strike that region. Therefore, he should repeatedly put dirt into the grave until it is completely covered. After performing the funeral, one should not observe a period of impurity or make water offerings. When a man carries or touches the corpse of an ascetic or digs a grave for him, he is puri-

fied immediately and takes a bath similar to the one taken at the end of a sacrifice. At every step a man obtains the reward of a horse sacrifice.

So said the Blessed Bodhāyana.

4. When an ascetic who was established in Brahman dies, his son, pupil, or a householder should bury him. The same person should perform an oblation to Nārāyaṇa[1] on his behalf.

5. There are no burnt offerings, no libations of water, no funerary offerings, and no feeding of Brahmins. He should perform all the offerings to Nārāyaṇa according to the rules of the funerary offerings made to a newly deceased person.[2]

6. Sages proclaim this to be the procedure even at the death of a simple ascetic.[3] On the eleventh day after death, a Pārvaṇa offering is prescribed.

7. One should never perform the Sapiṇḍīkaraṇa rite for them, because they do not fall into the ghostly state by the mere fact that they carried a triple staff.[4]

8. This alone is sufficient for a mendicant devoted to solitude, for no one does anything for him, and he does not do anything for anyone.[5]

9. There is, moreover, another procedure. He should do everything given before reciting just the Great Utterances. With the same Utterances he should place the corpse in the bier and dig the grave.

1. The Nārāyaṇabali is a special offering made after the death of certain individuals, including ascetics, and after certain types of deaths, such as suicide. For a description, see Sp, Ch. 23; for a detailed examination of the rite, see Krick 1977.

2. This type of offering is called the *ekoddiṣṭaśrāddha* and is made during the first eleven days after a person's death. The offerings are made only to that individual. On the twelfth day, the newly deceased is ritually associated with his ancestors in the ceremony known as Sapiṇḍīkaraṇa. After that ritual, which, as we are informed at Ch. 11.7, is not performed for ascetics, funerary offerings are made in common to the three previous generations of deceased ancestors: father, grandfather, and great grandfather. This common *śrāddha* is called Pārvaṇaśrāddha.

3. The first two verses addressed the death of an ascetic who had acquired the knowledge of Brahman. Here the same procedure is said to apply even when an ordinary ascetic dies.

4. A newly deceased person remains in a ghostly state (*preta*) until he is ritually conducted to the world of the fathers through the ritual of Sapiṇḍīkaraṇa. The deceased in that ghostly state is impure and hovers around the place of his former dwelling. He is then dangerous to his former relatives. The power of the triple staff is believed to conduct a newly deceased ascetic directly to the world of the fathers, bypassing this intermediary state.

5. The phrase is elliptic and ambiguous, and the various scribes appear to have tried to make sense by providing different readings. I think the overall sense is that an ascetic is totally independent and does not need the ritual services of others for his bliss after death.

10–11. He should again sprinkle water on the grave while reciting the same seven Great Utterances and place the corpse in the grave, reciting the mantra "May god Savitṛ spur you . . ." [TS 1.1.1.1].[6] Putting the bier away, he should place the staff on the deceased ascetic's side, reciting the mantra "Friend, protect me" [see Ch. 4.19], and lay the sling on his chest.

12. He should then place the water strainer on his mouth, reciting the mantra "The purifier with which the gods ever cleanse themselves . . ." [TB 1.4.8.6], and place the water pot in his right hand with the mantra "You, O Agni, who are wise . . ." [TS 2.5.12.3].

13. He should similarly place the begging bowl on his stomach, reciting the mantra "The earth has gone to the earth . . ." [ApSr 3.20.9], worship him with the Hotṛ mantras,[7] and sprinkle him with water reciting the seven Great Utterances.

14. He should finally fill the grave as he recites the mantra "Fire by fire is set alight . . ." [TS 1.4.46.3]; he should do so in such a manner that jackals and dogs would not be able to pull out the corpse.

15. A Brahmin should bury in the ground the bodies of ascetics who had previously maintained a sacred fire, while those of accomplished ascetics who had not maintained a sacred fire he should cremate.

16. He should also perform on their behalf the funerary offering for a newly deceased person, water libations, offerings of rice balls, and rites for the newly deceased, and, in their case, observe also the period of impurity. After one year, moreover, he should perform their Sapiṇḍīkaraṇa rite according to the prescribed rules. In the case of a mendicant who has attained Brahman, however, one should not perform any rite other than the Pārvaṇa offering [see Ch. 11.5 n. 2].

17. Atri:

After purifying himself by taking a bath, the son or a householder should perform the funeral of an ascetic. He should decorate the corpse with perfumes and garlands and place it on a bier.

18. Kindling a fire with chaff, he should carry it along for the ascetic's last rite. He should proceed toward the east or the north accompanied by the shouts of victory and the sound of drums and go to a pure place.

19. He should dig a grave as deep as the ascetic's staff while reciting the Great Utterances, sprinkle the grave with water reciting the seven Great Utterances, and make on it a wooden pyre.

20. According to his ability, he should use logs that are suitable for a sacrifice or others that are not objectionable. Then, with a pure mind, he should wash the corpse reciting the Gāyatrī verse.

6. The reading *piṣṭapraskanda* adopted in the edition is far from certain and its meaning, as well as that of the variant readings recorded in the mss, is far from clear.

7. These are the mantras of the ten Hotṛ contained in the TA 3.7. The full text is found in App. 1.12.

21. After laying the corpse on the pyre as he recites the mantra "O Viṣṇu, protect the oblation" [TS 1.1.3.1], he should place the water strainer on the mouth, reciting the mantra "The purifier with which the gods ever cleanse themselves . . ." [TB 1.4.8.6].

22. He should place the triple staff in the right hand, reciting the mantra "Viṣṇu traversed this . . ." [TS 1.2.13.1–2], and the sling in the left hand with the mantra "May that bright light born beyond the atmosphere . . ." [TS 4.2.5.2] and concluding with "Svāhā!"

23. Conversant with the rules, he should place the begging bowl on the stomach while reciting the Gāyatrī verse, and the water pot on the lap with the mantra "The earth has gone to the earth . . ." [ApSr 3.20.9].

24. The performer of the funeral should consecrate the corpse that has been laid on the pyre in the grave and on which his equipment has been placed and worship it, while reciting the Hotṛ mantras. He should then cremate the body until it is turned completely to ash.

25. Scriptures prescribe for a Brahmin the rites beginning with the impregnation ceremony and ending with cremation. Therefore, a householder performs the funerary rite of even an ascetic using the appropriate mantras.

26. When his father has proclaimed the Praiṣa formula [see Ch. 4.27 n. 26] after depositing the sacred fires in himself, the son should make the sacred fires descend once again[8] and cremate him according to the rules.

27. When a father who had been devoted to ritual activities even after renunciation dies, his sons should carry out his cremation and perform the funerary offerings, libations of water, and offering of rice balls on his behalf.

28. If, following the alternative method,[9] a person becomes an ascetic at the very beginning while he was still a vedic student, a householder should perform all his funerary rites in the presence of Viṣṇu.

29. After carrying, touching, or cremating the corpse of an ascetic, a person is purified by just taking a bath, and at every step he obtains the reward of a horse sacrifice.

30. Śaunaka:

In the case of an ascetic who had suppressed all his attachments and had been devoted to the practice of meditation, neither cremation nor the offering of water and rice balls should be performed.

8. The depositing of fires in the self or the fire drills was performed also when a Brahmin set out on a journey. According to the Vedic ritual texts, that Brahmin can reproduce his fires (literally make them descend) by using the mantra: "Descend again, O fire . . ." (TB 2.5.8.8). For this ritual, see AsSr 3.10.6; ApSr 6.28.12. Our source expects the son of the deceased ascetic to likewise reestablish the sacred fires that his father had deposited in himself prior to his renunciation.

9. For a discussion of this alternative, see Ch. 2.11–24.

31. The corpse of an ascetic devoted to meditation should be placed in a grave while just the syllable OṂ is recited. One should get everything done—sprinkling the corpse, digging the grave, and so forth—while reciting just that syllable.

32. After carrying or touching the corpse of an ascetic, a person is purified by just taking a bath, and at every step everyone who participates obtains individually the reward of a horse sacrifice.

33. This same procedure has been given by the Blessed Lord Yājñavalkya the Elder.[10]

146. That ends the eleventh chapter, entitled "The Procedure of an Ascetic's Funeral," of the *Collection of Ascetic Laws* composed by Yādava Prakāśa.

10. See App. 1.11 for this passage of Yājñavalkya the Elder.

Text

Introduction to the Critical Edition

This critical edition of Yādava Prakāśa's *Yatidharmasamuccaya* is based on sixteen manuscripts and two printed versions. They are described here according to the sigla ascribed to them in the critical apparatus.

Description of the Manuscripts

A1 Adyar Library and Research Center, Madras. Ms. no. 73570. *A Catalogue of the Sanskrit Manuscripts in the Adyar Library* (Madras, 1926), part I, p. 115. Palm leaf. Grantha script. 54 folios. Approximately 30.5 x 3.5 cms (lengths vary; folio 8 is 22.5 x 3.5 cms). Between 11 and 9 lines per page. Approximately 57 *akṣara*s per line. Complete. No date. A photocopy was used. Somewhat carelessly written with frequent corrections. Folios 47-48 are partly written in a different hand. A reader appears to have gone through the entire ms and made numerous marginal corrections. This was the original of Schrader's copy (Schr. 45) described below.

A2 Adyar Library and Research Center, Madras. Ms. no. 73486. *A Catalogue of the Sanskrit Manuscripts in the Adyar Library* (Madras, 1926), part I, p. 115. Palm leaf. Grantha script. 47 folios. Approximately 39 x 4 cms Between 10 and 11 lines per page. Between 55 and 71 *akṣara*s per line. Complete. The date in the colophon is given according to the Jupiter cycle, and without additional data it cannot to be translated into a unique date of the common era. Excellent condition. A photocopy was used. Two additional folios written in a different hand and containing astrological material are inserted at the end of the ms. Carefully written with few corrections. This was the original of the variants recorded in Schrader's copy (Schr. 45). Colophon:

श्रीनारायणगुरवे नमः । श्रीमते रामानुजाय नमः । श्रियै नमः । श्रीमते नारायणाय नमः । श्रीगोदायै नमः । करकृतमपराधं क्षन्तु-मर्हन्ति सन्तः । हेविलम्बि शरत्पुष्यमासि प्रथमातिथौ । मयेदं लिखितं सम्यग्यतिधर्मसमुच्चयम् । यदक्षरपदभ्रष्टं यत्पादप्रच्युतं यदा । तत्सर्वं क्षम्यतां यूयं कृपापूरवशंवदाः ॥

A3 Adyar Library and Research Center, Madras. Ms. no. 71573. *A Catalogue of the Sanskrit Manuscripts in the Adyar Library* (Madras, 1926), part I, p. 115. Palm leaf. Grantha script. 91 folios (many are in bits and pieces). 38 x 3 cms (difficult to measure because most edges are broken). Between 7 and 8 lines per page. The *akṣara*s per line cannot be accurately estimated because ends of folios are damaged. No date. Incomplete. A photocopy was used. Extremely poor condition. A significant section of almost every page cannot be read because of broken sections of palmleaf, and after Ch. 7 the ms becomes almost unreadable. The ms begins with Ch. 2. After the conclusion of Ch. 7 the ms inserts a large amount of extraneous material. This addition begins with the passage from Parāśara (Ch. 5.11). Most of this material, however, cannot be identified due to the poor condition of the ms A3 thus could be used only for Chapters 2–7 of the edition.

A4 Adyar Library and Research Center, Madras. Ms. no. VB 157. *Descriptive Catalogue of Sanskrit Manuscripts*. Vol. 13: Viśvabhāratī Collection—I. Compiled by Dr. E. R. Sreekrishna Sarma (Madras, 1976), p. 150, ser. no. 813E. Palm leaf. Telugu script. 31 folios. 42 x 3.5 cms 7 lines per page. 64 *akṣara*s per line. Complete. A photocopy was used. Good condition. Carefully written. According to Dr. David Pingree, the date of the Jupiter cycle given in the colophon corresponds plausibly with Wednesday, July 6, 1474. This is a rather early date for a South Indian palm leaf ms. Often, however, mss were copied together with their original dates. Thus, the date in a colophon is not necessarily an indication of the date of the ms in question. Colophon:

श्रीकृष्णाय नमः । श्रीनिवासब्रह्मणे नमः । श्रीमन्निलाद्रिपतये जगन्नाथाय नमः । जयवर्षे नभोमासि कृष्णपक्षेऽष्टमीतिथौ । बुधवारेऽग्निनक्षत्रे योगे व्याघातवर्जिते । श्रीनिवासमुदे तेन प्रेरितेन यथामति । लिखितो वरदार्येण यतिधर्मसमुच्चयः । कृत्वानवद्यं निगमान्तभाष्यं

निराकृतं येन भयं श्रुतीनाम् । प्रतारितानामबहुश्रुतैस्तं रामानुजं योगिनमाश्रयामः ।।

A5 Adyar Library and Research Center, Madras. Ms. no. PM 726. Paper. Telugu script. 31 folios. 34 x 21 cms Between 21 and 25 lines per page. 45 *akṣara*s per line. Complete. No date. A photocopy was used. Written in several hands with frequent errors and corrections. Some of the folios are ruled and the ms appears to be rather recent. This was probably the Telugu original of Schrader's copy of Chapters 1-6 (Schr. 46).

A6 Adyar Library and Research Center, Madras. Ms. no. VB 471. *Descriptive Catalogue of Sanskrit Manuscripts*. Vol. 13: Viśvabhāratī Collection—I. Compiled by Dr. E. R. Sreekrishna Sarma (Madras, 1976), p. 150, ser. no. 814. Palm leaf. Telugu script. 64 folios. 39.5 x 3.5 cms 8 lines per page. 58 *akṣara*s per line. Complete. A photocopy was used. Old and moth-eaten. This is a composite manuscript; it switches to the long recension (Y*) at Ch. 8.30 and back to the short recension at Ch. 10.128.

G1 Government Oriental Manuscripts Library, Madras. Ms. no. D 16207. Palm leaf. Grantha script. 20.5 x 4 cms 41 folios. Between 8 and 15 lines on a page. 30 *akṣara*s per line. A microfilm was used. The ms, as it now exists, is incomplete and ends at Ch. 8.7. The copy of it made by Schrader (Schr. 47), however, contains the whole text. The ms must have been seriously damaged sometime after Schrader's copy was made in 1910. I have used a microfilm of Schrader's copy for Chapters 8–11.

G2 Government Oriental Manuscripts Library, Madras. Ms. no. R 3105. Palm leaf. Grantha script. 50 folios. 40 X 4 cms 6 lines per page. Between 45 and 70 *akṣara*s per line. Complete. A microfilm was used. Good condition. Carefully and neatly written.

G3 Government Oriental Manuscripts Library, Madras. Ms. no. D 2951. *A Descriptive Catalogue of the Sanskrit Manuscripts in the Government Oriental Manuscripts Library*, Madras. Ed. by M. Raṅgācārya. Vol. V—Dharma-śāstra (Madras, 1909), p. 2189. Palm leaf. Grantha script. 29 folios. 40 x 3 cms 6 lines on a page. 55 *akṣara*s per line. A microfilm was used. Several folios, containing the passages 5.19–7.55 and 9.50–60, are missing. After Ch. 10.30 the ms departs completely from the text and appends sundry verses.

G4 Government Oriental Manuscripts Library, Madras. Ms. no. R 3196(g). Palm leaf. Grantha script. 6 folios. 21 x 2.5 cms Between 8 and 9 lines on a page. 33 *akṣara*s on a line. Incomplete:

contains only Ch. 8 and Ch. 9.1–9. The last folios of the ms appear to be loose folios written in a different hand and containing a different text on the procedure of renunciation.

G5 Government Oriental Manuscripts Library, Madras. Ms. no. D 2954. *A Descriptive Catalogue of the Sanskrit Manuscripts in the Government Oriental Manuscripts Library*, Madras. Ed. by M. Raṅgācārya. Vol. V—Dharma-śāstra (Madras, 1909), p. 2190. Palm leaf. Grantha script. 38 x 4 cms 7 lines on a page. 45 *akṣara*s per line. Contains only Chapter 11, which begins on p. 9 of the ms. The first eight pages contain a text on penances, beginning अथ संन्यासिनां प्रतिग्रहप्रायश्चित्तमाह. After Ch. 11, the ms contains a text on the procedure of renunciation that begins अथ संन्यासविधिरुच्यते.

G6 Government Oriental Manuscripts Library, Madras. Ms. no. D 2950. *A Descriptive Catalogue of the Sanskrit Manuscripts in the Government Oriental Manuscripts Library*, Madras. Ed. by M. Raṅgācārya. Vol. V—Dharma-śāstra (Madras, 1909), pp. 2188-89. Palm leaf. Kanarese script. 49 x 3.5 cms 8 lines on a page. 45–50 *akṣaras* per line. First two pages are lost. The ms begins at Ch. 1.14(21).

R1 University of Mysore Oriental Research Institute. Ms. no. P 2776. *Descriptive Catalogue of Sanskrit Manuscripts*. Ed. Dr. G. Marulasiddaiah (Mysore, 1979), vol. 3, ser. no. 8959. Palm leaf. Grantha script. 45 x 3.5 cms 61 folios. Between 5 and 9 lines on a page. 62 *akṣara*s on a line. Complete. Written in at least two different hands. Colophon:

> इति यतिधर्मसमुच्चयं समाप्तम् । हरिः ॐ । शुभमस्तु । यादृशं पुस्तकं दृष्ट्वा तादृशं लिखितं मया । अबद्धं वा सुबद्धं वा मम दोषो न विद्यते । The rest is unreadable on the microfilm.

R2 University of Mysore Oriental Research Institute. Ms. no. P 6872. *Descriptive Catalogue of Sanskrit Manuscripts*. Ed. Dr. G. Marulasiddaiah (Mysore, 1979), vol. 3, ser. no. 3961. Palm leaf. Grantha script. 39.5 x 3.5 cms 60 folios. Between 6 and 8 lines on a page. 70 *akṣara*s on a line. Complete. Carelessly written in at least two hands.

R3 University of Mysore Oriental Research Institute. Ms. no. P 3002. *Descriptive Catalogue of Sanskrit Manuscripts*. Ed. Dr. G. Marulasiddaiah (Mysore, 1979), vol. 3, ser. no. 8960. Palm leaf. Grantha script. Approximately 6 lines on a page. 50 *akṣara*s on a line. Complete. Carelessly written with frequent corrections.

R4 University of Mysore Oriental Research Institute. Ms. no. P 2031. *Descriptive Catalogue of Sanskrit Manuscripts*. Ed. Dr. G.

Marulasiddaiah (Mysore, 1979), vol. 3, ser. no. 8957. Palm leaf. Grantha script. 41 x 4 cms 89 folios. Approximately 6 lines on a page. 42 *akṣaras* on a line. Complete. Worm-eaten.

B Printed version in Devanāgarī characters edited by Srī Bhagavadācārya and published in Baroda in 1937 (76 pages). This is an extremely poor reprinting of the Grantha edition (M). The book is rare; I used the copy in the library of the Bhandarkar Oriental Research Institute, Pune.

M Printed version in Grantha characters edited by Mādapūsi Ramanujacāryāṃ and published in Madras in 1905 (139 pages). The editor states that he used sixteen mss in preparing his edition. These mss are not properly identified, and their variants are recorded only in Ch. 1. From Ch. 2 on the editor records few variants, listing them merely as *pāṭhāntara*. I have listed all variants recorded in this edition with the siglum M+. This is clearly not a critical edition, and a careful comparison of its readings with those of my mss shows that the editor has created a hybrid version. This edition is also rare; I used a microfilm of the copy in the British Library.

Other Manuscripts

Four mss in the Government Oriental Manuscripts Library, Madras (Ms. nos. D 2949; D 2952; D 2953; R 4957) and one ms in the University of Mysore Oriental Research Institute (Ms. no. P 2080) were too damaged and brittle to be copied or collated.

O. F. Schrader had several mss of the Ysam copied during his residence at the Adyar Library, Madras, early this century. These copies are now in the library of the University of Göttingen. Schr. 45 is a copy of A1, described above, prepared by V. Krishnamachari and N. Ramanatha Sastri and dated Dec. 12, 1911; this copy also contains variants from A2 recorded on the margins. Schr. 47 is a copy of G1 (both, for example, share the same lacuna at Ch. 6.3) made by K. Gopalaiyer and dated Nov. 26, 1909. Schr. 46 contains only Chapters 1-6 and is probably a copy of A5. Variant readings from a ms of the short recension are noted on this copy. Schr. 55 is an original ms containing extracts from the Ysam; see Klaus L. Janert and N. Narasimhan Poti, *Indische Handschriften* (Wiesbaden: Franz Steiner, 1979), 5: 450-51. This ms contains a variety of sundry material listed by Janert. The extracts from the Ysam are found on pp. 90–96 of the ms and follow the long recension (X*); most of the readings follow the subrecension X1*. I list here the chapter and verse numbers from the current edition according to the sequence in which they appear in this ms:

> **3**.65(1, a-d), 62(2), 63, 64, 73; जन्तुनिवारणं जलपवित्रं कार्पासतन्तुवस्त्रमित्यर्थः (cf. variant in A6 at 3.73n), अष्टाङ्गयोगक्रमलक्षणानि वक्ष्यन्ते (cf. 5.47); **5**.51, 52, 53(a-d), 54, 55, 60, 82-91, 106-12; **6**.35, हारीतः, **6**.47, 243, 257, 259, 304; **7**.106, 138-39, अयने विषुवे चैव ग्रसने चन्द्रसूर्ययोः । उपवासमकुर्वाणः यतिश्चान्द्रायणं चरेत् ॥ विष्णुः **7**.22, शातातपः **6**.243, 249, 250(1), देवलः **7**.110, 111(a-b), 73, गर्गः **7**.130-36; सनत्कुमारसंहितै [sic] । प्रपत्तेः किंचिदप्येवं परापेक्षा न विद्यते । सा हि सर्वत्र सर्वेषां सर्वकामफलप्रदा । श्रुतिः । पूर्णस्य पूर्णमादाय पूर्णमेवावतिष्ठते । सर्वं पूर्णं सहों वासुदेवोऽसि पूर्णः । **7**.140; ताम्बूले भर्तृहीनायाः . . . संभूय सुरासमम् [cf. App. 1.8]; **7**.141; इति यतिधर्मसमुच्चये जमदग्निः ।

Genealogical Relation of the Manuscripts

The following *stemma codicum*, in which Z* stands for the hypothetical original of the Ysam, presents the genealogy of the mss used to constitute the text:

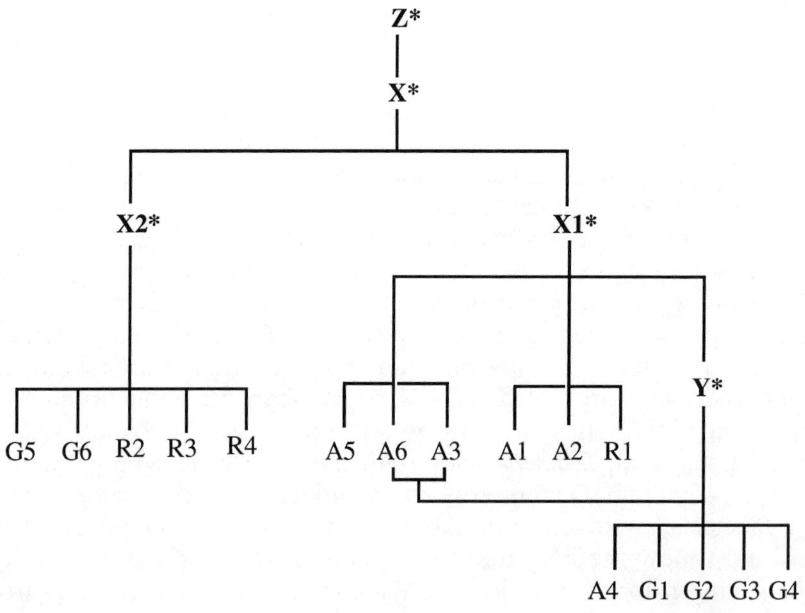

Recension X*

This recension contains the long version of the Ysam. Although the mss belonging to X* differ among themselves, their common readings stand in sharp contrast to those of the mss of Y*. I have identified two subrecensions of X*. The mss of X2* have numerous unique readings that differ substantially from those of X1*. Among the mss of X2*, G6, R2, and R3 appear to form a group with many unique readings, while R4 often has readings in common with mss of X1*. The subrecension X2* is also notable for several attempts to shorten the text, as at 2.48, 49; 3.65; and 5.136, 155. It shares this propensity with Y*, and in several places Y* and X2* show identical omissions, e.g., 5.117-19, 130-35, 137-43, 149-50. Among the mss of subrecension X1*, A1, A2, and R1 have many common readings and appear to be derived from a common ancestor. These three mss also share many common readings with Y* (e.g., 5.105; 6.54 and App. 1.4; 6.61; 7.129, 139), and it appears that the editor who made the short version used a ms derived from the same ancestor.

Recension Y*

This recension contains the short version of the Ysam. In contrast to the mss of X*, those belonging to Y* show a remarkable uniformity in their readings. I believe that all can be traced to a common source, which, as I will argue below, is the abbreviated version of the Ysam deliberately produced by an editor.

Composite Manuscripts

Two mss, A3 and A6, are hybrid versions of the two recensions. After Ch. 7, as we have seen, A3 appends a variety of other material from diverse sources regarding *yatidharma*. The scribe or editor of A3 appears to have used a variety of manuscript material, including some belonging to the two recensions. In the early sections, A3 follows recension X1*, but at 6.139 it switches to Y* until the end of Ch. 7. A similar switch between the two recensions is found also in A6, which follows X1* from the beginning until 8.30, Y* from 8.31 to 10.127, and again X1* from 10.128 until the end. Because the switching between recensions occurs quite suddenly in the middle of chapters, the presumption must be that these mss do not represent deliberate attempts to create hybrid versions. This is certainly true of A6. In all likelihood, some folios were missing in the exemplars used by the scribe, who then used other mss belonging to the short recension to supply the missing sections. The case is less clear with regard to A3, which frequently follows the readings of Y* even in those sections where it agrees overall with X1* (e.g., 2.15–17). It is possible that the scribe/editor of A3 used a ms of Y* to make a hybrid version of the entire text.

Constitution of the Text

The manuscript genealogy I have constructed is tentative at best and on its own does not provide an adequate basis for constituting the text. Most mss of the Ysam are in extremely poor condition, and it is very difficult to obtain a clear picture of the ms tradition from the available evidence. The constituted text presented here is the best that can be done without the discovery of new and significant mss.

The major issue to be resolved in constituting as far as possible the original text written by Yādava Prakāśa is the priority of the two recensions.[1] Numerous Indian texts, such as the *Mahābhārata* and the *Manusmṛti*, profess to be abridgments of earlier and longer versions. It is, nevertheless, a common scholarly assumption based on good evidence that most Indian texts, especially the Epics, Purāṇas, and Dharmaśāstras, were subjected to alteration principally by addition and accretion.[2] The assumption, therefore, is that longer versions are relatively more recent than shorter ones. The Ysam, however, proves to be an exception. The long recension, X*, in my estimate, is closer to the original than the short recension Y*, even though the priority of X* cannot be proved conclusively. The arguments I present taken together, however, suggest strongly that Y* is a later abridgment of the Ysam.

First, when the general principles of textual criticism, such as lectio difficilior and internal coherence, are applied, X* (especially X1*) most frequently presents the superior readings. An examination of 5.26, where Yādava explains the obscure half-verse 5.23c-d, shows how Y* and X2* have failed to understand the Sanskrit and attempted to emend the text. Likewise, the inability to perceive the reference to a later section (6.5) makes Y* delete the statement at 5.69.

1. Schrader, in the introduction to his edition of the Saṃnyāsa Upaniṣads, already noted the existence of the two recensions, calling them *textus ornatior* and *textus simplicior*, respectively (see SUS, p. xvii. See also Sprockhoff 1976, 308).

2. For a discussion of this issue, see Lariviere, NSm, pt. 2, pp. xii–xixiv.

Second, we find omissions in Y* that can be explained as scribal errors on the basis of X*, whereas it is difficult to see how these sections could be deliberate additions of X*. For example, Y* jumps from 3.28(1) to the end of 3.33, where we can see the editor combining the reading of 3.28(1) with the final two words of 3.33. A careful reader can readily see that the reading of X* is far superior.

We have seen, moreover, that A1, A2, and R1 have unique readings that set this group of mss apart from others belonging to X*. According to general editorial principles,[3] the divergence of this cluster from the tradition represented by the rest of the mss belonging to both subrecensions X1* and X2* must be presumed to be more recent than the divergence of X2* from X1*. We have also seen that the readings unique to this cluster are shared by Y*, in contrast to the other mss of X*, suggesting that the editor of Y* used a ms derived from the same ancestor as A1, A2, and R1. This feature is difficult to explain if Y* represents the original version from which X* diverged.

The uniformity of the readings of the mss belonging to Y* and their relatively small number further support the more recent origin of this recension.

A couple of pieces of external evidence also support the priority of X*. The only direct citation from the Ysam I have been able to trace thus far is in the *Śrīpāñcarātraparīkṣā* (p. 136) by Vedānta Deśika (1268–1369 C.E): यथोक्तं यतिधर्मसमुच्चये—फलपुष्पोत्पाटने प्रायश्चित्तविधानादद्भिः कर्तव्यमन्याहृतैर्वा. This passage, found in Ysam 6.73,[4] is preserved only in the long recension. There is a second reference to a passage of the Ysam in Deśika's Ybh. He says that Yādava Prakāśa disallows an option between a difficult and an easy course of action. This principle is laid down in Ysam 3.60, which again is missing in the short recension. So Vedānta Deśika, writing only a couple of centuries after Yādava, had before him the long recension. Deśika's testimony is all the more significant both because he assumed the leadership of the Śrī-Vaiṣṇava church in the early fourteenth century and because he was closely connected to the major figures of its early history. Deśika's maternal uncle, Ātreya Rāmānuja (1221–95 C. E.) was the teacher of Vatsya Varada, the author of the *Prameyamālā* and the *Yatiliṅgasamarthana* (see Olivelle 1986, 23). Varada was the

3. Katre (1954, 72) enunciates this principle clearly: "In comparison of variants, the larger arrays of manuscripts represent earlier divergences; the smaller always represent the later."

4. Deśika also cites at the same place a section of the passage from Vasiṣṭha, Ysam 4.21(4).

great-grandson of the sister of the great Rāmānuja, the founder of the sect and, according to tradition, initially a disciple of Yādava Prakāśa.[5] Deśika was thus in a position to obtain the best manuscripts of the Ysam. It is, of course, possible that the long recension was created out of the short before the time of Deśika, but, in view of the internal evidence given above, it is highly unlikely.

A careful examination of Y* makes it clear that it is a deliberately created edition and not the result of unintended scribal errors. Space does not permit me to explore fully the editorial principles followed by the editor of Y*, but several emerge from a close reading of the text: eliminating quotations that repeat what has already been said; deleting passages with difficult readings or where many mss have lacunae (e.g., 7.40; 9.82; 10.82); eliminating most of the explanatory material (e.g., 2.15); and rearranging verses for particular reasons. An example of the last is found in Ch. 3, where the editor places 3.46-50 after 3.56 and omits 3.57-58 (which appear to intrude into the flow of the discussion). Thus, verses dealing with the obligations to carry a staff are kept together, and the verses regarding tying a cord to the triple staff are placed last; the entire passage ends nicely with 3.59, which tells the ascetic not to tie a cord to a single staff.

Between the two subrecensions of the long version, X1* gives consistently superior readings. Among the mss of X1*, moreover, A3, A5, and A6 are the most reliable and give consistently superior readings. The most trustworthy portion of the constituted text is thus that part (until Ch. 6.138, where A3 switches to Y*) for which we have the evidence of these three mss. The constituted text from 6.139 to 8.30 is also by and large reliable, because we have the testimony of A5 and A6. The constitution of the remainder of the text was very difficult, because there I had to rely greatly on the mss of X2* and on A1, A2, and R1, the three least reliable mss of X1*. I am least certain about the constituted text of Ch. 11; here, the mss give widely divergent versions.

As a rule, I follow X1* when all its mss have the same reading. Where X1* presents divergent readings, I normally choose the readings shared by A5, A6, and the mss of X2*; in general, readings unique to A1, A2, R1, and the mss of Y* proved to be the least reliable. In the sections where it does not follow Y*, A6 proved to be the most reliable ms, giving consistently superior readings, especially of difficult passages (e.g., 3.24, 62; 5.26; 6.310; 7.75 the dual *yātaḥ;*

5. Although I believe that Y* is a later emendation of the Ysam, if we are to believe the date in the colophon of A4, it must have been made before 1474 C.E.

7.61-62). Metrical reasons sometimes forced the selection of a reading not supported by the majority of mss (e.g., 5.82; 6.64).

There are times, however, when one has to follow one's instinct. After working with this genre of literature for a lifetime, and after working closely with this text (including the manual collation of all the mss) for many years, I think I have developed a feel for Yādava's style—in art history they call it a connoisseur's judgment. Such judgments should be made judiciously and infrequently, but the connoisseur's touch is an essential part of an editor's repertoire.

The two printed versions were of little use in constituting the text. They follow X2* sometimes, the ms tradition of A1, A2, R1 at other times, and sometimes even Y*, as in Ch. 11. Further, they introduce new readings without any foundation in the available mss.

The Critical Apparatus

The critical apparatus lists all the significant variant readings, except obvious scribal errors. Longer variants that could not be conveniently listed at the foot of a page are placed in Appendix 1. Most Indian scribes, but especially those writing in Grantha and Telugu scripts, are altogether inconsistent in their notation of *anusvāra*s, *visarga*s (especially before conjunct consonants), and *avagraha*s; neither are they consistent in the use of sandhi. These variants are not noted in the critical apparatus. I have attempted to establish some consistency in these areas, except when the absence of sandhi is obviously used as punctuation. The spelling of the term *pārivrājya* is totally inconsistent, even within the same ms: *parivrājya, pārivrajya, parivrajya*. I have consistently used the standard *pārivrājya*.

Due to the exigencies of preparing camera-ready copy on a computer, I have been forced to place the entire critical apparatus for a verse or a prose passage at the bottom of the page on which the verse number appears. Thus, the variant readings of sections of some passages may be listed at the bottom of the following page when those passages span two pages.

Grammatical Peculiarities

We must, of course, assume that Yādava knew his Sanskrit. On the whole, correct grammar may be a reason to prefer a particular reading, yet there are times in this genre of literature, especially in verses quoted from sundry sources, when the established rules of Pāṇinian grammar are violated. I have not attempted to correct any of them; for example, accusative *mātrāṃ* when we would have expected the nominative (3.22) or *spr̥ṣṭvā* with instrumental (8.43). The most common such "error" is found in the gerund, where the *-ya* ending is used with uncompounded verbs: *gr̥hya* (8.44, 45; 9.34); *sthāpya* (10.31). There are several occasions when "double sandhi" is used in verses for metrical reasons (e.g., 6.156, 266).

यादवप्रकाशविरचितः

यतिधर्मसमुच्चयः

प्रथमं पर्व

पारिव्राज्यविधिः

ॐकारो वाचको यस्य योगकाले श्रुतो हरेः ।
तं श्रुतिश्रेणिनिःश्रेणिश्रयणीयं श्रयामहे ॥१॥
श्रीमाञ्जयति लोकानां नायको गरुडध्वजः ।
पाषण्डेभ्यस्त्रयी त्राता येन प्राग्यतिलिङ्गिना ॥२॥
संन्यासविषयाः सर्वाः समाहृत्य श्रुतिस्मृतीः ।
क्रियते **यादवेना**यं **यतिधर्मसमुच्चयः** ॥३॥
विधिः कर्तृदशा लिङ्गं प्रयोगो मुख्यकर्म च ।
अहोरात्रक्रियाचारो लिङ्गधर्मा गतिस्थितिः ॥४॥
प्रायश्चित्तानि संस्कार इत्येकादशपर्वकः ।
यतिधर्मः क्रमादत्र धर्मशास्त्रेभ्य उद्धृतः ॥५॥
वक्तारो धर्मशास्त्राणां **मनुर्विष्णुर्यमोऽङ्गिराः** ।

1. om Y* ; a)—अकारो R4 B M; c)—श्रुतीनां for तं श्रुति° A5; d)—श्रियामहे A1; समाश्रये R4 M+

2. d)—दृश्यते येन लिङ्गिना R4 M+

3. c–d)—om B; c)—ज्ञायते R4 M+

4. d)—धर्मो A1 2 R 1 2 4 B M; °स्थिती A4 B

5. a)—संस्कारा R4; b)—°पर्वकाः R4 M+; c)—°धर्माः M+; d)—सर्वशा° A1 2 R1 M+; उद्धृताः M+

वसिष्ठदक्षसंवर्तशातातपपराशराः ।।६।।
कात्यायनोशनोव्यासा आपस्तम्बो बृहस्पतिः ।
हारीतशङ्खलिखितयाज्ञवल्क्यात्रिगौतमाः ।।७।।
बोधायनो वृद्धदक्षः काश्यपः कपिलः क्रतुः ।
शाण्डिल्यो वृद्धजाबालो दत्तात्रेयश्च देवलः ।।८।।
गार्ग्यो वृद्धवसिष्ठश्च विश्वामित्रश्च गालवः ।
मेधातिथिर्भरद्वाजो जमदग्निश्च शौनकः ।
पैठीनसिः सत्यकामो वायुश्चेत्येवमादयः ।।९।।
एषां शास्त्रेषु संन्यासप्रदेशेष्वेव संचितः ।
धर्मोऽयं नान्यदेशेषु नेतिहासपुराणयोः ।।१०।।

तत्र संन्यासविधिरस्ति वा न वेति निरूप्यते ।।११।। तत्र केचिदाहुः[1] । श्रुतावदृष्टत्वात् श्रुतिविरोधे स्मृतीनामप्रामाण्यात् नास्त्येवेति[2] ।।१२।। तथा च **गौतमः**[1] ।

ऐकाश्रम्यं त्वाचार्याः प्रत्यक्षविधानाद्गार्हस्थ्यस्येति[2] ।।१३।। [GDh 3.36]

आह **बोधायनः**[1] ।

तस्य ह वा एतस्य चतुर्धा विभेदमेक आहुः[2] । अदृष्टार्थमेव चत्वार इति कर्मवाद ऐष्टिकसौमिकपाशुकदार्विकहौमिकानाम्[3] । तदेषा भवन्ति[4] । ब्रह्मचारी गृहस्थो वानप्रस्थः परिव्राजक इति[5] ।

6. om Y*; c)—°संवर्तः A1 °संवर्ताः A2 R3; d)—°शरौ A2

7. om Y*; b)—°म्बबृहस्पती A1 2 R1; c)—हारीतः A5 R2 3 B M; °लिखिता R4; °लिखितौ B M

8. om Y*; c)—शाण्डिल्य° R3 M+; °जाबालौ M+; °जाबाल्यौ R3; °जाबालिर्दत्ता° R4

9. om Y*

10. om Y*; a)—येषां A1 5; सर्वेषां for संन्यास° A6; b)—संचिताः A5; सन्ति नः B; सन्तितः M

11. वा om Y* A1 R1 4; विचार्यते R2 3 B M

12. 1)—तत्र om Y* A1 2 R1; अत्र R2 3 4 B M; 2)—यावज्जीवश्रुति° Y* A5 M+; स्मृतीनां प्रामाण्यं M+; नास्त्येव B M

13. 1)—च om A5; 2)—ऐका°...°चार्याः om A5; एके for ऐकाश्रम्यं A1 2 R1 2 3; °श्रम्यत्वादाचार्याः G1; एकाश्रम्य एव इत्याचार्याः R4; गार्हस्त्य इति B M

ब्रह्मचारी गुरुशुश्रूषुरामरणात्[6] । वानप्रस्थो वैखानसशास्त्रसमुदाचारेण वने मूलफलाशी तपःशीलः श्रामणकेनाग्निं समाधाय सवनेषूदकमुपस्पृशेत्[7] । अग्राम्यभोजी भैक्षमप्युपयुञ्जीत[8] । ग्रामं च न प्रविशेत्[9] । जटिलश्चीराजिनवासा नातिसंवत्सरं भुञ्जीत[10] । परिव्राजकः परित्यज्य बन्धूनपरिग्रहः परिव्रजेत्[11] । अरण्यं गत्वा मुण्डः शिखी वा कौपीनाच्छादनो वर्षास्वेकत्रस्थः[12] । काषायवासाः सन्नमुसले व्यङ्गारे भुक्तजने निवृत्ते शरावसंपाते भिक्षेत[13] । वाङ्मनःकायदण्डैर्भूतानामद्रोही[14] । पवित्रभृच्छौचार्थमुद्धृताभिरद्भिः कार्यं कुर्यात्[15] । अपविध्य दैविकाग्निकर्माण्युभयतः परिच्छिन्ना मध्यमं संश्लिष्यामह इति ब्रुवन्तः[16] । ऐकाश्रम्यं त्वाचार्या अप्रजननत्वादितरेषाम्[17] । तत्रोदाहरन्ति[18] ।

प्राह्लादिर्वै कापिलो नामासुरिरास[19] । स एतान्भेदांश्चकार
देवैः स्पर्धमानः[20] । तस्मान्मनीषी नाद्रियेतेति[21] ।

दृष्टार्थत्वात्[22] । तदेषाप्यनूद्यते[23] ।

एष नित्यो महिमेति[24] । [TB 3.12.9.7–8]

स ब्रूयात्[25] ।

येन सूर्यस्तपति . . . सांपराय इति[26] । [TB 3.12.9.7]
इमे ये नार्वाङ् न परश्चरन्ति न ब्राह्मणासो न सुतेकरासः ।
त एते वाचमभिपद्य पापया सिरीस्तन्त्रं तन्वते अप्रजज्ञय
इति[27] ।। [RV 10.71.9]
प्रजाभिरग्ने अमृतत्वमश्याम्[28] । [RV 5.4.10]
जायमानो वै ब्राह्मणस्त्रिभिर्ऋणवा जायते । ब्रह्मचर्येणर्षिभ्यो
यज्ञेन देवेभ्यः प्रजया पितृभ्य इति[29] । [TS 6.3.10.5]

एवमृणसंयोगवादीन्यसंख्यातानि भवन्ति निषेधाश्च[30] ।।१४।।
[BDh 2.11.9–33]

14. 1)—आह om Y*; 2–16)— om Y*; 2)—भेदमेक B M; 3)—अत्र दृष्टार्थ° R4 B M; ये चत्वार B M; कर्मवादी R4; गृहैष्टि° M+; °दार्विहौ° R2 B M; °सौरकानाम् A5; 4)—°षाभिवदन्ति B M; 5)—om R2 B M; 6)—°मरणम् A6 B M; 7)—वानप्रस्थो conj.

आपस्तम्बः[1] ।

> त्रयीं विद्यां ब्रह्मचर्यं प्रजातिं श्रद्धां तपो यज्ञमनुप्रदानम्[2] । य एतानि कुर्वते तैरित्सह स्मो रजो भूत्वा ध्वंसतेऽन्यत्प्रशंसन्निति[3] ॥१५॥ [ApDh 2.24.8]

तस्मात् श्रुतावदृष्टत्वात्प्रत्यक्षश्रुतिविरोधे स्मृतीनामप्रामाण्यान्न सन्त्यूर्ध्वरेतस आश्रमा इति ॥१६॥ अथ स्यात्[1] । अस्ति श्रुतिर्वाजसनेयिनां प्रत्यक्षा[2] ।

> एतमेव प्रव्राजिनो लोकमिच्छन्तः प्रव्रजन्तीति[3] । [BaU 4.4.22]
> तस्माद्ब्राह्मणः पाण्डित्यं निर्विद्य बाल्येन तिष्ठासेत् । बाल्यं च पाण्डित्यं च निर्विद्याथ मुनिरिति च[4] ॥१७ ॥ [BaU 3.5.1]

आचारं च दर्शयति[1] ।

> एतद्ध स्म वै पूर्वे विद्वांसः प्रजां न कामयन्ते । किं प्रजया करिष्यामो येषां नोऽयमात्मायं लोक इति[2] । [BaU 4.4.22]

---

following BDh & B M, om in all mss; °शास्त्र° om A5; श्रावणके° A5; °स्पृशेत् add in margin वनी नातिसंवत्सरं भुञ्जीत A1; 8)—भैक्षमुप° R4; भैक्षमपि युञ्जीत A2; 11)—परिव्रज्य बन्धू° A2; 12)—मुण्डी A1 2 R1; °कस्थम् A5; 13)—भुक्तवर्जिते R2 3 4 B M; निवृत्ते conj. following BDh, B M and marginal addition वृत्ते in A1 2, om in all mss; 15)—पात्रभृ° R3 4; पवित्रं बिभ्रत् शौ° B M; 16)—अपविद्धदै° A1 2 R1 3 4 M+; °विध्यादैवि° A5; दैविकानि कर्माणि R2 B M; मध्यमं add पदं A5; 17)—एकाश्रमत्वादाचार्यात्प्रजन° A1 2 [°चार्यः प्र° A2]; ऐकत्वाश्रम्यत्वाचार्यात् R4; एकाश्रमं A5; अप्रज° . . . [27] इति lacuna A6; अप्रजननार्थत्वादि° R5; °त्वादेतेषाम् R3; 19)—वै om A1 2 5 R1 4; कपिलो R2 5; नामाश्रमारि° A1 2 R1 [A1 corrected to नामासुरि°]; नामाश्रमणसुरि° R4; नामाश्रविरास A5; 21)—नाद्रियेत Y* A5 R1 4; 22–27)—om Y* ; 22)—अदृष्टत्वात् A5; 23)—°षाभ्यनूच्यते R4 M; 27)—°जज्ञय conj., all mss read °ज्ञीय; 29)—ब्रह्मचर्येण . . . पितृभ्य om Y*; 30—°योगवादीनि वचनान्यसंख्या° A1 2 R1; °योगादिवचनान्यसंख्या° A4 M+; °योगादीनि वचनान्यसंख्या° G1 2 3; सन्ति A5 6

15. 2)—त्रयी A1 2 R1 2; प्रजापतिं A6 G3 R2 3 4; 3)—य om G 1 2 3 B M; येतानि A5; तैरित्स° conj., all mss read तैरुत्स°

16. lacuna A6; °दृष्टत्वादिति प्रत्य° X2*; °दृष्टत्वाद्धि प्रत्य° M+; °श्रुति° om M

17. 1)—om Y* A1 2 R1; 2)— अस्मृति for अस्ति R4; 3)—एवमेव A1 2 6 G1 3 R1 2 3; प्रव्रजन्ति Y* A1 2 R1; 4)—ब्राह्मणः om A4 5; बाल्येन . . . निर्विद्य om G3

अग्निहोत्रं न जुहुवाञ्चक्रिर इति च[3] ।।१८।।

अत्रोच्यते[1] । किं पारिव्राज्यं पुरुषार्थं विधीयते उत पाणिग्रहणादिवदनुष्ठानान्तरार्थम्[2] । पुरुषार्थत्वे तु स स्वर्गः स्यादिति [PMS 4.3.7.15] न्यायेन स्वर्गार्थं वा स्यादन्यार्थं वा[3] । न तावत्स्वर्गार्थमपवर्गप्रकरणविरोधात्[4] । तथा हि सर्वत्रापवर्गप्रकरण एव पारिव्राज्यं विधीयते[5] । तेनापवर्गप्रकरण एव कथंचित्संबन्धो वाच्यः[6] । सोऽपि वा न शक्यते वक्तुं ज्ञानादेवापवर्गश्रुतेः[7] ।

तमेवं विदित्वाति मृत्युमेति । नान्यः पन्था विद्यतेऽयनायेति[8] ।। [VS 31.18]

विद्ययैव तदारोहति यत्र कामाः पराहताः ।
न तत्र दक्षिणा यन्ति नाविद्वांसस्तपस्विन इति[9] ।।१९।।
[SB 10.5.4.16]

अथ ज्ञानानुष्ठानाङ्गत्वेन विधीयत इति मतम्[1] । नैतत्[2] । ज्ञानानुष्ठानं गृहस्थानामपि संभवतीति न तदर्थमाश्रमान्तरविधिः कल्प्यः[3] । कल्प्यमानोऽपि नाश्रमान्तरं प्रापयेत्[4] । किंत्वाहिताग्निव्रतवद् गृहस्थानामेव किंचित्पारिव्राज्यं नाम व्रतं विदध्यात्[5] । तच्च प्रवृत्तगार्हस्थ्याविरोधी कश्चित्सङ्गत्यागात्मको धर्म इति गम्यते[6] । स्मृतिषु दृष्टानां धर्माणां श्रुतिविरोधान्न संग्रहः[7] । न च पारिव्राज्यशब्द एवाश्रमान्तरवचनोऽन्यत्र प्रसिद्धः अश्रौतत्वप्रसङ्गात्[8] । तथा च स्मृतिप्रसिद्धं पारिव्राज्यमियं श्रुतिर्विद्यास्तुतयेऽनुवदतीति स्यादित्थं महीयसी विद्या यद्बलाद्विहितान्यपि कर्माणि परित्यजन्तो न प्रत्यवयन्तीति[9] ।।२०।।

18. 1)—च om A5 R2 4 B M; 2)—एतद्धर्मं वै A1 2 R1; तत्पूर्वे A1 2 4 G2 3 R1; एषां R1 2 3 4 G6; 3)—न om A1 2 R1 3; च om Y*

19. 2)—°षार्थार्थं B M; °षार्थन्तरार्थं A5; °षार्थन्तरं A6; °ग्रहणवद° M+; °ष्ठानार्थम् B M; 3)—°षार्थार्थत्वे M; °षार्थे G2; सर्वार्थत्वशस्यत्वादि° for तु . . . स्यादि° A5; स्वर्गार्थमन्या° A4 G2 3 R2 B M; वा स्यादित्यन्या° A1 2 R1 4; °न्यार्थत्वं R4; 3–4)—इति न्यायेन . . . °रोधात् om G1; 7)—वा om A1 2 R1 2 3 M+; येन for वा न A6; 8)—तमेव G2 R2; 9)—अविद्य° A5; समाहिताः B M; तत्रादक्षका B M; न विद्वांस° Y* A1 2 R1 2 4; विद्वांस° for नाविद्वांस° A6; नातप° B M; इति च Y* B M

20. 3)—°स्थानां संभ° B M; संभवति A5 M+; न om A6 R2 3 4 M+; कल्प्यः om A6 R2 3 M+; 5)—om G3; °नामेव add ब्रह्मनिष्ठानां A4 G1 2 [A1 in margin]; 5–6)—पारि-

तस्मादग्निहोत्रादिवदसाधारणस्य गृहस्थेष्वसंभवतः श्रौतस्याश्रमधर्मस्याभावात् भिक्षाटनादीनां च संध्यावन्दनादिवदाचारत्वेनाश्रमधर्मार्थत्वात् स्वयमाश्रमधर्मत्वानुपपत्तेः न पारिव्राज्यं नामाश्रमोऽस्तीति केचिदाचार्या मन्यन्ते ।।२१।।

अत्रोच्यते[1] । अस्त्यसाधारणो धर्मो ज्ञानयोगो नाम[2] । तथा हि सत्यादीनि मानसान्तानि कर्माण्युपन्यस्य

तस्मान्न्यासमेषां तपसामतिरिक्तमाहुः । [MNU 538]

इति श्रुत्या संन्यासं विधाय

आत्मानं युञ्जीत । [MNU 540]

इति न्यासशब्दवाच्यं ज्ञानयोगं विधत्ते[3] । ज्ञानयोगो नाम केवलस्य ज्ञानमात्रस्यानुष्ठानम्[4] । न ह्यसौ गृहस्थानां संभवति अग्निहोत्रादेरप्यनुष्ठेयत्वात्[5] । अतस्तेषां कर्मयोग एव[6] । कर्मयोगो नाम ज्ञानकर्मसमुच्चयानुष्ठानम् ततो मोक्षः[7] । परिव्राजकानां तु ज्ञानयोगादेव मोक्षः[8] । अत एषां कर्माभावात्कर्मसंपादनं परेण दर्शयति[9] ।

तस्यैवं विदुषो यज्ञस्यात्मा । [MNU 543]

इत्यनुवाकेन इयमप्यहन्यहन्यनुष्ठेयैव परिव्राजकस्य विधीयते[10] । न स्तुतिमात्रमपूर्वत्वात्[11] ।।२२।।

व्राज्यं . . . कश्चित् om R4; 6)—प्रवृत्त° om X2* B M, पूर्ववृत्त° Y* M+, प्रवृद्ध° A1 2 R1 M+; °विरोधः A2 5; °विरोधं A6; °त्यागपरो A5; 7)—स्मृतिदृष्टा° B M; स्मृतिविरो° A5; संशयः R4; 8)—न तु M+; 9)—स्मृतिर्वि° M+; °स्तुतयो A2 G1; °द्याश्रुतये A5; °वदन्तीति A2 M+; कर्माण्यपरि° A6; प्रव्रजन्तो A5

21. गृहस्थेष्वेव संभ° A1 2 6 R1; °धर्माभा° M+; °धर्मत्वाभा° M+; °टनादीनि X2*; च om Y* A1 2 R1 B M; °श्रमार्थत्वात् A6; °श्रमधर्मत्वात् A5; °धर्मानुप° A1 2 M+; °श्रमधर्मोऽस्तीति Y* A1 2 R1 M+; °श्रमो नास्तीति R4

22. 2)—°धारणधर्मो R3 4; 3)—हि om Y* A1 2 R1; मानसान्तानि om A5; संन्यासमेषां वि° B M; संन्यासशब्द° A5 G1; अध्यासशब्द° A4 6; 5)—°होत्रादेरनुष्ठेय° A6; 6)—एव om Y*; 7)—कर्मसंन्यासश्च कर्मयोगानां [°योगिनां A4] for कर्मयोगो नाम Y*; 8)—om M+; परिव्राजिनां A1; ज्ञानादेव R4; 9)—अतस्तेषां Y* A1 2 R1 M+; 10)—°स्यात्मा add यजमान R4

ननु परिव्राजकानामपि संध्यावन्दनादिकर्माणि सन्ति[1] । सत्यम्[2] । तेषां समाचारत्वात् आश्रमधर्मार्थत्वमेव न मोक्षार्थत्वम्[3] । मोक्षार्थं तु ज्ञानयोग एव[4] । तदर्थानि संध्यावन्दनादीनि[5] । न हि संध्याहीनस्य तत्राधिकारः

संध्याहीनोऽशुचिर्नित्यमनर्हः सर्वकर्मसु ।

इति स्मरणात्[6] ।

आचारहीनं न पुनन्ति वेदाः ।

इति च[7] । जपतपोभिक्षाटनादीनामपि यमनियमेष्वन्तर्भावो वर्ण्यते[8] । यमनियमादीनां च योगाङ्गत्वं सर्वशास्त्रसिद्धम्[9] । अतस्तेषामपि ज्ञानयोग एवान्तर्भावः[10] ॥२३॥

तस्मात्परिव्राजकानां ज्ञानयोगो गृहस्थानां कर्मयोग इति स्थितम्[1] । तथा च

न कर्मणा न प्रजया धनेन त्यागेनैके अमृतत्वमानशुः । [MNU 227]

इति कर्मत्यागेनैवामृतत्वं श्रूयते[2] ।

वेदान्तविज्ञानसुनिश्चितार्थाः
संन्यासयोगाद्यतयः शुद्धसत्त्वाः ।
ते ब्रह्मलोके तु परान्तकाले
परामृतात्परिमुच्यन्ति सर्वे ॥ [MNU 229–30]

इति च[3] ।

23. 1)— °जकानां संध्या° Y*; °नादीनि A6 R2 3 4 M+; °कर्माणि om R2 3; भवन्ति A4 G2 3; 2)—सत्यं नास्ति M+; 3)—समयाचा° Y* A1 2 R1 B M; आचार° R2 3 M+; °कर्मार्थत्व° A4 6 G2 3 R2 3 M+; 4)—ज्ञानमेव A1 2 R1 M+; ज्ञानमात्रानुष्ठानमेव A4 G2 3 M+; 5)—एतदर्थानि M+; °नादीनीति B M; 6)—संध्यादिही° X2* G1 3 B M; संध्यावन्दनही° A4 G2; संध्यावन्दनादिही° M+; 7)—च om A4; 8)—जपदमतपो° A1 2 R1; °तपोदमभि° G1 M+; °क्षाटनादियम° A5; यम° om A6; वक्ष्यते Y* A5 R2 M+; 10)—ततस्ते° A4; ज्ञानेऽन्तर्भा°M+; °योगान्तर्भा° Y* A1 2 R1

तथा च भगवान्वासुदेवः[4] ।

ज्ञानयोगेन सांख्यानां कर्मयोगेन योगिनाम् इति[5] ।।२४।।

[BhG 3.3]

तदेवमसाधारणस्य धर्मस्य भावात् अस्ति पारिव्राज्यं नाम श्रौत आश्रमः[1] । तन्मूलत्वाच्च स्मृतीनां प्रामाण्यम्[2] । न चैष धर्मो गृहस्थानां संभवति भिक्षाचर्यं चरन्तीति सर्वत्र द्रव्यत्यागश्रवणात्[3] । तस्मादाश्रमान्तरमेव पारिव्राज्यमिति सिद्धम्[4] ।।२५।।

इति यादवप्रकाशेन विरचिते यतिधर्मसमुच्चये पारिव्राज्यविधिर्नाम प्रथमं पर्व ।।२६।।

24. 1)—इति च B M; स्थितः A2; सिद्धम् Y* M+; 2)—तथा च om Y*; अथ च R3 M+; °त्यागेनामृ° X2* B M; 3)—च omY* R4; 4)—तथा च om A6; वासुदेवः om Y*

25. 1)—°धारणधर्म° A5; धर्मस्य om B M (ed. notes धर्मस्य इति पदं लेखकप्रमादाल्लुप्तमिव); धर्मस्याभा° A1 R1 4 M+; श्रौताश्र° X2* A5; °श्रम इति R2 3 4 M+; 2)—°लत्वात्स्मृ° B M; तत्सत्त्वाच्च श्रुतीणां R4; प्रामाण्यम् om A5; 3–4)—om A6; 3)—नैष R2 3 B M; चरन्तिA4 G1 2; चरेति A1 2 R1; सर्वद्रव्य° G1 2 3; सर्वत्याग° B M; °त्याग एव श्रव° A1 2 5 R1; 4)—°न्तरमेवेति सिद्धम् A4 G1; °न्तरमेवेदं सिद्धम् G2; °व्राज्यं सिद्धम् A3

26. °यादव° . . . °चिते om Y*; भगवद्याद°A1 R1 M+; भगवद्यादवेन A2; भगवता याद° A3 6; °प्रकाशविर° A5 6 G6 R4; पारिव्राज्यं नाम A 1 2 5 R1

द्वितीयं पर्व

पारिव्राज्याधिकारिदशानिरूपणम्

अथाधिकारिदशा चिन्त्यते ॥१॥ वनवासादूर्ध्वमेव पारिव्राज्यम् न ब्रह्मचर्यादित्येकः पक्षः ॥२॥ तथा च श्रुतिः[1] ।

आचार्याय प्रियं धनमाहृत्य प्रजातन्तुं मा व्यवच्छेत्सीरिति[2] ॥३॥ [TU 1.11.1]

तथा[1] ।

जायमानो वै ब्राह्मण इति च[2] । [TS 6.3.10.5]

प्रजननं वै प्रतिष्ठा साधु प्रजायास्तन्तुं तन्वानः पितॄणामनृणो भवतीति च[3] ॥४॥ [MNU 525]

तथा च **मनुः**[1] ।

ऋणानि त्रीण्यपाकृत्य मनो मोक्षे निवेशयेत् ।
अनपाकृत्य मोक्षं तु सेवमानो व्रजत्यधः इति ॥५॥ [MDh 6.35]

आह **याज्ञवल्क्यः**[1] ।

अधीतवेदो जपकृत्पुत्रवानन्नदोऽग्निमान् ।

1. °कारदशा R2 3

2. न om A3

3. 1)—च om A6; 2)—इति om A5

4. 1)—तथा च A1 2 R1; 2)—ब्राह्मणस्त्रिभिर्ऋणवा जायत इति Y* A3 R4 B M [A1 in margin]; च om Y* X2* A3 B M; 3)—प्रतिष्ठा add लोके A5; साधुः A1 R2; भवति । तदेव तस्यानृणं तस्मात्प्रजननं परमं वदन्तीति च Y* A3 G6 R3 M+ [A1 adds in margin; G6 R3 M+ omit इति च]; च om A6 R2 4 B M

5. 1)—च om M R4; d)—पतत्यधः G6 R2 3 B M

शक्त्या च यज्ञकृन्मोक्षे मनः कुर्यात्तु नान्यथा इति ॥६॥
[YDh 3.57]

आहतुः **शङ्खलिखितौ**[1] ।

वनवासादूर्ध्वं परिणतवयसः कामतः पारिव्राज्यमिति[2] ॥७॥

आह **मेधातिथिः**[1] ।

पुत्रदारगृहक्षेत्रगोहिरण्यादिबन्धनैः ।
विरक्तो मानुषैर्भोगैर्दिव्यैश्च श्रुतिदर्शितैः ॥८॥
वेदाभ्यासेन यज्ञेन तपसा वीतकल्मषः ।
जन्मजन्मान्तराभ्यासाद्विशुद्धात्मा जितेन्द्रियः ॥९॥
इतिहासपुराणाभ्यां श्रुत्या च प्रतिबोधितः ।
यतते परमं स्थानं यतनात्स यतिर्भवेत् ।
तस्येयं परमा सिद्धिर्यतेर्नान्यस्य कस्यचित् इति ॥१०॥

केचित्तु ब्रह्मचर्याद् गृहाद्वनाद्वा यथाकामं पारिव्राज्यमित्याहुः ॥११॥

तथा च **जाबालिश्रुतिः**[1] ।

ब्रह्मचर्यं समाप्य गृही भवेत्[2] । गृही भूत्वा वनी भवेत्[3] । वनी भूत्वा प्रव्रजेत्[4] । यदि वेतरथा ब्रह्मचर्यादेव प्रव्रजेद् गृहाद्वनाद्वेति[5] ॥१२॥ [JU 64]

आह **यमः**[1] ।

चीर्णवेदव्रतो विद्वान्ब्राह्मणो मोक्षमाश्रयेत् ।

6. 1)—आह om A5; b)—°वान्नगदो A1 2; °वान्यागदो R4; d)—कुर्यादनन्यथा A1 2

7. Y* places 2.7–12 after 2.46; 1–2)—Y* reads एवं [om G1 2] शङ्खलिखितौ वनवासादूर्ध्वं परिणतवयसः कामतः पारिव्राज्यमाहतुः

8. 1)—आह om Y* A3; d)—स्मृति° B M

9. b)—हतकिल्बिषः G1 2

10. b)—स्मृत्या B M; e)—तस्यैवं A1 2 R1; f)—इति om A1 5

11. गृहस्थाद्वना° R1; गृहाद्वा [वनाद् om] A5; गृहाद्वा वनाद्वा G6 R2 3; यथाक्रमं G6 R2 3; °ज्यमाहुः A4 G1 2

12. 1)—जाबालश्रु° A4 5 M+; जाबालिः X2*A1 2 B M; 2)—गृही भवेत् om G6; 3)—om R4; 3–4)—गृहाद्वनी भूत्वा परिव्रजेत् [प्रव्र° A4] Y*; 4)—परिव्र° A2 G6 R4; 5)—यदि . . . प्रव्रजेद् om X2* A3 B M; यदि वा om Y*; परिव्र° A2 G1; गृहाद्वा वना° A4 5 G6 R2 3 B M

समः सर्वेषु भूतेषु स्थावरेषु चरेषु च ।।१३।।
जातपुत्रो गृहस्थो वा विजितात्मा जितेन्द्रियः ।
निःस्पृहः सर्वकामेभ्यः कृतकृत्यः परिव्रजेत् ।
वनस्थो वा तप्ततपाः परं पन्थानमाश्रयेत् इति ।।१४।।

अत्र यदि ब्रह्मचारी प्रव्रजेत् चीर्णव्रत एव प्रव्रजेत्[1] । यदि गृहस्थो जातपुत्र एव इष्टयज्ञश्च तानग्नीन्हृदि संहृत्येति पूर्वमुक्तत्वात्[2] । वानप्रस्थश्चेत्तप्ततपा एव प्रव्रजेत्[3] । इति गम्यते[4] । एतदुत्तरत्रापि योज्यम्[5] । एतद्विषयमेव **मानव**मपि वचनमृणानि त्रीण्यपाकृत्येत्यादि[6] ।।१५।।

केचिदाहुः[1]

ब्रह्मचारी गृहस्थो वा मृतदारो वनेचरः ।
ज्ञात्वा सम्यक्परं ब्रह्म त्यक्त्वा सङ्गान्परिव्रजेत् इति ।।१६।।

अत्र गृहस्थस्य मृतदारस्य पुत्रोत्पत्त्यादेः प्रागपि सति वैराग्ये पारिव्राज्यं गम्यते ।।१७।। आह **बृहस्पतिः**[1] ।

असारमेव संसारं दृष्ट्वा सारदिदृक्षया ।
प्रव्रजेदकृतोद्वाहः परं वैराग्यमास्थितः ।।१८।।
अन्योऽप्युत्पन्नसन्तान इष्ट्वा च विविधैर्मखैः ।
पतितार्धशरीरो वा वनादन्यः परिव्रजेत् इति ।।१९।।

13. आह om Y*; d)—च नित्यशः for चरेषु च Y*

14. a)—जाते पुत्रे R4; e–f)—om Y*; इति om Y*; Y* A1 2 B M add लिखितः [आह लि° B M]। सोऽधीतवेदतत्त्वार्थो गृहवासमशक्नुवन् । प्रव्रजेदकृतोद्वाहो गृहाज्जीर्णो वनादपि [वनाच्चीर्णो गृहादपि B M; add इति B M; see 2.27]

15. om Y* A3; 1)—परिव्रजेत् [both times] X2*; after 1st प्रव्रजेत् R3 adds गृहाद्वा वनाद्वा इति जाबालिः; 2)—एव om A5; समारोप्येति A1 2 R1; ऊर्ध्वमुक्त° A5; पूर्वमेवोक्त° R4; 3)—°प्रस्थश्च तप्त° G6 R4 ; °तपा om R4; एवाव्रजेत् G6; परिव्रजेत् R4; 6)—अत एत° R2; मानववच° X2* B M; वचनं च G6; °त्येत्यादीति A5; °त्येत्यादि वचनं X2*

16. om Y* A3; 1)—om A5; placed at end of 2.15 by X2*; क्रतुः for केचिदाहुः A1 2 R1 M+ [cf. 2.48]; a)—वा om G6; d)—इति om A5

17. om Y* A3; मृतदारस्य om A5

18. om Y* A3 [Y* inserts after 49]; a)—संसारमेव निःसारं Y*; b)—त्यक्त्वा Y*; d)—°माश्रितः Y*

19. om Y* A3; a)—अन्ये X2*; °सन्ताना R3 4; d)—इति om A5

अर्धशरीरं भार्या

पतत्यर्धं शरीरस्य भार्या यस्य सुरां पिबेत् । [VaDh 21.15]

इति दर्शनात्

अर्धो वा एष आत्मनो यत्पत्नी । [TS 6.1.8.5]

इति श्रुतेश्च ॥२०॥ आह **शङ्खः**[1] ।

एवं नीत्वा वने कालं द्विजो ब्रह्माश्रमी भवेत् ।
नानोपनिषदां ज्ञानात्प्राप्तवैराग्यपाटवः ॥२१॥
समाहृतेन्द्रियग्रामो विषयेभ्यः सुदूरतः ।
आत्मैकरामो मनसा निरस्य परिपन्थिनः ॥२२॥
योगाभ्यासेन बहुशो लब्धात्मा दृढबन्धनः ।
सर्वसङ्गनिवृत्तात्मा ब्रह्मचार्यपि सुव्रतः ॥२३॥
एतैर्गुणैरुपेतश्चेद् गृहस्थो वा प्रजापतेः ।
कृत्वेष्टिं विधिवद्दत्त्वा सर्ववेदसदक्षिणाम् ।
आत्मन्यग्नीन्समारोप्य द्विजो ब्रह्माश्रमी भवेत् इति ॥२४॥

एवं काश्चित् श्रुतयः स्मृतयश्च ब्रह्मचर्यादेव पारिव्राज्यं विदधति काश्चित्तु ऋणापकरणादेरूर्ध्वमेवेति[1] । एवं विरोधे सति केचिदाहुः[2] । अन्धपंग्वादीन्कर्मस्वनधिकृतानधिकृत्य ब्रह्मचर्यादुत्थानश्रुतयः स्मृतयश्च[3] ॥२५॥ तथा चाह **लिखितः**[1] ।

जन्मकोटिशतारब्धपुण्याप्तं देवकारितम् ।
वैराग्यं जायते यस्य तृष्णापि ब्रह्मणि स्थिरा ॥२६॥

20. om Y* A3

21. om Y* A3 d)—°पादपः X2* A 1 2 R1; °पाटलः A5

22. om Y* A3; a)—समाहृत्येन्द्रि° A1 2 6 R1; °ग्रामं A1 2 R1; d)—°बन्धिनः G6 R3

23. om Y* A3

24. om Y* A3; b)—प्रजायते R4 B M; e)—°ग्निं समा° R2 4; f)—इति om A5 R4

25. om Y* A3; 1)—स्मृतयश्च om G6; विदधति om G6; काश्चित् ऋणादेरू° G6; ऋणापाक° B M; °रणादूर्ध्व° A5; 2)—एवं om A5; 3)—°चर्याद्युत्थान° A2 5 6 R4; °श्रुतयश्च A1 2 G6 R1 2 3; स्मृतयश्च om A1 2 5 R1

26. om A3; Y* inserts after 2.61; 1)—तथा चाह om Y*; तथाह A5; च for चाह A1 2 R1; b)—°पुण्याद्दैवकारितम् G1 2; °पुण्याद्दैवेन कारितम् A4; °दैवकारितम् A6 G3; °देवतेरितम् M+

सोऽधीतवेदतत्त्वार्थो गृहवासमशक्नुवन् ।
प्रव्रजेद्ब्रह्मचर्याच्च गृहाज्जीर्णो वनादपि ॥२७॥
नीरुजश्च युवा चैव वसेद्गार्हस्थ्यमादृतः ।
अन्धः पङ्गुस्तथा कुष्ठी वृद्धो मौनं समाश्रयेत् इति ॥२८॥

अन्ये त्वाहुः[1]। उभयीषु श्रुतिस्मृतिषु विपरीतः किं न भवेत्[2]। अविरक्तः पारिव्राज्यं कर्तुमशक्नुवन्किं न गृही भवेत्[3] । न ह्यविरक्तः पारिव्राज्यं कर्तुं शक्नोतीति[4] ॥२९॥ तथा च **दक्षः**[1] ।

सत्त्वोत्कटाः सर्वे तेऽपि विषयैस्तु वशीकृताः ।
किं पुनः क्षुद्रसत्त्वैस्तु मानवैरत्र का कथा ॥३०॥
तस्मात्पक्वकषायेण कर्तव्यं दण्डधारणम् ।
इतरस्तु न शक्नोति विषयैर्ह्रियते यतः ॥३१॥
त्रिदण्डं लिङ्गमाश्रित्य जीवन्ति बहवो द्विजाः ।
यो हि ब्रह्म न जानाति त्रिदण्डार्हो न स स्मृतः इति ॥३२॥

आह **लिखितः**[1] ।

यः कृत्वा सर्वसंन्यासं प्रत्यापत्तिं भजेद् द्विजः ।
तं दास्ये योजयेद्राजा श्वपदेनाङ्कयेत्तथा ॥३३॥

27. om A3; Y* inserts after 2.61 [cf. 2.14]; a)—°धीततत्त्ववेदार्थो A5; b)—गृहवासी वशीभवन् G1 2 3; °समनश्नुवन् A1 2 M+; c)—°चारी च A5; d)—गृहे जीर्णो G1 2 3; गृहाच्चीर्णो A5 R2 B M

28. b)—°मादरात् Y* A1 2 3 R1 M+; c)—पङ्गुश्च कुष्ठी च R4; d)—इति om Y* A2 5

29. om Y* G6 R3 4 M+ [R3 writes it in margin; R4 inserts after दण्डधारणम् (2.31)]; 1)—before अन्ये R2 adds तथा च . . . वशीकृताः [cf. 2.30]; चाहुः B M; 2)—श्रुतिषु R4; विपरीतं R2 B M; भवेदिति A1 2 R1; 3)—विरक्तः A1 2 R1 M+; कर्तुमशक्नोति [°तीति R4] for कर्तुम° . . . भवेत् A1 2 R4; 4)—शक्नोति A1 2 R1 2 B M

30. तथा च om Y*; b)—परिष्कृताः A4 G1 2

31. d)—°यैर्व्यध्यते A1 2 R1

32. a)—त्रिदण्डलि° A6 B M; d)—न om R4; संस्मृतः A3 6 R4; इति om Y* A5

33. 1)—आह om Y* A5; लिखितः om A5 G1; a)—कृत्वैवं यस्तु संन्यासं Y* A1 2 3 R1; कृत्वैव A4 G1 2; b)—प्रत्यावृत्तिं A4 6 G1 2; भवेद् A5; c)—दण्डे A1 2 3 G6 R2 3; दण्डैर्यो° B M; d)—श्वपादे° A6 R4 B M; द्विजः for तथा G3

तस्मादाशयशुद्धिं प्राग्बहुकालं परीक्ष्य च ।
मनो न चलते धर्मादिति ज्ञात्वाथ संन्यसेत् इति ।।३४।।

आह **यमः**[1] ।

निवृत्तः कामरागादेः प्रशान्तो ब्रह्मतत्परः ।
स संन्यासेऽधिकारी स्यादितरो जीविकापरः इति ।।३५।।

न चानधिकृतविषया ह्युत्थानश्रुतिरिति युक्तं तेषामुत्तरत्र पृथगेव विधानात्[1] ।

अथ पुनर्व्रती वाव्रती वा स्नातको वास्नातको वा साग्निरनग्निको वेत्यादिना[2] ।।३६।। [JU 64]

आह **वृद्धजाबालिः**[1] ।

व्रतिको वाव्रतिको वा स्नातको वास्नातको वा आवसथ्यनावसथी वा अग्निहोत्र्यनग्निहोत्री वा ग्रामादग्निमाहृत्येत्यादि[2] ।।३७।।

यत्पुनरुक्तम्

अन्धः पङ्गुस्तथा कुष्ठी वृद्धो मौनं समाश्रयेत् ।

इति तदप्यविरुद्धम् अन्धादिशब्दानामन्यथा व्याख्याततत्वात् ।।३८।। तथा हि **मेधातिथिः**[1] ।

अद्यजातां यथा नारीं तथा षोडशवार्षिकीम् ।
शतवर्षां च यो दृष्ट्वा निर्विकारः स षण्ढकः ।।३९।।

34. c)—तस्मादिति B M; d)—इति om Y* A5

35. om Y*; 1)—आह च G6 R2 3; a)—निवृत्तका° A6; कर्मरा° G6 R2 3 B M; c)—संन्यासाधि°B M; d)—स्यादितरे B M; d)—°पराः B M; इति om A5

36. om Y*; 1)—चाधि° G6 R4; युक्तः R4; 2)—पुनरव्रती A1 2 3 5 R1; वाव्रती om X2* A3; वानग्निको for वास्नात° . . . °ग्निको A1 2 3; वास्नातको om G6 R1 4; साग्निको वानग्निको R1; साग्निकोऽनग्निको R4

37. om Y*; 1)—आह om A5 6; 2)—व्रतिकोऽव्रति° A5 R4; वाव्रतिको om G6 R2 3; स्नातकोऽस्ना° R4; वास्नातको om G6 R2 3; आवसथ्यनावसथी वा—om R4, R3 reads साग्निकोऽनग्निको वा, G6 reads साग्निरनग्निको वा, B M read साग्निको वानग्निको वा

38. यदुक्तम् A5; °रुक्तः A1 2 R1; वृद्धो . . . °श्रयेत् om R4; इत्यादि X2* B M

39. om Y*; 1)—तथाह A1 2 R1 3 4 M; b)—°र्षिकाम् G6; c)—दशवर्षां A1 5 6 R1 4; d)—पण्डकः R4

भिक्षार्थं गमनं यस्य विण्मूत्रकरणाय च ।
योजनान्न परं याति यः सदा पङ्गुरेव सः ।।४०।।
तिष्ठतो व्रजतो वापि यस्य चक्षुर्न दूरगम् ।
चतुर्युगाद्धयं मुक्त्वा परिव्राट् सोऽन्ध उच्यते ।।४१।।
हिताहितं मनोरामं वचः शोकावहं च यत् ।
श्रुत्वा यो न शृणोतीव बधिरः परिकीर्तितः इति ।।४२।।

न चान्धस्य पारिव्राज्येऽधिकारः

दृष्टिपूतं न्यसेत्पादम् । [MDh 6.46]

इति धर्मविधानात् ।।४३।। नापि पङ्गोः कुष्ठिनो वा[1]

पर्यटन्पुण्यतीर्थानि देवतायतनानि च ।
अध्वास्य सूर्यनिर्दिष्टः कीटवच्च महीं चरेत् ।।

इत्यादिधर्मविधानात्[2] ।।४४।। ब्रह्मचर्यविधानान्न षण्ढस्य पारिव्राज्यम्[1] । ब्रह्मचर्यं हि मैथुनवर्जनम्[2] । न हि षण्ढस्य मैथुनवर्जनमस्ति तस्य स्थाणुकल्पस्य मैथुने प्राप्त्यभावात्[3] । प्राप्तस्य हि वर्जनं व्रतम्[4] ।।४५।। तस्मादृणश्रुतिरविरक्तविषया[1] । विरक्तस्य तु पारिव्राज्यमेव[2] ।।४६।। तथा च **बृहस्पतिः**[1] ।

प्रव्रजेदकृतोद्वाहः परं वैराग्यमाश्रितः इति ।।४७।।

40. om Y*

41. om Y*

42. om Y*

43. Before न add अजितस्य A4 G2; °व्राज्याधि° R2 3 4 B M; पदं न्यसेत् A4; पदम् G2; धर्म° om Y*

44. om Y*; 1)—कुष्ठस्य A3 5; c)—अध्यास्य B M; सूर्यो A1 2 R1; d)—कटिवच्च B M; 2)—इति धर्म° X2* B M; इति इत्यादि° A1 2 R1

45. 1)—ब्रह्मचर्यविधानान् om G6; पारिव्राज्यम् om A3, °ज्यमस्ति A4; 2)— °वर्जम् X2* A5 6; 3)—न . . . °मस्ति om G6; °वर्जमस्ति R4; तस्य om A5; मैथुनप्रा° Y* G6; 4)—प्राप्तस्यैव वर्जनं X2* B M; प्राप्तस्य वर्जनं Y* A3; वर्जनं हि Y* A3; ब्रह्मचर्यव्रतं A5; वृतं R2 3 4; व्रतं भवति Y* A1 2 3 R1

46. 2)—तु om A4; एव om A4 R4; here Y* inserts 2.7–12

47. om Y*; b)—इति om A5

आह **क्रतुः**[1] ।

ब्रह्मचारी गृहस्थो वा मृतदारो वनेचरः ।
ज्ञात्वा सम्यक्परं ब्रह्म त्यक्त्वा सङ्गान्परिव्रजेत् इति ॥४८॥

आह **शङ्खः**[1] ।

सर्वसङ्गनिवृत्तात्मा ब्रह्मचार्यपि सुव्रतः ।
एतैर्गुणैरुपेतश्चेद् गृहस्थो वा प्रजापतेः ॥४९॥
कृत्वेष्टिं विधिवद्दत्त्वा सर्ववेदसदक्षिणाम् ।
आत्मन्यग्नीन्समारोप्य द्विजो ब्रह्माश्रमी भवेत् इति ॥५०॥

आह **दत्तात्रेयः**[1] ।

त्रिदण्डं वैष्णवं लिङ्गं विप्राणां मुक्तिसाधनम् ।
निर्वाणं सर्वधर्माणामिति वेदानुशासनम् ।
गृहवासविरक्तानां पुरा प्रोक्तं स्वयंभुवा इति ॥५१॥

उपकुर्वाणस्य ब्रह्मचारिणश्चतुर्ष्वाश्रमेषु इच्छाविकल्प इत्याचार्याः ॥५२॥

तथा च **वसिष्ठः**[1] ।

चत्वार आश्रमाः ब्रह्मचारिगृहस्थवानप्रस्थपरिव्राजकाः[2] । तेषां वेदमधीत्य वेदौ वा वेदान्वाचीर्णब्रह्मचर्यो यमिच्छेत्तमावसेदिति[3] ॥५३॥ [VaDh 7.1–3]

आह चा**पस्तम्बः**[1] ।

बुद्ध्वा कर्माणि यत्कामयेत तदारभेतेति[2] ॥५४॥ [ApDh 2.21.5]

48. a)—वेत्यादि X2* B M; b–d)—om X2* B M; d)—इति om A5; here Y* inserts 2.18

49. om Y*; 1)—आह om X2* B M; a)—°निवृत्तो वेत्यादि X2* B M; b–d)—om X2* B M

50. om Y* X2* B M; c)—°ग्निं A3; d)—इति om A5

51. om Y* [आह . . . °नुशासनम् Y* inserts after 2.63]; 1)—आह om X2* A3 B M; a)—वैणवं A1 2; वैणवी R1; लिङ्गमित्यादि X2*; b–d)—om X2*; e)—न गृहस्थोद्विर° A1 2 R1

52. om Y*; °चारिणश्च चतु° A1 5 R1; °तुर्थाश्रमेषु A1 2; °श्रमेष्वित्यादि विकल्प G6; इच्छया विकल्प R2 3 B M

53. Y* inserts after 2.63; 1)—चाह Y*; 2)—ब्रह्मचारी A1 2 3 G1 2 3; गृहस्थो वानप्रस्थः परिव्राजकः G1 2 3; °व्राजकानां R4; 3)—वेदौ वेदान्वा A1 2 3 4 G1 2 R1 B M; °च्छेत्तं वसेदिति G6 R2 4; यमिच्छे° . . . [55] °गुरुशुश्रूषया om A3

54. Y* inserts after 2.63; 1)—आहापस्तम्बः Y* X2* B M; 2)—कामयते X2*

आह भगवान्**व्यासः**[1] ।

गुरुशुश्रूषया विद्यां संप्राप्य विधिवद् द्विजः ।
स्नायीत गुर्वनुज्ञातो दत्त्वास्मै दक्षिणां हि गाम् ॥५५॥
नैष्ठिकं वा मुनेर्वापि पारिव्राज्यकमेव वा ।
यमिच्छेदाश्रमं विप्रो वसेत्तत्रैव संयतः इति ॥५६॥

आह **गौतमः**[1] ।

तस्याश्रमविकल्पमेके ब्रुवत इति[2] ॥५७॥ [GDh 3.1]

यदुक्तम् ऋणानि त्रीण्यपाकृत्येति तदपि श्रुतिस्मृतिभ्यां विरक्तस्य ब्रह्म-चर्यादेव पारिव्राज्यं विदधतीभ्यां व्यवस्थाप्यमानं रागवति पुरुष एवाव-तिष्ठते प्राप्तर्णापकरणार्थं वा ॥५८॥

तस्माद्विरक्तस्य ब्रह्मचर्याद् गृहाद्वनाद्वा पारिव्राज्यं सिद्धम् ॥५९॥ तथा च **बृहस्पतिः**[1] ।

परमात्मनि यो रक्तो विरक्तोऽपरमात्मनि ।
सर्वैषणाविनिर्मुक्तः स भैक्षं भोक्तुमर्हति ॥६०॥

आतुरस्यापि पारिव्राज्यम**ङ्गिरसो**क्तम्[1] ।

वनवासात्परिश्रान्तः प्रव्रजेद्विधिपूर्वकम् ।

55. 1)—Y* inserts after 2.63; आह च A5; भगवान् om Y*; a–d)—om Y*; a)—विद्याः G6 R3 B M; d)—दत्त्वातो R4

56. Y* inserts after 2.63; a)—मुनिं Y*; b)—परिव्राजकमेव Y*; c–d)—कामं विप्रो वसेत्तत्रैव संयम इति A4 G1 2; कामं विप्रो वसेत्तत्र यत्रैव च सुसंयत इति G3; इति om A5

57. om Y*; 2)—°कल्पमेते A5

58. om Y*; एतदपि A3; ब्रह्मचर्यादेव . . . [59] °रक्तस्य om G6; विदधति । आभ्यां A1 2 R2 3 4; °धतीभ्यामाभ्यां B M;

59. om Y*; °चर्याद्वा B M; °चर्यादेव G6 R2 3; गृहाद्वा वनाद्वा G6 R2 3; गृहस्थाद्वा वनाद्ववा A1 2 R1; गृहस्थाद्वनाद्वा R4

60. om Y*; b)—विरक्तो om G6; d)—add इति B M

व्याध्याविष्टो विरक्तो वा ब्रह्मवित्संन्यसेद् द्विजः ॥६१॥
प्रव्रजेद्ब्रह्मचर्याच्च प्रव्रजेच्च गृहादपि ।
वनाद्वा प्रव्रजेद्विद्वानातुरो वाथ दुःखितः ॥६२॥
उत्पन्ने संकटे घोरे चोरव्याघ्रादिगोचरे ।
भयभीतस्य संन्यासमङ्गिरा मुनिरब्रवीत् ॥६३॥

तथा च **शातातपः**[1] ।

संन्यस्तमिति यो ब्रूयात्प्राणैः कण्ठगतैरपि ।
स तु क्रतुसहस्रेण तुल्यं फलमवाप्नुयात् ॥६४॥

आह **दत्तात्रेयः**[1] ।

मुखजानामयं धर्मो विष्णोर्यल्लिङ्गधारणम् ।
बाहुजातोरुजातानामयं धर्मो न विद्यते ॥६५॥

इति यतिधर्मसमुच्चये पारिव्राज्याधिकारिदशानिरूपणं नाम द्वितीयं पर्व ॥६६॥

61. 1)—आहाङ्गिराः for आतु° . . . °सोक्तम् Y*; आतुरस्य पारि° A6; संन्यास अङ्गिरसोक्तः G6 R2 3 B M; a)—पवित्रान्तः A5; b)—परिव्र° R2 3; c)—व्याधिवि° A3 G3; d)—द्विज इति Y*; hereY* inserts 2.26–27

62. om A4 G1 2; d)—वा सुदुःखितः A1 2 R1

63. b)—°गोचरः G6; d)—here Y* inserts 2.51(1, a–d) and 2.53–56

64. 1)—आह शाता° Y*; तथा च om B M; b)—कण्ठस्थप्राणवानपि G6 R2 3 B M [कर्णस्थ° G6]; c)—स च G1 2 3; शतक्र° R4; सकृत्क्र° A1 2 R1; d)—तत्तुल्यं G3; फलमश्नुयात् G3; °यादिति Y* A3

65. 1)—After दत्तात्रेयः A3 M+ add द्विविधः खलु परिव्राट् ज्ञानाभ्यासशीलो [°सपरो M+] योगमारुरुक्षुरिति [cf. Ch 3.29]; b)—यद्विष्णोर्लि° Y* G6 R2 3 B M; विष्णो° . . . धर्मो om R4; d)—नायं धर्मो विधीयते Y* A3 R2; तद्दर्धो B M; न हि R3 B M; add इति A4 G2 3 6 R2 4; after विद्यते add पारिव्राज्यमातुरविरक्तविषयम् A3 A4 G2 [°ज्यमतिरिक्त° A3]

66. इति [A3 adds भगवता] यादवप्रकाशेन विरचिते A3 G1; °च्चये कर्तृदशा नाम Y*; नाम om X2*

तृतीयं पर्व

लिङ्गनिरूपणम्

अथ लिङ्गं निरूप्यते[1] । तच्च द्विविधं बाह्यं शारीरं च[2] । तत्र शारीरं यज्ञोपवीतं मुण्डत्वं शिखामात्रधारणं वेति[3] । बाह्यं दण्डकमण्डलुप्रभृति[4] । बाह्यं लिङ्गं मात्रा इत्युच्यते[5] ॥१॥

तत्र शारीरमुच्यते[1] । आह **वसिष्ठः**[2] ।

यज्ञोपवीत्युदकमण्डलुहस्त इति[3] । [VaDh 10.31]
मुण्डोऽमदोऽक्रोधोऽपरिग्रह इति च[4] ॥२॥ [VaDh 10.6]

आह **यमः**[1] ।

नित्यं स्थण्डिलशायी स्यादनित्यां वसतिं वसेत् ।
अरण्यनित्यो मुण्डः स्यान्मनसा ज्ञानमभ्यसेत् इति ॥३॥

आह **पैठीनसिः**[1] ।

अप्रतिष्ठो मुनिर्मुण्डो निर्ममो निष्परिग्रहः इति ॥४॥

आह **बोधायनः**[1] ।

अरण्यं गत्वा शिखी मुण्डो वेति[2] ॥५॥ [BDh 2.11.17–18]

1. 1)—अथ यतिलि° A4 G2; अथेतिलि° G1; 2)—बाह्यं add च R4; शारीरं बाह्यं च Y* A3; 3)—तत्र om Y* A3; यज्ञोपवीतं om R4; चेति G6 R4; 4)—बाह्यं add लिङ्गं R2 B M; 5)—बाह्यं om X2*; बाह्यमेव A1 2 3 R1; बाह्यलि° G1; मात्रा उच्यते A4 G1 2; उच्यते om A5; इत्युच्यन्ते G6 R4

2. 1)—om X2*; 3)—°दककमण्ड° Y* R2 3 4 B M; 3–4)—°हस्तो मुण्डो Y*; 4)—मुण्डोऽममो Y* R2 3 4; क्रोधो om Y* X2*; च om Y*

3. om Y*; c)—अरण्ये नित्यमु° M+; स्यान् om G6; d)—इति om X2* A5 B M

4. om Y*; b)—इति om A5

5. 2)—मुण्डी A1 2 5 R1

आह **क्रतु:**[1] ।

स्तुत्वा हंसं त्रिभिः सूक्तैर्मनो वैष्णवपौरुषैः ।
मुण्डः शिखी वा काषायी पात्री दण्डी गृहाद्व्रजेत् ॥६॥

आह **सुमन्तु:**[1] ।

मुनिर्मुण्डोऽपरिग्रह इति[2] ॥७॥

आह **गौतम:**[1] ।

मुण्डः शिखी वेति[2] ॥८॥ [GDh 3.21]

तस्मान्मौण्ड्यं शिखा वेति विकल्पः[1] । यज्ञोपवीतं तु सर्वेषां नित्यमेव[2] ॥९॥ तथा**त्रि:** पारिव्राज्यमेवाधिकृत्याह[1] ।

ब्रह्मसूत्रं त्रिदैवत्यं ब्रह्मविष्णुशिवात्मकम् ।
परित्यजन्ति विप्रा ये मोहात्तर्कोपजीविनः ।
स्वर्गापवर्गमार्गाभ्यां प्रच्युतास्ते न संशयः इति ॥१०॥

आहो**शना:**[1] ।

ब्रह्मसूत्रपरित्यागाद्ब्रह्मचारी गृही वनी ।
परिव्राट् चापि पतति तस्मात्तन्न परित्यजेत् इति ॥११॥

अथ बाह्यलिङ्गमुच्यते[1] । आह **दक्ष:**[2] ।

मेखलाजिनदण्डाद्यैर्ब्रह्मचारीति लक्ष्यते ।
गृहस्थो यष्टिवेदाद्यैर्नखरोमैर्वनाश्रमी ।
त्रिदण्डेन यतिश्चेति लक्षणानि पृथक्पृथक् ॥१२॥

6. om A3; a–b)—om Y*; a)—कृत्वा A1 2 R1; स्नात्वा R4; सूक्तैः om R2; d)—add इति Y* A1 2 R1

7. om Y* A3

8. om A3; 1)—आह om G6 R3 4

9. om A3; 1)—शिखी वेति G6 R4; शिखेति A5

10. om A3; 1)—तथा चात्रिः A6; तथाहात्रिः A5; परिव्राजकमधिकृत्यैवात्रिराह A1 2 R1; पारिव्राज्यमधिकृत्यात्रिराह Y*; परिव्राजकमेवा° B M; b)—°वात्मिकम् A6 R4; c)—ये विप्रा Y* A 5 R4; d)—°त्तर्कावलम्बिनः G1

11. om A3; 1)—आह om X2*; c)—वापि B M; च A2 R1; पतितः R4; d)—°त्यजेत् add आलोकनेन तेषां तु शुध्यते भानुदर्शनात् M+ [cf. 7.72]; इति om G6

12. om A3; 1–2)—बाह्यलिङ्गं [G6 adds तु] दक्षः X2* B M; a–d)—om Y*; c)—यष्टिदेवा° A5; d)—°रोमाद्वना° X2* B M; e–f)—यतिलक्षणानि G1 2; add इति Y*

आह **बृहस्पतिः**[1] ।

एवं संन्यसनं कृत्वा त्रिदण्डं सपवित्रकम् ।
केशसंमितमादाय पात्रं करकमेव च इति ॥१३॥

आहतुः **शङ्खलिखितौ**[1] ।

सर्वारम्भानुत्सृज्य त्रिदण्डकुण्डिकापक्ष्मपवित्रप्रयोजनापेक्षी मुण्डः काषायवासा भैक्षवृत्तिरिति[2] ॥१४॥

आहा**ङ्गिराः**[1] ।

यतेर्लिङ्गं प्रवक्ष्यामि येनासौ लक्ष्यते यतिः ।
ब्रह्मसूत्रं त्रिदण्डं च वस्त्रं जन्तुनिवारणम् ॥१५॥
शिक्यं पात्रं बृसी चैव कौपीनं कटिवेष्टनम् ।
यस्यैतद्विद्यते लिङ्गं स यतिर्नेतरो यतिः इति ॥१६॥

बृसी कूर्मासनम्[1] । आह **देवलः**[2] ।

काषायमुण्डत्रिदण्डकमण्डलुपात्रपवित्रपादुकासनकन्था मात्रा इति[3] ॥१७॥

आह **गालवः**[1] ।

अथ परिव्राजको लिङ्गी मुण्डः शिखी वा नित्यं यज्ञोपवीती काषायकर्पटः कौपीनाच्छादनार्थं वासो बिभृयान्नोत्तरीयं त्रिदण्डं जलपवित्रं कमण्डलुं कपालं कन्थां चेति[2] ॥१८॥

13. om Y* A3; 1)—आह om X2* B M; अथ A5; a)—संन्यासनंA1 2 R1; संन्यासं A5; c)—केश° . . . [23] सपवित्रकम् lacuna in A1 2 (but A1 inserts folio containing this section written in a second hand); शिक्यसंमि° R4; d)—सूत्रं A5 R1 B M

14. om A3; 1)—om Y*; आहतुः om X2* B M; 2)—सर्वार° . . . पक्ष्म° om Y*; एवं पवि° A4; एवं सपवि° G1 2 3; °क्ष्मपात्रपवित्र° B M; °पवित्रपात्रप्र° Y* A1; °क्ष्मजलपवि° A6

15. om A3; 1)—अङ्गिराः X2* A1 B M; c)—पवित्रं च M+

16. om A3; a)—बृसीं A1 5 G6 R1 3 M; d)—इति om Y* A6

17. om A3; 1)—om X2* B M; 2–3)—om Y*; आह om X2* B M; काषायी मुण्डी त्रिदण्डी R4; °त्रिदण्ड° om R1; °पवित्र° om R1

18. om A3; 1)—आह om X2* A1 B M; 2)—मुण्डी A1; शिखी . . . °नार्थं om R4; पवित्रोपवीती G3; °च्छादनं A5; °पवित्रमुपवीतं कम° B M; °पवित्रं सूत्रं कम° A6; कपालं om A1 R1; कन्धाश्चेति G1

आह **लिखितः**[1] ।

काषायमेव कार्पासं वासः कन्थां च धारयेत् ।
वल्कलं वाजिनं वापि कौशं शणमयं तु वा ॥१९॥
शिक्यं सकवचं पात्रं त्रिविष्टब्धेन संयुतम् ।
बद्धं जलपवित्रेण त्रिदण्डं वर्तुलासनम् ॥२०॥
शिखां यज्ञोपवीतं च शौचार्थमपि कुण्डिकाम् ।
सर्वदा धारयेद्गृच्छन्नासीनो वापि वा शुचिः इति ॥२१॥

आह **यमः**[1] ।

सूची पिप्पलकं चैव त्रिविष्टब्धमुपानहौ ।
कुण्डिका रज्जुशिक्यं च भैक्षभाजनमासनम् ।
कन्थां कर्पटकं दण्डं लघुमात्रापरिग्रहः इति ॥२२॥

आहो**शनाः**[1] ।

पात्रं तत्कवचं शिक्यं त्रिदण्डं सपवित्रकम् ।
आसनं कटिसूत्रं च कौपीनं कटिवेष्टनम् ।
यज्ञोपवीतं कन्थां च संगृह्यान्यत्परित्यजेत् इति॥२३॥

आह **क्रतुः**[1] ।

विंशतिं धारयेन्मात्रा दश वा पञ्च नित्यशः ।
कन्था सूच्यजिनं छत्रं पवित्रं कुण्डिकासनम् ॥२४॥
पात्रं शिक्याक्षसूत्राणि मृत्खनित्रमुपानहौ ।

19. om A3; 1)—आह om X2*A1BM; c)—चाजिनं B M; d)—कौशं वा A6; कौशेयं R4

20. om A3; a)—च कवचं Y* R1; स° om A5; c–d)—om G3

21. om A3; a–b)—om G3; c)—सर्वधा X2* A1 M; d)—°सीनोऽपिवा R1 G3; चाशुचिः A6; इति om R1

22. om A3; 1)—आह om X2* B M; a)—सूची च Y* R1 3; पिप्पलीकूर्चं त्रि° Y* R1; सूत्रं for चैव M+; e)—कन्थां sic in all mss; पवित्रकं A5 6 R4

23. om A3; 1)—आह om X2* B M; b)—त्रि° om G1; जलपवित्रकम् Y*; f)—इति om A1 2

24. 1)—आह om X2*; a)—विंशतिर्धार° A4 G2; मात्रान्दश all mss except A4 6 [M ed. notes मात्रानित्येव सर्वत्र पाठः]; d)—पवित्रं om G6

गुह्याच्छादस्त्रिपादी च पादुके दण्डपक्ष्मणी ।
योगपट्टो बहिर्वासो मात्राख्या विंशतिः स्मृताः ।।२५।।

आसां विंशतिमात्राणां पञ्चमात्रा नित्याः[1] । ताश्च उपवीतत्रिदण्डपवित्रपात्रकौपीनकटिवस्त्राख्याः[2] ।।२६।। तथा **विष्णुः**[1] ।

उपवीतं त्रिदण्डं च पात्रं जलपवित्रकम् ।
कौपीनं कटिवस्त्रं च न त्याज्यं यावदायुषम् इति ।।२७।।

पात्रग्रहणादेव तदङ्गभूतशिक्यकवचत्रिविष्टब्धानामपि ग्रहणमेव[1] । दशमात्रास्तु याः स्मृत्युक्ताः सूची पिप्पलकं चेत्यादि[2] । तत्र सूचीपिप्पलयोरेकीकरणेन दशत्वम्[3] । पिप्पलं सूत्रम्[4] ।।२८।।

द्विधाकारः परिव्राट्[1] । ज्ञानाभ्यासशीलो योगमारुरुक्षुरेकः अपरस्तु आरूढयोगस्तत्त्वदर्शी अव्यक्तलिङ्गोऽव्यक्ताचारोऽनुन्मत्त उन्मत्तवदाचरन्[2] ।।२९।।

तथा च **क्रतुना** द्वैविध्यं दर्शितम्[1] ।

पूर्वाह्णे विचरेद्योगी सम्यग्ज्ञानी तु पश्चिमे इति ।।३०।।

तत्र सम्यग्ज्ञानमभिप्रेत्य **क्रतु**रेवाह[1] ।

शीलं वृत्तं श्रुतं ज्ञानं वैराग्यं धर्मलक्षणम् ।

25. d)—°पक्षिणी R4; e)—योगपट्ट A6

26. 1)—पञ्चमात्रा तु नित्यशः A1 2 R1 3 M+ [but corrected in R3]; नित्यं धार्याः G6 R2 3 B M; °मात्रं च नित्यदा R4; 2)—ताः ततश्च G1; उपवीतत्रि° om Y* A3; उपवीतं त्रिदण्डं च जलपवि° R4; °पात्र° om A1 2 3 G6 R2 3 B M; °कौपीन° om A2 R4; °सूत्राख्याः A1 2 R1 4

27. 1)—तथा च A5 R4; आह वि° Y*; c)—कटिसूत्रं A1 2 6 G6 R3 4; कटिकूर्चं M+; c–d)—चात्याज्यं R2; d)—त्यजेद्या° A2; इति om X2* B M

28. 1)—om G6 R4; °हणात् शिक्य° A3; तदङ्गानामपि पञ्चमात्रधारणमवश्यं कर्तव्यमेव Y* [पञ्चमात्राणां धारणमव° A4]; °ब्धादीनामपि A1 2; 1–2)—ग्रहणम् । एवं दश° R2 3 B M; 2–4)—om Y*; 2)—पिप्पलकेत्यादि X2* B M; 3)—तत्र om A5; °लकयोरे° A6 B M; 4)—सूत्राणीति A3

29. om Y*; 1)—द्विधा च X2* B M; 2)—योगाभ्या° A1 2 R1 [A1 corrected sh to योगा°]; अपरः । आरू° A1 2 R1; अपरस्तत्त्व° R2; °रूढयोगत्वादव्यक्त° A1 2 G6 R1 3; °चारोऽनुन्मत्तवदा° G6

30. om Y*; 1)—कृतम् X2* A6

ऐश्वर्यं विद्यते यस्य मात्राभिस्तस्य किं फलम् ॥३१॥
ध्यानं शौचं तपः पूजां प्राणायामजपस्तुतीः ।
संध्यां भिक्षामुपस्थानं कुर्यादामरणान्तिकम् इति ॥३२॥

पञ्च नित्यश इति विधानात् भिक्षाविधानाच्च सम्यग्ज्ञानिनामपि पञ्चमात्राधारणमवश्यं कर्तव्यमेव ॥३३॥

अथैषामुपवीतादीनां लक्षणमुच्यते[1]। तत्र तावद्यज्ञोपवीतलक्षणम्[2] ॥३४॥ पारिव्राज्यमेवाधिकृत्य **दत्तात्रेयात्री** चाहतुः[1] ।

तन्तुत्रयमधोवृत्तं पुनश्चोर्ध्वं त्रिवृत्त्रिवृत् ।
कार्पासं तान्तवं कार्यं तथैकं चोत्तरीयकम् ॥३५॥
अधोवृत्तैस्त्रिभिः सूत्रैस्त्रिभिरूर्ध्वं त्रिवृत्कृतम् ।
ब्रह्मसूत्रं स्मृतं ब्राह्मं कार्पासं नवतान्तवम् ॥३६॥
संग्रहो नवसूत्रस्य द्विजानां मुक्तिसाधनम् ।
विना तेन भवेत्सद्यः सर्वधर्मबहिष्कृतः इति ॥३७॥

दण्डलक्षणमुच्यते[1] । **कपिल** आह[2] ।

अङ्गुलिपरिमाणमृजुं नासायतं वैणवं दण्डं दण्डान्वा धारयेदात्मसंमितं वा[3] ॥३८॥ अथाप्युदाहरन्ति[1] ।

31. om Y*; 1)—ततः G6 R3 4

32. om Y*; b)—प्रणायामं A1 2 3 5 R1 2; d)—इति om G6

33. om Y*; पञ्चविंशतिविधानात् R4

34. om Y*; 1)—अथैतेषा° X2* B M; °पवीतानां A1 R1

35. 1)—आह क्रतुः for पारि° . . . चाहतुः Y*; आहतुः A1 2 R1; b)—त्रिवृत्तवत् B M; c–d)—om G6; c)—कार्पासता° A1 2 3 4 R2 3 R1; धार्यं Y* A1 2 R1 M+; d)—तथैवं A3 G2

36. a–b)—om G6; त्रिवृत्त्रिवृत् A3 5 R4; वृतं त्रिवृत् A6; °कृतम् add इति Y* A1 2 3 R1; c)—यतो ब्राह्मं R4

37. d)—सर्वकर्म° Y* A1 2 3 R1; इति om Y*, add यज्ञोपवीते द्वे धार्ये वानप्रस्थगृहस्थयोः । यतिश्च ब्रह्मचारी च बिभृयादेकमेव तु ॥ A3 M+

38. 1)—उच्यते om Y* A1 2 R1; 3)—°प्रमाण° B M; °जुमूर्ध्वायतं G6 R2 4 B M; °जुं मूर्धायतं R3 M+; °जुमायतं A5; °यतं च A4; °यतं न G1 2; वैणवदण्डं G1; दण्डं add वा A5; दण्डान्वा om G6

अङ्कुरा यत्र दृश्यन्ते शुभाः पत्रविनिःसृताः ।
तत्तु पर्व विजानीयाच्छेषं मध्यमिहोच्यते ॥३९॥
त्रिपञ्चसप्तनवकं पर्व चैकादशं तथा ।
वर्जितो दण्ड इत्याहुर्यतेः सर्वत्र तस्य च ॥
अधस्तात्पर्वणोऽधस्तादूर्ध्वादूर्ध्वाङ्गुलिद्वयम् ॥४०॥

इदं गृहस्थानामप्यविरुद्धम्[1] । आह **दत्तात्रेयः**[2] ।

त्रिदण्डानङ्गुलिस्थूलान्वैणवान्मूर्धसंमितान् ।
सत्वचानव्रणान्सौम्यान्समसंनतपर्वकान् ॥
षडष्टदशपर्वाणो योनिहीनांश्च निर्व्रणान् ॥४१॥

दक्षः[1] ।

केशमात्रान्समग्रन्थींस्त्रिदण्डान्वैणवान्यतिः ॥४२॥

धारयेदिति[1] । **वृद्धदक्षः**[2] ।

त्रिदण्डं धारयेद्विद्वानूर्ध्वस्थोदपवित्रकम् ॥४३॥

हारीतः[1] ।

त्रिदण्डं पञ्चधा कृत्वा त्रिभागादूर्ध्वमेव च ।
वेष्टयेत्कृष्णगोवालरज्ज्वा तु चतुरङ्गुलम् ॥४४॥
ग्रन्थिधारात्रयोपेतं जलपूतेन चोपरि ।
गृह्णीयाद्दक्षिणे हस्ते गुरुदत्तं तु मन्त्रवत् ॥४५॥

जलपूतं जलपवित्रम्[1] । **वृद्धदक्षः**[2] ।

39. b)—शुभाः om Y*; पत्रशृङ्गविनिः° Y*; c)—तत्र X2* A5 B M; d)—°मिवोच्यते R4

40. a)—त्रिः A5; c)—वर्जितं A1 2 R1; सज्जितं दण्डं M+; d)—after च add एकादशनवद्वित्रिचतुःसप्तादीन्पर्वकान् Y* M+ [°सप्तादिपूर्विका G1; °सप्तादिप° M+], A3 adds this half-verse after 3.41; e)—अधस्त्रिप° R2 3 B M; f)—°लित्रयम् A6

41. 1)—om Y*; इतीदं G6; 2)—आह om Y* X2* B M; b–d)—वैणवा° . . . °व्रणान् om A6; b)—मूर्ध्नि A2 5 G1 3 R4; c)—सत्वक्कान° A4 G1 2 R4

42. 1)—आह दक्षः A1 2 R1; आह वृद्धदक्षः A3; b)—वैष्णवान् A3; °णवान्प्रति A5

43. 1)—om Y* A3 6; 2)—om Y*; b)—°स्थोऽथ पवि° A6 B M; °त्रकमिति A3

44. 1)—आह हारीतः A3

45. c)—°क्षिणहस्ते A5; d)—मन्त्रवित् G1; °वदिति A3

त्रिदण्डाग्रे च मूले च मध्ये सूत्रेण बन्धयेत् ।
अग्राद् द्विभागं हित्वा च तत्रैव चतुरङ्गुलम् ।।४६।।
गोवालदाम्ना बध्नीयादथ वा पञ्चबन्धनम् ।
रज्ज्वैव बन्धनं कुर्यात्पञ्चधा विभजेत्पुनः ।।४७।।

श्रीपाञ्चरात्रे **तत्वसागरसंहितायाम्**[1] ।

त्रिदण्डस्याग्रभागं तु संस्मरेत्परमेष्ठिनम् ।
द्वितीयं पुरुषात्मानं विश्वात्मानं तु मध्यमम् ।।४८।।
तुर्यं निवृत्तिपुरुषं सर्वात्मानं तु पञ्चमम् ।
त्रिदण्डं समुदायेन विष्णुरूपं स्मरेद्यतिः ।।४९।।

हारीतः[1] ।

विष्णुरूपं त्रिदण्डाख्यं सर्वदा धारेद्यतिः ।।५०।।

शौनकः[1] ।

ज्ञानदण्डो भवेद्धस्व आत्मदण्डस्तु मध्यमः ।
विष्णुदण्डस्तु दीर्घः स्यात्त्रिदण्डं धारयेद्यतिः ।।५१।।

प्रचेताः[1] ।

ब्रह्मसूत्रं त्रिदण्डं च शिखावद्बिभृयात्स्वयम् ।
वाहयेदितरेणाथ प्रायश्चित्ती भवेद्यतिः ।।५२।।
पौरुषेणैव सूक्तेन त्रिदण्डं चाभिषेचयेत् ।

46. 1)—om Y*; 2)—om Y* G6 R2 4 [G1 3 insert after 3.56]; a–d)—Y* inserts after 3.56; b)—सूत्रे च A1 2; c)—अग्रद्वि° A2 3; °भागमुत्सृज्य A4 G2 3; d)—तमेव A2 B M

47. Y* inserts after 3.56; a)—गोवालरज्ज्वा G6 R2 3; b)—°यादृश वा A3 5

48. Y* inserts after 3.56; 1)—°सागर° om G6; b)—om A5; परमेष्ठी तु संस्मरेत् Y* [तु om G3]

49. Y* inserts after 3.56; a–b)—om A3 6; om but inserted in margin R3; b)—तु मध्यमम् R4

50. om A6 G6; Y* inserts after 3.56; 1)—om Y* A3 R2 3 4; b)—सर्वधा A3 R4; सर्वथा B M

51. om R4; 1)—आह शौ° A3; d)—त्रिदण्डान् A4; यतिरिति A3

52. 1)—om X2* A6; आह प्र° A3; b)—°याद्यतिः A4; c)—वाहयन्त्वितरे° A5

सप्तभिर्वैष्णवीऋग्भिः प्राणायामशतं चरेत् ॥५३॥
स्नाने चावश्यके चैव भोजने जपकर्मणि ।
स्वाध्याये चापि निद्रायामुप दण्डेन बन्धयेत् ॥५४॥
त्रिदण्डधारणं चैकं वैणवं च तथा यतिः ।
कौपीनकटिवस्त्रादिधारणार्थं सदा वहेत् ॥५५॥
कुर्यान्मूत्रपुरीषे चेत्त्रिदण्डसहितो यतिः ।
शुद्ध्यर्थं सह दण्डेन चरेदाचमनक्रियाम् ॥५६॥

आह **वृद्धजाबालिः**[1] ।

अपां पूर्णाञ्जलिं निनीय दण्डं दण्डान्वा गृहीत्वेत्यादि[2] ॥५७॥

आह **बोधायनः**[1] ।

न चात ऊर्ध्वं शुक्लमम्बरं बिभृयात्[2] । एकदण्डी त्रिदण्डी वेति[3] ॥५८॥ [BDh 2.17.44—18.1]

आह **याज्ञवल्क्यः**[1] ।

एको वा तादृशो दण्डो गोवालरहितो भवेत् इति ॥५९॥

तस्माद्दण्डविकल्पः[1] । यत्नगौरवाद्भूयसीषु दृष्टत्वाच्च ऐकदण्ड्यात्त्रैदण्ड्यमेव शस्तम्[2] ॥६०॥ तथाह भगवान्**व्यासः**[1] ।

53. b)—त्रिदण्डमभि° Y* A1 2 R1 B M; c)—वैष्णवीभिः सप्तर्भिः X2*; वैष्णवै ऋग्भिः A3; वैष्णवै गृह्यात् A4 G2 3; वैष्णवैर्ग्राह्यात् G1

54. a)—d)—उप दण्डेनैव A5; योजयेत् M+; A1 in margin उपदण्डबन्धनम्

55. a–b)—om B M; b)—त्रिशिखं for च तथा Y* A5 [also A1 in margin]; विधि for यतिः A3; c)—कौपीनं A5 G1 2; °कटिसूत्रादि Y* X2* A3 M+; °कटिवस्त्राणि A6

56. a)—°पुरीषौ G2 3; च for चेत् A1 2 3 5 6 G1 R1 4; d)—कुर्यादाच° A1 2 R1 B M; add इति A3; here Y* adds 3.46–50

57. om Y*; 1)—आह वृद्ध° om X2*; °जाबालः A5

58. om Y*; 1)—आह om X2* B M; 2)—शुक्लाम्बरं R3 4 G6 B M

59. 1)—Before आह Y* adds दण्डस्य क्वचिद्विकल्पो [°कल्पं A4] दृश्यते । एकस्त्रयो वेति; आह om Y* X2* B M ; तथा चाह A3; a)—को वादृशो A4 G2; b)—°सहितो A1 2 3 R1 M+; इति om R2

60. 1)—om Y* A6; add एकस्त्रयो वेति A3; 2)—°सीषु स्मृतिषूक्तत्वा° Y* G6 R2 B M; °सीष्वपि A6; °सीषु add स्मृतिषु A3 [R3 also in margin]; °त्वाच्चेति A5; °त्वादैक° Y*; एकदण्डात्त्रिदण्डमेव A5 G6 R2 3 B M; °दण्ड्यं प्रशस्तम् Y*; प्रशस्तम् A3

त्रिदण्डधारणं शस्तं तथैकान्तनिषेवणम् ।
लघ्वाहारमनायासो यतीनां मुक्तिसाधनम् इति ॥६१॥

दण्डमात्राभेदादितरमात्राः संध्यावन्दनादयश्च धर्मा न भिद्यन्ते[1] । क्वचित्त्रिदण्डनाशे त्वेकदण्डो विधीयते[2] ॥६२॥ **अत्रिजाबालाव**ाहतुः[1] ।

नष्टे जलपवित्रे वा त्रिदण्डे वा प्रमादतः ।
गृह्णीयाद्वैणवं चैकं पालाशं वापि मध्यमम् ॥६३॥
ब्रह्मपत्रमभावेऽपि कुशस्तम्भमथापि वा ।
गृहीत्वा विचरेत्तावद्यावदन्यं न लभ्यते इति ॥६४॥

आह **हारीतः**[1] ।

नष्टे जलपवित्रे वा त्रिदण्डे वा प्रमादतः ।
एकं तु वैणवं दण्डं पालाशं मध्यमं तु वा ।
गृहीत्वा विचरेत्तावद्यावल्लब्धं त्रिदण्डकम् ॥६५॥
यत्नेनान्वेषयेन्नित्यमप्रमत्तः समाहितः ।
लब्धे त्रिदण्डे गृह्णीयाज्जलपूतमथोपरि इति ॥६६॥

आह **मेधातिथिः**[1] ।

यावन्न स्युस्त्रयो दण्डास्तावदेकेन पर्यटेत् ।

61. 1)—तथाह om Y* X2*B M; भगवान् om Y* A6

62. 1)—°मात्रस्य भे° Y* A3 G6 R2 3; °मात्रभे° A1 2 5 R1 B M [°मात्राभे° only A6 R4]; न om G1; भिद्यन्ते add इतरधर्मा उभयोरपि समानाः Y* [A1 also in margin]; 2)—क्वचिच्च दण्ड° A4 G1 3; °नाशेऽप्येक° Y*; त्वेकं दण्डं A5 R3 4; त्वेकदण्डं A6 G6; °दण्डोऽपि वि° B M

63. 1)—अत्रात्रि° A2; अत्रिजाबालौ om R2; °जाबाली A4 R3 4 B M; °जाबालिः G6; आहतुः om X2* B M [M cd. comments अत्रिबोधायनौ इति च अत्रिजाबालौ इति च पाठभेदः]; a)—च for वा R4; c)—वैष्णवं G6; त्वेकं Y* X2* B M; दण्डं for चैकं A6

64. a)—ब्राह्म° B M; °सत्रम° G1; °पवित्रमभा° A5; पि om A5; c)—लब्ध्वा चैव [वै A3] व्रजेत्ता° Y* A3; d)—यावल्लभ्येत्त्रिदण्डकम् A5; °वद्दण्डं G1; विद्यते G6; इति om A1 2 R1

65. om Y*; 1)—आह om X2* B M; a–d)—नष्टे जलपवित्रे वेत्यादि पालाशं मध्यमं वेत्यन्तं X2* B M; d)—बैल्वमेव वा A5; e–f)—°रेद्यावत्तावल्लभ्येत्त्रि° A5; लभ्यं A1 2 R1 3 4

66. om Y*; c)—बिभृयाज्ज° X2* B M; d)—इति om A6

तत्रापि वस्त्रमासज्य त्वग्रदेशेऽम्बुशुद्धये इति ।।६७।।

जमदग्निः[1] ।

त्रिदण्डे न तु बध्नीयात्कौपीनं कटिवेष्टनम् ।
यो मोहाद्बन्धनं कुर्यात्त्रिदण्डमवमन्यते ।।६८।।
त्रिदण्डमन्यदण्डेन संगतं चेत्प्रमादतः ।
प्रक्षाल्य मृज्जलैर्भिक्षुः प्राणायामत्रयं चरेत् ।।६९।।

कलौ युगे कुण्डिका न धार्या[1] । तथा च **देवलः**[2] ।

द्वापरादियुगे चैव पात्रभोजी यतिर्भवेत् ।
कलौ स्वपात्रे नैवाद्याद्धारयेन्न तु कुण्डिकाम् ।।७०।।

जलपवित्रलक्षणं **मेधातिथिर**ाह[1] ।

विकेशं सितमस्पृष्टमुभयं द्वादशाङ्गुलम् ।

अस्पृष्टमनुपयुक्तमित्यर्थः[2] ।

द्विगुणं त्रिगुणं वापि सर्वतोऽष्टाङ्गुलं तथा ।।७१।।
प्रादेशमात्रं वा सूक्ष्मं कार्पासकृतमव्रणम् ।
चण्डालाद्यकृतं चैव विद्याज्जलपवित्रकम् ।।७२।।

67. 1)—आह om Y* X2* B M; a)—त्रिदण्डास्ता° A2; c)—°सज्यादग्र° M+; d)—°सज्य अग्र° A6; °देशे तु सुद्धये Y* X2* B M

68. 1)—आह जम° A3; d)—M ed. comments इतरधर्मा उभयोस्समाना इति क्वचिदधिकपाठः [cf. 3.62n]

69. om X2* A5 6 B M [cf. 3.76n]; d)—चरेदिति A3

70. om Y* G6 R2 B M; A3 inserts after 3.73 [cf. 3.76n]; 2)—तथा च om R3 4; a)—°युगेष्वेव R4; b)—भवेद्यतिः A3; c)—नैवेद्यं R3 4; d)—तु om A3 6 R3 4; च for तु A5; कमण्डलुम् A6 R3 4; °कामिति A3

71. 1)—दत्तात्रेयः for मेधातिथिः Y*; आह om Y* X2* B M; b)—°भयद्वा° A1 2 3 4 G1 6 R1; °भया R4; 2)—अस्पृष्टमनवयुक्त° G1

72. om A3; a)—°मात्रो G1; सूक्ष्मका° A4 6 G1 3 6 R3 4; b)—कार्पासैः Y* A5 6; d)—add इति A5

आहा**ङ्गिराः**[1] ।

यतीनां त्रीणि शुक्लानि भवन्त्येतानि नित्यशः ।
यज्ञोपवीतं दन्ताश्च तथा जन्तुनिवारणम् इति ॥७३॥

पात्राण्याहा**त्रिः**[1] ।

मृद्दार्वलाबुनिर्वृत्तं वैणवं तान्तवौपलम् ।
तार्णं पात्रं तथा क्षौमं पात्रं पर्णपुटं तथा ॥७४॥
एतेषामेकमादेयमात्मशक्त्यनुरूपतः ।
लोभात्पात्रान्तरं गृह्णन्प्राणायामान्दशाचरेत् ॥७५॥

आह **क्रतुः**[1] ।

वेणुदारुशिलालाबुतृणपर्णमयानि च ।
मृन्मयं क्षौमपात्राणि गृह्णीयादात्मशक्तितः इति ॥७६॥

मनुः[1]।

अलाबुदारुपात्राणि मृन्मयं वैणवं तु वा ।
एतानि यतिपात्राणि मनुः स्वायंभुवोऽब्रवीत् इति ॥७७॥
[MDh 6.54]

शिक्यलक्षणं **हारीत** आह[1] ।

क्षौमं वा कुशसूत्रं वा सूत्रं कार्पासकं तु वा ।
तैरेव ग्रथितं शिक्यं पद्माकारसमन्वितम् ।

73. om Y*; 1)—om X2* B M; आह om A3; आह चाङ्गिराः A1 2 R1; d)—इति om M; here A3 inserts 2.70; A6 adds जन्तुनिवारणं जलपवित्रम्

74. 1)—पात्राण्याह om Y*; b)—दान्त° G3 R3 4; दान्तमौप° B M; c)—पार्णं for पात्रं A1 5 R1 B M; d)—पत्रपुटं R4

75. om Y*; a–b)—°कमादाय चात्म° X2* B M; °रूपत इति A1 2 R1

76. om Y*; 1)—आह om X2* B M; a)—वैणवं दारु° R4; c)—मृन्मयक्षौ° B M; क्षौमं A6; d)—M ed. comments त्रिदण्डमन्यदण्डेन . . . चरेत् [see 3.69] ॥ इति क्वचित्। अन्यत्र एतत्स्थाने कलौ युगे . . . कमण्डुलुम् [see 3.70]। इतीदं पद्यं दृस्यते

77. 1)—मनुः om Y* X2* A3 6; a–b)—om Y*; b)—वेणुतान्तवम् A5; तथा X2* B M; d)—इति om Y* A1 2 3 R1; M ed. comments कलौ युगे इत्यादिवाक्यमत्रैव स्थितं स्यात्

षड्भिर्वा पञ्चभिर्वापि मुष्टिभिः शिक्यलक्षणम् इति ॥७८॥

आसनलक्षणं स एवाह[1] ।

आसनं वर्तुलं प्रोक्तं सहस्तं दारुजं यतेः ।
शौचार्थमासनार्थं च निर्मितं मुनिभिः पुरा इति ॥७९॥

खनित्रलक्षणं **कपिल** आह[1] ।

चतुरङ्गुलमात्रमृत्तिकाखननपरिग्रहे न दोष इति[2] ॥८०॥

इति यतिधर्मसमुच्चये लिङ्गनिरूपणं नाम तृतीयं पर्व ॥८१॥

78. 1)—शिक्यलक्षणं om R2; °क्षणमुच्यते Y*; तथा शिक्य° A5; °क्षणमाह हारीतः A5 R2 3 B M; आह om Y* G6 R4; b)—कार्पासतन्तु वा A1 2 3 4 G1; f)—इति शिक्यलक्षणम् R2 B M

79. 1)—आसनलक्षणं om G6 R2 3

80. 1)—आह om X2*; आह कपिलः G1; 2)—°मात्रं मृ° A6 R1 2 4; न om G1

81. इति om A2 5 R4; यादवप्रकाशकृतौ यति°B M; लिङ्गं नाम Y*; नाम om G6 R1 2

चतुर्थं पर्व

संन्यासप्रयोगः

अथ प्रयोग उच्यते[1] । अथातः **शौनक**प्रोक्तं संन्यासविधिं व्याख्यास्यामः[2] । तत्र तस्मिन्ननुक्तान्यन्यत्रोक्तान्यपेक्षितानि तत्र तत्र निगद्यन्ते प्रयोगाङ्गानि[3] ॥१॥ तत्र पुरश्चरणमाह **कात्यायनः**[1] ।

कृच्छ्रचतुष्टयं कार्यमनाश्रमिभिः[2] । कृच्छ्रमेकमाश्रमिभिः[3] । एवं संन्यासयोग्यता भवति[4] । द्वादश्यां पौर्णमास्यां वा संकल्प्य वपनं कृत्वा देवश्राद्धं प्रथममृषिश्राद्धं द्वितीयं दिव्यश्राद्धं तृतीयं पित्र्यं चतुर्थं मातृकं पञ्चमं मानुषं षष्ठं भौतिकं सप्तममात्मनश्चाष्टममिति[5] ॥२॥

एवमाह भगवान्**वृद्धवसिष्ठः**[1] । पौर्णमास्यामित्यादि समानम्[2] ॥३॥ आह **शौनकः**[1] ।

पूर्वेद्युर्नान्दीमुखं कृत्वा ब्राह्मणान्भोजयेत्[2] । अथ पुण्याहं स्वस्ति ऋद्धिमिति वाचयित्वा केशश्मश्रुलोमनखानि वापयेदिति[3] ॥४॥

1. 1–2)—Y* reads संन्यासविधिं व्याख्यास्यामः; 2)—शौनकोक्तं A5 6 B M; संन्यास° om A2 R1; 3)—om Y*; before तत्र M+ adds तत्र पुरश्चरणमाह; तत्र तत्र तावदनुक्तान्यपेक्षि° R4; तत्र for तत्र तत्र A5 R4; अत्र for तत्र तत्र M+; °पेक्षितानि प्रयोगाङ्गानि तत्र निगद्यन्ते A3

2. om Y* [G3 inserts at 4.23]; 1)—तत्र पुरश्चरणमाह om X2* A1 2 R1 B M [for G3 cf. App. 1.2]; तत्र तत्र A5; 2)—°तुष्टयमनाश्रमिभिः कार्यम् X2* B M; 3)—om A2; °मेकं कार्यमाश्र° A3 G3; 4)—एवं कृते A3; 5)—after कृत्वा A1 [above line] adds पुण्याहवाचनं कृत्वा, M+ adds पुण्याहवाचनं; दैव° R4; द्वितीयं before ऋषिश्राद्धं G3 [same transposition in the rest of the list]; पित्र्यश्राद्धं R4; षष्ठमं A5 6; भौमं A3; °त्मनीयं चाष्ट° G6 R2 3 B M; °त्मानं चाष्ट° A5 6; परमात्मानं G3

3. om Y*

4. Y* reads शौनकः । तत्र पूर्वेद्युर्नान्दीमुखश्राद्धं कृत्वा कृच्छ्रचतुष्टयं कृत्वा ब्राह्मणान्भोजयेत् तदेव श्राद्धादीनि समाप्य पुण्याहं वाचयित्वा केशश्मश्रुलोमनखानि वापयेत्;

तत्राह भगवान्**जामदग्न्यो**ऽपि[1] ।

केशश्मश्रुलोमनखानि वापयेदिति[2] ॥५॥

आह **शौनकः**[1] ।

अथ यथाविधि स्नात्वा होमादिद्रव्यं वर्जयित्वा सर्वस्वं दद्या-
दिति[2] ॥६॥

आह **बोधायनः**[1] ।

यष्टयः शिक्यं कमण्डलुं जलपवित्रं पात्रमित्येतानि[2] ॥७॥
[BDh 2.17.11–12]

वसिष्ठः[1] ।

त्रिदण्डमासनं कन्थां शिक्यं पात्रं कमण्डलुम् ।
षण्णां परिग्रहं कुर्याच्छेषं वित्तं त्यजेद् बुधः ॥८॥
द्रव्यत्यागं प्रकुर्वीत मलशुद्धिर्विधीयते ।
अत्यागे पुत्रवित्तानां संन्यासं नैव कारयेत् इति ॥९॥

कात्यायनः[1] ।

त्रिदण्डं जलपवित्रं शिक्यं पात्रं कौपीनं काषायवस्त्रमग्निसंनिधौ संसाद्यानग्निमानग्निमुत्पाद्येति[2] ॥१०॥

बोधायनः[1] ।

अनग्नीनामग्न्युत्पादनमेकाग्निविधानेनेति[2] ॥११॥

---

1)—आह om X2*; 2)—°न्दीमुखान् A1 2 R1; °मुखं श्राद्धं A3; °जयेदिति R1; 3)—अथवा B M; °श्मश्रुलोमानि B M; °श्मश्रुनखलोमानि R4 M+. In place of the following section [4.5–39], Y* [except G3] has the reading given in App. 1.1, and G3 the reading given in App. 1.2; G3 gives all the citations from Śaunaka and a few of the others. The variants of G3 are incorporated in the critical apparatus.

5. om A3; 1)—तत्राह भगवान् om X2* B M; 2)—°लोमानि B M; °लोम° om R4

6. 1)—आह om X2*; 2)—अथ om A1 2; होमादिपूर्वं R4; इति om G3

7. 1)—आह om X2* B M; 2)—पात्रम् om A1 2 6 R1 3 4; °त्येतान् A3

8. d)—तु विसृजेद् बुधः M+ [A1 above line corrected to this reading]

9. a)—प्रकुर्वाणो A1 G6 R2 4 B M; °र्वाणे A2 R1 3; b)—मूल° R4; d)—इति om B M

10. 2)—त्रिदण्डजलपवित्रशिक्यपात्रकौपीनकाषायवस्त्राण्यग्नि° X2* [°वस्त्राग्नि° R4] A1 2 R1 B M; संस्थाप्यान° B M; संसाद्य अग्नि° A5; °नग्निमात्रमग्नि° R4; मुत्पादयेदिति A1 2 G6 R1 2 3 B M [see G3 in App. 1.2]

11. 2)—अनग्निनाग्न्यु° A1 2 R1 4; अनग्निमानग्न्यु° M+; °ग्निमुत्पा° B M; °विधिमाह इति B M; °विधिनेति A1 2 R1

शौनकः[1] ।

अथ दण्डादीन्संनिधाप्य देवायतने ग्रामे ग्रामसीमान्ते वा नदीपुलिने पुण्ये वा पूर्वं मनसा ब्रह्माञ्जलिं कृत्वा जपेत्[2] ।

ब्रह्मणे नमः[2] । इन्द्राय नमः[3] । सूर्याय नमः[4] । आत्मने नम इति[5] ।

अथाप उपस्पृश्य दर्भाञ्जलिं कृत्वा वेदादीञ्जपेत्[6] । अथ सक्तुमुष्टिं प्राश्याचमनं करोति[7] । अथ नाभिदेशमभिमन्त्रयेत्[8] ।

आत्मने स्वाहा[9] । अन्तरात्मने स्वाहा[10] । प्रजापतये स्वाहेति[11] ।

अथ पयो दधि सर्पिरिति त्रिवृत्प्राश्याचम्योपवसेत्[12] । अपो वा भक्षयेत्[13] । जपेच्च[14] ।

ॐ भूः सावित्रीं प्रविशामि । तत्सवितुर्वरेण्यम्[15] ।
ॐ भुवः सावित्रीं प्रविशामि । भर्गो देवस्य धीमहि[16] ।
ॐ सुवः सावित्रीं प्रविशामि । धियो यो नः प्रचोदयात्[17] ।
ॐ भूः सावित्रीं प्रविशामि । तत्सवितुर्वरेण्यं भर्गो देवस्य धीमहि[18] ।
ॐ भुवः सावित्रीं प्रविशामि । धियो यो नः प्रचोदयात्[19] ।
ॐ सुवः सावित्रीं प्रविशामि । तत्सवितुर्वरेण्यं भर्गो देवस्य धीमहि । धियो यो नः प्रचोदयात्[20] ।
ॐ भूर्भुवः सुवः सावित्रीं प्रविशामि । तत्सवितुर्वरेण्यं भर्गो देवस्य धीमहि । धियो यो नः प्रचोदयात्[21] ।

इत्यात्मानमाश्रमान्तरमुपनीय ब्रह्मभूतो भवतीति विज्ञायते[22] । अथाप्युदाहरन्ति[23] ।

आश्रमादाश्रमं गत्वा हुतहोमो जितेन्द्रियः[24] ।
भिक्षाबलिपरिश्रान्तः पश्चाद्भवति भिक्षुकः[25] ।।

स एव भिक्षुरानन्त्यायेति[26] ।।१२।।

12. 1)—आह शौ° A3; अथ शौ° A6; 2)—देवतायतने G6 R4; ग्रामे om A6; ग्राम° om R4; °मान्ते नदी° A3 G3; पुण्ये वारण्ये A3; पुण्ये वारण्ये वा A6; °ञ्जलिकृतो R4; 3)—नमः add सोमाय नमः R2 M+; 5)—अनतरात्मने G6 R2; नम add परमात्मने नम A3 G3 M+; इति

आह **शौनकः**[1] ।

अथ पुनरादित्यस्यास्तमयादाज्यं विलाप्य उत्पूय स्रुचि चतुर्गृहीतं गृहीत्वा समिद्धेऽग्नौ पूर्णाहुतिं जुहोति ॐ स्वाहेति[2] । अथ सायमग्निकार्यं कृत्वा उत्तरेणाग्निं तृणानि संस्तीर्य तेषु पात्राणि सादयित्वा दक्षिणेनाग्निं ब्रह्मायतने दर्भान्संस्तीर्य कृष्णाजिनमन्तर्धाय तां रात्रिं जागर्ति[3] । अथ ब्राह्मे मुहूर्ते उत्थाय यथाविधि स्नात्वा प्रातरग्निकार्यं करोति[4] । अथ व्याहृतीर्जपित्वान्तर्जले तिष्ठन्तरत्स मन्दीति सूक्तं जपेत्[5] । अथ ब्राह्मणानन्नेन परितोष्य पुण्याहं स्वस्ति ऋद्धिमिति वाचयित्वाग्निमुपसमाधायाज्याहुतिं जुहोति[6] ।

प्राणाय स्वाहा[7] । अपानाय स्वाहा[8] । व्यानाय स्वाहा[9] ।
उदानाय स्वाहा[10] । समानाय स्वाहेति[11] ।

अथ पुरुषसूक्तेन प्रत्यृचं समिदाज्यचरूञ्जुहोति[12] । अथ पुरुषसूक्तं जपित्वा प्रणीतापात्रं संस्तीर्य सौविष्टकृतेन जुहोति[13] । यथाकामं जयादिसौविष्टकृतं जुहोति[14] । अथाचार्यायाज्यपात्रं हिरण्यं धेनुं च दत्त्वा अन्यदपि यथाश्रद्धं दद्यात्[15] । अथाचार्यमुपतिष्ठेत सं मा सिञ्चन्त्विवति[16] । ततो या ते अग्ने यज्ञिया तनुरित्यात्मन्यग्नीन्समारोपयेत्[17] । अथाग्निपूर्वेऽन्तर्जले वा तिष्ठन् ॐ भूर्भुवः सुवः संन्यस्तं मयेति त्रिरुपांशु त्रिर्मध्यमेन स्वरेण त्रिरुच्चैः[18] । अथ अभयं सर्वभूतेभ्यो मत्तः स्वाहेति प्राङ्मुखोऽपां पूर्णाञ्जलिं निनयतीति[19] ॥१३॥

---

om R2; after इति G6 R2 3 add App. 1.3; 6)—अथ उपस्पृ° B M; दर्भाञ्जलिकृतो A6 R4; 7)—अथ om G3; 11)—इति om R4; 13)—om G3; भक्षयेत् add संन्यासाङ्गमुपवसामि M+; 15–17)—G3 om all ॐ; 18–21)—om G3; 18)—om R2; धीमहि add धियो यो नः प्रचोदयात् A5 6 B M; 19)—प्रविशामि add तत्सवितुर्वरेण्यं भर्गो देवस्य धीमहि A5 6 B M; 20)—om R2; ॐ . . . धीमहि om A5 M; सावित्रीं प्रविशामि om R4; 21)—सुवः om G6 R2 4; सावित्रीं प्रविशामि om A5 6 B M; 22)—इति जपित्वा आत्मा° A5; इति सावित्रीं प्रविश्य अथात्मा° A3; इति सावित्रीं प्रविस्य and om rest G3; ज्ञायते A1 2 G6 R1 2 3 B M; 23–26)—om G3; 24)—°होमे A1 2 R1; 26)—स एष A1 R1; भिक्षुरात्मानं तारयति B M

13. 1)—आह om X2*; 2)—°दित्यास्त° A1 2 R1 2 3 B M; उत्थाय B M; स्रुचि om A2 G6 R1 2 4; समिद्धेऽग्नौ om G3; ॐ om G3; ॐ स्वाहेति om R4; 3)—पात्राण्यासाद्य G3;

एवं **बोधायनो**ऽपि ॐ भूर्भुवः सुवः संन्यस्तं मयेत्यादि अपो निनय-तीत्यन्तमुक्त्वा[1] । [BDh 2.17.27–29]

अभयं सर्वभूतेभ्यो दत्त्वा यश्चरते मुनिः ।
तस्यापि सर्वभूतेभ्यो न भयं जातु विद्यते इति ॥१४॥
[BDh 2.17.30]

वृद्धवसिष्ठः[1] ।

संन्यस्तं मयेति स्वरक्रमेण त्रिर्वाचो वदन् ।
त्रिंशत्परांस्त्रिंशदपरांस्त्रिंशच्च परतः परान् ।
सद्यः संन्यसनादेव नरकात्त्रायते पितॄन् ॥१५॥
संन्यस्तं हि द्विजं दृष्ट्वा स्थानाच्चलति भास्करः ।

दक्षिणतोऽग्निं R4; दर्भान् om A5 6 R4; °जिनं वान्त° G3; °र्धाय एतां G6 R2 4 M; °र्धाय रात्रिं A1 2 R1; 4)—अथ om G3; after करोति add अथ संन्यासकर्माङ्गं प्राजापत्यस्थालीपाकेन यक्ष्ये इति सङ्कल्प्य विद्युदसि विद्यमे अग्निमुखान्ते ॐ प्रजापतये स्वाहा इति चरुणा हुत्वा G6 R2 M+; 5–6)—G3 reads अथ व्यहृतीर्जपित्वा ब्राह्मणेभ्योऽन्नं दत्वा पुण्याहं वाचयित्वाग्निमुप-समाधायेध्माज्यहोमं जुहोति; 6)—°णानन्ते B M; °णानन्ने A1 2; °णान्परि° X2*; पुण्याहं om X2* A6; पुण्याहं add वाचयित्वा A5; ऋद्धिं वाच° A5; °याज्यं जुहोति A3 6; °हुतीर्जुहोति R2 3; 7)—Before प्राणाय add अथ A5; 8–10)—om A6; 12)—उक्त्वा for अथ G3; आज्येनाथ R2; प्रत्यृचमाज्यं जुहोति G3; °चरुं A5; °चरूर्जुहो° A1 2 3 G6 R1 2 3 B M; 13)—om A5; अथ om G3 R4; प्राणीतामोक्षणं कृत्वा for प्रणीतापात्रं . . . जुहोति A1 2 G3 R1 B M; संस्पृश्य A3; संसृ-ज्य A6; स्विष्टकृतं G6 M+; सौविष्टकृतं R2; सौविष्टकृतौ A3; 14)—om A1 2 3 G3 R1 B M; यथाशाखं G6 R2 3 M+; स्विष्टकृतं A5 G6 M+; 15)—अथ om G3; अथाज्यपात्रं R4; °चार्याय हिरण्यमाज्यपात्रं धेनुं G6 R2 3; च om A6 G3 R4; °श्रद्धा A1 2; °श्रद्धया A5; °श्रद्धां R1; °श्राद्धं G3; 16)—[अथ A3] सं मा सिञ्चन्त्वित्याचार्यमुपतिष्ठते A3 G3 [°त्यादिनाचा° G3]; अथ om A5 B M; अथाचार्य उपदिशेत् R4; 17)—ततो om G3; अतो R4; अग्ने + सक्षय एहीत्यात्म° A1 2 R1; तनुरित्यग्निं A5; °न्यग्निं A6 R2 B M; °रोपयति G3; 18)—अथा° . . . तिष्ठन् om G3; °पूर्वे जले A1 2 R1; वा om A2 5; सुवः om A3 6 G6 R2 3; त्रिरुपांशूक्त्वा त्रिर्म° A3 6 G3; मध्यस्वरेण A1 2 G3 R1; स्वरेनोक्त्वा G3; त्रिरुच्चैः add उक्त्वा G3, add स्वरेणोक्त्वा A1 2 R1 B M; 19)—अथ . . . निनयतीति om A5; अथ om A1 2 R1; मत्तः स्वाहा A1 2 R1 B M; अपां पूर्णाञ्जलिं प्राङ्मुखो निनयति A1 2 3 G3 R1 [निनयतीति A3]; पूर्णामञ्जलिं R4

14. 1)—om A1 2 5 R1 B M; °नोऽपि add आह A6; a)—अथाभयं A5

15. 1)—प्राह [आह A5] वसिष्ठः A1 2 5 R1 B M; a)—न्यस्तं A2 3; स्वर° om G6 R3 4; नवक्रमेण A5; सयनक्रमेण A3; b)—त्रिर्वाचा A6 B M; वदेत् A3 6 B M; d)—°शत्परतः A2 5 R4; पुमान् A3

एष मे मण्डलं भित्वा परं ब्रह्माधिगच्छति ॥१६॥
विरक्तेन तु विप्रेण संन्यासाश्रममिच्छता ।
यत्र तत्र मृतश्चापि न स भूयो भविष्यति ॥१७॥

स एवाह[1] ।

अनाहिताग्निर्मृतपत्नीको वानेन विधिना संन्यासं कुर्यादिति[2] ॥१८॥

अथ **शौनकः**[1] ।

अथ युवा सुवासा इति काषायवासो गृह्णाति[2] । सखा मा गोपायेति त्रिदण्डं गृह्णाति[3] । तच्छंयोरावृणीमह इति यज्ञोपवीतं गृह्णाति[4] । यदस्य पारे रजस इति शिक्यं गृह्णाति[5] । ॐ इति पात्रम्[6] । येन देवाः पवित्रेणेति जलपवित्रम्[7] । येन देवा ज्योतिषोर्ध्वा उदायन्निति कमण्डलुं गृह्णाति[8] ॥१९॥

सप्तव्याहृतिभिः पात्रमिति **कात्यायनः** ॥२०॥ **वसिष्ठः**[1] ।

यज्ञोपवीतमिति उपवीतं समादाय हंसः शुचिषत् उदुत्यम् चित्रम् तच्चक्षुः नमो मित्रस्येति त्रिदण्डादिपञ्च अङ्गमित्युपस्थाय समिद्धमिति द्वाभ्यामग्निं विसृज्य ग्रामसीमान्तं गत्वा त्रिधा बद्धो वृषभो रोरवीतीति त्रिदण्डानादद्यात्[2] । पवित्रचतुष्टयत्रिकं जपित्वा त्रीणि पदा विचक्रम इति पदत्रयं गत्वा तद्विष्णोः परमं पदमित्युपस्थाय स्वयंभूरिति जपेत्[3] । जले मत्स्यादीनां स्थले

16. a)—हि om A3 5 6; तु for हि X2* B M

17. a)—च for तु R4; b)—संन्यासाच्छ्रेय इच्छता A1 2 3 R1; c)—यत्र कुत्र R2 3 B M; यत्र यत्र G6; तत्र तत्र A5; मृतं चापि A6; मृतं वापि A5; d)—तत्र श्रेयो for न स भूयो M+; भूयोऽपि जायते G6 R2 3 M; भविष्यतीति A3

18. 2)—वा न विधिना A5

19. 1)—अथ om X2* B M; 2)—अथ om G3; काक्षायवस्त्रं A3 G3; 3)—सभां for सखा B M; मे A1 2 G6 R1 3 B M; गोपायौजस्सखा योऽसीन्द्रस्य वज्रोऽसि वार्त्रघ्न शर्म मे भव यत्पापं तन्निवारयेति G3; गृह्णाति add च A6; 4)—गृह्णाति om A3 G3; 5)—गृह्णाति om A1 2 3 G3 R1; 6)—सप्तव्याहृतिभिः for ॐ इति G3 [cf. reading of Y* in App. 1.1]; पात्रम् add गृह्णाति A5; 7)—जल° om A2; °पवित्रम् add गृह्णाति A5; 8)—उदायन् om G3 ; गृह्णाति om G3, but adds: युवा सुवासा इति कौपीनं

पशुमृगसरीसृपादीनां सर्वप्राणिनामभयं दत्त्वा पुष्पमूलफलोपादान-द्रुमच्छेदमधुमांसानृतदानादानादीन्वर्जयेदिति[4] ॥२१॥

आह **कात्यायनः**[1] ।

स्वकीयं ग्रामं बन्धुजनं च परित्यज्यान्यग्रामं प्राप्य जपध्यानपरायणो भवेत्[2] । याचितायाचिताभ्यां भैक्षाभ्यां वर्तयेत्[3] । कामक्रोध-रागद्वेषादि वर्जयेत्[4] । यावदायुरेवं वर्तयन्ब्रह्म संपद्यते[5] । न च पुनर्जायत इति[6] ॥२२॥

शौनकः[1] ।

अथानवेक्षमाणो वाचं नियम्य प्राचीमुदीचीं वा दिशमभिप्रव्रजेत्[2] । शमदमादि यत्नेन कुर्यात्[3] । श्रवणमनननिदिध्यासनानि कर्त-व्यानि[4] । प्रणवमभ्यसेन्नित्यमिति[5] ॥२३॥

इति **शौनकीय**संन्यासविधिः समाप्तः ॥२४॥ आह **कपिलः**[1] ।

अनग्निस्तु मुण्डः शिखी वाहोरात्रमुपोषितः स्नात्वाप एवाप्सु पाणिना जुहोति[2] । आपो वै सर्वा देवताः सर्वाभ्यो देवताभ्यो जुहोमि स्वाहेति[3] । पुत्रैषणायाश्च वित्तैषणायाश्च लोकैषणा-याश्चाप्युत्थितोऽहं स्वाहेति[4] । ॐ भूर्भुवः स्वः संन्यस्तं मया[5] । इति त्रिरुपांशूक्त्वा त्रिर्मध्यमेन त्रिरुच्चैस्त्रिषत्या हि देवा इति विज्ञायते[6] । अभयं सर्वभूतेभ्यो मत्तः स्वाहा[7] । इत्यपां

21. 2)—यज्ञोपवीतमिति om A3; यज्ञोपवीतं for उपवीतं A3 5 6 B; पञ्च अङ्गमि° conj.; पञ्चाङ्गमि° Y* X2* A1 2 3 R1 B M; पञ्चकमिति° A5 6; 3)—पवित्रं B M; °तुष्टयं त्रिकं A5; जपन् X2* B M; 4)—°मृग° om A3 R2; °पादानं A5 R1; °द्रुम° om A6; °च्छेदन° A3 5 R2; °नृतवर्जितं दाना° X2*; °नृतवाददाना° A1 2 R1 B M; °नृतदानादानादि वर्ज° A3 5; °नृतदानादि वर्ज° A6; °नृतदानादीन्वर्ज° G6; °दानादानं वर्ज° R4; इति om A1 2 R1

22. 1)—आह om X2* A5 B M; 2)—स्वकं X2* B M; 3)—याचिताभ्यां A3; भिक्षाभ्यां R2 3 4; वर्तयेत X2* B M; 4)—°द्वेषादीन् A1 2 5 R1 B M; 5)—यावदायुषमेवं A1 2 R1; संर्वत° A6 R3 B M

23. 1)—आह शौ° A3 5 6; 2)—अथानपेक्ष° A1 2 R4; वाचं नियम्य om G3; दिशम-भिगम्य प्रव्रजेत् A1 2 R1 B M; दिशमभिव्रजेत् A6; दिशमभिप्रव्रजतीति G3; 5)—नित्यं प्रणव-मभ्यसेत् A5

24. इति om R2 B M; शौनकीयः A6; °संन्यासः समाप्तः A5; समाप्तः om X2*

पूर्णाञ्जलिं भूमौ निनीय दण्डं दण्डान्वा जलपवित्रं कमण्डलुं शिक्यं पात्रमित्येतानि समादाय पुत्रमित्रशत्रुज्ञातीनग्निसंनिधानं त्यजेदिति[8] ।।२५।।

आह **वृद्धवसिष्ठः**[1] ।

आहिताग्निस्तु प्रातरुत्थाय व्रीहियवाभ्यां वैश्वानरीं पाथीकृतिं तन्तुमतीं वा निर्वपेत्[2] । अथाहवनीयं गत्वा स्वर्गाय लोकाय स्वाहेति यज्ञपात्राणि जुहुयात्[3] । अयं ते योनिर्ऋत्विय इत्यात्मन्यग्निं समारोप्य दक्षिणाग्निं गत्वा अयमग्निं पुरीष्य इत्युलूखलमुसले जुहुयात्[4] । अयं त इत्यग्निं समारोप्य गार्हपत्यं गत्वा अयमग्निर्गृहपतिरित्यरणिं जुहुयात्[5] । अयं त इत्यग्निं समारोप्य वेदिमध्ये स्थित्वा सहस्रशीर्षा पुरुष इति जपेत्[6] । अद्भ्यः संभूत इत्युपस्थाय वेदाहमित्यात्मानमुपस्थाय पितृभ्यः पिण्डदानं कुर्यात्[7] । प्राच्यां दिशि पितरः सेन्द्रास्तृप्यन्ताम्[8] । त्रातारमिन्द्रमित्युपस्थाय पितृभ्यः पिण्डदानं कुर्यात्[9] । आग्नेय्यां दिशि साग्निकाः पितरस्तृप्यन्ताम्[10] । अग्निर्मूर्धेत्युपस्थाय पितृभ्यः पिण्डदानं कुर्यात्[11] । दक्षिणायां दिशि सयमाः पितरस्तृप्यन्ताम्[12] । असि यम इत्युपस्थाय पितृभ्यः पिण्डदानं कुर्यात्[13] । नैर्ऋत्यां दिशि सनिर्ऋतयः पितरस्तृप्यन्ताम्[14] । एष ते निर्ऋत इत्युपस्थाय पितृभ्यः पिण्डदानं कुर्यात्[15] । प्रतीच्यां दिशि सवरुणाः पितरस्तृप्यन्ताम्[16] । उरुं हि राजा वरुण इत्युपस्थाय पितृभ्यः पिण्डदानं कुर्यात्[17] । वायव्यां दिशि सवायवः पितरस्तृप्यन्ताम्[18] । वायो शतमित्युपस्थाय पितृभ्यः पिण्डदानं कुर्यात्[19] । उदीच्यां दिशि ससोमाः पितरस्तृप्यन्ताम्[20] । सोमो राजा इत्युपस्थाय

25. 1)—om A3; अन्यश्च कपिलः X2*; अन्यश्चाह कपिलः B M; 2)—स्नात्वा प्रणवाप्सु R4; 3)—जहोति A1 2 3; 4)—वित्तैषणायाश्च om R2; लोकेषणाया अप्यु° X2* A1 2 R1 B M; अप्युद्धृतो M+; 5)—om G6; ॐ om A6 R2 3 4; स्वः om A6; सुवः R1 2 3 M; 6)—om G6; °ध्यमेन स्वरेण A3; त्रिषद्यां B M; त्रिषद्या A3 R2; देवता R2 3 B M; 7)—om G6; मत्तः om A5; 8)—°पामञ्जलिं A5 6 R2 3 4; °मित्रक्षत्रशत्रु° A5; °ज्ञातिसन्निधानं A3 5 M+

पितृभ्यः पिण्डदानं कुर्यात्[21] । ऐशान्यां दिशि सेशानाः पितरस्तृप्यन्ताम्[22] । ईशानमित्युपस्थाय पितृभ्यः पिण्डदानं कुर्यात्[23] । ऊर्ध्वायां दिशि सब्रह्माणः पितरस्तृप्यन्ताम्[24] । ब्रह्म जज्ञानमित्युपस्थाय पितृभ्यः पिण्डदानं कुर्यात्[25] । अधरायां दिशि ससर्पाः पितरस्तृप्यन्ताम्[26] । नमोऽस्तु सर्पेभ्य इत्युपस्थाय पितृभ्यः पिण्डदानं कुर्यात्[27] ॥२६॥

पिण्डं दत्वा बन्धूननुमोदयतेत्युक्त्वा दर्भाननुशतं गृहीत्वा अत ऊर्ध्वं यज्ञोपवीतमसीत्यादि **शौनकीय**ोक्तं द्रष्टव्यम् ॥२७॥

आहिताग्नेरेव **कपिलो** विशेषमाह[1] ।

आहिताग्निश्चेत्प्राजापत्येष्टिं सर्वस्वदक्षिणां विधिवद्दत्त्वा अयं ते योनिर्ऋत्विय इत्यात्मन्यग्नीन्समारोप्य वेदिमध्ये स्थित्वा देवं नारायणं शङ्खचक्रगदाधरं पीतवाससं किरीटकेयूरकुण्डलधरं हारिणं विष्णुं ध्यात्वा गुर्वनुज्ञातः प्रैषमन्त्रमुदाहरेदिति[2] ॥२८॥

जामदग्न्यः[1] ।

ऋतं चेति द्वादशाहमनुतिष्ठन्हि मानवः ।

26. 1)—आह om X2*; 2)—पाथीकृतीं A1 2 R1 2 [add वा A1 2]; तन्तुमतीं om A5 R1; 4)—°न्यग्नीन्समा° A2 3 6 R1 4; °रोप्य add अथ B M; अयमग्निं . . . जुहुयात् om A3; °मुसलौ A1 2 R1; 5)—om A3; इत्यात्मन्यग्निं B M; °रोप्य add अथ B M; गार्हपत्यं . . . (6) समारोप्य om A6 R2; °रित्यथारणीन् R4; °रित्यरणीन् R1; 8)—om A3 G6 R3 4; 9)—om A3 G6 R3 4; पितृभ्यः . . . कुर्यात् om B M; 10)—om G6 R2 3; 11)—om A5 G6 R2 3; कुर्यात् om A6; 12)—om A5 G6 R2 3; 13)—om G6 R2 3; असि lacuma A1 2 R1, om in G6 R2 3 B M; कुर्यात् om A3 5 6; 15)—निर्ऋतिरि° A3 5 R2 3 4; कुर्यात् om A3 5 6; 16)—प्राच्यां R3; स° om R3; 17)—om A3; कुर्यात् om A5 6 G6 R1 2 4; 18)—om A3 5; 19)—om A5; कुर्यात् om X2* A1 3 6 R1; 20)—om A5; 21)—om A5; शतम् for राजा R3; कुर्यात् om A1 3 6 G6 R1 2 3; 23)—कुर्यात् om X1* X2* A3; 25)—कुर्यात् om X1* X2* A3; 27)—पिण्डदानं om A1 2 G6 R2 3; कुर्यात् om X1* X2* A3

27. इति पिण्डं B M; पिण्डं om A3 5 6 R1 4; दत्वा om R1 4, add शेषं व्रत्रेभ्य (unclear) आशिषं दत्वा A3 5 6; °मोदयनित्युक्त्व B M; शौनकोक्तं B M

28. 1)—आहिताग्नेरन्यो विशेषः कपिलः X2*; 2)—च for चेत् A5; प्राजापत्येष्टिं add विधिवत्कृत्वा B M; सर्वदक्षिणां G6; विधिवत्कृत्वा A3; °त्मन्यग्निं A5 R2 3; नारायणं add देवं A5; °मुच्चारयेदिति B M; इति om A1 2 5 R1

वेदार्थान्विधिवच्छ्रुत्वा संन्यसेदनृणो द्विजः ॥२९॥
केशश्मश्रून्वापयित्वा पुण्ये चैव जलाशये ।
वाचंयमोपवसति रात्रिं जागर्ति पर्वणि ॥३०॥
कृत्वा प्रजापतेरिष्टिं सर्ववेदसदक्षिणाम् ।
आत्मन्यग्नीन्समारोप्य या ते अग्ने य इत्यृचा ॥३१॥
अहं वृक्षस्येति तिष्ठेदन्तर्वेदि द्विजोत्तमः ।
वेदो ह वै ब्रह्मवृक्षो ब्रह्मभूयाय कल्पते ॥३२॥
सत्यं वदेत्यनुशास्ति पुत्रं वा शिष्यमेव वा ।
नानुशासनवादाभ्यां भिक्षां लिप्सेत कर्हिचित् ॥३३॥
ॐ भूर्भुवः सुवः संन्यस्तं मयेति त्रिरुपांश्वाह त्रिर्मध्यमं त्रिरुच्चैः ।
त्रिषत्या हि देवा इति वदन्ति ब्रह्मवादिनः ॥३४॥
त्रीणि पदेति त्रिदण्डं वैणवं धारयेद्यतिः ।
मानसं वाचिकं चैव कायिकं च विचक्षणः ॥३५॥
अग्निर्देवता गायत्री छन्द इति मन्त्रेणालाबुदारुपात्रं
गृह्णीयाद्भिक्षुको द्विजः ।
जलपवित्रं गृह्णीयात्प्राजापत्यमिति ऋचा ।
तेन पूतं पिबेत्तोयं पवित्रोपचितो मुनिः ॥३६॥
सर्वभूतेभ्यः स्वाहेति यो दद्यादभयाञ्जलिम् ।
तस्यैव सर्वभूतेभ्यो न भयं जातु विद्यते ॥३७॥

29. 1)—°दग्न्यः add आह B M

30. c)—°वाचंधर्म्योप° A1 2; d)—पर्वणि om A3; पार्वणं A5

31. d)—अग्नय A1 2 6 G6 R2 3 B M; अग्न R4

32. c)—सोऽहं वै ब्रह्मवृक्षश्च G6 R2 3 B M

33. a)—वेदेत्य° A2 G6 R2 3; °शास्ति हि G6 R3; °शास्तेह A3 5 6; °शाधि A1 2 R1; b)—पुत्रं शि° A2

34. c)—त्रिषद्या हि A3 5; त्रिषद्याद्या देवा B M; त्रिषत्या ह R3

35. b)—धारयेद् om A1 2 5 R1; °येद्यतिः add इति A3; c)—वाचकं A1 2 R1; वापि for चैव X2* B M; d)—कायकं A1 2 R1

36. 1)—°दारु° om B M; भिक्षुको द्विजः om X2*

37. a)—अथ सर्व° A3; c)—तेनैव X2* B M

ग्रामात्प्राचीमुदीचीं वा दिशं गत्वा तु वाग्यतः ।
स्नानं तु विधिवत्कृत्वा प्राणायामान्षडाचरेत् ।।३८।।

अथ यज्ञोपवीतमप्सु जुहोति भूः स्वाहेति[1] । त्रिदण्डानादत्ते सखा मे गोपायेति[2] । **परिशिष्टे** पूर्वयज्ञोपवीतप्रतिपत्तिविधानवाक्यमस्ति[3] ।।३९।।

अथापत्संन्यास उच्यते ।।४०।। तत्र **जाबालिः**[1] ।

यद्यातुरः स्यद्वाचा वा मनसा वापि संन्यसेत्[2] ।
एष पन्था ब्रह्मणानामिहानुविहितस्त्विति[3] ।।४१।। [JU 68–69]

आहा**ङ्गिराः**[1] ।

आतुराणां विशेषोऽस्ति न विधिर्नैव च क्रिया ।
प्रैषमात्रस्तु संन्यास आतुराणां विधीयते इति ।।४२।।

आह **लिखितः**[1] ।

व्याघ्राग्निदस्युसर्पाद्यैः संपन्नमरणस्तु यः ।
महता व्याधिना वापि पीडितो यो मुमूर्षति ।
तदैव कुर्यात्संन्यासं विधिनाविधिनापि वा ।।४३।।
संन्यस्तमिति यो ब्रूयात्कण्ठस्थप्राणवानपि ।
तारिताः पितरस्तेन स्वयं मुक्तिपथे स्थितः ।।४४।।
मुक्तो यः प्राणसंदेहात्कृतसंन्यसनो द्विजः ।

38. b)—वाग्यतः add आपत्संन्यासविधिः A6

39. 1)—यज्ञो° . . . [3] पूर्व° om G6 R4; 2)—अथ दण्डानादत्ते A3 5 6; सभां X2* B M; मा A3 5 6

40. °न्यासप्रयोगमुच्यते Y* R2 B M; °न्यासविधिरुच्यते A2

41. 1)—तत्राह A3; जाबालिः add आमनन्ति A3 5 6; 2)—वाचा मानसा वा संन्य° Y*; वा मनसा om A5 R4; 3)—ब्रह्मणा हानुवित्त इति A4; ब्राहाणो हाभ्यनुज्ञात इति G1 2 3; त्विति . . . [43] °सर्पाद्यैः om G6

42. 1)—om Y*; अथाङ्गिराः A5; अङ्गिराः X2* B M; d)—इति om Y*

43. 1)—om Y*; आह om X2* B M; शङ्खलिखितौ B M; b)—संप्राप्तमर° Y*; c–d)—वारिपीडितो B M; °डितो add वापि A5; यो om A2

44. b)—अपि . . . [45] कर्मचण्डालास् om G6; d)—मुक्तिपदे A3 4 5 G2 R4 B M; स्थितिः A6

पुनर्निवर्तते ये च तेन संव्यवहारिणः ।
सर्वे ते कर्मचण्डालास्तेषां दृष्टा न निष्कृतिः ॥४५॥
संन्यस्य चापदं तीर्णः सकाशे तु गुरोरथ ।
लब्ध्वा मन्त्रैस्त्रिदण्डादीन्गृहीत्वा योगमाचरेत् ॥४६॥
तेषां नाशे पुनः प्राप्ते गृहीत्वा मन्त्रवत्स्वयम् ।
समुद्रं गच्छ स्वाहेति नष्टानप्सु विनिक्षिपेत् ।
शिक्षेत यतिधर्मांश्च **लिखितस्य** वचो यथा इति ॥४७॥

आपन्नानां त्रिधा संन्यास उक्तः विधिनाविधिनापि वेत्युक्तत्वात्[1] । कथंचित्कर्तुं शक्तो विधिना कुर्यात्[2] । अशक्तः संन्यस्तं मयेति वाचा प्रैषमात्रमुच्चारयेत्[3] । तत्राप्यशक्तश्चेन्मनसैव सङ्गत्यागं कुर्यात्[4] । इत्यापत्संन्यासविधिः[5] ॥४८॥

इति यतिधर्मसमुच्चये संन्यासप्रयोगो नाम चतुर्थं पर्व ॥४९॥

45. a)—मुक्ता ये Y*; b)—°संन्यासिनो द्विजाः Y* A6; c)—पुनरावर्तते A5; °वर्त्यते Y*; यैश्च Y* R3; यश्च A1 2 G6 R1 2 B M; f)—दृष्ट्वा A1 2; दण्डादिनिष्कृतिः A5; मृष्टानि निष्कृ° G1; न om G2

46. a)—तीर्त्वा A5; b)—गुरोर्यथा R4

47. b)—मन्त्रवित् G2; d)—विनष्टानप्सु निक्षिपेत् Y*; e)—शिक्षंश्च A4 G1 2

48. 1)—त्रिविधः Y*; °धिना वेत्यु° A1 2 R1 B M; °धिनापीत्यु° G6 R2 3; °धिना वापीत्यु° R4; °धिना वापि वेत्यु° A6; 2)—कथंचिच्छक्तो X2* B M; शक्तोऽपि G1 3; 3)—तदशक्तौ G1 2 3; तदशक्तो A4; वाचा om A4 G2 B M; प्रैषमन्त्रमु° G1 2 3; प्रैषमु° G6 R2 3 B M; °च्चारयति R4; 4)—तत्कर्तुमशक्तोऽपि मनसा सर्वस्वस्य [सर्वस्व G1 2] त्यागं कुर्यात् Y*; 5)—om X2* G1 2 3

49. इति यादवप्रकाशीये यति° Y*; इति यादवीये यति° A3; संन्यास° om Y*

पञ्चमं पर्व

मुख्यकर्मविधिः

अथ यतीनां मुख्यकर्मोच्यते ।।१।। तत्राहो**शनाः**[1] ।

ब्रह्मचार्युपकुर्वाणो नैष्ठिकोऽप्यपरस्तथा ।
सदारो न्यस्तदारश्च वानप्रस्थो द्विधा स्मृतः ।।२।।
भिक्षू द्वौ भिक्षुसंन्यासी वेदसंन्यासिकस्तथा ।
बहुधा गृहिणो भिन्नाः शालीनादय एव ते ।।३।।
द्विधैवाश्रमिणां भेदश्चतुर्णां **मनुर**ब्रवीत् ।
तेषां यो भिक्षुसंन्यासी तस्येदं शृणुताधुना ।।४।।
इहामुत्रोपभोगेषु विरक्तः प्रव्रजेद् द्विजः ।
वैश्वानरीं निरूप्येष्टिं सर्ववेदसदक्षिणाम् इति ।।५।।

एवं परिव्राजकस्य द्विधा भेदोऽभ्युपगतः ।।६।। केचित्तु चतुर्विधत्वं वर्ण-यन्ति[1] ।

चतुर्विधा भिक्षवस्तु कुटीचकबहूदकौ ।
हंसः परमहंसश्च यो यः पश्चात्स उत्तमः इति ।।७।।

1. अथ om A5; °कर्मोपलिख्यते R4

2. 1)—तत्र शौनकः X2* B M; d)—स्मृताः A5 G1 2 6 R3

3. b)—वेदन्यासी तु वा तथा Y* A3; °संन्यस्तकस्तथा G6 R4; °न्यासक° A1 2 R1

4. a)—द्वेधै° A1 2 R1; द्विधा वाश्र° G6 R2 3 M+; द्विधा चाश्र° R4; भेदं A3 5 G1 M+; d)—तस्यैव G6 R2 3 B M; तस्यैतं R4

5. om G6; a)—इहामुत्र च भो° A4 5 G1 2; इहामुत्रेषु भो° G3; b)—°जेद्बुधः R2 3 B M; d)—दत्वा सर्वस्वदक्षिणामित्यादिना Y*

6. om G6; परिव्राजस्य A2 G3; भेदाभ्युपगमः A5; भेदाभ्युपगमात् Y*

7. om G6; 1)—केचिच्च A1; तु om A3; चतुर्विधं A6 R2 3 4; b)—°हूदकाः A5; d)—इति om A5

एतदपि पाञ्चरात्रसिद्धं सांख्यसिद्धं च न वेदसिद्धमिति केचिदाहुः ॥८॥

आपस्तम्ब इमं पक्षं प्रतिषेधति[1] ।

सर्वतः परिमोक्षमेके[2] । सत्यानृते सुखदुःखे वेदानिमं लोकममुं च परित्यज्यात्मानमन्विच्छेत्[3] । बुद्धे क्षेमप्रापणम्[4] । तच्छास्त्रैर्विप्रतिषिद्धम्[5] । बुद्धे चेत्क्षेमप्रापणमिहैव न दुःखमुपलभेत[6] । एतेन परं व्याख्यातमिति[7] ॥९॥ [ApDh 2.21.12–17]

आहा**त्रिः**[1] ।

शिखिनश्च श्रुताः केचित्केचिन्मुण्डास्तु भिक्षुकाः ।
चतुर्धा भिक्षवो विप्राः सर्वे चैव त्रिदण्डिनः इति ॥१०॥

आह **पराशरः**[1] ।

तत्र परिव्राजकाश्चतुर्विधा भवन्ति[2] । कुटीचका बहूदका हंसाः परमहंसाश्चेति[3] । तत्र कुटीचका नाम पुत्रादिभिः कुटीं कारयित्वा कामक्रोधलोभमोहमदमात्सर्यादीन्परित्यज्य विधिवत्संन्यासं कृत्वा त्रिदण्डजलपवित्रकाषायवस्त्रधारिणः स्नानशौचाचमनजपस्वाध्यायब्रह्मचर्यध्यानतत्पराः पुत्रादेरेव भिक्षाकालेऽन्नं यात्रामात्रमुपयुञ्जानास्तस्यां कुटौ नित्यं वसन्त आत्मानं मोक्षयन्ते[4] । बहूदका नाम त्रिदण्डकमण्डलुपक्ष्मपवित्रशिक्यकाषायवस्त्रधारिणो वेदान्तार्थावबोधकाः साधुवृत्तेषु ब्राह्मणेषु भिक्षाचर्यं चरन्त आत्मानं मोक्षयन्ते[5] । हंसा नाम त्रिदण्डजलपवित्रशिक्ययज्ञोपवीतिनो गोमूत्रगोमयाहारा एकरात्रत्रिरात्रमासोपवासपक्षोपवासकृच्छ्रचान्द्रायणसान्तपनमहासान्तपनपराकतुलापुरुषादीनि व्रतानि चरन्तो गोद्विजाढ्येषु पुण्येशु देशेषु वसन्त आत्मानं मोक्षयन्ते[6] । परमहंसा नाम त्रिदण्डजलपवित्रशिक्ययज्ञोपवीतिनोऽन्तर्वासोबहिर्वासधारिणो ग्रामैकरात्रवासिनो नगरतीर्थावसथेषु पञ्चरात्रिका भिक्षाकाले

8. om Y* G6; च om R3

9. om Y* G6; 1)—पक्षं om R4; 2)—°क्षमेते A3 6 R4; °क्षमित्येके A5; 4)—बुद्धेः A5; 5)—तच्छा . . . [6] °प्रापणम् om A6; तच्छास्त्रैः प्रति° B M; 6)—चेत् om A1 2 R1

10. om X1* [A1 puts in margin] R4; 1)—om G6; अत्रात्रिः G1 2 3

शीर्णपर्णपुटं कृत्वा ब्राह्मणकुलादेव भैक्षं गृहीत्वाष्टौ ग्रासानेव भुञ्जानाः संध्योपासनतत्परा नित्यं वृक्षमूले वसन्त आत्मानं मोक्षयन्त इति[7] ॥११॥

तत्र **मनुः** वेदसंन्यासिकानामाह[1] ।

एष धर्मोऽनुशिष्टोऽन्यो यतीनां नियतात्मनाम् ।
वेदसंन्यासकानां तु कर्मयोगं निबोधत इति ॥१२॥ [MDh 6.86]

ऋणानि त्रीण्यपाकृत्येति त्रयः श्लोका अस्मिन्नवसरे पठ्यन्ते केषुचित्प्रदेशेषु[1] ।

ब्रह्मचारी गृहस्थश्च वानप्रस्थोऽथ भिक्षुकः ।
एते गृहस्थप्रभवाश्चत्वारः पृथगाश्रमाः ॥१३॥
सर्वेऽपि क्रमशस्त्वेते यथाशास्त्रं निषेविताः ।
यथोक्तकारिणं विप्रं नयन्ति परमां गतिम् ॥१४॥
सर्वेषामपि चैतेषां वेदश्रुतिविधानतः ।
गृहस्थ उच्यते श्रेष्ठः स त्रीनेतान्बिभर्ति हि ॥१५॥
यथा नदीनदाः सर्वे सागरे यान्ति संस्थितिम् ।

11. 1)—आह om A5 6 G6 R2 4; 2)—ततः B M; चतुर्धा B M; 3)—कुटीचकबहूदकहंसपर° R1 2 B M; 4)—कामक्रोधादीन्परि° Y*; °दण्डकमण्डलुजलपवित्रशिक्यकाषा° A6; °काषायधारिणः B M; °पवित्रपात्रधारिणः Y*; °धारणस्नान° A1 2 R4; पुत्रादपि R4; 5)—त्रिदण्ड° . . . [6] हंसा नाम om G3; °पात्र° for °पक्ष्म° A4; °पक्ष्मपात्रपवि° A3 G2; वेदार्थाव° A3; ब्राह्मणेषु om A1 2 R1 4; ब्राह्मणकुलेषु A4 5 [also A6 in margin]; भैक्षचर्या A3 4 G2; 6)—°शिक्यपात्रकाशायवस्त्रधारिणो यज्ञो° Y* A3 B M; एकरात्रं त्रिरात्रं Y* A5; °त्रिरात्र° om R4; °त्रिरात्र° add षड्रात्र Y*; °मासोपवासादिपराक° A4; °मासोपवासादिपराको गोद्विजा° G1 2 3; °कृच्छ्रातिकृच्छ्रचा° A3 5 6; °कृच्छ्रादिचा° R4; °महासान्तपन° om R4; गोद्विजमेध्येषु B M; पुण्यदेशेषु Y* A5 G6; 7)—°न्तर्वासब°Y* G6 R2 3 B M; °बहिर्वस्त्रधा° A6; नगर° . . . °रात्रिका om Y*; पञ्चरात्रं त्रिरात्रं त्रिकालस्नानं भिक्षा° A5; जीर्णपर्ण° A2; कृत्वा om A2; संध्यावन्दनतत्परा Y* A3 R4; इति om A5

12. 1)—तत्र om Y* R4; °संन्यासिनाम् X1* R2; °संन्यासिकानाह A4 G2 3; मनुः om A5; मनुः placed after आह Y* A1 2 R1; a–d)—om Y*; c)—°न्यासिकानां A5 R2

13. om Y*; शौनकः for त्रयः श्लोका X2* M+; अस्मिन्नेवावसरे G6 R2 4 M+; a)—गृहस्थो वा R4

14. om Y*; c–d)—°कारिणो विप्रास्ते यान्ति X2* B M

15. a)—सर्वेषामेव [°मेवं G2 3] वैतेषां Y*; सर्वेषामेवमपि A3; d)—एको for एतान् A3 G3

तथैवाश्रमिणः सर्वे गृहस्थे यान्ति संस्थितिम् ॥१६॥
चतुर्भिरेतैरपि तु नित्यमाश्रमिभिर्द्विजैः ।
दशलक्षणको धर्मः सेवितव्यः प्रयत्नतः ॥१७॥
धृतिः क्षमा दमोऽस्तेयं शौचमिन्द्रियनिग्रहः ।
ह्रीर्विद्या सत्यमक्रोधो दशकं धर्मलक्षणम् ॥१८॥
दश चिह्नानि धर्मस्य ये विप्राः समधीयते ।
अधीत्य चानुवर्तन्ते ते यान्ति परमां गतिम् ॥१९॥
दशलक्षणकं धर्ममनुतिष्ठन्हि मानवः ।
वेदान्तान्विधिवच्छ्रुत्वा संन्यसेदनृणो द्विजः ॥२०॥
संन्यस्य सर्वकर्माणि कर्मदोषानपानुदन् ।
नियतो वेदमभ्यस्य पुत्रैश्वर्ये सुखं वसेत् इति ॥२१॥
[MDh 6.87–96]

एवमेव कुटीचक इति केचिदाहुः[1] । दश चिह्नानि धर्मस्येति चिह्नग्रहणमाश्रमधर्मं प्रति शेषत्वख्यापनार्थम्[2] । ततश्च सर्वैराश्रमिभिः स्वं स्वं धर्ममनुतिष्ठद्भिर्धृत्यादिदशधर्मोपेतैर्भवितव्यमिति भावः[3] ॥२२॥

तत्र भिक्षुसंन्यासिनामाश्रमधर्म उच्यते[1] । आह **क्रतुः**[2] ।
सांख्यं योगो हरेर्भक्तिरप्रमादो विरागता ।
एतत्सारमतः शेष आश्रमो धर्म उच्यते इति ॥२३॥

16. c–d)—om A5
17. a)—चतुर्भिरपि तु त्वेतैर्नि° [कृत्वैतैर्नि° A6] A5 6 R4; तैः for तु G6 R2 3 B M
18. a)—दयास्तेयं A2 6 G6 R1 4 B M; दमास्तेयं Y* R2 3
19. G3 has several folia missing here. The missing text runs from here until Ch. 7.53; c)—चानुतिष्ठन्ति Y*
20. Y* omits 5.20–46, but inserts 5.23–45b after 5.49; b)—°नुतर्प्यन्हि B M; °नुतिष्ठन्ति मानवाः G6 R4; d)—°सेद्विधिवद् द्विजः A1 2 R1 M+
21. om Y*; d)—पुत्रैश्वर्यैः B M; B M place इति in next sentence: इत्येवं
22. om Y*; 1)—एवं कुटी° X2* B M; कुटीचकधर्म B M; कुटीचकस्थितिरिति A1 2; 3)—स्वस्वधर्म° A3 R3 4; स्वधर्म° A6 G6 R2
23. 1)—तत्र om Y*; °संन्यासधर्म X2*; °संन्यासाश्रमधर्म B M; °संन्यासिनामाह मनुः Y*; उच्यत इति A5; 2)—om A4 5 G2; आह om X2*; a)—सांख्ययोगौ A1 3 5 6 R1; हरौ

एतदुक्तं भवति[1] । सांख्यं तत्त्वज्ञानम्[2] । योगोऽष्टाङ्गः षडङ्गो वा[3] । हरेर्भक्तिरीश्वरोपासनं परमात्मनि स्नेहः[4] । अप्रमादः सदा प्रतिबुद्धताः[5] । विरागता विषयेष्वस्नेहता[6] ॥२४॥ तथाह **बृहस्पतिः**[1] ।

परमात्मनि यो रक्तो विरक्तोऽपरमात्मनि ।
सर्वैषणाविनिर्मुक्तः स भैक्षं भोक्तुमर्हति इति ॥२५॥

एतत्सारमतः शेष इति[1] । एष एव प्रधानधर्म आश्रमस्य[2] । शेषस्तु धर्मः संध्यावन्दनादिलक्षण आश्रम एव आश्रमधर्मः स्वरूपमेव[3] । तन्निष्ठ आश्रमनिष्ठ एव स्यात् नाश्रमधर्मनिष्ठः[4] । संध्यावन्दनादयो व्यापारा आश्रमधर्माङ्गत्वमापन्ना न स्वयमाश्रमधर्माः[5] ॥२६॥ तथाह **दक्षः**[1] ।

संध्याहीनोऽशुचिर्नित्यमनर्हः सर्वकर्मसु ।
यदन्यत्कुरुते कर्म न तस्य फलभाग्भवेत् इति ॥२७॥

तत्र सांख्यमुच्यते[1] । आह **यमः**[2] ।

पञ्चविंशतितत्त्वज्ञो यत्र तत्राश्रमे रतः ।
प्रकृतिज्ञो विकारज्ञः स दुःखात्परिमुच्यते ॥२८॥
मनो बुद्धिरहङ्कारः खानिलाग्निजलानि भूः ।

भक्ति° R4; c–d)—एष सारतमो धर्मश्शोष आश्रम उच्यते R4; सारमशेषाणामाश्रमो Y* M; सारतमः शेष A1 2 5 G6 R 2 3 B; इति om X2* Y* A5 B M

24. 1)—तदुक्तं A5; 3)—योगमष्टाङ्गमीश्वरोपासनं A4 G2; षडङ्गो वा om A4 G2; 4)—हरिभ° A5; ईश्वरोपासनं om Y*; 5)—°प्रति° om A5 6 R4; °प्रबुद्धता A1 2 R1; 6)—विरागो R2 3 4 B M; °ष्वस्नेहः A1 2 R1; °ष्वनासक्तिः X2* B M

25. 1)—om R3 4; तथा च Y* A5 G6 R2 B M

26. 1)—om X2* B M; एतत्सारमिति Y*; एतत्सारतमश्शेष इति । एतत्सारम् A1 2 R1; 2)—एतदेव G6; एतत्प्रधा° A5; प्रधानमाश्र° Y*; आश्रमधर्मस्य A5; 3)—शेषो धर्मस्तु X2* B M; एष तु धर्मः Y*; आश्रम एव . . . [5] व्यापारा om Y*; आश्रम एव om G6 R2 B M; °धर्माङ्गमेव G6 R2 B M [R3 आश्रम एव धर्मस्वरूपमेव corrected to अश्रमधर्माङ्गमेव]; 4)—आश्रमनिष्ठ repeated A1 2 R1; आश्रमधर्म एव A5; आश्रमधर्मनिष्ठश्च [°निष्ठः R4] स्यात् X2* B M; नाश्रममात्रनिष्ठः G6 M; आश्रममात्रनिष्ठः R2; अनाश्रमधर्मोमात्रनिष्ठा R4

27. 1)—तथा च B M; तथा चाह Y*; च om A6; b)—°कर्मस्विति Y*; c–d)—om Y*; c)—धर्मं G6 R4

28. 2)—आह om X2* B M; b)—यत्राश्रमे A4 G6 R2 3 M; °श्रमोऽन्यतः R4

एताः प्रकृतयस्त्वष्टौ विकाराः षोडशापरे ॥२९॥
श्रोत्राक्षिरसनाघ्राणं त्वक्च सङ्कल्प एव च ।
शब्दरूपरसस्पर्शगन्धवाक्पाणिपायवः ।
उपस्थपादाविति च विकाराः शोडश स्मृताः ॥३०॥

सङ्कल्पः अन्तःकरणानां वृत्तयः ।

चतुर्विंशकमित्येतज्ज्ञानमाहुर्मनीषिणः ।
पञ्चविंशकमव्यक्तं षड्विंशः पुरुषोत्तमः ।
एतज्ज्ञात्वा तु मुच्यन्ते यतयः शान्तबुद्धयः ॥३१॥
अशब्दमरसस्पर्शमरूपं गन्धवर्जितम् ।
निर्दुःखं सुसुखं शुद्धं तद्विष्णोः परमं पदम् ॥३२॥
अजं निरञ्जनं शान्तमव्यक्तं ज्ञानमक्षरम् ।
अनादिनिधनं ब्रह्म तद्विष्णोः परमं पदम् इति ॥३३॥

बृहस्पतिः[1] ।

तदेतत्परमं भूतं यस्माद्भूतान्यनेकशः ।
पृथिव्या इव भाण्डानि प्रभवन्ति विशन्ति च ॥३४॥
तदेतत्परमं ज्योतिस्तस्यान्ये विस्फुलिङ्गवत् ।
विक्षिप्तं सूर्यचन्द्राग्निविद्युत्ताराग्रहादिषु ॥३५॥
स एष परमानन्दो याश्चान्याः सुखविप्रुषः ।

29. a)—°हङ्काराः A1 2 R1; c)—एषां R4

30. a)—before श्रोत्रा° add अत्र [A3 तत्र] विकाराः A1 2 3 G1 2 R1 B M; °रसनं घ्राणं Y*; b)—त्वचस्सङ्कल्प A3 6; c–d)—शब्दस्पर्शरसगन्धरूपवाक्पा° Y*; °रसगन्धस्पर्श° A1 2 3 R1; e)—उपस्थपादावपि च Y*; च om A2 R1; f)—add इति G1 2

31. 1)—om X2* Y* B M; वृत्तय इति A5 6; a)—°शतिकमि° A3; °शतिमि° A5; °शमि° G1; °शतिरि° X2* B M; c)—°शतिकं व्यक्तं A6; °शतिमव्यक्तं A5; d)—°षोत्तमं A5; e)—°त्वाथ X2* B M; °त्वा विमुच्य° Y* A3

32. a–b)—अशब्दरूपमस्पर्शं रसगन्धविवर्जितम् Y* A3; °रसमस्पर्श° R4; c)—तु सुखं A5 6; सुखसंशुद्धं A3; रूपं for शुद्धं X1*; d)—पदम् add उच्यते R4

33. b)—ज्ञानमक्षयम् A2 M+; d)—इत्यादि X1*

34. 1)—आह बृह° A3 G1 2; a–d)—om Y*; c)—पृथिव्यामिव X2* B M

35. om Y*; b)—विष्फु° A1 R2 3; विष्णुलि° A2 5 R1 4 M+; सर्वलि° G6; d)—°दिषु add च G6

पिबन्ति पुण्यकर्माणो ब्रह्मेन्द्रपितृमानवाः ॥३६॥
नानात्वैकत्वभावेन सर्वभावस्थितं प्रभुम् ।
इदं तु परमैकत्वं परा सत्ता परा गतिः ॥३७॥

इत्युपक्रम्यान्ते च[1] ।

य एवं ब्रह्म जानाति संसारात्स विमुच्यते इति ॥३८॥

आह **शौनकः**[1] ।

पृथिव्यापस्तथा तेजो वायुराकाश एव च ।
पञ्चैतानि विजानीयान्महाभूतानि पण्डितः ॥३९॥
श्रोत्रं चक्षुः स्पर्शनं च रसनं घ्राणमेव च ।
बुद्धीन्द्रियाणि जानीयात्पञ्चैवास्मिञ्छरीरके ॥४०॥
मनो बुद्धिस्तथैवात्मा ह्यव्यक्तं च तथापरम् ।
इन्द्रियेभ्यः पराण्याहुश्चत्वारि कथितानि तु ॥४१॥
शब्दं रूपं तथा स्पर्शं रसं गन्धं तथैव च ।
इन्द्रियार्थान्विजानीयात्पञ्चैव सततं बुधः ॥४२॥
हस्तपादावुपस्थं च जिह्वा पायुस्तथैव च ।
कर्मेन्द्रियाणि पञ्चैव नित्यमस्मिञ्छरीरके ॥४३॥
चतुर्विंशतिरेतानि तत्त्वानि कथितानि तु ।
मत्वात्मानं तद्रहितं पुरुषं पञ्चविंशकम् ॥४४॥

36. om Y*; a)—एव A3 5; b)—°विभ्रमाः M+

37. b)—सर्वतोवस्थि° B M; सर्वभावव्यवस्थितम् [om प्रभुम्] Y*; विभुम् A6; d)—परसत्ता Y*; सक्ता G6; सन्ता A1 2

38. 1)—om Y*; अन्ते च om A2; a)—य om G6; b)—संसारद्धि A1 5 R1; संसाराच्च A2; संसाराब्धेः R4 M+; संसारं विप्रमु° A6; प्रमु° A1 2 5 R1; इति add पर्यन्तम् B M

39. 1)—आह om X2* B M; a–d)— om Y*

40. om Y*

41. om Y* R2; a)—तथा चात्मा G6 R3 4; b)—सव्यक्तं R4; परात्परम् G6 R2 B M; d)—चत्वार्येवेतराणि G6 R3 B M; चत्वारि इतराणि R4

42. om Y* R2; a)—शब्दो R3 B M; स्पर्शो G6 R4 B M; b)—रसो G6 R4 B M; गन्धस्तथैव R3 B M; c–d)—om G6 R3 4

43. om Y* R2; a–b)—om G6 R3; a)—हस्तौ A3; b)—च om A2

44. a)—°शतिमेतानि Y*; c)—तदाहितं G2; d)—°शतिम् A6

यज्ज्ञात्वा तु विमुच्यन्ते यतयः शान्तबुद्धयः ।
एतत्तत्परमं गुह्यमेतदक्षरमुत्तमम् ॥४५॥

अशब्दमरसस्पर्शमित्यादि **याम्य**पाठ एव[1] । एवमन्यत्रापीतिहासपुराणेषु **मानव**ादिषु वेदान्तेषु च सांख्यशब्दवाच्यं तत्त्वज्ञानमन्वेषणीयम्[2] ॥४६॥

अथ ज्ञानतत्त्वस्य योग उच्यते[1] । सोऽष्टाङ्ग उक्तः **पातञ्जले**[2] ।

यमनियमासनप्राणायामप्रत्याहारधारणाध्यानसमाधयोऽष्टाङ्गानि[3] । तत्र अहिंसासत्यास्तेयब्रह्मचर्यापरिग्रहा यमाः[4] । शौचसंतोषतपः-स्वाध्यायेश्वरप्रणिधानानि नियमाः[5] । स्थिरसुखमासनम्[6] । प्राण-गतिविच्छेदः प्राणायामः[7] । स्वविषयासंप्रयोगे चित्तस्वरूपानुकार एवेन्द्रियाणां प्रत्याहारः[8] । देशबन्धश्चित्तस्य धारणा[9] । तत्र प्रत्य-यैकतानता ध्यानम्[10] । तदेवार्थमात्रनिर्भासं स्वरूपशून्यमिव समाधिः[11] ॥४७॥ [Ys 2.29—3.3]

एषामष्टानामङ्गानां प्रत्याहारादीनि स्वरूपाङ्गानि देवदत्तस्येव हस्तादीनि इतराणि साधनत्वेनाङ्गानि[1] । तेषामन्तरङ्गविरोधेऽन्तरङ्गाण्येव पालनी-यानि[2] ॥४८॥ तथा च भगवान्**व्यासः**[1] ।

45. a)—यं ज्ञात्वा A3 4 G6 R4 B M; °त्वा परिमुच्यन्ते B M; c–d)—om Y*; c)—य एतत्प° G6 R2 3 B M; य एतत्तु परं R4

46. om Y*; 1)—°त्यादि वाद्यपाद्य A2 R1 [A1 also but corrected to याम्यपाठम्]; पूर्वपाठ A3; °पाठमेव G6 R2 3 M; याम्यपरमेव R4; एव om A1 2 R1; 2)—एवम् om X2* B M; °पुराणादिषु X2* B M; मानवेषु G6 R2 3 B M; च om A2; °वाच्यतत्त्व° A1 2 R1

47. 1)—ज्ञात° A2 4 G6 R4; योगमुच्यते R4; 2)—सो om A1 2; उक्तः om A4 G2; °ष्टाङ्गयुक्तः X2* G1 B M; पातञ्जले om Y* G6 R2 3 B M; पातञ्जलीयः R4; पातञ्जलेयः A1 2; 3)—°ध्यानधारण° A1 2 4 5 B M; °ध्यान° om G2; 4)—तत्र om Y* B M; अत्र R4; °सत्यास्तेय° conj., all mss read सत्यमस्तेयं [except A3 सत्यमस्तेय]; °ग्रहौ R1 B; °ग्रहः A2 M [also A1 but corrected]; 5)—शौचं X2* A1 2 R1 B M; °संतोष° om Y*; संतोषः M; संतोषं G6; ईश्वरप्रणिधानतपःस्वाध्याया X2* A1 2 R1 B M; 6)—स्थिरं A6 G6 R3 4; 8)—इवेन्द्रि° R1 M+; एव om A1 2; 9)—देशबन्धश्च तत्र तस्य धारणा R4; सा धारणा A2; 11)—समाधिरिति Y*

48. om Y*; 1)—°ष्टाङ्गानां X2*; °ङ्गादीनि A5; °दत्तस्यैव X2* A1 2 R1; हस्तपादादीनि B M; 2)—तेषामन्तरङ्गाण्येव A6 R2

यमान्यतेत सततं बाधित्वापीतरान्बुधः ।
यमान्पतत्यकुर्वाणो नियमान्केवलं भजन् इति ॥४९॥

तानीमान्यङ्गानि व्याख्यायन्ते स्मृतिषु नानाप्रकारेण[1] । तत्र तावत्**क्रतुः**[2]

योगाङ्गैर्वा यमादिभिः[3] । [see 6.23]

इत्युक्त्वाह[4] ।

धृतिः क्षमा दमोऽस्तेयं शौचमिन्द्रियनिग्रहः ।
ह्रीर्विद्या सत्यमक्रोध एतद्धर्मस्य लक्षणम् ॥५०॥
अहिंसा समतास्तेयं क्षमादमशमादयः ।
तुष्टिरद्रोहताकल्कं निर्वैरत्वं यमाः स्मृताः ॥५१॥
विकल्पो दम्भ आलस्यं सङ्गः कर्मफलं भयम् ।
परिग्रहो ममत्वं च त्यागश्चोपयमाः स्मृताः ॥५२॥

एषां त्यागस्त्याग इत्यर्थः[1] ।

कामरागद्वंद्वनिद्रामोहक्षुत्पापचेतसाम् ।
द्वेषाहङ्कारलोभानां विजयाः संयमाः स्मृताः ॥५३॥
संनतिः शीलमास्तिक्यं योगो वृत्तं श्रुतं क्रिया ।
औदासीन्यं मृदु स्थैर्यं वैराग्यं च परा यमाः ॥५४॥
अप्रार्थनमसंकल्पमस्पर्शनमदर्शनम् ।
ध्यानं प्रसादमाधुर्यं मौनं संनियमान्विदुः ॥५५॥

49. 1)—चाह A3 5; a)—सेवेत Y* A3; b)—°त्वा त्वितरा° Y*; °त्वापि तान्बुधः A5; °त्वा च तान्बुधः R4; d)—Y* inserts here 5.23—45b [see 5.20]

50. Y* omits 5.50–65; 1)—तान्यङ्गानि नानाव्या° X2*; व्याख्यायन्ते placed at end A3; नानाप्रकारेण om X2*; 2–4)—om X2*; तत्र तद्योगान्तैर्वा [तावद्यो° A1 2R1] यमादिभिः इत्युक्तत्वात् A1 2 R1 B M; a)—before धृतिः add क्रतुः X2*

51. omY*; a)—सत्यमस्तेयं X2* B M; b)—°शमदमादयः A5; c)—जन्तोरद्रो° G6 R2 3 M+; जन्तुष्वद्रो° R4; °ष्टिरमोहता° A3 6; कल्मं A5 M; कल्पं R2; d)—निर्विरक्तं B M

52. om Y* G6 R2 3; d)—त्यागश्चैव यमः स्मृतः R4

53. om Y* A3 G6 R2 3; 1)—त्यागस् om R4; a)—°रागद्वयं B M; °निद्रां A1 2 R1 B M; c)—द्वेषालङ्कार° A6; d)—च जयाः A6

54. om Y*; a)—संततिः A6; b)—योगवृत्तं A6; क्रियाः A5; d)—परे B M; परो यमः [धमः G6] X2*

55. om Y*; c)—ज्ञानप्र° G6 R2 3; ज्ञानं R4 B M; प्रसादं A6 R3; °दमायुष्यं M+; d)—मानं R4; तं नियमं X2* R1 B M; तन्नियमान् A1 2; विदुः add एवं नानात्वं X2*

शौनकः[1] ।

दश व्रतानि सर्वेषां यतीनां विहितानि वै ।
अहिंसा सत्यमस्तेयं ब्रह्मचर्यापरिग्रहौ ॥५६॥
अक्रोधो गुरुशुश्रूषा शौचं दुर्वृत्तिवर्जनम् ।
वाङ्मनःकायचेष्टासु प्रमादस्य च वर्जनम् इति ॥५७॥

आह **बोधायनः**[1] ।

अथैतानि व्रतानि भवन्ति[2] । अहिंसा सत्यमस्तेयं मैथुनस्य च वर्जनं त्याग इति[3] । पञ्चैवोपव्रतानि भवन्ति[4] । अक्रोधो गुरुशुश्रूषाप्रमादः शौचमाहारशुद्धिश्चेति[5] ॥५८॥ [BDh 2.18.2–3]

यमः[1] ।

अथादित्यो यमो राजा यतीनां भावितात्मनाम् ।
जगाद विहितान्धर्मान्वेदसंन्यासिनामपि ॥५९॥
अहिंसा सत्यमक्रोधो ब्रह्मचर्यं तपः श्रुतम् ।
अस्तेयाव्यभिचारौ च धर्मो दशविधः स्मृतः ॥६०॥

तपसो वाङ्मनःकायभेदेन भिन्नत्वाद्दशविधत्वम्[1] ।

संतोषो गुरुशुश्रूषा ह्यप्रमादः क्षमा दया ।
मौनमाहारशुद्धिश्च शौचमष्टौ व्रतानि च ॥६१॥

ननु हिंसाभेदादहिंसापि भिद्यते[1] । हिंसा च दशविधा[2] । तथा हि उद्वेगकरणं सन्तापकरणं रुजाकरणं शोणितोत्पादनं पैशुन्यं सुखापनयनमतिक्रमः सङ्कोचो हितप्रतिषेधो वध इति[3] ॥६२॥ अप्रसिद्धांश्च भेदान् **वृद्धजाबालिर**ाह[1] ।

56. om Y*; 1)—om A1 2 3 R1 B M

57. om Y*; b)—दुर्जप्ति° A5 6; °वर्जितम् G6 R3 4; d)—इति om A5

58. om Y*; 1)—आह om X2*; 3–4)—om A1 2 R1 B M; त्याग इति om X2*; संभवन्ति R2; 5)—°चमाचारश्चेति A2 B M

59. om Y*; 1)—om X2* B M; आह यमः A3; वक्ति यमः A1

60. om Y*; d)—°विधाः A5

61. om Y*; 1)—तपसः करणत्रयभिन्नत्वाद्द° X2*; b)—°श्रूषा अप्रमा° A5; क्षमादयः B M; दमः A5

62. om Y*; 1–2)—ननु हिंसा दशविधा X2*; 3)—पैशुण्यकरणं X2* A5 6; वध om A6

हन्ता चैवानुमन्ता च विशस्ता क्रयविक्रयी ।
संस्कर्ता चोपकर्ता च खादकश्चाष्ट घातकाः इति ॥६३॥

सत्यं **वायुर**ाह[1] ।

न धर्मयुक्तमनृतं हिनस्तीति मनीषिणः ।
तथापि तन्न वक्तव्यं प्रसङ्गोऽप्येष दारुणः ॥६४॥

अस्तेयं च स एवाह[1] ।

असद्वादो न कर्तव्यो यतिना धर्मलिप्सुना ।
न चैवापद्गतेनापि स्तेयं कार्यं कदाचन ॥६५॥

ब्रह्मचर्यभेदं **बृहस्पतिर**ाह[1] ।

स्मरणं कीर्तनं केलिः प्रेक्षणं गुह्यभाषणम् ।
संकल्पोऽध्यवसायश्च क्रियानिवृत्तिरेव च ॥६६॥
एतन्मैथुनमष्टाङ्गं प्रवदन्ति मनीषिणः ।
विपरीतं ब्रह्मचर्यमेतदेवाष्टलक्षणम् ॥६७॥

अपरिग्रहं **लिखित** आह[1] ।

संस्कृतां न वदेद्वाणीं बालवन्मूकवच्चरेत् ।
न द्रव्यसंचयं कुर्यान्मात्रामप्यन्यकालिकाम् ॥६८॥

शौचमुपरि व्याख्यास्यते **गर्गेण** [see 6.5] ॥६९॥ स्वाध्यायं **यम** आहः[1] ।

63. om Y*; 1)—अप्रतिषिद्धांश्च A6 R4; अक्रोधसि° B M; °सिद्धान्भे° A1 2 R1 B M; आह before वृद्ध° X2* B M; c)—संस्मर्ता M; चापकर्ता X2* [च om R2 3] A1 2 R1; चैव कर्ता B M; d)—घातक° A1 2 3 5 G6 R1 2 M; पातकाः B M

64. om Y*; 1)—before सत्यं add अहिंसा X2*; a–d)—om A3; b)—मनीषिणां A1 B M; महर्षिणां A2; c)—कर्तव्यं R4; d)—प्रसङ्गो एष G6

65. om Y* A3; 1)—स एवास्तेयमाह X2*; b)—यतीनां धर्मलिप्सुनाम् A6 G6 R3 4; c)—before न add न धर्मयुक्तमनृतं R3

66. a)—स्मारणं R3; b)—प्रेषणं A6

67. a)—एवं मैथु° G6 R2 3 B M; c–d)—om X2*; विपरीतं om A1 2; c)—°ष्टाङ्ग-लक्षणम् A2; d)— add इति Y* A3

68. 1)—अपरिग्रहं om Y*; आह लिखितः Y*; आह om A3; a)—संस्कृतानां न G2; d)—मात्रमप्य° Y* A2; मात्रामकालिकाम् R4; °कालिकमिति Y*; °कालिकीम् R1 B M; °काल-कीम् A1 2

69. om Y* X2* [M ed. comments इदं क्वाचित्कम्]; °मुपरिष्टाद्व्या° B M

जप्येनापि नयेत्कालं ध्यानश्रान्तो यतिः सदा ।
ध्यानेन जपविश्रान्तः पुनर्ध्यायेत्पुनर्जपेत् ॥७०॥
चत्वारः पाकयज्ञास्तु विधियज्ञसमन्विताः ।
सर्वे ते जपयज्ञस्य कलां नार्हन्ति षोडशीम् ॥७१॥
विधियज्ञाज्जपो यज्ञो विशिष्टो दशभिर्गुणैः ।
उपांशु स्याच्छतगुणः सहस्रो मानसः स्मृतः इति ॥७२॥

मनुः[1] ।

अधियज्ञं ब्रह्म जपेदाधिदैविकमेव च ।
आध्यात्मिकं च सततं वेदान्ताभिहितं च यत् ॥७३॥
[MDh 6.83]

वेदान्ताभिहितं प्रणवः[1] । **आपस्तम्बः**[2] ।

स्वाध्याय एवोत्सृजमानो वाचमिति[3] ॥७४॥ [ApDh 2.21.10]

बोधायनः[1] ।

सायंप्रातरग्निहोत्रमन्त्राञ्जपेत्[2] [BDh 2.18.20] । योऽग्निहोत्री भूत्वा प्रव्रजति तस्यायं विधिः[3] ॥७५॥

ईश्वरप्रणिधानं **कपिल** आह[1] ।

प्रातःस्नानं जपो मौनं नित्यमेकान्तशीलता ।
नमस्कारोपवासौ च भक्तिर्विष्णौ तथा गुरौ ॥७६॥
आस्तिक्यं ब्रह्मसंस्पर्शः प्राणायामरतिस्तथा ।
त्रैकाल्यमर्चनं विष्णोः परमं मुक्तिसाधनम् ॥७७॥

70. a)—जपेनापि B M; b)—ध्यानैः शान्तो Y* A3

72. a)—जपयज्ञो A4 6 G6; जपयज्ञाद् A5; जपतियज्ञो R2 3; c)—°गुणं R3 4 B M; d)—इति om Y* X2* A5

73. 1)—om Y* R4; a)—°यज्ञाद् A4; जपादाधि° Y* A2 R1; d)—वेदान्तं चिन्तयेत्सदा M+; add इति Y* A3

74. om Y*; 1)—वेदान्तं प्र° M+; °भिहितः X2*; प्रणवं A2 5 6

75. om Y*; 2)—सायंप्रातः om A1 2 5 R1; °होत्रमन्त्रान् only in A3, conj. (haplology?); °होत्रं X2* A5 B M; °होत्रान् A1 2 6; 3)—प्रव्रजितस्यायं X1*; प्रव्रजेत्तस्यायं A3

76. 1)—ईश्वरप्रणिधानं om Y*; आह कपिलः Y*; a)—प्राणायामं A5; c–d)—om A2

77. om A2; a)—°स्पर्शं Y* A3 5; c)—विष्णोः . . . [5.78a] °मर्चनं om A6 R1; विष्णोः . . . [5.78] °विष्णोः om A5; d)—परं मुक्तिप्रसाधनम् Y* A3; add इति Y* A3

अत्रिः[1] ।

त्रैकाल्यमर्चनं विष्णोर्देवानां च तदात्मनाम् ।
नमस्कारार्चनादीनि कुर्यान्नान्यस्य कस्यचित् इति ॥७८॥

आह **क्रतुः**[1] ।

ईश्वरो भगवान्विष्णुः परमात्मा महानजः ।
शास्ता चराचरस्यैको यतीनां परमा गतिः ॥७९॥

पुनः स एवाह[1] ।

ध्यायतेऽर्चयते योऽन्यं विष्णुलिङ्गमुपाश्रितः ।
कल्पकोटिशतैश्चापि गतिस्तस्य न विद्यते ॥८०॥

अथापि स एवाह[1] ।

पूजां पुरुषसूक्तेन वेदगुह्यस्तवैः स्तुतिम् ।
ॐ इत्येकाक्षरं ध्यायेदधियज्ञं तथा जपेत् ।
त्रिकं पुरुषसूक्तं च चतुष्कं प्राणसंयमैः ॥८१॥

त्रिकं प्रणवव्याहृतिगायत्र्यः[1] । ता एव सशिरस्काश्चतुष्कम्[2] । आसनं **शङ्ख** आह[3] ।

शून्ये गृहे देवगृहे गुहायां गिरिगह्वरे ।
यत्र वा रमते बुद्धिस्तत्रासीत प्रसन्नधीः ॥८२॥
योगशास्त्रोक्तमार्गेण कृतासनपरिग्रहः ।
योगं युञ्जीत सततं संध्यासु तु विशेषतः ॥८३॥

78. om Y*; 1)—om A2; अत्रिराह A3; a–b)—om A2; विष्णोर्यतीनां A1 5 R1 M+; तथात्म° A3; b–c)—om R4; d)—इति om A5 B M

79. 1)—आह om X2* B M; क्रतुराह A3 5 G1 2; b)—महात्मजः G6; सनातनः Y*; c)—चराचरस्वामी B M

80. 1)—om Y* A3; d)—न before गति° Y*; विद्यत इति Y*

81. om Y*; 1)—om A1 2 R1; अथ स एव R2 3 4; अथ स एवाह G6 B M; f)—°संयमः G6 R4 B M; °संक्रमः R2

82. 1–2)—om Y*; 1)—प्रणवत्रिव्या° R2 3; 2)—एता A3; 3)—आह om X2*; a)—गेहे Y* A3; d)—°त्रासीनः Y* A1 2 R1; °त्रासन्न A6

83. c)—योगं कर्माणि A 2 R1 [A1 also but corrected]; d)—संध्यास्वपि X2* B M; संध्यासु च A1 2 5 R1

विश्वामित्रः[1] ।

ततो निवातके रम्ये निम्नोन्नतविवर्जिते ।
कुशाजिनसुचेलानामुपर्युपरि विन्यसेत् ॥८४॥
पद्मासनं तु तत्रैव कृत्वाङ्गानि समं नयेत् ।
प्राणायामांस्ततः कुर्याद्यावत्कालं समाहितः ॥८५॥

प्राणायामप्रत्याहारधारणाध्यानानां लक्षणं **शङ्ख** आह[1] ।

प्राणायामैर्दहेद्दोषान्धारणाभिश्च किल्बिषान् ।
प्रत्याहारेण संसर्गान्ध्यानेनानैश्वरान्गुणान् ॥८६॥
सव्याहृतिं सप्रणवां गायत्रीं शिरसा सह ।
त्रिः पठेदायतप्राणः प्राणायामः स उच्यते ॥८७॥
संयमश्चेन्द्रियाणां हि प्रत्याहारः प्रकीर्तितः ।
मनःसंयमनं तज्ज्ञैर्धारणेति निगद्यते ॥८८॥
ब्रह्मणि ध्यानयोगेन देवदेवस्य दर्शनम् ।
ध्यानं प्रोक्तं प्रवक्ष्यामि ध्यानयोगमतः शुभम् ॥८९॥

ध्यानं समाधिः[1] । ध्यानयोगस्तु ध्यानम्[2] । तदाह[3] ।

हृदिस्था देवताः सर्वा हृदि प्राणाः प्रतिष्ठिताः ।
हृदि ज्योतींषि सूर्यश्च हृदि सर्वं प्रतिष्ठितम् ॥९०॥
स्वदेहमरणिं कृत्वा प्रणवं चोत्तरारणिम् ।
ध्याननिर्मथनाभ्यासाद्विष्णुं पश्येद्धृदि स्थितम् ॥९१॥

84. 1)—आह वि° Y* A3; a)—निवाते रम्ये तु Y* A3 R1; रम्ये तु A1 2 [see 6.55]; b)—°वर्जितः G1

85. b)—समाहितः A5; c)—प्राणायामं ततः Y* A1 2 5 R1; d)—add इति Y* A3

86. 1)—प्राणा° . . . लक्षणं om Y*; आह शङ्खः Y*; a–d)—om Y*; d)—°नानीश्व° B M

87. a)—°हृतिकां Y* A3 6; c)—°यतः प्राणः A1 2 G1 2 6 R2 3; °प्राणः om A6

88. c)—तद्व्रद्धार° Y* A1 2 R1; तच्चेद्धा° A5; After this verse G6 R2 3 add 5.98c–d, ब्रह्म प्रणवः [here R3 adds 5.106], and 5.92[2–3], 96, 98a–b, and यत्तु सातपवर्षेण . . . न संशयः [see 5.105n]

89. om Y*; c–d)—om X2*

90. om Y*; 2)—ध्यानम् om X2*

91. om Y*; a)—स्वं A6; c)—ज्ञाननिर्म° M+;

ॐकारेण ब्रह्म ध्यायेदन्यांस्त्यक्त्वा शब्दादीनित्यभिप्राय:[1] । तथा च श्रुति:[2] ।

ॐ इत्यात्मानं युञ्जीतेति[3] ।।९२।। [MNU 540]

तथा

अन्या वाचो विमुञ्चथ[1] । [MuU 2.2.5]

इत्युक्त्वाह

ॐ इत्येव ध्यायतात्मानमिति[2] । [MuU 2.2.6]

नानुध्यायेद्बहूञ्छब्दान् । [BaU 4.4.21]

इति च[3] ।।९३।। आह **यम:**[1] ।

द्वे ब्रह्मणी वेदितव्ये शब्दब्रह्म परं च यत् ।
शब्दब्रह्मणि निष्णात: परं ब्रह्माधिगच्छति ।।९४।।

शब्दब्रह्म प्रणव:[1] । **यम: शङ्खश्च**[2] ।

रविमध्ये स्थित: सोमस्तस्य मध्ये हुताशन: ।
तेजोमध्ये स्थितं तत्त्वं तत्त्वमध्ये स्थितोऽच्युत: ।।९५।।

विश्वामित्र:[1] ।

प्रसीदति मनो यावत्तावच्चित्तं नियम्य तु ।
चिन्तयेद्धृदि मध्ये तु प्रदीप्तं सूर्यमण्डलम् ।।९६।।
तस्य मध्ये स्थितं सोममग्निं ब्रह्म महच्छिखम् ।
सर्वविघ्नप्रशान्त्यर्थं हृत्पद्मे देवमच्युतम् ।।९७।।
शुद्धस्फटिकसंकाशं चतुर्बाहुमनुस्मरेत् ।
तत: स निष्कलं ध्यायेद्ब्रह्मपूर्वमतन्द्रित: ।।९८।।

ब्रह्मपूर्वं प्रणवपूर्वं नारायणमित्यर्थ:[1] ।

92. 1)—om Y*; 3)—om X2* [but see 5.88n]; इति om B M

93. om Y*; 1)—om X2*; 2)—इत्युक्त्वाह om X2*; इत्याह A5; ॐइत्येवं A5 6 G6; °ध्यायथात्मा° A6 R1; °ध्यायेदात्मा° A3 5 R4; 3)—om X2*; च om A5 6

94. om Y*; 1)—आह om A2 R1

95. om Y*; 2)—यमशङ्खौ X2* B M; d)—तस्य मध्ये A1 2 3 B M

96. आह विश्वा° Y* A3; b)—निशाम्यति X2*; नियम्य यत् A5

97. om Y*; b)—महच्छिवम् B M

98. a–b)—om X2*; °बाहुं किरीटिनम् Y* A3; c)—ततस्सन्नि° X2*; ततस्तन्नि° A1 2 5 R1 B M; स om A4; ततश्च निष्क° A3

सर्वं सर्वात्मकं तत्त्वं विष्ण्वाख्यं परमं पदम् ।
पुनः पुनः स्वचित्तस्थं निर्मलं यन्निरामयम् ॥९९॥
तद्ब्रह्म चाहमेवास्मि सर्वगं त्वात्मनः परम् ।
निरस्य विषयासक्तिं संनिरुध्य मनो हृदि ॥१००॥
यदा यस्य मनोभावं तदेवं परमं पदम् ।
वीक्षितां बुद्धिमादद्यात्पुनरप्यात्मनीश्वरे ॥१०१॥
न निर्वेदं मुनिर्गच्छेन्निरुन्ध्यादेव मानसम् ।
तावदेव निरोद्धव्यं हृदि यावत्क्षयं गतम् ॥१०२॥
एतज्ज्ञानं च ध्यानं च शेषोऽन्यो ग्रन्थविस्तरः ।
इन्द्रियेषु निरुद्धेषु मनसि स्पन्दवर्जिते ।
आत्मा प्रकाशते शुद्धो बोधाकारो निराकुलः इति ॥१०३॥

लिखितः[1] ।

विचार्य च पुराणार्थान्वेदान्तान्भक्तिमास्थितः ।
विष्णुं सदा हृदि ध्यायेत्साकारं निष्कलं तु वा ॥१०४॥
इदं तु सर्वधर्माणां यद्योगेनात्मदर्शनम् ।
श्रेष्ठमेतद्विरोध्यन्यत्त्यजेदावश्यकादृते ॥१०५॥

बृहस्पतिः[1] ।

क्षमा तीर्थं दमस्तीर्थं तीर्थमिन्द्रियनिग्रहः ।

99. 1)—ब्रह्म प्रणवः for ब्रह्म° . . . °त्यार्थः X2*; °पूर्वकं G1; नारायणम् om Y*; a–d)—om Y* X2*; c–d)—om A6

100. om Y* X2* A6; a)—यद् A3; °वास्मिन् A1 2

101. om Y* X2* A3; a–b)— om A6; b)—तदेव A5

102. omY* A3; b)—मानसा R2; c–d)—om X2*

103. om Y*; a–d)—om A3; a)—च ज्ञेयं च G6 R3; c–f)—om X2*; e)—प्रकाशते om A1 2 R1 B M; f)—बोधकरो A1 2 3 B M; बोधादरो R1; A1 in margin इतीरितः

104. om Y*; 1)—लिखित आह A3; a)—स for च A3 5 6; b–d)—om G6

105. om Y*; a–c)—om G6; c)—श्रेष्ठमन्यद्वि° A1 2 R1; d)—here Y* A1 2 3 R1 add आह [om Y*] पराशरः । आग्नेयं वारुणं ब्राह्मं वायव्यं दिव्यमेव च । आग्नेयं भस्मना स्नानं वारुणं ह्यवगाहनम् [हृदवगा° A3] ॥ आपो हि ष्ठेति च [om A1 2 R1] ब्राह्मं वायव्यं गोरजः स्मृतम् । यत्तु सातपवर्षेण दिव्यं स्नानं तदुच्यते । तत्र स्नात्वा तु गङ्गायां स्नात एव न संशयः ॥

सर्वभूतदया तीर्थं ध्यानतीर्थमनुत्तमम् ॥१०६॥
एतानि पञ्च तीर्थानि सत्यं षष्ठं तु सर्वदा ।
देहे तिष्ठन्ति सर्वत्र तेषु स्नानं समाचरेत् ॥१०७॥
न तथा पुष्करे स्नातो गङ्गायां कुरुजाङ्गले ।
मुच्यते पुरुषः पापैर्यथा स्नातः क्षमादिषु ॥१०८॥
निगृहीतेन्द्रियग्रामो यत्र यत्र वसेन्नरः ।
तत्र तत्र कुरुक्षेत्रं नैमिषं पुष्करं तथा ॥१०९॥
इदं तीर्थमिदं नेति ये नरा भेदवादिनः ।
तेषां विधीयते तीर्थगमनं तत्फलं च यत् ॥११०॥
सर्वं ब्रह्मेति यो वेत्ति नातीर्थं तस्य किंचन ।
जाग्रत्स्वप्नसुषुप्तेषु ब्रह्मण्येव स वर्तते ॥१११॥
स एव परमो धर्मो ये त्वन्ये तस्य बिन्दवः ।
यज्ञं दानं तपो वेदास्तीर्थरूपेण संस्थिताः ॥११२॥

योगं योगाङ्गानि च प्राणायामप्रत्याहारधारणाध्यानसमाधीन्**क्रतुः** स्तौति[1] ।

रत्नैर्ब्रह्माण्डमापूर्य वेदविद्भ्यो निवेदिते ।
क्षयिष्णु तत्फलं दृष्टं न विष्णोः स्मरणं सकृत् ॥११३॥
पञ्चाग्निजलमध्यस्थाः खस्थाश्चैवाग्निधूमपाः ।
प्राणायामस्थितस्यैते कलां नार्हन्ति षोडशीम् ॥११४॥
त्वक्पत्रपुष्पशाकाम्बुफलमूलानिलादनैः ।
द्वादशाब्दैस्तत्त्वशुद्धिः प्रत्याहारेण वत्सरात् ॥११५॥

106. 1)—आह बृह° Y* A3 B M; a)—तपस्तीर्थं G6 R3 4; d)—ज्ञानती° A4 6

108. a)—स्नानाद् Y*; c)—मुच्यते सर्वपापैस्तु M+

109. b)—यत्र तत्र A6 G1 2 R4; वसन्नरः A1 2 R1; d)—पुष्कराणि च Y*

110. c–d)—तीर्थं तदनन्तफलं A1 2; च om A6

111. b)—न तीर्थं A5 R4; d)—वर्तयेत् G6

112. a)—स एष A3 G1 2; b)—धर्मबि° Y* A3; c–d)—om X2*; यज्ञदानत° Y* A3

113. om Y*; 1)—om X2*; क्रतुः om A6; d)—तत्परं सकृत् A3

114. om Y* A1 2 5 R1 B M; c)—°यामे स्थितस्यैते A3

115. om Y* A1 2 5 R1 B M; a)—°शाखा° X2*; b)—मूलादिखादनैः R4; c)—°ब्देन त्वशुद्धिः R2 M+; °ब्दे तत्त्व° G6; °शुद्धिं A3 6 R3

सुस्थेयं शक्तिचक्रासिबाणाश्रयहितैषिणा ।
धारणायां तु योगस्य दुःस्थेयमकृतात्मभिः ॥११६॥
शक्यतेऽग्नौ हिमे युद्धे स्वाध्याये तपसि व्रते ।
पापध्वंसिन्यवस्थातुं न स्थाने क्षणमप्यलम् ॥११७॥
कुष्ठज्वरगरव्याधीन्मर्षयन्तीह मानवाः ।
ये जना दुःसहा लोके योगनिश्चलकारकाः ॥११८॥
त्यक्तबन्धस्य शुद्धस्य समाधिस्थस्य योगिनः ।
विरजाकाशकल्पस्य सा काष्ठा वैष्णवी गतिः ॥११९॥
रवीन्दुवह्निद्युतयः शुद्धस्फटिकनिर्मलाः ।
तरन्ति तमसः पारं योगाङ्गैस्तोषिते हरौ ॥१२०॥
मनोवाग्देहजान्दोषानज्ञानोत्थान्प्रमादतः ।
सर्वान्दहति योगाग्निस्तूलराशिमिवानलः ।
भक्तियुक्तो हरिं पश्येद्योगदीपिकया सदा ॥१२१॥

योगावसानं **हारीत** आह[1] ।
आत्मलाभसुखं यावत्तावद्ध्यानमुदाहृतम् ।
श्रुतिस्मृत्युदितं कर्म तदूर्ध्वं च समाचरेत् ॥१२२॥
निष्कलध्यानाशक्तौ ध्यानं **बृहस्पति**राह[1] ।

116. om Y* X2* [M ed. notes सुस्थेया इत्यादि तोषिते हरावित्यन्तं बहुषु कोशेषु नास्ति । किंतु तत्स्थाने श्लोकाविमौ दृश्येते and gives 5.114–15; a)—सुस्थेया B M; °शक्ति° lacuna B M [M ed. notes अत्राक्षराणि मूलकोशेषु गलितानि]; b)—°बाणायुध° B M; c)—धारणा या B M A1 R1; d)—दुःस्थेया ह्यकृ° B M; दुःस्थेयं कृता° A1 2 R1; सुस्थेय° A5

117. om Y* X2*; b)—बुध्यंये तापसव्रते A5; c)—तापध्वंसि° A5

118. om Y*X2*

119. om Y* X2*

120. om X2*; b)—°कसन्निभाः Y* A3; c)—तपसः A1 2 B M

121. a)—°वाक्कक्कायजा° A1 2 5 R1 B M; b)—प्रमादजान् Y* A3; c)—योगेन Y*; d)—तुषराशि° G1; f)—सदेति Y* A3

122. 1)—योगावसानमुच्यते । आह हारीतः Y* A3; a)—आज्ञाला° A1 2 R1; आत्मलाभं B M; सुखी A1 2 R1 B M; b)—तत्त्वध्या° A2; d)—न for च A1 2 R1 B M; °चरेदिति Y* A3

ब्रह्मण्येव निराकारे ध्यानं कर्तुमशक्नुवन् ।
प्राणायामेन संशुद्धस्तन्मूर्तिध्यानमाचरेत् ॥१२३॥
सव्याहृतिं सप्रणवां गायत्रीं शिरसा सह ।
त्रिः पठेदायतप्राणः प्राणायामः स उच्यते ॥१२४॥
प्राणायामैर्दहेद्दोषान्मनोवाक्कायसंभवान् ।
प्रत्याहारेण संसर्गान्ध्यानेनानीश्वरान्गुणान् ॥१२५॥
ध्मायमानं यथा भ्रस्येद्धातूनां संभृतं मलम् ।
तथेन्द्रियकृतो दोषः प्राणायामेन दह्यते ॥१२६॥
आधानं रोधमुत्सर्गं वायोस्त्रिस्त्रिः समभ्यसेत् ।
ब्रह्माणं केशवं शंभुं ध्यायन्मुच्येत बन्धनात् ॥१२७॥
रक्तं पितामहं ध्यायेद्विष्णुं नीलोत्पलप्रभम् ।
श्वेतं त्रिलोचनं शंभुं संसारार्णवतारणम् ॥१२८॥
योगाभ्यासपरो नित्यमेवं यो वर्तते यतिः ।
प्राप्तवैराग्यसर्वस्वः स याति परमां गतिम् ॥१२९॥
वासुदेवः परं ब्रह्म परमात्मा जगन्मयः ।
तस्यैव मूर्तयस्त्वेता भिद्यन्ते ह्याख्यया त्रिधा ॥१३०॥
नारायणं जगद्योनिं सर्वलोकेश्वरं हरिम् ।
चिन्तयेदन्वहं भक्त्या सर्वकारणकारणम् ॥१३१॥

123. 1)—निष्कलध्यानाशक्तौ om Y* X2* B M; ध्यानं om Y*; आह बृहस्पतिः Y*; d)—मूर्ध्नि ध्या° A1 2 R1 B M; °चरेदिति Y*

124. om Y* X2*; a)—°हृतिकां A1 2 R1 [A1 cor.]; c)—आयतः प्रा° A1 2 3 5 R1

125. om Y* X2*; d)—°नैश्वरान् A3

126. om Y* X2*; a)—ध्माय° conj., धयाया° all mss; यदा A1 2 R1 M; c)—तदेन्द्रि° A1 2 3 R1 M

127. om A4 R4; c–d)—om G6 R2; d)—ध्यायेन्मु° A5 G1 2 R3

128. om A4 G6 R2 4; b)—नीलोत्पलं A1 R1 3; °प्रभुम् R3; c)—त्र्यक्षं A5; पारं चैव for शंभुं A5 6

129. c)—°सर्वः G6; d)—सा यतिः R2; गतिमिति Y*

130. om Y* X2*; d)—°न्तेऽभिख्यया B M

131. om Y* X2*

शङ्खचक्रधरं सौम्यं चतुर्बाहुं किरीटिनम् ।
श्रीवत्सकौस्तुभोरस्कं दिव्यरत्नविभूषितम् ॥१३२॥
पीताम्बरमुदाराङ्गं प्रसन्नेन्दुनिभाननम् ।
श्यामलं पुण्डरीकाक्षं स्फुरन्मकरकुण्डलम् ॥१३३॥
संतापनाशनं सद्यः कालमेघमिवोदितम् ।
सर्वतेजोमयं पुण्यं शरण्यं शरणार्थिनाम् ॥१३४॥
चिन्तयेत्पुण्डरीकाक्षं नारायणमनामयम् ।
मनसा षोडशैः सम्यगुपचारैः प्रयत्नतः इति ॥१३५॥

आह **दत्तात्रेयः**[1] ।

अष्टादशोपचारेण भगवान्पुरुषोत्तमः ।
हृदयेऽग्नौ तथादित्ये पूज्यते च मुमुक्षुभिः ॥१३६॥
पलाशैः पद्मकुसुमैरर्चनं शस्यते हरेः ।
एवमभ्यर्च्य देवेशं नारायणमतन्द्रितः ॥१३७॥
तद्रूपं चिन्तयेद्योगी प्रणवेन समाहितः ।
साकारं वा यथायोगं नित्यं मनसि धारयेत् ॥१३८॥
आदित्यवर्णं पुरुषं पुण्डरीकनिभेक्षणम् ।
शङ्खचक्रगदापाणिं पीतनिर्मलवाससम् ॥१३९॥
किरीटचारुकेयूरकटकादिविभूषितम् ।
श्रीवत्सवक्षसं श्रीशं कौस्तुभोद्भ्राजिवक्षसम् ॥१४०॥
श्यामलं वा हृषीकेशं पुण्डरीकाक्षमच्युतम् ।
हृत्पद्मकर्णिकामध्ये स्थितमासीनमेव वा ॥१४१॥

132. om Y* X2*
133. om Y* X2*
134. om Y* X2*
135. om Y* X2*; b)—नारायणमयं हरिं A1 2 R1 B M; d)—समर्चयेत् M+
136. om Y*; 1)—आह om X2*; d)—पूज्येत मुमु° A2; हि for च R4; add इत्यादि X2*
137. om Y* X2*
138. om Y* X2*
139. om Y* X2*
140. om Y* X2*
141. om Y* X2*

एवं संचिन्तयद्देवं सर्वलोकमहेश्वरम् ।
समस्तक्लेशहन्तारं कार्यकारणसंस्थितम् ॥१४२॥

योगाभ्यासफलं **शङ्ख** आह[1] ।

सर्वेषु योगशास्त्रेषु वेदान्तेषु च निष्ठितः ।
सदा तद्भावयेद्योगी तैस्तैर्ब्रह्म विशेषणैः ॥१४३॥
पुनः पुनरनिर्विण्णो ज्योतिस्तल्लभते ध्रुवम् ।
सौम्यमानन्दमद्वैतं बहुशस्तत्प्रकाशितम् ।
तन्मयत्वेन लब्ध्वासौ परं निर्वाणमृच्छति ॥१४४॥

आह **याज्ञवल्क्यः**[1] ।

इज्याचारदमाहिंसादानस्वाध्यायकर्मणाम् ।
अयं तु परमो धर्मो यद्योगेनात्मदर्शनम् ॥१४५॥

आह **विश्वामित्रः**[1] ।

एवं हि ध्यायतस्तस्य ब्रह्मनिष्ठस्य योगिनः ।
सांख्यमानन्दमद्वैतं परं ब्रह्म प्रकाशते ॥१४६॥
प्रकाशितेन तत्त्वेन मुक्तिरुक्ता मनीषिणाम् ।
नान्येन योगहीनेन कर्महीनेन लभ्यते ॥१४७॥
तस्मात्कर्म च कर्तव्यं यथाकालं दिने दिने ।
ज्ञानयुक्तं च तत्कर्म कर्तव्यं मोक्षकाङ्क्षिभिः ॥१४८॥

142. om Y* X2*; c)—°हर्तारं A6

143. 1)—यो° . . . फलं om Y* X2*; आह शङ्खः Y*; आह om X2*; a)—योगेषु सर्वशास्त्रेषु A5; d)—विशेषणः G6 R2 3

144. a)—पुनः om A6 R2; b)—लभ्यते A2 5; इति ध्रुवम् A1 2 R1; ध्रुवमिति X2* A6 B M; after ध्रुवम् A1 adds विश्वामित्रः । एवं हि . . . योगिनः [see 5.148a–b]; c–f)—om X2*; c)—सौख्यम् Y* A3; d)—तं प्रका° A5 6; cor. to परं ब्रह्म प्रकाशते A1; f)—°णमिच्छति A6; add इति A3 4 G2

145. 1)—आह om G6 R2 3; a)—इत्या° B M; °चारधर्मा° G6; d)—add इति Y* A3

146. 1)—आह om G6 R2 4; a)—एवं तु A4; हि om A6; c)—सौख्यम् A3 5 R3 4 B M

147. a–b)—om G6 R3 4; c)—नायोगवेदहीनेन R2; वेदहीनेन A5 G6 R3 4 M+; d)—कर्महीनेन om G6

148. a)—च om A3; d)—add इति Y* A3 G6 R2 3 B M

बृहस्पतिः[1] ।

एवं भावयतस्तस्य व्यपैत्यज्ञानवासना ।
ज्ञानदीपोदयश्च स्यात्तमः सूर्योदये यथा ॥१४९॥
कुर्याच्छुद्धिमशुद्धस्य सर्वेणानेन चेतसः ।
तस्मिंस्तु विमलीभूते लयो ब्रह्मणि नान्यथा ॥१५०॥

मुक्तस्वरूपं **मेधातिथिर**ाह[1] ।

विमुक्तः परमप्येति सरितः सागरं यथा ।
तदाख्यस्तन्मयो भूत्वा स पुनर्नेह जायते ॥१५१॥
साधिभूताधिदैवस्य साधियज्ञस्य चैव हि ।
आत्मा भवति सर्वस्य तथैवाध्यात्मिकस्य च ॥१५२॥
स ब्रह्मा स शिवो विष्णुः शक्रः सोऽहर्पतिर्यमः ।
हुताशो निर्ऋतिर्वायुरीशानः सर्वभूतराट् ॥१५३॥
वेदा यज्ञास्तथा देवाः पशवो दक्षिणादयः ।
श्रद्धादयो हविः कालः क्रिया कर्ता धृतिर्विधिः ।
सर्वात्मा सर्वभूतेशः सर्वस्यायतनं च सः इति ॥१५४॥

सांख्ययोगं तत्फलं च **क्रतुर**ाह[1] ।

कर्मेन्द्रियाणि मनसा बुद्धिं ज्ञानेन शोधयेत् ।
वृत्तिं संशोधनेनैव विद्याविद्ये गुरोर्गिरा ॥१५५॥

149. om Y* X2*; c)—°दीपाद° A1 5 R1; °पोदयश्च स्यात् lacuna in B M, broken A2 [M ed. comments अत्राक्षराणि गलितानि मूलकोशेषु]; °दयः स्या° A1 R1; °यश्चास्य A5

150. om Y* X2*; c)—तस्मात्तु A1 2 R1 B M

151. 1)—मुक्तस्वरूपं om X2*; मुक्तिस्व° G2; आह om X2*; a)—मुक्तं G1 2; मुक्तिं A4; मुक्तः A3; परमं A3 4

152. om R4; a)—°देवस्य A3 5 G6; b)—वै स हि A2 R1; d)—°त्मिकस्तथा A1 2 R1

153. om R4; a)—सरितो for स शिवो R2; विष्णुः om A4; b)—स शक्रः G1 2 6 R2 3; स सोमोऽह° A4; सोमोपति° A5 6; सोमोऽह° G2; सोमहाप° R2 3; सोमः पति° A1 2 R1

154. om R4; c)—श्राद्धा° Y* R2 3 4 B M; श्रद्धादया A1 2 3 R1; e)—सर्वे ते सर्व° G6 R2; सर्वलोकेशः Y* A3 G6 R2 3; d)—इति om Y* A3 G6 R2

155. 1)—सांख्य° . . . च om R4; आह om X2*; b)—शोधयेदित्यारभ्य [omits वृत्तिं . . . (5.160b) भावयेत्] X2*; c)—वृत्ति° conj., वृत्ति° all mss, वित्ति° B M; विष्णोराराधनेनैव A6; °संरोध° R1; °धनं चैव A1 2 R1 B M; °धनं नैव G1 2; d)—गिरः Y*

राज्ञी बुद्धिर्गुणोऽमात्यः प्रतिहारो मनो मतम् ।
सेनापतिमहङ्कारं कारयेदभिमानतः ।।१५६।।
दशग्रामाधिपतयस्तेषां संकल्पनं विना ।
त्रिभिरावरणैर्युक्तं पाञ्चभूतं महत्पुरम् ।।१५७।।
योगैश्वर्यासनारूढो राजेव पुरुषः स्थितः ।
पश्यते गुणवैषम्यं सर्वं ज्ञात्वा तु साक्षिवत् ।।१५८।।
भावनाकल्पनाचिन्ताभयविक्षेपवर्जितः ।
संबन्धमर्थधर्मांश्च देशजातिगुणाश्रयान् ।।१५९।।
सर्वभावान्परित्यज्य सदस्मीत्येव भावयेत् ।
दिवारात्रौ सदैकाकी भूत्वा मनसि चिन्तयेत् ।
ततो रागक्षयादात्मा परे विशति तत्क्षणात् इति ।।१६०।।

इति यतिधर्मसमुच्चये मुख्यकर्मविधिर्नाम पञ्चमं पर्व ।।१६१।।

156. om X2*; a)—राजा A5 M+; राज्ञा A6; राज्ञो A1 2 R1 B M; गुणामात्याः A1 2 G1 2 R1 B M; b)—प्रतीहारो A5 B M; मतः A3 5; d)—°मानितः A4 G2

157. om X2*; b)—संकल्पकं मनः G1 2; पुनः for विना A4; d)—महत्पदम् B M

158. om X2*; a)—°र्यसमारूढो A4 G2; b)—स पुरः स्थितः Y*; c)—पश्यतो A1 2 5 R1; दृश्यते A3; d)—ज्ञात्वानुसाक्षि° Y*

159. om X2*; b)—°वर्जितं Y* B M; °वर्जनम् A1 2 R1; c)—संबन्धवर्णधर्मांश्च Y*

160. a–b)—om X2*; a)—सर्वान्भा° Y* A3; b)—सदास्मी° A5; c)—°रात्रं A4 B M; तदेकाग्रो R4; d)—तूष्णीमासीत चिन्तयन् Y* A3; f)—पुरे X2* A5 B M; °क्षणम् R4; इति om A5

161. इति add यादवप्रकाशीये Y* A1 2 R1, add यादवीये A3, add यादवप्रकाशविरचिते B M; °कर्म नाम G1 2; °विधिर्नाम om A4; °विधानं नाम A5; °विधं नाम A6; नाम om G6 R2 3

षष्ठं पर्व

अहोरात्रक्रिया

अथ यतीनामहोरात्रक्रियोच्यते[1] । तत्रानुक्तमपेक्षितं ब्रह्मचारिधर्माद् गृहीतव्यम्[2] ।

इतरेषां चैतदविरोधि[3] । [GDh 3.10]

इत्यनुज्ञानात्[4] । तत्राप्यसंभवे गृहस्थधर्मेभ्यो गृहीतव्यम्[5] ।।१।। तथा च भगवान्**व्यासः**[1] ।

सर्वाश्रमाणां धर्माः स्युर्येऽविरुद्धाः परस्परम् ।
सर्वाश्रमाणां ते सर्वे साधारण्यमवाप्नुयुः इति ।।२।।

विश्वामित्रः[1] ।

उषःकाले समुत्थाय शौचं कृत्वा विधानतः ।
दन्तकाष्ठमथाचम्य पर्ववर्जमतन्द्रितः ।।३।।
कृतस्नानो जपेत्तावद्यावदादित्यदर्शनम् ।
उत्तिष्ठ ब्रह्मणेत्यादिरुत्थाने मन्त्र ईरितः ।।४।।

गर्गः[1] ।

अथ भिक्षूणां नियमसंयमशौचप्रायश्चित्तं व्याख्यास्यामः[2] । तत्र पूर्वं मूत्रशौचम्[3] । मृत्तिकया पर्वत्रयपूरणं कृत्वा लिङ्गं चतसृभिः प्र-

1. 1)—°क्रिया उच्यन्ते X2*; 2–5)—om Y*; 2)—अत्रानु° A2 6 R1 4 B M

2. 1)—आह भग° Y*; a–b)—स्युरविरु° A6 G6 R3 4; d)—°प्नुयात् A5; इति om A5; अवाप्नुयुः इति . . . [6] प्राणायामत्रयं कृत्वा G1 om

3. 1)—आह विश्वा° A3 4 G2; c)—°मनाचम्य R4; d)—दर्पव° B M

4. c–d)—°त्यादि उत्थाने X2* B M; add इति A3 4 G2; in place of c–d A1 2 R1 give the entire mantra उत्तिष्ठ . . . अनु मेऽमं साथाम् [TA 4.2] and conclude: इति मन्त्रेण उत्थाय हरिध्यानं कुर्यात्

क्षालयेत् सव्यहस्तं द्वादशभिः द्वौ हस्तावष्टाभिर्मृत्तिकाभिः[4] । एवं यथोक्तं लिङ्गमूत्रशौचं कृत्वा पश्चाद् गुदशौचमाचरेत्[5] । प्रथमा प्रसृतिरेका दातव्या द्वितीया च तृतीया च तदर्धार्धेन[6] । एवं यथो-क्तक्रमेण विंशत्या मृत्तिकाभिर्गुदशौचं कृत्वा द्विगुणेन सव्यहस्तं प्रक्षा-लयेत् द्वौ हस्तावष्टाविंशत्या[7] । मृत्तिकात्रयेण पादौ प्रक्षाल्य हस्तौ चाचम्य प्राणायामत्रयं कृत्वा पुनराचामेत्[8] ॥५॥

मृत्तिकाभावे वालुकाभिर्यदा शौचं करोति तदा द्विगुणं कुर्यात्[1] । स्वस्थावस्थो भिक्षुः शौचशैथिल्यं न कुर्यात्[2] । शौचशैथिल्ये प्रत्य-वायो भवति[3] । तत्प्रत्यवायनिराकरणाय प्राणायामत्रयं कृत्वा पुनराचामेत्[4] ॥६॥

ब्राह्मे मुहूर्ते उत्थाय वसुरण्वो विभुरिति ।
अनेन परमात्मानं ध्यायेदहरहर्हृदि ॥७॥
तत आवश्यकं कृत्वा पूर्वमादाय मृत्तिकाम् ।
शौचं चतुर्गुणं कुर्याद्विहिताद् गृहमेधिनः ।

5. om G1; 1)—आह गर्गः A3; शौचमाह गर्गः Y* A1 2 R1 B M; 2)—om A4 G2 6 R2; in place of नियम° . . . °स्यामः R3 4 read संनियमप्रायश्चित्तं; 3)—मूत्र° om A4 G2; 4)—सव्यं हस्तं A3 4 G2; मृत्तिकाभिः om A4 G2; 5)—एवमेव R4; लिङ्ग° om X2* B M; °मूत्र° om A3 4 G2; पश्चाद् om G6 R3; समाचरेत् A5 G6; °चमारभेत् A4 G2; 6)—प्रथमा and तृतीया om G6; 1st च om A4 6 G2 6; तदर्धेन A5 B; तदर्धमर्धं A4; तदर्धार्धे G2; 7)—एवमुक्तक्र° X2* B M; विंशतिमृ° X2* B M; सव्यं प्रक्षा° A5 6 R4; °विंशतिमृत्तिकया A1 2; 8)—at beginning add मृत्तिकाभिर्गुदशौचं कृत्वा द्विगुणेन सव्यं प्रक्षालयेत् । द्वौ पादावष्टाविंशत्या A5 6; °त्रयेण तु A3 4 G2; प्रक्षाल्य add पुनर्मृत्तिकात्रयेण A1 2 R1 B M; हस्तौ om X2*, add प्रक्षाल्य A1 2 R1 B M; आचम्य for चाचम्या X2* A1 2 B M; add इति A1 2 3 4 5 G2 6 R1 B M

6. om G1; 1)—यदा . . . तदा om X2*; कुर्यात् for करोति A5 6; तद् for तदा A5; 2)—°वस्थायां A4 G2; °वस्थासु X2*; °वस्थे A6; भिक्षुः om X2* A4 6 G2; कृत्वा for न कुर्यात A4 G2; कुर्यादिति R1; 3)—शौचशैथिल्ये om A 1 2 4 G2 R1 B M; शौच° om G6; प्रत्यवायी A1 2 4 R1 B M; 4)—तत्र for तत्प्र° . . . °णाय A4 G2; °वायनिवारणाय A5 G6 R1; °वायपरि-हाराय A1 2 B M; add इति A1 2 3 4 5 G2 B M

7. om Y*; a)—चोत्थाय B M; b)—वसुरण्वो conj.; all mss read वसुरण्यो; A1 2 R1 B M give the whole mantra वसुरण्यो विभूरसि . . . ॐ इत्यात्मानं युञ्जीतेति [MNU 539–40]; c)—मन्त्रेण पर° A1 2 R1 B M; d)—°हरहरेवं हृदि A1 2 R1 B M

आददानस्तु वै पश्चात्सचेलो जलमाविशेत् ॥८॥

देवलः[1] ।

शोधयेच्च चतुर्लिङ्गमङ्गुलिनां त्रिपर्वकम् ।
यथा मृत्तिकया पूर्णं सा संख्यैका मृदः स्मृता ॥९॥
हस्तं द्वादशभिः सव्यमष्टाभिः संहतौ करौ ।
गुदशौचं ततः कुर्याद्विंशतिस्तु मृदो गुदे ॥१०॥
प्रथमा प्रसृतिर्देया उत्तरे तु तदर्धके ।
चत्वारिंशत्करे सव्ये करयोः साष्टविंशतिः ॥११॥
पादयोश्च त्रिरेकस्मिन्द्विगुणं वालुका यदि ।
द्विराचम्य त्रिराचम्य प्राणानप्याचमेत्पुनः इति ॥१२॥

स एवाह[1] ।

विण्मूत्रकरणात्पूर्वमादद्यान्मृत्तिकां सदा ।
आददानस्तु वै पश्चात्सचेलो जलमाविशेत् ॥१३॥

आह **जमदग्निः**[1] ।

अन्यदेव दिवाशौचमन्यद्रात्रौ विधीयते ।
अन्यथा बाधमानेषु स्वस्थादिषु यथोदितम् ॥१४॥
यथोदितं दिवाशौचमर्धं रात्रौ विधीयते ।
आतुरस्य तदर्धं स्यात्तदर्धं पथि गच्छतः ॥१५॥

8. om Y*; a)—आवश्यकं add कर्म A1 2 R1; c)—शौचं om A1 2; d)—at end A1 2 5 R1 B M add उभे मूत्रपुरीषे तु पूर्वमादाय मृत्तिकाम् ; e)—°दानश्च X2*; f)—सवासा A3

9. om Y*; a)—शोधयेत चतु° X2* A1 2 R1; B M शोधयेत्तच्चतु° [also A1 as corr.]; शोधयत् चतु° A5; d)—स्मृताः A3 6 G6 R2 4 B; स्मृतौ A1 2 R1

10. om Y*; a)—हस्तौ B M; हस्ता A1 2 R2; d)—गुदे मृदः G6 R3 4

11. om Y*

12. om Y*; a)—पादयोस्तु B M; c–d)—folio with text up to 6.23b missing in A3; इति om A5 [see trans. n.8]

13. Y* inserts after 6.21; 1)—आह देवलः Y*; d)—सवासा Y*; add इति Y* G6 R2 B M

14. 1)—om A5; आह om X2* B M; a–d)—om Y*; d)—यथोदितः R2 3

15. a)—यथोदितं om R1; तथा शौचं Y*; d)—at end A1 2 R1 B M add देवलः [Y* inserts it after 6.21]

देवलः[1] ।

एको द्वौ वा त्रयो मूत्रे पुरीषे चाथवा पुनः ।
प्राणायामान्यतिः कुर्याद्देशकालाद्यपेक्षया ॥१६॥

स एवाह[1] ।

ध्याने दैवतपूजायां भोजने दन्तधावने ।
अवश्यकार्ये स्नाने च षट्सु मौनं विधीयते ॥१७॥

वायुः[1] ।

आकर्णप्रावृतशिरा अप्सु यानगतस्तथा ।
अधौतपादस्तिष्ठन्वा जल्पन्मुक्तशिखोऽपि वा ।
यज्ञोपवीतेन विना स्वाचान्तोऽप्यशुचिर्भवेत् ॥१८॥

देवलः[1] ।

विरिक्तवान्तविण्मूत्रकरणेष्वथ संध्ययोः ।
स्नात्वान्तरान्तरादित्यं प्राणायामत्रयं चरेत् ॥१९॥
एकेन प्रणवेनैव प्राणायामा निशि स्मृताः ।
मध्याह्नकाले नैकेन काष्ठस्थो नाचमेद्यतिः ॥२०॥

16. Y* X2* A5 6 om [but Y* insert after 6.21, and X2* A6 insert after 6.20]; 1)—आह दे° Y*; a)—एकं Y* A1 2 R1; b)—द्वौ पुरीषे तु वा पुनः X2* A6; चाथवापि वा A1 2 R1 B M; c)—यतः A1 2 R1

17. 1)—om Y*; स एव A1 2 R1; d)—add इति Y*

18. om Y*; a)—आकण्ठ° A1 M+; °शिरो R2 3 4; b)—ततः A5; e)—विनाप्याचान्तो A1 2 R1

19. om Y*; 1)—om X2* A5; a)—विरिक्त° only A6; विरक्त A1 2 5 R1 2, विरक्तो G6 R3 4 B M; °वान्ति° B M; c)—स्नात्वा भुक्त्वा [lacuna] कादित्य A5; स्नात्वा हुत्वादनामेत्य A 6; °रानित्यं B M

20. om Y*; b)—प्राणायामो R3 4 B M; निशा A5; स्मृतः R3 4 B M; c)—स्नानकाले तु संप्राप्ते X2*; ध्यानकाले तु नैकेन A6; स्नानकाले ध्यानकाले तु M+; d)—here X2* A6 B M add दिवा कीर्त्येत सावित्रीं सा निशायां न चोच्यते इति । प्रणवप्राणायामा अष्टत्रिंशत्संख्याता इत्याहुः । प्राणायामविधानश्लोकः [°श्लोका उच्यन्ते A6] । न भूमौ पात्रमादध्यान्न त्रिदण्डं कदाचन [कथंचन A6] । आचम्य चासून्संयम्य [चासूनायम्य A6] त्रिराचामेत्पुनस्तथा [पुनः पुनः A6] । निवेदनं करिष्यंश्च संध्योपासनमेव च । अन्येष्वाचमनेष्वेवं सकृदेवेति केचन । देवलः । एको . . . [see 6.16] देशकालाद्यपेक्षया । विण्मूत्रसर्जने [°मूत्रोत्सर्जने A6 R4] शौचं सर्वत्रैवं विधीयते । आतुरस्य तदर्धं स्यात्तदर्धं चाध्वनि स्मृतम् । अतोऽर्धमातुरस्योक्तं पथि पादस्तु कथ्यते । यथोदितं दिवाशौचमर्धं रात्रौ विधीयते [see 6.15a–b] ।

गर्गः[1] ।

ब्रह्मचारी यतिश्चैव अन्तर्लिङ्गं न शोधयेत् ।
अन्तर्लिङ्गस्य शौचेन तयोश्चान्द्रायणं चरेत् ॥२१॥

ततो दन्तधावनं कृत्वा स्नानं कुर्यात्[1] । **क्रतु**राह[2] ।

यतिर्योगी ब्रह्मचारी शतायुः सत्यवाग्व्रती ।
सती च दानशीलश्च स्नाताः शुद्धाश्च ते सदा ॥॥२२।
प्राक्शौचं नैव च स्नायाद्ब्राह्मं वा स्नानमिष्यते ।
वृद्धातुराणामुष्णाभिर्योगाङ्गैर्वा यमादिभिः ।
अब्लिङ्गैर्वारुणं स्नानं कुर्यान्मन्त्रैः सदा यतिः ॥२३॥

दक्षः[1] ।

उषःकाले तु संप्राप्ते शौचं कृत्वा यथाविधि ।
ततः स्नानं प्रकुर्वीत दन्तधावनपूर्वकम् ॥२४॥
अत्यन्तमलिनः कायो नवद्वारसमन्वितः ।
स्रवत्येव दिवारात्रं प्रातःस्नानं विशोधनम् ॥२५॥
उपर्युषसि यत्स्नानं संध्यायामुदितेऽपि वा ।
प्राजापत्येन तत्तुल्यं सर्वपापप्रणाशनम् ॥२६॥
प्रातरुत्थाय यो विप्रः संध्यास्नानं समाचरेत् ।

21. om A 5 6 R4 [A1 2 R1 insert after 6.27]; 1)—om G6 R2 3; आह गर्गः Y*; b)—अन्तर्लिङ्गे Y*; d)—°यणं व्रतम् A4 G2 6 R2 3; add इति Y*; after चरेत् G6 R3 M add एको . . . [see 6.16] अपेक्षया, Y* inserts आह देवलः and 6.13, then आह देवलः and 6.16

22. om A1 2 5 R1; 1)—ततः for कृत्वा X2* B M; कुर्यात् om X2* B M; 2)—स्नानं क्रतु° A6; आह om X2* B M; a–d)—om Y*

23. om A1 2 5 R1; a–b)—om A6, प्राक्पायुशौचमाग्नेयं ब्राह्मं वा Y*; स्नायात् [lacuna] स्नानमादेयं B M [M ed. comments अत्र मूलकोशेषु पंक्तिर्गलिता; this half-verse is corrupt and readings in mss are uncertain]; e–f)—Y* reads स्नानं प्रोक्तं तु मुनिभिः समर्थो वारुणं चरेत् । अब्लिङ्गैर्वारुणैः [वारुणं G1] स्नानं शौचं कुर्याच्चतुर्गुणमिति; e)—वारुणैः R3; स्नानं add ततः R2

24. om Y* A1 2 5 R1; 1)—आह दक्षः A6

25. om Y* A1 2 5 R1; b)—नवछिद्रसम° A3

26. om Y* A1 2 5 R1; d)—°प्रशमनम् G6

सप्तजन्मकृतं पापं त्रिभिर्वर्षैर्व्यपोहति ।।२७।।
ध्यायेन्नारायणं देवं स्नानादिषु च कर्मसु ।
प्रायश्चित्तं हि सर्वस्य दुष्कृतस्येति वै श्रुतिः ।।२८।।
गुणा दश स्नानपरस्य साधो रूपं च तेजश्च बलं च शौचम् ।
आयुष्यमारोग्यमलोलुपत्वं दुःस्वप्ननाशश्च तपश्च मेधा ।।२९।।

कपिलः[1] ।

प्रातःस्नाने चासमर्थो नाभेरधः प्रक्षाल्य जलार्द्रेण कर्पटेन सशिरस्कमङ्गममलं कृत्वान्तर्वासो विपरिधाय संध्यामुपासीत[2] । नित्यं मध्याह्नादर्वागूर्ध्वं वा स्नायात्[3] । अथाचम्य प्राणायामत्रयं कृत्वा पुनराचामेत्[4] ।।३०।।

विश्वामित्रः[1] ।

प्रातःस्नाने त्वशक्तश्चेत्कापिलस्नानमाचरेत् ।
तस्मिन्नप्यसमर्थश्चेन्मन्त्रस्नानं समाचरेत्। ।।३१।।

अङ्गिराः[1] ।

स्नानकाले तु संप्राप्ते वस्त्रार्धं परिधापयेत् ।
तस्यार्धं जपकाले तु कटिवेष्टनशाटिकाम् ।।३२।।

27. om Y*; a–b)—om A 1 2 5 R1; d)—at end A1 2 R1 add देवलः । गर्गः and then insert 6.21

28. om Y*; a)—ध्यायन्ना° R3; d)—°कृतस्येति निष्कृतिः R4

29. om Y*; a)—काल्ये for साधो X2* B M; सौधो A1 2 R1; d)—°नाशं च A5; मेधाः X2* A5

30. 1)—आह कपिलः Y*; 2)—°स्नानासमर्थो B M; नाभिसमं X2*; जलार्द्रकर्प° Y* R3 B M; जलान्ते R2; जलार्दितवस्त्रेण G6; °ङ्गसंमार्जनं कृत्वा वासो R4; °मङ्गं संपीड्यामलं X2* A3 B M; °मङ्गं संपीड्यान्तर्वासो Y*; °वासोऽपि परि° A1 2 R1 4; 3)—°गूर्ध्वं वा only A6, others omit वा ; स्नानात् A1 2 3 R1 3 4 B M; 4)—अथाचम्य om Y* B M; कुर्यात् for कृत्वा . . . °मेत् B M; पुनः om Y*

31. om Y*; a)—स्नानेऽप्य° A5 B M; b)—मध्याह्ने स्नानमा° A6; c–d)—om A3 5; c)—कपिलन्नप्यस° A1 2 R1 M; तस्मिन्नप्यशक्तश्चेन् A3 6

32. 1)—om Y*; b)—°धारयेत् B M; d)—°टिका A5 6; °टिकेति Y* A3

एवं सवनत्रये स्नानं कुर्यात्[1] । मार्जनमन्त्राः पठ्यन्ते अव ते हेड उदुत्तमं दधिक्राव्ण आपो हि ष्ठेति तिसृभिः[2] । हिरण्यवर्णा इति चतस्रः पवमानानुवाकश्च मार्जने विहिताः[3] ॥३३॥

अथ मन्त्राचमनम्[1] । तत्र **क्रतुः**[2] ।

चतुष्केणाप आचम्य द्रुपदाद्यघमर्षणैः ।
मार्जयित्वा च पूताद्भिः पितृदेवांश्च तर्पयेत् इति ॥३४॥

अस्यार्थः चतुष्केणैव मन्त्रेण चतुष्कृत्वः पिबेदप इति[1] । **मनुः**[2] ।

दशभिः प्रणवैर्युक्तां सप्तव्याहृतिपूर्विकाम् ।
गायत्रीं शिरसोपेतामाहुः पापप्रणाशिनीम् इति ॥३५॥

अयं वेदगुह्योऽनुवाकश्चतुष्कः[1] । प्रणवव्याहृतिगायत्र्यः सशिरस्काश्चतुष्क इत्येके[2] । **देवलः**[2] ।

त्रिपदेत्यनयैवर्चा साघमर्षणसूक्तया ।
प्रोक्ष्याङ्गं चुलुकैर्विष्णुस्तर्प्यो द्वादशनामभिः ॥३६॥
प्रणवाद्यैर्नमोऽन्तैस्तु प्रतिमन्त्रं यतिः शुचिः ।
तर्पयेदेकहस्तेन पूर्वं द्वादशनामभिः ॥३७॥

ॐ केशवाय नम इत्यादि[1] । अथ देवतर्पणं पितृतर्पणं च[2] ।

गोशृङ्गमात्रमुद्धृत्याञ्जलिना तर्पयेत्सुरान् ।

33. om Y*; 1)—संध्यात्रये X2* B M; 2–3)—°मन्त्रः R3 4; पठ्यन्ते om X2*; A1 2 R1 B M give part or all of the text of these mantras and omit तिसृभिः and चतस्रः; चतसृभिः A5; पवमानः सुवर्जन इत्यनुवाकश्च A1 2 5 R1 B M

34. omY*; 1)—अथ om A5; 2)—तत्र om X2* A5 B M; b)—A1 2 R1 B M give the whole mantra; °मर्षणैश्च R1; c)—च om A1 2 R1 B M; d)—पितॄन्दे° A5 R4; इति om X2* A5 B M

35. omY*; 1)—अस्यार्थः om A1 2 R1 B M; °कृत्वा A5 G6 R2; इति om A5 G6 R3; 2)—मनुराह A3; b)—°पूर्वकाम् A3 G6; d)—इति om X2* B M

36. omY*; 1)—°गुह्यश्चतु° G6; °वाकचतुष्कं A5; 2)—सशिरश्चतु° A1 2 3 R1; सशिरस्कश्चतु° A5 6 R3; °तुष्क इष्यते G6 R3 M+; °तुष्क उच्यते R4; a)—त्रिपदाप्यन° A1 2 R1 B M; द्रुपद इत्यन° R4;

37. Y inserts at 6.55

पितॄंश्च तर्पयेत्पश्चात्पूर्ववत्सुकृताञ्जलिः ॥३८॥
पैतृकं देवतीर्थेन तथा यज्ञोपवीतिना ।
अन्ते महर्नमो वाच्यं तर्पयामीति चोच्चरेत् इति ॥३९॥

ॐ भूस्तर्पयामि[1] । ॐ भुवस्तर्पयामि[2] । ॐ सुवस्तर्पयामि[3] । ॐ भूर्भुवःसुवर्महर्नमस्तर्पयामीति[4] । ॐ भूः स्वधोम्[5] । ॐ भुवः स्वधोम्[6] । ॐ सुवः स्वधोम्[7] । ॐ भूर्भुवःसुवर्महर्नमः स्वधोम्[8] । स्वधान्तमेतत्[9] ॥४०॥ स्नानं समाप्य त्रीन्प्राणायामान्कृत्वा मन्त्राचमनादि संध्योपासनं पूर्ववत्[1] । आचमनादिषु पञ्चसु जलपवित्रस्य संबन्धः[2] । विद्यमाने जलपवित्रेऽन्येनाचमनमार्जनतर्पणादित्योपस्थानकुण्डिकापूरणसावित्रीजपान्यः करोति तदास्य सर्वं निष्फलं भवति[3] ॥४१॥ **मेधातिथिः**[1] ।

स तेनाचमनं कुर्यान्मार्जनं तर्पणं तथा ।
उपस्थानं सहस्रांशोः कुण्डिकायाश्च पूरणम् इति॥४२॥

गालवः[1] ।

सदा जलपवित्रेण मार्जनाचामतर्पणम् ।
उपस्थानं रवेश्चापि यो यतिः कुरुते न च ।
सर्वं तन्निष्फलं तस्य प्रायश्चित्तमथाचरेत् ॥४३॥

अत्रिः[1] ।

उद्धृतासु स्रवन्तीषु ह्रदेषु विमलेषु च ।

38. 1–2)—omY*; 1)—ॐ om X2* A3 6; a–d)—Y* inserts at 6.55; b)—°ञ्जलिं G1 2; c)—तर्पयेद्भिक्षुः A4 6 G2; d)—सुवृताञ्जलिः B M

39. Y* inserts at 6.55; d)—नोच्चरेत् Y* A1 2 3 5 R1 4; इति om Y* A5 6

40. omY*; 4)—°वर्महस्तर्प° A1 2 B M; °वर्महर्जनस्तर्प° A3 5; इति om A6 R2 3 4; 5)— om A2; 8)—°हर्जनः स्व° A3; नम इति स्व° A1 2 6 R1; स्वधोम् om A1 2 6 R1; स्वधोम् नम इति A3; 9)—om A5

41. omY*; 1)—संध्योपसनादि A5 6; 3)—तदा तस्य A5 6 R1; places सर्वं after भवति A2 B M

42. omY*; a)—तेन चाच° for स तेनाच° A2

43. omY*; f)—प्रायश्चित्तं समाचरेत् R2

वस्त्रपूता न कर्तव्या आपः शुद्धा इति श्रुतिः ॥४४॥

हारीतः[1] ।

स्नात्वा चाचम्य विधिवत्तिष्ठन्नासीन एव वा ।
बिभ्रज्जलपवित्रं चाप्यक्षसूत्रं करद्वये ॥४५॥
तद्वत्पवित्रे गोवालकृते दुष्कृतनाशने ।
उदयाद्विधिवत्संध्यामुपास्य त्रिकजप्यवत् ॥४६॥
मित्रस्य चर्षणीत्याद्यैरुपस्थाय रविं त्रिभिः ।
प्रातः सायं चोपतिष्ठेद्वारुणीभिश्च पञ्चभिः ॥४७॥
त्रिकालं दद्यादर्घ्यं तु लोहितार्काय सो यतिः ।
भुक्तोत्तरे च तद्दद्यात्परमात्मपरायणः ॥४८॥

भुक्तोपस्थानमुद्वयेन भिक्षाकाले हंसमन्त्रेण[1] ।

दिवाकरोदये दद्यात्सावित्र्यार्घ्यं समाहितः ।
जपमध्यगते भानौ जपान्तेऽर्घ्यं प्रदापयेत् ॥४९॥

देवलः[1] ।

उपस्थानं प्रकुर्वीत भास्करस्य त्रिसंध्यकम् ।
प्रदक्षिणं ततः कुर्याज्जानुभ्यां शिरसा नमेत् ॥५०॥
न नामग्रहणं कुर्यादात्मनः प्रणमेद्रविम् ।
पूर्ववत्तर्पयित्वाथ जपेत्सम्यक्समाहितः इति ॥५१॥

44. omY*; 1)—अत्रिराह A3; d)—शुद्धिरिति G6 R4; स्मृतिः A1 3 G6 R4 B M

45. omY*; 1)—om X2*; a)—स्नात्वाचम्य A5 6 R4; °चम्याथ R4; c)—वाप्यक्ष° B M; च अक्ष° G6; d)—°सूत्रे B M

46. om Y*; a)—गोवालैः R2 3; गोवाले A6 G6 R4; °कृतदु° A3 G6 R4 B M; c)—संध्याद्युपा° A2 R1; संध्याप्युपास्या B M; संध्या उपास्या G6 R2 3

47. om Y*

48. om Y*; a)—त्रिकालमर्घ्यं दद्यात्तु A5; b)—संयतिः R2 3; स यति R4; संपातिः G6; संयमी B M; c)—भुक्तोत्तरे A1 2 5 R1; °त्तरेण तद्दद्यात् R4

49. om Y*; 1)—भुक्तोप° A1 2 5 R1; भिक्षोप° R4; °मन्त्रोपस्थानम् A2 B M; °मन्त्रेणोपस्थानम् A1 R1; c)—जल° R2; °मध्ये R2 B M; °मध्यं A1 2 R1;

50. om Y*; 1)—om A5

51. om Y*; d)—इति om A5 R2 B M

बोधायनः[1] ।

वारुणीभिः सायंसंध्यामुपतिष्ठेत मैत्रीभिः प्रातः ॥५२॥ [BDh 2.18.21]

शौनकः[1] ।

सुप्तोत्थितोऽभिध्यायेत्[2] । अथ कृतावश्यक्रियः शुद्ध आचान्तो दन्तधावनपूर्वकमुपर्युषसि यथाविधि स्नात्वापोमन्त्रवदापो हि ष्ठेति तिसृभिर्मार्जयित्वा पूर्वाभिमुखो गायत्र्याप ऊर्ध्वं विक्षिप्य दर्भ-पाणिरादित्योदयात्तिष्ठन्गायत्रीमभ्यसेत्[3] । अथ जपध्यानस्तुतिभि-रहःशेषं समापयेत्[4] ॥५३॥

कपिलः[1] ।

भूम्यां पादौ प्रतिष्ठाप्य जप्यं भोजनमर्चनं च कुर्यात्[2] । अथ तिष्ठन्प्राङ्मुख आसीनो वा पवित्रपाणिरक्षसूत्रैरङ्गुलिभिर्वा यथाशक्ति त्रिकं जपेत्[3] । त्रिसंध्यं प्राणायामत्रयं कुर्यात्[4] । अज्ञा-तप्राणिवधशुद्धये जलपवित्रेणाचमनमार्जनतर्पणकमण्डलुपूरणादि कुर्यात्[5] । सजलाञ्जलिरादित्योपस्थानमिति[6] ॥५४॥

एवं संध्योपासनं कृत्वा ततः पूर्वोक्तं योगमाचरेत्[1] । **विश्वामित्रः**[2] ।

कृतस्नानो जपेत्तावद्यावदादित्यदर्शनम् ।
ततो निवातके रम्ये निम्नोन्नतविवर्जिते ॥

52. om Y* B M

53. 1)—आह शौ° Y* A3; 2)—सुप्त्वो° A5 R3; °तोऽपि ध्या° Y*; 3)—अथ om X2* B M; अथाधिकृतावश्यकः कृतशुद्ध (°शौचः G1) Y*; °पर्युषसीति A1 2 R1; स्नात्वा° . . . (4) जप-ध्यान° om G6; स्नात्वा मन्त्रवदापो° Y*; °मन्त्रमापोहि° B M; °हिष्ठा मयो भुव इति Y* B M; उत्क्षिप्य B M; प्रक्षिप्य A5; °दित्योदये B M; तिष्ठन् add प्राङ्मुख आसीनो A6; 4)—अथ om Y* A5; °पयेदिति Y* A3

54. 1)—आह क° Y* A3; 2)—जपं Y* R2 B M; च न R1; 3)—अथ om Y*; अक्षसू° . . . °भिर्वा om Y*; त्रिकं om Y* X2* B M; 4)—Y* reads मध्याह्ने (°ह्न G1) स्नानगतस्त्रीन-सून्वधतः (°सून्यतः G1 2); 5)—om Y*; सपवि° X2*; जल° om A6; °चमनार्चनतर्प° A6 G6 R3 4; °त्रेण वाचमनतर्प° R2; °रणादिकं A3 5 6; 6)—om Y*; सजलाञ्जलिरिति आदि° A2 R1; सजलाञ्जलिनादि° X2* B M; at end Y* A1 2 R1 add प्राणिवधशुद्धये षड्जलाञ्जलिनादि-त्योपस्थानमिति, and Appendix 1.4.

इत्यादि[3] ।।५५।। एवं योगं कृत्वा तस्यैवं विदुषो यज्ञस्येत्युक्तकर्मसंपादनं च कृत्वा ततो योगाद्विरम्य जपित्वा गत्वा ग्रामैकरात्रचारी चेद् ग्रामान्तरं गच्छेत्[1] । तदाह **शङ्खः**[2] ।

आत्मलाभसुखं यावत्तावद्ध्यात्वा शनैः शनैः ।
विरम्य योगात्प्रणवं जपेत्स्वाध्यायमेव च ।
अन्यत्र विहरेद् ग्रामाद् ग्रामान्तरमिति स्थितिः ।।५६।।

यदि ग्रामान्तरं न गच्छेत्तदा स्तुतिजपध्यानादि कुर्वन्नासीत[1] । तदाह **बृहस्पतिः**[2] ।

उशसः पूर्वमुत्थाय कृतावश्यक्रियः शुचिः ।
गायत्रीमभ्यसेत्तावद्यावदादित्यदर्शनम् ।।५७।।
प्राणायामैर्जपैर्ध्यानैः स्तुतिभिश्चेतिहासकैः ।
पुराणैर्वेददृष्टैश्च किंचिदह्नोऽवशेषयेत् ।।५८।।

इति प्रातःकाल्यं समाप्तम् ।।५९।।

अथ मध्याह्नकर्मोच्यते[1] । तत्राह **शौनकः**[2] ।

अथ यथाविधि स्नात्वाचम्य आपो हि ष्ठा मयो भुव इति तिसृभिर्मार्जयित्वान्तर्जलगतोऽघमर्षणेन षोडशप्राणायामान्धारयित्वोत्तीर्य वासः पीडयित्वा मृदम्भसा जङ्घयोः शौचं कृत्वा अन्य-

55. Y* inserts at beginning आह देवलः, verses 6.37, 38a–b, 39, then adds आह मेधातिथिः 1)—प्रातःसंध्यो° A1 2 R1; संध्योपासनं om Y*; संध्यामुपास्य X2*; ततः om G6 R2 3, add संध्यां Y*; पूर्वोक्तयो° X2* A3 5; °चरेदिति Y*; 2)—om Y*; आह विश्वा° A3; a–d)—om Y* X2* B M; c)—see 5.84; निवाते रम्ये च A1 2 3 6 R1 [A6 तु]; 3)—om Y* X2* B M

56. 1)—om Y*; यज्ञस्यात्मेत्यु° A5 6; °क्तकर्म संपाद्य [समाप्य R4] योगाद्विरम्य ग्रामैक° X2* B M; 2)—तदाह om X2* B M; आह Y*; d)—वा B M; e)—विचरेद् B M; f)—स्मृतिः A1 2 R1 M+; add इति Y* A3

57. om Y*; 1)—यदि न [om R2] गच्छेद् [गतश्चेद् R4] ग्रामान्तरं स्तुति° X2*; 2)—तदाह om X2* B M; तथाह A1 2 R1

58. om Y*; a)—प्राणायामजपध्यानस्तु° A1 2 R1; d)—कंचिद° A1 2; °ह्नोविशेष° A1 2 5 R1 4; °ह्नोपशेष° R2; °ह्नोविशेषतः G6; add इति A2 R1

59. om Y*; °कालीनं X2* B M; °कालः समाप्तः A1 2 R1; समाप्तम् om X2*

त्प्रयतं कौपीनं बहिर्वासश्च परिधाय अप आचम्य ॐ भूर्भुवः सुवरिति जलपवित्रमादाय तर्पयति ॐ भूस्तर्पयामीति[3] ॥६०॥

पूर्ववत्सुकृताञ्जलिरित्यन्तम्[1] [see 6.38] । अथ उदु त्यं चित्रमिति द्वाभ्यामादित्यमुपतिष्ठते[2] । प्राणायामान्षड् धारयित्वा गायत्र्याष्टशतं जपेदिति[3] ॥६१॥ **बोधायनः**[1] ।

उदु त्यं चित्रमिति द्वाभ्यामादित्यमुपतिष्ठते[2] । ॐ इति ब्रह्म ब्रह्म वा एतज्ज्योतिः य एष तपति एष वेदो य एष तपति वेद्यमेतद्य एष तपति[3] । एवमेवैष आत्मानं तर्पयति[4] । आत्मने नमस्करोति[5] । आत्मा ब्रह्म[6] । आत्मा ज्योतिरिति[7] । अथ सावित्रीं सहस्रकृत्व आवर्तयेत् शतकृत्वोऽपरिमितकृत्वः[8] । ॐ भूर्भुवःसुवरिति जलपवित्रमादायापो गृह्णाति[9] ॥६२॥ [BDh 2.17.39–42]

हारीतः[1] ।

स्नात्वा ह्याचम्य विधिवज्जलपूतास्रवेण वै ।
वारिणा तर्पयित्वा तु मन्त्रवद्भास्करं नमेत् ॥६३॥

क्रतुः[1] ।

उदु त्यं चित्रं तच्चक्षुः शिवसंकल्पं पौरुषम् ।
सूक्तं च वैष्णवं भिक्षुः स्नात्वार्कस्याग्रतो जपेत् ॥६४॥

60. 1)—माध्याह्निककर्मो° A1 2 4 R4 B M; 2)—om G6; तत्राह om R2 3 4; आह Y*; तत्र A5; 3)—ओपोहिष्ठेति A5; °यित्वा जलेऽघम° Y*; °यित्वा त्वन्तर्ज° R4; °यित्वा तज्जल° A1 2; जङ्घाशौचं Y* A3; प्रयतः Y* A1 2 3 R1 B M; कौपीनं च बहि° A3 R4; च om X2*; अप आचम्य ॐ om Y*; तर्पयेत् A2 4 B M; तर्पयतीति A2 4 B M; ॐ. . . °मीति omY*

61. 1)—om Y*; °लिपर्यन्तम् B M; at end Y* A1 2 R1 B M add जलपवित्रं विना तर्पयतीति [तर्पयति G1; all preceding om A4 G2] वचनात् । उद्धृतासु. . . श्रुतिः [see 6.44] इत्यत्रिवचनात्; 2)—at beginning Y* adds आह शौनकः; °तिष्ठेत G6 R2 3 B M; 3)—om X2* A2 3 B M; गायत्र्यष्ट° A6 R1; जपेत् A6

62. om Y*; 1–3) om X2* A2 3 B M; 1)—आह बोधा° A5; 2)—द्वाभ्यामुप° A5; 3)—वा om R4; 8)—अथ om A1 2 R1 B M; अर्थः A5 R2; गृह्णातीति R4

63. om Y*; 1)—om A3; a)—चाचम्य G6 R2 3; त्वाचम्य R4; b)—च A6

64. om Y*; 1)—om A3 R4; b)—देवसं° B M; °कल्पं च A2 3 5 6 G6 R1 2 3 4; d)—तस्याग्रतो A5; नमेत् X2*

प्रातः सायं चोपतिष्ठेत्सूर्यं मैत्रैश्च वारुणैः ।
भुक्ते ग्रामेऽह्नि भिक्षार्थी हंसमन्त्रेण पर्यटेत् ॥६५॥
त्रिभिस्त्रिभिर्वाच्यलिङ्गैः पावमान्यघमर्षणैः ।
मार्जयित्वा सुपूताद्भिर्गायत्र्यष्टशतं जपेत् ॥६६॥

विश्वामित्रः[1] ।

मध्याह्ने च ततः स्नात्वा सावित्रीं च समाहितः ।
जपं कृत्वा तु मेधावी वैदिकं किंचिदाचरेत् ॥६७॥
वैष्णवं पावमानं च वारुणं रौद्रमेव च ।
सौरं चोपनिषच्चैव जप्त्वा शुद्ध्यर्थमात्मनः ।
ध्यानं च विधिवत्कृत्वा ततो भिक्षां समाचरेत् ॥६८॥

हारीतः[1] ।

आसीनः प्राङ्मुखो मौनी प्राणायामत्रयं चरेत् ।
गायत्रीं च यथाशक्ति जप्त्वा ध्यायेत्परं पदम् ।
स्थित्यर्थमात्मनो नित्यं भिक्षाटनमथाचरेत् ॥६९॥

देवलः[1] ।

ऋग्वेदादीञ्जपेन्मन्त्रान्स्तोकांश्च प्राङ्मुखो यतिः ।
तेषां च नास्त्यनध्यायो नित्यकर्म हि तत्स्मृतम् ॥७०॥
वैदिकेन विधानेन पूजां कुर्याद्धरेस्ततः ।
अभावे वेदमन्त्राणां पाञ्चरात्रोदितेन वा ॥७१॥

मनुः[1] ।

अह्नि रात्रौ च यान्जन्तून्हिनस्त्यज्ञानतो यतिः ।

65. om Y*; a–b)—प्रातः स्नात्वा चोपतिष्ठेत मैत्रैश्च A5; चोपतिष्ठन्सूर्यं A2 B M; c–d)—om A2 B M

66. om Y*; a–b)—om A2 B M; d)—°यत्र्याष्ट° G6 R2 3

67. 1)—आह विश्वा° Y*; a)—तथा A1 2 R1; b)—सावित्र्या तु Y*; d)—°दारभेत् A3 G1 2 6 R2 3 B M; °दाहरेत् A2 R1

68. a–d)—om Y*; f)—add इति Y*

69. om Y*

70. om Y*; 1)—om A5; d)—नित्यं A1 2 5

71. om Y*; d)—पञ्च° A5 6 R1 2 3; °रात्रोक्तमानवाः A2 R1

तेषां स्नात्वा विशुद्ध्यर्थं प्राणायामान्षडाचरेत् ॥७२॥
[MDh 6.69]

कथं पूजां प्रकुर्वीतेति[1] । पुरुषसूक्तेन वेदगुह्यैरन्यैर्मन्त्रैश्च फलपुष्पोत्पाटने प्रायश्चित्तविधानात् अद्भिः कर्तव्यमन्याहृतैर्वा[2] ॥७३॥ **आपस्तम्बः**[1] ।

स्वाध्याय एवोत्सृजमानो वाचं ग्रामे प्राणवृत्तिं प्रतिलभ्यानिहोऽनमुत्रश्चरेत्[2] । तस्य मुक्तमाच्छादनं विहितम्[3] । सर्वतः परिमोक्षमेके[4] ॥७४॥ [ApDh 2.21.10–12]

मनुः[1] ।

अधियज्ञं ब्रह्म जपेदाधिदैविकमेव च ।
आध्यात्मिकं च सततं वेदान्ताभिहितं च यत् ॥७५॥
[MDh 6.83]
संयोगं च वियोगं च वियोगस्य च साधनम् ।
जीवेश्वरप्रधानानां स्वरूपाणि विचिन्तयेत् ॥७६॥
इतिहासपुराणाभ्यां ध्यानाध्ययनसंपदा ।
आमध्याह्नदिनं प्राप्य मध्याह्नेऽप्येष वै विधिः ॥७७॥
स्नानस्य विधिकर्मान्ते प्रदायार्घ्यं यथोदितम् ।
उदु त्यं चित्रमित्याभ्यामुपस्थाय ततो जपेत् ॥७८॥

इति मध्याह्नस्नानं समाप्तम् ॥७९॥

72. 1)—om A3; आह देवलः Y*; a)—अह्ना रात्र्या Y*; यान्मन्त्रान् A6; b)—यदि R4; c)—ज्ञात्वा A5 R4; d)—add इति Y*

73. om Y*; 1)—अथ पूजां X2* B M; पूजां om A3; 2)—अन्यैश्च A1 2 R1; कर्तव्या X2* B M; वा om G6

74. om Y*; 2)—स्वाध्याय एवो° conj. following R4 B M; all other mss read स्वाध्याये नैवो°; मूकवच्चरेत् X2* A1 6 M+; 3)—तच्च A1 2 B M; मुख्यमा° R4; 4)—°क्षमित्येके A1 2 R1; °क्षमेते A5

75. om Y*; 1)—मनुराह A3; d)—वेदैरभिहितं G6 R3; तत् A5

76. om Y*

77. om Y*; c)—आमध्याह्नाद्दिनं A3 R4 [°द्दिवा R4]; आमध्याह्नादिदिनं R3

78. om Y*; b)—प्रदर्श्यार्घ्यं A2 R1; यथोचितम् A1 R1 B M; d)—उपस्थानं A6; add इति A3

79. om Y* X2*; इति om A6; माध्याह्निक° B M

अथ भिक्षाटनमुच्यते[1] । तत्रो**शना**:[2] ।

माधूकरमसंक्लृप्तं प्राक्प्रणीतमयाचितम् ।
तात्कालिकोपपन्नं च भैक्षं पञ्चविधं स्मृतम् ॥८०॥
मनःसङ्कल्परहितान्गृहांस्त्रीन्पञ्च सप्त वा ।
गत्वा मधुवदुद्धारो यत्तन्माधूकरं स्मृतम् ॥८१॥
शयनोत्थानतः प्राग्यत्प्रार्थितं भक्तिसंयुतैः ।
तत्प्राक्प्रणीतमित्याह भगवानु**शना** मुनिः ॥८२॥
भिक्षाटनसमुद्योगात्प्राग्येनापि निमन्त्रितम् ।
अयाचितं च तद्भैक्षं भोक्तव्यं **मनुर**ब्रवीत् ॥८३॥
उपस्थाने च यत्प्रोक्तं भिक्षार्थं ब्राह्मणेन हि ।
तात्कालिकमिति प्रोक्तं तच्च प्राश्यं मुमुक्षुणा ॥८४॥
सिद्धमन्नं भक्तजनैरानीतं यन्मठं प्रति ।
उपपन्नं तदित्याहुर्मुनयो मोक्षकाङ्क्षिणः ॥८५॥
भिक्षाः पञ्चविधा ह्येताः सोमपानसमाः स्मृताः ।
आसामिहैकतमया वर्तयञ्छुद्धिमाप्नुयात् ॥८६॥

विश्वामित्रः[1] ।

भैक्षप्रतिकृतीरेता विदुर्माधूकरे स्थिते ।
शक्तो माधूकरे त्वेताः कुर्वन्किल्बिषमाप्नुयात् ॥८७॥

80. 1)—om Y*; 2)—om G6 R3; आहोश° Y*; तत्राहोश° A3; a)—°संक्षिप्तं B M; c)—°कोपपन्ने A3 6 G6 R2 3; °कोपक्लृप्तं A2 B M

81. a–b)—°ल्पहीनांस्त्रीन्पञ्च सप्त वाथ वा [वा तथा A4] Y*; d)—°करः स्मृतः A1 2 R1

82. a)—°नोत्थापनात् A1; °नोत्थायनं A2; पश्चात्प्रा° X2* B M; भक्ति° om R4

83. b)—प्राक्केनापि A3 6; °मन्त्रितः B M; c)—तु Y*

84. b)—भिक्षार्थे A3 5 G6 R2 4; वै G1 2; तु A4; d)—तदव्यक्तं Y* [A4 cor. तदत्तव्यं]; °मुक्षुणां G6 R2 3

85. a)—शुद्धमन्नं R2; c)—उपक्लृप्तं B M; d)—जघन्यं भैक्षपञ्चके A3 5 6 R4

86. a)—भिक्षोः G1 2; °विधा एताः Y* G6 R4; त्वेताः R4; c)—°कतमं यो A1 2 R1; d)—add इति Y* A3

87. om Y* A3; 1)—om A5; आह विश्वा° A1 2 R1 B M; b)—°धूकरैः स्मृतैः A2 B M

एकान्नं मधु मांसं चेत्येवमादयो निषेधा अनेनैकवाक्यत्वान्माधूकरसमर्थ-स्यैव द्रष्टव्या:[1] [see 10.59] । समर्थस्याप्यनुग्रहार्थमेकान्नं न दुष्यति[2] ॥८८॥

आह **मेधातिथि:**[1] ।

एकान्नं न तु भुञ्जीत न शूद्रान्नं न बह्वपि ।
अशक्तोऽनुग्रहार्थं वा विप्रादेकान्नभुग्भवेत् ॥८९॥

कात्यायन:[1] ।

याचितायाचिताभ्यां तु भैक्षाभ्यां वर्तयेद्यतिः ॥९०॥

अङ्गिरा:[1] ।

व्याधितानां यतीनां तु वृद्धानां दीर्घरोगिणाम् ।
एकान्नाशनदोषेण नैनस्तेषां तु विद्यते ॥९१॥

बोधायन:[1] ।

यात्रामात्रं भुञ्जीतेति[2] ॥९२॥ [BDh 2.18.12]

कपिल:[1] ।

असाङ्केतिकतात्कालिकादिप्रशस्तान्नं भुञ्जीत[2] । प्रेतान्नं वर्जयेद्यति-रिति[3] ॥९३॥

88. 1)—add आह विश्वामित्रः Y* A1 2 R1 B M; च वर्जयेदित्येव° Y*; चेत्यादयो G6; निषिद्धाः R4; °करासमर्थ° A1 2 5 R1 4; 2)—एकान्नं before अनुग्रहा° X2*; न om A6

89. 1)—आह om X2* A6; a)—नैव X2*; b)—°न्नमनापदि R4; c)—भेषजार्थं M+; d)—यतिरेका° B M; भवेदिति B M; then Y* G6 R2 3 add अशक्तो [अशक्तौ G1 2] भेषजार्थं वा यतिरेकान्नभुग्भवेदिति; Y* X2* [except R4] B M add further आहारस्य चतुर्भागमर्धं वाप्याह-रेद्यतिः [यदि R3 B M] । युवा चैवारुजश्चैव प्रसङ्गं तत्र वर्जयेत् । अन्नसङ्गाद्बलं दर्पो विषया-सक्तिरेव च [half-verse om A4] । कामः क्रोधः तथा लोभः पतनं नरके ततः । ज्ञानेन मुच्यते जन्तुस् [भिक्षुस् Y*] तपसा स्वर्गमश्नुते । नरकं विषयासङ्गात्त्रयो मार्गास्तपस्विनाम् ॥

90. 1)—आह कात्या° A4 G1; b)—add इति Y* B M

91. 1)—आह अङ्गि° Y*; here A1 2 R1 B M add अशक्तौ [अशक्तो B M] . . . एकान्न-भुग्भवेदिति [see 6.89n]; a)—°तानां तु भिक्षूनां Y*; c)—एकान्नभोजने चापि [°जनेनापि A4] Y* B M; d)—add इति Y*

92. om Y*; 2)—°मात्रं add तु A3

93. 1)—आह कपि° Y*; 2)—om A6 R4; °ङ्केतिकं A5 G1 2 6 R2 3; °ङ्केतितं A1 3 R1; °ङ्केतित° A2 B M; भुञ्जीतेति A1 2 5 R2 4 B M; 3)—इति om Y* X2* A3; here Y* X2* [except R4] A3 B M add नक्तात्परं चोपवास उपवासादयाचितम् । अयाचितात्परं भैक्षं तस्माद्भैक्षेण वर्तयेत् ॥ Then X2* [except R4] B M add प्राजापत्यसहस्रं च भैक्षं च तुलया धृतम् । प्राजापत्यसहस्राद्धि भैक्षमेवातिरिच्यते ॥ while Y* A3 add दधिभिक्षाः पयोभिक्षा ये वायाचितभोजनाः [°चायाचि° A3] । सर्वे ते भैक्षभिक्षस्य कलां नार्हन्ति षोडशीम् ॥

यमः[1] ।

चरेन्माधूकरं भैक्षं यतिर्म्लेच्छकुलादपि ।
एकान्नं न तु भुञ्जीत बृहस्पतिसमादपि ॥९४॥
ब्राह्मणेभ्यः परं नास्ति वासुदेवात्परो न च ।
वर्णाश्रमात्परो नास्ति नास्ति वेदसमा श्रुतिः ।
नास्ति भैक्षसमा शुद्धिस्तपो नानशनात्परम् ॥९५॥
भैक्षं माधूकरं यत्तन्महापातकनाशनम् ।
तस्मात्तेनैव वर्तेत शुद्धे पात्रेऽथ निर्व्रणे इति ॥९६॥

अथ माधूकरधर्माः[1] । तत्र कालं **मनुराह**[2] ।

विधूमे सन्नमुसले व्यङ्गारे भुक्तवर्जिते ।
वृत्ते शरावसंपाते भिक्षां नित्यं यतिश्चरेत् ॥९७॥
[MDh 6.56]

क्रतुः[1] ।

पूर्वाह्णे विचरेद्योगी सम्यग्ज्ञानी तु पश्चिमे ।
मध्याह्ने भिक्षयन्भिक्षुस्तेन ह्याप्नोति किल्बिषम् ॥९८॥

पञ्चदशघटिकाया ऊर्ध्वं पादोनचतस्रो मध्याह्नः यत्प्रतीचीनं सङ्गवात्प्राचीनं मध्यन्दिनादिति लिङ्गदर्शनात् ॥९९॥ **कपिलः**[1] ।

94. 1)—om Y* A6; c)—तु न R4; d)—समेष्वपि Y*; then Y* A3 add प्राजापत्यसहस्रं . . . °रिच्यते [see 6.93n]

95. b–c)—om Y* A3; परं न G6 R2; d)—श्रुतिः add वासुदेवात्परो नास्ति न वर्णाश्रमतः परम् A3

96. d)—इति om Y*

97. 1)—अथ om X2*; माधूकरकालः [°कालं G6] X2*; अथैतस्य माधूकरस्य धर्म उच्यते Y*; °धर्मा उच्यन्ते A3; 2)—तत्र कालं and आह om X2*; after आह add ततः षष्ठे विभागे तु सप्तमे [B M add further वा समाहितः] A1 2 5 R1 B M; d)—add इति Y*

98. om Y*; 1)—om G6 R2 3; c)—भिक्षयेद्धि° A1 2 R1; d)—प्राप्नोति A3

99. om Y*; पादोनाश्चतस्रो A1 2 3; पादोनायाश्चतस्रो A6; यत्प्राचीनं सङ्गवान्प्रतीचीनं A5; इति om R2

अत्यन्तं बुभुक्षितो न जघन्यं कालमुदीक्षेतेति[2] ।।१००।।

भैक्षदेशनियमे **बोधायनः**[1] ।

अथ भैक्षचर्या[2] । ब्राह्मणानां शालीनयायावराणां प्रवृत्ते वैश्वदेवे भिक्षां लिप्सेतेति[3] ।।१०१।। [BDh 2.18.4]

विष्णुः[1] ।

भैक्षं चरेद् गृहस्थेषु यायावरगृहेषु च ।
श्रेष्ठा तु प्रथमा चेयं वृत्तिरत्रोपदिश्यते ।।१०२।।
अत ऊर्ध्वं गृहस्थेषु साग्निकेषु चरेद्यतिः ।
श्रद्दधानेषु दान्तेषु श्रोत्रियेषु महात्मसु ।।१०३।।
अत ऊर्ध्वमशूद्रेषु त्वदुष्टापतितेषु च ।
भैक्षचर्या त्वियं तस्य त्रिप्रकारा प्रकीर्तिता ।।१०४।।

मेधातिथिः[1] ।

ब्राह्मणक्षत्रियविशां मध्ये तद्भैक्षमाचरेत् ।
तत्राप्यसंभवे पूर्वादाददीतोत्तरोत्तरात् ।।१०५।।
सर्वेषामप्यभावे तु भक्तत्रयमनश्नतः ।
भैक्षं शूद्रादपि ग्राह्यं रक्ष्याः प्राणास्तु भिक्षया ।।१०६।।
धर्मार्थकाममोक्षाणां प्राणाः संस्थितिहेतवः ।
तान्निघ्नतां किं न हतं रक्षतां किं न रक्षितम् ।।१०७।।
प्राणायामशतं कुर्याच्छतार्धं पादमेव वा ।

100. Y* inserts after addition below; 1)—om R4; आह कपि° Y* A3; 2)—here Y* A1 2 R1 B M add [आह Y*] याज्ञावल्क्यः । अप्रमत्तश्चरेद्भैक्षं सायाह्ने नाभिलक्षितः । रहिते भिक्षुकैर्ग्रामे यात्रामात्रमलोलुप इति ।।

101. 1)—°देशः । बोधा° X2*; °नियम उच्यते and om बोधायनः Y*; 2–3)—om Y*; 3)—°राणामप्रवृत्ते A5 G6 R4

102. 1)—आह विष्णुः Y*; d)—वृत्तिरस्यापदि° Y*

103. a)—तत A5; अथ G6; c)—शान्तेषु B M

104. a)—तत A5; ऊर्ध्वं तु शू° A2 R1; b)—अदुष्टा° for त्वदुष्टा° A5; d)—add इति Y*

105. 1)—°तिथिराह Y*; d)—°रोत्तरम् A1 2 3 R1 B M; °रोत्तरः A5; °रोत्तराः A6

106. d)—here Y* adds अत्यल्पमतिशुष्कं च भैक्षमन्नं सुधासमम् । तस्मात्सर्वप्रयत्नेन भैक्षमन्नं चरेद्यतिः ।।

107. om Y*; c)—°घ्नता B M; d)—रक्षता B M

शूद्रविट्क्षत्रभैक्षेषु ह्यापत्सु च विशुद्धये ।
अज्ञानादर्धमेतस्य प्रायश्चित्तं विशुद्धये ॥१०८॥

क्रतुः[1] ।

न क्रियायोगचरणं शौचाशौचं शुभाशुभम् ।
पृच्छेन्माधूकरे भैक्षे शीलं वृत्तं श्रुतं कुलम् ।
पात्रे तु पतिते भैक्षे शौचाशौचं विनश्यति ॥१०९॥

वृद्धजाबालिः[1] ।

न वर्णविचयं कुर्यान्न च पृच्छेच्छुभाशुभम् ।
पात्रे तु पतिते भैक्षे शौचाशौचं न चिन्तयेत् ॥११०॥

विनश्यतीति वा पाठः[1] । **अत्रिः**[2] ।

न ज्ञातीनां कुले भिक्षेत्[3] । अन्तेवासिपरिपन्थिज्ञातीश्वरप्रेतसूतकगृहेषु भिक्षामुपलभ्य न गृह्णीयात्[4] । आत्मना संस्कृतं परबाधाकरं च वर्जयेत्[5] ॥१११॥

कपिलः[1] ।

सुजीर्णश्च कृशो रोगी प्रशान्तो विकलेन्द्रियः ।
शिष्यबन्धुसुतभ्रातृसखिभ्यो भैक्षमाचरेत् ॥११२॥
अश्वशय्यासनादीनां बाह्यानां स्पर्शलक्षणैः ।
याजनाध्यापनव्याख्यावस्त्रभाण्डपरिग्रहैः ॥११३॥

108. om Y* A2; b)—वार्धमेव B M; d)—इहापत्सु विशु° A5; तु A3 6 R1; e–f)—om A6 B; f)—विधीयते X2* M

109. 1)—om Y*; a)—न om A5; °चरणे Y*; शौचाचारं A5; e–f)—om X2* A6; f)—शौचाचारं A5; add इति Y*

110. om Y* A3; a–d)—om A1 2 R1; b)—°शुभे R4; d)—°शौचाचारं A5

111. om Y*; 1)—om A1 2 3 R1 B M; °तीति पाठान्तरम् X2*; 2)—अत्रिराह A3; 3)—न om A3; भिक्षेत R2 3 4; भिक्षुः A6; 4)—°परिबन्धि° X2* B M; 5)—आत्मनः R2 3 4 B M; आत्मसं° G6; संस्तुतं R2 B M

112. 1)—कपिल आह Y*; a)—सुजीर्णोऽथ Y*; योगी A2 R4 B M; b)—शताब्दो A3 6; d)—°स्वसृभ्यो Y*; add इति Y*; then Y* adds तथा सारपद्धतौ । नैकान्नं भिक्षुरश्नीयात्सदा भैक्षेण वर्तयेत् ।

113. om Y*; a)—यश्चशय्या° A1 2 R1

मैथुनेक्षणसङ्कल्पैः सङ्करी स्याद्यतिः कृतैः ।
तस्मात्पुत्राद्भैक्षमिच्छेद् गृहेऽरण्येऽपि वाश्रयन् ॥११४॥

स एवाह[1] ।

सुजीर्णोऽतिकृशो रोगी शताब्दो विकलेन्द्रियः ।
शिष्यबन्धुसुतभ्रातृसुहृद्भ्यो भैक्षमाचरेत् ॥११५॥
कुब्जवामनकुण्डाश्च छिन्नपंग्वन्धरोगिणः ।
भिक्षादोषैर्न लिप्यन्ते यदि राजा न पालयेत् ॥११६॥

गृहसंख्यां **वसिष्ठ** आह[1] ।

सप्तागाराण्यसंकल्पितानि चरेद्विधूमे सन्नमुसले एकशाटीपरिवृतोऽजिनेन वा[2] ॥११७॥ [VaDh 10.7–9]

देवलः[1] ।

सर्वं वा विचरेद् ग्रामं पूर्वोक्तानामसंभवे ।
नियम्य प्रयतो वाचमभिशस्तांश्च वर्जयेत् ॥११८॥
श्रोत्रियस्य कदर्यस्य वदान्यस्य च वार्द्धुषेः ।
मीमांसित्वोभयं देवाः सममन्नमकल्पयन् ॥११९॥
तान्प्रजापतिरित्याह मा कृध्वं विषमं समम् ।
श्रद्धापूतं वदान्यस्य हतमश्रद्धयेतरत् ॥१२०॥
उद्यतं चाप्यभोज्यान्नं यच्च व्याधिप्रकोपनम् ।
निराकृतान्नं वान्येन नाददीत विचक्षणः ॥१२१॥

114. om Y*; d)—वाश्रयेत् X2* B M

115. 1)—om Y*; c–d)—[न A4] पुत्रमित्रगुरुभ्रातृपत्निभ्यो भैक्षमाचरेदिति Y*

116. a)—कुब्ज° . . . [117] चरेद् om A2; d)—यत्र A1 R1; add इति Y* A3

117. 1)—आह om X2*; आह वसि° B M; 2)—चरेद्भैक्षं विधू° Y*; वेति Y* B M

118. 1)—आह देवलः Y* A3; then X2* [except R4] B M add दधिभिक्षा . . . भैक्षभिक्षायाः . . . षोडशीम् ॥ [see 6.93n]; X2* [except R4] further adds आह याज्ञवल्क्यः । अप्रमत्तश्च° . . . °लोलुप इति ॥ [see 6.100n]; d)—add इति Y*

119. om Y*; d)—°कल्पयत् G6 R2 4; °कल्पयेत् A3

120. om Y*; a)—इत्याह om R4

121. om Y*; a)—उद्यतान् A3 5 6; वाप्य° X2* B M; c)—निराकृतान्नं conj.; all mss read निराकृतानां

अत्रिः[1] ।

अथ भैक्षविधिं कृत्स्नं वक्ष्ये वर्ज्यांश्च नित्यशः ।
यमकुर्वन्पतत्याशु यतिः कुर्वन्विमुच्यते ॥१२२॥
माधूकरेण वर्तेत न कुर्यादितराः सदा ।
ताः सर्वाः कुत्सिता वृत्तिरनिन्द्या मन्त्रणादृते ॥१२३॥
माधूकरमसंक्लृप्तमुपपन्नं यदृच्छया ।
तदश्नीयादनिन्द्यान्नं निःस्पृहेणैव चेतसा ॥१२४॥
षट् त्रीन्वापि च सप्ताष्टौ नित्यं भिक्षुर्गृहांश्चरेत् ।
माधूकरमिदं श्रेष्ठमूर्ध्वं वा कामतश्चरेत् ॥१२५॥
कणयावकपिण्याकशाकतक्रपयोदधि ।
भिक्षां सर्वरसोपेतां हिंसावर्जं समाहरेत् ॥१२६॥
व्रताविरुद्धं यद्यस्य तस्य तद्भक्षणं भवेत् ।
हितं मितं सदाश्नीयाद्यत्सुखेनैव जीर्यते ।
धातुः प्रकुप्यते येन तदन्नं वर्जयेद्यतिः ॥१२७॥
कुटुम्बसङ्कटं चैव लोभेनोपहतं गृहम् ।
पीडयान्नं प्रयच्छेत तस्मात्तद्वर्जयेद् गृहम् ॥१२८॥
शाठ्यं वाप्यथ दैन्यं वा लक्ष्यते यद्गृहे क्वचित् ।
वर्जयेत्तद्गृहं भिक्षुः काकजग्धं यथा हविः ॥१२९॥
उदक्याचोदितं ह्यन्नं द्विजान्नं शूद्रचोदितम् ।

122. 1)—आहात्रिः Y*; a)—सर्वं R4; b)—वर्ज्यं च A1 2 3 B M; d)—कुर्वंश्च मु° Y*

123. Folios of G6 containing 6.123–63 are lost; b)—इतरत् B M; इतरात् G1; इतरस् A1 2 6 R1; c)—ताः om A1 2 R1 B M; सर्वदा A1 2 B M; सर्वात् R1

124. om Y*; a)—°रमनाक्षिप्तमु° B M

125. om Y*; a)—त्रीन्वा पञ्च M+; c–d)—om A6

126. om Y*; d)—समाचरेत् A2 3 R 2 3 B M

127. b)—तद्भिक्षणं A3 M+; c–f)—Y* inserts after addition below; c)—समश्नी° A1 2 R1 B M; d)—जीर्यति Y*; f)—परिवर्जयेत् R4; after f) Y* A1 2 R1 B M add पथ्यं मितं च शुद्धं च रस्यं हृदयनन्दनम् । स्निग्धं दृष्टिप्रियं सोष्णमन्नं भोज्यं मनीषिभिः ॥

128. b)—°पहृतं A5; c–d)—om R4; c)—पीडयन्न प्रय° B M

129. b)—वक्ष्यते A5; d)—हविर्यथा R2 3

प्राण्यङ्गे चायसे वापि क्लृप्तान्नं वर्जयेद्यतिः ॥१३०॥
पित्रर्थं कल्पितं पूर्वं देवार्थं वान्यकारणात् ।
वर्जयेत्तादृशीं भिक्षां परबाधाकरीं तथा ॥१३१॥
नोत्पन्ना संततिः काचिद्यत्र स्त्रीपुंसयोर्गृहे ।
नाश्नीयात्तद्गृहे भिक्षुर्भुक्त्वा चान्द्रायणं चरेत् ॥१३२॥
दृष्टं भ्रूणहपाषण्डैः कुष्ठ्यादिभिरुदक्यया ।
श्वषण्डकाकचण्डालैरन्यैर्वान्तेऽवसायिभिः ॥१३३॥
पश्यंश्चैतान्न भिक्षेत भिक्षंश्चान्द्रायणं चरेत् ।
एतैर्न चापि संभाषेन्मार्गप्रश्नाद्भयाद्विना ॥१३४॥
महापातकिनः सर्वान्पतितान्परिवर्जयेत् ।
सर्वेषु व्यवहारेषु भोजनार्थे विशेषतः ॥१३५॥
कृते देशं त्यजेद् ग्रामं त्रेतायां द्वापरे कुलम् ।
कर्तारं तु कलौ दुष्टं त्यक्त्वा भैक्ष्यं चरेद्यतिः ॥१३६॥
कर्ता चैवानुमन्ता च प्रेरकश्चानुमोदकः ।
पुण्ये चैव तथा पापे भवन्ति फलभागिनः ॥१३७॥
सगोत्रमसगोत्रं वा यद्गृहे सूतकं भवेत् ।
न तावच्छुध्यते भूमिर्यावत्तत्स्यादनिर्दशम् ॥१३८॥
न तत्र कर्म कुरुते पितृदेवादिकं क्वचित् ।

130. b)—द्विजानां A4 G2 R2; c–d)—A1 2 R1 read प्राश्यंगवेऽपि सुप्तान्नं वर्जयेद्यतिः

131. b)—दैवार्थं Y*; c)—तादृशीं वर्जयेद्वि° Y*; d)—°बाधकरं A4 G1; °बाधाकरं R4

132. b)—यथा R4; c)—भिक्षां A3 5 6 R2 3

133. om A1 2 R1; a)—यद्दृष्टं R4; भ्रूणघ्न° Y*; b)—पतितैर्वाप्युदक्यया A4; [lacuna] रुदक्यया G1 2; कुष्ठरोगादुदक्यया X2* B M; c)—पाषण्डकाक° X2* B M; d)—°न्ताव-सायिभिः A6 R2 3 B M; °न्तावसादिभिः A5; °न्तासमादिभिः A3; °न्तरवासिभिः R4

134. a–b)—om A1 2 R1; a)—पश्येच्चैतान्न A5; पश्यंश्चेत्तान्न R2 B M; पश्यंश्च तान्न R4; b)—भुक्त्वा चान्द्रा° X2* B M; d)—मनाक्प्र° B M

135. c–d)—om Y*

136. om Y*; c)—दृष्ट्वा A1 2 R1

137. om Y*

138. a)—°गोत्रसमगोत्रं A3; c–d)—om Y*; d)—हि स्यादनि° R4

भिक्षां भिक्षुर्न भिक्षेत भिक्षंश्चान्द्रायणं चरेत् ॥१३९॥
न ज्ञातीनां कुले भिक्षुर्न चेश्वरगृहे क्वचित् ।
न शिष्यबन्धुमित्रादीन्भिक्षां लिप्सेत कर्हिचित् ॥१४०॥
नाश्नन्ति पितरो देवा नाश्नन्ति वृषलीपतेः ।
स्त्रीजितस्यापि नाश्नन्ति तदन्नं वर्जयेद्यतिः ॥१४१॥
वर्णानामाश्रमाणां च स्वधर्मो वीरसंज्ञितः ।
ये तु तस्मिन्प्रवर्तन्ते वीरास्ते विप्रकीर्तिताः ।
यस्तं लोपयते धर्मं तं वीरघ्नं यतिस्त्यजेत् ॥१४२॥
अथ दिग्वाससीं कन्यां गर्भिणीं मलिनां तथा ।
प्रमत्तां मुदितां क्रुद्धामन्नं भोक्तुं समुद्यताम् ॥१४३॥
गर्भभर्तृद्रुहां चैव स्वैरिणीं कामचारिणीम् ।
अवीरां कुष्ठिनीं चान्धां पुनर्भूं कृत्रिमां तथा ॥१४४॥
मुक्तकेशीं सुखासीनां सरागां विस्मयान्विताम् ।
शठां दीनां दुराचारां सखेदां व्याधिपीडिताम् ॥१४५॥
निर्लज्जां वर्धकीं श्रान्तां प्रेष्यां क्लीबां सुनिष्ठुराम् ।
भिक्षां भिक्षुर्न भिक्षेत पाययन्तीं स्तनं शिशुम् ॥१४६॥

कपिलः[1] ।

कुटुम्बसङ्कटं सोपरोधं वा गृहं न विशेत्[2] । सुप्तां मत्तां प्रमत्तां प्रमुदितां सखेदां सुखासीनामन्तर्वत्नीं व्याधितां भर्तृगतां सरागामन्नं

139. a–b)—om Y* A3; b)—°दैवा° M; देवादीनां A5; °देवगृहे यतः X2* B M; c–d)—Y* A3 read तद्गृहं वर्जयेद्भिक्षुर्भुक्त्वा [भिक्षां A3] चान्द्रायणं d)—भुक्त्वा X2*; add इति R2 3

140. a)—भिक्षेन्न B M; b)—°कुले A3 R4; c–d)—om A3; °मित्रारीन् Y*

141. om Y* A3

142. om Y* A3; b)—°संज्ञिकः A1 2; °संज्ञकः R3 B M; °संस्थितः A6; d)—ते वीरा B M

143. At beginning Y* A3 add आहात्रिः [A3 places this after वर्ज्याः] । अथ स्त्रीषु वर्ज्याः । a)—असंस्कृतां तु यां कन्यां Y* A3; c)—रुदितां A1 2 R1 B M; मथितां R4; d)—भोक्तुमन्नं Y* A3

144. a)—At beginning R4 adds तथा; °भर्तृगृहां A4; °भर्तृगृहं G1; °भर्तृ[lacuna]हश्चैव G2; नैव B M; c)—अधीरां A2 6 R1 2 4; d)—कृत्तिकां Y*; कृत्तकां A3 6

145. b)—सुरागां A1 2 B M; विशयान्विताम् Y*; d)—सुखेदां Y*

146. a)—बन्धकीं R2 3 B M; d)—शिशुं स्तनं G1; add इति Y* A3

भोक्तुमुद्यतां बाललग्नस्तनां भिक्षां न याचेत[3] । रजस्वलाप्रयुक्तां नग्नवधूहस्तगतामवज्ञोपहतां कुमार्यानीतां भिक्षां न याचेत न गृह्णीयाच्च[4] ।।१४७।।

क्रतुः[1] ।

प्रत्यक्षलवणं मांसं मधु शावकसौतकम् ।
मूर्खाभिशस्तपतितक्लीबान्नानि च वर्जयेत् ।।१४८।।
अधीरां स्वैरिणीं कुष्ठीं गर्भभर्तृद्रुहामपि ।
कन्यां धात्रीं पुनर्भूं च नग्नां भिक्षेत न क्वचित् ।।१४९।।

वृद्धजाबालिः[1] ।

द्वावेवाश्रमिणौ भोज्यौ वानप्रस्थो गृही तथा ।
अभोज्यमन्नमन्येषामितरेषां च लिङ्गिनाम् इति ।।१५०।।

अथ भिक्षाचर्या[1] । तत्राह **शौनकः**[2] ।

अथ सप्तव्याहृतिभिर्गोवालरज्ज्वा सोदकया पात्रं प्रक्षाल्य हंसः शुचिषदित्यादित्यमुपस्थाय वाग्यतः प्रसन्नात्मा च गच्छेदिति[3] ।।१५१।।

शङ्खलिखितौ[1] ।

147. 1)—om A5; आह कपि° Y* A3; 2)—om Y* A3; प्रविशेत् R2 3 B M; 3)—om X2*; मुक्तां प्र° A2 R1; भुक्तां प्र° A1 B M; प्रमुदितां सखेदां om Y* A3; °र्वतिं A3 6; व्याधितां om Y* A3; व्याधिगतां A1 2 R1; भर्तृगतां om A1 2 R1 B M; भोक्तुमन्नं समुद्यतां Y* A3; भिक्षां न याचेन्न गृह्णीयात् Y* A3; याचेत add न गृह्णीत A5; 4)—X2* B M places this before 2, and M inserts it here also; न वधू° Y*; तथावज्ञो° X2* B M; भिक्षां om A1 2 R1; न गृह्णीयाच्च om A 1 2 R1; न याचेन्न [याचयेन्न A3 G1] गृह्णीयाच्च Y* X2* A3; add इति Y* A3

148. 1)—om Y* A3; b)—°सौतिकम् M A6; °सौत्रिकम् A1 2 R1; °सूतकम् G1 2; c)—मुखा° A1 2 5 R2 3; °पतित° om Y*

149. om Y* X2* A3

150. 1)—om A2; आह वृद्ध° Y* A3; °बालः A5; a)—°मिणां R2; °मिणामभो° R3; d)—तु R3 4 B M

151. 1–2)—°चर्यामाह Y*; °चर्यामाह । तत्राह A1 2 R1; तत्र om A3; तत्राह om X2* B M; 3)—at beginning A2 B M add पार्थिवानामेकैकभिक्षाभाजनं; अथ omY* X2* A3; सोदकेन Y* A1 2 3 R1; °त्याद्युप° A1 2 R1; सन्प्रस° X2* B M; सुप्र° A6; प्रसन्ना च A2 R1; सन्नात्मा A3; च om Y* A1 3 5 R1; चरेदिति A1 5 R1; गच्छेदिति om A6 R4

काष्ठालाबुविदलपार्थिवानामेकैकं भैक्षभाजनम्[2] । तस्य गोवाल-रज्ज्वा सोदकपाणिना परिघर्षणं कृत्वा साधुवृत्तेषु ब्राह्मणेषु भैक्ष-चर्यां चरेत्[3] ।।१५२।।

अत्रिः[1] ।

सव्येनादाय पात्रं तु त्रिदण्डं दक्षिणे करे ।
उपस्थानं रवेः कुर्याद्ध्यात्वा चैकत्वमात्मनः ।।१५३।।
जपेद्विरजसं मन्त्रं देवं ध्यायन्समाहितः ।
योऽसौ विष्ण्वाख्य आदित्ये पुरुषोऽन्तर्हृदि स्थितः ।।१५४।।
सोऽहं नारायणो देवः पुरुषो लोकसाक्षिकः ।
एवं ध्यात्वात्मनात्मानं पुरुषं विश्वभावनम् ।।१५५।।
प्रदक्षिणं ततः कृत्वा नमस्येत्तिमिरापहम् ।
नमस्कृत्य पुनर्भूमौ समारोहेदुपानहौ ।।१५६।।
शौचार्थं विचरेद्भिक्षुः पादत्राणे तु न त्यजेत् ।
उदपात्रं तथा भिक्षां विना दुष्यत्युपानहौ ।।१५७।।
उपानहाववष्टभ्य व्रजेद्भिक्षुः स्मरन्हरिम् ।
विष्णुस्तिर्यगधोर्ध्वं मे वैकुण्ठो विदिशो दिशः ।।१५८।।
पातु मां सर्वतो रामो धन्वी चक्री च केशवः ।
स मां रक्षतु गोविन्दः सोमपो हव्यकव्यभुक् ।।१५९।।
विष्णुस्तार्क्ष्यासनोऽनन्तश्चक्री वामनरूपधृक् ।

152. 1)—आहतुः शङ्ख° Y* A3; °खितावाहतुः A1 2 R1; 2)—°बुबिल्वपा° A1 2 R1 B M; 3)—सोदकेन Y* A3; °घर्षणं । प्रत्यहं शौचं साधुगृहेषु ब्राह्म° A3 4 G2; ब्राह्मणेषु om A6; ब्राह्मणकुलेषु A5; भैक्षां X2* B M; चरेदिति Y* A3

153. 1)—om A6; आहात्रिः Y* A3

154. b)—ध्यायेत् A1 2 3 R1 B M

155. a)—सोऽयं A1 2 B M

156. a)—प्रदक्षिणान् G2

157. om Y*; a)—विचरन् A2 5 R1; विहरेद् A3; भिक्षां A5 6 R4; b)—°त्राणं A2 5 R1; c)—उदपात्रे R3 4 A1 B

158. b)—भिक्षां A1 2 R1

159. om Y* A3; b)—सोमपा A1 2 R1

योऽसौ सर्वगतः सूक्ष्मः परमात्मा सनातनः ।।१६०।।
निर्गुणो निष्कलश्चैव श्वेतमूर्तिधरोऽव्ययः ।
अनाद्यन्तः सदानन्ते फणामणिविभूषिते ।
श्वेते क्षीरार्णवे मध्ये स मां रक्षतु माधवः ।।१६१।।
सबाह्याभ्यन्तरं देहमापादतलमस्तकम् ।
सर्वायुधः सर्वशक्तिः पातु मां गरुडध्वजः ।।१६२।।
स मां रक्षतु सर्वात्मा माधवः परमेश्वरः ।
यस्य नाभ्यम्बुजाज्जातो ब्रह्मा सर्गकरः प्रभुः ।।१६३।।
एवं ध्यायन्नेकवासा उपवीती च पर्यटेत् ।
वासो हि ब्रह्मणा सृष्टं सर्वधर्मप्रसिद्धये ।
वस्त्राभावे क्रियाः सर्वा निष्फलाः परिकीर्तिताः ।।१६४।।

देवलः[1] ।

आत्मानं ब्रह्मस्वरूपसंस्थानं कृत्वा नमो ब्रह्मण इत्येतैर्नमस्कारं कृत्वा विरजसं मन्त्रं जपित्वा आ सत्येनेति प्रदक्षिणं कृत्वा ये ते पन्थान इति जपित्वा वाग्यतः परिव्रजेत्[2] ।।१६५।।

यमः[1] ।

मेध्यं भैक्षं चरेन्नित्यं सायाह्ने वाग्यतः शुचिः ।
एकवासा अवासा वा मन्दगामी युगान्तदृक् ।।१६६।।
एक एव चरेद्भैक्षमेकदृष्टिरलोलुपः ।

160. om Y* A3; c–d)—om X2; c)—सर्वमतः A2 R1 B M

161. om Y* X2* A3; c)—सदानन्तो A5 B M; सदानन्दो A1 2; सदानन्दे R2

162. om R4; placed after 6.163 Y* R2 3 B M; c)—निराधारः सर्व° A5

163. om Y*; a–b)—om X2*; c)—नाभ्यन्तरे B M

164. a)—ध्यायेन्नेक° A5 G1 2 M; ध्यायेदेक° A4; c)—वासोभिर्ब्रह्म° A1 2 5 R1; f)—add इति Y* A3

165. 1)—om R2; आह देव° Y* A3; 2)—नमो . . . प्रदक्षिणं कृत्वा om A4 G2; नमो . . . जपित्वा om R4; नमस्कृत्वा X2* B M; before विरजसं add यमः M+; विरजा° A1 2; विरजस° A3; विरज R1; °मन्त्रान् A3 G1 R1; ये ते conj. following B M, all mss read एते; जपित्वा om A1 2 R1; व्रजेत् X2* B M

166. om Y* A3; 1)—om X2* A6 B M; c)—द्विवासा वा G6 R2 3 B M

तृप्तिप्रयोजनो न स्याद्योऽनग्निरनिकेतनः ।।१६७।।

मेधातिथिः[1] ।

ऊर्ध्वं जान्वोरधो नाभेः परिधायैकमम्बरम् ।
द्वितीयमन्तर्वासश्च परिधाय रविं ततः ।।१६८।।
उपस्थायाथ भैक्षार्थं पात्री दण्डी गृहान्व्रजेत् ।
तिष्ठेत्संदर्शने द्वारि याच्य भिक्षामधोमुखः ।।१६९।।
वाग्यतः सुप्रसन्नात्मा स्वपन्ध्यायन्दिवापि च ।
अदृष्टोपक्रमे काले तूर्ष्णीं गोदोहसंमितम् ।।१७०।।
यदि नोद्यमते कश्चिद्दृष्ट्वाप्यन्यगृहं व्रजेत् ।
तावत्प्रतिश्रुते तिष्ठेद्यावद्भैक्षं प्रदीयते ।।१७१।।

क्रतुः[1] ।

दृष्टिपूतपदन्यासी मौनी तु सुमतिः शमी ।
एकवस्त्र्येकपात्री च निःसङ्गः सुप्तवच्चरेत् ।।१७२।।
चतुःषडष्टकाले वा यतिश्चान्द्रायणेन वा ।
पञ्चसप्तगृहेभ्यो वा भिक्षामिच्छेत्क्रियावताम् ।।१७३।।
भवत्पूर्वं सकृद्याचेत्तिष्ठन्भिक्षामधोमुखः ।
गोदोहमात्रमाकाङ्क्षन्निष्क्रान्तो न पुनर्व्रजेत् ।।१७४।।

167. om Y* A3; c)—तृप्तिं A1 2 R1; °योजनेनान्यादनग्नि° R2 B M; °योजनेनास्या-दनग्नि° G6 R3; °योजन स्याद्यो A1 2 5 R1

168. 1)—आह मेधा° Y* A3; °तिथिराह A1 2 R1; d)—तथा A5

169. a)—भिक्षार्थं G1; b)—after व्रजेत् A6 adds यमः and 6.166a–b; c)—तिष्ठन् X2* B M; °दर्शयन्देहं Y* A1 2 3 R1; d)—याचेद्धि° Y* A1 2 R1 B M

170. b)—स्वाध्यायध्यानसंयुतः X2* B M; वा A5; c–d)—om Y* A3; d)—तिष्ठन् A5; °संमितः X2*

171. om Y* A3; b)—दृष्ट्वात्वल्पेतरं A6; दृष्ट्वाप्यल्पेतरं A1 2 5 R1 [A1 cor.]; दृष्ट्वाप्यल्पतरं R4

172. om Y* A3; 1)—om B M; b)—तु om G6; c)—°वस्त्रैक° X2* A5 B M

173. om Y* A3; a)—चतुष्टमष्ट° A1 2 R1; °कालेर्वा A5 6 R1; b)—°द्रायणेन च A1 2 R1; °द्रायणेऽपि वा G6 R2 3 B M

174. om Y* A3 [c–d inserted after 6.185]; a)—at beginning M+ adds क्रतुः

बोधायनः[1] ।

भवत्पूर्वं प्रचोदयात्[2] । गोदोहनमाकाङ्क्षेत्[3] ॥१७५॥ [BDh 2.18.5–6]

देवलः[1] ।

भिक्षाकाले सदा कार्यं यतीनां छत्रधारणम् ।
वर्षमाणे तु पर्जन्ये न तु घर्मार्कतापनात् ॥१७६॥

अत्रिः[1] ।

एकवस्त्र्येकपात्री च सदैकाकी व्रजेद्यतिः ।
एककालं चरेद्भैक्षं न जघन्यं कथंचन ॥१७७॥
ऊर्ध्वं न तिर्यग्दूरं वा निरीक्षेत्पर्यटन्यतिः ।
युगमात्रं महीपृष्ठं भिक्षुर्गच्छेद्विलोकयन् ॥१७८॥
न वीक्षेद् द्वाररन्ध्रेण भिक्षालिप्सुर्गृहान्तरम् ।
न कुर्याद्घोषणं तत्र न द्वारं ताडयेद्यतिः ॥१७९॥
अतिक्रम्य गृहं पूर्वं प्रविशेन्न पुनस्तु तत् ।
प्रविश्य भिक्षामादाय त्रिंशत्प्राणायमांश्चरेत् ॥१८०॥
नैव सव्यापसव्येन भिक्षाकाले चरेद् गृहम् ।
अनिन्द्यातिक्रमं कृत्वा प्राणायामशतं चरेत् ॥१८१॥
पूर्वासंकल्पितगृहं स्वयं विवृतमाश्रयेत् ।
देशकालविभागेन सामर्थ्यापेक्षयापि च ॥१८२॥
अनागते परे भिक्षौ भिक्षार्थं प्रविशेद् गृहम् ।

175. om Y* A3; 3)—गोदोहनकालमा° A1 2 R1; गोदोहमात्रमा° G6 R3; गोदोहमात्रकालमा° B M

176. a)—धार्यं G1; d)—add इति Y* A3

177. 1)—आहात्रिः Y* A3; a)—°वस्त्रैक° A5 G1 B; b)—चरेद्य° Y* A3; d)—कदाचन A1 2 R1 G6

178. c)—महीं प्रेक्षन् Y* A1 2 R1 [A3 is damaged here]; d)—गच्छेत्पुरः शुचिः Y* A1 2 3 R1

179. a)—°रन्ध्राणि X2*; b)—भिक्षां A1 2 R1 2 3 B M; d)—द्वारान् G1 2; °येदपि Y* A3

180. b)—पुनश्चरेत् A5; d)—प्राणायामांश्च° A2 G1 6; प्राणयमांश्च° A1 G2 R1 2 3 B M

182. a)—°ल्पितं A5 R2 B M; गेहं B M; b)—°माविशेत् Y* A3

प्रविश्य भैक्षभुग्गेहं निष्प्रकम्पेन चेतसा ॥१८३॥
गृहिणीदर्शने वापि वह्न्यागारेऽपि वा स्थितः ।
सव्येनादाय पात्रं तु त्रिदण्डं दक्षिणेन तु ॥१८४॥
प्रणवादि भवत्पूर्वं भिक्षां देहीति याचयेत् ।
भिक्षार्थं चोदनं कृत्वा शक्तो नोपविशेत्क्वचित् ॥१८५॥
न चान्यद्वस्तु याचेत तृप्तिलोभेन किंचन ।
कृत्वा भिक्षां दृष्टिपूतां दातुश्च करसंस्थिताम् ॥१८६॥
त्रिदण्डं दक्षिणे त्वंसे यतिः संधाय पाणिना ।
उत्पाट्य पात्रकवचं दक्षिणेन करेण तु ।
पात्रं वामकरे स्थाप्यं न क्वचिद्दक्षिणे करे ॥१८७॥

लिखितः[1] ।

नैकान्नं म्रियमाणोऽपि भुञ्जीतापि निषादजात् ।
माधूकरेण वर्तेत सत्त्वशुद्धिकरं हि तत् ॥१८८॥
नैकस्मिन्नापि कुत्रापि प्रत्याख्यातो गृहे पुनः ।
प्रविशेद्भैक्षसमये न च गेहान्तरेण वा ।
अन्यार्थं पूर्वक्लृप्तं वा भिक्षां नैवाददीत च ॥१८९॥

काश्यपः[1] ।

चतुरङ्गुलान्तरितः समपादो निश्चलस्तिष्ठेत्[2] । काष्ठपाषाणमृण्मयवर्जमशुचिरिति न जुगुप्सेत शुचिरिति मत्वा गृह्णीयात्[3] । मुखमण्डलं न कदाचिन्निरीक्षेत[4] । हस्तमात्रं चक्षुषा पश्येत्[5] । तथाग्रतो युगमात्रावलोकी[6] । पार्श्वं पृष्ठतश्च मुहुर्मुहुर्नावलोकयेत्[7] ।

183. b)—भिक्षार्थे X2* A1 2 B M; c)—भैक्षकृत् A1 2 R1; देहं G1

184. b)—बाह्यागारे A1 2 R2 B M; वाह्यागारे R1 [reading uncertain, many mss drop the nasal and read वह्यागारे]; d)—च for last तु X2* B M

185. a)—जपन्पू° B M; b)—वाचयेत् A1 2 6 R1; c)—चोदनां Y* A1 2 3 R1; at the end Y* A3 add गोदोहकालम् [गोदोहमात्रकालम् G1] आकाङ्क्षन्निष्क्रान्तो न पुनर्व्रजेत् [see 6.174]

186. c–d)—om X2*; °संमिताम् B M

187. a–b)—om X2*; e)—स्थाप्य A6 G6 R3; f)—add इति Y* A1 2 R1

188. om Y* A3; a)—क्रियमाणो X2*; श्रयमाणो A1 2; श्रीयमाणो R1 B M

189. om Y* A3; a)—°स्मिन्यत्र कु° G6 R2 3 B M; °स्मिन्नह्नि A5; °स्मिन्कुत्रापि R4; e)—°क्लृप्तां X2*; f)—चेत् G6 R2 3; चेदिति R4

विवृतद्वाराणि प्रविशेत्[8] । अपद्वाराणि न प्रविशेत्[9] । द्वारं न हन्यात् न घोषयेत्[10] । क्षिप्रं न निर्गच्छेत्[11] । चिरं न तिष्ठेदिति[12] ।।१९०।।

देवलः[1] ।

ग्रामे प्रविष्टे भिक्षार्थे यदि विघ्नो भवेत्क्वचित् ।
पुनर्भैक्षं न भिक्षेत बहिर्ग्रामाद्विनिर्गतः ।।१९१।।

जमदग्निः[1] ।

पञ्चाहं सप्तरात्रं वा यस्मिन्भिक्षा न लभ्यते ।
तद् गृहं वर्जयेन्नित्यं चण्डालगृहवद्यतिः ।।१९२।।
तद्दिनानि गृहस्थस्य निराशो भिक्षुको व्रजेत् ।
स्वाध्यायं होमदानं च सर्वमादाय गच्छति ।।१९३।।

स एवाह[1] ।

आहारमात्रादधिकं यतिर्भैक्षं तु नाहरेत् ।
अन्यायेन तु पक्वान्नं चोरवद्दण्डमर्हति ।।१९४।।

वृद्धजाबालिः[1] ।

एकपात्रेण भुञ्जीत निर्दिष्टं व्रतमुत्तमम् ।
नैव दोषो द्विपात्रेण त्वशक्तो व्याधिपीडने ।।१९५।।

190. 1)—आह काश्य° Y* A3; 2)—तिष्ठन् Y* A3; 3)—°षाणतृणमय° X2* B M; अशुचिरि न जुगुप्सेत om X2* B M; मत्वा om G6; 4)—न मुख° G1; न om Y*; कदाचिन् om Y* A3; 5)—चक्षुषा om X2* A1 2 R1 B M; पश्येदिति Y* A3; 6–12)—om Y* A3 but add यत्किंचिद्दीयमानं . . . जायते [see 6.200]; 6)—तथा om X2* B M; तस्मादग्रतो A1 2 R1; 7)—पार्श्वतः X2* B M; 9)—विशेत् G6 R3 4; 10)—X1* places न हन्यात् after घोषयेत्, after which A1 2 R1 add न कृन्तेत्, A5 adds न तु, and A6 adds न तु दिष्ठेत् [blurred and unclear] A6; 11)—पुनर् for क्षिप्रं न A6; 12)—om A6; चिरकालं A5

191. 1)—आह दे° Y* A3; a)—भिक्षार्थं X2* B M; d)—add इति Y* A1 2 3 R1 B M

192. 1)—आह जम° Y* A3; c)—वर्जयेद्दुष्टं Y* A1 2 3 R1

193. b)—व्रजन् G1 2 6 R2 3; c)—°ध्यायहोम° A6

194. 1)—om Y* X2* B M; b)—न यतिर्भैक्षमाहरेत् [°चरेत् A1 2] Y* A1 2 3 R1; c)—तु om G1 2

195. 1)—आह जाबालिः Y* A3; a)—एतत्पात्रे° A1 2 M+; d)—अशक्तो A5 R4; °शक्तौ R1; °पीडिते Y*

शक्तश्च नीरुजश्चैव नैकपात्रेण वर्तयन् ।
पात्रलोभी स दुष्टात्मा नरकं प्रतिपद्यते ।।१९६।।
लोभमानस्तु यो भिक्षुः पात्रपूरणमिच्छति ।
दाता स्वर्गमवाप्नोति भोक्ता भुञ्जीत किल्बिषम् ।।१९७।।
निमन्त्रितस्तु संन्यासी यदा भिक्षां समाचरेत् ।
लोभं तत्र प्रकुर्याच्चेत्पतत्येव न संशयः ।।१९८।।
देहि देहीति यो ब्रूयाल्लवणव्यञ्जनादि वा ।
गोमांसतुल्यं तद्भैक्षं भुक्त्वा चान्द्रायणं चरेत् ।।१९९।।
यत्किंचिद्दीयमानं तु गृहिणीकरसंस्थितम् ।
न गृह्णात्यल्पबुद्ध्या चेत्काकयोनिषु जायते ।।२००।।

कपिलः[1] ।

भिक्षित्वा न चिरमासीत[2] । नेत्युक्ते चादोषमनाः परिवर्तेत[3] । नैकपात्रपूरणमन्विच्छेत्[4] ।।२०१।।

भरद्वाजः[1] ।

पूर्णा दर्वि परापत इति जपित्वा पुनर्नम इति परिवर्तेत[2] ।।२०२।।

अथ भोजनविधिः[1] । तत्र **शौनकः**[2] ।

तत उपावृत्य शुचौ देशे पात्रं न्यस्य पादौ प्रक्षाल्याचम्य त्रीन्प्राणायामान्धारयित्वाप आचम्य ॐ इति वारिणा भैक्ष्यं प्रोक्ष्य गायत्र्याभिमन्त्र्य इदं विष्णुर्विचक्रम इति विष्णवे हविर्निवेदयेत्[3] । उदु त्यं चित्रमिति द्वाभ्यामादित्याय ब्रह्म जज्ञानमिति ब्रह्मणे

196. om Y* A3; b)—वर्तयेत् B M; वर्जयन् A5 6; c)—°लोपी A5

197. b)—°पूरणमृच्छति Y*

198. om Y* A3; b)—समाहरेत् A1 2 R1

199. b)—लवणं A1 2 4 R1 4; °नादिकम् A3; c)—तद् om Y*; भक्षं वै A4

200. om Y* A3 [see insert at 6.190]; d)—add इति A2 B M

201. om Y* A3; 3)—चादुष्टमनाः A6 G6 R2 3; वादुष्टमनाः B M; परिवर्तेत om A6; 4)—नैव पात्र° A1 2 R1 B M

202. 1)—आह भर° Y* A3; 2)—जपित्वा om A6; निवर्तेत Y* A3 G6 R2 3 B M; add इति G6 R2 3 B M

भूतेभ्यो नम इति भूतेभ्यो निवेदयेत्[4] । अथ शेषमौषधवत् प्राश्नीयात्[5] ॥२०३॥

बोधायनः[1] ।

अथ भैक्षचर्याया उपावृत्य पात्रं शुचौ देशे न्यस्य हस्तं पादं च प्रक्षाल्याचम्य उदु त्यं चित्रमित्यादित्यस्याग्रे निवेदयेत्[2] । ब्रह्म जज्ञानमिति ब्रह्मणे इदं विष्णुरिति विष्णवे भूतेभ्यो नम इति भूतेभ्यो निवेदयेदिति[3] । विज्ञायते[4] । आधानप्रभृति यजमान एवाग्नयो भवन्ति[5] । तस्य प्राणो गार्हपत्यः अपानोऽन्वाहार्यपचनः व्यान आहवनीयः समानोदानौ सभ्यावसथ्यौ[6] । पञ्च वा एतेऽग्नय आत्मस्था आत्मन्येव जुहोति[7] । स एवात्मयज्ञ आत्मनिष्ठ आत्म-प्रतिष्ठित आत्मानं क्षेमं नयतीति विज्ञायते[8] । भूतेभ्यो दयापूर्वं संसृज्य शेषमद्भिः संस्पृश्य औषधवत्प्राश्नीयात्[9] ॥२०४॥

[BDh 2.18.7–10]

यमः[1] ।

न भैक्षपात्रे भुञ्जीत पात्रे नाचमनं चरेत् ।
कृतत्रेताद्वापरेषु पात्रभोजी यतिर्भवेत् ।
कलौ न पात्रे भुञ्जीत धारयेन्न च कुण्डिकाम् ॥२०५॥

भरद्वाजः[1] ।

यत्किंचिज्जीर्णपर्णं पतितं पात्रं लब्ध्वा तत्राश्नीयान्न तैजसे कदा-चन[2] । तैजसपात्रे भोजनं कृत्वा प्राजापत्यं समाचरेत्[3] । ग्रामान्ते

203. 1)—°विधिरुच्यते Y* A3; 2)—आह for तत्र Y* A3; तत्र om X2* B M; 3)—तत om X2* A6 B M; देशे उपन्यस्य A6; प्रक्षाल्याचमनं कृत्वा A1 2 R1; त्रीन् om Y*; °यित्वाचम्य Y*; अप आचम्य om A3; आचम्य om A6; प्रोक्ष्य om A6; इदं . . . इति om A6; हविर् om G6; 4)—उदु . . . दित्याय Y* A1 2 3 R1 place after ब्रह्मणे; चित्रमित्याभ्या° R4; चित्रमि-त्यादित्याय A5; भूतेभ्यो नम इति om A5 R2; शेषं भूतेभ्यो A6; निवेदयेत् om A3 4 G2; 5)—अथ om Y* X2* B M

204. om Y* A3; 2)—अथ om X2*; हस्तेन A2 R1; हस्त B M; पादौ A1 2 R1 B M; च om X1* B M; °त्याराध्यादित्य° A6; °स्याग्रं X2* A5 6; 3)—विष्णुर्विचक्रम इति A5 6 R1; 4)—इति वि° R1 2 B M; 6)—उदानसमानौ X2* B M; 7)—एते पञ्च A6; आत्मने स्वाहा for आत्मस्था X2*; 8)—आत्मप्रतिष्ठित om A6; 9)—°पूर्वं संविभज्य X2* B M

205. om A5 6 R4; e)—X2* B M place पात्रे before न

विजनेऽरण्ये तटाके विजने नदीपुलिने पुष्करिणीषु गत्वा तदन्नमुपयुञ्जीत[4] । तीर्थदेशे प्रक्षालनं कृत्वा सान्तर्धानं पात्रं स्थापयेत्[5] । मृत्तिकात्रयेण तु पादौ प्रक्षाल्य हस्तौ च तथैव प्रक्षाल्याचम्य प्राणायामान्षडाचरेत्[6] । प्रणवेन गायत्र्या अन्नसूक्तं जपित्वा परमात्मस्वरूपं ध्यात्वा अमृतोपस्तरणमसीत्यपः प्राश्य प्राणाहुतिं जुहोति[7] । भोजनमध्ये यत्किंचित्सूक्ष्मकेशमक्षिकाभिहतं च तदन्नं पिण्डमात्रमुद्धृत्य हस्तप्रक्षालणं कृत्वा भोजनं करोति[8] । मुखे केशं लग्नं तत्क्षणात्क्षिपेद् ग्रासमास्येन द्वादशगण्डूषैर्मुखप्रक्षालणं कृत्वा भोजनं करोति[9] ॥२०६॥

बृहस्पतिः[1] ।

सुगुप्तवाङ्मनश्चक्षुर्गुप्तगुह्यः कृताह्निकः ।
सुगुप्तभैक्षमाहृत्य सुगुप्तं भोजनं चरेत् ॥२०७॥
न स्पृशेद्वामहस्तेन भुञ्जानोऽन्नं कदाचन ।
न पादौ न शिरोपस्थं न पद्भ्यां भोजनं स्पृशेत् ॥२०८॥
न किंचिद्भेषजादन्यत्तत्तथा दन्तधावनात् ।
विना भोजनकालेन न भक्ष्यान्भक्षयेद्यतिः ॥२०९॥

206. 1)—om A5 G6 R2 3; आह भ° Y* A3; 2)—जीर्णपतितं पर्णपुटं लब्ध्वा Y* A3; पत्रं G6 R2 3; तैजसे कदाचन om A3; 3)—°पात्र A4 G2 R4; 4)—2nd विजने om X2* B M; गत्वा om Y* A3; after उपयुञ्जीत M+ adds गंगातोयं च भैक्षं च वैष्णवानां विशेषतः । आजन्म हन्ति यत्पापं दृष्टिपूतं हविर्यथा ॥ 5–7)—om Y* A3; 6)—तु om A5 R4; हस्तं A2 R1; च om A6; तथैव प्रक्षाल्यom X2* B M; तथैव om A5 6; after आचरेत् A5 6 add पात्रक्षालणं [°प्रक्षालणं A6] कृत्वा सान्तर्धानं पात्रं स्थापयेत्; 7)—°हुतीर्जुहोति A5 6; 8)—यत्किंचित् om R2 3; °क्षिकादिभिर्हतं Y* G6 R2 3; चेत्तदन्नं A4; चेदन्नं तत्पि° X2* A3 6 G1 2; °हतमन्नं तत्पि° BM [see 10.68]; °मुत्सृज्य A1 2 R1 B M; after कृत्वा A1 2 R1 add मृत्तिकां किंचिन्निक्षिप्य; 9)—om Y*; at beginning add बृहस्पतिः R2 3; मुखान्ते A3; तत्केशं R2; लग्नं add यदि A1 2 R1 B M; क्षणं प्रक्षिपेत् A5; आस्ये X2*; °गण्डूषणं X2*; करोत्येव A6; करोति च A5

207. 1)—om A5 R2 3; आह बृह° Y* A3; c–d)—गुप्तभैक्षं समाहृत्य गुप्तं भोजनमाचरेत् A5

208. b)—कथंचन Y* A3; c)—शिरोवस्ति Y* A3 M+; d)—कराभ्यां भोजने X2* B M

209. om Y* A3; a)—भेषजादन्यत् conj. following G6; all other mss have divergent and corrupt readings, which some have attempted to correct: देहजां दद्यात् A1 2

विष्णुः[1] ।

भैक्षं यवाग्रं भुञ्जीत पयो घृतमथापि वा ।
सुपक्वं फलमूलं वा शाकपिण्याकसक्तु वा ।।२१०।।
इत्येते ह्यशनाकारा योगिनः सिद्धिकारकाः ।
तत्प्रयुञ्ज्यादहरहः परमेण समाधिना ।।२११।।
अपः पीत्वा सकृत्तूष्णीं भुञ्जानः प्राक्समाहितः ।
प्राणायेति तु भुञ्जीत प्रथमामाहुतिं यतिः ।।२१२।।
अपानाय द्वितीया स्याद्व्यानायेति ततः परा ।
उदानाय चतुर्थी स्यात्समानायेति पञ्चमी ।।२१३।।
इत्थं प्राणाहुतीर्हुत्वा शेषं भुञ्जीत वाग्यतः ।
अपः पुनः सकृत्प्राश्य त्वाचम्य हृदयं स्पृशेत् ।।२१४।।

यमः[1] ।

विधूमे सन्नमुसले वृत्ते वा यज्ञसंस्तरे ।
न श्ववृत्तिसमाकीर्णे न तापससमाकुले ।।२१५।।
नाभुक्तवति लोके वा भैक्षं भिक्षेत भिक्षुकः ।
यात्रामात्रं तु गृह्णीयात्केवलं प्राणधारणम् ।
यथालब्धं च नाश्नीयात्कामं भुञ्जीत न क्वचित् ।।२१६।।

R1; सदा दद्यात् A6; भेषजानद्यात् R4; भुक्षजादद्यात् A5; a–b)—भेषजादन्यप्पादनाद्दन्त° R2 3 [unclear and much corrected]; तत्तदा A1 R1; d)—न om A5 6

210. आह विष्णुः Y* G6 R2 3 B M; a)—यवागूं G6 R4 M+; वायोन A4; वावाम G2; यावाम G1; यावाग्रपां A5; c)—च B M; d)—°सक्तवः Y*

211. a)—इत्येते ह्यशुभाहारा Y* G6 R2 3; इत्येते ह्यस्य शुभाहारा A3 M+; b)—om A5; c–d)—om Y* A3; c)—तद्भक्षयेदह° G6 R2 3 B M

212. om Y* A3

213. om Y* A3; a)—द्वितीया om A5; द्वितीयां A2 R4; b)—परम् R2 3 4 B M; परः G6; c)—चतुर्थीति X2* B M; d)—पञ्चमं A5; पञ्चमा A6 G6

214. om Y* A3; a)—इदं A5; °हुतिं X2*; कृत्वा R4

215. 1)—om A5; आह य° Y* A3; c)—न om R1; स्ववृत्ति° R4 M+; चवृत्ति° A1 2 M+

216. a)—वा om A2; c–d)—G6 R2 3 place after 6.217; धारकम् B M; c–f)—om Y* A3; c)—अथ लब्धं A5; यथाबलं G6; समश्नीयात् X2* B M

भैक्षस्यागमशुद्धस्य प्रोक्षितस्य हुतस्य च ।
यावतो ग्रसते ग्रासांस्तावद्भिः क्रतुभिः समाः ॥२१७॥
प्रोक्षितं प्रणवेनैव हुतमाध्यात्मिकाग्निषु ।
प्राणादिषु दशार्धेषु स्वाहाकारैः पृथक्पृथक् ॥२१८॥
प्राणश्चक्षुर्दिवं सूर्यो व्यानः श्रोत्रं निशा शशी ।
अपानो वाङ्गनो वह्निः समानोऽपो मनोऽशनिः ॥२१९॥
उदानो वायुराकाशस्तृप्यन्त्वन्नं समाहितः ।
दत्वैषां भक्षयंस्तृप्तिं मुच्यते स ऋणत्रयात् ॥२२०॥

भैक्षस्य भोजनं सर्वत्रोक्तं प्रक्षाल्य भोजनम्[1] । आह **संवर्तः**[2] ।

अष्टौ भिक्षाः समादाय स मुनिः पञ्च सप्त वा ।
अद्भिः प्रक्षाल्य तत्सर्वं भुञ्जीत सुसमाहितः ॥२२१॥

कपिलः[1] ।

अथ ग्रामादागत्य एकपात्रेण भैक्षमुदकेन प्लाव्य सकृद्भुञ्जीत[2] । न केनचित्सह संभाषेत किंचन[3] । न किंचन याचेदौषधादन्यत्[4] । एवं वर्तमानो यावज्जीवं भिक्षुको मुक्तो भवेत्[5] ॥२२२॥

दोषाशङ्कायामिदं द्रष्टव्यम्[1] । **क्रतुः**[2] ।

चतुष्कैः प्रोक्षयेद्भिक्षां तल्लिङ्गैर्बलिमाहरेत् ।

217. Y* A3 insert after 6.221; b)—भुक्तस्य Y* A3; c)—याचतो Y* A3; d)—तावन्तः G6 R2 3 B M

218. om Y* A3; from here to 6.246b om R2 3 [see insert after 6.250] a)—before प्रोक्षितं G6 R2 3 add यमः; b)—°त्मिकादिषु X2*; here G6 R2 3 insert 6.213c–d; c)—प्राणादिषु om G6; प्राणाहुतिदश° A5; d)—°कारे A5 R4

219. om Y* A3; a)—दिवा X2* B M; b)—दिशं A1 2 R1; दिशि A5

220. om Y* A3; c)—तृप्तो B M; d)—हि for स R4

221. 1)—om Y*; सर्वत्र प्रक्षाल्योक्तम् for सर्वत्रो° . . . भोजनम् X2* B M; 2)—आह om X2* B M; संवर्त आह A5 6; a)—अष्टभि° A5; b)—सप्त पञ्च B M; d)—after this Y* A3 insert 6.217; then Y* A1 2 3 R1 insert 6.225.

222. Y* A3 omit 6.222—55 and give instead 6.239, 6.240a–b, 6.241c–d, आह क्रतुः 6.252a–d, 6.233, in that order; 1)—कपिलश्च G6 R2 3; 2)—ग्रामादाहृत्य A1 2 R1; °केनाप्लव्य A6; 3)—न om A5; किंचन om X2* B M; 5)—भवेदिति B M

विष्णुब्रह्मार्कभूतेभ्यो दद्याद्वा किंचिदर्थिने ।।२२३।।
पद्ममूर्ध्वमुखं कृत्वा प्राणाद्यैः पूरकादिभिः ।
प्रादेशमात्रे ब्रह्माग्नौ हुत्वान्नं मुच्यते मलैः ।।२२४।।
न स्वादयीत भुञ्जानः षड्रसान्नैव कीर्तयेत् ।
सत्कृतासत्कृते तुल्यो नाभिनन्देत न द्विषेत् ।।२२५।।

स एवाह[1] ।

नोत्सृजेन्नातिभुञ्जीत न निन्देन्नाधिकं हरेत् ।
गोब्राह्मणार्कसोमाग्निमरुदापो न कुत्सयेत् ।।२२६।।

कपिलः[1] ।

व्रताविरुद्धं यत्किंचित्पर्युषितमपि गृह्णीयादाप्याययितुकामः प्राणायामत्रयं कृत्वा पुनराचामेत्त्रिर्द्विर्वा प्रक्षाल्य देशं पात्रं वा यन्त्रमारोप्य प्रणवेनाभ्युक्ष्य त्रिकेणाभिमन्त्रयेद्भिक्षाम्[2] । इदं विष्णुरिति ग्रासमात्रमपि पूजयेत्[3] । नानिवेद्यं भुञ्जीत[4] । भूतबलिदानादिकमर्थिने संविभागशीलतापि प्रशस्ता[5] ।।२२७।।

सुखं जीवन्ति मुनयो भैक्षवृत्तिमुपाश्रिताः ।
अद्रोहाः सर्वभूतानां सारङ्गा इव षट्पदाः ।।२२८।।

सोम एवान्नमश्नीयादिति ध्यात्वा योऽन्नमत्ति सोऽमृतमत्ति[1] । प्राणाय स्वाहेति प्राणेऽन्नमत्ति[2] । अपानाय स्वाहेत्यपानेऽन्नमत्ति[3] । व्यानाय स्वाहेति व्यानेऽन्नमत्ति[4] । उदानाय स्वाहेत्युदानेऽन्नमत्ति[5] ।

223. om Y* A3; 1)—G6 R2 3 read अतिदोषशङ्कायामेवान्नस्य प्रक्षालणमिति द्रष्टव्यम्; a)—चतुष्केन R4; d)—किंचन दक्षिणे A1 2 R1

224. om Y* A3; b)—प्रणवाद्यैः A5; d)—कृत्वान्नं A1 2 R1

225. Y* A1 2 3 R1 insert after 6.221; d)—नाभिनन्देन्न विद्विषेत् A3

226. om Y* A3; 1)—om X2*; a)—नोत्सृजेत and om नातिभुञ्जीत R4; °जेन्नाभिनन्देत G6 R2 3; b)—निन्द्यान्नाधि° X2* B M; नातिभोजयेत् X2*; °धिकां A1 2 R1

227. om Y* A3; 1)—om A5; 2)—°तमपि add यद् A6; त्रिभिर्वा R4; भिक्षां च A1 2 R1 B M; 5)—°लिदानामर्थिने A1 2 R1; °नादिमर्थिने A6; °शीलता च प्र° A5

228. om Y* A3; b)—भैक्षमुपा° A1 2 R1; भैक्षमन्नमुपा° B M; d)—G6 R2 3 B M insert here 6.255, 6.257 [B M repeat these two passages also at 6.255, 257], and the text in App. 1.5; but the editor of M comments that this section is not found in many mss [see the same addition in A6 and R4 at 6.229].

समानाय स्वाहेति समानेऽन्नमत्ति[6] । यो योऽन्नमत्ति स सोऽग्निः[7] । यदन्नमद्यते तत्सर्वं सोमः[8] । प्रक्षाल्य पात्रं त्रिकेणाभिमन्त्रितं प्रतिगृह्णीत[9] । प्रतिमुच्यते भुक्त्वा पापादिति[10] ।।२२९।।

विश्वामित्रः[1] ।

माधूकरे यथापूर्वं चतुर्थायोत्सृजेद्यतिः ।
शेषेषु च चतुर्ष्वेव यतिस्तन्न विसर्जयेत् ।।२३०।।
उदु त्यं चित्रमित्याभ्यामादित्याय निवेदयेत् ।
ब्रह्म जज्ञानमित्युक्त्वा ब्रह्मणेऽन्नं निवेदयेत् ।
इदं विष्णुरित्यनेन विष्णवेऽथ निवेदयेत् ।।२३१।।
ततस्तु सर्वभूतेभ्यो बलिं दत्त्वा चतुर्थकम् ।
ग्रासमात्रं तु दातव्यं सूर्यादीनां यथाक्रमम् ।।२३२।।
यः परान्नं समाहृत्य त्यजत्यन्नं दिने दिने ।
तस्य दोषेण युज्येत प्रायश्चित्ती भवेद्यतिः ।।२३३।।
अपि चास्य कुतो दानं दत्त्वा चास्य कुतः फलम् ।
दाता प्रतिग्रहीता च प्रेत्य वै नरकं व्रजेत् ।।२३४।।

229. om Y* A3 G6 R2 3; 1)—B M add at beginning विश्वामित्रः; A6 omits 1–7, and यदन्नमद्यते [8], but includes this section in the repetition noted at 8; °श्रीरन्नदमिति A5; °श्रीरन्नाद इति R4; 4–6)—om R4; 7)—सो om B M; 7–8)—ह्यग्निमयमन्नमद्यते A1 2 B M; योऽन्नमत्ति सोऽश्नीया आन्नमत्ति हैतुकीरिति R4; 8)—यदन्नमत्त्यहेतुक इति A6; then A6 R4 give text of App. 1.5; 10)—पापादिति conj. following B M; पापानि R1; पादानि A2 5; पादानि cor. पापानि A1; पदानि गत्वा स नियुञ्जीत । ततो देवं चतुर्भुजं चिन्तयेत् । निद्रायामप्यदोषः A6 [phrase 10 appears to be corrupt, and the reading is very uncertain]

230. om Y* A3; a–d)—om X2*; a)—दयापूर्वं A6; यदापूर्वं A1 2 R1; b)—चतुर्था-चोत्सृ° A5 6; चतुर्थायोन्नमुत्सृजेत् B M; c)—च om A5; च यथातुष्टि B M; d)—यतिस्तं तं वि° A6; विलङ्घयेत् B M

231. om Y* X2* A3; d)—ब्रह्मणेऽथ A6; ब्रह्मणे नि° A5; e–f)—om A5 B M; e)—विष्णुर्विचक्रम इत्यनेन A1 2 R1; विष्णवे निवे° A1 2 R1

232. om Y* A3; a–b)—om X2*; a)—ततस्तु om A5; c)—°मात्रं om G6

233. om Y* A3 [but inserted at 6.222]; a)—पुरान्नं B M; b)—भुनक्त्यन्नं A1 B M; भुञ्जत्यन्नं A2; भु[lacuna]त्यन्नं R1; चत्यन्नं A5; c)—युञ्जीत A6; d)—भवेदपि A1 2 5 R1

234. om Y* A3; a)—दानात् A1 2 R1;

हारीतः[1] ।

उत्पाटयेच्च कवचं दक्षिणेन करेण वै ।
पात्रं वामकरे स्थाप्य दक्षिणेनानुश्लेषयेत् ॥२३५॥
यावदन्नक्षुधार्तिः स्यात्तावद्भैक्षं समाचरेत् ।
ततो निवृत्य तत्पात्रं संस्थाप्याचम्य संयमी ॥२३६॥
चतुरङ्गुलैः प्रच्छाद्य ग्रासमात्रं समाहितः ।
सर्वव्यञ्जनसंयुक्तं पृथक्पात्रे निवेदयेत् ॥२३७॥
सूर्यादिदेवभूतेभ्यो दत्त्वान्नं प्रोक्ष्य वारिणा ।
भुञ्जीत पर्णपुटके न पात्रे वाग्यतो यतिः ॥२३८॥
वटार्काश्वत्थपत्रेषु कुम्भीतिन्दुकपत्रयोः ।
कोविदारकरञ्जेषु न भुञ्जीत कदाचन ॥२३९॥
न च कांस्ये तु भुञ्जीत त्वापद्यपि कदाचन ।
पलाशाः सर्व उच्यन्ते यतयः कांस्यभोजिनः ॥२४०॥
कांस्यकस्य च यत्पापं गृहस्थस्य तथैव च ।
कांस्यभोजी यतिः सर्वं प्राप्नुयात्किल्बिषं तयोः ॥२४१॥

यमः[1] ।

235. om Y* A3; from 6.235 to 6.250(2) मेधातिथेस्तु स्वयं omitted in A6 [possibly a missing page]; 1)—om X2*; b)—करेण च X2*; d)—°नुश्लेषयेत् conj., mss read °नुशेषयेत् X2* A5 R1; °नुशोषयेत् A2 B M; °नुशेषयेत् cor. °नुशोषयेत् A1. The conj. reading is supported by a near-identical verse cited in Ypra 57.22 and PaM I, 560.

236. om Y* A3 6; a)—यावतान्नक्षुधार्तः X2*; यावतान्नक्षु° R1; यावदान्नक्षु° A5; b)—समाहरेत् R1

237. om Y* A3 6; a)—चतुरङ्गुलप्रमाणाच्च G6 R2 3; °ङ्गुलिभिर्गृह्य B M; °ङ्गुलं R4; c)—सव्यञ्जनरसं युक्तं A1 2; सव्यञ्ज° R1

238. om Y* A3 6; d)—पलाश for न प्रात्रे A1; मुनिः X2*

239. om A3; G6 R2 3 insert after 6.250; Y* A3 insert at 6.222; a)—°पर्णेषु A5; °पात्रेषु R4; b)—°पर्णयोः A5 R4; c)—°रञ्जेन A1 2 R1

240. om Y* A3 6 [A3 inserts a–b at 6.222]; G6 R2 3 insert after 6.250; a–b)—om B M; भुञ्जीयादापद्यपि M+; भञ्जीत आपद्यपि A1 2; ह्यापद्यपि R4 [accepted reading confirmed by 6.250]; d)—°भोजनाः B M

241. om Y* A3 6 [A3 inserts c–d at 6.222] A6; a)—तु A2 5 R1; c)—सर्वे A5

हिरण्मयानि पात्राणि कृष्णायसमयानि च ।
यतीनां तान्यपात्राणि भैक्षे वा भोजनेऽपि वा ।।२४२।।
सुवर्णरूप्यपात्रेषु ताम्रकांस्यायसेषु च ।
भिक्षां दत्त्वा न धर्मोऽस्ति गृहीत्वा नरकं व्रजेत् ।।२४३।।

लिखितः[1] ।

न भैक्षपात्रे भुञ्जीत पात्रे नाचमनं चरेत् ।
कृतत्रेताद्वापरेषु पात्रभोजी यतिर्भवेत् ।।२४४।।
कलौ न पात्रे भुञ्जीत धारयेन्न च कुण्डिकाम् ।
भुञ्जीत पर्णपुटके पर्णपृष्ठे न जातुचित् ।।२४५।।
पलाशपद्मकदलीदलाभावे ह्यभोजनम् ।
अभावेऽप्यन्यपात्राणां न कांस्ये नैव राजते ।।२४६।।
नापि कार्ष्णायसे नापि सौवर्णे नापि ताम्रके ।
न प्राण्यङ्गे नैव भूमौ न कुशादितृणेषु वा ।।२४७।।
पलाशपर्णे भुञ्जीत पाणिपात्रेऽथ वापदि ।
पलाशपद्मपत्रेषु गृही भुक्त्वैन्दवं चरेत् ।
यतिर्वनस्थश्च ततो लभते चैन्दवं फलम् ।।२४८।।

मेधातिथिः[1] ।

सुवर्णकांस्यरूप्येषु ताम्राब्जाश्ममयेषु च ।

242. om Y* A3 6; G6 R2 3 insert after 6.250; 1)—om R4; b)—कृष्णायससमानि A5; c)—नान्यपा° R4

243. om Y* A3 6

244. om Y* A3 6; G6 R2 3 insert after 6.250

245. om Y* A3 6; a–b)—G6 R2 3 insert after 6.250; b)—तु B M; न च . . . [246] राजते om R1

246. om Y* A3 6; a)—पलाशपद्म° om A1 2; पलाशपत्र° B M; b)—°भावे . . . [247] तृणेषु वा om G6 R2 3

247. om Y* A3 6; a)—कृष्णा° B M; d)—कुशस्तरणे तथा G6 R2 3; °तृणेन R4; च for वा A5; then G6 R2 3 add लिखितः and insert 6.242a–d

248. om Y* A3 6; R2 3 insert after 6.250; a)—°पत्रे G6; °पात्रे R2 3; b)—वा यदि B M; c)—°पत्रे च R2 3; °पात्रे च G6

भुञ्जन्भिक्षुर्न दुष्येत दुष्यते तु परिग्रहात् ॥२४९॥

सुवर्णादीनि पात्राणि भैक्षाय भोजनाय वा स्वयं न परिग्राह्याणीति **यमलिखितयोर**भिप्रायः[1] । **मेधातिथे**स्तु स्वयं परिग्रहेऽपि परकीयेषु तेष्वापदि भुञ्जानो न दुष्यतीति मतम्[2] । परकीयानामप्यभावे पाणिपात्रभोजनम्[3] । कांस्यादिषु पर्णाभावमात्रेण न भोक्तव्यं किंतु मुमूर्षावस्थाप्राप्तौ **हारीतेन** त्वापद्यपि कदाचनेत्युक्तत्वात्[4] ॥२५०॥ बलिदानस्य विनियोगम**त्रि**राह[1] ।

निवेद्यं नार्थिने दद्याद्यथेष्टं नोत्सृजेत वा ।
प्रक्षिपेत्तज्जले विद्वान्निखनेद्वा महीतले ॥२५१॥

भिक्षान्नस्य दानं भोजनविघ्ने समुत्पन्ने तस्यान्नस्य विनियोगं च **क्रतु**राह[1] ।

माधूकरं समाहृत्य ब्राह्मणेभ्यो ददाति यः ।
स याति नरकं घोरं भोक्ता चान्द्रायणं चरेत् ॥२५२॥
प्रायश्चित्तव्रतापत्सु भैक्षमुक्तं द्विजातिषु ।
तद्देयं स्तेयमन्येषां यतीनां तु मखैः समम् ॥२५३॥

यतेः सकृद्भोजनं **शाण्डिल्य** आह[1] ।

249. om Y* A3 6; a)—सौवर्ण° X2*; °रौप्यकांस्येषु G6 R2 3;; °रौप्येषु A1 R4; c)—लिप्येत X2*

250. om Y* A3; 1)—om A6; सौवर्ण° X2*; भैक्षार्थं X2* B M; भैक्षं वा भो° A5; च for वा A1 2 R1 B M; 2)—मेधातिथेस्तु स्वयं om A6; स्वयमेव A5; स्वयमपरि° R3; before परिग्रहे A6 add भोजनावस्थायां न; परकेषु A1 2 R1; परकीयेष्वापदि R4; परकीयेषु तेषु om G6 R2 3; 3)—°नामभावे X2* A6; पाणिभो° A1 2 R1 3 B M; 4)—किंतु om A1 2 R1 4 B M; °प्राप्ताविति [प्राप्ततेति G6] द्रष्टव्यं G6 R2 3; °प्राप्ताविति R4; नापद्यपि X2*; आपद्यपि A5; °क्तत्वाच्च A5; after this G6 R2 3 add App. 1.6 [this addition repeats much of the text already given in these mss and is probably a scribal error]

251. om Y* A3; 1)—भिक्षान्नस्य भोजनविघ्ने समुत्पन्ने विनि° B M; °दानविनि° A1 2 R1; विधानस्य विनि° A5; विनियोगम् om G6; a)—नैवेद्यं A1 G6 B M; b)—°जेत्तथा R2 3 4

252. om Y* A1 2 3 R1 B M [but A3 insert a–d at 6.222]; ; 1)—भिक्षितान्नस्य A5; तस्य विनि° G6 R2 3; च om G6 R2 3; d)—after this A1 2 R1 B M add सुवर्णादीनि पात्राणि भैक्षाय [भिक्षायै B M] भोजनाय च

253. om Y* A3; a–b)—स्वयं न परिग्राह्याणि सत्सु भैक्षं द्विजातिषु A1 2 R1 B M; c)—तद्धेयं A1 R1 B M; स्नेहमन्ये° A5

ग्रामं गत्वा तु सायाह्ने भैक्षमाहृत्य वाग्यतः ।
अष्टौ ग्रासान्समश्नीयात्प्रत्यहं सकृदेव तु ॥२५४॥

वृद्धजाबालिः[1] ।

न क्वचिन्निशि भुञ्जीत भुक्त्वा भुञ्जीत नो पुनः ।
भुञ्जानो निशि संन्यासी पतते नात्र संशयः ॥२५५॥
संध्याकाले तु संप्राप्ते निशि भुञ्जीत यो यतिः ।
उपस्थानं च जप्यं च प्राणायामो बलिस्तथा ।
सर्वे ते निष्फलास्तस्य प्रायश्चित्तं विधीयते ॥२५६॥

द्विर्भोजने **वसिष्ठः**[1] ।

ब्राह्मणकुले यल्लभते तद्भुञ्जीत सायं प्रातर्मधुमांसवर्जं न च तृप्येदिति[2] । (VaDh 10.24–25)

तदेतदशक्तविषयम्[3] ॥२५७॥

अथ भोजनोत्तरक्रिया[1] । तत्र **शौनकः**[2] ।

प्राश्याप आचम्य वाङ्म आसन्नसोः प्राण इति जपित्वाचम्य उद्वयं तमसस्परीत्यादित्यमुपस्थाय सप्तव्याहृतिभिर्गोवालरज्ज्वा सोदकेन पात्रं प्रक्षाल्य त्रीन्प्राणायामान्धारयित्वा गायत्र्याष्टशतं जपेत्[3] । जपध्यानाभ्यां शिष्टकालं नयेत्[4] । अथास्तमितभास्करां सायंसंध्यामातारकोदयमुपासीनो गायत्रीजपं कुर्यात्[5] । अथ यावदवशमुपागतस्तावद्ध्यायेत्[6] । सुप्तोत्थितोऽपि ध्यायेत्[7] ॥२५८॥

254. om Y* A3; a)—तु om G6; c)—अष्ट R1; d)—हि A1 2 B M

255. 1)—आह वृद्ध° Y* A3 R3; आह जाबालिः R2; a–d)—G6 R2 3 insert at 6.228; b)—यो यतिः G6 R2 3; वा पुनः Y*; d)—पतत्येव न A1 2 R1 B M

256. om Y* A3; a)—संध्या° conj. following reading of 10.85, all mss read अन्यकाले; तु om R2

257. om G6 R2 3; 1)—द्विर्भोजने om Y* A3; आह व° Y* A3; 2)—न conj., missing in all mss; 3)—एतदश° A1 2 B M; after this A5 6 add इति भोजनविधिः

258. 1)—भोजनक्रि° Y* A3; भोजनान्तरक्रि° A6; °क्रियोच्यते Y* A1 2 R1; 2)—तत्र om X2*; आह for तत्र Y*; 3)—प्राश्याचम्य Y*; प्राणः अक्ष्योश्चक्षुः कर्णयोः श्रुतं बाह्वोर्बलमूर्वोरोज अरिष्टा विश्वाङ्गानि तनूस्तनुवा मे सह इत्यङ्गानि स्पृशेत् । अनन्तरं सावित्र्यार्घ्यं

यमः[1] ।

सुवर्णस्याथ रूप्यस्य यज्ञेषु चमसस्य च ।
यतीनां चैव पात्राणामद्भिः शौचं विधीयते ॥२५९॥

लिखितः[1] ।

भुक्त्वोपस्थाय मार्तण्डं पुराणानि सदा पठेत् ।
भावशुद्ध्या हरौ भक्तिः पुराणश्रवणाद्भवेत् ॥२६०॥

शङ्खलिखितौ[1] ।

काष्ठालाबुविदलपार्थिवानामेकं भैक्षभाजनम्[2] । तस्य गोवालरज्ज्वा सोदकया परिघर्षणम्[3] । प्रत्याह्निकं शौचम्[4] । नात्राचामेत्[5] । न भूमौ क्षिपेत्[6] । नाशुचिभिः संस्पृशेत्[7] । भुक्त्वाचान्तः पुनराचम्य द्रव्याण्यभ्युक्षेत्[8] । रज्जुशिक्यं यथान्यदविरुद्धं स्यात्[9] ॥२६१॥

शङ्खः[1] ।

भुक्त्वा सूर्यमुपस्थाय प्राणानायम्य चासने ।
गायत्र्यष्टशतं जप्त्वा ध्यायेन्नारायणं पुनः ॥२६२॥
दिनशेषं पुराणाद्यैर्नीत्वोपास्य च पश्चिमाम् ।
संध्यां ततोऽभ्यसेद्योगं निद्रान्तेऽपि पुनस्तथा ॥२६३॥
एवं दिने दिने कुर्वन्ध्यानमेव प्रधानतः ।
कर्माण्यपि च कुर्वाणो ब्रह्मभूयाय कल्पते ॥२६४॥

दत्वा आचम्य उद्वयं तम इत्यादित्यमुप° G6 R2 3 M+; आचम्य om B M; सोदकया B M; सोदकेन सोदकया G6 R2 3; त्रिः प्रा° A1 2 R1 B M; °यामान्कृत्वा A1 2 R1 B M; गायत्र्यष्ट° A6 B M; 4–7)—om Y*; 5)—अर्धास्तमित° A5 G6; अथार्धास्तमित° A6; अस्तमित° R4; अथास्तमिते A1 2 B M; °भास्करे A1 2 G6 B M; °कोदयादुपा° X2* A5; 6)—अथ om B M; यावदवकाशमु° G6 R2 3 B M; 7)—om A5; °त्थितोऽभिध्या° A1 2 R1 B M

259. om Y*

260. om Y*

261. om Y*; 2)—भैक्ष° om G6 R4; 3)—तस्य om X2*; 7)—°चिभिः सह A5; संस्पर्शयेत् R2 3 4

262. om X2*; 1)—आह शङ्खः Y*; b)—चासीनो G1 2; c)—गायत्र्याष्ट° Y* A1 2 R1; जपित्वा G1

263. om Y*; X2*; a)—पुराणाद्यैः om A6

264. om Y*; X2*

विश्वामित्रः[1] ।

भुक्त्वा पुनरुपस्थानमुद्वयं तमसस्परि ।
भिक्षाटनविधिर्भिक्षोः प्रोक्तः पञ्चविधो मया ॥२६५॥
य एवं वर्तते भिक्षुः स यतिः साश्रमी स च ।
संध्यामुपास्य विधिवद्ध्यानकर्म समाचरेत् ॥२६६॥
मैत्रीभिर्ऋग्भिः पूर्वायां संध्यायामुपतिष्ठते ।
मध्याह्नसंध्यां सौरीभिः सायं वरुणदेवतैः ॥२६७॥
सेयं सारस्वती ज्ञेया संध्या याभ्युदयाश्रया ।
शाङ्करी चैव मध्याह्ने अपराह्णे तु वैष्णवी ॥२६८॥
एवं ध्यानं सदा कार्यं ब्राह्मणेन विपश्चिता ।
जपयज्ञार्थसिद्ध्यर्थं ध्यानमेतन्मयोदितम् ॥२६९॥
गवां वालपवित्रैस्तु यः संध्यां समुपासते ।
यत्कृतं दुष्कृतं तेन तस्य सद्यो विनश्यति ॥२७०॥
दर्भेषु दर्भपाणिः सन्प्राङ्मुखः सुसमाहितः ।
सहस्रकृत्वः सावित्रीं शतकृत्वोऽपि वा जपेत् ॥२७१॥
ॐकारपूर्विकास्तिस्रो महाव्याहृतयोऽमलाः ।
त्रिपदा चैव गायत्री विज्ञेया परमं पदम् ॥२७२॥
पवित्रं धारयेन्नित्यं कौशेयं दक्षिणे करे ।
भुञ्जानस्तु विशेषेण सोऽन्नदोषैर्न लिप्यते ॥२७३॥

265. om Y*; c)—भिक्षादने A1 2 R1 B M; भिक्षाटने M+; d)—भोक्तुं पञ्च° R4; यमाः G6 R4

266. om Y*; a)—य om G6 R2 3; b)—संयमी B M

267. om Y*; a)—त्रयोभिर्ऋ° A6; पूर्वस्यां A1 2 R1 B M; पूर्वं स्यात् A5; d)—°दैवतैः A1 2 5 B M

268. om Y*; a)—सायं A6 G6 R4; स्वेयं A1 2 R1; स्वयं B M; सरस्वती all except R2 3; c)—शङ्करी A2 B M; माध्याह्ने G6 R2 3

269. om Y*

270. om Y*

271. om Y*; b)—तु समा° G6 R3 4

272. om Y*; a)—°पूर्वका° A6 M

273. a)—धारयन् G6 R4; c–d)—°षेण अन्न° X2* A6; °षेणान्नदोषैर्न विद्यते A1 2; °षेण नान्नदोषैर्विलिप्यते B M; न विद्यते A5

उपवीती त्रिदण्डी च शिखी पीठी कुसुम्भवान् ।
श्रुतिस्मृत्युक्तकर्माणि यानि तानि समाचरेत् ।
अनुतिष्ठन्सदा योगं यतिः सिध्यति नान्यथा ॥२७४॥

मेधातिथिः[1] ।

गोवालरज्ज्वा सोदक्या पात्रं प्रक्षालयेत्स्वयम् ।
भुक्त्वा व्याहृतिभिश्चैव गायत्र्या प्रणवेन वा ॥२७५॥
प्राणायामत्रयं कृत्वा गायत्र्यष्टशतं जपेत् ।
अर्थमात्रं वदेत्किंचिद्वक्तव्यं यदि विद्यते ॥२७६॥
ध्यानेन दिनशेषं यत्ततोऽव्यग्रः समापयेत् ।
लोहितार्कमुपासीत संध्यामातारकोदयात् ॥२७७॥
तावद्ध्यायेत्पुनर्यावन्निद्रावशमुपागतः ।
सुप्तोत्थितः पुनर्ध्यायेत्तिष्ठन्संध्यां पुनर्जपेत् ॥२७८॥

भरद्वाजः[1] ।

अमृतापिधानमसीति चुलुकं गृहीत्वा प्रणवेन दन्तधावनं करोति[2] । उच्छिष्टमन्नं पात्रं चाप्सु प्रक्षिप्याचम्य प्राणायामत्रयं कृत्वा पुनराचम्य वाङ्ग आसन्निति जपित्वा आपो हि ष्ठेति मार्जयित्वा उद्वयं तमसस्परीत्युपस्थानं कुर्यात्[3] । प्रणवेन पात्रं प्रक्षालयेत्[4] । गायत्र्यष्टशतं जपेत्[5] । गोवालं गृहीत्वा प्रणवेनैव शुष्कं पात्रं मार्जयेत्[6] । दिशः प्रदिश इति बन्धनं कृत्वा गायत्र्या स्थापयेत्[7] । लोहितार्कमुपासीत[8] । एवं यथोक्तविधानेन भोजनं कृत्वा भिक्षुः परां गतिं प्राप्नोतीति[9] ॥२७९॥

274. om Y*; a)—उपवीतं त्रिदण्डं A5; b)—कुण्डी [मुण्डी G6] कुशी भवन् X2* A6 [R3 cor. मुण्डी to कुण्डी]; पीठी च कुण्डवान् B M; e)—अनुतिष्ठेत् X2* A5 M+

275. om Y* X2*; d)—om A1 2 R1 B M

276. om Y*; a–b)—om X2*; a)—om A1 2 R1 B M; b)—गायत्रष्ट° A1 2

277. om Y*; b)—समाचरेत् G6 R3 [but R3 cor. समापयेत्]; c–d)—om X2*

278. om Y* X2*; b)—निद्राया समुपा° A1 B M; निद्राय समुपा° A2 R1; निद्रावश° om A5

279. om Y*; 3)—वाप्सु A1 2 R2 4 B M; आसन्नसोरिति X2*; °स्थानं कृत्वा A2 B M; 4)—प्रोक्षयेत् R4; 6)—शुष्क X2*; 7)—प्रदिश आदिश A1 2 R1 B M; 8–9)—°तार्कामु° A1

अथ सायंसंध्योपासनम्[1] । तत्र **शौनकः**[2] ।

स्नानादि सायमेवं स्यात्समाप्य सकलं विधिम् ।
अर्घ्यं च पूर्ववद्दद्याल्लोहितायति भास्करे ॥२८०॥
वारुणीभिरुपस्थानं ततः संध्याविधिक्रिया ।
ध्यायन्नासीत चैतावद्यावन्निद्रावशंगतः ।
ध्यायेत्पुनः प्रबुद्धश्चेद् ब्रह्मभूयाय कल्पते ॥२८१॥

रात्रिवसनदेशं **हारीत** आह[1] ।

भुक्त्वा पात्रे यतिर्नित्यं क्षालयेन्मन्त्रपूर्वकम् ।
न दुष्येत्तस्य तत्पात्रं यज्ञेषु चमसं यथा ॥२८२॥
अथाचम्य निरुद्धासुरुपतिष्ठेत भास्करम् ।
जपध्यानेतिहासैस्तु दिनशेषं समापयेत् ।
कृतसंध्यस्ततो रात्रिं नयेद्देवगृहादिषु ॥२८३॥

शाण्डिल्यः[1] ।

वेदं विहाय कर्माणि सर्वाण्येव तु संन्यसेत् ।
ग्रामाद्बहिः कुटीं कृत्वा वृक्षमूलेऽपि वा वसेत् ॥२८४॥

क्रतुः[1] ।

शून्यागारे गुहायां वा वह्न्यागारे सुरालये ।
वसेदसङ्गो निःशङ्को निर्मलो योगमास्थितः ॥२८५॥

R1; °पासित्वैव यथो° A 1 2 5 R1 B M; एवंविधा° G6 R2 4; °विधिनानेन A1 2 R1; परमां G6; गतिमाप्नो° A1 2 R1 4 B M; at the end A5 6 R1 add इति भोजनोत्तरक्रिया

280. om Y*; 1)—सायं om A5 G6 R3 [R3 adds in margin]; °सनमुच्यते A1 2 R1 B M; 2)—तत्र om X2*

281. om Y*

282. Y* inserts after 7.137; 1)—रात्रिवसनदेशं om X2* B M; रात्रिअवसानं देशं R4; आह om X2*; a)—पात्रं X2*; पात्रे यद्भिक्ष्यं A6

283. om Y*; c)—°हासैश्च R2 3 4

284. 1)—रात्रिवासस्थानमुच्यते आह शा° Y*; a–b)—सर्वाणि कर्माण्येव A4; d)—वापि G1; वसेद्यतिः G2; वसेदिति A4 G1

285. 1)—आह क्रतुः Y*; c)—वसेदसङ्ग A1 2 R1; d)—add इति Y*

खट्वादिनिषेधमास्तरणं स्थण्डिलशायित्वं वासदेशं च **वसिष्ठ** आह[1] ।

एकशाटीपरिवृतोऽजिनेन वा गोप्रलूनैस्तृणैरवस्तृतशरीरः स्थण्डिलशायी नित्यं वसतिं वसेत्[2] । ग्रामान्ते देवगृहे शून्यागारे वृक्षमूले वा मनसा स्वाध्यायमधीयानोऽरण्यनित्यो न ग्राम्यपशूनां संदर्शने विचरेत्[3] ॥२८६॥ [VaDh 10.9-16]

स एवाह[1] ।

न च तृप्येत्[2] । ग्रामे वसेत्[3] । अजिह्मोऽशठोऽसङ्कुसुकः[4] ॥२८७॥

[VaDh 10.25-27]

असहवासमावसथार्हत्वानर्हत्वे च **दक्ष** आह[1] ।

एको भिक्षुर्यथोक्तस्तु द्वावेव मिथुनं स्मृतम् ।
त्रयो ग्रामः समाख्यात ऊर्ध्वं तु नगरायते ॥२८८॥
नगरं तु न कर्तव्यं ग्रामो वा मिथुनं तु वा ।
एतत्त्रयं प्रकुर्वाणः स्वधर्माच्च्यवते यतिः ॥२८९॥
राजवार्तादि तेषां च भिक्षावार्ता परस्परम् ।
स्नेहपैशुन्यमात्सर्यं संनिकर्षाद्भविष्यति ॥२९०॥
तपोजपैः कृशीभूता व्याधिता वसथार्हकाः ।
वृद्धा ग्रहगृहीताश्च ये चान्ये विकलेन्द्रियाः ॥२९१॥
नीरुजश्च युवा चैव भिक्षुर्नावसथार्हकः ।
वसन्नावसथे भिक्षुर्मैथुनं यदि सेवते ।
स दूषयति तत्स्थानं वृद्धान्संपीडयेदपि ॥२९२॥

286. 1)—खट्वा° . . . च om Y*; आह वसिष्ठः Y*; चाह वसिष्ठः X2*; आह om A1 R1; 2)—°प्रसूनैः Y*; °प्रशूनैः A6; °पलूनैः B M; तृणैः om Y*; वा स्तृत° R4; स्तृत° Y* G6 R2 3 B M; °शरीरे A2 M; स्थण्डिलशायी om R4; नित्यं om Y*; नित्यां X2* A6; नित्यं add वा A5; 3)—om Y*

287. om Y* X2*; 2)—न तु च A1 2 R1 B M; 4)—अजीर्णो A1 2 R1 A6

288. om Y*; 1)—°समावधानार्ह° A1 2 R1; °समावनधानार्ह° A5; °समालयानार्हतवं B M

289. om Y*; b)—न ग्रामो मि° A1 2 B M; ग्रामं A5

290. om Y*; a)—°र्तादिदोषां R4; वेषां A5; d)—°र्षाच्च जायते A5

291. om Y*; d)—ये येऽन्ये A1 2 R1 B M; वान्ये A6

292. om Y*; c–d)—om X2* A6

कपिलस्तु सहवासमनुमोदते[1] ।

गुरुवृद्धतपस्विन आगतानभिवदेत्[2] । चतुर्भुजवत्पश्येत्[3] । करणे यथाशक्ति संविभागशीलतापि प्रशस्ता[4] । अनुद्वेगकारिभिस्तपस्विभिः समानशीलैः सह संवसेत्[5] ॥२९३॥

शौनकः[1] ।

शरणं न कुर्यान्न च कारयेत्[2] । कृतं प्रविशेत्[3] । अथ ब्रह्मोपासीत[4] । तच्चित्त एव शयीत[5] । अनिन्दके देवगृहे वा प्रविष्टो यथाकथंचिच्छर्वरीं नयेत् जाग्रदेव सुषुप्तः[6] । आसीनोऽथाचम्य प्राणायामत्रयं कृत्वा पुनराचामेत्[7] । काष्ठारोपितकमण्डलुना रात्रावाचामेत् दिवा स्रवन्त्या[8] । अभिरुचितं प्रभूतोदकं पुण्यस्थानं न त्यजेत्[9] । न तीर्थलोलुपः[10] ॥२९४॥

वायुः[1] ।

निशान्तेऽभ्युद्धृता आपः शुद्धे पात्रे यथाविधि ।
अहोरात्रोषितास्तास्तु त्याज्या मेध्या अपि स्वयम् ॥२९५॥

अथ ग्रासवासादिनिमित्तं भिक्षावागते गृहस्थस्य कर्तव्यमुच्यते[1] । तत्र **वृद्धजाबालिः**[2] ।

चतुर्वेदोऽपि यो विप्रः सोमयाजी शतक्रतुः ।
तस्मादपि यतिः श्रेष्ठस्तिलमेरुवदन्तरम् ॥२९६॥
आसनं शयनं वापि यतिं दृष्ट्वा त्यजेन्न यः ।

293. om Y*; 1)—सहवासं [R2 adds तु] कपिलः X2*; 5)—तपस्विभिः om A1 2 R1 B M; संवदेत् A5; संविशेत् A6

294. 1)—आह शौ° Y*; 2–7)—om Y*; 2)—च om X2*; 3)—कृतं add न R4; 6)—अनिद्रके A1 2 B M; जाग्रत एव R2 3; 8)—काष्ठारोपित° om Y*; स्रवन्त्यां all except Y*; प्रभूतदण्डं A5 [from स्थानं न until व्रतज्येष्ठो at 6.300 omitted in A5; probably a scribal oversight, as a new scribe takes over here]; 10)—न om G6; add इति Y*

295. 1)—आह वा° Y*; a)—°न्तेऽप्युद्धृता X2*; d)—स्वयम् om A1 2 R1; add इति Y*

296. 1)—अथ संन्यासिदर्शने गृहस्थस्य वक्तव्यमुच्यते Y*; ग्राम° A5 R3 4 B M; 2)—तत्र om Y* X2*; आह वृद्ध° Y*; d)—after this G6 R2 3 M+ add सूर्यखद्योतयोर्यद्वन्मेरुसर्षपयोरपि । अन्तरं हि महद्दृष्टं तथा भिक्षुगृहस्थयोः ॥

स मूढात्मा मृतस्तस्मात्तिर्यग्योनिषु जायते ॥२९७॥
दुर्वृत्ते वा सुवृत्ते वा यतौ निन्दां न कारयेत् ।
यतीनां द्विष्यमाणस्तु नरकं प्रतिपद्यते ॥२९८॥

दत्तात्रेयः[1] ।

त्रिदण्डरूपधृग्विप्रः साक्षान्नारायणात्मकः ।
यस्तं पूजयते भक्त्या विष्णुस्तेन प्रपूजितः ॥२९९॥
सगुणो निर्गुणो वापि व्रतज्येष्ठो युवापि सः ।
संपूज्योऽभिक्षुभिर्भिक्षुः स्वधर्मे संस्थितो यतिः ॥३००॥
अष्टाक्षरेण मन्त्रेण नित्यं नारायणात्मना ।
नमस्यो भक्तिभावेन विष्णुरूपी त्रिदण्डधृक् ॥३०१॥
त्रिदण्डं वैष्णवं लिङ्गं विप्राणां मुक्तिसाधनम् ।
निर्वाणं सर्वधर्माणामिति वेदानुशासनम् ॥३०२॥
काणादशाक्यपाषण्डैस्त्रयीधर्मो विलोपितः ।
त्रिदण्डधारिणा पूर्वं विष्णुना रक्षिता त्रयी ॥३०३॥

जमदग्निः[1] ।

शुष्कमन्नं पृथक्पाकं यतये यः प्रयच्छति ।
स मूढो नरकं याति तेन पापेन कर्मणा ॥३०४॥
यतिश्च ब्रह्मचारी च पक्वान्नस्वामिनावुभौ ।
तयोरन्नमदत्वा तु भुक्त्वा चान्द्रायणं चरेत् ॥३०५॥

297. a)—शयनं यानं Y* X2*; d)—°योनौ च X2*

299. 1)—आह द° Y*; a)—°धृद्विप्रः B M; c)—यस्तु A1 2 5 B M; d)—तेनैव पूजितः G6 R2 3

300. c)—स पूज्यो Y*; d)—यदि R4

301. Y* inserts after 6.303; c)—मनसा for नमस्यो B M

302. om Y*

303. om Y*; c)—°धारणात् A1 2 R1 B M; d)—विष्णुना प्रभविष्णुना A1 2 5 R1 B M; after this Y* A1 2 R1 B M add द्वे रूपे वासुदेवस्य चलं चाचलमेव [त्वचलमेव Y*] च । चलं संन्यासिनां रूपमचलं ब्रह्मसंस्थितम् [A1 in margin प्रतिमादिकम्] ॥; then Y* inserts 6.301.

304. 1)—om A6; आह जम° Y*

305. a)—यती च A1 2 G6 R1

यतिहस्ते जलं दद्याद्भैक्षं दद्यात्पुनर्जलम् ।
तद्भैक्षं मेरुणा तुल्यं तज्जलं सागरोपमम् ॥३०६॥
यतिर्यस्य गृहे भुंक्ते तत्र भुंक्ते हरिः स्वयम् ।
हरिर्यस्य गृहे भुंक्ते तत्र भुंक्ते जगत्त्रयम् ॥३०७॥
संचितं यद् गृहस्थस्य पापमामरणान्तिकम् ।
निर्दहिष्यति तत्सर्वमेकरात्रोषितो यतिः ॥३०८॥
अपचन्तं परित्यज्य पचन्तं यस्तु भोजयेत् ।
दैवे कर्मणि पित्र्ये च वृथा तस्य परिश्रमः ॥३०९॥
अदुष्टापतितं साधुं यो यतिं परिवर्जयेत् ।
स तस्य सुकृतं दत्वा दुष्कृतं प्रतिपद्यते ॥३१०॥
दुर्वृत्तो वा सुवृत्तो वा मूर्खः पण्डित एव वा ।
काषायदण्डमात्रेण यतिः पूज्यो युधिष्ठिर ॥३११॥

अत्रिः[1] ।

भैक्षदाता सदा भिक्षोः सलिलं दक्षिणे करे ।
दत्वा भिक्षां प्रयच्छेत पात्रे सव्ये करे स्थिते ॥३१२॥
तृप्त्यर्थं पितृदेवानां तत्प्रदानेऽम्बु कल्पितम् ।
तदन्नेनैव दत्तेन भवेत्तदुपपादितम् ॥३१३॥
भैक्षं संस्कृत्य यो दद्याद्विष्णुरूपाय भिक्षवे ।
कृत्स्नां वा पृथिवीं दद्यात्तेन तुल्यं न तद्भवेत् ॥३१४॥

307. om Y*; c–d)—om X2*; c)—यतिर्यत्र B M; गृहे यस्मिन्हरिर्भुंक्ते A6

308. om Y*

309. om Y*; c–d)—om A1 2 5 R1 B M

310. om Y* X2*; a–b)—om A1 2 5 R1 B M [this half-verse is found only in A6, but it is required, I believe, by the sequence of verses]; after this verse G6 R2 3 add द्वे रूपे . . . रूपमचलं प्रतिमादिकम् [see 6.303n]

311. om Y*; c)—काषायमात्रवेषेण A1 2 R1 B M; काषायमात्रधारेण A6

312. 1)—om A1 2 6 G6 R1 3 B M; आहात्रिः Y*; a–d)—om X2*; a)—भैक्षदस्तु B M; भैक्षदा A2; भिक्षादाता A5; d)—सव्यकरे A5 G1 2

313. om Y* X2*

314. a)—at beginning G6 R3 add अत्रिः; a)—संस्मृत्य B M; b)—भिक्षुरूपाय विष्णवे R4; c)—वा om R3; d)—तत्फलम् G1 2; तज्जलम् A4

पात्रासनं तथा दण्डं शिक्यं जलपवित्रकम् ।
संन्यासिने प्रदायैव गोदानफलमाप्नुयात् ।।३१५।।
व्याधितानां च भिक्षूणां कुर्यादाश्रममण्डपम् ।
पथ्याद्यैर्वा परिचरेत्सोऽनन्तफलमश्नुते ।।३१६।।

वृद्धजाबालिः[1] ।

पृथक्कृता तु या भिक्षा घ्राता मार्जारमूषकैः ।
वातोपवाता शुष्कान्ना मधुमांससमा भवेत् ।।३१७।।
पर्युषिता तु या भिक्षा या च नैवेद्यकल्पिता ।
सा गृह्णतो न दोषाय दाता तु नरकं व्रजेत् ।।३१८।।
भिक्षोः पाणौ जलं दद्याद्भैक्षं दद्यात्पुनर्जलम् ।
सा भिक्षा पर्वतैस्तुल्या तज्जलं सागरोपमम् ।
एवं दत्तं तु यद्भैक्षं तेन तृप्यन्ति देवताः ।।३१९।।

जाबालिः[1] ।

यतिहस्तगतं द्रव्यं यो गृह्णाति नरः क्वचित् ।
स मूढो नरकं याति तेन पापेन कर्मणा ।।३२०।।
त्रिदण्डमप्पवित्रं च भैक्षभाजनमासनम् ।
संन्यासिने ददानो हि गोसहस्रफलं लभेत् ।।३२१।।
पात्रं चतुर्विधं युक्तं यो ददाति त्रिदण्डिने ।
पूरयित्वा हविष्यान्नैरात्मानं च निवेदयेत् ।।३२२।।

315. a)—दण्डः A1 2 6 R1 2 3 B M; c)—प्रदायेह G1 2

316. om Y*; a)—तु G6 R2 3 B M; c)—यः पथ्या° G6; वा om G6; °द्यैर्यः R4; d)—सोऽनन्तं B M

317. om Y*; 1)—om X2*; b)—आखुमार्जा° G6 R2 3; घ्राणमार्जा° R4; °मूषिकैः A2 6 G6 R2 3

318. om Y*

319. om X2* [G6 R2 3 insert after 6.324]; e)—यैर्भैक्षं A1 2 R1; f)—तृप्यन्तु G6 R2 3; add इति Y*

320. 1)—आह वृद्धजाबालिः Y*; b)—येन गृह्णाति यो नरः A1 2 R1 B M

321. om X2* [G6 R2 3 insert after 6.324]; a)— °दण्डं च पवि° A1 2 B M; °दण्डं जलपवि° G6 R2 3; b)—भिक्षा° A5; d)—भवेत् A5 G6

322. om Y*

ये के च नरकस्थाने पच्यन्तेऽप्यतिपापिनः ।
उद्धरंश्चात्मनात्मानं स गच्छेत्परमां गतिम् ॥३२३॥
यावन्ति यतिपात्राणि यावन्त्यन्नानि तत्र च ।
तावद्वर्षसहस्राणि स्वर्गलोके महीयते ॥३२४॥

इति यतिधर्मसमुच्चये अहोरात्रक्रिया नाम षष्ठं पर्व ॥३२५॥

323. om Y* X2*; a)—एके A1 2 R1; c–d)—om A6; उद्धरन्स्वात्म° B M

324. b)—ताव° A5; °न्नानि दीयते A1 2 B M; यत्र R2; d)—दाता स्वर्गे A5 6; at the end G6 R2 3 insert 6.321 and 319.

325. At the end G6 R2 3 add: एकासने गृहस्थाद्यैः प्रमादादपि संविशेत् । गृहस्था नरकं यान्ति स्वनिष्ठापि वृथा भवेत् ॥ ब्रह्मचारिसहस्रेण वानप्रस्थायुतेन च । गृहस्थानां तु कोटेस्तु यतिरेको विशिष्यते ॥

सप्तमं पर्व

आचारः

अथाचारः[1] । तत्र **मनुः**[2] ।

अनग्निरनिकेतः स्याद् ग्राममन्नार्थमाश्रयेत् ।
उपेक्षकोऽसंचयिको मुनिर्भावसमन्वितः ॥१॥ [MDh 6.43]
कपालं वृक्षमूलानि कुचेलमसहायता ।
समता चैव सर्वस्मिन्नेतन्मुक्तस्य लक्षणम् ॥२॥ [MDh 6.44]
नाभिनन्देत मरणं नाभिनन्देत जीवितम् ।
कालमेव प्रतीक्षेत निर्वेशं भृतको यथा ॥३॥ [MDh 6.45]
दृष्टिपूतं न्यसेत्पादं वस्त्रपूतं जलं पिबेत् ।
सत्यपूतां वदेद्वाचं मनःपूतं समाचरेत् ॥४॥ [MDh 6.46]
अतिवादांस्तितिक्षेत नावमन्येत कंचन ।
न चैनं देहमाश्रित्य वैरं कुर्वीत केनचित् ॥५॥ [MDh 6.47]
क्रुध्यन्तं न प्रतिक्रुध्येदाक्रुष्टः कुशलं वदेत् ।
सप्तद्वारावकीर्णां च न वाचमनृतां वदेत् ॥६॥ [MDh 6.48]
अध्यात्मरतिरासीनो निरपेक्षो निरामिषः ।

1. 1)—om A1 2; अथ सदाचारः G6 R2 3; अथ सदाचार उच्यते Y* A3 B M; 2)—तत्र om X2*; तत्राह Y* B M; क्रतुः A1 2 R1; a)—सहस्रैकं for अनग्नि° . . . °स्याद् A1 2 R1 [A1 cor.]; c)—संकुसुको M; संकुसंको B

2. a)—कपाल A4 G2 6 R2; c)—सवत्र X2*

3. a)—om A6; d)—निर्देशं B M; निर्वेदं A1 2 R1 [A1 2 cor.]; भृशको A1 2

4. b)—पिबेज्जलम् A1 2 R1 B M; c)—°पूतं Y* A6; वाणीं A1 2 5 R1 B M; वाक्यं Y*

5. b)—किंचन G6 R2; c)—चैतं R4; °मासाद्य Y* A3 B M; °माहृत्य A1 2 R1

6. b)—°दाक्रुष्टं A1 2 G6 R1 B M; °दाकृष्टं Y*; °दाक्रुष्ट A3

आत्मनैव सहायेन सुखार्थं विचरेद्दिवा ॥७॥ [MDh 6.49]
न चोत्पातनिमित्ताभ्यां न नक्षत्राङ्गविद्यया ।
नानुशासनवादाभ्यां भिक्षां लिप्सेत कर्हिचित् ॥८॥ [MDh 6.50]
न तापसैर्ब्राह्मणैर्वा वयोभिरपि वा श्वभिः ।
आकीर्णं भिक्षुकैर्वान्यैरगारमुपसंव्रजेत् ॥९॥ [MDh 6.51]
अभिपूजितलाभांस्तु जुगुप्सेतैव सर्वशः ।
अभिपूजितलाभैस्तु यतिर्मुक्तोऽपि बध्यते ॥१०॥ [MDh 6.58]
अल्पान्नाभ्यवहारेण रहःस्थेनासनेन च ।
ह्रियमाणानि विषयैरिन्द्रियाणि निवर्तयेत् ॥११॥ [MDh 6.59]
इन्द्रियाणां निरोधेन रागद्वेषक्षयेण च ।
अहिंसया च भूतानाममृतत्वाय कल्पते ॥१२॥ [MDh 6.60]
अवेक्षेत गतीर्नृणां कर्मदोषसमुद्भवाः ।
निरये चैव पतनं यातनां च यमक्षये ॥१३॥ [MDh 6.61]
विप्रयोगं प्रियैश्चैव संप्रयोगमथाप्रियैः ।
जरया चाभिभवनं व्याधिभिश्चोपपीडनम् ॥१४॥ [MDh 6.62]
देहादुत्क्रमणं चास्मात्पुनर्गर्भे च संभवम् ।
योनिकोटिसहस्रेषु सृतीश्चास्यान्तरात्मनः ॥१५॥ [MDh 6.63]
अधर्मप्रभवं चैव दुःखयोगं शरीरिणाम् ।
धर्मार्थप्रभवं चैव सुखसंयोगमक्षयम् ॥१६॥ [MDh 6.64]

7. om Y* A3; d)—सुखार्थी X2* A5; न चरे° A1 2 R1

8. om Y* A3

9. b)—वासभिः R1 2 3 [R3 cor.]; d)—°संविशेत् Y* A3 G6 R2 3

10. a)—at beginning A5 6 add उत्तरत्र; °लाभांश्च Y* A3

11. a)—अल्पेनाभ्य° G6 R2 3 4 [R3 cor.]; b)—°स्थानास° R4; गृहस्थेनास° G6; c)—प्रीयमाणानि Y* A1 2 3 [A1 2 cor.]

12. b)—वा R4

13. om Y* A3; a)—अपेक्षेत R4; गतिं G6 R2 4; b)—कामद्वेष° R4; °मुद्भवां X2* A2 6 R1; °मुद्भवान् A5; d)—यातनाश्च B M

14. om Y* A3; a)—प्रियैश्चैवं R2 3; b)—सुप्रयो° A1 2 R1 B M

15. om Y* A3; a)—तस्मात् A1 2 B M; b)—च om A2; संभवः R2; संभवे A1 2 R1

16. om Y* A3

सूक्ष्मतां चान्ववेक्षेत योगेन परमात्मनः ।
देहेषु चैवोपपत्तिमुत्तमेष्वधमेषु च ॥१७॥ [MDh 6.65]

विष्णुः[1] ।

मानावमानौ यावेतौ प्रीत्युद्वेगकरौ नृणाम् ।
तावेव विपरीतार्थौ योगिनः सिद्धिकारकौ ॥१८॥
मानावमानौ यावेतौ तावेवाहुर्विषामृते ।
अवमानोऽमृतं तत्र मानस्तु परमं विषम् ॥१९॥

उत्तरत्र[1] ।

यथा चैवावमन्यन्ते जनाः परिवदन्ति च ।
तथा युक्तश्चरेद्योगी सतां धर्ममदूषयन् ॥२०॥

पुनस्तत्रैवः[1] ।

सारभूतमुपासीत येन मुक्तिमवाप्नुयात् ।
क्रियान्या बहुधा या तु योगविघ्नकरी हि सा ॥२१॥
काम्यानि यानि कर्माणि प्रतिषिद्धानि यानि च ।
तानि तानि परित्यज्य नित्यं कर्म समाचरेत् ॥२२॥

यमः[1] ।

यश्चास्य दक्षिणं बाहुं चन्दनेनानुलिम्पति ।
सव्यं वास्य च यस्तक्षेत्समौ ताववधारयेत् ॥२३॥
एवमस्य भवेद्भावो नित्यमेव प्रियाप्रिये ।
इष्टे वा यदि वा द्वेष्ये समः सर्वत्र वर्तयेत् ॥२४॥
समः साधौ च पापे च शत्रौ मित्रे च वै समः ।

17. om Y* A3

18. 1)—om A5; आह विष्णुः Y* A3; a–d)—om Y* A3 6 R4; c)—तौ चैव A5

19. om Y* A3

20. om Y* A3; c)—तावयुक्त° A1 2 G6 B M; d)—स्थलं मा मम [मम मा A2] दूषयन् [दूषयेत् A2] A1 2; स्थलं मम न दूषयेत् [दूष्यते B] B M

21. 1)—om Y* X2* A3; °त्रैवाह A1 2 R1 B M; d)— °करी सदा A1 2 R1 B M

22. d)—नित्यकर्म X2* A2 B M; add इति A3 5 G1 2 B M

23. 1)—om A5 G6 R2 3; आह यमः Y* B M; आह कपिलः A3; a–d)—om Y* A3; b)— °नुलिप्यति A5 R4 B

24. om Y* X2* A3; c)—इष्टो B M; द्वेष्यः B M

शीतोष्णसुखदुःखेषु समः सङ्गविवर्जितः ॥२५॥
न प्रहृष्यति सन्माने नावमाने च कुप्यति ।
रागद्वेषौ समौ यस्य स मुनिः सर्वनिःस्पृहः ॥२६॥
श्रुत्वा स्पृष्ट्वा च दृष्ट्वा च भुक्त्वा घ्रात्वा च यो नरः ।
न हृष्यति ग्लायति वा स विज्ञेयो जितेन्द्रियः ॥२७॥
न पाणिपादचपलो न नेत्रचपलो भवेत् ।
न च वाक्चपलश्च स्यादिति शिष्टस्य लक्षणम् ॥२८॥

तथा[1] ।

अन्नाच्छुद्धागमाच्छुद्धाद्विशेषरसवर्जितात् ।
निर्मलं जायते सत्त्वं मलिनं मलिनाद्भवेत् ॥२९॥
मांसशोणितसंघातं मेदोमज्जास्थिसंचयम् ।
नखरोमसमायुक्तं वसाप्रभृतिकर्दमम् ॥३०॥
पूर्णं मूत्रपुरीषाभ्यां दुर्गन्धं चर्मबन्धनम् ।
देहोऽनिलमयं धाम मलाधारमसारकम् ॥३१॥
चित्रभित्तिप्रतीकाशमपां फेनोपमं परम् ।
नित्यानित्यसमायुक्तं रागद्वेषसमुच्चयम् ॥३२॥
एकस्तम्भं नवद्वारं त्रिस्थूणं पाञ्चभौतिकम् ।

25. a–b)—om Y* A3

26. a)—°ष्यति माने R 2 3 4; सममाने G6; b)—नापमाने B M; न for च Y* X2* A3; c–d)—om Y* A3

27. b)—पीत्वा घ्रा° Y* A3; c)—म्लायति Y* A3; ग्लायति om G6; यः स A3 G1 2; च स A4

28. a)—पादपाणि °A3 G6 R2 3; b)—न च दृक्चपलो X2*; after भवेत् Y* A1 2 R1 B M add न च त्वक्चपलो वापि न घ्रानचपलो भवेत्; c)—न श्रोत्रचपलो वा A3; वाक्चपलो वा Y* B M; d)—at end A1 2 R1 insert 7.37–38

29. om Y* A3; 1)—om X2*; a)—अन्नाच्चैवागमाच्चैव X2*; °गमाद्विशे° A6; b)—°वर्जनात् G6 R4

30. om Y* A3

31. om Y* A3; d)—°धारस्त्वसारकम् A6

32. om Y* A3; a)—चित्तभि° A6; b)—°काशं पापमन्त्रोपमं A1 2 R1

प्रीतिप्राकारसंयुक्तं मनःप्रबलनायकम् ।।३३।।
दशेन्द्रियभटाकीर्णं व्याधिश्वापदसेवितम् ।
विशेषविषयाक्रान्तं चेतनाधिष्ठितं पुरम् ।।३४।।
जराशोकसमाविष्टं रोगायतनमातुरम् ।
रजस्वलमनित्यं च भूतावासमिमं त्यजेत् ।।३५।।
स्नानं जपं तथा ध्यानं शौचमाहारलाघवम् ।
य एतत्पञ्चकं कुर्यान्मुक्तो भवति नान्यथा ।।३६।।
पुराणश्रवणाभ्यासं भक्तितो नित्यमाचरेत् ।
पुराणश्रवणे भक्तिर्मूर्खस्यापि प्रजायते ।।३७।।
भक्त्याविच्छिन्नया मुक्तिस्तस्मात्पौराणमभ्यसेत् ।
तदभ्यासात्परं ब्रह्मभावमापद्यते मुनिः इति ।।३८।।

वसिष्ठः[1] ।

परिव्राजकः सर्वभूताभयं दत्वा प्रतिष्ठेत[2] । [VaDh 10.1]
तथाप्युदाहरन्ति[3] ।
अभयं सर्वभूतेभ्यो दत्वा चरति यो मुनिः ।
तस्यापि सर्वभूतेभ्यो न भयं जातु विद्यते ।।३९।। [VaDh 10.2]
अभयं सर्वभूतेभ्योऽदत्वा यस्तु निवर्तते ।
हन्ति जातानजातांश्च [द्रव्याणि प्रतिगृह्य च] ।।४०।। [VaDh 10.3]

33. om Y* A3; b)—त्रिस्थानुं X2*; d)—°प्राकारकारकम् A1 2 R1 [A2 cor. प्राबल्य°]; प्राबल्यकारकम् B M

34. om Y* A3; a–b)—om A1 2 R1 B M; A5 [long lacuna] देवसेवतिम्; b)—°श्वा-पदसे° only in A6; °चापादिसे° X2* A1 2 5 R1 B M; °चापाधिसे° M+; d)—पुरः A1 2 R1

35. om Y* A3; d)—भूतायासम् R2 4 B M

36. om Y* A3; a)—ध्यानं जपं A5

37. A1 2 R1 place 7.37–38 after 7.28; a)—before पुराण° A5 M+ add तथा; c)—°श्रवणाद्भक्ति° R2; d)—प्रवर्तते A5 6 R4 M+

38. a)—युक्तस्तस्मा° A1 2 R1 B M; b)—पौराण्यमभ्य° Y* A3; c–d)—om X2*; परं भावमापद्येत दृढं मुनिः Y* A1 2 R1 B M; °पद्यते यतिः A3

39. 1)—आह वसि° Y* A3; 2–3)—om Y* A3; 2)—प्रतिष्ठते B M; 3)—om X2*; a–d)—om R4; b–c)—om A5 6; b)—यश्चरते मुनिः B M; यतिः A3

40. om Y* X2* A3; d)—conj. following VaDh; all mss [except A6] and B M leave lacuna [M ed. comments अत्र ग्रन्थपातः]; A6 प्रतिगृह्णाति यस्सदा

एकाक्षरं परं ब्रह्म प्राणायामः परं तपः ।
उपवासात्परं भैक्षं दया दानाद्विशिष्यते ॥४१॥ [VaDh 10.5]

तथोत्तरत्र[1] ।

अव्यक्तलिङ्गोऽव्यक्ताचारोऽनुन्मत्त उन्मत्तवेषः[2] । अथाप्युदाहरन्ति[3] ।

न शब्दशास्त्राभिरतस्य मोक्षो
न लोकचित्तग्रहणे रतस्य ।
न भोजनाच्छादनतत्परस्य
न चैव रम्यावसथप्रियस्य ॥४२॥ [VaDh 10.18–20]
नाध्येतव्यं न वक्तव्यं न श्रोतव्यं कथंचन ।
एतैः पूर्वं सुनिष्पन्नो यतिर्भवति नान्यथा ॥४३॥
पारिव्राज्यं गृहीत्वा तु यः स्वधर्मे न तिष्ठति ।
श्वपदेनाङ्कयित्वा तं राजा राष्ट्रात्प्रवासयेत् ॥४४॥

उत्तरत्र[1] ।

लाभपूजानिमित्तं हि व्याख्यानं शिष्यसंग्रहः ।
एते चान्ये च बहवः प्रपञ्चाः कुतपस्विनाम् ॥४५॥
ध्यानं शौचं तथा भिक्षा नित्यमेकान्तशीलता ।
भिक्षोश्चत्वारि कर्माणि पञ्चमं नोपपद्यते ॥४६॥

41. om Y* A3; a)—ॐ इत्येका° X2* A1 2 R1 B M; एका° om A5; परं om A1 2 R1 2 3 B M; d)—यदा दाना° A2; तथा दाना° A5; दानाद् om A6

42. om Y* A3; 1–3)—om X2*; 1–2)—तथेति आचारोऽनुत्तमवेषेण A1 2 R1 B M; तथे [lacuna] चारोनुत्त [lacuna] मवेषेण A5; the mss are corrupt; only A6 has the reading adopted; conj. following VaDh; A6 reads °रोऽनुत्तमवेषेण; 3)—तथाप्यु° A5; c)—°दन-गर्वितस्य X2* A6; d)—at the end G6 R2 3 B M add: एकान्तशीलस्य दृढव्रतस्य पञ्चेद्रिय-प्रीतिनिवर्तकस्य । अध्यात्मविद्यारतमानसस्य मोक्षो ध्रुवो नित्यमहिंसकस्य ॥

43. Y* A3 insert after 7.50; a)—न कर्तव्यं Y*; c)—एतैः सर्वे A3; सु° om A5; d)—नान्यथा A6 add पारिव्राज्यं कथंचन

44. Y* A3 insert after 7.50

45. om Y* A3; 1)—om X2*; a–b)—°निमित्तं हि व्याख्यानं om A1 2 R1, and A5 leaves lacuna

46. c)—एते चत्वारि A1 2; यतेश्चान्ये A5; येतेश्चान्ये R1; d)—add इति Y* A3; add तथा A5

अत्रात्मव्यतिरेकेण द्वितीयं यदि पश्यति ।
ततः शास्त्राण्यधीयन्ते श्रूयते ग्रन्थविस्तरः ॥४७॥
अग्निं स्वात्मनि संस्थाप्य द्विजः प्रव्रजितो भवेत् ।
वेदाभ्यासपरो नित्यमात्मविद्यापरायणः ॥४८॥
संसेव्य चाश्रमान्सर्वाञ्जितक्रोधो जितेन्द्रियः ।
ब्रह्मलोकमवाप्नोति वेदशास्त्रार्थविद् द्विजः ।
आश्रमेषु तु सर्वेषु प्रोक्तः प्राणान्तिको विधिः ॥४९॥

शातातपः[1] ।

आरूढो नैष्ठिकं धर्मं यस्तु प्रच्यवते यतिः ।
प्रायश्चित्तं न पश्यामि येन शुद्ध्येत्स आत्महा ॥५०॥
पारिव्राज्यं गृहीत्वा तु गृहस्थो यो भवेत्पुनः ।
षष्टिर्वर्षसहस्राणि विष्ठायां जायते कृमिः ॥५१॥
इह पूर्वं प्रतिज्ञाय संन्यासं न करोति यः ।
मिथ्यावचनदग्धोऽसौ सोऽन्धे तमसि मज्जति ॥५२॥
यस्तु प्रव्रजितो भूत्वा पुनः सेवेत मैथुनम् ।
षष्टिर्वर्षसहस्राणि विष्ठायां जायते कृमिः ॥५३॥
शून्यागारेषु घोरेषु भवत्याखुः सुदारुणः ।
सोऽचिराज्जायते गर्भे श्वा स्याद् द्वादशजन्मसु ॥५४॥

47. om Y* A1 2 3 R1 [but see 7.51n]; c)—after अधीयन्ते A5 leaves a large lacuna until end of 7.51b; d)—श्रूयते conj., all mss read श्रूयन्ते

48. om Y* A1 2 3 R1; a)—अग्नीन् G6 R4

49. om Y* A1 2 3 R1; e)—तु om G6; च R4

50. 1)—आह शाता° Y* A1 2 3 R1 B M; b)—नरः G6 R2 3; द्विजः A1 2 R1; यदि G1 2; d)—Y* A3 add इति and insert 7.44, 7.43

51. b)—यो गृहस्थो A1 2 4 R1 B M; यो om G1 2; भवेन्नरः A1 2 R1 B M; भवेद् द्विजः G6 R2 3; d)—at end G6 R2 3 insert 7.53 and A1 2 R1 add वसिष्ठः अत्रात्मव्यतिरेकेण + [see 7.47]

52. om Y* A1 2 5 R1 [Y* inserts after 7.55]; a–b)—om B M

53. om Y* A1 2 R1 4 B M; inserted after 7.51 by G6 R2 3; a)—यः प्रव्रज्य गृहात्पूर्वं G6 R2 3

54. om A1 2 5 R1; c)—श्रयते R3; श्रितते A3 6; भयते R4

भासो विंशतिवर्षाणि नववर्षाणि सूकरः ।
अपुष्पो विफलो वृक्षो जायते कण्टकावृतः ।।५५।।
ततो दावाग्निना दग्धः स्थाणुर्भवति कामुकः ।
ततो वर्षशतान्यष्टौ द्वे च तिष्ठत्यचेतनः ।।५६।।
पूर्णे वर्षसहस्रे तु जायते ब्रह्मराक्षसः ।
क्षुत्पिपासापरिश्रान्तः क्रव्यादो रुधिराशनः ।
क्रमेण लभते मोक्षं कुलस्योत्सादनेन च ।।५७।।
संन्यासं पातयेद्यस्तु पतितः संन्यसेच्च यः ।
संन्यासविघ्नकर्ता च त्रयस्ते पतिताः स्मृताः ।।५८।।
बिन्दुला नाम चण्डालाः परिव्राजकरूपिणः ।
तेषां जातान्यपत्यानि चण्डालैः सह वासयेत् ।।५९।।

हारीतः[1] ।

विधिना बुद्धिपूर्वेण यः संन्यस्य गृही भवेत् ।
स एवारूढपतितः सर्वधर्मबहिष्कृतः ।।६०।।
पारिव्राज्यं परित्यज्य गृहस्थो यो भवेत्पुनः ।
षष्टिर्वर्षसहस्राणि विष्ठायां जायते कृमिः ।।६१।।

इत्यादिपरं **शातातपेय**पाठवत्[1] ।

आरूढपतितो हन्याद्दश पूर्वान्दशापरान् ।
तानेव तारयेद्विप्रो यतिः सम्यग्व्यवस्थितः ।।६२।।

55. om A1 2 5 R1; b)—नववर्षाणि om G6; शत° A3; d)—at end Y* inserts 7.52.

56. om Y* A1 2 5 R1; b)—कार्मुकः G6 R3; कानने B M

57. om Y* A1 2 5 R1; a)—°हस्रेषु G6 R3; f)—°सादनेन conj. following B M; °सेधनेन X2* [this word damaged in A6]; at end A6 adds ये च संतानजा ह स्युर्येऽपि स्युः कर्मसंभवाः । संन्यासस्तान्दहेत्सर्वान्तुषाग्निरिव काञ्चनम् ।।

58. om Y* A1 2 5 R1; a)—न्यासं संपात° R2 B M; न्यासं संपादये° R3 4; स संपात° G6; b)—पतितं A3 R2; c)—संन्यासे A3

59. om Y* A1 2 3 5 R1

60. om Y* A1 2 3 5 R1 [Y* A3 insert at 7.145]; b)—संन्यासी G1; d)—सर्वकर्म° Y* R4

61. Only in A6; all other mss omit.

62. om Y* A3; 1)—om A1 2 G6 R1 2 3; इत्यादिक्रमो शातातपपाठवत् A5; इत्यादि [damaged] शातादपियावत् R4 [see 7.51]; d)—यदि G6 R3 B M

तस्मात्सर्वप्रयत्नेन त्रिदण्डं धारयेद्यतिः ।
नेह भूयः स जायेत यतिधर्मस्य पालनात् ॥६३॥
सर्वेषामाश्रमाणां तु त्रिदण्डी ह्युत्तमाश्रमी ।
स एवास्य नमस्यः स्याद्भक्त्या सन्मार्गवर्तिनः ॥६४॥
त्रिदण्डरूपधृग्विप्रः साक्षान्नारायणात्मकः ।
यस्तं पूजयते भक्त्या विष्णुस्तेन प्रपूजितः ॥६५॥
अष्टाक्षरेण मन्त्रेण नित्यं नारायणात्मना ।
नमस्यो भक्तिभावेन विष्णुरूपी त्रिदण्डधृक् ॥६६॥
एवं वः कथितो विप्राः सन्मार्गोऽयं सनातनः ।
प्राप्ते कलियुगे घोरे इतोऽन्ये क्षुद्रलिङ्गिनः ॥६७॥
संभविष्यन्ति ते सर्वे गौतमाग्निविदीपिताः ।
वेदार्थं चान्यथा सर्वं प्रवक्ष्यन्ति कलौ युगे ॥६८॥
नग्नाः प्रच्छन्नबौद्धाश्च विनिन्दन्ति त्रयीमयम् ।
रात्रौ वेदरहस्यानि पठिष्यन्त्यल्पमेधसः ॥६९॥
भक्षयिष्यन्ति शूद्रान्नं वयं मुक्ता इति स्थिताः ।
अन्यानपि स्वधर्मस्थान्प्रेरयिष्यन्ति ते कलौ ॥७०॥
एकवेणुं समाश्रित्य जीवन्ति बहवो द्विजाः ।
नरके रौरवे घोरे कर्मत्यागात्पतन्ति ते ॥७१॥
तस्मात्तान्नालपेत्प्राज्ञो न निरीक्षेत वापि तान् ।

63. om Y* A3

64. om Y* A3; a)—सर्वेषां ह्याश्र° A2 B M; c)—एवैभिर्नम° X2* B M; d)—°वर्तिभिः X2* B M

65. om Y* X2* A3

66. om Y* X2* A3; c)—विष्णुभावेन A2 5 B M

67. om Y* A3; a)—स एव क° G6 R3 4; स एष वः A5; b)—सन्मार्गयस्सना° A5 R2 3; °मार्गोयस्सना° A6; °मार्गीयस्सना° G6 R4; d)—यतिलि° A1 2 R1 B M; भिक्षुलि° G6

68. om Y* A3; c)—वेदार्थान् G6 R2 3; वेदान्तं A2

69. om Y* A3; b)—त्रयीमयीं R4; त्रयीमयां G6

70. om Y* A3

71. om Y* A3; c)—रौरवे नरके A5 B

आलोकने च तेषां तु शुध्यते भानुदर्शनात् ॥७२॥
नग्नं वानुपनीतं वा यः श्राद्धे भोजयेद् द्विजम् ।
रेतोमूत्रपुरीषाणि स पितृभ्यः प्रयच्छति ॥७३॥
प्रेरणादथ वा लोभादेकदण्डं समाश्रितः ।
भूयो निर्वेदमापन्नस्त्रिदण्डं धारयेद् बुधः ॥७४॥

पराशरः[1] ।

द्वाविमौ पुरुषौ यातो भित्त्वा वै सूर्यमण्डलम् ।
परिव्राड्योगयुक्तश्च रणे चाभिमुखो हतः ॥७५॥
संन्यस्तं तं द्विजं दृष्ट्वा स्थानाच्चलति भास्करः ।
एष मे मण्डलं भित्वा परं ब्रह्माधिगच्छति ॥७६॥

कात्यायनः[1] ।

कामक्रोधादिकान्दोषान्वर्जयेद्यावदायुषम् ।
एवं संवर्तयन्नित्यं ब्रह्म संपद्यते यतिः ॥७७॥

उशनाः[1] ।

त्यक्तसङ्गो जितक्रोधो लघ्वाहारो जितेन्द्रियः ।
पिधाय बुद्ध्या द्वाराणि मनो ध्याने निवेशयेत् ॥७८॥

व्यासः[1] ।

यत्पूर्वमभिनिर्दिष्टमात्मज्ञानं मया पुरा ।

72. om Y* A3; a)—तस्मादेतान्नालपेत A1 2 R1 B M; b)—नेक्षेत A1 2 B M [A1 cor.]; c)—°कनेन तेषां G6 R2 3; च om A5

73. om Y* A3; b)—द्विजः A5 R4

74. om Y* A3; d)—धारयेत्पुनः X2*

75. om Y* X2*; 1)—om A3; a–b)—पुरुषौ लोके सूर्यमण्डलभेदिनौ A3; पुरुषावेतौ A1 2 B M; d)—स्थितः A1 2 R1

76. om Y* X2* A3 [Y* A3 insert at 7.145]; c)—मे हृदयं Y*; d)—ब्रह्म प्रयास्यति Y*; at end A5 adds याच्या ॥०॥ मुनिरिति; R1 adds याज्ञवल्क्यः; B M add verses in App. 1.7 in parenthesis; they are missing in X1* and X2* but given by Y* [App. 1.8].

77. Y* A3 insert at 7.145; 1)—आह कात्या° Y*; a)—रागद्वेषादीन्वर्ज° Y*; c–d)—om G6; एवं वर्तयन्ब्रह्म संपद्यत इति Y*; स वर्त° A1 R3 B M; °वर्तयेन्नि° A5 6 R2

78. om Y* X2* A3 [Y* A3 insert after 7.145]; 1)—आहोशनाः Y*; a)—मुक्तसङ्गो B M; c)—बुद्धिद्वाराणि B M

तत्सर्वं यत्नतोऽभ्यस्येत्सर्ववित्सङ्गवर्जितः ॥७९॥
लोकयात्रां प्रयत्नेन वर्जयेदात्मचिन्तकः ।
नानोपनिषदो यत्नादभ्यस्येन्मुक्तिहेतुकीः ॥८०॥

आपस्तम्बः[1] ।

अथ परिव्राजकः[2] । अत एव ब्रह्मचर्यात्परिव्रजति[3] । तस्योपदिशन्ति[4] । अनग्निरनिकेतः स्यादशर्माशरणो मुनिः[5] । स्वाध्याय एवोत्सृजमानो वाचं ग्रामे प्राणवृत्तिं प्रतिलभ्यानिहोऽनमुत्रश्चरेत्[6] ॥८१॥ [ApDh 2.21.7–10]

बृहस्पतिः[1] ।

आत्यन्तिकं ब्रह्मचर्यमाश्रमत्रयवासिनाम् ।
स्वदारनियमादेव गृहस्थो ब्रह्मचर्यवान् ॥८२॥

उत्तरत्र[1] ।

न ज्ञातिपुत्रमित्रादीन्न प्रशस्तान्द्विजातिषु ।
देशान्तरेऽपि तान्दृष्ट्वा न च तैः सह संविशेत् ।
अवश्यं भाविनी तत्र रागद्वेषादिषु स्थितिः ॥८३॥

तथैव[1] ।

न तीर्थवासी नित्यं स्यान्नोपवासपरो यतिः ।
न चाध्यापनशीलः स्यान्न व्याख्यानपरो भवेत् ॥८४॥

शङ्खः[1] ।

चन्दनेनोक्षितं बाहुं वास्यैकं वापि तक्षतः ।

79. om Y* A3 G6; d)—सर्वसङ्गविवर्जितः G6 R2 3 B M

80. om G6; Y* A3 insert after 7.117[but G1 om c–d]; a)—°यात्राः G6 R3 B M; c–d)—om R2 3 4; c)—युक्तादभ्य° A1 2; d)—°हेतुकः A1 2 3 4; °हेतुकाः A5; °हेतुः R1; °हेतवे B M; at the end A1 2 R1 B M add आपस्तम्ब आह and 7.54–55; 7.52

81. om Y* X2* A3; 3)—°चर्यवान्परि° A6; प्रव्रजन्ति A5; °व्रजेत् B M

82. Y* A3 insert at 7.145; 1)—om A1 2 R1; a)—आत्यन्तिकब्र° A2 B M

83. om Y* A3; 1)—om X2*; a)—°मित्रादि न G6 R2 3 B; b)—नाप्रश° A1 2 R1; °स्तद्विजा°; °जादिषु A4; d)—संवसेत् Y*; e–f)—om X2*; भाविनो A1 2 6 R1; स्थितः A1 2

84. om Y* A3 [all insert a–d at 7.117]; 1)—om X2*; d)—°परो यतिः Y* A5

कल्याणं वाप्यकल्याणं तयोरपि न चिन्तयेत् ।
सर्वभूतहितो मैत्रः समलोष्ठाश्मकाञ्चनः ॥८५॥

लिखितः[1] ।

नानध्यात्मग्रन्थरतिर्न च ज्यौतिषिको भवेत् ।
न व्याधिविषवेतालांश्चिकित्सेद्धर्मतोऽपि च ॥८६॥
न शिष्यसंग्रहं कुर्यान्न स्वविद्यां प्रकाशयेत् ।
संस्कृतां न वदेद्वाणीं बालवन्मूकवच्चरेत् ॥८७॥

उत्तरत्र[1] ।

संन्यस्य यतिधर्मांश्च कुर्वाणो वत्सरत्रयम् ।
योगनिष्ठः सदा भूत्वा मोक्षं प्रेत्य स विन्दति ॥८८॥
तस्मादैश्वर्यमाकाङ्क्षेत्तद्विष्णोः परमं पदम् ।
कैवल्याश्रममासाद्य चरेद्दिनमपि द्विजः ॥८९॥

शङ्खलिखितौ[1] ।

भैक्षवृत्तिरसंविभागरुचिरभिशस्तपतितवर्जं निन्दकोपहतान्नजीवी कौपीनाच्छादनमात्रावरणपरितुष्टः परिपक्वकषायः कालकाङ्क्षी सदायुक्त आत्मरतिरसंनिधानशीलः कुहककल्कदम्भवर्जितः सदा नैकग्रामवासी सङ्गदोषान्परित्यज्य पर्यटनशीलः स्यात्[2] । आत्मज्ञानविवेकार्थकुशल ऊर्ध्वं वार्षिकाभ्यां नैकस्थानवासाभिरुचिरुद्धृताभिरद्भिर्मूत्रपुरीषशौचाचमनादि कुर्यात्[3] ॥९०॥

85. om Y* A3; a–d)—om X2*; a–b)—चन्दनोक्षित° A1 2 R1 B M; °बाहुं A1 R1; °बाहुः A2; बाहौ B M; वा तस्यैकं A1; e)—सर्वभूतेष्वपि सुहृत् X2*

86. om Y* A3 [all insert a–d at 7.117]; a–d)—om X2*; b)—ज्योति° Y* A3 R1; c–d)—M+ reads लोक° . . . °चिन्तकः [see 7.80]; व्याधिभूतवे° Y* B M

87. om Y* X2* A3

88. om Y* A3; 1)—om X2*

89. om Y* A3; c)—°मारोप्य G6; d)—°मपि त्रयम् A2 B M

90. om Y* A3; 2)—°वर्जं om A5 6 G6 R4; निन्दितोप° A5 B M; °कोपहृतान्नं वर्जी G6 R2 3; °हतान्नवर्जं B M; °हतान्नाजीव A1 2 R1; °हतानां जीवी A6; कालाकाङ्क्षी X2* A6; °रतिः संनिधा° A1 2 R1; °रतिः संविधा° B M; कुहककल्क° om B M; कुंभिंनकल्क° A1 2 R1; कुहकलुब्धकदम्भजीवननैरपेक्ष्यः (°ननैरपेक्ष्यः om R4) G6 R3 4; कुहककल्कजीवननैरपेक्ष्यः R2; सदा

तथा[1] ।

वाग्बाणान्दुर्जनैर्मुक्तान्सहते यो न कुप्यति ।
भावेन च सुसंहृष्टः स दमस्तस्य बुद्धिजः ॥९१॥
शीतोष्णादीनि च द्वन्द्वान्दुर्जनप्रहितानि च ।
यथा धारयते बुद्ध्या सा तितिक्षा क्षमा स्मृता ॥९२॥
इष्टानिष्टेषु भूतेषु व्यसनाभ्युदयेषु च ।
उपशान्तः परां प्रज्ञां प्राप्तः शमदमात्मकः ॥९३॥
तपोज्ञानदमैश्वर्यैः सर्वदा यो न कुप्यति ।
वाग्बाणाभिहतस्तीक्ष्णैर्धीरः सोऽत्र न मुह्यति ॥९४॥
यो यतिर्मृदुभावेन मोक्षधर्मं चरेदिह ।
भवबन्धं विहायाशु सोऽमृतत्वाय कल्पते ॥९५॥

तथैव[1] ।

चातुर्वर्ण्यं चरेद्भैक्षं पतितेषु च वर्जयेत् ।
नियतेन्द्रियवाक्चक्षुः पूर्वं पूर्वं विवर्जयेत् ॥९६॥

वृद्धदक्षः[1] ।

वाग्दण्डोऽथ मनोदण्डः कर्मदण्डस्तथापरः ।
एतैर्दण्डैस्तु दण्डी स्यान्न तु वैणवधारणात् ॥९७॥

---

om A5 G6 R2 3; 3)—°वेककुशल X2* B M; °स्थानाभिरु° A2 B M; °द्धृताद्भिर्मू° G6 R2 3; °पुरीषाचम° A1 2 5 R1 B M; at end A1 2 5 R1 B M add उत्तरत्र । शीतोष्णवर्षवातादि नात्यन्तं परिहरेत् । आत्मनः प्रतीकारमात्रं कुर्यात् ।

91. om Y* A3; 1)—om X2* B M; b)—कुप्यतीति A1 2 R1 B M; d)—सदमन्त्व-र्थबुद्धिजः A1 2 R1

92. om Y* A3; a)—°दीनिव A1 2 B M; °दीन्न च R4; c)—यया B M; तथा A6

93. om Y* A3; c)—परं A1 2 5 R1; d)—°त्मकम् M; °त्मिकाम् B

94. Y* A3 insert at 7.145; a)—ततो B M; °बलैश्वर्यैः X2* B M; b)—सदा A6; c)—लोकपारुष्ययुक्तोऽपि X2 B M; d)—मुच्यते Y*

95. Y* A3 insert at 7.145

96. om Y* A3; 1)—om X2*; b)—विवर्जयेत् B M; c)—°वाग्भिक्षुः B M; °वाग्द्रिक्षुः A1 2 R1

97. Y* A3 insert at 7.145; b)—कामदण्डस्तथैव च A5; तथेतरः R4; तथापरं G6; c)—°स्त्रिदण्डी Y* X2*; d)—वेणुभिर्न भवेद्यतिः A5

वाग्दण्डो मौनसंयोगः कर्मदण्डस्त्वहिंसनम् ।
मनसः स तु दण्डः स्यात्प्राणायमस्य धारणम् ।।९८।।

कपिलः[1] ।

स्वस्त्याशिषं वर्जयेत्[2] । शरणं न कुर्यान्न कारयेत्[3] । कृतं प्रविशेत्[4] । अथ ब्रह्मोपासीत[5] । तच्चित्त एव शयीत[6] । अनिन्दके देवगृहे वा प्रविष्टो यथाकथंचिच्छर्वरीं नयेत् जाग्रदेव सुषुप्तः[7] । आसीनोऽथाचम्य प्राणायामत्रयं कृत्वा पुनराचामेत्[8] । काष्ठारोपितकमण्डलुना रात्रावाचामेत् दिवा स्रवन्त्या[9] । अभिरुचितं प्रभूतोदकं पुण्यस्थानं न त्यजेत्[10] । न लोलुपो नेतिहासपुराणव्याख्यानपरः[11] ।।९९।।

उत्तरत्र[1] ।

निर्जन्तुकैः स्वपतितैरिन्धनैरसहिष्णुरग्निमिन्धीत[2] । बीजशून्यमूलफलभक्षणे न दोषः[3] । चेतनाचेतनमल्पप्रयोजनाय न द्रुह्येत्[4] । कमण्डलुजलपवित्रकुसीदतैजसादिसंग्रहे न दोषः[5] । कोपितोऽपि न कुप्येत्[6] । तोषितोऽपि न तुष्येत्[7] । मर्तुं नेच्छेन्न जीवितुं वा[8] । अदग्धं पात्रं न त्यजेत्[9] । शौचार्थं पूतिकाकरणात्क्षणमपि सद्यः संनिहितोदके जपनीयं जपेत्[10] । ततश्चतुर्भुजं चिन्तयेत्[11] । नैकदेवतापक्षपातित्वं दर्शयेत्[12] । संनिकृष्टं साश्रयं शरणं संत्यजेत्[13] । सुरूपां स्त्रियं दृष्ट्वा न क्वचित्प्रेक्षेत[14] । संकोचयेदक्षिणी[15] । ॐ इति नैव कम्पयेत्[16] ।।१००।।

98. Y* A3 insert at 7.145; a)—मौने A5; b)—कामद° A5; c)—मानसः B M; य तु A5; मनस्भूषणदण्डः R4; d)—धारणात् X2* A5

99. om Y* X2* A3; 7)—अनिन्दके conj. following 6.294; एके A1 2 5 6 R1; शून्यागारे B M; 9)—काष्ठा° . . . °चामेत् om A5; 9–10)—स्रवन्त्या महारुचि° A1 2 R1 B M [°महा° om A1 2 R1]; स्रवन्त्यामधिरु° A5 6; adopted reading follows 6.294.

100. om Y* A3; 1)—om X2*; 2)—स्वपचितै° A5; स्वयंपति° R4; °तितैरसहि° A6; °धनैरग्निमि° B M; °मिन्धेत B M; °मिन्धेत् A5; 3)—बीजवधशू° A6; °शून्य° om X2*; 4)—च न R4; द्रोहेत् X1*; 5)—°कुसीदकादिसंग्रहे X2*; 6)—कोपितो न X2* A1 R1; 7)—तोषितो न A1 2 5; 8)—मर्तुं जीवितुं वा नेच्छेत् A1 2 R1 B M; नेच्छेज्जीवितुं X2*; 9)—[initial अ of अदग्धं is combined in sandhi with preceding वा in most mss]; दग्धं B M; दण्डं A1 6

तथैव[1] ।

सर्वेन्द्रियाणां संकोचो दृष्टादृष्टकरो यतेः ।
अप्रमत्तेन कर्तव्यः सुखमत्यन्तमिच्छता ॥१०१॥
गीतानां गानशीलस्य प्राणायामपरस्य च ।
नैवोक्षन्ति च पापानि जन्मान्तरकृतान्यपि ॥१०२॥

क्रतुः[1] ।

बीजघ्नं तैजसं पात्रं शुक्लोत्सर्गः सिताम्बरम् ।
दिवास्वापो वृथाजल्पो यतीनां पतनानि षट् ॥१०३॥
चिरस्थितानि द्रव्याणि संचयादीनि सर्वदा ।
तृणमृद्दारुतोयाश्मपत्रमूलफलानि च ।
अप्रयुक्तं न गृह्णीत प्रयुक्तं न च संचयेत् ॥१०४॥
दासीदासं गृहं यानं गोभूधान्यधनं रसम् ।
प्रतिगृह्याप्रतिग्राह्यं हन्यात्कुलशतद्वयम् ॥१०५॥

वृद्धजाबालिः[1] ।

आतिथ्यश्राद्धयज्ञेषु देवयात्रोत्सवादिषु ।
कुतूहलेषु सर्वेषु न गच्छेद्यतिरात्मवान् ॥१०६॥

R1; दण्डपात्रे G6; अदग्धपात्रे R2 3 4; 10)—°करणं X2*; क्षणमपि om G6 R2 3; संनिहितेन दण्डो नियतं जपेत् R4; जपनीयं conj. following A6; other mss read: नियतं X2* B M; जम A5; म्मपनीं A1 2 R1; 11)—तप्येच्चतु° X2*; ततश्चतुष्कं A1 2 R1; 13)—संनिकृष्टं om X2*; स्वाश्रयं R2 3; नाश्रयं B M; 14)—सुरमां A1 2; दृष्ट्वा add क्षणादपि R2; किंचित् A1 2 R1 B M; 15)—संकोचेद° X2*; 16)—न for नैव A2 B M

101. om Y* A3; 1)—om X2*; d)—°मिच्छतः A1 2 R1

102. om Y* A3; a)—शीतानां A6 R3 4; श्रुतानां A1 2 R1 2 M; c)—नैवोक्षयन्ति A6; नैवेक्षिपन्ति R2 3; नैव क्षिपन्ति G6 R4; नैवोक्षिपन्ति M; नैवाक्षिप्यन्ति B; च om X2* A5 6 B M; पापादीनि A5; d)—°कृतानि च A5

103. Y* A3 insert at 7.145; 1)—om G6 R3 4

104. om Y* A3; a)—चिरस्थितानां द्रव्यानां X2* B M; f)—न om A5

105. Y* A3 insert at 7.145; a)—दासदास्य A1 2 R1; दासदासी B M; b)—°धान्यं गृहं रसम् X2*

106. Y* A3 insert at 7.145; 1)—om X2*; आह वृ° Y* A3; a)—आतिथ्यं Y* A3; c)—कुतूहलेन Y* A3 5; सर्वत्र Y* A3

उत्तरत्र[1] ।

यस्तु दानपरो भिक्षुर्वस्त्रादीनां च संग्रही ।
उभौ तौ मन्दबुद्धित्वात्पूतीनरकपातिनौ ॥१०७॥

दत्तात्रेयः[1] ।

आदाय वैष्णवं लिङ्गं यस्तु त्यजति मूढधीः ।
स याति नरकं घोरं तीव्रं सङ्कटदारुणम् ॥१०८॥

देवलः[1] ।

तुल्यारिमित्रो निष्परिग्रहो ब्रह्मचारी मङ्गल्यव्यवहारो संस्कारो जीवशिक्षारत्नधनधान्यविषयोपभोगसंपर्केर्ष्यादर्पमायामोहहर्षविरोधविस्मयविवादत्रासवितर्कादिवर्जनमिति यतिधर्माः[2] ॥१०९॥

आहारमौषधं चैव सद्गृहस्थगृहे यतिः ।
प्रत्यहं चैव भिक्षेत यथा शेषं न तिष्ठति ॥११०॥
आहारमौषधं चैव तत्कालार्थाधिकं यतिः ।
आत्मार्थं धारयेन्मोहान्नरकं प्रतिपद्यते ॥१११॥
आददीत प्रवृत्तेभ्यः साधुभ्यो धर्मसाधनम् ।
नाददीत निवृत्तेभ्यः प्रमादादपि किंचन ॥११२॥

गर्गः[1] ।

सर्वधर्मान्परित्यज्य यतिधर्मं समाश्रयेत् ।

107. Y* A3 insert at 7.118 with ascriptiton जाबालिः; 1)—om X2*; d)—°शायिनौ A4 G2 3; °शालिनौ A5; °शाधिनौ A3; °यायिनौ G6 R3 4; °यामिनौ A6; °पात्रिणौ B

108. Y* A3 insert at 7.145; d)—तीव्र° A1 2 5 R1B M; °संवेददारु° A1 2 R1

109. om Y* A3; 2)—माङ्गल्य° B M; संस्कारो om B M; °पर्केदर्प° A1 2; °पर्के [lacuna] दर्प° R1; °पर्केषु दर्प° B M; °त्रासवितर्जतर्कादि° A1; °त्रासवि [lacuna] तर्कादि° A2; °त्रासवित [lacuna] तादि° A5; °त्रासवि [damaged] र्कादि R1; °त्रासवितर्जतास्त्रीवर्जनमिति R2; °त्रासवितर्कज्ञद्रीवर्ज° R4; °त्रासवितर्कतद्रिंवर्ज° A6 G6 R3; यति° om A5 R2; °धर्मः A1 2 R1 B M

110. om Y* A3; at the beginning A5 R1 add तथा

111. om Y* A3; b)—तत्कालार्थं हितं X2* B M; तत्कालार्थं गृहे A1 2 R1; श्रुतिः R1; c–d)—धारयेन्नित्यं नरकं X2*

112. om Y* A3

यतिधर्मात्परिभ्रष्टो न धर्मफलमश्नुते ॥११३॥

वृद्धवसिष्ठः[1] ।

पुष्पमूलफलपाटनाग्रच्छेदनमधुमांसदानादानानि वर्जयेत्[2] ॥११४॥

मेधातिथिः[1] ।

त्रिदण्डं कुण्डिकां शिक्यं भैक्षभाजनमासनम् ।
कौपीनाच्छादनं वासः षडेतानि परिग्रहः ॥११५॥
स्थावरं जङ्गमं बीजं तैजसं विषमायुधम् ।
षडेतानि न गृह्णीयाद्यतिर्मूत्रपुरीषवत् ॥११६॥
भिक्षाटनं जपः स्नानं ध्यानं शौचं सुरार्चनम् ।
कर्तव्यानि षडेतानि सर्वदा नृपदण्डवत् ॥११७॥
रसज्ञानं क्रियावादो ज्योतिषं क्रयविक्रयौ ।
विविधानि च शिल्पानि वर्जयेत्परदारवत् ॥११८॥
नटादिप्रेक्षणं द्यूतं प्रमदां सुहृदस्तथा ।
भक्ष्यभोज्यमुदक्यां च षण्ण पश्येत्पुरीषवत् ॥११९॥
स्कन्धावारे पुरे सार्थे खले गोष्ठे तथा गृहे ।
न वसेत यतिः षट्सु स्थानेष्वेतेषु कर्हिचित् ॥१२०॥
रात्र्यध्वानं च यानं च स्त्रीकथा लौल्यमेव च ।

113. om Y* X2* A3 [Y* A3 insert at 7.145]; b)—यतिधर्मान् A6; मोक्षधर्मं A3; समाचरेत् A1 2 R1 B M; c)—मोक्षधर्मात् A3

114. Y* A3 insert at 7.145; 1)—आह वृद्ध° Y* A3; 2)—°मूल° om G6; °फल° om A1 2 R1 B M; °टनतृणाग्र° R4; °टनार्दनच्छे° Y* A3; °मांसदानानि G6 R2 3; °मांसहृतदत्तादानानि A6; °मांसहृतान्दत्तादानानि R4; °दानादि A5; °मांसहरणादि Y* A3

115. 1)—Y* A3 insert at 7.145; c)—°दनं भिक्षोः M; °दनं भिक्षा B; d)—°ग्रहेत् X2*

116. Y* A3 insert at 7.145; a)—जङ्गमं चैव B M

117. a)—जपं A1 2 4 5 6 G3 6 R1 2 3; शौचं for स्नानं Y* A3; d)—यतीनां नृप° A5; at the end Y* A3 insert 7.84, 86a–b, 80, 86c–d, 107; then Y* B M add नादृष्टां . . . गिरा [see 7.145]

118. a)—रसदानं G1 2 3; °वादं G2 3; °वादौ A5; °वाद A3; °वादे A1 2 R1; °दानं G1

119. c)—भैक्ष्यं Y* X2* A3

120. om Y* A3; a)—सौधे B M; b)—च नो गृहे X2*; ह्यसद्गृहे B M; c)—वस्तव्यं यतिभिः षट्सु X2*

मञ्चकं शुक्लवस्त्रं च यतीनां पतनानि षट् ॥१२१॥
रागद्वेषौ मदं मानं दम्भं द्रोहं परात्मसु ।
षडेतानि यतिर्नित्यं मनसापि न चिन्तयेत् ॥१२२॥
आसनं पात्रलोपश्च संचयः शिष्यसंग्रहः ।
दिवास्वापो वृथाजल्पो यतेर्बन्धकराणि षट् ॥१२३॥
एकाहात्परतो ग्रामे पञ्चाहात्परतः पुरे ।
वर्षाभ्योऽन्यत्र यत्स्थानमुक्तं तद्दुष्टमासनम् ॥१२४॥
उक्तानां यतिपात्राणामेकस्यापि न संग्रहः ।
भिक्षोर्भैक्षभुजश्चापि पात्रलोपः स उच्यते ॥१२५॥
पात्रस्यापि त्रिदण्डादेर्द्वितीयस्य परिग्रहः ।
कालान्तरोपभोगार्थं सोऽपि स्याद् द्रव्यसंचयः ॥१२६॥
शुश्रूषालाभपूजार्थं यशोऽर्थं वा परिग्रहः ।
शिष्याणां न तु कारुण्यात्स ज्ञेयः शिष्यसंग्रहः ॥१२७॥
विद्या दिवा प्रकाशत्वादविद्या रात्रिरुच्यते ।
विद्याभ्यासप्रमादो यः स दिवास्वाप उच्यते ॥१२८॥
आध्यात्मिकां कथां मुक्त्वा भिक्षायात्रां सुरस्तुतिम् ।
अनुग्रहं पथिप्रश्नं वृथाजल्पोऽन्य उच्यते ॥१२९॥
अजिह्वः षण्ढकः पङ्गुरन्धो बधिर एव च ।

121. Y* A3 insert at 7.123; c)—मञ्चकंश्चेत्वस्त्रं A5

122. om Y* A3

123. X2* inserts at 7.124; d)—एते षट् बन्धकारिणः X2*; यतीनां पतनानि षट् Y* A3; then Y* A3 insert 7.121

124. om Y* A3; c–d)—°स्थाने चोत्तरं दुष्टमासनम् X2*; °नमासनं तदुदाहृतम् B M; then X2* inserts 7.123

125. om Y* A3; b)—°कस्याधिकसंग्रहः R4

126. om Y* A3; a)—त्रिदण्डादेः om R4; c)—°न्तरेऽपि भोगार्थं X2*

127. om Y* A3; a)—°लोभ° A6; c–d)—om A6

128. om Y* A3; c)—°भ्यासे B M

129. om Y* A3; a–b)—om R2; a)—°त्मिकीं B M; b)—भैक्षचर्यां B M; नरस्तुतिम् R4; c)—अनुग्रहकरप्रश्नाद् B M; प्रतिप्रश्नं A2 5; d)—°जल्पः स B M; at the end Y* A1 2 3 R1 add 6.76

मुग्धः स उच्यते भिक्षुः षड्भिरेतैर्न संशयः ॥१३०॥
इदं मृष्टमिदं नेति योऽश्नन्नपि न सज्जते ।
इदं तीक्ष्णमिदं स्वादु तमजिह्वं प्रचक्षते ॥१३१॥
अद्यजातां यथा नारीं तथा षोडशवार्षिकीम् ।
शतवर्षां च यो दृष्ट्वा निर्विकारः स षण्ढकः ॥१३२॥
भिक्षार्थमटनं यस्य विण्मूत्रकरणाय च ।
योजनान्न परं याति य सदा पङ्गुरेव सः ॥१३३॥
तिष्ठतो व्रजतो वापि यस्य चक्षुर्न दूरगम् ।
चतुर्युगाद्भयं मुक्त्वा परिव्राट् सोऽन्ध उच्यते ॥१३४॥
हिताहितं मनोरामं वचः शोकावहं च यत् ।
श्रुत्वा यो न शृणोतीव बधिरः स तु कीर्तितः ॥१३५॥
संनिधौ परकीयाणां समौनोऽविकलेन्द्रियः ।
सुप्तवद्वर्तते योऽपि स भिक्षुर्मुग्ध उच्यते ॥१३६॥
श्रद्धया परयोपेतः परमात्मपरायणः ।
स्थूलसूक्ष्मशरीराभ्यां मुच्यते दशषट्कवित् ॥१३७॥

जमदग्निः[1] ।

धान्यवृक्षलतावल्लीः स्थावरं जङ्गमं तथा ।
उत्पाटयेद्यो मूढात्मा नरकं प्रतिपद्यते ॥१३८॥

130. a)—अनिह्वः A1 2 R1 B M; पण्डकः X2* A1 2 G3 R1 [A1 cor.]; c)—स मुग्ध उच्यते X2*; मुग्धश्च A6; इत्युच्यते A5 [A3 gives pratīkas of each half-verse in 7.130–37]

131. d)—तमजिह्मं R1 4 B

132. a)—तथा A3; b)—°वार्षिकाम् A5 6 R4; c)—दशवर्षां A1 2 5 R1 4; d)—पण्डकः X2* G3 R1

133. d)—च for सः G6 R4

134. b)—दृष्टिर्न दूरगाम् X2*; c)—°गात्परं त्यक्त्वा G1 2 3

135. b)—शोककरं X2*; c)—श्रुत्वापि न Y*; प्रकीर्तितः Y*

136. a)—विषयाणां हि Y* A1 2 R1 B M; परकृत्यानां X2*; b)—समर्थो Y* A1 2 R1 B M; समौनावि° A5 6; c)—यो हि Y* A1 2 R1 B M; d)—भिक्षुर्मन्द A2 M

137. After this verse Y* A3 B M add महाभारते and 3.61; 6.17, 282

138. a–d)—om Y* A3; c)—उत्पाटयन्यो R3

एकान्नी द्विप्रती चैव भैक्षजीवस्त्रिसंग्रही ।
चत्वारः पतिता ह्येते यतयो नात्र संशयः ॥१३९॥
ताम्बूलाभ्यञ्जने चैव कांस्यपात्रे च भोजनम् ।
यतिश्च ब्रह्मचारी च विधवा च विवर्जयेत् ॥१४०॥
द्वे एते समवीर्ये तु सुरा ताम्बूलमेव च ।
तस्मात्सर्वप्रयत्नेन ताम्बूलं वर्जयेद्यतिः ॥१४१॥

शौनकः[1] ।

न स्वगुणं कीर्तयेत्[2] । त्रासितोऽपि न कुप्येत्[3] । पूजितोऽपि न मुदं व्रजेत्[4] । त्रिषवणं दण्डवत्स्नानमाचरेत्[5] । तथा न लङ्घयेत नदीं न बाहुभ्यां तरेत्[6] । मृत्युं जीवितं वा न काङ्क्षेत्[7] । रात्रौ न चरेत्संध्ययोश्च[8] । ताम्बूलभक्षणं वर्जयेत्[9] । अभ्यङ्गं द्विरन्नं न लिप्सेत[10] । आतिथ्यश्राद्धयज्ञेषु देवयात्रोत्सवेषु न गच्छेत्[11] । सार्थ-समवायेषु वानप्रस्थगृहस्थाभ्यां प्रीतिं च वर्जयेत्[12] ॥१४२॥

पैठीनसिः[1] ।

स्तूयमानो न तुष्येत[2] । निन्द्यमानो न कुप्येत्[3] । सममेव वर्तेत विद्यया तपसा च तदुभयं प्राप्येति[4] ॥१४३॥

सत्यकामः[1] ।

सर्वधर्मान्परित्यज्य मोक्षधर्मं समाश्रयेत् ।
मोक्षधर्मात्परिभ्रष्टः संस्कारं प्रतिपद्यते ॥१४४॥

139. om Y* A1 2 3 R1; a)—एकान्ना G6 R2 3 B M; °प्रतिश्चैव R4; regarding द्विप्रती M ed. comments: इदमशुद्धमिव [see note to trans.]

140. a)—at beginning A5 6 add तथा; °भ्यञ्जनं A1 2 3 R1 2; d)—चैव वर्जयेत् A5

141. om Y* A3; a)—द्वौ A5 6; यत् for तु B M;

142. om Y* A3; 3–4)—om X2*; 5)—दण्डवत् om G6 R2 3; जवत् R4; 6)—तथा om X2*; लज्जयेत B M; 2nd न om A1 2 R1; न नदीं R4 B M; 8)—संध्ययोश्च om A1 2 R1 B M; 9)—om G6 R2 4; °क्षणं च A5; 10–12)—om A5; 10)—असङ्गं च A1 2 R1 B M [A1 अभ्यङ्गं cor. to असङ्गं]; नाभ्यङ्गं X2*; 11)—°यज्ञदेव° X2*; 12)—सार्ध° A1 2 M; °गृहिभ्यां B M

143. om Y* A3; 2)—तुष्येत् R2 3 4; 3)—कुप्येत A1 2 B M; 4)—सममेव वर्तेत om X2*; विद्यातपसी तदु° X2*

144. Y* A3 insert at 7.145; 1)—आह सत्य° Y* A3; b)—समाचरेत् R3; आचरेत् G6; d)—संसारं Y* A3; नरकं A5

नादृष्टां भूमिमातिष्ठेन्नासूर्यं मार्गमाव्रजेत् ।
न हिंस्यात्सर्वभूतानि कर्मणा मनसा गिरा ॥१४५॥

इति यतिधर्मसमुच्चये आचारो नाम सप्तमं पर्व ॥१४६॥

145. Y* A3 insert at 7.117; see App. 1.8]; a)—न दुष्टां G6 R4; After this verse Y* A1 2 3 R1 add जाबालिः । अमावास्यां यतिः प्रातर्न कुर्याद्दन्तधावनम् । भुक्तोच्छिष्टविनाशार्थमपराह्ले समाचरेत् । गृहस्थः . . . शुनां योनिषु जायते [see 8.47] । कुण्डिकां रज्जुसंलग्नामन्यथा दुष्यते यतिः । वसिष्ठः । न कुर्याद्भोजने सङ्गं न चेले न त्रिविष्टपे । नागारे . . . मोक्षवित्तु सः [see 8.68]; [Y* A3 B M add here further यात्रामात्रं . . . यथालब्धं तदश्नीयात्कामं भुञ्जीत न क्वचित् see 6.216] । पलाशपद्म° . . . फलम् [see 6.248]; After this Y* A3 add the section given in App. 1.8.

146. इति यादवप्रकाशीये यतिधर्मसमुच्चये यतीनामाचारविधिर्नाम Y*; समाचारो M; सदाचारो B

अष्टमं पर्व

लिङ्गधर्मप्रायश्चित्तविधिः

अथ लिङ्गधर्मा वपनादयः सप्रायश्चित्ता उच्यन्ते[1] । तत्र **शौनकः**[2] ।

शिखावर्जमृतुसंधिषु वापयेत्[3] । न रोमाणि वापयेत्[4] ॥१॥

देवलः[1] ।

ऊर्ध्वं सितचतुर्दश्याः प्रतिपत्तोऽधरा तिथिः ।
ऋतुसंधिः स विज्ञेयो वपनं तत्र कारयेत् ॥२॥

लिखितः[1] ।

ऋतुसंधिषु सर्वत्र चातुर्मास्यान्तरं विना ।
पौर्णमास्यां शिखावर्जं मुण्डयेत शिरो यतिः ॥३॥
अलाभे व्याधिपीडायां राजचोराद्युपद्रवे ।
वापयेत्पौर्णमास्यादि यावत्स्यात्कृष्णपञ्चमी ॥४॥

1. 1)—यतिलिङ्ग° G1 2 3 4; यतिधर्मलिङ्ग° A4; °धर्मा उच्यन्ते । वप° A1 2 R1; °धर्म उच्यते । वप° B M; 2)—आह for तत्र A4 G1 2 3; आहोशनाः G4; तत्र om G6 R4; 3)—पौर्णमास्यां शिखा° A4; 4)—om Y*; वापयेत् om G6 R4

2. 1)—om Y*; a)—°चतुर्दश्यां X1* R4; b)—प्रतिपत्तेरधरा A1 2 R1; प्रतिपत्तिमधरा A5; प्रतिपत्ताधरा R2; प्रतिपत्तोया G1 2; प्रतिपत्तोयथा G4; प्रतिपच्चोत्तरा R4; mss attempt to correct the reading. The accepted one is found in A4 6 G3 6 R3 and is clearly uncertain. Editors of B and M have corrected the reading to प्रतिपद्यधरा following the reading of the prose passage at 5[1]. I have assumed that the word is प्रतिपद् with the ablative suffix तस्. d)—तत्र om R2 3; वपनं कारयेद्यतिरिति A4; add इति G1 2 3 4

3. 1)—आह लिखितः Y*

ऋतुसंधिकालः सितचतुर्दश्या ऊर्ध्वं प्रतिपद्यधरा तिथिः या सा ज्ञेया[1] । अपरपक्षादिप्रतिपत्पञ्चदश्योः संधिमदहोरात्रं यत्तस्मिन्वपनं कुर्यादित्यर्थः[2] ॥५॥ **देवलः**[1] ।

चातुर्मास्यानन्तरं केशश्मश्रूण्यपनयेत् नाधोरोमाणि[2] ॥६॥

मनुः[1] ।

कृत्तकेशनखश्मश्रुः पात्री दण्डी कुसुम्भवान् ।
विचरेन्नियतो नित्यं सर्वभूतान्यपीडयन् ॥७॥ [MDh 6.52]

देवलः[1] ।

मौण्ड्यं शिखाविकल्पो वा यदि लुम्पेत्प्रमादतः ।
प्राजापत्येन कृच्छ्रेण शुध्यते नात्र संशयः ॥८॥

गालवः[1] ।

त्रिस्थानलोमवपनं कृत्वा प्राजापत्यं कृत्वा प्राणायामशतं कुर्यात्[2] ॥९॥

जमदग्निः[1] ।

कक्षोपस्थादिवपने प्रायश्चित्ती भवेद्यतिः ।
प्राजापत्यत्रयं कृत्वा प्राणायामशतानि च ॥१०॥

इदं कक्षोपस्थादिवपनसमुच्चये प्रायश्चित्तम्[1] । **मेधातिथिः**[2] ।

कक्षोपस्थशिखावर्जमृतुसंधिषु वापयेत् ।
न त्रैमुण्ड्यमतिक्रामेद्भिक्षुः संवत्सरे क्वचित् ॥११॥
वपनानन्तरं स्नात्वा मृद्भिर्द्वादशभिर्यतिः ।

5. om Y* X2*; 2)—संधि [lacuna] होरात्रं B M [M ed. comments अत्र ग्रन्थपातः]; संधिमहो° A1 2; संधिं दशरात्रं A6

6. 1)—आह लिखितः Y*; 2)—चतुर्दश्यान° M+; °श्मश्रूणि वापयेत् Y* R4; add इति Y*

7. 1)—आह मनुः Y*; b)—कुटुम्भवान् R4; d)—add इति Y*

8. 1)—om G6 R3 4; आह दे° Y* R2 B M; a)—°विकल्पं Y* B M; °विकल्पेर्वा A1 2 R1; M ed. comments अनन्वितमिव

9. 1)—om Y*; 2)—°वपनं कृतं चेत्प्राजापत्येन शुध्यति प्राणा° Y*; 2nd कृत्वा om X2*; °शतं च R2 3 4; add इति Y*

10. 1)—om A5; आह जम° Y*; c)—कुर्यात् G2 3 4; d)—चेति Y*

11. 1)—om Y*; 2)—°तिथिराह A1 2 R1 B M; c)—तत्र मुण्डमतिक्र° G1

प्राणायामत्रयं कृत्वा वारुणीभिश्च मार्जयेत् ॥१२॥
स्नात्वोत्तीर्य च शेषेण जङ्घाशौचं मृदम्भसा ।
अपवित्रीकृतो भिक्षुः कौपीनस्राविवारिणा ॥१३॥
कुर्यान्मूत्रपुरीषे चेद् द्विगुणं स्नानमाचरेत् ।
मुहूर्तद्वयमस्नात्वा पिबन्खादंश्च षड्गुणम् ॥१४॥
गृहीतं यदि दण्डाद्यमविनष्टं तु न त्यजेत् ।
समुद्रं गच्छ स्वाहेति विनष्टं प्रक्षिपेज्जले ॥१५॥
प्रक्षिप्य चान्यदादद्याद्गायत्र्या प्रणवेन वा ।
तच्छंयोरित्युपवीतमब्लिङ्गाभिः कमण्डलुम् ॥१६॥
कुण्डिकामिषुमात्रोर्ध्वां निक्षिपेच्च विहायसि ।
सोदकां रज्जुसंलग्नामन्यथा दुष्यते यतिः ॥१७॥
अरण्ये त्रीनिषुक्षेपान्त्रिदण्डेन विना व्रजेत् ।
न दुष्येद्दुष्यति ग्रामे गृहाद् गृहमपि व्रजन् ॥१८॥

तथा[1] ।

प्रगृहीतान्त्रिदण्डादीनविनष्टान्यदि त्यजेत् ।
एकरात्रोषितः कुर्यात्प्राणायामशतानि च ॥१९॥

12. d)—वारुणीभिः प्रमार्ज° A1 2 5 R1 B M

13. om Y*; c)—अपवित्रकरो X2*; d)—कौपीनश्रावि° A2; कौपीनं श्रावि° A1; कौपीनः संविवा° A5; कौपीनं <u>ग्रापिधारिणा</u> [blurred] A6

14. om Y*; c–d)—om A1 2 R1

15. om Y* A1 2 R1; a)—यत्र A5; दण्डादिरवि° A5 6; b)—न तु R2 4; न तु तं त्यजेत् G6 R3; मरुतस्त्यजेत् B M [M ed. comments सन्दिग्धम्]; d)—निक्षिपे° A5

16. om Y* A1 2 R1

17. om Y* A1 2 R1; a)—कुण्डिकाभि [lacuna] मात्रो° B M [M ed. comments: ग्रन्थ-पातः]; c)—रज्जुसंयुक्ताम् A5

18. om A1 2 R1; a)—वने यतिरिषुक्षेपत्रि° G1 2 3 4 [°षुक्षेपं त्रि° G1 4]; वपने यदि विक्षिप्य त्रि° A4; त्रिषु निक्षेपं G6 R4; a–b)—अरण्ये त्रिषु निक्षेपाश्शंरुद व्रजेत् R2; आरभ्य त्रिषु निक्षिप्ता [lacuna] वर्जयेत् B M [M ed. comments: ग्रन्थपातः]; b)—त्यजेत् G1; c–d)—om X2* B M; d)—गृहान्गृह° G1 2 3 4; add इति Y*

19. om Y* A1 2 R1; 1)—om X2* B M; तथा च A5; a–b)—om X2* B M

गालवः[1] ।

विद्यमानेन जलपवित्रेणाचमनतर्पणोपस्थानानि न करोति यः तस्य सर्वं निष्फलं भवेत्[2] । तस्य प्रायश्चित्तं विधीयते[3] ।

प्राणायामांस्त्रिशतं कृत्वा जपेत्त्रिकशतत्रयमिति[4] ।

जलपवित्रं विनापः प्राश्य दश प्राणायामान्धारयेत्[5] ॥२०॥

अत्रिः[1] ।

गन्धवर्णरसैर्दुष्टमस्वच्छं केशदूषितम् ।
विना वस्त्रं पिबन्नम्भः प्राणायामान्दशाचरेत् ॥२१॥

तत्र[1] ।

उद्धृतासु स्रवन्तीषु ह्रदेषु विमलेषु च ।
वस्त्रपूता न कर्तव्या आपः शुद्धा इति श्रुतिः ॥

इति तेनैव पूर्वमेव परिहृतम्[2] [see 6.44] ॥२२॥ **गालवः**[1] ।

जलपवित्रादानं बन्धनं च प्रणवेन कुर्यात्[2] । त्रिदण्डजलपवित्र-वियोगं न कुर्यात्[3] । प्रमादात्करणे आचम्य प्राणायामत्रयं कृत्वा पुनराचामेत्[4] । स्नानभोजनकाले तु त्रिदण्डवियोगं न कुर्यात्[5] । प्रमादात्करणे आचम्य प्राणायामत्रयं कृत्वा पुनराचामेत्[6] । प्रागुदक्शिरसं विष्णोः स्थानमसीति त्रिदण्डं स्थापयेत्[7] । अधःपतने उत्तिष्ठ ब्रह्मणस्पत इति जपेत्[8] । अन्यदण्डेषु दण्डान्स्पृष्ट्वा विष्णोर्मनसा पूतेस्थ इति प्रक्षाल्य प्राणायामांस्त्रीन्कुर्यात्[9] । अज्ञानात्करणे प्रणवेन प्रक्षाल्य प्रणवं दशधावर्तयेत्[10] ॥२३॥

20. om Y* A1 2 R1; 2)—विद्यमाने जले स्नानाचमनतर्पणोपस्थानानि न करोति प्रीत्या स प्राणाया [lacuna] सर्वं B M [M ed. comments ग्रन्थपातः]; °तर्पणमुपस्थानं न A6; °तर्पणं स्नानं न A5; न om R2; यः तस्य om R2; 3)—विधीयते om X2* B M; 4)—इति om R4; 5)—विना दश B M

21. om Y* A1 2 R1; 1)—अत्र B M; c)—पिबेन्नम्भः A5; पिबेन्नाम्भः X2* B M; d)—at end B M add गालवः । जलपवित्रदानबन्धनं प्रणवेन कुर्यात्

22. om Y* X2*; 1)—om B M; 2)—परिहृता A1 2 R1 B M

23. 2)—om Y*; 3)—त्रिदण्डान्जल° A5; त्रिदण्डं जल° M; °वित्रयोगं A6; न om G1 2 3 4; 4)—प्रमादाद्वियोगक° A1 2 R1 B M; प्रमादकरणे Y*; अप आचम्य A4 G1 2 3; कृत्वा add वारुणीभिश्च मार्जयेत् G2; पुनराचमनं चरेत् G1 3 4; कृत्वा चाचामेत् G6 R4;

गर्गः[1] ।

दण्डसंघर्षणं कृत्वा वनस्पते वीड्वाङ्ग इति जपित्वा विष्णोर्मनसा पूतेस्थ इति प्रक्षाल्य प्राणायामांस्त्रीन्कुर्यात्[2] । अज्ञानात्कृत्वा प्रणवेन प्रक्षालयेत्[3] । प्रणवं दशकृत्व आवर्तयेत्[4] ॥२४॥

गालवः[1] ।

कमण्डलुजलपवित्रपात्रसंघर्षणे सद्यस्त्यागो विधीयते[2] ॥२५॥

अत्रिः[1] ।

पात्रस्नेहसंघर्षणं न कुर्यात्[2] । अज्ञानात्कृतेऽपवित्रतां व्रजेत्[3] ॥२६॥

स एवाह[1] ।

अभिन्नमदुष्टं वा पात्रं त्रिदण्डादीन्वा त्यक्त्वा अहोरात्रमुपोष्य गायत्र्यष्टशतं जपेत्[2] । भिन्नपात्रं धारयित्वोपवासत्रयं चरेत्[3] ॥२७॥

जमदग्निः[1] ।

शौचभेदे शतं कुर्यात्पात्रभेदे तथैव च ।
भिन्ने त्वन्यधृते पात्रे उपवासत्रयं चरेत् ॥२८॥

उत्तरत्र[1] ।

पूयशोणितमांसैस्तु विण्मूत्राभ्यां तथापि वा ।

5-6)—om A6; °काले तु त्रिदण्डवियोगे प्राणायामत्रयं कुर्यात् Y*; 5)—°कालेऽपि A5; त्रिदण्ड° om A5; 6)—अप आचम्य A1 2 R1 B M; कृत्वाचामेत् G6 R2 3; 7)—प्रागुदगग्रं Y*; °सीति मन्त्रेण R4; त्रिदण्डान् A5; स्थापयेद्यतिः A2 B M; 8)—अतस्त्रिदण्डपतने A5; full text of mantra in A1 2 R1; इति add मन्त्रं A1 2 R1 B M; 9)—अन्यदण्डेन Y* B M; प्रणायामत्रयं A1 2 R1 4 B M; 10)—करणे om Y*; करणेन G6 R3; प्रक्षालयेत् Y*; दशधा° om A4 G1 2 4; द्वादशाव° G3; दशावर्त° A1 2 G6 R1 2 B M

24. om Y*; 2)—वीड्वाङ्ग A1 2 R1 2 4 B M give whole mantra; त्रीन्प्राणायामान् G6 R2 3; प्राणायामत्रयं R4; 3–4)—om X2*

25. 1)—om Y*; 2)—°पवित्रे A1 2 6 R1; °पात्र° om A5 6; °र्षणे कृते Y*; add इति X2* B M

26. om Y* X2*; 2)—पात्रे A5

27. 1)—om Y* X2*; 2)—वा om Y*; त्रिदण्डं त्यक्त्वा Y*; गायत्र्याष्टोत्तरशतं Y*; गायत्र्याष्ट° A1 2 R4; 3)—भिन्नं X2* A4; add इति Y*

28. 1)—आह जम° A4; a–d)—om Y*; b)—ज्ञानभेदे A1 2 R1 B M; मात्राभेदे X2*; c)—भिन्नेऽप्यन्यद्धृत्वा A1 2 R1 B M [°न्यधृते B M]; पात्रम् A1 2 G6 R1 3; पात्र A5 6 R4

रेतोऽश्रुश्लेष्मभिः स्पृष्टं पात्रं यदि यतिस्त्यजेत् ॥२९॥
श्वकाकाखुगवोष्ट्रांश्च जम्बुकं वानरं तथा ।
चण्डालं पतितं स्पृष्ट्वा हस्तस्थं पात्रमुत्सृजेत् ॥३०॥
मज्जामूत्रपुरीषैस्तु शुक्लकीलालशोणितैः ।
स्पृष्टं दण्डं त्यजेद्भिक्षुः शेषं संस्कारमर्हति ॥३१॥
न दण्डेन विना ग्रामे गृहाद् गृहमपि व्रजेत् ।
प्राणायामांस्तथा कुर्याद्वने चाध्वव्यतिक्रमे ॥३२॥
यद्यदण्डो गृहं गच्छेद्वनं वा त्रीषुमात्रतः ।
नीडं प्रतिनिवर्तेत प्राणायामांस्त्रयस्त्रयः ॥३३॥
त्रिदण्डासनपात्रादेर्न वियोगः कथंचन ।
वियोगात्पतते भिक्षुः प्रायश्चित्तं तदुच्यते ॥३४॥
त्रिदण्डस्य वियोगे तु प्राणायामशतं चरेत् ।
शतार्धं कुण्डिकायाः स्यात्पात्रे वै षोडश स्मृताः ॥३५॥
पवित्रे चाष्ट विज्ञेयाः शिक्ये षट् च प्रकीर्तिताः ।
चत्वारश्चासने ज्ञेयाः पवित्रीकरणं त्विदम् ॥३६॥

सत्यकामजाबालौ[1] ।

अथ भिक्षूणां प्रायश्चित्तं व्याख्यास्यामः[2] । पात्रं क्रोशमात्रं त्यक्त्वा व्रजति चेत्प्रायश्चित्तेन युज्यते[3] । त्रिंशत्प्राणायामान्कृत्वा जपेत्त्रि-

29. 1)—om Y* X2*; a)—पूतमांसैस्तु A5; b)—°भ्यामथापि G1; c)—रेतोऽसृगश्रु° A5 6; स्पृष्ट्वा Y*

30. a)—श्वकाककरभोष्ट्रांश्च Y* A6 B M; c)—om A6; d)—वस्त्रस्थं पात्रकं त्यजेत् Y* A6 [from here until 10.128 A6 switches to recension Y*]

31. c)—स्पृष्ट्वा A6; d)—at end Y* A6 B M add अत्रिः [om B M] । श्वकाककरभोष्ट्रैश्च दण्डादौ दूषिते यतिः । दण्डान्मृद्भिर्द्वादशभिरद्भिः [A6 °शभिर्दण्डान्] संशोध्य यत्नतः । दण्डं मन्त्रेण गृह्णीयाज्जप्त्वा पौरुषसूक्तकम् । इतरेषां तु राजेन्द्र सद्यस्त्यागो विधीयते [8.42]

32. c)—प्राणायामत्रयं Y* A6; d)—चोर्ध्वं व्यति° Y* X2* A6

33. om Y* A6; b)—त्विषुमा° R2 B M; त्रीषु निर्गतः R4; c)—नीखुं A1 2 R1; गच्छेन्प्रति° R4

34. b)—वियोगं Y* A6; d)—विधीयते Y* A6

35. c)—कुण्डिकायां Y* A6 G6 R4 B M

36. b)—षट् परिकी° R4; c)—चत्वारस्त्वासने Y* A6; d)—add इति Y* A6

कशतत्रयम्[4] । त्रिदण्डं पात्रासनं वा त्यक्त्वा समुद्रगाया नद्याः पारं व्रजति चेदुपवासत्रयं कृत्वा प्राणायामशतं चरेत्[5] ॥३७॥

उत्तरत्र[1] ।

स्त्रीशूद्रे दण्डान्तरं गते प्राणायामांस्त्रीन्कुर्यात्[2] । खरोष्ट्रेऽन्तरं गते प्राणायामान्षडाचरेत्[3] । श्वानसूकरचण्डालेष्वन्तरं गतेषु प्राणायामान्द्वादश धारयेत्[4] । विहितातिक्रमं कृत्वा प्राणायामान्द्वादश धारयेत्[5] ॥३८॥

दक्षः[1] ।

दण्डान्पात्रं परित्यज्य एकरात्रोषितो यतिः ।
दण्डान्मन्त्रेण गृह्णीयाद्भिक्षापात्रं परित्यजेत् ॥३९॥

अत्रिः[1] ।

यदि भूमौ क्षिपेद्दण्डान्पात्रं वापि कदाचन ।
षोडशासुयमान्कुर्यादष्टौ षड् द्वादशापि वा ॥४०॥

देवलः[1] ।

दण्डादौ दूषिते विष्ठाक्रव्यादाद्यैर्महामुने ।
किं तत्र वद कर्तव्यं संस्कारो येन जायते ॥४१॥
दण्डान्मृद्भिर्द्वादशभिरद्भिः संशोध्य यत्नतः ।
जप्त्वाथ पौरुषं सूक्तमद्भिः संशोधयेदपि ।
इतरेषां तु राजेन्द्र सद्यस्त्यागो विधीयते ॥४२॥

37. 1)—सत्यकामः [जाबाल om] Y* A6; °बालिः A1 2 R1; 2–4)—om A6 G1 3 4; 5)—त्रिदण्डान् A5; आसनं पात्रं Y* A6; पात्रमासनं B M; चेद् om X2*; चेत्तदोपवास° Y* A6

38. 1)—om Y* X2* A6; 2)—°शूद्रेऽन्तरं Y* A6; °न्तरे X2* B M; 3)—°न्तरे B M; गते च A6; 3–4)—षडाचरेत् . . . प्राणायामान् om A6; 4)—श्वसूक° G1; 5)—om A1 2; गत्वा A6; द्वादशैव तु धारयेदिति Y* A6

39. Y* A6 insert after 8.40; 1)—om Y* A6; a)—पात्रं यतिस्त्यक्त्वा Y*; पात्रं यतिर्वापि त्यक्त्वा A6; b)—यदि Y* A6; d)—भिक्षामात्रं Y* A6

40. 1)—om Y* A6; a)—यदि om A6; यतिर्भूमौ Y* B M; a–b)—दण्डान्वा पात्रं वा A6; कथंचन G6 R3 4; d)—वेति Y* A6

41. om Y* A6; a)—दण्डादि R4; c)—न तत्र A5; d)—यत्र A1 2 R1 B M

42. om Y* A6; c)—जप्त्वा तु A5

शुक्लोच्छिष्टाश्रुविण्मूत्रश्लेष्मशूद्रगवानलैः ।
त्यजेत्पात्रपवित्रादीन्स्पृष्ट्वा वा तस्करादिभिः ॥४३॥
गृह्य शूद्रादिवर्णेभ्यः क्रमाद्दण्डादिकं यतिः ।
शतं शतार्धं पञ्च च प्राणायामान्दशापि च ॥४४॥

अत्रिः[1] ।

उपानच्छत्रवस्त्रादि भिक्षायाः साधनं तथा ।
गृह्य शूद्राच्छतं कुर्याद्वैश्यादर्धशतं तथा ।
क्षत्रियात्पञ्चविंशच्च हीनविप्राद्दशैव तु ॥४५॥

वृद्धजाबालिः[1] ।

त्रिदण्डमप्पवित्रं च त्यक्त्वा भिक्षुर्गृहान्तरे ।
जपेत्पुरुषसूक्तं च प्राणायामान्दशाचरेत् ॥४६॥

देवलः[1] ।

गृहस्थः परपाकाशी पात्रलोपी च भिक्षुकः ।
दशवर्षसहस्राणि तिर्यग्योनिषु जायते ॥४७॥
पात्राभावे यतेर्नित्यं पात्रं पर्णपुटं भवेत् ।
तत्पात्रं तावदेव स्याद्यावन्मुख्यं न लभ्यते ॥४८॥

कपिलः[1] ।

सूचीनखनिकृन्तने जलपवित्रपात्रे अन्तर्वासोबहिर्वाससी चाशक्तौ धारयेत्[2] ॥४९॥

अत्रिः[1] ।

त्यक्त्वा यज्ञोपवीतं तु षट् कृच्छ्राणि समाचरेत् ।
गायत्रीसहितान्येव पुनश्चाप्युपनाययेत् ॥५०॥

43. om Y* A6; b)—°शूद्रश्लेश्म° G6 R3; °शूद्र° om R3; °गवाननैः A1 2 R1; °गखाननैः M+; °गवाशनैः B M; d)—स्पृष्टान्वा R4; चेत्तस्क° G6 R2 3

44. om Y* A1 2 6 R1; a)—ग्राहि A5; c)—पञ्चाशत् X2* B M [M ed. comments अत्र पञ्चविंशरिति वर्तितव्यम् see note to trans.]; d)—वा R4 B

45. om Y* A6; c)—ग्राह्य G6 R2 3; ग्राह्यं R4; d)—°दर्धं द्विशतं G6 R3

46. 1)—वृद्ध° om A6; a–d)—om Y* A6; a)—तु R4 B M

47. om Y* A6; b)—पात्रलोभी R2 3 4

48. b)—पर्णपत्रपुटं भवेत् G6 R3 4; d)—तु लभ्यत इति Y* A6

49. om Y* A6; 1)—om X2* A5; 2)—चाशक्तो R3 B M; °शक्तौ add प्राणायामान् X2*

50. om Y* A6 [all insert a–d at 8.52]; b)—समापयेत् G6; d)—°नायनमिति Y* A6

वृद्धजाबालिः[1] ।

हीनो यज्ञोपवीतेन यदि स्याद्ध्यानभिक्षुकः ।
तस्य क्रिया निष्फलाः स्युः प्रायश्चित्तं विधीयते ॥५१॥
गायत्रीसहितानेव प्राजापत्यान्षडाचरेत् ।
पुनः संस्कारमाहृत्य धार्यं यज्ञोपवीतकम् ॥५२॥
कुर्यात्त्रिदण्डग्रहणं कालक्षेपं न कारयेत् ।
एवं न याति नरकं सुगतिं चापि गच्छति ॥५३॥

इदमेव यज्ञोपवीतत्यागात्मकं पारिव्राज्यं कृतवतां प्रायश्चित्तम्[1] ।

हारीतः[2] ।

विना यज्ञोपवीतेन यत्कृतं भोजनादिकम् ।
तत्पापप्रशमायालं प्रायश्चित्तं ब्रवीमि वः ॥५४॥
तेषां तु भोजनादीनां प्रत्यहं सुसमाहितः ।
सहस्रार्धैरसुयमैर्विधिपूर्वकृतैः शुचिः ॥५५॥
योगाभ्यासरतस्येह नश्यन्ते पातकानि तु ।
तस्माद्योगरतो भूत्वा ध्यायेन्नित्यं क्रियान्तरे ॥५६॥

स एवाह[1] ।

अज्ञानेन तु विप्रेन्द्रो विना यज्ञोपवीतकम् ।
कृत्वा मूत्रपुरीषाणि प्राणायामान्षडाचरेत् ॥५७॥
नित्यं यज्ञोपवीती स्यादृते त्वावश्यकक्रियाम् ।
कुर्वन्नावश्यकं कर्म निवीतं पृष्ठतः क्षिपेत् ॥५८॥

51. 1)—om Y* A6; b)—यदि . . . [8.52a] °सहितानेव om X2*

52. b)—समाचरेत् Y* A5 6; c)—°माश्रित्य B M; d)—add इति Y* A6

53. Y* A6 insert after 8.68; b)—°क्षेमं B M

54. 2)—om A1 2 5; a–d)—om A5; c)—°प्रशमार्थं च B M; °प्रशमायार्थं A1 2;

55. om Y* A6;

56. om Y* A6; d)—गृहान्तरे G6 R2 3 M+

57. om Y* A6; 1)—om X2*; a)—च X2*; विप्रेन्द्र B M;

58. At beginning A6 G1 3 4 add मेधातिथिः; b)—°क्रियाः X2*; c)—कृत्वा for कर्म A5; d)—निवीतः A1 2 R1; add इति Y* A6

अथ वस्त्रमुच्यते[1] । तत्राह **गौतमः**[2] ।

कौपीनाच्छादनार्थं वासो बिभृयात्[3] । प्रहीणमेके निर्णिज्य[4] ॥५९॥

[GDh 3.18–19]

बृहस्पतिः[1] ।

कौपीनाच्छादनार्थं च बिभृयाज्जीर्णमम्बरम् ।
प्रहीणमेके निर्णिज्य बहिस्त्याज्यं तु यद्भवेत् ॥६०॥

हारीतः[1] ।

कौपीनाच्छादनं वासः कन्थां शीतनिवारिणीम् ।
पादुके चापि गृह्णीयात्कुर्यान्नान्यस्य संग्रहम् ॥६१॥

जाबालिः[1] ।

कार्पासं धारयेद्वस्त्रं पटं वल्कलवर्जितम् ।
नान्यथाचमने शुध्येत्संध्योपासन एव च ।
काषायमेव कार्पासं वासः कन्थां च धारयेत् ॥६२॥

शङ्खलिखितौ[1] ।

त्रिदण्डपवित्रपाणिर्विपरिधानं कुशचीरवल्कलवासाः शीतत्राणार्थं कम्बलमेके[2] ॥६३॥

यद्यपि काषायमित्यविशेषेणोक्तं तथापि गैरिकाख्यधातुना रक्तं कर्तव्यम्[1] । तथा हि पारिव्राज्यलिङ्गधारणं गृहस्थस्य प्रतिषेधयन्नेतज्ज्ञापयति **वृद्ध-जाबालिः**[2] ।

न धारयेद्धातुवस्त्रं शिक्यं चापि न धारयेत् ।

59. 1)—वस्त्रविधिरुच्यते Y* A6; 2–4)—om Y* A6; 2)—तत्राह om X2*; 3)—कौपीनार्थं R4; 4)—°णमेकं A1 5 R4 B M; °णमेक R2 3; निर्णिज्येत् G6 R2; निर्णिज्येत R3 4

60. c)—°णमेकं A1 2 5 R1 B M; d)—त्यक्तं Y* A6; च A1 2 R1; add इति Y* A6

61. 1)—om A6; गौतमः Y*; b)—°निवारणं Y*; d)—add इति Y* A6

62. om Y* A6 [but all insert 1, a–b and e–f at 8.64]; b)—पट्टवल्क° Y* A6 B M; सूक्ष्मतन्तुवर्जि° X2*; c)—°चमनं G6 R4; नान्यशौचमनः A1 2 R1 B M; d)—°सनमेव A5 R4

63. 2)—त्रिदण्ड . . . लवासाः om Y* A6; °पाणि A1 2 B M [M ed. comments here and after कम्बलमेके—उभयत्र ग्रन्थपातः]; विपरिधावनं A1 2 R1 B M; शीतार्थं Y* A6; कम्बलमित्येके A5; कम्बलमेकमिति Y* A6

न धारयेत्त्रिविष्टब्धमेतत्स्नातकलक्षणम् ॥६४॥

दत्तात्रेयः[1] ।

मोक्षाश्रमे स्मृतं वस्त्रं रक्तं गैरिकधातुना ।
धार्यं यज्ञोपवीतं तु सितं नवगुणान्वितम् ॥६५॥

एतासु विहितास्वपि मात्रासु सङ्गो न कर्तव्यः[1] । तथा च **देवलः**[2] ।

सममृत्काञ्चनः स्वमात्रास्वप्यसक्तो मध्यस्थः[3] ॥६६॥

मनुः[1] ।

मात्रासङ्गाद्विनिर्गतः इति[1] ॥६७॥

वसिष्ठः[1] ।

न कुट्यां नोदके सङ्गो न चेले न त्रिपुष्करे ।
नागारे नासने नान्ने यस्य वै मोक्षवित्तु सः ॥६८॥
[VaDh 10.23]

इति यतिधर्मसमुच्चये लिङ्गधर्मप्रायश्चित्तविधिर्नाम अष्टमं पर्व ॥६९॥

64. 1)—यद्यपि . . . तथापि om Y* A6; गैरिकाख्येन धातुना काषायेण रक्तं Y* A6; 2)—तथा हि om Y* A6; तथापि G6 R2 3; प्रतिषेधन्नेत° Y*; प्रतिषिद्धं नैतज्ज्ञा° A6; प्रतिषेधादेत° B M; °पयतीति Y* A6; वृद्धजाबालिः om Y* A6; a–d)—om Y* A6; c–d)—om A5; then Y* A6 add 6.62 [except c–d]

65. 1)—om A5; a–b)—om A5; b)—रक्तं यद्धातुरञ्जितं A4; रक्तं यद्धातुवर्जितं A6 G1 2 3 4; d)—add इति Y* A6

66. om Y* A6; 2)—तथा च om X2*; च om R1; 3)—सममृत्काञ्चनः conj. [often Grantha and Telugu mss omit the visarga before a conjunct consonant beginning with a sibilant]; समदृक्काञ्चन A1 2 R1; समताकाञ्चन A5 [possibly also R3 but there much crossed out and unclear]; समृत्तिकाञ्चन R4; समृत्काञ्चन G6; सममृत् om R2; आसनवस्त्रकाञ्चनमात्रा° B M; °स्व° om B M; °मात्रास्वसक्तो A1 2 R1 B M

67. om Y* A6

68. a)—कुट्ये Y*; b)—त्रिविष्टपे B M [see 7.145n]; d)—add इति G2 3 4 M; at end Y* A6 insert 8.53.

69. यादवप्रकाशीये यति° A4 G1 2 4; लिङ्गधर्म° om X2*; °प्रायश्चित्त° om B M; नाम om X2*;

नवमं पर्व

गतिस्थितिनिरूपणम्

अथ यतीनां गतिस्थितिर्निरूप्यते[1] । तत्र **गौतमः**[2] ।

ऊर्ध्वरेता ध्रुवशीलो वर्षासु[3] ।।१।। [GDh 3.11–12]

मेधातिथिः[1] ।

उदितेऽन्यत्र मध्याह्ने अन्यत्रास्तमिते रवौ ।
दृश्यते त्वनिकेतः स्यात्सूर्यवत्सङ्गवर्जितः ।।२।।
देवालयाग्न्यागारेषु त्वेकदेशे निशां नयेत् ।
अन्यत्र मरणत्रासान्महतश्चाप्युपद्रवात् ।।३।।
वार्षिकांश्चतुरो मासान्बहिर्ग्रामात्समापयेत् ।
तत्राप्युपक्रमे हेतू पूर्वोक्तावनिवारितौ ।।४।।

अत्र वर्षास्वेकत्र वस्तव्यमन्यथा न वस्तव्यमिति प्रतीयते[1] । तत्राल्पानुग्रहं **मनु**राह[2] ।

ग्रैष्महैमन्तिकान्मासानष्टौ प्रायेण पर्यटेत् ।

1. 1)—गतिस्थिती A4 G1 2 B; °स्थितिरुच्यते A6; 2–3)—om Y* A6; 2)—om R4; तत्र om G6 R2 3

2. b)—त्वन्यत्रा° A5 G6 R3 4; c)—त्वनिकेतत्वात् G1

3. a–b)—देवालयेऽग्न्या° X2*; देवालये शून्यागारे एक° A6; देवालयाग्न्यागारे तु एक° A5; वेश्मशून्याग्न्यागारेषु A4; वेशून्याग्न्यागारेषु G1 2 4 [°पैशू° G1]; देवशून्याग्न्यागारेषु G3; चैकदेशे G6 R4 B M; वैकदेशे R2 3; d)—°प्युपप्लवात् Y* M+

4. a–b)—om A6; b)—समाचरेत् A1 2 B M; समाश्रयेत् G3; c)—हेतुः A5 6 G6 R2 3; हेतु G1; d)—add इति Y* A6

दयार्थं सर्वभूतानां वर्षास्वेकत्र संवसेत् ॥५॥

अत्र प्रायेणेति सूचितमनुग्रहं **क्रतु**र्विशिनष्टि[1] ।

ग्रामे दिनं पुरे त्रीणि नगरे पञ्च सप्त वा ।
तिष्ठेदेकत्र वर्षासु व्रजेत्सूर्योदिते पथि ॥६॥

लिखितः[1] ।

परे ब्रह्मणि संन्यस्य कुर्वन्कर्माणि शक्तितः ।
योगाभ्यासप्रधानस्तु जपशीलः क्षमापरः ॥७॥
पर्यटेत्पुण्यतीर्थानि देवतायतनानि च ।
कृच्छ्रचान्द्रायणादीनि कुर्याच्छुद्ध्यर्थमात्मनः ॥८॥
अनन्धोऽव्याधितोऽपङ्गुः षड्रात्रं न वसेत्क्वचित् ।
धर्मधीरन्यदेशाच्चेद्वसेद्वा सार्वकालिकम् ॥९॥
श्रावणं मासमारभ्य यावन्मासचतुष्टयम् ।
वसेयुः सर्वयतय एकत्रैवेति निश्चयः ॥१०॥

देवलः[1] ।

न चिरमेकत्र वसेदन्यत्र वार्षिकात्[2] । श्रावणादिचतुर्मासिको वार्षिकः[3] । तस्मिन्न यायी स्यात्[4] ॥११॥

गालवः[1] ।

शून्यागारे वृक्षमूले वा वर्षास्वेकत्र निवसेत्[2] ॥१२॥

5. 1)—om Y* A6; तत्र X2*; 2)—मनुः for तत्रा° ··· °राह Y* X2* A6; अत्राल्पा° B M; a)—ग्रीष्म° B M; b)—पर्यटन् Y* A6; c)—यदार्थं G1 2 4; यदर्थं A4; दातारं A6; d)—add इति Y* A6

6. 1)—क्रतुः for अत्र . . . °शिनष्टि Y* A6; क्रतुः om A5; d)—सूर्योदये X2*

7. a)—विन्यस्य G1; न्यस्य A6; संत्यज्य G6; b)—वर्तितः A1 2 R1; c–d)—om A4 6 G1 2

8. a)—पर्यटेत्पुण्यतीर्थाति om A6 G2 [A6 leaves lacuna]; पर्यटन् X2* G1; b)—तीर्थानि विविधानि च G1

9. b)—षड्रात्रान् G6 R2 3; d)—om A6; वसेत्तत्रादितः क्वचित् A4

10. d)—निश्चयमिति Y* A6

11. om Y* A6; 2)—वार्षिकान् R2 3 4 B M; 3–4)—om X2*

12. 1)—आह गालवः G3; 2)—वा om G1 6 R4; °कत्र वसेत् A5; °कत्रातिवसेत् A1 2; add इति Y* A6

विश्वामित्रः[1] ।

वर्षाभ्योऽन्यत्राप्येकत्र वसेदेव[2] ॥१३॥

वृद्धमनुः[1] ।

धर्मवृद्धो त्वामरणादेकत्रापि वसेत्[2] । अन्यत्र व्रजनशीलः स्यादि-
त्याचार्याः[3] ॥१४॥

प्रकारं देशं **यम** आह[1] ।

ग्रामैकरात्रवासी स्यान्नगरे पञ्चरात्रिकः ।
एकत्र निवसेन्मासांश्चतुरो वार्षिकान्मुनिः ॥१५॥
जले जीवाः स्थले जीवा आकाशे जीवमालिका ।
जीवमालिकाकुले लोके वर्षास्वेकत्र संवसेत् ॥१६॥
अध्वा सूर्यस्य निर्दिष्टः कीटवच्च चरेन्महीम् ।
अश्वस्तननिधानस्तु सुमतिः सुसमाहितः ॥१७॥
भयं प्राणान्तिकं त्यक्त्वा विण्मूत्रोत्सर्गमेव च ।
नान्यत्र विचरेद्रात्रौ न मध्याह्ने न संध्ययोः ॥१८॥
एकाकी विचरेन्नित्यं मुक्तात्मा त्वसहायकः ।
एकस्य हि समः पन्था जायतेऽन्यत्र जीयते ॥१९॥
दृष्टिपूतं न्यसेत्पादं वस्त्रपूतं जलं पिबेत् ।
सूनृतामीरयेद्वाचं सर्वसत्त्वहितं चरेत् ॥२०॥
एकशाट्येकभक्तश्च एकपात्री च भिक्षुकः ।

13. om Y* A6

14. om Y* A6; 2)—°वृद्धो भूत्वा G6 B M; °वृद्धो मरणा° B M; 3)—A5 adds ग्रामैकरात्रो चेत्

15. 1)—om R2; यमः for प्रकारं . . . आह Y* A6 G6 R3 4; a)—°रात्रीवासी A1 2 6 R1; °रात्रावासी A5; c–d)—मासान्वार्षिकान्चतुरो मुनिः Y* A6; चत्वारो A5 G6

16. om Y* A6; b)—°मालिकाः A1 G6 R1; c)—देशे X2*

17. om Y* A6; b)—महीं चरेत् B M; चरेन्मुनिः R2; c)—°विधानस्तु B M

18. om Y* A6

19. om Y* A6; a)—विचरन्नित्यं G6 R3; d)—°तेऽन्योत्र X2*; जीर्यते G6 R3 4 B M

20. om Y* A6; a–b)—om X2*; पदं न्यसेत् A1 2 R1; d)—सर्वभूत° R4

एकैकं विचरेद् ग्रामं तत्पुराणमृषिव्रतम् ॥२१॥
नित्यं स्थण्डिलशायी स्यादनित्यां वसतिं वसेत् ।
अरण्यनित्यो मुण्डी स्यान्मनसा ध्यानमभ्यसेत् ॥२२॥
भैक्षदेशं नृपज्ञातिपुत्रमित्रादियोषितः ।
उपकारकथाश्चैव मनसापि न चिन्तयेत् ॥२३॥
आगच्छ गच्छ तिष्ठेति स्वागतं सुहृदं प्रति ।
सन्मानमपि न ब्रूयान्मुनिर्मोक्षपरायणः ॥२४॥
यतीनां व्रतवृद्धानां स्वधर्ममनुवर्तिनाम् ।
विष्णुरूपेण वै कुर्यान्नमस्कारं दिने दिने ॥२५॥
यो भवेत्पूर्वसंन्यासी तुल्यो वा धर्मतो यतिः ।
नमस्कारार्चनादीनि कुर्यान्नान्यस्य कस्यचित् ॥२६॥
स्वधर्मस्थान्यतीन्वृद्धान्देवांश्च प्रणमेद्यतिः ।
नान्यमाश्रमिणं कंचित्प्रशस्तमपि तं नमेत् ॥२७॥
सायंप्रातर्न तृप्येत न प्रसज्जेत भोजने ।
नेन्द्रियार्थेषु सज्जेत कदाचिदपि कामतः ॥२८॥
पन्थानमपि पृच्छेच्च भिक्षां देहीति च द्वयम् ।
तावदेव व्याहरणं शेषमन्यन्निषिध्यते ॥२९॥

अत्रिः[1] ।

गूढधर्माश्रितो विद्वानज्ञानचरणे स्थितः ।
अमूढो मूढरूपेण चरेद्धर्ममदूषयन् ॥३०॥

21. om Y* A6; a)—त्वेक° A1 R1
22. om Y* A6; c)—मुण्डः X2*
23. om Y* A6; a)—°देशे R4; °देश A5; °देशः G6; c)—उपचार° R2; °कथां A5
24. om Y* A6
25. om Y* A6; at beginning add वसिष्ठः X2* B M; b)—स्वस्वधर्मानु° G6 R2 3;
26. om Y* A6;
27. om Y* A6; a)—धर्मस्थान्यतिवृद्धांश्च B M; d)—मा नमेत् R4
28. om Y* A6; d)—नामतः A5
29. b)—स्वयम् A1 2 R1 B M; d)—add इति Y* A6
30. b)—°ज्ञानकरणे A1 2 G6 R1 2 3 B M; d)—add इति Y* A6

कपिलः[1] ।

वृद्धातुरवद्यथाकथंचित्स्थितिं संपादयेत्[2] ॥३१॥

बृहस्पतिः[1] ।

नैवाददीत पाथेयं यतिर्वै यदनापदि ।
पक्वमापत्सु गृह्णीयाद्यावदह्नोपयुज्यते ॥३२॥

जमदग्निः[1] ।

अरण्ये निर्जने देशे चोरव्याघ्राकुले पथि ।
कृत्वा मूत्रपुरीषं च द्रव्यहस्तो न दुष्यति ॥३३॥
भूमौ निधाय तद् द्रव्यं शौचं कृत्वा यथाविधि ।
उत्सङ्गे गृह्य तद् द्रव्यमाचान्तः प्रयतः शुचिः ॥३४॥

गालवः[1] ।

योजनाधिकगमने द्वादश प्राणायामान्धारयेत्[2] ॥३५॥

अथ चातुर्मास्यकाल उच्यते[1] । आषाढ्यां पौर्णमास्यामारभ्य कार्त्तिक्यामुत्थानम्[2] । अथवा श्रावण्यामारभ्य मार्गशीर्ष्याम्[3] । अन्ये त्वेवमाहुः[4] । वर्षासु ध्रुवशील इत्यनेन ऋतुविधानात् मासद्वयेन व्रतसमाप्तिरिति[5] ॥३६॥ **जाबालिः**[1] ।

ग्रैष्महैमन्तिकान्मासानष्टौ भिक्षुर्विपर्यटेत् ।

31. om Y* A6; 2)—°तुरवत्पथि युक्ताः कथंचित्स्थितिं G6 R3 4

32. 1)—om A6; after बृहस्पतिः R4 adds अत्रिः; a–b)—om A6; b)—यतिः किंचिदनापदि Y* X2*; d)—add इति Y* A6

33. a)—निर्जले A1 2 6 R1 B M; b)—°कुलेऽपि च Y* A6; c)—मूत्रं पुरीषं च A1 G6 B M; °पुरीषे R2 3 4

34. c)—उत्सर्गे Y* A6 G6; उत्सहे R2 3; उत्सर्पेत् M+; ग्राह्य A6; d)—स्वाचान्तः A4 G2; प्राचान्तः X2*; add इति Y*

35. 1)—om Y* X2* A6; 2)—°धिगमने X2* A6 G1 2; °धिगमे A4 G3; प्राणायामान्द्वादश धारयेदिति Y* A6

36. 2–5)—om Y* A6; 2)—आषाढपौर्णमासमार° X2*; 3)—अथ श्राव° B M; 4)—अत्रैवमाहुः A5; त्वाहुः X2*; 5)—वर्षासु om B M

दयार्थं सर्वभूतानां वर्षास्वेकत्र संवसेत् ॥३७॥
चातुर्मास्यान्वसेद् ग्रामे श्रद्धाभक्तिसमन्वितः ।
स्थितिभङ्गमकुर्वन्हि शाश्वतं पदमाप्नुयात् ॥३८॥
यावद्वर्षत्यकालेऽपि यावत्क्लिन्ना च मेदिनी ।
ग्रामे सीमाधिकं नेयाद्विस्तीर्णे क्रोशतः परम् ॥३९॥

मेधातिथिः[1] ।

प्रशस्तां मृत्तिकां शुष्कां गृह्णीयाच्छुचिशुक्रयोः ।
द्वादश्यां मृदमादाय शुभां किंचिदपीडयन् ॥४०॥
यावद्वर्षत्यकालेऽपि यावत्क्लिन्ना च मेदिनी ।
तावन्न विचरेद्भिक्षुः स्वधर्ममनुपालयन् ।
आषाढादि वसेन्मासांश्चतुरः कार्त्तिकोदयात् ॥४१॥

अत्रिः[1] ।

चातुर्मास्यविधिं वक्ष्ये यतीनां नियतात्मनाम् ।
यमाश्रित्य सदा मुक्तो भविष्यति न संशयः ॥४२॥
शुक्लमासादिकः कालो यावदाषाढपूर्णिमा ।
तत्र पुण्येऽह्नि कस्मिंश्चित्सङ्कल्पदिवसेऽपि वा ॥४३॥
शर्कराश्मलतावल्लीलोष्टादिरहितां शुभाम् ।
शुष्कां साधारणीं भूमिं गत्वा ससिकतां यतिः ॥४४॥
स्मरन्वराहरूपेण धारयन्तं महीं हरिम् ।

37. om Y* A6

38. om Y* A6

39. om Y* A6; c)—ग्रामसी° X2* B M; °मादिकं A2 B M; °मान्तिकं R2 3

40. 1)—om G6; आह मेधा° A4 6 G1 2; d)—शुभं G1 R2 B M; कर्मानुपालयन् X2* B M [°लयेत् R2]; °पीडयेत् A2 6

41. a–d)—om X2* G3; f)—चत्वारः A6; कार्तिकादिति G1 2 3; कार्तिकाविति A6; कार्तिका इति A4

42. 1)—om X2*; आहात्रिः Y* A6 B M; a)—°विधीयन्ते X2*; c–d)—समान्मुक्तो X2*; मुक्ता भविष्यन्ति Y* A6

43. a)—शुक्र° Y* X2*; °सादिकालो यं Y* X2* A6

44. a–b)—°वल्लीजन्त्वादि° Y* X2*; °लोष्टैर्विरहितां B M; शुचिम् Y* A6; शिवाम् R4

सर्वभूताधिवासेन वासुदेवेन पावनीम् ।।४५।।
अधिवासितासि देवि त्वं प्रणवेन स्वयंभुवा ।
पवित्रत्वाय यस्मात्त्वं देवदेवेन निर्मिता ।।४६।।
प्रणवेन तथा पृथ्वी देवि त्वमधिवासिता ।
अधिवास्य क्षमामेवं मन्त्रैः सप्रणवैस्ततः ।।४७।।

अश्वक्रान्त इत्यारभ्य पदे पदे, उद्धृतासि, भूमिर्धेनुः, मृत्तिके हन, त्वया हतेन, मृत्तिके देहि, गन्धद्वाराम्, ईश्वरीम् ।।४८।।

येनोद्धृतासि देवि त्वं क्रोधरूपेण दंष्ट्रिणा ।
त्वया सह स मां पातु केशवो धरणीधरः ।।४९।।
आधारः सर्वभूतानां त्वं देवि वसुधे स्मृता ।
पालनी पावनी धात्री सर्वभूताभयंकरी ।।५०।।
विष्णुक्रान्तासि देवि त्वं विश्वक्रान्तासि मेदिनी ।
पाहि मां सर्वभूतेभ्यो विष्णुना सह माधवी ।
इति विज्ञाप्य युक्तात्मा माधवीं लोकधारिणीम् ।।५१।।
मृत्तिके ब्रह्मदत्तासि काश्यपेनाभिमन्त्रिता ।
मृत्तिके जहि तत्सर्वं यन्मया दुष्कृतं कृतम् ।।५२।।
इदं विष्णुरिति द्वाभ्यां शुभां गृह्णीत मृत्तिकाम् ।
अथ दर्भकरस्तेषु चासीनः प्राङ्मुखो यतिः ।

45. d)—पावनी X2* G1 A6

46. a)—अधिष्ठितासि A6 R2 3; अधिव्याप्तासि R4; पृथ्वि त्वं Y* A6; b)—देवादीनां स्व° Y* A6; d)—देवि देवेन R3

47. a)—पृथ्वि A6 G6 R2 3 B; b)—मया त्वम° Y* A6; °वासिते A5

48. om Y* A6; उद्धृतासीति A1 2 R1 B M; धेनुरिति A1 2 R1 B M; हन मे पापम् A1 2 R1 B M [पापम् om A1 R1]; A1 2 R1 B M give full texts of the mantras; Y* A6 give full texts of अश्वक्रानते and उद्धृतासि

49. b)—विष्णुना X2* A1 2 R1 B M [R1 adds दंष्ट्रिणा]

50. b)—वसुधा A5; c)—यात्री A1 M

51. om A6; until end of 9.60 om G3 [page missing?]; b)—विष्णुक्रान्तेसि A4 G1 2

52. d)—मया यद्दुष्कृतं A4 6 G2; add इति X2*

वार्षिकं व्रतमेतत्तु चातुर्मासिकमाहरेत् ॥५३॥
माधवश्चतुरो मासान्सर्वभूतहिताय वै ।
स्वापं यास्यति शेषाङ्के लक्ष्म्या सह जगत्पतिः ॥५४॥
सुप्तश्चैवोत्थितो यावन्न भवेत्स सनातनः ।
अहं तावन्निवत्स्यामि सर्वभूतहिताय वै ॥५५॥
ध्रुवा द्यौरित्यृचं जप्त्वा ततो भूमिं च संस्पृशेत् ।
अनेनैव विधानेन आषाढे मासि भिक्षुकः ॥५६॥
द्वादश्यां शुक्लपक्षस्य पौर्णमास्यामथापि वा ।
उत्तराषाढयुक्तायां यदि खण्डा तु पूर्णिमा ॥५७॥
मृदं गृहीत्वेदं विष्णुरिति तामानयेन्मृदम् ।
अनेनैव तु मन्त्रेण तीर्थान्संपूजयेत्ततः ॥५८॥
नमस्कृत्य विधानेन वृद्धानुक्रमतो यतीन् ।
ज्यायसे यतये दद्याद्यवीयान्मृत्तिकां यतिः ॥५९॥
पिण्डमेकमथ द्वौ वा मन्त्रेणानेन पूजयेत् ।
गृहाण मृत्तिकां भिक्षो सर्वपापहरां शिवाम् ॥६०॥
युष्मानस्मानियं देवी विष्णुना सह रक्षतु ।

53. a)—विष्णुस्त्रीणि पदानि द्वा° A4 6 G2 [°पदा A4 G1]; °रिति च G6 R2 3; b)—शुभां om Y* X2* A6; स्वयं A5; after मृत्तिकाम् A1 2 R1 add text of mantra; c)—°करस्त्वेवं A5; °करो देशेस्वासीनः R4; d)—वासीनः G1; f)—°कमारभेत् X2*

54. om A5

55. om A5; a)—सुप्त एवोत्थितो B M

56. a)—A1 2 R1 give text of mantra; द्यौर्ऋचं R4; ऋचं om A1 2 R1; जपित्वा G6; c)—इत्यनेन A4; इत्यनेनैव G2; d)—त्वाषाढे A1 2 G6 R3 4 B M; आषाढे . . . [6.57] मन्त्रेण om A6

57. d)—यद्यखण्डा A4 G1 2 6 B M; लङ्घा R2 3; च A4 G2

58. a)—मृदं om G2, placed after विष्णुरिति in A4; b)—तु नयेन् A4 G1 2; d)—वृद्धान्संपू° A4 6 G1 2; तीर्थाणि A5; संपूरयेत् A1 2 R1 B M

59. b)—वृद्धाननुक्र° A1 2 R1 4

60. a)—°कमथो A1 2 R1 B M; द्वौ वा om A5; हृत्वा A1 2 R1 B M; d)—सर्वकल्याणधारिणीम् A4; शुभाम् A5; after this X2* A4 6 B M add युष्मत्पादप्रसादेन मम रक्षां करोत्वियम् । गृहाण मृत्तिकां भिक्षो [कुम्लैति मृत्तिकां भित्वा B M] सर्वकल्यानधारिणीम् [सर्वपापहरां सुभां A4 6]

मृदमित्थं गृहीत्वा तां तया स्नानादि साधयेत् ॥६१॥
आहृत्य मृत्तिकामेवं तत्कालहृतया मृदा ।
कुर्यान्मृच्छौचकर्माणि यावन्मासचतुष्टयम् ॥६२॥
श्वोभाविनीं प्रतिपदमारभ्य श्रावणीं यतिः ।
न प्रयायाच्चतुर्मासान्वपनं कारयेन्न च ॥६३॥
आरम्भोत्थानदिनयोर्वापयेद्वपनेऽपि तु ।
अधःकण्ठशिखाक्षिभ्रूरोमाणि न हि जातुचित् ॥६४॥
द्वादश्यां पौर्णमास्यां वानारम्भो विघ्नतो यदि ।
स्थानाभावाद्व्रजेत्तावद्यावत्स्यात्कृष्णपञ्चमी ॥६५॥
प्रायश्चित्तेन युज्येत तदूर्ध्वं हि व्रजन्यतिः ।
कृच्छ्रमेकं चरेद्भिक्षुर्यदि व्याजेन गच्छति ॥६६॥
विस्तीर्णे ग्रामसीमान्ते क्रोशादूर्ध्वं व्रजेद्यदि ।
त्रिंशत्प्राणायामान्कृत्वा जपेत्त्रिकशतत्रयम् ॥६७॥

इदं प्रायश्चित्तं तस्मिन्नेवाहनि पुनः प्रत्यागतस्य[1] । तत्रैव रात्रिमध्युषितस्य तु प्रायश्चित्तं **वृद्धजाबालि**राह[2] ।

ग्रामे सीमाधिकं नेयाद्विस्तीर्णे क्रोशतः परम् ।
यदि कश्चित्प्रमादेन क्रोशमात्राधिकं व्रजेत् ।
प्राजापत्येन शुध्येत षोडशासुयमैस्तथा ॥६८॥

61. a)—युष्मानियं G6; c)—गृहीत्वा तु Y* A6; गृहीत्वाथ A1 2 R1B M; d)—तथा A6 R3 4 M+; यथा A5; स्नानानि Y* A1 2 5 6 R1; स्नायात्ततः परम् A1 2 R1 B M

62. c)—कारयेत्सर्वकर्माणि Y*

64. b)—वपने वपनेऽपि तु A4 G2; c–d)—गुह्यकण्ठ° A6; अधःकर्ण° X2* G1; °शिखा-कुक्षि° B M; °शिखाभ्रू° G6; न तु A4; हि om B M

65. a–b)—वानारम्भो conj.; वा आरम्भो A5 M; °मास्यामारम्भो A1 2 R1; वा नार-भेद्विघ्नतो Y* A6; त्वारम्भो X2* [G6 om वा]

66. c–d)—om R4

67. a–b)—om R4; b)—व्रजेद्यतिः Y* A6 G6 R2 3; c)—प्राणायमान् A4 5

68. 1)—पुनः om A4 5; 2)—तत्रैव . . . प्रायश्चित्तं om Y* A6; तत्रैव om X2*; त्रिरात्रि° X2* B M [G6 त्रिरात्र°]; रात्रिमध्ये उषितस्य A1 2 R1 B M; आह om X2* A4 6 G1 3; आह वृ° G2; a)—ग्रामसी° B M; °धिकं नैव A1 2 B M; c)—किंचित् Y* A6; d)—भवेत् G1; f)—तथेति Y* A6

वायुः[1] ।

वर्षाभेदं तु यः कुर्याद् ब्राह्मणो योगदीक्षितः ।
तप्तकृच्छ्रेण शुद्धात्मा विरजा जायते पुनः ॥६९॥
शारीरं दृश्यते यत्र भयं कस्यांश्चिदापदि ।
दुर्भिक्षे राष्ट्रभङ्गे वा वर्षास्वपि तमुत्सृजेत् ॥७०॥
चोरैरुपद्रुतं देशं दुर्भिक्षव्याधिपीडितम् ।
चक्रेणान्येन वाक्रान्तं वर्षास्वप्याशु तं त्यजेत् ॥७१॥

अत्रिः[1] ।

वर्षर्तौ तु विना विघ्नं शरणं संत्यजेद्यदि ।
जपेत्त्रिकसहस्रं वै प्राणायामशतं तथा ॥७२॥
वर्षाकाले विना विघ्नं विशेत्स्थानान्तरं यदि ।
जपेत्त्रिकसहस्रं वै प्राणायामशतत्रयम् ॥७३॥
स्थितियोग्यान्बहून्ग्रामान्यदि वर्षासु लङ्घयेत् ।
प्रत्येकं तु चरेत्कृच्छ्रं ततः पापात्प्रमुच्यते ॥७४॥
समुद्रज्येष्ठादिभिर्मन्त्रैश्चतुर्भिः शिरसोदकम् ।
चतुर्दिशं जलैर्वापः सं नः शिशीहि मन्त्रतः ॥७५॥
क्षुराभिमन्त्रणं कुर्याद्व्याधितस्यातुरस्य च ।
आपञ्चम्याः प्रशस्ताः स्युर्यतेः क्षौरादिकाः क्रियाः ॥७६॥
द्वादश्यां कार्त्तिके मासि पौर्णमास्यामथापि वा ।

69. 1)—om A6; a)—पक्षभेदं G6 M+; b)—यो न दीक्षितः A5; c)—उक्तकृच्छ्रेण B M; नवकृच्छ्रेण G1

70. a)—शरीरं X2*; d)—समुत्सृजेत् Y* A6

71. b)—दुर्भिक्षं A5 G2 R2; c)—वाक्रान्ते Y* A6; d)—तत्त्यजेत् A5 R4 B M

72. 1)—om A5; b)—°जेद्यतिः Y* A6 R4; c)—तु Y* A6 B M; d)—°शतत्रयम् Y* A6 M+

73. om X2*; b)—यतिः A6; d)—°शतद्वयं G1 3

75. d)—सं नः शिशीहि most mss and B M have diverse readings [B inserts a question mark] through a failure to recognize the mantra; मन्त्रितः A1 2 5; मन्त्रितम् G1

76. a)—om A1 2 5 R1 4; °मन्त्रणैः A6; b)—°तस्याध्वगतस्य Y* A6

कृतवापो मृदं शिष्टामुर्विंति प्रक्षिपेज्जले ।।७७।।
श्वोभूतेऽथ त्रयोदश्यां प्रतिपद्यपि वा क्वचित् ।
उत्थायेष्टं व्रजेद्देशं तदा त्रीणि पदेत्यृचा ।।७८।।
महि त्रीणामृचस्तिस्रो ये ते पन्थान इत्यपि ।
जपित्वैता ऋचो गच्छेदारभ्य प्रागुदक्च वा ।।७९।।

गौतमः[1] ।

न द्वितीयामपर्तु रात्रिं ग्रामे वसेत्[2] ।।८०।। [GDh 3.21]

अपगते ऋतौ द्वितीयां रात्रिं ग्रामे न वसेत्[1] । एकस्मिन्ग्रामे दिनद्वयं न वसेदित्यर्थः[2] । ग्रामग्रहणादरण्ये न दोष इति **मस्करी**[3] ।।८१।। न द्वितीयामपर्तु रात्रिमिति यद्यपि ऋतुरविशेषितः तथापि वार्षिको ग्राह्यः[1] । ऊर्ध्वं वार्षिकाभ्यां नैकस्थानं विधीयत इति **शङ्खः**[2] । यौ च श्रावणभाद्रपदौ अशक्तस्य तौ[3] । चत्वारो मासाः **देवलः**[4] ।

न चिरमेकत्र वसेदन्यत्र वार्षिकात्[5] । श्रावणादयश्चत्वारो मासा वार्षिकाः[6] [see 6.11] ।

इति **विश्वरूपः**[7] ।।८२।।

77. d)—उर्विंति conj., all उर्वीति; A1 2 R1 B M add text of mantra TS1.1.2.2.

78. a)—°भूते तु R2; °भूते यत्त्रयो° G1; b)—°पद्यथवा Y* A6; c)—उत्थायेवं A5; उत्थाय यथेष्टं R4; d)—तथा Y* A6 R4; पदेति च R4

79. b)—यतः पन्थानमिति B M

80. 1)—om X2* A5 6; 2)—°यामपर्तौ X2* B M; add इति Y* A6

81. om Y* A6; 1)—om X2*; ऋतौ न A5; न conj. following B M, om A1 2 5 R1; 3)—इति om G6 R2; इत्यर्थः R3 4; मस्करी conj. following B M [these, however, mistakenly take this as the first word of the next sentence], all mss read मस्करिः

82. om Y* A6; this passage is garbled in the mss, and I am not sure whether I have been able to restore the original; 1)—°यामपर्तौ B M; °यामपररात्रिं A1 2 R1; रात्रिं ग्रामे वसेदित्यत्र ऋतुश्च यद्यपि [B M add न] विशेषतः [विशेषितः B M; विशे then crossed out letters A5] A1 2 5 R1 B M; तथापि om A1 2 R1; 2)—नैकग्रामवासीति X2*; 3)—तौ for यौ G6 R2 3; तौ om X2* A5; 4)—mss place चत्वारो मासाः at the end of preceding sentence, putting the daṇḍa after it; 5)—वार्षिकान् G6 B M

सत्यकामजाबालौ[1] ।

ग्रामे नगरे पुरे वा प्राप्ते वर्षाकाले स्थितिमेव करोति भिक्षुस्तस्मिन्नेव स्थाने ऊर्ध्वकालं क्षणमपि स्थितिं न कुर्यात्[2] । अज्ञानात्स्थितिं कृत्वा प्राजापत्यं समाचरेत्[3] ॥८३॥

पुनर**त्रिः**[1] ।

जपित्वैता ऋचो गच्छेदारभ्य प्रागुदक्च वा ।
ग्रामैकरात्रं विहरेद्दीर्घमासीत वा क्वचित् ।
अन्धवज्जडवच्चापि बधिरोन्मत्तमूकवत् ॥८४॥
नामगोत्रादिचरणं देशं वंशं श्रुतं कुलम् ।
वयो वृत्तं व्रतं शीलं ख्यापयन्नैव सिद्ध्यति ।
प्रख्यापनाद्यतेर्हानिः पुण्यस्य स्यान्न संशयः ॥८५॥
गूढधर्माश्रितो विद्वानज्ञातचरिते स्थितः ।
अमूढो मूढरूपेण चरेद्धर्ममदूषयन् ॥८६॥

इति यतिधर्मसमुच्चये गतिस्थितिनिरूपणं नाम नवमं पर्व ॥८७॥

83. 1)—सत्यकामः [जाबाल om] Y* A6; 2)—पुरे नगरे A4 6 G1; नगरे om G1; वापि A4 6 G1 2; भिक्षुकः Y* A6; स्थानादू° Y*; 3)—ऊर्ध्वं . . . [84] आरभ्य om A6; add इति Y*

84. 1)—पुनः om Y* X2*; a–b)—om X2*; गच्छेदित्यारभ्य A4; तु वा A5; c)—°रात्रिं A1 2 R1

85. a)—°गोत्रे च चरणं X2*; b)—पात्रं for वंशं G1; d)—ख्यापयेन्न च A1 2 R1 M; ख्यापयेन्नैव X2* A5 B; f)—पुण्यस्यास्य न A4 6 G1 2

86. a–b)—om Y* A6; c)—आरूढोरूढरूपेण G1 2

87. यादप्रकाशीये यति° Y* A6

दशमं पर्व

प्रायश्चित्तविधिः

अथ प्रायश्चित्तान्युच्यन्ते[1] । तत्र **वायुः**[2] ।

प्रायश्चित्तानि कार्याणि यान्यकामकृतानि च ।
कृतानि कामतश्चापि तत्र चेत्यपरे विदुः ॥१॥
पापं तु त्रिविधं ज्ञेयं वाङ्मनःकायसंभवम् ।
संततं स्यादहोरात्रं येनेदं दह्यते जनः ॥२॥
न कर्माणि न चाप्यायुस्तिष्ठतीति परा श्रुतिः ।
प्रायश्चित्तं क्षणेनाथ प्रयुञ्ज्यादायुषि स्थिते ॥३॥
अभ्यासाद्रमते पापे वर्धते दिनसंख्यया ।
अभ्यासे बुद्धिपूर्वे च प्रायश्चित्तेन शोधयेत् ।
शोधयेत्तावदात्मानं यावच्चित्तं प्रसीदति ॥४॥
यदि स्यात्पातकं किंचिद्योगी कुर्यात्प्रमादतः ।
योगमेव निषेवेत नान्यां कुर्वीत निष्कृतिम् ॥५॥
प्राणायामप्रत्याहारध्यानयोगसमन्वितः ।
नश्येत्प्रमादजो दोषो व्रतैर्नान्यैरनुष्ठितैः ॥६॥

1. 1)—उच्यन्ते om X2* A5; 2)—तत्र om X2*; आह for तत्र Y* A6; a–d)— om A5; b)—यतिना [om G2] यानि कानिचित् A4 G2; यानि काम° A6; [lacuna]धान्यकानि च G1

2. om A5; c)—सततं R3 4; स्याद्दिवारात्रं Y* X2* A6; d)—येन यन्नश्यते [यन्नह्यते A4 G2] Y* A6; दृश्यते A1 2 R1 B

3. a)—om A5; कर्माणि च न चाप्यायुस् X2*; वाप्यायुस् A6; d)—स्थिताविति Y* A6

4. add मेधातिथिः Y* A6; a)—पापो R4, यत्र Y* A6; b)—वर्तते A5; d)—प्रायश्चित्तैर्न Y* A6; e–f)—om Y* A6

5. a–b)—om Y* A6; a)—पापकं A1 2 R1; b)—यो हि A2; d)—नान्यत्कु° G1

6. om Y* A6; b)—°योग° om G6; °न्वितं A1 2 R1; d)—व्रतिना° A5; व्रतेना° G6 R3

अभ्यासे बुद्धिपूर्वे च व्रतानुष्ठानं प्रमादकृते योग इत्युक्तम्[1] । तदाह **हारीतः**[2] ।

योगाभ्यासरतस्येह नश्यन्ते पातकानि तु ॥७॥ [see 8.56]

अत्रिः[1] ।

चान्द्रायणं पराकं वा कृच्छ्रं सान्तपनादि वा ।
न शक्नोति यतिः कर्तुं स कुर्यात्प्राणसंयमम् ॥८॥
यत्पापं नश्यते पुंसामेकाह्नोऽभोजनेन तु ।
जपात्त्रिकसहस्रस्य तत्पापं नश्यति ध्रुवम् ॥९॥
जपात्त्रिकसहस्रस्य यत्पापं नाशयेद् द्विजः ।
प्राणायामशतेनैव तत्पापं नश्यतेऽखिलम् ॥१०॥
प्राणायामसहस्रेण यत्पापं नश्यते द्विजैः ।
क्षणमात्रेण तत्सम्यग्घरेर्ध्यानात्प्रणश्यति ॥११॥
प्राणायामाज्जपाद्ध्यानान्नान्यद्भिक्षोर्विशोधनम् ।
तस्मात्तान्येव कुर्वीत यतिः शुद्ध्यर्थमात्मनः ॥१२॥
प्राणायामशतं भिक्षुर्यः करोति दिने दिने ।
पितृमातृगुरुघ्नोऽपि त्रिभिरेभिर्विमुच्यते ॥१३॥

जमदग्निः[1] ।

प्राणायामैश्च ध्यानैश्च जपैश्च सततं कृतैः ।
दह्यन्ते सर्वपापानि पावकेनेन्धनं यथा ॥१४॥

7. 1–2)—om Y* A6; 1)—अभ्यास X2*; तु X2*; इत्यत्रोक्तम् A1 2 R1; उक्तम् om R2 3 4; 2)—तदाह om X2*; तथाह A1 2 R1; a)—°भ्यासात्तु तस्येह Y*; °भ्यासरतेनैव A6

8. b)—च G6 R2 3; c)—कुर्यात् X2*; d)—न for स X2*

9. b)—°काह्नाभो° X2* G2 3 B M; d)—नश्यते X2*; द्विज G6 R2 3

10. om Y* R 2 3 A6; a–b)—जपात् . . . नश्यते om R4

11. a–b)—om R2 3; b)—द्विजाः G6 R2 3 B M; द्विज R4; c)—तत्सर्वं A6; d)—गुरोर्ध्यानात् G1

12. a)—°यामाद्धरेर्ध्या° A4; °यामजपध्या° A1 2 G1 R4; c)—तस्मान्नान्येन Y* A6

13. c)—गुरुमातृपितृघ्नो R4; d)—त्रिभिर्वर्षैर्वि° Y* A6; त्रिभिरेतैर्वि° R4; त्रिभिरेभिः स मुच्यते A1 2 R1 B M

14. om Y* X2* A6

व्यासः[1] ।

उपपातकेषु सर्वेषु पातकेषु महत्सु च ।
रजन्याः पादमेकं तु ब्रह्मध्यानेन शुध्यति ॥१५॥

गालवः[1] ।

ईश्वरदर्शनं सर्वप्रायश्चित्तमिति[2] ॥१६॥

वायुः[1] ।

भवेद्योगोऽप्रमत्तस्य योगो हि परमो मतः ।
न हि योगात्परं किंचिन्नराणां विद्यते हितम् ॥१७॥
पवित्राणां पवित्रं तत्पावनानां च पावनम् ।
तस्माद्योगं प्रशंसन्ति तत्क्षमस्य मनीषिणः ॥१८॥

जमदग्निः[1] ।

अथ वा यद् गुरुर्ब्रूयात्तत्कार्यमविशङ्कया ।
निग्रहेऽनुग्रहे वापि गुरुः सर्वत्र कारणम् ॥१९॥

वायुः[1] ।

व्यतिक्रमेत्तु यः कश्चिद्वाङ्मनःकायकर्मभिः ।
सभ्याः सर्वे विनिश्चित्य यद् ब्रूयुस्तत्समाचरेत् ॥२०॥

अत्रिः[1] ।

उपपातकिनो भिक्षोस्तथा लघ्वशनं जपः ।
मौनं कालत्रयस्नानं विहितानि विशेषतः ॥२१॥
सहस्रासुयमान्कृत्वा प्रणवस्यायुतं जपेत् ।

15. om X2*; a)—उपपातकसर्वेषु B M (A2 cor.); c)—प्रबुध्य राजनीपादम् M+; d)—add इति G2 3

16. om X2*; 2)—°रसंदर्शनं Y* A6; पूर्वप्राय°

17. om Y* A6; a–b)—om X2*; d)—विद्यते क्वचित् X2*

18. om Y* A6; a)—च for तत् X2*; b)—तु A5; c–d)—om X2*; क्षमेषु B M

19. om Y* A6

20. 1)—om A6; a)—यत्किंचिद् Y* A6; d)—add इति Y* A6

21. om Y* A6; 1)—om X2*; b)—लघ्वाहारो जपस्तपः M+; c)—°त्रये G6 R3 4

ततस्त्रिकसहस्राणां विधिना पञ्चविंशतिः ।
अरण्ये व्रतमेतत्तु कृत्वा भिक्षुर्विशुध्यति ।।२२।।

अथ संध्यातिक्रमप्रायश्चित्तमुच्यते[1] । तत्र **देवलः**[2] ।

संध्यालोपोऽनातुरस्य यदि जातः प्रमादतः ।
जपात्त्रिकसहस्रस्य शुध्यते नात्र संशयः ।।२३।।

गर्गः[1] ।

भिक्षुः संध्यामतिक्रम्य प्रायश्चित्तेन युज्यते ।
जपेत्त्रिकसहस्रं तु प्राणायामशतं तथा ।।२४।।

गालवः[1] ।

अर्धोदित उपस्थानं कुर्यात्[2] । कालातिक्रमं कृत्वा प्राणायामान्द्वादशैव तु धारयेत्[3] ।।२५।।

अथ भिक्षाटनप्रायश्चित्तम्[1] । तत्र **देवलः**[2] ।

उपस्थानं कृत्वा चिरकालं न तिष्ठेत्[3] । चिरकालं स्थित्वा प्राणायामान्षोडशाचरेत्[4] । उपस्थानं कृत्वा देवतावृद्धादीनां नमस्कारं न कुर्यात्[5] । अज्ञानात्कृत्वा षोडश प्राणायामान्धारयेत्[6] । उपस्थानं कृत्वा भिक्षाग्रहं न व्यतिक्रमेत्[7] । व्यतिक्रमं कृत्वा

22. om Y* A6; a)—सहस्रसंयमान् G6 R4; कुर्यात् B M; c–d)—ततो दशसहस्राणि गायत्रीं विधिना जपेत् B M; तत्र त्रि° A1 2 R1; f)—add इति G6 R2 3

23. 1)—अथ om X2* A6; °क्रमे A4 R4; उच्यते om X2*; 2)—om A4 G6; तत्र om Y* X2* A6; a–d)—om A6; a)—°लोपे A1 2 R1; d)—add इति Y*

24. om A6; a)—संध्यातिक्रमं कृत्वा Y*; b)—°श्चित्तौ G1; शुध्यति G6 R2 3; d)—प्राणायामांस्तु शोडशेति Y*; then Y* adds जमदग्निः । यदि किंचित्प्रमादेन उपस्थानं तु विस्मरेत् । जपेत्त्रिकसहस्रं तु प्राणायामशतं तथेति ।।

25. om A6; 2–3)—B M give as verse अर्धोदित उपस्थानात्कालातिक्रमणेऽपि च । प्राणायामान्द्वादश च धारयेद्यतीनां वरः ।। 2)—अथोदित G1; °दितमुप° A1 2 R1; °स्थाने A5; 3)—°क्रमे प्राणा° X2*; द्वादशेति [तु धारयेत् om] Y*

प्राणायामांस्त्रिंशच्चरेत्[8] । उपस्थानं कृत्वा एकभिक्षां न समाचरेत्[9] । यदि समाचरेत्प्राजापत्यं समाचरेत्[10] ॥२६॥

भरद्वाजः[1] ।

संभाषणादीन्परिहरेत्[2] । अज्ञानात्कृत्वा प्राणायामत्रयं कुर्यात्[3] । सव्येनादाय पात्रं त्रिदण्डं दक्षिणे न क्वचिदपि परिवर्तयेत्[4] । अज्ञानात्परिवर्तनं कृत्वा त्रीन्प्राणायामांश्चरेत्[5] । सव्येनादाय पात्रं दक्षिणस्थत्रिदण्डे न संश्लेषयेत्[6] । संश्लेषणं यदा करोति तदा प्राणायामान्षडाचरेत्[7] । भिक्षार्थं चोपस्थानं कृत्वा प्रविश्य नोपविशेत्[8] । क्वचिदुपविशन्प्राणायामान्द्वादश धारयेत्[9] । यदि भिक्षुः प्रमादेन शूद्रोदक्याचोदितं गृह्णाति भैक्षं प्राणायामान्षोडश धारयेत्[10] । त्रिदण्डं बहिः स्थाप्य भिक्षां न याचयेत् न च गृह्णीयात्[11] । यदि गृह्णीयात्प्राणायामान्षोडश धारयेत्[12] । त्रिदण्डं कराद्विहाय भिक्षां न याचयेत् न गृह्णीयात्[13] । अज्ञानात्कृत्वा प्राणायामशतं चरेत्[14] ॥२७॥

26. 1–2)—om A6; 1)—अथ om X2*; °श्चित्तमुच्यते Y*; 2)—तत्र om Y* X2*; 3)—चिरकालं न तिष्ठेत् om G6; 4)—चिरकालस्थितौ G6 R3 4; यदि तिस्ठेत्प्राणा° B M; षोडशप्राणायामानाचरेत् X2*; षडाचरेत् A2 B M; षोडश धारयेत् A5; 5–8)—om Y*; 5–10)—om A6; 5)—°वृद्धादीन्न नमेत् A1 2 R1; °वृद्धादीन्नमेत् B M; °वृद्धादीन्नमस्कुर्यात् R4; न om R2 3; 6)—अज्ञानादकृत्वा B M; 7)—भिक्षां न A5; नातिक्रमेत् A1 2 B M; 8)—व्यतिक्रमे तु X2* B M; यदि कुर्यात् A1 2 R1 [adopted reading only in A5 and clearly uncertain]; 9)—कृत्वा om A2 R1; च न A5; 10)—यदि समाचरेत् om A5; आचरणे तु प्राजा° X2*; add इति Y*

27. 1–12)—om A6; 3)—°यामान्षोडशाचरेत् Y*; after कुर्यात् R4 adds passage in App. 1.9; 4–7)—om G1; 4)—पात्राणि A1 2 R1 B M; प्रात्रं तु Y*; त्रिदण्डं om A5; दक्षिणेन त्रिदण्डं X2*; दक्षिणे करे [then omits न . . . (6) त्रिदण्डे] Y*; क्वचित्परि° A5 R4; 5)—परिवर्तने च त्रीन् X2*; यदि परिवर्तनं कुर्यादज्ञानतः A1 2 R1 B M [adopted reading only in A5]; प्राणायामांस्त्रीन् A5; 6)—सव्यापसव्यस्थपात्रत्रिदण्डं [°पात्रदण्डं R4] न संश्ले° X2*; पात्रं add त्रिदण्डं A5; 7)—संश्लेषणं कृत्वा प्राणा° X2*; यदा [यदि B M] संश्लेषणं करोति A1 2 R1 B M; यदि Y*; यदा न A5; षोडशाचरेत् Y* R4; 8)—भिक्षार्थी गृहं प्रविश्य नोपविशेत् Y*; भिक्षार्थमुप° X2*; 9)—क्वचिद् om Y*; °पवेशने X2*; °पविशेत् A2 B M; °दशाचरेत् G1; समाचरेत् A4 G2; 10)—om A1 2 4 G2 R1 B M; द्वादश A5 G1; 11–12)—भिक्षाग्रहणे for भिक्षां . . . गृह्णीयात् Y*; 11)—याचेत् G6 R2 4 B M; न च गृह्णीयात् om X2* A1 2 B M;

देवलकाश्यपौ[1] ।

श्वखरोष्ट्राखुमार्जारभासवानरसूकरान् ।
नीलीकाष्ठाग्निचयने नरास्थि ग्रामकुक्कुटम् ॥२८॥
सृगालं च कृतघ्नं च शूद्रं मद्यपमेव च ।
त्यक्तोपवीतं नग्नं च पाषण्डानुगतं द्विजम् ॥२९॥
विश्रम्भघातिनं चैव देवब्राह्मणनिन्दकम् ।
अगारदाहिनं चैव धर्मविक्रयिणं तथा ॥३०॥
अमेध्यनिचयं षण्ढं स्पृष्ट्वा देवलकं यतिः ।
स्थाप्य पात्रं शुचौ देशे शुभं गच्छेज्जलाशयम् ॥३१॥
शौचं कृत्वा यथान्यायं क्षालयेच्च मृदम्भसा ।
यत्स्यादुपहतं चाङ्गं मृद्भिर्द्वादशभिर्यतिः ॥३२॥
अद्भिः संशोध्य तत्सर्वं तथा स्नानं समाचरेत् ।
आचम्य प्रयतो भुक्त्वा प्राणायामान्षडाचरेत् ॥३३॥
आपो हि ष्ठेति तिसृभिर्मार्जयित्वा पुनः पुनः ।
जलेऽघमर्षणं कृत्वा पुनः स्नानं समाचरेत् ॥३४॥
भिक्षाधारं समादद्यात्त्रिकेणाभ्युक्ष्य वारिणा ।

12–14)—प्राणा° . . . अज्ञानात्कृत्वा om G1; 12)—om R3; यदि गृह्णीयात् om A5; तु षोडश A4; 13–14)—त्रिदण्डेन विना भिक्षाग्रहणे प्राणायाम° Y* A6; 13)—त्रिद° . . . याचयेत् om R3; बहिः स्थाप्य G6 R2 4; न गृह्णीयात् om R2; नाश्नीयात् R4; न च A5; 14)—धारयेत् A5; चरेदिति A4 G1 3

28. 1)—देवलः काश्यपश्च Y* A6; c)—°चयनं Y* A6; °चयन X2* B M [the reading of this pāda is uncertain]; d)—ग्रामांश्च कुक्कुटान् A5

29. c)—°पवीतान् G2; नग्नं त्यक्तोपवीतं R4; d)—°षण्डानां गतं G6 R2 3

30. b–c)— om G1; c)—अङ्गार° A1 2 R1 G6

31. a)—after षण्ढं M+ adds अश्वविक्रयिणं तथा । नकुलं वायसं वेश्यामपविद्धां त्यजेत्तथा । मद्यभाण्डं चयावन्तचिताकाष्ठं चितान्तथा । पापिष्ठं धर्मभेत्तारं; b)—दृष्ट्वा R4

32. om Y* A6

33. a–b)—om Y* A6; b)—ततः X2* B M; स्नानं om G6; सर्वं R2 3; c–d)—om R2; c)—भूत्वा G1 R3

34. om G1 R2; b)—ततः पुनः Y*A6; c)—जलाघम° A1 2 R1; d)—प्राणायामान्समाचरेत् Y* A6

निमज्जयेत्पुनस्तोये शुद्ध्यर्थं सकरे तथा ।।३५।।
एवमेषां तु संस्पर्शे भिक्षा भिक्षोर्विशुद्ध्यति ।
यदि पात्रेऽन्यसंसर्गस्तदा शुध्यति नान्यथा ।।३६।।
यदि पात्रेऽन्यसंस्पृष्टिः श्वकाकादिभिरन्त्यजैः ।
यदा च चरते तत्र तदा चान्द्रायणं चरेत् ।।३७।।

जमदग्निः[1] ।

श्वकाकक्रोडवेश्याविट्खरोष्ट्रस्पर्शने यतिः ।
सभैक्षस्तु जले मग्नः शुध्येज्जप्त्वाघमर्षणम् ।।३८।।

वृद्धजाबालिः[1] ।

भिक्षामटन्यः संन्यासी शुनोऽमेध्यं च वा स्पृशेत् ।
भिक्षां गृहीत्वा स्नात्वा च प्राणायामान्षडाचरेत् ।।३९।।
भिक्षां पवित्रां कुर्वीत गायत्र्या प्रणवेन च ।
वारुणेन तु मन्त्रेण प्रोक्षितं तु ततः शुचिः ।।४०।।

गर्गः[1] ।

पतिते पात्रे भिक्षां गृहीत्वा प्राणायामांस्त्रिंशच्चरेत्[2] ।।४१।।

गालवः[1] ।

मत्स्यमांसं यद्गृहे पच्यते तद्गृहं वर्जयेत्[2] । तत्र गृहीत्वा प्राणायामान्द्वादश धारयेत्[3] ।।४२।।

35. a)—समादध्यात् A1 2 R1; c–d)—om Y* A6; तोयैः A5; सकरः X2* B M; तदा A1 2 R1 B M

36. b)—भिक्षोस्तु शुद्ध्यति Y* A6; c–d)—om Y* A6; c)—यतिपात्रे A5 [also A1 but cor.]; संसर्गे X2*; d)—तथा R2 3

37. a)—यतिः पात्रं क्वचित्स्पृष्टं Y* A6; पात्रान्य° X2*; c)—यथा तु A5; यद्वा A1; तत्र om R4; b)—तथा A5; d)—add इति Y* A6

38. om Y* A6; a)—श्वपाक° G6 R3 4

39. 1)—वृद्ध° om Y* A6; a)—भिक्षाटनस्य संन्यासी R2 3; c)—स्नात्वाथ R4; d)—add इति Y* A6

40. om Y* A6 G6

41. om Y* A6 G6 R2 3; 2)—त्रिंशत्प्राणायामांश्चरेत् R4

42. 1)—om A1 2 6 B M; 2)—दृश्यते A1 2; पश्यते R1; दृश्येते B M; 3)—तत्र [G1 add हि] भिक्षां Y* A6; °यामांश्च A6; add इति Y* A6

देवलः[1] ।

ग्रामाद्बहिस्तथा ग्रामे यदि भिक्षां समाचरेत् ।
उभयत्र च गृह्णानश्चरेत्सान्तपनव्रतम् ।।४३।।

जमदग्निः[1] ।

ग्रामे प्रविष्टे भिक्षार्थं यदि भिक्षा न लभ्यते ।
ग्रामे द्वितीये भिक्षित्वा तप्तकृच्छ्रं समाचरेत् ।।४४।।
पात्रे तु पतिते भैक्षे एकभिक्षां समाचरेत् ।
प्राणायामशतं कुर्याच्छुध्यर्थं यतिरात्मनः ।।४५।।
भिक्षां माधूकरीमश्नन्नैवेद्यमपि वर्जयेत् ।
प्राजापत्येन कृच्छ्रेण शुध्यते नात्र संशयः ।।४६।।
भिक्षां माधूकरीमश्नन्नैवेद्ये तु विसर्जिते ।
परतोऽन्नमभुञ्जानस्त्रिरात्रेणैव शुध्यति ।।४७।।

गालवः[1] ।

परान्नं भिक्षान्नं चैकस्मिन्नह्नि भुक्त्वा गायत्रीमयुतं जपेत्[2] ।।४८।।

देवलः[1] ।

पात्रे कृत्वा निवेद्यं तु यदि मन्त्रं न विन्यसेत् ।
जपात्त्रिकसहस्रस्य विरजा जायते यतिः ।।४९।।
उदक्याशवचण्डालचोरनग्नकपालिनः ।
पतितान्पिशुनान्स्पृष्ट्वा भिक्षां भिक्षुः परित्यजेत् ।।५०।।
पतितान्नं सकृद्भुक्त्वा प्रायश्चित्तं चरेद्यतिः ।

43. c)—उभयत्रापि A5; तु A4; d)—°पनं व्रजेदिति Y* A6

44. a)—प्रविष्टो B M; भिक्षार्थे Y* A5 6; c)—द्वितीये om G6; द्वये तु A5; द्वितीयादि A6

45. b)—समाचरन् R2 3; °चरेदिति A6

46. om G1; b)—°वेद्यं च X2*; विवर्ज° R3

47. b)—निवेद्य A6 G2; नैवेद्यं च विसर्जयेत् R4; विवर्जिते R3; विसर्जयन् A5; c)—°तोऽन्नं न भुञ्जानस् Y* A6; d)—°रात्रेण विशुध्यति X2*

48. om Y* A6; 1)—om A5; 2)—गायत्र्यायुतं R4; °युतं च A5

49. 1)—om Y* A6; b)—मन्त्रेण न त्यजेत् Y* A6; d)—add इति Y* A6

50. om Y* A6; c)—पैशुनान् G6 R2 3; d)—परित्यजेत् om R4

वज्रकृच्छ्रत्रयं कृत्वा शुध्यते नात्र संशयः ॥५१॥
यवप्रसृतिमात्रं तु गवां मूत्रेण संपचेत् ।
अमावास्यायामश्नीयाद्वज्रकृच्छ्रमिदं महत् ॥५२॥
प्राजापत्यं तु वा कृच्छ्रं चरेत्पतितभोजने ।
अज्ञानात्तु सकृद्भुक्त्वा प्राजापत्येन शुध्यति ॥५३॥
प्राणायामशतं कुर्यात्पादकृच्छ्रं समाचरेत् ।
त्रिरात्रं शङ्खपुष्पं वा पक्वाढ्यं पयसा पिबेत् ॥५४॥

हारीतः[1] ।

शङ्कास्थाने समुत्पन्ने भक्ष्यभोज्यस्य संकरे ।
आहारशुद्धिं वक्ष्यामि तन्मे निगदतः शृणु ॥५५॥
अक्षारलवणां कृत्वा पिबेद् ब्रह्मसुवर्चलाम् ।
त्रिरात्रं शङ्खपुष्पं वा पयसा सह पाययेत् ॥५६॥
पालाशबिल्वपत्राणि कुशान्पद्मानुदुम्बरान् ।
क्वाथयित्वा पिबेदापस्त्रिरात्रेण विशुध्यति ॥५७॥
कपिलापञ्चगव्येन विधियुक्तेन वा पुनः ।
पीत्वा शुद्धिमवाप्नोति अभक्ष्यान्नस्य भक्षणात् ॥५८॥

अत्रिः[1] ।

एकान्नं मधु मांसं चाप्यन्नं विष्ठादिदूषितम् ।
हन्तकारमनैवेद्यं प्रत्यक्षलवणानि च ॥५९॥

51. om Y* A6

52. om Y* A6; a)—यवं X2* B M; d)—°कृच्छ्रं त्विमं R3

53. om Y* A6

54. om Y* A6; d)—पक्वार्घ्यं X2*

55. om Y* A6

56. om Y* A6; a)—°लवणं A5 B M; चैव for कृत्वा B M; b)—°वर्चलम् B M; c–d)—om X2*

57. om Y* A6; d)—°रात्रेणैव शुध्यति A5

58. om Y* A6; a)—कपिलापन्न° B M; b)—°युक्तोऽथ A1 2 B M; c)—शुचिमवा° R3

59. om Y* A6; a–b)—च अन्नं A5; विष्ठाविदू° B M; c)—हरेरप्यनिवेद्यं X2* B M; °कारं निवेद्यं च A5; d)—°लवणं तथा G6 R2 3 B M; °लवणादि च R4

एषामेकं यतिर्भुक्त्वा प्राजापत्यं समाचरेत् ।
मधुमांसाशनैर्भुक्त्वा पराकं तु समाचरेत् ।
त्रिकस्य च जपेल्लक्षं जपश्चेद्वत्सरं जपः ।।६०।।
अपःप्राण्यङ्गभोक्ता यो मधुमांसस्य चापदि ।
जपेत्त्रिकसहस्रं वै प्राणायामशतं तथा ।।६१।।

वृद्धजाबालिः[1] ।

दयापूर्वमदत्तं च दत्त्वा च प्रतिगृह्य च ।
दत्त्वा सौम्यं महत्कृच्छ्रं प्राजापत्यमथापि च ।।६२।।
भिक्षुर्भुंक्ते य एकान्नं दाक्षिण्याल्लौल्यतोऽपि वा ।
प्राजापत्येन कृच्छ्रेण प्राणायामशतेन च ।।६३।।

देवलः[1] ।

व्रणात्क्रिमिसमुद्भूते भक्षणे मधुमांसयोः ।
उपवासत्रयं कृत्वा प्राणायामशतं चरेत् ।।६४।।

गालवः[1] ।

मांसं मधु वा भक्षयित्वा पराकं कुर्यात्[2] । ताम्बूलं भक्षयित्वाहोरात्रमुपवसेत्[3] । बुद्धिपूर्वे प्राजापत्यं चरेत्[4] ।।६५।।

जमदग्निः[1] ।

एकान्नं मधु मांसं च नवश्राद्धं च सौतिकम् ।
अभोज्यानि यतीनां तु प्रत्यक्षलवणं तथा ।
एकैकातिक्रमे तेषां प्राजापत्येन शुध्यति ।।६६।।

60. om Y* A6; d)—पराकेन विशुध्यति X2*; e)—जपो R3 4; f)—वत्सरं जपेत् B M

61. om Y* A6; a)—अथ प्राण्य° R2 3 B M

62. om Y* A6; a)—यदापूर्वं G6 R2; सदापूर्वं R3; c)—शुध्येत्सौ° X2*; d)—वा G6 R2 4

63. om Y* A6; a)—भुंक्तेऽथ B M

64. om Y* X2* A6; a)—प्राणात् A1 2 R1

65. Before this Y* A6 add अत्रिः and विना . . . दशाचरेत् [8.21c–d] and उद्धृतासु . . . श्रुतिरिति [8.22]; 1)—om A4 G2; 2)—om X2*; वा om Y* A6; 3)—ताम्बूलभक्षणेऽहोरा° Y* A6; 4)—कुर्यात् Y* A6

66. om Y* A6; 1)—om A5

क्रतुः[1] ।

श्वाखुमार्जारकाकानां केशकीटास्थिवाससाम् ।
दूषितान्नं यतिर्भुक्त्वा पञ्चगव्येन शुध्यति ॥६७॥

भरद्वाजः[1] ।

भोजनमध्ये यत्किंचित्सूक्ष्मकेशकीटमक्षिकाभिहतं चेत्यादि[2] ॥६८॥

देवलः[1] ।

क्रव्यादाशुद्धिसंपाते भुञ्जानस्य कथंचन ।
पूर्वं त्यक्त्वा भोजनं तु पश्चात्स्नानं समाचरेत् ।
जपेत्त्रिकसहस्रं तु प्राणायामशतं चरेत् ॥६९॥

जमदग्निः[1] ।

भुञ्जानस्य तु विप्रस्य कदाचित्प्रस्रवेद् गुदम् ।
उच्छिष्टताशुचित्वं च तस्य शौचं कथं भवेत् ॥७०॥
पूर्वं कृत्वाथ शौचं तु तत्र पश्चादुपस्पृशेत् ।
अहोरात्रोषितः स्नात्वा पञ्चगव्येन शुध्यति ॥७१॥
भैक्षशेषं तु यत्किंचिद्यदि भिक्षुः समुत्सृजेत् ।
ग्रासे ग्रासे तु कर्तव्याः प्राणायामास्त्रयस्त्रयः ॥७२॥
सकर्दमं तु वर्षासु प्रविश्य ग्रामसङ्कटम् ।
जङ्घयोर्मृत्तिकास्तिस्रः प्रदद्यात्सप्त पादयोः ॥७३॥

67. 1)—om A6; a)—°र्जारकाकैश्च X2* B M; °र्जारकानां च A5; °र्जारकादीनां G1; b)—कृमिकी° X2*; °वायसैः B M; c)—दूषितं तु यतिर् G6 R2 3; d)—add इति A6 G1 2

68. om Y* X2* A6; 2)—°क्षिकाभिहतं conj. following 6.206; °क्षिकाविह° A1 2 B M; °काभह° R1; °काविहतश्चे° A5; °हतमित्यादि A2 B M

69. 1)—om A4; a)—°व्यायादाशुचि° Y* X2* A6; c)—च Y* A6; e–f)—om Y* A6, instead they add सत्यकामजाबालौ। त्रिदण्डग्रहणं कृत्वा पुत्रमित्रादिभिः संभाषणं न कुर्यात् ।अज्ञानात्कृत्वोपवासमेकं कृत्वा प्राणायामशतं चरेदिति ।

70. 1)—om A6; a–b)—भुञ्जानस्य प्रस्रवेद् om A6; a)—न for तु A1 2 R1; d)—सत्यं for तस्य G1

71. a–b)—om A6; b)—ततः Y*; c)—विना for स्नात्वा A6

72. a)—च G6 R2 3; यः कश्चिद् Y* A6

देवलः[1] ।

केशश्मश्रुगतं तोयं पात्रे तु पतितं यदि ।
त्यजेद्भिक्षां तथा पात्रं त्यक्त्वा चोपवसेद्यतिः ॥७४॥
विरिक्तवान्तविण्मूत्रस्कन्दनैकान्नजग्धिषु ।
स्नात्वा भिक्षाटनादेत्य प्राणायामास्त्रयस्त्रयः ॥७५॥

जमदग्निः[1] ।

घ्रात्वा गन्धं सुरायाश्च तथा मूत्रपुरीषयोः ।
क्रव्यादपूतिगन्धं वा प्राणायामास्त्रयस्त्रयः ॥७६॥
छर्दिमूत्रपुरीषं वा दृष्ट्वा तु सहसा यतिः ।
प्राणायामेन शुध्येत कृत्वा तद्द्विगुणं चरेत् ॥७७॥

गालवः[1] ।

पूतिविण्मूत्रक्रव्यादसुरागन्धाघ्राणं कृत्वा प्राणायामांस्त्रींस्त्रीन् कुर्यात्[2] ॥७८॥

नियमांस्तु सदा कुर्याद्यमांस्तेभ्योऽभिपालयेत् ।
आपत्कालेऽप्यशक्तौ वा पानेऽपां भेषजादने ॥७९॥
हविषि ब्राह्मणेच्छायां पुष्पमूलफलादने ।
दध्नि दुग्धे गुरोर्वाक्ये त्वक्पत्रे दन्तधावने ।
नियमातिक्रमो नास्ति ब्राह्मणानामनुज्ञया ॥८०॥
तेषां पुण्याहघोषेण कार्यं पापापनोदनम् ।
अकामकृतपापेभ्यस्तत्कृत्वा विप्रमुच्यते ॥८१॥

74. om X2*; 1)—om B M; b)—तु om Y*; यतिः A5

75. om Y* A6; a)—विरक्तो X2*; विरक्त° M; विरक्तवान्न° A2 B; °मूत्रः X2; b)—स्कन्दने स्पन्दनेऽपि च X2*; c)—भुक्त्वाटना° A1 2 5 R1

76. om Y* A6 G6 R2 3; a)—सुरायास्तु A5; c)—°गन्धे च B M

77. om Y* A6; a)—तु X2*; d)—कृत्वा तु द्वि° X2*; चिरेण द्वि° B M

78. 2)—om X2*; °क्रव्यादादिसुराघ्राणं Y* A6; °यामांस्त्रीन्कुर्यात् Y* A6

79. a–b)—om X2*; तेभ्योऽपिपा° Y* A6; तेभ्योऽनुपा° B M; c)—°शक्तो X2*; d)—पाने भैषजवादने Y* A6 [भैषज्य° A6]

80. d)—अमन्त्रे Y*; अमन्ते A6; त्वक्पात्रे A1; त्वत्पात्रे A2 R1; त्वपत्रादन्त° X2* B M [अपत्रा° R4]

81. om Y* A6; d)—कृत्वापि मुच्यते X2* R1

बोधायनः[1] ।

अथ यत्रोपनिषदमाचार्या ब्रुवते तत्रोदाहरन्ति[2] । स्थानमौनासनं सवनोपस्पर्शनं चतुर्थषष्ठाष्टमकालव्रतयुक्तत्वं कणपिण्याकयावकदधिपयोव्रतत्वं च[3] । तत्र मौनयुक्तस्त्रैविद्यवृद्धैराचार्यैर्मुनिभिरन्यैर्वाश्रमिभिर्बहुश्रुतैर्दन्तैर्दन्तान्संधायान्तर्मुख एव यावदर्थं संभाषेत एवं न यत्र लोपो भवतीति विज्ञायते[4] । स्थानमौनवीरासनानामन्यतमेन संप्रयोगो न त्रयं सन्निपातयेत्[5] । यत्र गतश्चेद्यावन्मात्रमनुव्रजेदापत्सु न यत्र लोपो भवतीति विज्ञायते[6] । स्थानमौनवीरासनोपस्पर्शनचतुर्थषष्ठाष्टमकालव्रतयुक्तस्य[7] ॥८२॥

अष्टौ तान्यव्रतघ्नानि आपो मूलं घृतं पयः ।
हविर्ब्राह्मणकामाय गुरोर्वचनमौषधम् ॥८३॥ [BDh 2.18.15–19]

देवलः[1] ।

यदि कश्चित्प्रमादेन स्वापाचारं तु विस्मरेत् ।
जपेत्त्रिकसहस्रं तु शुध्यते नात्र संशयः ॥८४॥

अथ रात्रिजानामपराधानां निष्कृतिरुच्यते[1] । तत्र **वृद्धजाबालिः**[2] ।

संध्याकाले तु संप्राप्ते निशि भुञ्जीत यो यतिः ।
उपस्थानं च जप्यं च प्राणायामो बलिस्तथा ॥८५॥

82. om Y* A6; 2)—यज्ञीयोपनि° B M; तत्रोदाहरन्ति om X2*; 3)—°स्पर्शनं च A5; °चतुर्थषष्ठाष्टम° conj., °चतुष्षष्ठकाल° A1 2 5 R1; °चतुष्षष्ठाष्टकाल° X2* B M; °व्रतकालयुक्त° A1 2 R1; °पयोघृतत्वं X2* B M; 4)—मुनिभिरन्यैर्वा om A1 2 R1 B M; यन्त्रलोपो A1 2 R1 2 4; यज्ञलोपो G6 R3 B M; 5)—सन्निपातयेत् conj; त्रयं सन्निपातयेत् om A1 2 R1 B M; सन्निपातो A5; सन्निपतेत् X2*; 6)—यत्रगतश्चेद् conj; यन्त्रगतश्चेद् A5; यज्ञगतश्चेद् R2 3; यन्त्रितश्चेद् G6 R4; यत्र लोपो conj; यन्त्रलोपो A5 G6 R4; यज्ञलोपो R2 3; 7)—यज्ञोपनिषद्व्रतनिष्ठस्य for स्थान° . . . °युक्तस्य X2*; स्थान . . . स्पर्शन° om A1 2 R1 B M; °चतुर्थषष्ठाष्टम° conj; °चतुष्षष्ठाष्ट° A1 2 5 R1 B M [conj. based on BDh ed.; passage corrupt in mss]

83. c)—°काम्या च B M; d)—add इति Y* A6

84. om Y* A6; a)—किंचित् X2* A5; b)—स्वापाचारं conj., साध्वाचारं R4, all others स्वापचारं; विस्मरन् M

85. 1)—अथाहोरात्रयोरपरा° Y* A6; उच्यते om X2*; 2)—तत्र om Y* X2* A6; d)—बलिं X2*; बलं A1 R1; जपं A2 B M

सर्वे ते निष्फलास्तस्य प्रायश्चित्तं विधीयते ।
एकरात्रोपवासश्च प्राणायामाश्च षोडश ॥८६॥

जमदग्निः[1] ।

आहारग्रहणे रात्रौ प्राणायामा दश स्मृताः ।
जलमृद्ग्रहणे चापि निशायां तद्वदाचरेत् ॥८७॥
गृहीतनाशे धर्मेण स्रवन्तीषु सरित्सु च ।
सकृद् गृह्णन्न लिप्येत देवतायतनेषु च ॥८८॥
रात्रौ तु क्षरणे स्नात्वा द्वादशासुयमांश्चरेत् ।
प्राणायामैर्विशुद्धात्मा विरजा जायते यतिः ॥८९॥

शौनकः[1] ।

पूर्वसंभोगान्न स्मरेत्[2] । प्रमादात्स्मरणे आचम्य प्राणायामत्रयं कृत्वा पुनराचामेत्[3] । प्रमादात्स्त्रीदर्शने प्राणायामानाचरेत्[4] । स्वप्नसंभोगे त्रिकसहस्रं जप्त्वा प्राणायामान्द्वादश धारयेत्[5] । संभोगे स्वप्नक्षरणे द्वादश तु धारयेत्[6] । मेहमानो द्वयं कृत्वा पुनराचामेत्[7] ॥९०॥

कपिलः[1] ।

स्वप्नसंभोगे स्नात्वा त्रिकसहस्रं जपेत्[2] । कण्डूयनरुधिरक्षरणे उपवासः[3] ॥९१॥

86. c)—°रात्रोषितस्तस्य A6; d)—°यामांश्च A2 G1 2 R1; °यामांस्तु A6; add इति Y* A6

87. a)—°ग्रहण A1 2 R1; b)—शतं Y* A6; चरेत् A6; c)—वापि X2* A4 B

88. d)—add इति Y* A6

89. om Y* A6; a)—तु A5; संरक्षणे [om च] A1 2 R1; c–d)—om X2*; प्राणा° . . . [90] स्मरणे om A5

90. 1)—om G6; 2–3)—पूर्वसंभोगस्मरणे अप आचम्य Y* A6; 3)—अप आचम्य R2 3; °चामेदिति Y* A6; 4–7)—om Y* A6; 4)—°याममाचरेत् A1 R1 2; °यामोचरेत् A2; °यामांश्चरेत् B M; 5)—जपित्वा R2 4; 6–7)—om X2*; 6)—°करणे A1 2 R1 B M; द्वादश om A5, add तु A1 2 R1; 7)—मेह° conj. following B M, मोह° A1 2 5 R1

91. 2)—स्वप्ने Y* A6; °स्त्रीसंभोगे Y* A5 B M; after जपेत् Y* A6 add असंभोगस्वप्नक्षरणे [°स्मरणे A6] द्वादशैव [A6 G1 adds तु] धारयेदिति; 3)—om Y* A6

गालवः[1] ।

कामाद्रेतउत्सर्गे त्रीन्पराकान्धारयेत्[2] । अकामतः स्वप्ने स्त्रीसंभोगे द्वादश प्राणायामान्धारयेत्[3] । निद्रायां प्रमादात्क्षरणे द्वादश प्राणायामान्धारयेत्[4] । प्राणायामांस्त्रींस्त्रीन्गुह्यप्रमाददर्शने धारयेत्[5] । स्वप्ने एतद्दर्शने अघमर्षणम्[6] । सदा चाप्रयत्नोत्सर्गं कृत्वा रेतस षोडश प्राणायामान्धारयेत्[7] । प्रयत्नेन रेतःसेकं कृत्वा चान्द्रायणं चरेत्[8] ॥९२॥

जाबालिः[1] ।

शुक्लोत्सर्गं यदा कुर्यात्कामादभ्यासतोऽपि वा ।
पराकत्रयसंयुक्तं प्राणायामशतं चरेत् ॥९३॥
दिवा तु स्कन्दयेद्रेतः प्रायश्चित्ती प्रमादतः ।
स त्रिरात्रोपवासेन प्राणायामशतं चरेत् ॥९४॥
स्कन्न इन्द्रियदौर्बल्यात्स्त्रियं दृष्ट्वा प्रमादतः ।
तेन धारयितव्याः स्युः प्राणायमास्तु षोडश ॥९५॥

वायुः[1] ।

शुक्लोत्सर्गं यदा कुर्यात्क्वचिद्भिक्षुस्तु कामतः ।
प्राजापत्यत्रयं कुर्यात्प्राणायामशतानि च ॥९६॥

92. 2–3)—om Y* A6; 2)—रेतस उत्सर्गे X2* B M; रेतोत्सर्गे A5; स धार° B M; °कानाचरेत् R2 3 4; 3)—स्वप्ने स्त्रीसंभोगे om X2*; प्राणायामाः द्वादश [धारयेत् om] X2*; 4–7)—om A1 2 R1 B M; 4)—निद्राक्षरणे X2*; अघमर्षणत्रयं कुर्यात् A5; धारयेदिति Y* A6; 5)—om A5; प्रमादात्स्त्रीगुह्यदर्शने त्रीन्प्राणायामानाचरेत् Y* A6; 6)—om Y* A5 6; 7)—om Y* A6; सदा चाप्र° only in R4, others unclear and corrupt; सदाचारप्रयत्नो° A5; रेतस om A5; 8)—यत्नतः B M; प्रयत्न X2* A2; रेतसेके X2*; कृत्वा om X2*; चरेदिति A4 G1; कुर्यादिति A6 G2; this whole passage is corrupt, and my reconstruction is tentative.

93. Y* A6 insert at 7.145; 1)—वृद्धजा° A4 6 G2; b)—प्रमादाभ्या° B M

94. om A2 G1 B M; c)—स om X2* A1 6 R1 B M; °रात्रमुप° X2* B M; °वासेनैव A6; d)—add इति Y* A6

95. om Y* A6; a)—स्कन्न इन्द्रि° conj., all mss read स्कन्नेन्द्रि°; °न्नेन्द्रियस्तु दौर्ब° B M; c)—सारयि° A1 2 R1; साधयि° B M

96. 1)—om A5; b)—भिक्षुस्स Y* A6; d)—°यामायुतानि X2* M+; Y* [not A6] adds दिवा स्कन्दे तु भिक्षूणां प्रायश्चित्तं विधीयते । त्रिरात्रमुपवासश्च प्राणायामशतानि चेति ।

वृद्धपराशरः[1] ।

वासुदेव प्रसुप्तोऽसि यावन्नोदयते रविः ।
अहं तावन्निवत्स्यामि सर्वभूतहिताय वै ॥९७॥
सप्तऋषयः प्रतिहिताः शरीरे
सप्त रक्षन्ति सदमप्रमादम् ।
सप्तापः स्वपतो लोकमीयुस्तत्र
जागृतो अस्वप्नजौ सत्रदौ च देवौ ॥९८॥ [VS 34.55]

आभ्यां मन्त्राभ्यां शयीत[1] । यदि न कुर्यात्प्राणायामषट्कं कृत्वा पुनरपि मन्त्राभ्यां शयीत[2] । उत्तिष्ठेत्युत्थानं प्रातःकाले कुर्यात्[3] । यदि न कुर्यात्प्राणायामत्रयं कृत्वा पुनरुत्तिष्ठेदिति[4] ॥९९॥

अथ नियमातिक्रमे प्रायश्चित्तानि[1] । तत्र **वायुः**[2] ।

व्रतानि यानि भिक्षूणां तथैवोपव्रतानि च ।
एकैकातिक्रमे तेषां प्रायश्चित्तं विधीयते ॥१००॥
उपेत्य तु स्त्रियं कामात्प्रायश्चित्ती भवेद्यतिः ।
प्राणायामसमायुक्तं कृच्छ्रमब्दं समाचरेत् ॥१०१॥
ततश्चरितनिर्वेदः कृच्छ्रध्याने समाहितः ।
भूयो निर्वेदमापन्नश्चरेद्भिक्षामतन्द्रितः ॥१०२॥

97. a)—प्रसुप्तोऽसि conj. following A5 R4; प्रसुप्तोऽस्मि Y* A1 2 6 G6 R1 2 3 B M [M ed. comments अस्य श्लोकस्यात्र सङ्गतिरन्वेषणीया]

98. a)—आहुः सप्तऋषयः । A1 2 5 R1 B M [M ed. comments इदमशुद्धमिव]; प्रहिताः X2* A1 2 5 R1 B M; b)—रक्षन्ति om G6 R2 3; c)—स्वप्नापः M A1 2; d)—जाग्रते A1 2 5 R1 2 3 4. The readings of this mantra in all the mss are corrupt; I have reconstructed it with the help of the VS reading.

99. 1)—रात्रौ शयीत Y* A6; 2)—om A5; न om A1 2 R1; °यामान्षट् कृत्वा Y* A6; कुर्यात् X2*; 3)—उत्तिष्ठ ब्रह्मणस्पत इत्यु° Y* A6; 4)—यदि न कुर्यात् om A1 2 R1; न कुर्याद्यदि X2* M; °यामान्षट् कृत्वा A4; पुनर्मन्त्रेणोत्तिष्ठेत् Y* A6; °ष्ठेद्यतिः A1 2 R1 B M

100. 1)—यमाद्यति° G6 R2 3 B M; नियमाद्यति° R4; °क्रमप्रायश्चित्तम् X2*; यमनियमप्रायश्चित्तमुच्यते Y* A6; 2)—om Y* A6; तत्र om X2*; a–d)—om Y* A6

101. om Y* A6; a)—स्त्रियः G6 R4

102. om Y* A6; a–b)—निर्वेदकृच्छ्रो B M; कृच्छ्रश्रान्ते A5; कृच्छ्रस्यान्ते X2*; d)—भिक्षुरतन्द्रितः A5

कपिलः[1] ।

सकृत्संभोगे द्वादशरात्रमुपवासः त्रिकलक्षं जपश्च[2] । अभ्यासे त्रिरात्रं संवत्सरं जपेत्[3] । सकृदन्त्यजां गत्वारण्ये बिल्वादीनि स्वयंपतितानि प्रक्षाल्योपयुञ्जीत ब्रह्मावर्तयन्यावत्स मृत्युतः शुद्धो भवति[4] ।।१०३।।

जाबालिः[1] ।

उपेत्य तु स्त्रियं कामात्प्रायश्चित्ती भवेद्यतिः ।
प्राणायामसमायुक्तमब्दं सान्तपनं चरेत् ।।१०४।।

गालवः[1] ।

सकृत्साधारणीं गत्वा ब्रह्महत्याप्रायश्चित्तं चरेत्[2] ।।१०५।।

अत्रिः[1] ।

महापातकजाद्दोषाच्छुद्ध्यर्थं वर्तयेद्यतिः ।
त्रिकलक्षं जपेद्योगी प्राणायामायुतं तथा ।
ततः शतसहस्राणि प्रणवानां जपेद्यतिः ।।१०६।।
स्त्रीसंभोगे सकृन्मोहाद्विधिनानेन शुध्यति ।
कामतो वा तथाभ्यासे प्रायश्चित्तेन शुध्यति ।।१०७।।

वायुः[1] ।

यदेतद् द्रविणं नाम प्राणा ह्येते बहिश्चराः ।
स तस्य हरति प्राणान्योऽस्य संहरते धनम् ।।१०८।।
एवं कृत्वा स दुष्टात्मा भिन्नवृत्ताश्रमो यतिः ।
ततो निर्वेदमापन्नश्चरेच्चान्द्रायणव्रतम् ।

103. om Y* A6; 2)—जपः B M; जपेत् X2*; 3)—वत्सरं A2 B M; °त्सरं add त्रिकं X2*; 4)—°वर्तयेत्यावत्स A5; °वर्तयन्नावत्स A1 2 R1; °वर्तयन्तावत्स B M; यावत्संवत्सरं मृत्युतः X2*

104. 1)—वृद्धजा° Y* A6; a)—स उपेत्य स्त्रियं Y* A6; स्त्रियः R4; b)—प्रायश्चित्तीयते यतिः Y* A1 5 R1; d)—add इति Y* A6

105. 2)—°रणीं स्त्रियं Y* A6; add इति A6

106. om Y* A6; d)—प्राणानामायमं A1 2 R1 B M; e)—तत्र A1 2 R1

107. om Y* X2* A6; a)—°संभोगे om A1 2 R1; स्त्रीसकृद्गमने मोहाद्वि°` B M

108. om Y* A6; 1)—om X2*; c)—स om G6 R2 3; d)—यो यस्य हरते X2*

विधिना शास्त्रदृष्टेन संवत्सरमिति श्रुतिः ॥१०९॥
ततः संवत्सरस्यान्ते भूयः प्रक्षीणकल्मषः ।
भूयो निर्वेदमापन्नो भिक्षां भिक्षुः समाचरेत् ॥११०॥

गालवः[1] ।

धनगोभूमितिलादीनां बुद्धिपूर्वं परिगृह्य पतितवत्प्रायश्चित्तं कुर्यात्[2] ॥१११॥

जमदग्निः[1] ।

लब्धद्रव्यं परित्यज्य उपवासत्रयं चरेत् ।
गायत्रीमयुतं जप्त्वा मुच्यते सर्वपातकैः ॥११२॥

स एवाह[1] ।

भूमिर्गावो हिरण्यं वा यतेर्यस्य परिग्रहः ।
तादृशं कश्मलं दृष्ट्वा सवासा जलमाविशेत् ॥११३॥

वायुः[1] ।

प्राणायामशतं कुर्यादुपवासे वदन्मृषा ।
असद्वादो न कर्तव्यो यतिना धर्मलिप्सुना ॥११४॥

गालवः[1] ।

अनृतमुक्त्वा त्रिरात्रमुपवसेत्[2] । धर्मयुक्तमनृतमनूच्याहोरात्रमुपोष्य प्राणायामशतं कुर्यात्[3] ॥११५॥

जमदग्निः[1] ।

वाङ्मनःकायहिंसायां चरेषु स्थावरेषु च ।

109. om Y* A6; a)—तुष्टात्मा A1 2 5 R1; b)—°श्रयो B M

110. om Y* A6

111. om Y* A6; 1)—om A5; 2)—Y* A6 insert at 10.115; धनधान्यगो° Y* A6; °भूतिला° A1 2 R1 B M; °भूमिजीवादीनां X2*; °तिलान्बुद्धि° Y* A6; add इति Y* A6

112. Y* A6 insert at 10.115; 1)—om A5; b)—उपवासं समाचरेत् A1 2 R1 B M; d)—सर्वदोषैर्प्रमुच्यते A5

113. om Y* A6; a)—om R2 3 4; d)—सचेलो A5

114. om Y* A6; b)—°पवसेद्वदन् B M

115. 1)—om Y* A6; 2)—°वसेदिति A6; 3)—°नृतमुक्त्वाहो° Y* A6; here Y* A6 insert 10.111–12.

येन येनोपरुध्येत तेन तेन विशोधयेत् ॥११६॥
वाक्संप्रयोगे वाग्दण्डः प्राणदण्डस्तु मानसे ।
कर्मदण्डः शरीरस्य बुद्ध्या निर्वेदमादिशेत् ॥११७॥
वाग्दण्डो हन्ति वै ज्ञानं मनोदण्डः परां गतिम् ।
कर्मदण्डस्तु लोकांस्त्रीन्हन्यादपरिरक्षितः ॥११८॥
वाग्दण्डं मौनमातिष्ठेत्कर्मदण्डस्त्वभोजनम् ।
मनसः स तु दण्डः स्यात्प्राणायामस्य धारणम् ॥११९॥
समुत्पन्नेषु दोषेषु स्यादनेन तु निष्कृतिः ।
अतीव चिरकाले तु द्विगुणं व्रतमाचरेत् ॥१२०॥

गालवः[1] ।

चतुष्पदान्मृगान्हत्वा व्रतं चान्द्रायणं चरेत् ।
कर्कटचित्ररोमादीन्दशरात्राण्युपवसेत् ॥१२१॥
कामादेव तु हिंसीत यदि भिक्षुः पशून्मृगान् ।
कृच्छ्रातिकृच्छ्रे कुर्वीत चान्द्रायणमथापि वा ॥१२२॥

जमदग्निः[1] ।

कृकलासे क्षीरगले मण्डूके गृहगोलिके ।
कुररादिषु भूतेषु दशाहं चार्धभोजनम् ॥१२३॥

116. om Y* A6; a)—°हिंसायाः G6 R3 4; °हिंसानां B M; d)—तेनापि रोधयेत् X2*

117. om Y* A6; a)—वाक्संयोगे तु A2 B M [A2 om तु]; वाग्दण्डं A1 2 R1; b)—मनोदण्डस्तु A1 2 R1 B M; d)—बुद्धिनिर्वे° G6 R3 4

118. om Y* A6

119. om Y* X2* A6; a)—वाग्दण्डो B M

120. om Y* A6; a)—दण्डेषु X2*; b)—उपवासस्तु A1 2 R1 B M; c)—अत्रिः for अतीव X2*

121. om Y* A6 [but see 10.126]; b)—यतिश्चान्द्रा° X2*; c–d)—the readings vary widely and do not follow the meter; my conjectural reconstruction assumes that it is set in verse; कर्कटकचित्र° all mss; °रोमादीन्हत्वा दशाहोरात्राण्युप° A1 2 R1 M+[A2 om हत्वा]; °रोमादीन्द्वादशाहोरात्राण्युप° A5; °रोमादीन्हत्वाहोरात्रानुप° G6 R2 3; °रोमादीनामहोरात्रानुप° R4; °रोमादीन्हत्वाहोरात्राण्युप° B M

122. om Y* A6; c)—°कृच्छ्रौ A1 2 R1

123. 1)—om Y* A6; a)—कृकलास A2 B M; b)—गोधिके X2* A2 B M; c)—कुररादिषु G6 R2 3; कुकुरादिषु A2; कुक्कुटादिषु B M; d)—दशाहं…[124] भूतेषु om A1 2 5 G6 R1

मार्जारे मूषके सर्पे स्थूलमत्स्येषु पक्षिषु ।
नकुलादिषु भूतेषु चरेच्चान्द्रायणं व्रतम् ।
पिपीलिकायां सूक्ष्मायां प्राणायामास्त्रयस्त्रयः ॥१२४॥
सूक्ष्मास्थिमद्वधे भिक्षोः प्रायश्चित्तं विधीयते ।
त्रिंशत्प्राणायामान्कृत्वा एकाहं त्वर्धभुग्भवेत् ॥१२५॥

गालवः[1] ।

पर्णमूलाङ्कुरपुष्पाणां छेदनं कृत्वा त्रिंशत्प्राणायामान्धारयेत्[2] ॥१२६॥

दत्तात्रेयः[1] ।

नग्नं वानुपनीतं वा विप्रं दृष्ट्वा प्रमादतः ।
मृद्भिर्द्वादशभिः स्नात्वा वासोभिः सह शुध्यति ॥१२७॥

हारीतः[1] ।

नग्नं वानुपनीतं वा यः श्राद्धे भोजयेद् द्विजम् ।
रेतोमूत्रपुरीषाणि स पितृभ्यः प्रयच्छति ॥१२८॥
प्रेरणादथ वा लोभादेकदण्डं समाश्रितः ।
भूयो निर्वेदमापन्नस्त्रिदण्डं धारयेद् बुधः ॥१२९॥
प्राजापत्यं चरेत्कृच्छ्रं नियतो माससंख्यया ।
उपस्पृशंस्त्रिषवणं गायत्रीं च सदा जपेत् ॥१३०॥
अथ चेत्त्वरते कर्तुं दिवसं मारुताशनः ।

124. a)—क्रिमिके सर्पे X2* B M; d)—at end Y* A6 add: यूकायां मत्कुणे चैव मूशके पञ्च निर्दिशेत् [निर्विशेत् A4] । मूलाङ्कुरेषु पर्णेषु पुष्पेषु च फलेषु च । स्थावराणां चोपमर्दे प्राणायामास्त्रयस्त्रय इति ।

125. om Y* A6; d)—तदर्धभु° A1 2 R1

126. 1)—om A5; 2)—पुष्पपर्ण° A6; °पुष्पछेदनं X2*; त्रीन्प्राणा° A4 6 G2; त्रीन्त्रीन्प्रा° G1; at end Y* A6 add चतुष्पदान्मृगान्हिंसित्वा चान्द्रायणं चरेद्यतिः [see 10.121] । अथ परिशिष्टप्रायश्चित्तमुच्यते ।

127. 1)—after दत्तात्रेयः X2* inserts 10.128; c)—मृद्भिश्च दशभिः R4

128. om Y* [here A6 reverts to recension X1*]; 1)—om X2*; a–d)—om A1 2 R1 B M [inserted at 10.126 by X2*]; b)—°येद्यतिम् R2 3 G6; भोजयिष्यति R4

129. om Y*

130. om Y*

रात्रौ स्थित्वा जले व्युष्टः प्राजापत्यफलं लभेत् ।।१३१।।
गायत्र्यष्टसहस्रं तु जपं कृत्वोत्थिते रवौ ।
मुच्यते सर्वपापेभ्यो यदि न भ्रूणहा भवेत् ।।१३२।।
सर्वेषामेव पापानां सङ्करे समुपस्थिते ।
दशसाहस्रमभ्यस्य गायत्री शोधनं परम् ।।१३३।।
सव्याहृतिं सप्रणवां गायत्रीं शिरसा सह ।
त्रिः पठेदायतप्राणः प्राणायामः स उच्यते ।।१३४।।
प्राणायामान्धारयेत्त्रीन्यथाविधि समाहितः ।
अहोरात्रकृतं पापं तत्क्षणादेव नश्यति ।।१३५।।
कर्मणा मनसा वाचा यदह्ना कुरुते द्विजः ।
आसीनः पश्चिमां संध्यां प्राणायामेन शुध्यति ।।१३६।।
सहस्रपरमां देवीं शतमध्यां दशावराम् ।
गायत्रीं यो जपेन्नित्यं न स पापेन लिप्यते ।।१३७।।
सव्याहृतिकाः सप्रणवाः प्राणायामास्तु षोडश ।
अपि भ्रूणहतं मासात्पुनन्त्यहरहः कृताः ।।१३८।।
दुरितानां दुरिष्ठानां पापानां महतां तथा ।
कृच्छ्रं चान्द्रायणं चैव सर्वपापप्रणाशनम् ।।१३९।।

संवर्तः[1] ।

संन्यासात्प्रच्युतानां तु निष्कृतिं श्रोतुमर्हथ ।
संन्यस्य दुर्मतिः कश्चित्प्रत्यापत्तिं भजेत्तु यः ।।१४०।।

131. om Y* A6; c)—जलेभ्युष्टः A1 2 R1 2; व्युसः A5; व्युष्य B M; d)—भवेत् R2 3
132. om Y*; a)—गायत्र्याष्ट° G6 R2 3; d)—न यदि R4
133. om Y*; c)—°स्रमभ्यस्त X1*
134. om Y*
135. om Y*
136. om Y*
137. om Y*
138. om Y*; c)—भ्रूणहनं G6 R4
139. om Y*
140. om Y*; c)—संन्यासाद् G6 R3 4

स कुर्यात्कृच्छ्रमश्रान्तं षण्मासात्प्रत्यनन्तरम् ।
यतेर्विपत्तौ संदृष्टः प्रायश्चित्तविधिक्रमः ।।१४१।।

स एवाह[1] ।

चतुर्विद्योपपन्नस्य ब्रह्मघ्नो गुरुघातिनः ।
सेतुबन्धपथे युक्तं प्रायश्चित्तं विनिर्दिशेत् ।।१४२।।
सेतुबन्धपथे भिक्षां चातुर्वर्ण्यं समाचरेत् ।
ख्यापयंश्च स्वकर्माणि छत्रोपानहवर्जितः ।।१४३।।
अहं दुष्कृतात्मा वै महापातककारकः ।
वेश्मद्वारेषु तिष्ठामि भिक्षार्थी ब्रह्मघातकः ।।१४४।।
गोकुलेषु च गोष्ठेषु ग्रामेषु नगरेषु च ।
पर्यटंश्चैव तीर्थानि पुण्यं गत्वा तु सागरम् ।।१४५।।
सेतुबन्धं ततः पश्येल्लङ्कामार्गं महोदधेः ।
दशयोजनविस्तीर्णं शतयोजनमायतम् ।।१४६।।
राघवस्य समादेशान्नलसंचयसंचितम् ।
सेतुबन्धं ततो दृष्ट्वा राजानं पृथिवीपतिम् ।
यजन्तमश्वमेधेन दृष्ट्वा सद्यः शुचिर्भवेत् ।।१४७।।

देवलः[1] ।

रजस्वलां तु नारीं वा वेश्यां वा मद्यपां तु वा ।
शवोपस्करकाष्ठं वा स्पृष्ट्वा स्नात्वा द्वयं जपेत् ।।१४८।।

स एवाह[1] ।

यूकोत्पत्तिः शरीरे चेत्प्रायश्चित्तं विधीयते ।

141. om Y*; b)—षण्मासान् G6 R3 4 B M

142. om Y*; 1)—om X2*; b)—गुरुकामिनः R3 4; गुरुगामिनः G6; c)—°पथा G6 R4; °पथं R2 3

143. om Y*; c)—आख्याय च X2*; ख्यापयन्तु A5

144. om Y*; d)—भिक्षातु X2*; भिक्षार्थं B M

145. om Y*; a)—च तिष्ठामि A1 2 R1 B M; c)—पर्यटनेव G6 R3 4

146. om Y*

147. om Y*

148. 1)—om R4; a)—तु यां नारीं Y*; b)—मद्यपायिनीम् X2*; d)—स्नात्वायुतं A4

कृत्वोपवासमेकं तु प्राणायामान्षडाचरेत् ॥१४९॥

गर्गः[1] ।

भिक्षवः परस्परं न गृह्णीयुः[2] । प्रमादाद् ग्रहणे मित्रस्य चर्षणी धृत इति जपेयुः प्राणायामास्त्रयश्च[3] ॥१५०॥

गालवः[1] ।

कण्डूयनरुधिरक्षरणेऽहोरात्रमुपवासः[2] ॥१५१॥

जमदग्निः[1] ।

मातरं पितरं पुत्रं मनसापि न चिन्तयेत् ।
यदि स्नेहो भवेत्तेषु प्राणायामास्तु षोडश ॥१५२॥

सत्यकामजाबालौ[1] ।

एकवषट्कारस्वाहास्वधावषट्कारं करोति कारयेद्वा सर्वं तन्निष्फलं भवति[2] । तस्य प्रायश्चित्तं विधीयते[3] । स्वयमेव प्रयुञ्जानः प्राजापत्यत्रयं कृत्वा प्राणायामान्द्वादश धारयेत्[4] ॥१५३॥

अनुक्तानां सर्वेषां प्रायश्चित्तं **सत्यकाम** आह[1] ।

विहितातिक्रमं कृत्वा प्राणायामान्द्वादश धारयेत्[2] ॥१५४॥

149. 1)—om Y* X2*; a)—रक्तोत्पत्तिः Y*

150. 1)—om A1 2 R1; 2)—om G1; 3)—मित्रस्य . . . जपेयुः om A4 G2; प्राणायामान्द्वादशाचरेत् A4 G2 [षोडशा° G2]; प्राणायामत्रयं च R4; at end Y* adds भिक्षवः परस्परं किंचिन्न पूरयेयुः । गृहस्थादिपूरणे प्राणायामांस्त्रींश्चरेयुः [त्रिंशच्चरेयुः G1] । भिक्षवः परस्परमङ्गसंमर्षणं [°संघर्षणं G1] न कुर्युः । अज्ञानात्संमर्षणे [संघर्षणे G1] मित्रस्य चर्षणी धृत इति जपेयुः प्रणायामत्रयं चरेयुरिति ।

151. 2)—उपवास इति Y*; at end Y* adds passage in App. 1.10.

152. om Y*; c)—गुरुस्नेहो A1 2 R1; d)—at end R4 adds: संनिधौ मातृमरणे यतेः कार्यं हि दाहनम् । स्नात्वोपोश्य विमुच्येत शमीमूलं व्रजेद्यतिः । एवं पितुरपुत्रस्य कृत्वा मुक्तो यतिर्भवेत् । पुत्रं प्रतिनिधिं कृत्वा कृतकृत्यः पिता श्रुतेः । न स्नानमाचरेद्भिक्षुः पुत्रादिनिधने श्रुते । पितृमातृक्षयं श्रुत्वा स्नात्वा शुध्यति साम्बरः ।

153. om Y*; 2)—कारयेद्वा . . . भवति om A5; सर्वं निष्फलं A6; भवेत् A1 2 R1 B M; 3)—विधीयते om X2*; 4)—स्वधर्मे च G6 R3 4; स्वधर्मेण R2 B M; स्वमेव A2; स्वधर्मेव A1

154. 1)—°क्ततानां च G6 R2 3; °क्तानामपि B M; सत्यकाम . . . [155] अशक्तस्य om A6; 2)—°क्रमे प्राणा° A1 2 R1 B M; °येदिति Y*

अशक्तस्य देशकालाद्यपेक्षया गुरूणि लघूनि प्रायश्चित्तानि व्यवस्थापनीयानि[1] । ऋषीणां मतभेदात्तु विकल्प इति केचित्[2] ।।१५५।। तथान्येऽपि धर्मास्तत्प्रायश्चित्तं च गृहस्थधर्मादेव योजनीयम् ।।१५६।।

इति यतिधर्मसमुच्चये प्रायश्चित्तविधिर्नाम दशमं पर्व ।।१५७।।

155. 1)—अथ देश° Y*; °कालापेक्षया X2*; प्रायश्चित्तानि om G6; 2)—°भेदेन विकल्प X2* B M; °भेदात्तुल्यविकल्प एवेति Y*; केचित् om G1

156. तथान्येऽपि धर्माः । अत्रानुक्तं प्रायश्चित्तं गृहस्थ° Y*; च om A1 2 5 R1 4; at the end Y* adds त्रिकमिति प्रणवव्याहृतिगायत्रीत्युच्यते [°गायत्रय उच्यन्ते G1]; see 5.82.

157. यादवप्रकाशीये यति° Y*

एकादशं पर्व

यतिसंस्कारविधिः

अथ यतीनां संस्कारविधिरुच्यते[1] । तत्र **बोधायनः**[2] ।

यतीनां प्रेतसंस्कारविधिं वक्ष्याम्यशेषतः ।
स्नात्वा गृहस्थः शुद्धात्मा यतिसंस्कारमाचरेत् ॥१॥
शिक्ये शरीरमारोप्य गन्धमाल्यैरलंकृतम् ।
घोषितं जयशब्देन दुन्दुभीनां रवेण च ।
प्राचीमुदीचीं वा गत्वा शुद्धदेशं समाश्रयेत् ॥२॥

नदीतीरेऽश्वत्थवृक्षे देवगृहे गोष्ठे ब्रह्मवृक्षस्याधस्ताद्वा व्याहृतिभिर्दण्डायामप्रमाणं देवयजनं खात्वा सप्तव्याहृतिभिः प्रोक्ष्य पुरुषसूक्तेन स्नापयित्वा गन्धादिभिरलंकृत्य विष्णो रक्षस्वेति निदधाति[1] । इदं विष्णुर्विचक्रम इति दक्षिणहस्ते दण्डं निदधाति[2] । हंसः शुचिषदित्यृचा हृदयदेशे जपेत्[3] । पुरुषसूक्तं भ्रुवोर्मध्ये जपेत्[4] । ब्रह्म जज्ञानमिति मूर्ध्नि देशे जपेत्[5] । भूमिर्भूमिमगादिति मूर्धानं भेदयेत्[6] । गायत्र्याभिमर्षणं[7] । प्रणवेन देवयजनं पूरयेत्[8] । पुनः पुनर्गायत्र्या देशसंस्कारः[9] । सृगालकाकादिबाधो यदि दोषमापादयेत्कर्तुस्तद्देशेऽनावृष्टिर्भविष्यति[10] । तस्मात्पुनः पुनः पूरयेत्[11] । तस्मिन्प्रच्छादयेत्[12] । नाशौचं नोदकक्रिया[13] । यतेर्वहनखनन-

1. 1)—अथ om Y*; यतिसंस्कारविधिः [om उच्यते] X2* G5; 2)—from here Y* has a radically different version given in App. 1.11 [B M give Y* as the main entry and then add the longer recension as पाठभेद]; तत्र om X2* G5 B M; तत्राह A1 2 R1

2. c)—प्राच्यामुदीच्यां A6; वा om R2; गत्वा तु G5

स्पर्शनाच्च सद्योऽवभृथस्नानं भवति[14] । पदे पदेऽश्वमेधफलं पुरुषः प्राप्नोति[15] ।

इत्याह भगवान्**बोधायनः**[16] ॥३॥

ब्रह्मनिष्ठे मृते पुत्रः खनेच्छिष्योऽथवा गृही ।
तस्य तेनैव कर्तव्यो नारायणबलिस्तथा ॥४॥
न वह्निर्नोदकं श्राद्धं नापि ब्राह्मणतर्पणम् ।
सर्वं नारायणोद्दिष्टमेकोद्दिष्टवदाचरेत् ॥५॥
यतिमात्रे मृतेऽप्येतद्विधानं कवयो विदुः ।
अहन्येकादशे प्राप्ते पार्वणं तु विधीयते ॥६॥
सपिण्डीकरणं चैषां न कुर्वीत कदाचन ।
त्रिदण्डग्रहणादेव प्रेतत्वं नैव गच्छति ॥७॥
एतदेव हि पर्याप्तं भिक्षोरेकान्तशीलिनः ।
न चास्य क्रियते कश्चित्क्रियते न स कस्यचित् ॥८॥
अथापरो विधिर्दृष्टो व्याहृतिभिस्तु पूर्ववत् ।
ताभिरेव निधायैनं ताभिः कृत्वा तथावटम् ॥९॥

3. 1)—चैत्यवृक्षे X2* G5 B M [°वृक्ष G5 R4]; देवगृहगोष्ठेषु X2* G5 B M; °धस्ताद्व्याहृ° A6; रक्ष स्वाहेति B M; 2)—दक्षिणे X2 G5; 3)—हृदयं स्पृशन्जपेत् A1 2 R1; °देशं B M; 4)—जपेत् om A5; 5)—ऊर्ध्वदेशे G5 6 R1 2 3; ऊर्ध्वदेशं B M; मूर्धदेशं R4; 6)—भिन्दयन् R4; 10)—श्वसृगाल° G5 6 R3; सृगालश्वका° B M; सृगालश्वादि° R2; °बाधो conj.; °कादिबाधदोषे कर्तु° X2* B M; °कादिबाधदोषस्तद्देशे G5; °बाधा यदि X1*; भवति R4 B M; 12)—तत्र° B M; 14—वहनात्खनननात्स्पर्शनाच्च B M; 16)—इत्याह भगवान् om B M; इति भग° X2* G5; इत्याह बोधायनः इति A6

4. [Y* inserts 4–15 in App. 1.11] a–b)—मृते तस्मिन्खनेत्पुत्रोऽथवा गृही Y*; d)—°बलिस्तदा M A6

5. a–b)—सर्वं नारायणोद्दिष्टवदाचरेत् G1 2; b)—°ब्राह्मणभोजनतर्पणम् R4;

6. a–b)—यतिमात्रेऽप्येवम् । परिव्राजि मृते तस्मिन्विधानं कवयो विदुः Y*

7. a)—चैव Y* G5 6 R2 3 B M; नैव R4; b)—न कदाचन भिक्षुके R4; c)—°ग्रहणमात्रेण Y*; d)—जायते A1 2 R1; विद्यते A4

8. c–d)—om X2* B M; c)—म्रियते Y* A6; d)—जायते न च Y* G5; नस्य [नास्य?] A1 2 R1

9. a)—विनिर्दिष्टो Y*; b)—व्याहृतिभिरित्यादि पूर्व° B M; तु om X2*; व्याहृतिभिः पृथक्पृथक्पूर्ववत् G5; d)—यथावटम् X2* G5 R1 B M; ततोऽवटम् G1

सप्तव्याहृतिभिश्चैव प्रोक्ष्य तच्चावटं पुनः ।
पिष्टप्रस्कन्दमन्त्रेण देवो वः सवितादिना ॥१०॥
दत्वा शिक्यं तु निक्षिप्य पार्श्वे दण्डं तु निक्षिपेत् ।
सखा मेत्यादिना शिक्यं हृदयेऽस्य विनिक्षिपेत् ॥११॥
येन देवाः पवित्रेण मुखे जलपवित्रकम् ।
त्वं नो अग्न इति न्यस्य कुण्डिकां दक्षिणे करे ॥१२॥
भूमिर्भूमिमगान्मन्त्रमुक्त्वा पात्रं तथोदरे ।
होतृभिः समुपस्थाय प्रोक्ष्य व्याहृतिसप्तकैः ॥१३॥
पूरयेदवटं मन्त्रमग्निनाग्निः समिध्यते ।
यथा सृगालाः श्वानो वा नोद्धरेयुः पुनस्तथा ॥१४॥
प्राक्साग्निकानां भिक्षूणां निदध्याद्वा बिले क्षितौ ।
निरग्नीनां दहेद्विप्रः संसिद्धानां कलेवरम् ॥१५॥
एकोद्दिष्टं जलं पिण्डमाशौचं प्रेतसंस्क्रियाः ।
एतेषां तु विधानेन कुर्यादब्दे सपिण्डताम् ।
न कुर्यात्पार्वणादन्यद् ब्रह्मभूताय भिक्षवे ॥१६॥

अत्रिः[1] ।

पुत्रो गृहस्थः शुद्धात्मा यतिसंस्कारमाचरेत् ।

10. b)—तं चावटं Y*; c)—विषप्र° G5 6 R2 3 B M; विश्वप्र° A4 G2; विष्ट° G1 R4; °प्रस्कन्न° B M; °मात्रेण G5 R2 3 [reading of pāda uncertain; see tr.]; d)—सविता त्विति Y*

11. a)—देहं B M; शिक्ये X2* G5 B M; b)—पात्रे A4 G2; मात्रे G1; c)—दण्डं Y*; d)—हृदये च X2* G5 B M; च निक्षि° A6; हृदयेषु यदस्य च Y*

12. a–b)—पवित्रेणेति A1 2; R1 gives text of the mantra, ending इति मन्त्रेण; जल-पवित्रम् A1 2

13. a–b)—°मिमगादिति पात्रं A1 2; c–d)—तदन्तस्थमुपस्थाय प्रोक्ष्य व्याहृतिसप्तकैः Y*; d)—व्याहृतिभिश्च सप्तकैः B M

14. a)—मन्त्रश्चाग्नि° G5 R4 A B; मन्त्रस्त्वग्नि° Y*; मन्त्रं चाग्नि° G6 R3; c–d)—om A1 2 R1

15. a–b)—om A1 2 R1; °कानां हि तनुं X2* G5 B M; c)—निरग्निना A1 2 R1; d)—संस्थितानां B M

16. b)—°संस्क्रियां X2* A6; d)—कुर्यादग्निसपि° X2* G5 B M; f)—°भूयाय G5 6 R2 3 B M

शिक्ये शरीरमारोप्य गन्धमाल्यैरलंकृतम् ॥१७॥
तुषाग्निमत्र चोत्पाद्य संस्कारार्थं यतेर्हरेत् ।
घोषितं जयशब्देन दुन्दुभीनां रवेण च ।
प्राचीमुदीचीं वा गत्वा शुद्धदेशं समाचरेत् ॥१८॥
खात्वा व्याहृतिभिर्भूमिं दण्डायामप्रमाणकम् ।
सप्तव्याहृतिभिः प्रोक्ष्य तत्र दारुचितिर्भवेत् ॥१९॥
याज्ञीयैस्तु यथाशक्ति काष्ठैरन्यैरनिन्दितैः ।
ततः शरीरं प्रक्षाल्य सावित्र्या शुद्धमानसः ॥२०॥
विष्णो हव्यं रक्षस्वेति दारुचित्यां निधाय तत् ।
पवित्रमित्यनेनैव पवित्रं स्थापयेन्मुखे ॥२१॥
त्रिदण्डं दक्षिणे पाणाविदं विष्णुरिति न्यसेत् ।
सव्ये शिक्यं यदस्येति स्वाहान्तेन निधाय तत् ॥२२॥
सावित्र्या चोदरे पात्रं गुह्यस्थाने कमण्डलुम् ।
भूमिर्भूमिमगादिति स्थापयेद्विधिकोविदः ॥२३॥
श्वभ्रे काष्ठेऽथ निक्षिप्तं सर्वसाधनसंयुतम् ।
शरीरं होतृभिः कर्ता अभिमन्त्र्योपतिष्ठते ।
तुषाग्निना दहेद्देहं यावद्भस्मीभविष्यति ॥२४॥

18. a)—दुष्टाग्नि° A1 2 R1 [A1 cor. तुष्टाग्नि°]; °ग्निमात्रमुत्पाद्य B M; b)—हरेद्यतेः R4; c–f)—X2* G5 B M read प्रागुदग्देशे [°देश G5 R3 4; add वा R2 B M] रणदुन्दुभिजयशब्दादि पूर्ववत् [see 11.2]

19. b)—°प्रमाणतः X2* G5 B M

20. c)—शरीरं om X2* G5 B M; d)—विधिवत्सावि° G5; सावित्र्या add शरीरं B M, add आमन्त्र्य R4

21. c)—A1 2 R1 give text of the mantra and end इति मन्त्रेण; c)—पवित्रं त इत्यने° A5 6 R3; पवित्रं तमित्यने° G5; d)—धारयेन्मुखे A1 2 5 R1; स्थापेत्करे B M

22. b)—विष्णुर्विचेत्यृचा G6 R3 4; विष्णुर्विचक्रमेत्यृचा G5 R2 B M; after न्यसेत् A1 2 R1 add text of the mantra; d)—after स्वाहान्तेन B M leave a lacuna [M ed. comments अत्रात्यशुद्धं कोशान्तसंवादात् शोधनीयम्]

23. d)—स्थापयेदितिकोविदः G5 R2

24. a)—श्वभ्र G5 6 R3 4; काष्ठेषु G5 R4; e–f)—om A6

अथाप्युदाहरन्तीमं वेदार्थनिपुणा बुधाः ।
निषेकादिश्मशानान्ता विधयो ब्राह्मणे स्मृताः ।
तस्माद्यतेश्च संस्कारं मन्त्रवत्कुरुते गृही ।।२५।।
आत्मन्यग्नीन्समारोप्य यः प्रैषमवदद्यतिः ।
तस्य पुत्रो विधानेन ह्यवरोप्याग्निना दहेत् ।।२६।।
अपि होत्रविधानेन गायत्र्या प्रणवेन वा ।
कर्मनिष्ठे तु संन्यस्ते पितर्युपरते सुतैः ।
दहनं तस्य कर्तव्यं श्राद्धं पिण्डोदकक्रियाः ।।२७।।
आदावेव विकल्पेन ब्रह्मचारी यतिर्भवेत् ।
तस्य सर्वं गृहस्थेन कर्तव्यं सन्निधौ हरेः ।।२८।।
यतीन्वहन्दहन्स्पर्शन्स्नानमात्रेण शुध्यति ।
पदे पदेऽश्वमेधस्य फलं प्राप्नोति मानवः ।।२९।।

शौनकः ।

सर्वसङ्गनिवृत्तस्य ध्यानयोगरतस्य च ।
न तस्य दहनं कार्यं नैव पिण्डोदकक्रियाः ।।३०।।
निदध्यात्प्रणवेनैव ध्यानभिक्षोः कलेवरम् ।
प्रोक्षणं खननं चैव सर्वं तेनैव कारयेत् ।।३१।।

25. e)—संस्कारं om G6; संस्कारा R4; f)—विधिवत् R4; कुरुतेमहि X2* G5 B M

26. a)—°न्यग्निं A 5 6 B M; b)—यतिर्यदि विपद्यति B M; c)—तस्य पुत्रो om A5; d)—समारोप्याग्निना दहेत् A1 2 5 R1; ह्यवरोऽप्यग्निना B M; ह्यपरोऽप्यग्निना G5; ह्यपरोऽह्यग्निना R4

27. [Y* inserts in App. 1.11] a)—अग्निहोत्र° A4 G2 M; अग्निहोत्रि° B; अपिवाथविधा° R4; b)—च B Ṁ; c)—च X2*; e)—संस्कारः तस्य कर्तव्यः A1 2 R1; f)—श्राद्धपिण्डादिकाः क्रियाः Y*; °क्रिया A1 6 G6 R1 2 3

28. d)—हरेत् R4; परे B M

29. [Y* inserts in App. 1.11] a)—यतिं वहन्स्पृशन्देहं Y*; दहन् om R2; d)—फलमाप्नोति Y* A2

30. d)—°क्रिया A1 2 6 R1

यतीन्वहन्स्पृशन्वापि स्नानमात्रेण शुध्यति ।
अश्वमेधफलं सर्वे पृथक्पृथगवाप्नुयुः इति ॥३२॥

एतमेवाह भगवान्**वृद्धयाज्ञवल्क्यः** ॥३३॥

इति यादवप्रकाशीये यतिधर्मसमुच्चये यतिसंस्कारविधिर्नाम एकादशं पर्व ॥३४॥

32. om X2* G5 B M; d)—इति om A5

33. एतदेवाह A1 2 R1; एतमेव भग° X2*; after this A1 2 R1 add passage in App. 1.12.

34. om G6 R3 and in its place read यतिधर्मसमुच्चयं संपूर्णम्; यादवप्रकाशविरचिते M before यति°, A1 2 R1 after °समुच्चये; संस्कार° for यतिसंस्कार° Y* R2 B M; at end X2* [except R4] adds passage in App. 1.13; B M place this passage after 11.33.

APPENDIX 1

Long Variant Readings

1

Ch. 4.4: reading of Y*

अथ यथाविधि स्नात्वा होमादिद्रव्यं शिक्यं पात्रं कौपीनं काषायवस्त्रमग्निसन्निधौ संसाद्यानग्निमानप्यग्निमुत्पाद्यापराह्णे प्रणवेन प्राणाहुतिं हुत्वा ब्रह्मरात्रमुषित्वापरेऽह्नि पुरुषसूक्तेन द्वादशाज्याहुतीर्जुहुयात्[1] चरुं च । आहिताग्निश्चेत्प्राजापत्येष्टिं विधिवत्कृत्वा सर्वस्वदक्षिणां दत्वा अयं ते योनिर्ऋत्विय इत्यात्मन्यग्निं समारोप्य वेदिमध्ये शङ्खचक्रगदाखड्गशार्ङ्गधरं नारायणं श्रियः पतिं ध्यात्वा गुर्वनुज्ञया प्रैषमन्त्रमुदाहरेत् । ॐ भूर्भुवःस्वः संन्यस्तं मयेति त्रिरुपांशु त्रिर्मध्यमस्वरेणोक्त्वा त्रिरुच्चैरुक्त्वा अभयं सर्वभूतेभ्यो मत्तः स्वाहेत्यपां पूर्णाञ्जलिं प्राग्भूमौ निनयेत्[2] । युवा सुवासा इति कौपीनं काषायवस्त्रं गृह्णीयात् । सखा मा गोपायेति त्रिदण्डं गृह्णीयात् । तच्छं योरावृणीमह इति यज्ञोपवीतम् । यदस्य पारे रजस इति शिक्यम् । सप्तव्याहृतिभिः पात्रम् । येन देवाः पवित्रेणेति जलपवित्रम्[3] । येन देवा ज्योतिषोर्ध्वा इति कमण्डलुं गृह्णीयात् [see 4.19]। स्वकीयं ग्रामं बन्धुजनं च परित्यज्यान्यग्रामं प्राप्य जपध्यानपरायणो याचितायाचिताभ्यां तु भैक्षाभ्यां[4] वर्तयेत् । रागद्वेषादि वर्जयेत् । यावदायुषमेवं वर्तयन्ब्रह्म संपद्यते न च पुनरावर्तत इति [see 4.21]।

1. षोडशाज्या° G2
2. निनयति G2
3. येन . . . जलपवित्रम् om A4
4. तु भैक्षाभ्यां om A4

2

Ch. 4.4: reading of G3 [variants are incorporated in the critical apparatus]

अथ यथाविधि...दद्यात् [4.6]; अथ दण्डादीन्...इति सावित्रीं प्रविष्य [4.12]; अथ पुनरादित्यस्या°...निनीयति [4.13]; युवा...कमण्डलुम् [4.19]; अथानवेक्षमाणो... दिशमभिप्रव्रजतीति [4.23(2)]; अथ कात्यायनप्रोक्तं संन्यासविधिः [°विधिं ?] व्याख्यास्यामः । पुरश्चरणं कृच्छ्रचतुष्टयं...अष्टमं परमात्मानमिति [4.2]; पयोदधिसर्पिरिति त्रिवृत्प्राश्योपवसेत् । त्रिदण्डं...अग्निमुत्पाद्य [4.10]; अपराह्णे प्रणवेन प्राणाहुतिं हुत्वा [from here G3 follows Y* in App. 1.1]

3

Ch. 4.12: reading of G6 R2 3

अथ संन्यासविधिः । अष्टौ देवादीनि[5] श्राद्धादीनि नान्दीमुखविधानेन करिष्य इति संकल्प्य तीर्थं गत्वा जलाञ्जलिना तर्पयेत् । अष्टौवस्वेकादशरुद्रद्वादशादित्येभ्यो[6] नमः । मरीच्यङ्गिरसपुलस्त्यपुलहक्रतुप्रचेतोवसिष्ठभृगुनारदेभ्यो[7] नमः । हिरण्यगर्भविराट्प्रजापतिभ्यो नमः । सनकसनन्दनसनातनकपिलासुरिपञ्चशिखेभ्यो नमः । पृथिव्यप्तेजोवायुराकाशेभ्यो नमः । क्रव्यवाहनानलसोमार्यमाग्निष्वात्तसोमपबर्हिषद्भ्यो नमः । गौरीपद्माशचीमेधासावित्रीविजयाजयादेवसेनास्वधास्वाहाभ्यो नमः[8] । परमात्मने नम इति संतर्प्य दैवर्षिदिव्यमानुषभौतिकपितृमातृपरमात्मश्राद्धेषु भवद्भिः क्षणः कर्तव्यः । ॐ तथा प्राप्नोतु भवन्तः प्राप्नुवाम इति वाचयित्वा प्रतिश्राद्धं विप्रद्वयं विश्वेदेवार्थं संवृणीय अशक्तौ विश्वेदेवव्यतिरेकेन विप्रद्वयं वा वरयित्वा पादप्रक्षालणस्नानादि कारयित्वा स्वाग्निमुपसमाधाय अग्निमुखान्तं संस्कारं विधाय ॐ अष्टौवस्वेकादशरुद्रद्वादशादित्येभ्यः स्वाहा । मरीच्यङ्गिरःपुलस्त्यपुलहक्रतुप्रचेतोवसिष्ठभृगुनारदेभ्यः स्वाहा । हिरण्यगर्भविराट्प्रजापतिभ्यः स्वाहा । सनकसनन्दनसनातनकपिलासुरिपञ्चशिखेभ्यः स्वाहा । पृथिव्यप्तेजोवाय्वाकाशेभ्यः स्वाहा । क्रव्याडनलसोमार्यमाग्निष्वात्तसोमपबर्हिषद्भ्यः स्वाहा । गौरीपद्माशचीमेधासावित्रीविजयाजयादेवसेनास्वधास्वाहाभ्यः स्वाहा । परमात्मने स्वाहा । अग्नये स्विष्टकृते

5. देवादिश्रा° G6 R3
6. °कादशादित्येभ्यो R3
7. °ङ्गिरसोपु° G6
8. गौरी°. . . °नमः om R3

स्वाहेत्युपवीत्येवान्नेन जुहुयात् । अदितेन्वमंस्था [?] इत्यादि विधाय ब्राह्मणानासनेषूपवेश्य अमृतोपस्तरणमसि प्राणे निविष्टोऽमृतं जुहोति[9] । अमृतापिधानमसीत्याद्युच्चारणं कुर्वन्भोजयित्वा दक्षिणां दत्वा उत्तरतः प्रागग्रान्दर्भान्संस्तीर्य ॐ अष्टवस्वेकादशरुद्रद्वादशादित्येभ्यो नम इत्यादिना अष्टौ पिण्डानुपवीत्येव[10] दद्यात् । ॐ देवादिश्राद्धकर्माङ्गं पुण्याहं कर्म करिष्य इति संकल्प्य पुण्याहं वाचयित्वा स्नात्वा यथोक्तकारिणं भिक्षुं भगवन्तं वा[11] गुरुत्वेन स्वीकृत्य संकल्पेन संन्यासाश्रममाश्रयिष्यामीति ।

4

Ch.6.54: reading of Y* A1 2 R1

क्रतुराह । सदा जलपवित्रं च गृहीत्वा मन्त्रवित्तमः । तेनैव पूरयेद्भिक्षुरुदकेन कमण्डलुम् ।। तेनैवाचमनं कुर्यान्मार्जनं तर्पणं तथा । उपस्थानं च सूर्यस्य कुर्यात्पञ्च यथाविधि ।। ततः प्रदक्षिणं कृत्वा जानुभ्यां शिरसा नमेत् । कालेष्वन्येषु बध्नीयाद्दण्डाग्रे सूत्रलम्बितम् । ऊर्ध्वं न बिभृयाज्जातु कदाचिच्छुष्कमम्बरम् । दिवाकरोदये . . .प्रदापयेदिति [6.43]। आह **गालवः** । सदा जलपवित्रेण. . .प्रायश्चित्तमथाचरेत् [6.49]। त्रिंशत्° . . . °शतत्रयमिति [9.67c–d] ।

5

Ch. 6.228: reading of G6 R2 3 B M; Ch. 6.229: reading of A6 and R4

याज्ञवल्क्यः[1] । संनिरुध्येन्द्रियग्रामं रागद्वेषौ प्रहाय च । भयं मुक्त्वा च भूतानाममृतीभवति द्विजः ।। कर्तव्याशयशुद्धिस्तु भिक्षुकेण विशेषतः । ज्ञानोत्पादनिमित्तत्वात्स्वातन्त्र्यकरणाय[12] च ।। अवेक्ष्य गर्भवासं च कर्मणां गतयस्तथा । आधयो व्याधयः क्लेशा जरारूपविपर्यया:[13] । भवो जातिसहस्रेषु[14] प्रियाप्रियविपर्ययः[15] ।। **अत्रिः** । ज्ञातवेदान्तसारार्थो[16] विरक्तो भवसागरे । कैवल्याश्रममासाद्य ब्रह्मदर्शन-

9. जुहोमि G6
10. °पसृत्येव R2
11. om G6
12. ज्ञानोत्पत्तिनि° A6; ज्ञानोपातनि° R4
13. °पर्ययौ B M; °पर्ययः A6
14. भवेज्जाति° R2 3
15. °पर्यया: R4
16. ज्ञान° R4 B M

तत्परः ॥ कृत्स्नं स्वधर्ममातिष्ठेत्प्रतिषिद्धादि[17] वर्जयेत् । अहिंसा सत्यमस्तेयं ब्रह्मचर्यापरिग्रहौ [5.56.c–d]॥ [18]भावशुद्धिर्हरौ भक्तिः सन्तोषं चापि मार्दवम् । आस्तिक्यं ब्रह्मसंस्पर्शः[19] स्वाध्यायः समदर्शिता ॥ अनुद्धतिरदीनत्वं प्रसादस्थैर्यमार्जवम् । विरागो गुरुशुश्रूषा[20] श्रद्धा शान्तिर्दमः क्षमा[21] ॥ उपेक्षा धैर्यमाधुर्ये तितिक्षा करुणा तथा । ह्रीस्तपो ज्ञानविज्ञाने योगो लघ्वशनं रतिः ॥ स्नानं सुरार्चनं ध्यानं प्राणायामो बलिः स्तुतिः । भिक्षाटनं जपः संध्या त्यागः कर्मफलस्य च ॥ एष स्वधर्मो विख्यातो यतीनां नियतात्मनाम् । भेदभेदोपमर्दश्च वागारम्भो गृहाश्रयः ॥ स्वाहा स्वधा वषट्कारो विषयाणां च सन्निधिः । स्तुतिर्निन्दा क्रियावादः परमर्माभिघट्टनम्[22] ॥ तृष्णा क्रोधोग्रता लोभमोहौ प्रियाप्रिये । अहङ्कारो ममत्वं च चिकित्सा कर्मसाहसः ॥ प्रायश्चित्तव्रतादेशो मन्त्रौषध्यस्तथा विषम् । नृत्तं गीतं वाद्यवादो हर्षशोकौ प्रतिग्रहः ॥ एकान्नं मदमात्सर्यं[23] गन्धपुष्पादिभूषणम् । ताम्बूलाभ्यञ्जने क्रीडा भोगाकाङ्क्षा रसायनम् ॥ राजवार्तादिकं प्रश्नं भैक्षभोगाङ्गनाकथा । कल्पनं कुत्सनं स्वस्ति ज्यौतिषं क्रयविक्रयौ ॥ काम्यकमपहासश्च सङ्गस्नेहविकत्थनम् । साङ्केतिकं प्रमादश्च गुरुवाक्यातिलङ्घनम् ॥ संधिश्च विग्रहो यानं मञ्चारोहः सिताम्बरम् । शुक्लोत्सर्गो दिवास्वापो भैक्षभुक्तिश्च तैजसे ॥ बीजायुधनिकेतानां ग्रहणं संस्कृता च वाक् । कार्पण्यालस्यशाठ्यानि तैक्ष्ण्यं हिंसा च मैथुनम् ॥ प्रतिषिद्धानि चैतानि समाजोत्सवदर्शनम् । विशेषतो न कार्यं स्याद्यानि चान्यानि वै यतिः ॥ श्रुतिस्मृतिनिषिद्धानि नाचरेत्तानि सर्वशः । अतः परं प्रवक्ष्यामि त्वाचारो यो यतेः स्मृतः ॥ अभ्युत्थानं प्रियालापो गुरुवत्प्रतिपूजनम् । यतीनां व्रतवृद्धानां कार्यं धर्मपरात्मनाम् ॥ विष्णुरूपेण कार्यं च नमस्कारो विधानतः । त्रैकाल्यमर्चनं विष्णोर्देवानां च तदात्मनाम् । नमस्कारार्चनादीनि कुर्यान्नान्यस्य कस्यचित् [5.78] ॥ कणयावकपिण्याकशाकतक्रपयोदधि [6.126a–b] । स्थानं वीरासनं मौनमष्टग्रासस्तु भोजनम् । स्नानं च त्रिषु कालेषु त्रिरात्राभोजनादिकम् ॥ सत्त्वशुद्धिकरा ह्येते योगसिद्धिकरास्तथा । नियमांस्तु सदा कुर्याद्यमांस्तेभ्योऽपि पालयेत् [10.79a–b] ॥ **गौतमः** । नाविप्रमुक्तमोषधि-

17. प्रतिषिद्धानि A6 R4
18. भाव° . . . प्रासादस्थैर्यमार्जवम् om A6;
19. °संस्पर्शं R4
20. अस्तेयो गुरु° A6
21. दमः शमः A6
22. °मर्मावघ° A6 R4
23. °मात्सर्ये A6 R4

वनस्पतीनामङ्गमुपाददीत [GDh 3.19] । उत्तरत्र । वर्जयेद्बीजवधं समो भूतेषु हिंसानुग्रहयोरनारम्भी [GDh 3.22–24] ।। **बोधायनः** । अनग्निरनिकेतः स्यादशर्माशरणो मुनिः [BDh 2.18.22] । भिक्षामद्यते ।।

6

Ch. 6.250: addition in G6 R2 3. Since much of the addition consists of repetition of passages of Chapter 6 already given, I list the verse numbers of the critical edition in the order they appear in the addition.

239; 240a–b; 241c–d; आह **क्रतुः** 252a–b; 218 [om G6 R3]; 252c–d; 233; **यमः** 218–21

7

Ch. 7.76: reading of B M [see App. 1.8 for Y*]

याज्ञवल्कयः । यस्य गेहे यतिर्नित्यं मुहूर्तमपि विश्रमेत् । किं तस्यान्येन धर्मेण कृतकृत्यो भवेद्धि सः । ब्राह्मणानां च[24] कोट्यस्तु यतिरेको विशिष्यते ।। ब्रह्मा विष्णुश्च रुद्रश्च ससाध्या मरुतस्तथा[25] । सकृद्भुक्तेन यतिना पितृदेवाः सवासवाः । सर्वे ते तृप्तिमायान्ति दश वर्षाणि पञ्च च ।। सूर्यखद्योतयोर्यद्वन्मेरुसर्षपयोर्यथा[26] । अन्तरं हि महद्दृष्टं तथा भिक्षुगृहस्थयोः ।। तस्य श्राद्धे विशेषेण पुण्येषु दिवसेषु च । नाम चोद्दिस्य दातव्यं यतीनां मुक्तिसाधनम् ।। **महाभारते** श्राद्धप्रकरणे भगवद्वचनम् । यत्र भिक्षुरहं तत्र तं च मां[27] विद्धि पाण्डव । पूजिते पूजितोऽहं वै पूजिताः सर्वदेवताः ।। सकृदेकेन भुक्तेन कोटिकोटिगुणं[28] भवेत् । किं पुनर्बहुभिर्भुक्तैस्तेभ्यः संख्या न विद्यते ।। संक्रान्तौ ग्रहणे चैव व्यतिपाते दिनक्षये । श्राद्धकालः स विज्ञेयो भिक्षौ तु गृहमागते ।। काले वा यदि वाकाले भिक्षुर्यस्य गतो गृहम्[29] । पितॄनुद्दिश्य दातव्यं पितॄणां तृप्तिमिच्छता ।। **शातातपः** । वटौ तु समदत्तं स्याद् गृहस्थे द्विगुणं भवेत् । वानप्रस्थे तु त्रिगुणं[30] यतौ दत्तमनन्तकम् ।।

24. प्राणिनां चैव A4;
25. ससाध्या मरुतः om with lacuna G1 2 3; वसवो for ससाध्या A4
26. °पयोरिव Y*
27. तं चाहं G1 2 3
28. कोटिकोटिशतं A4 G1 2
29. यतिर्यस्य गतो गृहे A4 G1 2
30. शतगुणं for तु त्रिगुणं Y*

8

Ch. 7.145: reading of Y* and A3 [partiallly]. Passages in this addition that occur elsewhere in the text are referred to by chapter and verse numbers.

10.93; 10.101; **वसिष्ठः** । यदा ग्रामद्वये भिक्षुः चरेद्भिक्षां प्रमादतः । स्वधर्मकुशलोऽलस्यः[31] चरेत्सान्तपनं व्रतम् ।। **देवलः** । पुनर्भैक्षं च ताम्बूलमेकादश्यां तु भोजनम् । नोद्धृतानामपां पानं सुरापानसमं भवेत् ।। **वृद्धदत्तात्रेयः** । प्राङ्मुखोदङ्मुखोऽश्नीयात्कदाचित्पश्चिमे मुखः । दक्षिणाभिमुखो भिक्षुर्नाश्नीयाद्वै कदाचन ।। 7.113 [here ends the addition of A3]; 9.27; अपि शास्त्रसमायुक्तान्शौचाचारसमन्वितान् । वानप्रस्थगृहस्थाद्यान्न नमस्येद्यतिः क्वचित् ।। **शङ्खः** । स्त्रीसङ्गं च दिवास्वप्नं रात्रिसंचारमेव च । प्रसह्य रेतः पतनं सर्वथा वर्जयेद्यतिः ।। **अग्निवैश्ये** । काषायामुपवीतं च तथा जन्तुनिवारणम् । भिक्षुश्चैव पुनर्ग्राह्यं त्रिदण्डं न पुनर्ग्रहीत् । यस्य गेहे . . . भवेद्धि सः [App 1.7, v. 1] ।। **भाष्कलश्रुतौ** add rest of App. 1.7; 7.76–78; 7.60a–d; यच्च प्रव्रजितापत्यं या चैषां बीजसंततिः । विदारा नाम चण्डाला जायन्ते नात्र संशयः ।। आरूढपतितं विप्रं चण्डालाच्च विनिःसृतम् । उद्भिज्जं कृमिदष्टं च स्पृष्ट्वा चान्द्रायणं चरेत् । 7.108a–d; संन्यस्य सर्वकर्माणि स्वकार्यनिरतोऽस्पृहः । संन्यासेनेह हन्त्येनः प्राप्नोति परमां गतिमिति ।। आह **भृहस्पतिः** 7.83a–d; आहतुः **शङ्खलिखितौ** 7.94c–d; 7.95; आह **याज्ञवल्क्यः** । संनिरुध्ये° . . . भवति द्विजः [App. 1.5] । आह **अत्रिः** । आस्तिक्यं . . . धैर्यमार्जवम् [App. 1.5] । अस्नेहो गुरुशुश्रूषा क्षान्तिः सत्यं दमः शमः । भिक्षाटनं जपो . . . यतीनां नियतात्मनाम् [App. 1.5] । एकान्तं मधुमांसानि गन्धपुष्पादिभूषणम् । ताम्बूलाभ्यञ्जने क्रीडा भोगाकाङ्क्षा रसायनम् । शुक्लोत्सर्गो दिवास्वापो भैक्षभुक्तिश्च तैजसे । कार्पण्यालस्यशाठ्यानि . . . नाचरेत्तानि सर्वश इति [App. 1.5] । आह **दक्षः** 7.97–98; आह **कपिलः** 7.103a–d; 7.105; 7.106; 7.115–117; 7.114; 7.138; 7.140 [om A4]; ताम्बूलो[32] भर्तृहीनानां[33] यतीनां ब्रह्मचारिणाम् । एकैकं मांसतुल्यं स्यात् संभूय तु सुरासमम् । 7.141; आह **वायुः** । आरूढपतितस्याथ प्रायश्चित्तं वदामि वः । चान्द्रायणं नरः कुर्याद्वर्षमेकं समाहितः ।। पुण्यतीर्थाभिगामी च पुण्याश्रमनिवास्यपि । ततः पुनर्गुरून्गत्वा संन्यसेद्विगतस्पृहः ।। 7.145; 7.144.

31. Unclear reading: कुशलोलुस्स A3

32. ताम्बूलाभ्यञ्जनं चैव A4;

33. भर्तृहीनानां conj. (see reading in Schrader ms 55 p. 188 above); भकृस्त्रीणां [unclear] G1 2 3; कस्त्रीणां A4

9

Ch.10.27: reading of R4

भिक्षाकाले तु केनापि नमस्कारः कृतो यदि । तदन्नं तु परित्यज्य भुक्त्वा चान्द्रायणं चरेत् ।। शिखिभ्यो या तु रत्नेभ्यो त्रिदण्डिभ्यश्च दापयेत् । ताननादृत्य यद्दत्तं <u>कव्यमन्येभ्य आसंरम्</u> [unclear] ।। यस्मिन्गृहे विवाहादि यस्मिन्प्रेतादिकर्म च । तद्गृहान्न विशेद्भिक्षुः प्रायश्चित्ती भवेद्यतिः ।। मौञ्जीबन्धे विवाहे च सीमान्ते पिण्डकर्मणि । कदाचिदपि नाश्नीयादन्नं माधूकरं क्वचित् । स कृत्वा प्राकृतं कृच्छ्रं शुध्यते नात्र संशयः ।। पात्रे कृत्वा तु नैवेद्यं यदि मन्त्रं न विन्यसेत् [see 10.49] । प्राणायामशतं कृत्वा जपेत्त्रिकशतत्रयम् ।। यतिपात्राणि मृद्वेणुदार्वलाबुमयानि च । तेषामद्भिः स्मृतं शौचं चमसानामिवाध्वरे ।। यथा हि सोमसंयोगात् चमसो मेध्य इष्यते । अपां तथैव संयोगात् नित्यो मेध्यः कमण्डलुः ।। ततः परं ततः शौचं तत आचमनक्रिया । तत आराधनं चैव कुर्यादेवाविचारयन् । गृहीणां त्रीणि पात्राणि यतीनामेव च विपर्यये । पतितौ तावुभौ मनुरब्रवीत् ।। गृहस्थैः सह यो भुंक्ते यदि भिक्षुः प्रमादतः । प्राजापत्येन कृच्छ्रेण शुध्यते नात्र संशयः ।। गन्धं घ्रात्वा सुरायास्तु तथा मूत्रपुरीषयोः । क्रव्यादपूतिगन्धे च प्राणायामो विधीयते ।। छर्दिमूत्रपुरीषं च दृष्ट्वा तु सहसा यतिः । प्राणायामेन शुध्येत चिरेण द्विगुणं भवेत् [see 10.76–77] । धृत्वात्रोपवसेद्भिक्षुः <u>स्रजधा</u>दिविभूषणम् [unclear] ।। यदा पूर्वं तु दत्वा च भुक्त्वा च प्रतिगृह्य च । चरेत्सौम्यं महाकृच्छ्रं प्राजापत्यमथापि वा ।। पुत्रादिभिश्चेत्संभाषां यदि कुर्यात्प्रमादतः । उपोष्य रजनीमेकां प्राणायामशतं चरेत् ।। तान्दृष्ट्वा दुःखितश्चेत्स्यादश्रुपातं करोति च । उपवासत्रयं कृत्वा प्राणायामशतं चरेत् ।। स्वकाये स्वयमुत्पात्य शोणितं तु यदि क्वचित् । प्राणायामत्रयं कृत्वा तथाचम्य विशुध्यति ।। प्रत्युत्तिष्ठेद्यतीन्वृद्धान्नमस्कृत्वा तथा<u>सत</u> [unclear] । एकैकातिक्रमे तेषां प्राणायामान्दश स्मृताः । **देवलकाश्यपौ** ।

10

Ch. 10.151: reading of Y*

सत्यकामः । परस्मै पाकं कुर्वन्प्राजापत्यमेकं कृत्वा प्राणायामशतं चरेत् ।[34] भिक्षुराजगामित्वं [sic] कृत्वोपवासत्रयं कृत्वा प्राणायामशतं चरेदिति । **मनुः** । प्राणायामान्धारयेत त्रीन्यथाविध्यतन्द्रितः । अहोरात्रकृतं पापं तत्क्षणादेव नश्यति ।।

34. G1 add आत्मनः पाकं कारयन्प्राजापत्यद्वयं कृत्वा प्राणायामशतं चरेत्

सव्याहृतिकां . . . उच्यते [10.134] । आसने सम्यगासीनो वामेनापूर्य चोदरम् । कुम्भकेन त्रिरावृत्तिर्दक्षिणेन विरेचयेत् । **हारीतः** । सव्याहृतिकाः . . . प्रणाशनमिति [10.138–39] । **गालवः** । बहूनि सूक्ष्मपापानि कृत्वा संकीर्णमात्मनः । मन्यमानोऽथ[35] गायत्र्या दशसाहस्रकं जपेत् । सर्वेषामेव . . . परमिति [10.133] । **व्यासः** । उपपातकेषु सर्वेषु . . . शुध्यति [10.15] । ईश्वर° . . . प्रायश्चित्तमिति [10.16] ।

11

Ch. 11.1: Y* recension of the 11th chapter. Variants in Y* of sections in common with the critical edition are given in the critical apparatus.

आह **वृद्धयाज्ञवल्क्यः** । अथ विप्रो गृहस्थस्तु यतिसंस्कारमाचरेत् । अग्निमुत्पाद्य माल्याद्यैरलंकृत्यास्य देहकम् ।। आरोप्य शिक्यं तं चाग्निं[36] नीत्वा ग्रामात्ततो बहिः । प्रशस्तैर्मङ्गलैर्युक्तं वाद्यादिध्वनिभिस्तथा ।। दिशं प्राचीमुदीचीं वा न्यस्य देशे शुचौ मृतम् । खात्वा व्याहृतिभिर्भूमिं दण्डायामप्रमाणकम् ।। अथ प्रोक्ष्य च तं देशं व्याहृतिभिश्च सप्तभिः । याज्ञिकैर्दारुभिस्तत्र चितां कृत्वा शुभैस्तथा[37] ।। देहं प्रक्षाल्य सावित्र्या चितायां तं विनिक्षिपेत् । विष्णो हव्यमिति न्यस्य मुखे जलपवित्रकम् ।। पवित्रं त इति न्यस्य[38] दण्डं दक्षिणहस्तके । इदं विष्णुरिति प्रास्य शिक्यं सव्यकरे यतेः ।। यदस्य पारे रजसः शिक्यमित्यादिनैव तु[39] । सावित्र्या चोदरे पात्रं गुह्यस्थाने कमण्डलुम् ।। भूमिर्भूमिमगान्मन्त्रमुक्त्वाथाप्युपतिष्ठते । पञ्चभिर्दशहोत्राद्यैः षड्भिरित्यपरे जगुः । अग्निना च दहेत्तेन नास्ति कर्मोदकादिकम् ।। गच्छन्तमनुगच्छन्ति वहन्ति च दहन्ति च । स्नानमात्रेण शुद्धाः स्युरश्वमेधफलं च ते । तस्य ये बान्धवास्तेषां सद्यः शौचं विधीयते ।। यतीनां . . . चरेत् [11.1] । पौरुषेणैव सूक्तेन यतेः स्नानं समाचरेत् । शिक्ये शरीरमारोप्य गन्धमाल्यैरलंकृतम् [see 11.2a–b] । घोषयित्वा तु वाद्यादीन्नृत्यगेयानि कारयेत् ।। नदीतीरे पर्वतसमीपे गोष्ठे अश्वत्थमूले पलाशच्छायायां[40] वा शुद्धे देशे परिव्राजकं निधाय तस्य दण्डायामप्रमाणं देवयजनं भूः स्वाहा भुवः स्वाहा सुवः स्वाहा भूर्भुवः

35. मन्यमानो गायत्र्या G1 2
36. शिक्ये A4; शिक्यं चाग्निं G1 2
37. शुभैस्ततः A4
38. न्यसेत् G1 2
39. च G1
40. अश्वत्थपलाशच्छायां G2

सुवः स्वाहेति खात्वा सप्तव्याहृतिभिर्देवयजनं संप्रोक्ष्य यतेर्देहं सावित्र्या प्रोक्ष्य कूर्मासनं येन देवा ज्योतिषोर्ध्वा [gives the whole mantra] इति कूर्मासने[41] निधाय तस्योपरि परिव्राजकं विष्णो हव्यं रक्षस्वेति निधाय पवित्रं ते विततं [whole mantra] इति मुखे जलपवित्रं दत्वा इदं विष्णुर्विचक्रम इति दक्षिणहस्ते दण्डं दत्वा यदस्य पारे [whole mantra] इति शिक्यं दत्वा सप्तव्याहृतिभिः पात्रमुदरे दत्वा पुरुषसूक्तं भ्रुवोर्ब्रह्म जज्ञानं मूर्ध्नि भूमिर्भूमिमगान्माता [whole mantra] इति गुह्यस्थाने कमण्डलुं न्यस्य हंसः शुचिषद् [whole mantra] इति हृदयदेशं स्पृष्ट्वा संजप्य पुरुषसूक्तेन भ्रुवोर्मध्ये जपित्वा ब्रह्म पश्चात्परिव्राजकमभिमुखीकृत्य दशहोतृभिरुपस्थानं कुर्यात् । ब्राह्मण एकहोता [whole mantra] । अग्निर्होतेत्यनुवाकेन च यतिं स्पृष्ट्वोपस्थाय तुषाग्निना[42] दहेत् । संन्यासी कर्मनिष्ठश्चेत्संस्कारं कृत्वा पिण्डोदकक्रियां कुर्यात् । ज्ञाननिष्ठश्चेत्समुद्रे त्वामिति लवणेन निखनेत् । यतिं वहन् . . . मानवः [11.29] । ब्रह्ममिष्ठे . . . कलेवरम् [11.4–15] । अपि होत्रविधानेन. . .पिण्डोदकक्रियाः [11.27] । ब्रह्मचारी यतिश्चेत्स्याच्छ्राद्धं नारायणार्पणम् । बलिमेकादशेऽन्येषां कुर्याद्दर्शे सपिण्डताम् ।। अथ नारायणबलिः कृष्णपक्षे क्रियते । पूर्वेद्युर्ब्राह्मणाण्षण्णिमन्त्र्य द्वादशाथवा । अथोत्तरेद्युर्द्वादश्यां नदीतीरादिके शुचौ ।। कृत्वा कर्म प्रणीतान्तमेवमावाहयेद्धरिम् । द्वाभ्यामृग्भ्यां नृसूक्तस्य सप्तव्याहृतिभिस्तथा । स्नापयित्वा नृसूक्तेन गन्धाद्यैरर्चयेत्ततः ।। अष्टाक्षरेण संतर्प्य तथा द्वादशनामभिः । विष्णोर्नुकं परो मात्रे द्वाभ्यां चैव तु पञ्चतः ।। उपहृत्वा तु तैरेव नामभिः केशवादिभिः । गुडपायसमन्नं च घृतमन्नं निवेदयेत् ।। देवस्य त्वेति मन्त्रेण विष्णवे हविरग्रतः । जपेच्च व्याहृतिभिश्च सप्त स्वाहाथ विष्णवे ।। दत्वाचमनवारीणि व्याहृतिभिस्ततो द्विजान् । उपवेश्यासने चैतानलंकृत्य च शक्तितः ।। अग्नौ करिष्यामीत्येताननुज्ञाप्याथ चोदिते । तिलाज्यमिश्रं हस्तेन जुहुयान्मन्त्रकैश्चरुम् ।। पञ्चविंशतिभिः सिद्धैर्मासिश्राद्धे स्वधा नमः । नारायणाय स्वाहेति प्रत्येकमनुषज्य च ।। ब्राह्मणान्भोजयित्वा तान्दत्वा तेभ्यस्तु दक्षिणाम् । कृत्वा प्रदक्षिणं तांश्च अनुज्ञाप्यान्नशेषकम् ।। दक्षिणेनाग्निमास्तीर्य प्रागुदग्दर्भकांस्ततः । विश्वेदेवादिकैस्तेषु बलिं दशभिरावपेत् ।। ततः स्विष्टकृदाज्यं तु कुर्यादावनदानतः । पुत्राद्या विधिमेतं तु कृत्वा सिद्धिमवाप्नुयुः ।।

41. कूर्मासनं A4
42. कपालाग्निना A4

12

Ch. 11.33: reading of A1 2 R1

भूमिर्भूमिमगान्मन्त्रमुक्त्वा पात्रं तथोदरे [see 11.13] । प्रणवेन व्याहृतिभिर्दग्ध्वा यतिशरीरकम् । होतृभिः समुपस्थानं दहनानन्तरं चरेत् ॥ चित्तिसृगित्यारभ्य सर्वं च मे भूयादित्यन्तमेभिर्मन्त्रैरुपस्थानं कुर्यात् । After this sundry texts from Chapters 9 and 7 are added: **गौतमः** । ऊर्ध्वरेता ध्रुवशीलो यतिर्नियमितेन्द्रियः [9.1] । **मेधातिथिः** 9.2 **देवलः** 9.3–4 and 9.5(1); **क्रतुः** 9.6; 9.7a–d; 9.8; 9.12; 9.15a–d; 9.16; 9.17a–b; 9.20; 9.26–29; **अत्रिः** 9.5a–d; 7.103a–d; 7.104–105; यतेर्न प्रतिग्राह्यं स्यात् हन्याद्धर्माणि वै मुनिः ॥ 7.106a–d; 7.109–12; 7.113a–d; 7.114.

13

Ch. 11.33: reading of X2* B M

दहनपक्षः । पुत्रोऽन्यो वा गृहस्थः स्नात्वाचम्य नवघटे पञ्चरत्नानि प्रक्षिप्य प्रणवेन तीर्थोदकमुपरि नारायणः परं ब्रह्मेत्यादिनाभिमन्त्र्य तेनैव यतिं स्नाप्य[43] गन्ध-पुष्पधूपदीपादीनष्टाक्षरेण दत्वा गायत्र्या प्रणवेन वा तप्ते पात्रे तुषाग्निमुत्पाद्य[44] शिक्यस्थं यतिदेहमिदं विष्णुरिति विमानमारोप्याग्निसहितो जयमङ्गलशब्देन प्रतीचीमुदीचीं वा दिशं गत्वा नदीतीरे वा अश्वत्थाधस्ताद्वा शुचौ देशे भूर्भुवः स्वरिति दण्डप्रमाणं गर्तं खात्वा सप्तव्याहृतिभिः प्रोक्ष्य तत्र याज्ञिककाष्ठचितिं कृत्वा तस्यां विष्णो हव्यं रक्षस्वेति यतिदेहं निधाय इदं विष्णुरिति दक्षिणहस्ते त्रिदण्डं यदस्य पार इति सव्ये शिक्यं पवित्रं त इति मुखे जलपवित्रं गायत्र्या उदरे पात्रं प्रणवेन पृष्ठे आसनं गुह्ये कमण्डलुमन्यदपि मात्रादिकं पार्श्वे विन्यस्य ॐ इति अग्निनाग्निरित्यादि सखा सख्या समिध्यसे इत्यन्तमन्त्रेणाग्निं मूर्ध्नि दत्वा होतृभिः पञ्चभिः षड्भिर्वा दशहोतृभिः अष्टोत्तरप्रणवेन चोपतिष्ठेत् । ततः प्रदक्षिणीकृत्य निःशेषं दहन्नारायणः[45] परं ब्रह्ममेति स्नात्वा तेनैव सन्तर्प्य शान्तेऽग्नौ च शुष्केणास्थिभस्मानि तीर्थोदके निक्षिपेत् । एकादशेऽह्नि पार्वणश्राद्धम् । अस्थिसंचयनादिप्रेतकार्यं सपिण्डीकरणं च द्वादशेऽह्नि नारायणबलिं च द्वादशेऽह्नि

43. संस्नाप्य R2 3
44. °मुत्पाद्याकृतं [°दालंकृतं ?] G6 R3
45. दग्ध नारा° G6 R3

कुर्यात् । कर्तुः स्नानमात्रेण शुद्धिः अश्वमेधफलं च । अपरः संस्कारविशेषः । शुद्धो गृहस्थः स्नात्वा पुरुषसूक्तेन यतिदेहं स्नाप्य शिक्ये समारोप्य गन्धमाल्यादि अष्टाक्षरेण दत्वा जयशब्दसहितं नदीतीरे गिरिसमीपे अश्वत्थच्छायायां वा परिव्राजकं निधाय व्याहृतिभिर्दण्डप्रमाणं खात्वा सप्तव्याहृतिभिः प्रोक्ष्य यतिदेहं सावित्र्या प्रोक्ष्य येन देवा ज्योतिषा इति कूर्मासनं निधाय तस्योपरि[46] विष्णो हव्यं रक्षस्वेति निधाय पवित्रं ते विततमिति जलपवित्रं मुखे इदं विष्णुरिति दक्षिणहस्ते त्रिदण्डं यदस्य पार इति शिक्यं वामहस्ते सप्तव्याहृतिभिरुदरे पात्रं भूमिर्भूमिम-गान्माता मातरमप्यगाद्भूयास्म पुत्रैः पशुभिर्यो नो द्वेष्टि स भिद्यतामिति गुह्यस्थाने कमण्डलुं च दत्वा हंसः शुचिषदिति हृदये पुरुषसूक्तेन भ्रूमध्ये ब्रह्म जज्ञानमिति ऊर्ध्वदेशे जप्त्वा भूमिर्भूमिमिति मूर्धानं भित्वा गायत्र्याभिमर्श्य लवणेन प्रच्छाद्य प्रणवेन देवयजनं पूरयेत् ।

46. add यतिं R3

APPENDIX 2

Index of Authors Cited

APPENDIX 3

Index of Citations

This list contains the first pāda of each half-verse and the first words of each significant sentence in prose quotations. An 'n' after a number indicates that the citation is found in the critical apparatus of that passage.

इन्द्रियार्थान्विजानीयात् ५.४२
इन्द्रियेभ्यः पराण्याहुः ५.४१
इन्द्रियेषु निरुद्धेषु ५.१०३
इमे ये नार्वाङ् न १.१४
इष्टयज्ञश्च तानग्नीन् २.१५
इष्टानिष्टेषु भूतेषु ७.९३
इष्टे वा यदि वा द्वेष्ये ७.२४
इह पूर्वं प्रतिज्ञाय ७.५२
इहामुत्रोपभोगेषु ५.५

ईश्वरदर्शनं सर्वप्रायश्चित्तम् १०.१६; App. 1.10
ईश्वरीम् ९.४८
ईश्वरो भगवान्विष्णुः ५.७९

उक्तानां यतिपात्राणाम् ७.१२५
उच्छिष्टताशुचित्वं च १०.७०
उच्छिष्टमन्नं पात्रम् ६.२७९
उत्तराषाढयुक्तायाम् ९.५७
उत्तिष्ठ ब्रह्मणेत्यादिः ६.४
उत्तिष्ठेत्युत्थानं प्रातःकाले १०.९९
उत्थायेष्टं व्रजेद्देशम् ९.७८
उत्पन्ने संकटे घोरे २.६३
उत्पाटयेच्च कवचम् ६.२३५
उत्पाटयेद्यो मूढात्मा ७.१३८; App. 1.8
उत्पाट्य पात्रकवचम् ६.१८७
उत्सङ्गे गृह्य तद् द्रव्यम् ९.३४
उदक्याचोदितं ह्यन्नम् ६.१३०
उदक्याशवचण्डाल° १०.५०
उदपात्रं तथा भिक्षाम् ६.१५७
उदयाद्विधिवत्संध्याम् ६.४६
उदानाय चतुर्थी स्यात् ६.२१३
उदानाय स्वाहेति ६.२२९
उदानो वायुराकाशः २.२२०; App. 1.6
उदितेऽन्यत्र मध्याह्ने ९.२; App. 1.12
उदु त्यं चित्रं तच्चक्षुः ६.६४
उदु त्यं चित्रमिति ६.६२
उदु त्यं चित्रमिति ६.२०३
उदु त्यं चित्रमित्याभ्यामादि° ६.२३१
उदु त्यं चित्रमित्याभ्यामुप° ६.७८
उद्धरंश्चात्मनात्मानम् ६.३२३
उद्धृतासि ९.४८
उद्धृतासु स्रवन्तीषु ६.४४; ८.२२; १०.६५n
उद्भिज्जं कृमिदष्टं च App. 1.8
उद्यतं चाप्यभोज्यान्नम् ६.१२१
उपकारकथाश्चैव ९.२३
उपपन्नं तदित्याहुः ६.८५
उपपातकसर्वेषु १०.१५; App. 1.10
उपपातकिनो भिक्षोः १०.२१
उपर्युषसि यत्स्नानम् ६.२६
उपवासत्रयं कृत्वा १०.६४; App. 1.9
उपवासात्परं भैक्षम् ७.४१
उपवीतं त्रिदण्डं च ३.२७
उपवीती त्रिदण्डी च ६.२७४
उपवेश्यासने चैतान् App. 1.11
उपशान्तः परां प्रज्ञाम् ७.९३
उपस्थपादाविति च ५.३०
उपस्थानं रवेश्चापि ६.४३; App. 1.4
उपस्थानं रवेः कुर्यात् ६.१५३
उपस्थानं सहस्रांशोः ६.४२
उपस्थानं कृत्वा १०.२६
उपस्थानं च जप्यं च ६.२५६; १०.८५
उपस्थानं च सूर्यस्य App. 1.4

ध्यानेन दिनशेषं यत् ६.२७७
ध्यायतेऽर्चयते योऽन्यम् ५.८०
ध्यायन्नासीत चैतावत् ६.२८१
ध्यायेत्पुनः प्रबुद्धश्चेत् ६.२८१
ध्यायेन्नारायणं देवम् ६.२८
ध्रुवा द्यौरित्यृचं जप्त्वा ९.५६

न कर्मणा न प्रजया धनेन १.२४
न कर्माणि न चाप्यायुः १०.३
न किंचन याचेत् ६.२२२
न किंचिद्द्वेषजादन्यत् ६.२०९
न कुट्यां नोदके सङ्गः ८.६८
न कुर्यात्पार्वणादन्यत् ११.१६
न कुर्याद्घोषणं तत्र ६.१७९
न कुर्याद्भोजने सङ्गम् ७.१४५n
नकुलं वायसं वेश्याम् १०.३१n
नकुलादिषु भूतेषु १०.१२४
न केनचित्सह ६.२२२
नक्तात्परं चोपवासः ६.९३n
न क्रियायोगचरणम् ६.१०९
न क्वचिन्निशि भुञ्जीत ६.२५५
नखरोमसमायुक्तम् ७.३०
नगरं तु न कर्तव्यम् ६.२८९
न गृह्णात्यल्पबुद्ध्या चेत् ६.२००
नग्नं वानुपनीतं वा यः ७.७३; १०.१२८
नग्नं वानुपनीतं वा विप्रम् १०.१२७
नग्नाः प्रच्छन्नबौद्धाश्च ७.६९
न च कांस्ये तु भुञ्जीत ६.२४०; App. 1.6
न च तृप्येत् ६.२८७
न च त्वक्चपलो वापि ७.२८n
न च पुनर्जायते ४.२२
न च वाक्चपलश्च स्यात् ७.२८
न चात ऊर्ध्वं शुक्लम् ३.५८
न चाध्यापनशीलः स्यात् ७.८४
न चान्यद्वस्तु याचेत ६.१८६
न चास्य क्रियते कश्चित् ११.८; App. 1.11
न चिरमेकत्र वसेत् ९.११, ८२
न चैनं देहमाश्रित्य ७.५
न चैवापद्गतेनापि ५.६५
न चोत्पातनिमित्ताभ्याम् ७.८
न ज्ञातिपुत्रमित्रादीन् ७.८३; App. 1.8
न ज्ञातीनां कुले भिक्षुः ६.१४०
न ज्ञातीनां कुले भिक्षेत् ६.१११
नटादिप्रेक्षणं द्यूतम् ७.११९
न तत्र कर्म कुरुते ६.१३९
न तत्र दक्षिणा यन्ति १.१९
न तथा पुष्करे स्नातः ५.१०८
न तस्य दहनं कार्यम् ११.३०
न तापसैर्ब्राह्मणैर्वा ७.९
न तावच्छुद्ध्यते भूमिः ६.१३८
न तीर्थलोलुपः ६.२९४
न तीर्थवासी नित्यम् ७.८४
न त्रैमुण्ड्यमतिक्रामेत् ८.११
न दण्डेन विना ग्रामे ८.३२
नदीतीरे पर्वतसमीपे App. 1.11
नदीतीरेऽश्वत्थवृक्षे ११.३
न दुष्येत्तस्य तत्पात्रम् ६.२८२
न दुष्येद्दुष्यति ग्रामे ८.१८
न द्रव्यसंचयं कुर्यात् ५.६८
न द्वितीयामपर्तु ९.८०, ८२
न धर्मयुक्तमनृतम् ५.६४
न धारयेत्त्रिविष्टब्धम् ८.६४
न धारयेद्धातुवस्त्रम् ८.६४

सकर्दमं तु वर्षासु १०.७३
स कुर्यात्कृच्छ्रमश्रान्तम् १०.१४१
स कृत्वा प्राकृतं कृच्छ्रम् App. 1.9
सकृत्संभोगे द्वादशरात्रम् १०.१०३
सकृत्साधारणीं गत्वा १०.१०५
सकृदन्त्यजां गत्वारण्ये १०.१०३
सकृदेकेन भुक्तेन App. 1.7, 8
सकृदूह्लन्न लिप्येत १०.८८
सकृद्भुक्तेन यतिना App. 1.7, 8
सखा मा गोपायेति ४.१९
सखा मेत्यादिना शिक्यम् ११.११; App. 1.11
सगुणो निर्गुणो वापि ६.३००
सगोत्रमसगोत्रं वा ६.१३८
संकल्पोऽध्यवसायश्च ५.६६
संकोचयेदक्षिणी ७.१००
संक्रान्तौ ग्रहणे चैव App. 1.7, 8
संग्रहो नवसूत्रस्य ३.३७
सजलाञ्जलिरादित्योपस्थानम् ६.५४
संचितं यद् गृहस्थस्य ६.३०८
स तस्य सुकृतं दत्वा ६.३१०
स तस्य हरति प्राणान् १०.१०८
सती च दानशीलश्च ६.२२
स तु क्रतुसहस्रेण २.६४
स तेनाचमनं कुर्यात् ६.४२
सत्कृतासत्कृते तुल्यः ६.२२५
सत्त्वशुद्धिकरा ह्येते App. 1.5
सत्त्वोत्कटाः सर्वे तेऽपि २.३०
सत्यं वदेत्यनुशास्ति ४.३३
सत्यपूतां वदेद्वाचम् ७.४
सत्यानृते सुखदुःखे ५.९
स त्रिरात्रोपवासेन १०.९४
सत्वचानव्रणान्सौम्यान् ३.४१
सदा चाप्रयत्नोत्सर्गं कृत्वा १०.९२
सदा जलपवित्रं च App. 1.4
सदा जलपवित्रेण ६.४३; App. 1.4
सदा तद्भावयेद्योगी ५.१४३
सदारो न्यस्तदारश्च ५.२
स दूषयति तत्स्थानम् ६.२९२
सद्यः संन्यसनादेव ४.१५
संततं स्यादहोरात्रम् १०.२
संतापनाशनं सद्यः ५.१३४
संतोषो गुरुशुश्रूषा ५.६१
संधिश्च विग्रहो यानम् App. 1.5
संध्याकाले तु संप्राप्ते ६.२५६; १०.८५
संध्यां ततोऽभ्यसेद्योगम् ६.२६३
संध्यामुपास्य विधिवत् ६.२६६
संध्यां भिक्षामुपस्थानम् ३.३२
संध्यालोपोऽनातुरस्य १०.२३
संध्याहीनोऽशुचिर्नित्यम् १.२३; ५.२७
संनतिः शीलमास्तिक्यम् ५.५४
संनिकृष्टं साश्रयम् ७.१००
संनिधौ परकीयाणाम् ७.१३६
संनिधौ मातृमरणे १०.१५२n
संनिरुध्येन्द्रियग्रामम् App. 1.5, 8
संन्यस्तं हि द्विजं दृष्ट्वा ४.१६
संन्यस्तं तं द्विजं दृष्ट्वा ७.७६; App. 1.8
संन्यस्तमिति यो ब्रूयात् २.६४; ४.४४
संन्यस्तं मयेति स्वर° ४.१५
संन्यस्य चापदं तीर्णः ४.४६
संन्यस्य दुर्मतिः कश्चित् १०.१४०
संन्यस्य यतिधर्मांश्च ७.८८
संन्यस्य सर्वकर्माणि कर्म° ५.२१
संन्यस्य सर्वकर्माणि स्व° App. 1.8

Abbreviations and Bibliography

Abh Vedānta Deśika, *Alepakamatabhaṅgavāda*; 65th chapter of the *Śatadūṣaṇī*. Ed. and tr. in Olivelle 1987.

AnSS Ānandāśrama Sanskrit Series, Poona.

ApDh *Āpastamba Dharmasūtra*. Ed. G. Bühler. 3rd ed. BSS 44, 50, 1932. Ed. with Haradatta's commentary *Ujjvalā* by U. C. Pāṇḍeya. KSS 93, 1969. Tr. G. Bühler. SBE 2, 1879.

App. Appendix.

ApSr *Āpastamba Śrautasūtra*. Ed. with Rudradatta's commentary by R. Garbe 1882–1902. 3 Vols.; Reprint. Delhi: Munshiram Manoharlal, 1983.

BaU *Bṛhadāraṇyaka Upaniṣad*. Ed. in EPU. Tr. in TPU.

BDh *Baudhāyana Dharmasūtra*. Ed. E. Hultzsch. 2nd ed. Abhandlungen für die Kunde des Morgenlandes, XVI.2, 1922. Ed. with Govinda Svāmī's commentary by U. C. Pāṇḍeya. KSS 104, 1972. Tr. G. Bühler. SBE 2, 1879.

Belvalkar, S. K. and Ranade, R. D. 1927. Reprint 1974. *History of Indian Philosophy*—II. *The Creative Period*. New Delhi: Oriental Books Reprint Corporation.

BhG *Bhagavad Gītā*. Ed. and tr. by J. A. B. van Buitenen. Chicago: Chicago University Press, 1981.

Bodhāyanīyabrahmakarmasamuccaya. Poona: Āryabhūṣaṇamudraṇālaya, 1970.

Bouillier, V. 1979. *Naître renonçant: une caste de sannyāsī villageois au Népal central*. Nanterre: Laboratoire D'Ethnologie.

Bronkhorst, J. 1993. *The Two Sources of Indian Asceticism*. Schweizer Asiatische Studien, Monographien, Bd. 13. Bern: Peter Lang.

BU *Brahma Upaniṣad*. Ed. in SUS. Tr. in Olivelle 1992.

ChU *Chāndogya Upaniṣad*. Ed. in EPU. Tr. in TPU.

conj. conjectural reading.

cor. corrected, correction

Dasgupta, S. N. 1922. *A History of Indian Philosophy*. Vol. 2; Cambridge: Cambridge University Press.

Derrett, J. D. M. 1974. "Modes of Sannyāsis and the Reform of a South Indian Maṭha Carried Out in 1584." *Journal of the American Oriental Society* 94: 65–72.

Devaṇṇabhaṭṭa, *Smṛticandrikā.* Ed. and tr. J. R. Gharpure. Collections of Hindu Law Texts. Bombay: 1917.

Dīgha Nikāya of the *Sutta Piṭaka.* Ed. T. W. Rhys Davids and J. E. Carpenter. 3 vols. PTS, 1890–1911. Tr. T. W. and C. A. F. Rhys Davids. SBB 2–4, 1899–1921.

Douglas, Mary. 1984. *Purity and Danger: An Analysis of the Concepts of Pollution and Taboo.* London: ARK Paperbacks.

_______. 1982. *Natural Symbols: Explorations in Cosmology.* New York: Pantheon Books.

Dumont, L. 1960. "World Renunciation in Indian Religions," *Contributions to Indian Sociology* 4: 33–62.

EPU *Eighteen Principal Upaniṣads.* Ed. V. P. Limaye and R. D. Vadekar. Poona: Vaidika Saṃśodhana Maṇḍala, 1958.

GDh *Gautama Dharmasūtra.* Ed. with Haradatta's commentary. AnSS 61, 1910. Ed. with Maskarin's commentary by Veda Mitra. New Delhi: Veda Mitra & Sons, 1969. Tr. G. Bühler. SBE 2, 1879.

GOS Gaekwad's Oriental Series, Baroda.

Harpham, G. G. 1987. *The Ascetic Imperative in Culture and Criticism.* Chicago: University of Chicago Press.

Heesterman, J. C. 1964. "Brahmin, Ritual and Renouncer," WZKSA 8: 1–31

HOS Harvard Oriental Series, Cambridge, Mass.

JU *Jābāla Upaniṣad.* Ed. in SUS. Tr. in Olivelle 1992.

Kane, P. V. 1962–75. *History of Dharmaśāstra.* I.1 1968, I.2 1975, II.1–2 1974, III 1973, V.1 1974, V.2 1962. Poona: Bhandarkar Oriental Research Institute.

Katre, S. M. 1954. *Introduction to Indian Textual Criticism.* 2nd ed.; Poona: Deccan College.

KauU *Kauṣītaki Upaniṣad.* Ed. in EPU. Tr. in TPU.

Krick, H. 1977. "Nārāyaṇabali und Opfertod," WZKS 21: 71–142.

KSS Kashi Sanskrit Series, Varanasi.

Markaṇḍeya Purāṇa. Ed. J. Vidyasagara. Calcutta: Saraswati Press, 1879.

Matsumoto, S. 1968. "Yādavaprakāśa." *Journal of Indian and Buddhist Studies* University of Tokyo, 17,1: 21-24.

MBh *Mahābhārata.* Ed. V. S. Sukthankar et al. 19 vols. Poona: Bhandarkar Oriental Research Institute, 1927–59. Tr. van Buitenen. 3 vols. Chicago: Chicago University Press, 1973–78.

MDh *Mānava Dharmaśāstra* (*Manusmṛti*). Ed. with the commentaries of Medhātithi, Sarvajñanārāyaṇa, Kullūka, Rāghavānanda, Nandana,

Rāmacandra, and Govindarāja by V. N. Mandlik. 3 vols. Bombay: Ganpat Krishnaji's Press, 1886. Tr. G. Bühler SBE 25, 1886.

MK *Mīmāṃsā Koṣa*. Ed. Kevalānanda Sarasvatī. 7 vols. Wai: Prājña Pāṭhaśālā Maṇḍala, 1952–66.

MNU *Mahānārāyaṇa Upaniṣad*. Ed. and tr. J. Varenne. 2 vols. Série in-8, 11–12. Paris: Institut de Civilisation Indienne, 1960.

ms(s) manuscript(s)

MS *Maitrāyaṇīya Saṃhitā* of the *Yajur Veda*. Ed. L. von Schroeder. 4 vols. Leipzig: F. A. Brockhaus, 1881–86.

MuU *Muṇḍaka Upaniṣad*. Ed. in EPU. Tr. in TPU.

NPU *Nāradaparivrājaka Upaniṣad*. Ed. in SUS. Tr. in Olivelle 1992.

NSm *Nāradasmṛti*. Ed. and tr. Richard W. Lariviere. 2 pts. University of Pennsylvania Studies on South Asia, vols. 4–5 (Philadelphia: University of Pennsylvania, 1989).

Nyāyakośa. Ed. B. Jhalakīkar. 2nd ed.; Poona: Bhandarkar Oriental Research Institute, 1978.

Olivelle, P. 1975. "A Definition of World Renunciation. " WZKS 19: 75–83.

_______. 1981. "Contributions to the Semantic History of Saṃnyāsa." *Journal of the American Oriental Society* 101: 265–74.

_______. 1986–87. *Renunciation in Hinduism: A Medieval Debate*. Vol. 1, 1986: *The Debate and the Advaita Argument*. Vol. 2, 1987: *The Viśiṣṭādvaita Argument*. De Nobili Research Library, Vols. 13-14. Vienna: University of Vienna Institute for Indology.

_______. 1990. "Village vs. Wilderness: Ascetic Ideals and the Hindu World." In *Monasticism in the Christian and Hindu Traditions*, ed. A. Creel and V. Narayanan, 125–60. Lewiston, N.Y.: Edwin Mellen.

_______. 1992. *Saṃnyāsa Upaniṣads: Hindu Scriptures on Asceticism and Renunciation*. New York: Oxford University Press.

_______. 1993. *The Āśrama System: The History and Hermeneutics of a Religious Institution*. New York: Oxford University Press.

om omission, omitted.

PaM Mādhava. *Pārāśaramādhavīya*. Ed. V. S. Islampurkar. 3 vols. in 6 parts. Bombay: Bombay Sanskrit Series, 1893–1919.

Pāṇini, *Aṣṭādhyāyī*. Ed. and tr. O. Böhtlingk 1887. Reprint Hildesheim: Olms, 1964. Tr. S. C. Vasu 1891. 2 vols. Reprint. Delhi: Motilal Banarsidass, 1962.

PG *Pāraskara Gṛhyasūtra*. Ed. M. P. Puṇatāmakara. KSS 11, 1920. Tr. H. Oldenberg. SBE 19, 1886.

PMS *Pūrva Mīmāṃsāsūtra* of Jaimini. Ed. with the commentaries of Śabara and Kumārila. 7 vols. AnSS 97, 1971–81. Tr. G. Jha. 3 vols. GOS 66, 70, 73, 1973–74.

Raghavan, V. 1967. "The Upadeśasāhasrī of Śaṅkarācārya and the Mutual Chronology of Śaṅkarācārya and Bhāskara," WZKS 9: 137-39.

Rhys Davids, T. W. 1903. Reprint 1971. *Buddhist India*. Delhi: Motilal Banarsidass.

RV *Ṛgveda Saṃhitā*. Ed. with Sāyaṇa's commentary by F. Max Müller. 6 vols. London: Wm. H. Allen & Co., 1849–74. Tr. Geldner 1951–57.

SanGr *Śāṅkhāyana Gṛhyasūtra*. Ed. S. R. Seghal. 2nd ed. Delhi: Sri Satguru Publications, 1987. Tr. H. Oldenberg. SBE 19, 1886.

SB *Śatapatha Brāhmaṇa*. Ed. A. Weber 1855. Reprint. Chowkhamba Sanskrit Series 96. Varanasi: 1964. Tr. J. Eggeling. SBE 12, 26, 41, 43, 44, 1882–1900.

Shastri, A. M. 1972. "The Bhikṣusūtra of Pārāśarya," *Journal of the Asiatic Society* (Calcutta; issued 1975) 14, nos. 2-4: 52-59.

Singh, S. 1958. *Vedāntadeśika: A Study*. Chowkhamba Sanskrit Studies, 5; Varanasi: Chowkahmba Sanskrit Series Office.

SBE Sacred Books of the East, Oxford.

Smith, H. D. 1975. *A Descriptive Bibliography of the Printed Texts of the Pāñcarātrāgama*. Vol. 1. GOS 158, 1975.

Sp Rudradeva, *Saṃnyāsapaddhati*. Ed. P. Olivelle. Madras: Adyar Library and Research Centre, 1986.

Sprockhoff, J. F. 1976. *Saṃnyāsa: Quellenstudien zur Askese im Hinduismus. I—Untersuchungen über die Saṃnyāsa-Upaniṣads*. Abhandlungen für die Kunde des Morgenlandes 42,1. Wiesbaden: Franz Steiner.

Śrautakośa. English Section. Ed. R. N. Dandekar. 2 vols. in 4 pts.; Poona: Vaidika Saṃśodhana Maṇḍala, 1958–82.

Srinivasachari, P. N. 1934. *The Philosophy of Bhedābheda*. Adyar Library Series, 74; Madras: Adyar Library and Research Centre.

Srinivasa Chari, S. M. 1961. *Advaita and Viśiṣṭādvaita: A Study Based on Vedānta Deśika's Śatadūṣaṇī*. Bombay: Asia Publishing House.

SUS *Saṃnyāsa Upaniṣads*. Ed. F. Otto Schrader. Madras: Adyar Library, 1912.

SvU *Śvetāśvatara Upaniṣad*. Ed. in EPU. Tr. in TPU.

TA *Taittirīya Āraṇyaka*. Ed. with Sāyaṇa's commentary. 3rd ed.; 2 vols. AnSS 36, 1967.

TB *Taittirīya Brāhmaṇa*. Ed. with Sāyaṇa's commentary. 3 vols. AnSS 37, 1898.

TPU *The Thirteen Principal Upanishads*. Tr. R. E. Hume. 2nd ed. Oxford: Oxford University Press, 1931.

TS *Taittirīya Saṃhitā*. Ed. with Sāyaṇa's commentary. 9 vols. AnSS 42, 1900–08. Tr. A. B. Keith. HOS 18–19, 1914.

TU *Taittirīya Upaniṣad*. Ed. in EPU. Tr. in TPU.

Turner, B. S. 1984. *The Body and Society*. Oxford: Basil Blackwell.

VaDh *Vasiṣṭha Dharmasūtra*. Ed. A. A. Führer. 3rd. ed. BSS 23, 1930. Tr. G. Bühler. SBE 2, 1879.

VaiDh *Vaikhānasa Dharmasūtra*. Ed. and tr. W. Caland. Bibliotheca Indica 242, 252. Calcutta: Asiatic Society of Bengal, 1927–29.

Vaidyanātha Dīkṣita, *Smṛtimuktāphala*. Ed. J. R. Gharpure. Collection of Hindu Law Texts 25. Bombay: 1937–40.

Varadachari, K. C. 1950. "The Philosophy of Yādavaprakāśa." *Siddha-Bhāratī* (Hoshiarpur: Vishveshvaranand Vedic Research Institute) Vol.1, Ser. 2: 109-14.

ViDh *Viṣṇu Dharmasūtra* (*Viṣṇusmṛti*). Ed. with Nandapaṇḍita's commentary by V. Krishnamacharya. 2 vols. Adyar Library Series 93. Madras: 1964. Tr. J. Jolly. SBE 7, 1880.

Vidyarnava, R. B. S. C. 1979 (reprint of 1918). *The Daily Practice of the Hindus*. New Delhi: Oriental Books Reprint Corporation.

Viṣṇusaṃhitā. Ed. M. M. T. Ganapati Sastri. Reprint. Sri Garib Dass Oriental Series 98. Delhi: Sri Satguru Publications, 1990.

von Hinüber, O. 1992. *Sprachentwicklung und Kulturgeschiche*. Mainz/Stuttgart: Akademie der Wissenschaften und der Literatur and Franz Steiner Verlag.

VS *Vājasaneyi Saṃhitā*. Ed. A. Weber. Berlin: Ferd. Dümmler's Verlagsbuchhandlung, 1852.

WZKSA Wiener Zeitschrift für die Kunde Südasiens

Yāska, *Nirukta*. Ed. V. K. Rajavade. Poona: Bhandarkar Oriental Research Institute, 1940.

Ybh Vedānta Deśika, *Yatiliṅgabhedabhaṅgavāda*; 64th chapter of the *Śatadūṣaṇī*. Ed. and tr. in Olivelle 1987.

YDh *Yājñavalkya Dharmaśāstra*. Ed. with Vijñāneśvara's commentary by U. C. Pandey. KSS 178, 1967.

Ydhs Viśveśvara Sarasvatī, *Yatidharmasaṃgraha*. Ed. V. G. Apte. AnSS 60, 1928.

Yls Varadācārya. *Yatiliṅgasamarthana*. Ed. and tr. in Olivelle 1987.

Ypra Vāsudevāśrama, *Yatidharmaprakāśa*. Ed. and tr. P. Olivelle. 2 vols. De Nobili Research Library 3–4. Vienna: University of Vienna Institute for Indology, 1976–77.

Ys *Yogasūtras* of Patañjali. Ed. with the commentaries of Vyāsa, Vācaspati Miśra, and Vijñānabhikṣu. KSS 110, 1935. Tr. J. H. Woods. HOS 17, 1914.

Ysam Yādava Prakāśa, *Yatidharmasamuccaya*.

Index